ENVIRONMENTAL
Ethics

ENVIRONMENTAL
Ethics

Theory in Practice

RONALD L. SANDLER

Oxford   New York
Oxford University Press

Oxford University Press is a department of the University of Oxford. It furthers the University's objective of excellence in research, scholarship, and education by publishing worldwide. Oxford is a registered trademark of Oxford University Press in the UK and certain other countries.

Published in the United States of America by Oxford University Press
198 Madison Avenue, New York, NY 10016, United States of America.

For titles covered by Section 112 of the US Higher Education
Opportunity Act, please visit www.oup.com/us/he for the
latest information about pricing and alternate formats.

Library of Congress Cataloging-in-Publication Data

Names: Sandler, Ronald L., author.
Title: Environmental ethics : theory in practice / Ronald L. Sandler.
Description: New York : Oxford University Press, 2017.
Identifiers: LCCN 2016050474 | ISBN 9780199340729 (pbk.)
Subjects: LCSH: Environmental ethics.
Classification: LCC GE42 .S2625 2017 | DDC 179/.1—dc23
LC record available at https://lccn.loc.gov/2016050474

9 8 7 6 5 4 3 2
Printed by Webcom Inc., Canada

To the students of PHIL 1180:

Environmental Ethics

TABLE OF CONTENTS

LIST OF BOXES

LIST OF TABLES, FIGURES, AND IMAGES

LIST OF ABBREVIATIONS

CAFO	Concentrated Animal Feed Operation
CBA	Cost-Benefit Analysis
CBD	Convention on Biological Diversity
DEFRA	Department for Environment, Food, and Rural Affairs (United Kingdom)
EPA	Environmental Protection Agency (United States)
ESA	Endangered Species Act (United States)
FAO	Food and Agricultural Organization (United Nations)
GDP	Gross Domestic Product
GM/GMO	Genetically Modified/Genetically Modified Organism
GMST/GMSAT	Global Mean Surface Temperature/Global Mean Surface Air Temperature
IEA	International Energy Agency
IK	Indigenous Knowledge
INDC	Intended Nationally Determined Contributions
IPCC	Intergovernmental Panel on Climate Change
IUCN	International Union for Conservation of Nature
MDEQ	Michigan Department of Environmental Quality
NASA	National Aeronautics and Space Administration (United States)
NGO	Non-Governmental Agency
NOAA	National Oceanic and Atmospheric Administration (United States)
NPS	National Park Service (United States)
PPP	Purchasing Power Parity
OECD	Organisation for Economic Cooperation and Development
TEK	Traditional Ecological Knowledge
UDHR	Universal Declaration of Human Rights
UN	United Nations
UNDRIP	United Nations Declaration on the Rights of Indigenous Peoples
UNEP	United Nations Environment Programme

UNESCO	United Nations Educational, Scientific, and Cultural Organization
UNFCCC	United Nations Framework Convention on Climate Change
UNICEF	United Nations International Children's Emergency Fund
USFWS	United States Fish and Wildlife Service
USD	United States Dollars
USDA	United States Department of Agriculture
WCED	World Commission on Environment and Development
WHO	World Health Organization

PREFACE

> By and large, our present problem is one of attitudes and implements. We are remodeling the Alhambra with a steam-shovel, and we are proud of our yardage. We shall hardly relinquish the shovel, which after all has many good points, but we are in need of gentler and more objective criteria for its successful use.
>
> Aldo Leopold, *A Sand County Almanac*, 1949

The natural world is magnificent. It is filled with unique and amazing forms of life that constitute astoundingly complex and varied ecological systems. It is comprised of awesome landscapes and wonderful seascapes. It provides a bounty of material goods and ecosystem services. It enriches people's lives, culturally, aesthetically, recreationally, and spiritually.

Environmental concerns arise from the observation that these goods and values are being diminished and lost. The cumulative environmental impacts of modern technology, population growth, and increased consumption include resource depletion, pollution accumulation, habitat destruction, species extinctions, and climate change. These are, in turn, detrimental to people, particularly those with limited resources and who have immediate dependencies on ecological systems. The field of environmental ethics provides critical perspectives for helping to understand the social, cultural, and attitudinal dimensions of environmental problems.

Theories of environmental ethics aim to provide guidance on how we ought to address environmental issues by identifying the full range of environmental goods and values at stake and articulating how we ought to respond to them. Different theories support different approaches to environmental decision-making. They thereby have different implications for which policies and practices we ought to adopt. If the primary thing we should care about is human welfare and the goal is to maximally satisfy human preferences, then the practical implications for everything from species conservation to what we should eat are different than if we should care about all living things and the goal is to protect the flourishing of diverse life forms. This is why determining which theories of environmental ethics are well justified and which are not has such practical importance.

GOALS AND AIMS

The intended audience for this textbook is undergraduate environmental ethics students. It has three interrelated goals:

- Help students develop the analytic skills and critical perspectives for effectively identifying and evaluating the social and ethical dimensions of environmental issues.
- Provide students with an accessible but rigorous introduction to the field of environmental ethics, including its subject matter, methods, and theories.
- Encourage students to develop an informed, well-justified ethical outlook and approach to decision-making regarding environmental issues.

Accomplishing these goals requires studying both the theoretical aspects of prominent theories of environmental ethics and their implications for environmental issues. Therefore, this textbook is replete with illustrative examples and cases for students to consider.

STRUCTURE AND APPROACH

The organization of this textbook is based on the approach to teaching environmental ethics that I have found to be most effective:

1. Clarify what environmental ethics is and why it matters, and demonstrate the importance of developing well-justified theories of environmental ethics (Chapter 1).
2. Provide the basic resources for analyzing ideas and views on environmental issues, and preemptively address commonly made mistakes when thinking about environmental ethics (Chapters 2 to 3).
3. Distinguish and separately discuss theories of environmental values or what things we ought to care about (Chapters 4 to 7, 11 to 13) from normative theories or how we ought to care about them (Chapters 8 to 12).
4. Consider challenges to theory-oriented approaches to environmental ethics (Chapter 14).
5. Emphasize the relationship between environmental issues and social justice issues (Chapters 14 to 16).
6. Incorporate examples and cases at every stage to motivate the theoretical issues and explore the practical implications of different views and theories.

This approach enables students to develop well-reasoned, empirically sound, and practically informed views on environmental values and environmental decision-making at the same time as they are studying different theories of environmental ethics. It also encourages them to continually revise and improve their views as challenges, concerns, and additional considerations are introduced.

FEATURES

This textbook has many features intended to help promote student learning, several of which distinguish it from other environmental ethics texts:

- *Extensive use of cases and issues to ground theoretical discussions and demonstrate the practical implications of theories.* The environmental issues discussed include (but are not limited to): species conservation, ecological restoration, global climate change, intergenerational justice, environmental activism, environmental justice, concentrated animal feed operations, crop agriculture, fisheries management, genetic modification, hunting, wildlife viewing, ecological economics, zoos and aquaria, wilderness preservation, water scarcity, population growth, pollution and waste management, consumption, sustainable development, energy access, eco-tourism, food security, and environmental rights.

- *Incorporation of both classic and contemporary cases and examples.* Iconic cases frequently referred to in the environmental ethics literature are discussed—for example, the spotted owl, Tellico dam, and Hetch Hetchy controversies. However, there is also an emphasis on very recent and cutting edge issues. For instance, the genomic technologies and applications covered include recombinant DNA techniques and genetically modified crops, as well as conservation cloning, deextinction, and gene drives; and the examples of exposure to environmental hazards include the Bhopal chemical disaster, as well as an extensive discussion of the ongoing lead contamination of Flint, Michigan's water supply.

- *Integration of both food ethics and technology ethics.* Technology is a contributing factor to many environmental problems, and novel technologies are often pro-posed to help address environmental problems. Agriculture and food production are a critical aspect of the human-nature relationship and are arguably the most environmentally impactful activities in which people engage. Environmental ethics is thus intertwined with agricultural and food ethics, as well as with the philosophy and ethics of technology. Therefore, this textbook includes discussion of many prominent issues in food and agricultural ethics—including genetic engineering, food systems, food waste, and eating animals—as well as criti-cal reflections on technological power, technologically oriented approaches to problem-solving, and the role of technology in human life.

- *Emphasis on the social justice dimensions of environmental problems.* This textbook includes several chapters in which the relationship between social justice and the environment is in the foreground. These include chapters on environmental justice, food security, and ecofeminism. Social justice considerations also arise frequently throughout the textbook and are prominent in many of the issues discussed, such as environmental rights, creation of ecological parks and reserves, and traditional ecological knowledge.

- *Accessible, charitable, and fair presentation of views and theories.* The aim of this textbook is not to defend any particular theory of environmental ethics or to tell students what they ought to think on any particular environmental issue. I strive to present all the theories discussed—and the arguments for them and concerns raised about them—as clearly, accurately, and charitably as possible. I also point out what are commonly regarded as the most promising positions on an issue, indicate when a view or argument has widely recognized flaws, highlight aspects of views that are influential or widely accepted, and suggest questions or perspectives that might be helpful for thinking through issues.
- *Extensive use of prompts to promote learning.* Each chapter includes several text boxes. The boxes are of a variety of types and are intended to foster idea generation, critical reflection, and appreciation of practical implications. They include: (1) extended discussions of cases, (2) thought experiments, (3) theoretical issues that are related to or build upon topics discussed in the main text, (4) exercises in which students are asked to apply theories or reflect on how theoretical issues intersect with practice issues. They typically conclude with a set of questions for students to consider.
- *An array of learning tools and aids.* In addition to the learning prompts found in the text boxes, this textbook includes review questions, discussion questions, key terms and additional reading lists at the end of each chapter, extensive internal cross-referencing to help make connections across topics, a glossary of key terms and concepts, and over thirty images, illustrations, tables, and graphs.

ACKNOWLEDGMENTS

This textbook is based on the environmental ethics course that I have taught at Northeastern University almost every semester since 2003. I love teaching the course, in no small part because of the engaged and thoughtful students with whom I have the privilege of exchanging ideas and discussing environmental issues. I am grateful to them for sharing their questions, experiences, perspectives, and knowledge with me. This textbook is the product of what I have learned from them about teaching environmental ethics. It is dedicated to them.

I am deeply indebted to my colleague John Basl. It was enormously valuable for me to be able to discuss the organization and content of this textbook on a regular basis with someone else who frequently teaches environmental ethics. John also read a draft of the manuscript from beginning to end, and it is much improved from his comments and suggestions. I am grateful to Christopher Preston, Kyle Powys Whyte, and Rory Smead for providing extremely helpful feedback on sections of the manuscript, to Christopher Bosso and Lee Breckenridge for answering my many questions about environmental policy and law, and to the reviewers—Michael Boring, Estrella Mountain Community College; Matt Ferkany, Michigan State University; William

Grove-Fanning, Trinity University; Larry D. Harwood, Viterbo University; Ned Hettinger, College of Charleston; Kenneth Itzkowitz, Marietta College; James Justus, Florida State University; William P. Kabasenche, Washington State University; Joel Kassiola, San Francisco State University; and Lauren Hartzell Nichols, University of Washington—for their thoughtful suggestions on how to improve the manuscript. Jodie Ly and Sorell de Silva provided valuable research assistance on this project. Jodie helped at the start of the project with tracking down sources and developing cases and examples. Sorell helped at the conclusion with organizing references, fact-checking, building the glossary, formatting the manuscript, and constructing the tables. Sorell also gave me excellent advice regarding passages that needed to be written more clearly, as well as terminology and ideas that required further explication. I am thankful to both of them for their hard work.

Some of the material in this textbook is drawn from work that I published elsewhere, including in *Food Ethics: The Basics* (Routledge, 2015), *The Ethics of Species* (Cambridge University Press, 2013), *Character and Environment* (Columbia University Press, 2007), "Global Climate Change and Species Preservation" in Byron Williston, ed., *Environmental Ethics for Canadians* (Oxford University Press, 2016), and "Environmental Virtue Ethics: Value, Normativity, and Right Action" in Allen Thompson and Stephen Gardiner, eds., *The Oxford Handbook of Environmental Ethics* (Oxford University Press, 2016). I thank the publishers of those works for permission to draw upon them here, and I am grateful to all my friends and colleagues who provided feedback on the material both before and after publication. I am particularly indebted to Philip Cafaro, who has pushed me to clarify, refine, and (sometimes) change my views on topics ranging from virtue theory to species conservation.

I am grateful to everyone at Oxford University Press who helped to make this textbook a physical (and virtual) reality: Robert Miller for suggesting the project to me and for his truly incredible patience as it was completed; Alyssa Palazzo, Nicole Argyropoulos, and Jenelle Emmert for their help and guidance on preparing the manuscript, securing permissions, and working through the production process; and Elizabeth Bortka for copyediting that cleaned and significantly improved the manuscript.

Most of all, I thank my family, particularly my wife, Emily, for her support and encouragement, and my children, Elijah and Ruth, for making every day a good day. (Elijah and Ruth also consulted on choices for several of the images used in the textbook.)

One final note. The focus of this textbook is contemporary environmental ethics in what is often called the analytic tradition. There are many other traditions, areas of environmental philosophy, and approaches to environmental ethics that are not covered here. This is in no way intended to be a statement on their worth or value. Even in a textbook as long as this one, it is not possible to cover everything.

PART I: DOING ENVIRONMENTAL ETHICS

CHAPTER ONE

WHAT IS ENVIRONMENTAL ETHICS?

ETHICS CONCERNS HOW WE ought to live. Ethical questions are about what actions we ought to perform, what policies we ought to adopt, what kind of people we ought to be, and what sort of society we ought to have. The need for ethics arises from the fact that we—individually and collectively—confront multiple possibilities. Therefore, we must make choices. We have to choose what career to pursue, who to spend time with, whether to have children, how to spend our money, where to live, what policies to support, what to eat, and so much more. Moreover, we are self-aware and deliberative. So we do not always choose arbitrarily, unreflectively, or based on instinct. Much of the time we aim to make informed, reasoned choices. That is, we aim to choose well.

The point of **ethical theory** is to provide guidance for choosing well regarding our actions, practices, and policies. It aims to provide an account of what sorts of things matter (or have value) and how things matter (or how we ought to consider them given their value), as well as provide methods and resources, such as rules, principles, or guidelines, to help make decisions in concrete situations.

With respect to the natural environment, many people, particularly those of us in affluent, highly industrialized nations, have not been choosing well. The limits of earth's natural resources are being stretched; thousands of species go extinct each year; nearly 800 million people are chronically malnourished; the land, air, and water are being polluted; and people are increasingly cut off from the beauty and wonder of the nonhuman world. We need **environmental ethics** because we need to improve our decisions about and interactions with the natural environment. We need to see more

2

clearly what in the environment matters and how it matters. The central questions of environmental ethics are, therefore, these:

1. What is the proper way to understand the relationship between ourselves and the nonhuman environment, including the organisms that populate it?
2. What values emerge from that relationship or are possessed by environmental entities, such as species, ecosystems, organisms, and landscapes?
3. What principles, rules, or other forms of guidance regarding action, character, and policy do those environmental values justify?
4. What do those principles and rules imply for how we ought to interact with the environment, as well as how we should live more generally?

Theories of environmental ethics are distinguished by how they answer these questions. The central aim of this textbook is to characterize prominent, influential, and promising theories of environmental ethics and demonstrate their implications for practice and policy. The goal is not to advocate for a particular environmental ethic. It is to present the considerations that have been raised for and against different approaches to environmental ethics, and indicate where errors of reasoning or mistakes of fact commonly occur, in order to help the reader evaluate for herself which of them (or which combination of them) are well justified.

✳ BOX 1.1

THE CALIFORNIA WATER CRISIS
AND ENVIRONMENTAL ETHICS

One of the most prominent environmental issues in the United States in recent years has been a severe, multi-year drought in California. There has not been enough water in the state's system for farmers to use as much as they would like for their crops and residents to use as much as they would like in their households, while leaving sufficient amounts for the ecological integrity of riparian and wetland ecosystems. As a result, there have been "water wars" between cities, agricultural interests, and environmentalists. Urban residents want to protect their lifestyles—for example, green golf courses, long showers, and clean cars. Farmers want to protect the state's agricultural economy and, for family farmers, the continuity of their way of life. Environmentalists want to protect at-risk species, such as the delta smelt and Chinook salmon.

(cont.)

BOX 1.1 *(cont.)*

Images 1.1   In summer 2016, over 90 percent of the state of California was in a prolonged drought (NDMC 2016), which stressed the state's water system and severely depleted many of its key reservoirs, such as the Lake Oroville Reservoir.

Source: California Department of Water Resources

(cont.)

BOX 1.1 *(cont.)*

One question regarding the drought is, "How should this scarce natural resource be allocated?" This is an evaluative and normative question. It is about what things have value, which claims are legitimate, what would be a fair outcome, and how to adjudicate when interests conflict.

Another question is, "What (in addition to reduced rainfall and snowfall) generated the situation?" Was it the result of inefficient use of resources? Poor planning and water infrastructure design? Or was it the product of deeper cultural and attitudinal factors, such as conceptualizing the natural environment as a mere resource, the pursuit of perpetual economic growth, the tendency to modify ecological systems to suit human ends, and faith in human ingenuity to engineer solutions to whatever problems arise?

Yet another question is "What should be done to prevent the situation from occurring again in the future?" Should people do more to accommodate their lifestyles to ecological limits—for example, foregoing lawns and refraining from growing water-intensive crops? Should the engineering and control-oriented approach to water management be expanded—for example, pumping in water from further away, desalinating ocean water, and engineering drought-tolerant crops? Should efforts be made to address the macro scale factors contributing to the problem, such as global climate change and population growth?

Thus, analyzing, evaluating, and responding well to this case involves:

- Thinking about how we understand our relationships to the nonhuman environment;
- Identifying all the ways in which the nonhuman environment is important and valuable;
- Determining how we ought to respond to those different values;
- Developing resources for adjudicating conflicts between legitimate values, both in the short term and the long run, as well as between humans and nonhumans;
- Reconsidering how we should approach environmental problems;
- Improving practices, social systems, attitudes, and policies in order to prevent environmental problems from arising in the future.

The California water crisis is not unique in involving these elements. They are part of all types of environmental challenges—for example, ecosystem management, species conservation, resource allocations, pollution control and remediation, and environmental justice—and, as discussed above, they are the purview of environmental ethics.

1.1 WHAT ARE ENVIRONMENTAL ISSUES?

Environmental ethics is often associated with wilderness. It is conceived as being about managing the land and sea, and how we ought to behave when we are out in nature, hiking in woods, or paddling on rivers. Some environmental issues are like this. Land use issues dominated early North American environmentalism, for example, and creation of ecological parks, off-road vehicle use, road building, deforestation, wildlife protection, natural resource management, and species preservation are crucial environmental issues around the world.

However, our pressing environmental challenges are not limited to those concerning the protection of places, management of resources, or treatment of flora and fauna "out there." Beginning with the Industrial Revolution but amplified by rapid population growth, the post-WWII chemical revolution, and ongoing urban migration, environmental issues began to increasingly arise "right here," in people's communities. Issues associated with industrial production systems include manufacturing and consumer waste disposal, ambient air quality, water pollution from input intensive agriculture, sustainable development, and environmental justice.

In addition to the environmental problems that are "out there" and "right here" are problems that are "everywhere," such as climate change and ozone depletion. These problems are global in the sense that their causes and effects are distributed around the world. Greenhouse gas emissions contribute to global climate change regardless of where they occur and the effects of climate change are manifest, often most acutely, in lower-income countries with small per capita emissions. Globalization also ties people to environmental issues geographically distant from them. The global food system links the food preferences of people in North America and China to fisheries depletion and aquatic habitat destruction in oceans around the world, and biofuel standards in the European Union incentivize deforestation to create palm oil plantations in Indonesia and Malaysia, for example.

Environmental issues are ubiquitous, and our behaviors, practices, and policies connect us to them. This is perhaps most clearly the case with our consumption patterns. Take for example food, which, whether it is grown or caught, depends upon ecological systems for its production. Some foods are much more ecologically intensive than are others. Beef production requires greater water and energy inputs than does chicken production, which in turn requires more inputs than does vegetable production (for the same nutritional and caloric output). Fish that is flown to market typically involves much greater greenhouse gas emissions than do in-season locally-sourced foods. Of course, it is not only our food choices and policies that are ecologically significant. How we travel, how we take our recreation, how large our homes are, how we dispose of our waste, how much energy we use, how many children we have, and the causes that we support are ecologically relevant as well. Moreover, we do not make decisions about such things in a vacuum. Institutions and policies structure the options that we have and frame the choices that we make.

For these reasons, environmental ethics is relevant in both the private and the public spheres, and it is relevant to both our mundane daily choices (e.g., what to eat) and our occasional decisions (e.g., whom to vote for).

1.2 WHY ENVIRONMENTAL ETHICS?

An implication of environmental considerations permeating almost all human activities is that environmental issues are not really distinct from **interpersonal ethics,** or ethics between people. For example, satisfying human rights requires that the ecological conditions necessary for people to meet their basic needs for nutrition, water, and shelter are maintained. Social justice involves addressing health inequalities resulting from unequal exposures to pollution and other environmental hazards, as well as ensuring that indigenous peoples are empowered to protect and manage their ancestral lands. Political stability can be undermined by ecological degradation, which can result in food shortages and refugees. Poverty alleviation and economic development frequently involve accessing natural resources, agricultural expansion, and ecotourism.

Moreover, accomplishing environmental goals is often impossible without attending to interpersonal considerations. For example, successfully establishing ecological reserves requires working with local communities to administer them, as well as ensuring economic and food security so as to eliminate the need for deforestation and poaching. Promoting environmental justice involves empowering communities in local permitting and land use decision-making processes, as well as incorporating distributional considerations into pollution regulation and enforcement. Responding to climate change requires aggressive energy policy reform, as well as addressing overconsumption and population growth.

Given that social and environmental issues—and environmental ethics and interpersonal ethics—are so intertwined, why break out the study of environmental ethics? Why have courses, textbooks, and research dedicated to it, rather than just incorporate it into the study of ethical theory more generally?

One reason is that the environmental side of ethics is comparatively underdeveloped. The history of Western ethics is dominated by interpersonal ethics, by questions about how we ought to treat other people and organize human societies. As a result, there are a large number of questions concerning the value of nature and the importance of ecological relationships that have been under-studied. Environmental ethics requires us to reflect on the ethical significance of things that are not alive (e.g., landscapes), are alive but not sentient (e.g., plants), are sentient but not human (e.g., animals), and are collectives (e.g., species and ecosystems). Thus, there are distinctive questions that arise when we begin to consider the ethical significance of the ecological world, which have not been sufficiently addressed in theories of interpersonal ethics.

Environmental issues also often have some distinctive features. Many of our most pressing environmental problems—such as habitat loss, climate change, and pollution—are **longitudinal collective action problems**. Take, for example, polar bear conservation. Polar bear populations are threatened due to sea ice reductions caused by increases in air temperature that are the result of the accumulation of greenhouse gases in the atmosphere (Section 13.5). The increased concentration of those gases is the product of the activity of billions of people over decades. Thus, the challenge of polar bear conservation involves collective action over time. It is a different sort of ethical problem than one that concerns the discrete actions of a single individual, such as whether to stretch the truth to gain an advantage or give more money to charity. Not all environmental problems are longitudinal collective action problems (and not all longitudinal collective action problems are environmental problems). However, many of the most crucial ones are, and attention to their distinctive features is needed to adequately understand and address them.

Furthermore, despite increases in environmental concern and awareness over the past several decades, appreciation of the importance of environmental considerations continues to lag behind interpersonal ethics. As Aldo Leopold, an influential ecologist and ethicist put it, "A farmer who clears the woods off a 75 percent slope, turns his cows into the clearing, and dumps its rainfall, rocks, and soil into the community creek, is still (if otherwise decent) a respected member of society" (1966, 204). There remains a sense that environmental ethics is secondary or elective, in comparison to interpersonal ethics. Therefore, another reason for focusing in on environmental ethics is to raise its salience within ethics more generally.

Environmental problems such as biodiversity loss, food insecurity, and climate change are among the greatest challenges that we face. These problems often have distinctive structures and raise distinctive value questions, which have traditionally been under-addressed within predominant ethical outlooks. These are the reasons why environmental ethics merits special attention. Perhaps in the future this will not be the case, and the questions and problems of environmental ethics will be sufficiently appreciated, understood, and incorporated into people's ethical outlooks that there will be no need for it to be studied separately. In many ways this would be a successful outcome. Unfortunately, we are not there yet.

Why focus, as this textbook does, on theories of environmental ethics? The reason is that different theories have different implications for how we ought to address environment issues. If the basis for environmental ethics is human welfare and the goal is to maximize satisfaction of human preferences, the practical implication for everything from ecosystem management to individual lifestyles is different than if all living things have value and the goal is to protect the flourishing of diverse life forms. Different value and normative systems support very different prescriptions about how we should live, what policies we should support, and how we should treat the biological world. It is the same as with interpersonal ethics. Identifying the most justified theory of justice is important because different theories—for example, libertarian, egalitarian, communitarian, or liberal—have different implications for how we should arrange our social, political, and economic systems, what our institutional goals should be, and what policies we should use to try to accomplish them. Moreover, even in cases where there is general convergence between theories of environmental ethics—for example, that we ought to reduce pollution, promote sustainability, and use resources efficiently—there tends to be considerable divergence on the details—such as how much pollution reduction, what form of sustainability, and how to allocate scarce resources.

We need to decide how to live. Quite a lot of how we live involves or is related to ecological systems and nonhuman organisms. Different theories of environmental ethics provide different accounts of how we should take those systems and organisms into consideration, and so what our policies, lifestyles, and behaviors should be. Therefore, we need to try to identify which theories are well justified and which are not.

1.3 THREE BASES FOR ENVIRONMENTAL ETHICS

Theories of environmental ethics aim to describe our moral relationships to the ecological and biological world. There are three dimensions of this relationship that form the basis for environmental ethics (Table 1.2). The first, and most widely recognized, is that we are dependent upon **ecosystem services** and **natural resources**. We need the clean air, fertile soil, pollinators, and potable water that are provided by ecological systems and processes. We use trees, minerals, fossil fuels, and animals to construct our homes, roads, electronics, and clothing, as well as to power our economies. We are vulnerable to environmental hazards and rely upon ecological systems for protection from disease vectors and natural disasters. In these and other ways our life, health, and socioeconomic systems are environmentally dependent. If we damage ecological systems or deplete or pollute resources faster than they can be repaired or replenished then current and future people will be harmed. Thus, one of the primary sources of environmental concern and bases for environmental ethics is that if we do not take care of the environment it will come back to harm us. Overfishing and depletion of freshwater aquifers will contribute to food insecurity. Destruction of wetlands will contribute to greater exposure to hurricanes and cyclones. Degradation of the ozone layer will contribute to increased rates of cancer. Air pollution will contribute to heart and lung disease. Deforestation will contribute to more frequent landslides.

However, our relationship to the environment is not limited to physical dependence, vulnerability, and economic resources. Ecological systems, biological diversity, and individual organisms can significantly enrich human life when we relate to them in appropriate ways. Many people have a spiritual connection with nature,

THREE BASES FOR ENVIRONMENTAL ETHICS			
HUMAN – NATURE RELATIONSHIP	Human Dependence and Vulnerability	Contribution to Human Flourishing	Moral Agent - Moral Patent
ILLUSTRATIVE TYPES OF VALUE	Instrumental Value/Economic Value	Cultural Value/ Aesthetic Value	Intrinsic Value/ Inherent Worth
ILLUSTRATIVE TYPES OF LANGUAGE	Natural resources/ Ecosystem Services	Enrichment/ Self-Realization	Duties/ Responsibilities
ILLUSTRATIVE FORMS OF RESPONSIVENESS	Conservation/ Wise Use	Appreciation/ Engagement	Preservation/ Respect

Table 1.2   This table summarizes three dimensions of the human-nature relationship that are frequently taken to justify environmental awareness and consideration. Each relationship is associated with particular types of value, language, and responsiveness. These bases for environmental ethics are not mutually exclusive, but as we will see in the chapters that follow, alternative approaches to environmental ethics prioritize different ones.

both in general and to particular places and species. Some draw creative inspiration, both artistic and scientific, from the natural world. Landscapes and natural phenomena are often beautiful and enable aesthetic experiences. People frequently find respite, renewal, and recreation in nature. The natural environment is often central to cultural traditions, practices, rituals, and identity. Appreciation of the natural world, openness to it, engagement with it, and study of it can contribute not just to our survival, but to our flourishing. This is a second basis for environmental ethics.

The third basis for environmental ethics concerns values in nature separate from humans. One of the perennial and central issues in environmental ethics is whether the environment matters (or has value) independent of its being useful to people or cared about by people. As we will see, there are many different accounts of which parts of the biological world have human-independent value, as well as what sort of value they possess. For instance, are collectives and systems as a whole valuable—for example, species and ecosystems? Are individual organisms—for example, plants and nonhuman animals? Does their being valuable mean that they ought to be afforded rights? Or just that they should not be harmed unnecessarily? If there is value in nature independent of humans, then it is a basis for direct consideration of and responsibilities toward the nonhuman environment.

To see the differences between these three bases for environmental ethics, consider the arguments made for maintaining water levels sufficient for salmon to run in rivers in the western United States, rather than allocating more water for agriculture, industry, or energy production. One argument in favor of maintaining the water flows and protecting the salmon is economic. It is good for tourism and the fishing industry for salmon to be able to swim upriver and spawn in large numbers. This rationale conceives of salmon as a natural resource. Another argument is that it is crucial to the traditions and practices of Native American communities in the region. This rationale conceives of the salmon as culturally significant and enriching. Yet another argument is that the salmon are a distinctive form of life crucial to the ecological integrity of the rivers. This rationale conceives of the salmon and their ecosystem as mattering independent of their usefulness or roles in human practices. As this example illustrates, the bases for concern for the natural environment are not mutually exclusive. The same environmental entity—in this case the salmon—are economically important, provide basic resources, are culturally significant, and are thought to be valuable in themselves. It is for this reason that a full accounting of environmental goods and values is crucial to environmental ethics. If the salmon are conceived of as only a natural resource, when they are in fact valuable in other ways as well, the result could be misinformed and poorly justified water allocation and ecosystem management policies.

As the discussion above indicates, the bases for environmental ethics are both *aspirational* and *proscriptive*. That is, environmental ethics is not only about what we ought not do to the environment or the ways in which it will come back to hurt us if we do not take adequate care of it. Environmental ethics also concerns the ways in which positive relationships with the natural environment can contribute to individual and social accomplishment and flourishing. A complete environmental ethic will provide an affirmative vision for how we should live with and relate to the ecological and biological world, not only a list of prohibitions.

1.4 THE RADICALNESS OF ENVIRONMENTAL ETHICS

Environmental ethics is radical in the sense that it challenges fundamental features and assumptions of conventional ethical perspectives and worldviews. First, by inquiring into whether there are human-independent values in the ecological world, environmental ethics requires that we reconsider the predominant **anthropocentric** or human-centered orientation of ethics. The idea that we could have responsibilities to the natural world itself is a departure from standard Western conceptions of ethics, which focuses on how we ought to consider and treat other people. Questioning anthropocentrism also involves reevaluating prevalent views about humanity's relationship with nature more generally—for example, the idea that humans have a unique or special status in the order of things. In this way, environmental ethics raises fundamental questions concerning the sort of creatures we are and our place in the world.

Second, as discussed earlier, many environmental problems are large-scale collective action problems. The seemingly mundane choices that we make, such as what to eat and how to get to work, cumulatively have implications for people decades from now and on the other side of the world because of how they relate to such things as climate change, pollution, and food security. Environmental ethics therefore requires rethinking the nature of ethical responsibility, as well as developing resources for analyzing and addressing problems involving multiple agents and diffuse causal relationships over time. Many of the things that we might have considered outside of ethics, such as what cars we drive and where we go on vacation, turn out to be proper objects of ethical evaluation.

Third, several approaches to environmental ethics challenge the idea that individuals—persons, animals, and organisms—should be the primary focus of ethical concern. The idea that individuals are what ultimately matter is often called **individualism**, and it is the predominant view in Western ethical traditions. It is individual people who are thought to have rights or be due consideration. However, several theorists believe that for environmental ethics a more collectivist approach is needed, one on which the primary objects of concern are ecosystems, species, and communities. These **holistic** approaches to environmental ethics require reconsidering whether the prevalent individualistic orientation of ethics is justified.

Finally, environmental ethics requires reevaluating familiar and entrenched features of our social organization and cultural practices. In the 150 years since the Industrial Revolution, those of us living in industrialized nations have significantly diminished and degraded our ecological resource base, and have created an array of ecological problems and challenges. Part of environmental ethics involves critically assessing cultural practices, social structures, value orientations, and outlooks that have enabled or contributed to this. For example, **ecofeminism** and the **environmental justice movement** highlight forms of domination, power, and privilege that are pervasive in Western culture and have contributed to ecological exploitation and social injustices. **Deep ecology** is critical of the ascendency of faith in techno-science, and highlights ways in which ideologies with a strong human-nature dichotomy can alienate people from deep engagement with and appreciation of the natural world. **Nonanthropocentrism** challenges the presumption that human beings are exceptional and elevated above the rest of nature, which is merely a resource for our use. Several theories of environmental ethics, both anthropocentric and nonanthropocentric, challenge economic dogma regarding the need for continual economic growth, as well as consumeristic conceptions of human flourishing that prioritize material success. Many theories also are critical of structural features of economic and political systems that make responding to ecological challenges difficult and that make ecologically problematic activities seem either innocuous or impossible to avoid.

So while environmental ethics is ultimately about our relationships with and treatment of the nonhuman environment, it involves asking challenging questions about ourselves, our worldviews, our ways of life, and our social, political, and economic systems.

1.5 SUMMARY

The primary questions addressed in this chapter were:

- What are environmental issues and environmental ethics?
- Why is studying and evaluating theories of environmental ethics important?

In the course of discussing these questions, this chapter explicated the central questions of environmental ethics, indicated the broad array of environmental issues that we face, and described the primary bases for environmental ethics. It also indicated the ways in which environmental ethics is intertwined with interpersonal ethics, as well as elucidated some distinctive features of environmental ethics and environmental issues. Finally, it showed how thinking critically about environmental issues, relationships, and values leads to questioning fundamental features and assumptions of conventional Western perspectives and worldviews, such as the growth paradigm and a strong human-nature dichotomy.

Overall, this chapter has been about the "what" of environmental ethics. The next chapter focuses on the "how."

KEY TERMS (SEE GLOSSARY FOR DEFINITIONS):

anthropocentric	ethics
deep ecology	holism
ecofeminism	individualism
ecosystem services	interpersonal ethics
environmental ethics	longitudinal collective action problems
environmental justice movement	natural resources
ethical theory	nonanthropocentrism

REVIEW QUESTIONS

- What are the three bases for environmental concern discussed in this chapter and how do they differ from each other?
- Why does environmental ethics involve reassessing our worldviews, attitudes, behaviors, lifestyles, and social systems?
- What are some of the distinctive value questions raised by environmental ethics?
- What makes something a longitudinal collective action problem?
- What does it mean to say that environmental ethics is both aspirational and proscriptive?
- What are the central questions of environmental ethics?

DISCUSSION QUESTIONS

- Do you find the reasons given for separating out the study of environmental ethics compelling? Why or why not?
- Do you believe that the three bases for environmental ethics discussed are of equal importance or is one more important than the others? Are there other bases for environmental concern than these three?
- Do you agree that the questions and challenges posed by the study of environmental ethics are radical? Why or why not?

FURTHER READING

Environmental ethics began to emerge as a distinct area of inquiry in the 1970s, which was a time of growing environmental awareness and concern. Rachel Carson's *Silent Spring* was published in 1962, an event that is often used to mark the beginning of the modern environmental movement, particularly in the United States. Much of the early work in the field involved clarifying the ethically distinctive features of environmental issues and questions, as well as discussing the extent to which new ethical outlooks and theories were needed. Here are several prominent and influential works that address these issues:

Attfield, Robin. *The Ethics of Environmental Concern*. Columbia University Press, 1983.

Hargrove, Eugene. *Foundations of Environmental Ethics*. Prentice Hall, 1989.

Leopold, Aldo. *A Sand County Almanac and Sketches Here and There*. Oxford University Press, 1968.

Naess, Arne. "The Shallow and the Deep: Long-Range Ecological Movements." *Inquiry* 16 (1973): 95–100.

Norton, Bryan. *Toward Unity among Environmentalists*. Oxford University Press, 1991.

Plumwood, Val. *Feminism and the Mastery of Nature*. Routledge, 1993.

Passmore, John. *Man's Responsibility for Nature: Ecological Problems and Western Traditions*. Charles Scribner's Sons, 1974.

Rolston, Holmes, III. *Philosophy Gone Wild: Environmental Ethics*. Prometheus Books, 1989.

Routley (Sylvan), Richard. "Is There a Need for a New, an Environmental, Ethic?" *Proceedings of the XVth World Congress of Philosophy* 1, no. 6 (1973): 205–10.

Singer, Peter. *Animal Liberation*. HarperCollins, 1975.

Taylor, Paul. *Respect for Nature: A Theory of Environmental Ethics*. Princeton University Press, 1986.

Warren, Karen. "The Power and Promise of Ecological Feminism." *Environmental Ethics* 12, no. 2 (1990): 125–46.

CHAPTER TWO

METHODS OF ENVIRONMENTAL ETHICS

ETHICS IS ULTIMATELY ABOUT how we *should* live, and particular ethical claims are about what *ought* to be the case or what we *ought* to do. We *ought* to volunteer in our communities. We *ought* to reduce our ecological impacts. We *ought* to be honest. This chapter is about how we can evaluate such prescriptive claims—ought and should claims—in a rigorous way by means of justification, reasoning, and evidence. By the end of this chapter it should be clear that ethics, including environmental ethics, is not just a matter of opinion. Ethical beliefs are open to evaluation and some are more informed and well reasoned than others. First, however, it is crucial to be able to distinguish evaluative and prescriptive claims from other types of claims, so that is where this chapter begins.

2.1 DESCRIPTION, EXPLANATION, PREDICTION, AND PRESCRIPTION

The distinctive feature of ethical claims is that they are **evaluative** and **prescriptive**. They aim to accurately depict what we *should* do, rather than *describe* what we have done in the past, *explain* why we did it, or *predict* what will happen in the future. To see the difference between description, explanation, prediction, and prescription consider the following set of claims:

1. Ninety percent of the world's fisheries are fully or overexploited.
2. This is the result of enormous global demand for seafood, proliferation of industrial fishing methods, global distribution systems, short-term economic incentives, and inadequate regulatory oversight.

3. The massive biological depletion from overfishing and its cascading effects through aquatic ecosystems are bad because they reduce biological diversity, diminish ecosystem services, and harm people, particularly local and traditional fishing communities.
4. Policies and regulatory capacity ought to be established to ensure long-term sustainability and fair access to fisheries.
5. It will be difficult to effectively regulate most fisheries due to the absence of strong institutional authority, inadequate governmental resources, the vast areas and complex supply chains involved, the power of industrial fishing interests, and rising demand due to growth in population and affluence.
6. It is unlikely that there will be substantial increases in fisheries sustainability and fair access to them.

Claim (1) is **descriptive**. It characterizes the way the world *is*. It is also an **empirical claim**. Whether it is true or not is determined by scientific investigation—that is, observation, measurement, experimentation, analysis, and modeling. The only way to find out whether a fish population is robust or depleted is to study it—for example, to monitor catch volume and fish size and age over time. It is true that 90 percent of the world's fisheries are fully exploited (~60 percent) or overexploited (~30 percent). The evidence for it is data collected by researchers, regulators, nongovernmental organizations, and fishing groups that has been synthesized by the United Nations Food and Agricultural Organization (FAO 2014, 37).

Claim (2) is also an empirical claim. However, in addition to being descriptive, it is **explanatory**. It proposes causal explanations for why the world is the way it is—in this case, factors that contributed to fisheries becoming so exploited. These causal explanations are not, however, **justifying**. That is, even if they are true, they do not justify overfishing. They merely explain why it occurs. This is also the purview of science, both physical sciences and social sciences. If we want to assess whether a proposed causal explanation is correct, we need to conduct observations, run experiments, analyze data, or otherwise test it. In this case, the factors cited in (2) are widely recognized as common causes of fisheries depletion. Enormous demand creates economic incentives for overfishing; industrial fishing fleets and global distribution systems make it possible and cost-effective; and lack of oversight enables it.

Claims (5) and (6) are not descriptive, since they do not depict the way the world is now or has been in the past. They are **predictive**, in that they concern what might happen in the future. Predictive claims are projective. They involve inferences from what is the case now to what will be the case in the future. For example, meteorologists predict the weather in the future based on present conditions, data on what followed similar conditions in the past, and knowledge about the relevant systems and processes. Their predictions of the weather are more reliable than mine because they have better data, more experience, superior models, and access to greater processing power. Moreover, it is standard scientific practice to make one's data and methods available for others to evaluate. This helps to ensure that they are sound. Therefore, not all predictions are equally speculative. We should be more confident of some predictions (including probabilistic ones) than others. In environmental discourse it is sometimes claimed that scientific prediction is not any better than common sense prediction. This is false for the reasons just discussed. Scientifically scrupulous expert predictions are better predictions, since they are based on more reliable data and methods. It is true that no one knows the future with absolute certainty, but that does not imply that no prediction is better than any other.

Claims (3) and (4) are not strictly descriptive or predictive. They are **evaluative** and **prescriptive**. They are claims about the *value* of things and what *ought* to be done. Claim (3) not only describes the effects of overfishing, it judges them to be *bad*. Claim (4) does not predict what will happen in the future, but asserts that fisheries *ought* to be managed more sustainably and justly. These claims are consistent with the fact that many fisheries currently are not being managed well. They are also consistent with the fact that it will be difficult to accomplish good management in the future, and might not be done successfully in many cases. The fact that something is not the case now and unlikely to be the case in the future does not imply that it should not be the case. Child abuse is bad and we should try to stop all instances of it, even though it does occur and it is unlikely that we will be able to eliminate it completely. Unfortunately, things are not always as good as they could be, and people do not always behave as they should. This is why prescriptive ethics is needed. It provides an account of how things ought to be, how they could be better, even if that is different from how they are now or the course that they are on for the future.

2.2 ENVIRONMENTAL ETHICS AND ENVIRONMENTAL SCIENCE

As discussed above, the fact that something *is* a particular way or that it is predicted that it *will* be that way does not imply that it is *good* or *ought* to be that way. An implication of this is that evaluative and prescriptive claims do not fall within the purview of the empirical sciences. Therefore, environmental sciences, such as ecology, climatology, ecological economics, environmental sociology, and environmental psychology, cannot themselves settle ethical questions. They provide information about what our social and ecological worlds are like now, as well as about future possibilities, including how our behaviors and policies could influence which of those possibilities are realized. However, since they are social, biological, and physical sciences, they are concerned with description, explanation, and prediction. Their subject matter does not include what ought to be.

Prescriptive claims depend upon value judgments and normative principles—claims about which things matter and how we ought to care about them—and this is the purview of **ethical evaluation and theory**. When scientists make prescriptive claims, which they often do, the claims always involve an appeal to what has value or to a principle that goes beyond the scientific findings. To see this, consider the follow-ing set of claims regarding global climate change:

1. The global means surface air temperature (GMST) has been increasing ~0.15–0.2 degrees Celsius per decade since the 1970s.
2. The dominant cause of the increase in GMST is the buildup of greenhouse gases, principally carbon dioxide, but also other gases such as methane and nitrous oxide, in the atmosphere since the Industrial Revolution.
3. The buildup of greenhouse gases has been the result of human activities, such as burning fossil fuels, deforestation, and animal agriculture, which have been driven by economic and population growth.
4. On our current emissions trajectory (given official international emissions reduction commitments), it is projected that by 2100 there will be a further increase in GMST of greater than 3 degrees Celsius.
5. The impacts of such a large and rapid increase in GMST are predicted to include: species extinction rates several orders of magnitude above background historical rates, hundreds of millions of environmental refugees due to such things as sea level rises and food insecurity, increases in the frequency and severity of extreme weather events and natural disasters, increases in political and military conflicts over natural resources as well as due to human migrations, and a proliferation of invasive species and disease vectors.
6. The impacts of global climate change, should they occur, will be very bad for current people, future generations, and nonhuman species, and will dramatically increase social injustices.
7. The detrimental impacts of climate change need to be avoided so far as is possible.
8. People ought to act now to aggressively mitigate future greenhouse gas emissions.
9. Countries ought to put policies into place that promote alternative energies and reduce overconsumption and population growth.
10. Individuals ought to become politically active to push for policies that would ac-complish these goals, and they ought to decrease their own emissions by reducing their consumption and energy usage as much as is feasible.

The first of these claims (1–3) are the purview of the empirical sciences. They aim to describe what the GMST was in the past, what it is now, and explain (causally) how it has come to be this way. The next set of claims (4–5) are predictive. They aim to project what will happen in the future under certain conditions (i.e., given a partic-ular future greenhouse gas emissions scenario). These claims are also the purview of the sciences, albeit with different methodologies, since they are not observational and make greater use of modeling. Claims (6–7), however, shift to ethical evaluation. They are not only about what could happen, but also involve claims about value and justice. In this case, the impacts are claimed to have widespread disvalue and to be unjust, and because of this they need to be avoided. Finally, claims (8–10) involve prescriptions regarding what sort of behaviors and policies ought to be adopted to avoid the impacts of climate change. They are about what our goals ought to be and how we ought to go about accomplishing them. Claims (6–10), the evaluative and prescriptive claims, cannot be scientifically determined. As discussed earlier, even when we know what is the case and what is likely to be the case, we do not yet know what ought to be the case. Justifying prescriptive claims involves value analyses and normative principles, which are the domain of ethical theory.

Although they are not scientifically determinable, prescriptive claims do need to be empirically informed in a number of respects. First, value claims are often empirically dependent. For example, the claim that wolves should be valued because of the role they play in their ecosystems depends in part on the facts about their behavior and their impacts on the systems. The claim that salmon have cultural value to the Lower Elwha Klallam Tribe depends upon the facts about the historical relationship between their culture and the species. Thus, the legitimacy of evaluative claims very often depends upon empirical or scientific information. Historically, one of the reasons given in support of the claim that we ought not care about how we treat nonhuman animals was that they cannot feel pain. However, there is now very strong physiological and behavioral evidence that this is mistaken. For instance, many nonhuman animals (e.g., mammals and birds) have the type of nervous system that makes the experience of pain possible and they exhibit avoidance and reactive behaviors in response to the sort of stimuli that cause pain in us. Thus, scientific investigation, observation, and analogical reasoning have undermined a key empirical claim in a prominent argument against caring about the welfare of animals (see Section 7.1).

Second, application of ethical principles to concrete situations requires a thorough understanding of the relevant facts about the situations. Suppose that the following normative rule is well justified: We ought not be concerned about nonnative species unless they are likely to be ecologically disruptive, detrimental to native species, or economically problematic. Applying this principle to determine if we should be concerned about a particular population—for example, ruddy ducks in the United Kingdom or Japanese knotweed in the United States—requires knowing if the species is nonnative and what its ecological and economic impacts are. As discussed earlier, facts without principles do not generate prescriptive guidance on concrete issues; but neither do principles without facts.

Third, well-justified prescriptions require understanding what the available courses of action are and what their outcomes are likely to be. Suppose we reach the conclusion that we ought to aggressively reduce greenhouse gas emissions, but that we ought to do so without compromising the ability of people to lift themselves out of poverty. Developing ethically responsible policies will require a thorough understanding of the causes of global poverty, the barriers to addressing it, and how different policies are likely to affect emissions as well as economic development and income distributions in the future. For example, one of the primary barriers to reducing poverty is energy access. About 1.3 billion people, 18 percent of the global population, lack access to electricity (IEA 2016). Therefore, lifting people out of poverty while reducing emissions will require widely distributed, reliable, low-emission methods of electricity production. Which types of energy sources and policies are conducive to bringing this about are descriptive and predictive questions spanning the physical and social sciences, and they are crucial to developing well-justified policy prescriptions.

Fourth, prescriptions need to be informed by the facts about us. For example, an ethic that requires people to care about strangers in the same way as they care about their own children will be at odds with human psychology and fails to appreciate the role of the parent-child relationship in human life. Environmental ethics is about the nonhuman world, but it aims to describe the norms that are justified *for us* to follow and the way in which *we* ought to live. The ethical norms for asocial, emotionless, self-reliant, or nonbiological beings would be very different from those for human beings.

So while ethical claims are distinct from descriptive, explanatory, and predictive claims, and are not determinable by the scientific method, it is impossible to do practical ethics well without a strong empirical understanding of ourselves and the world. Environmental ethics must be informed by environmental and biological sciences, as well as social and political sciences.

✳ BOX 2.1

GLOBAL CLIMATE CHANGE

Many people regard global climate change as the world's most pressing environmental problem. It also intersects with and exacerbates many other environmental challenges. As a result, it is discussed frequently throughout this textbook. Therefore, it is important to be clear on what it is and why it is regarded as so important.

The global mean surface temperature of earth has been increasing for the past one hundred years. Since 1970 it has been doing so at a rate of ~0.15–0.2 degrees Celsius each decade (Hansen et al. 2010). The causal process underlying this, the greenhouse effect, is well established. Energy from the sun enters the earth's atmosphere as shortwave radiation. Some is absorbed or captured, and some is reflected back out by the atmosphere and the earth's surface. The energy that is absorbed heats the earth and is then radiated as longwave radiation. Some types of gas molecules in the atmosphere absorb the longwave radiation and re-emit part of it back toward the earth. In this way, heat is "trapped" by the atmosphere, thereby making the earth warmer than it would be if those gas molecules were not there. None of this is scientifically contested. Without

(cont.)

BOX 2.1 *(cont.)*

the greenhouse effect, the earth's surface temperature would be around −18 degrees Celsius (0 Fahrenheit) instead of 15 degrees Celsius (59 Fahrenheit).

The more heat-trapping molecules (or greenhouse gases) that there are in the atmosphere, the greater the greenhouse effect, and the greater, all other things being equal, the global mean surface air temperature (GMST) of the planet. There are many greenhouse gases—methane, nitrous oxide, and perfluorocarbons—and they absorb and re-emit radiation at different rates. Carbon dioxide is by far the most abundant greenhouse gas. Although its global warming potential (or rate at which it absorbs and re-emits heat) is much lower than that of other greenhouse gases, its abundance makes it the greatest cumulative contributor to the greenhouse effect.

The concentration of greenhouse gases in the atmosphere has increased dramatically since the start of the Industrial Revolution. The concentration of carbon dioxide in the atmosphere is now greater than 400 parts per million, up from ~280 ppm at the start of the industrial revolution. The primary source of the carbon dioxide increase is the combustion of hydrocarbons or fossil fuels, principally oil, natural gas, and coal. There are other contributing causes to the increasing GMST (Figure 2.1). Nevertheless, greenhouse gases emitted as

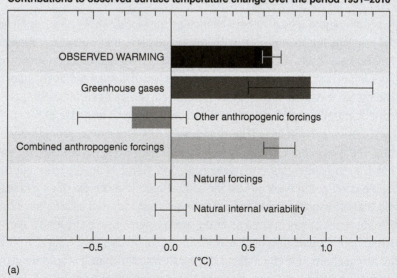

Contributions to observed surface temperature change over the period 1951–2010

(a)

(cont.)

BOX 2.1 *(cont.)*

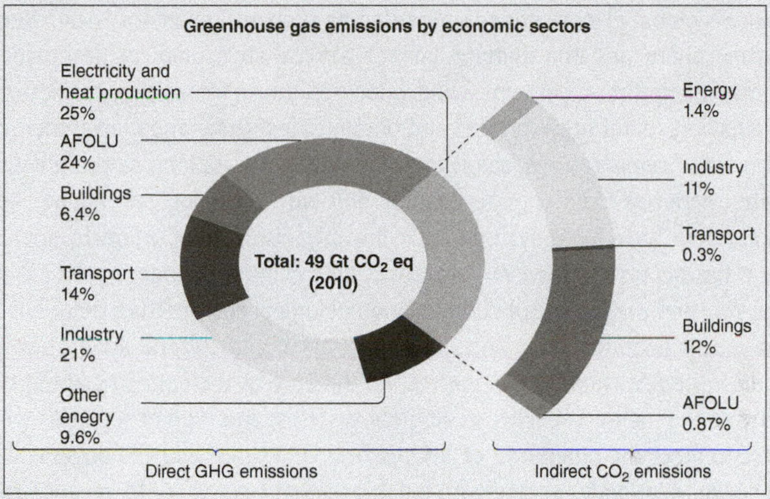

(b)

Figures 2.1 The above figure (a) indicates the contribution of different sources to observed GMST increases from 1951 to 2010. The black lines indicate the likely ranges of contribution and the bars are the midpoints of those ranges. Although there is considerable uncertainty involved—which is why the ranges are so large—it is clear that anthropogenic greenhouse gas emissions are by far the greatest contributor to observed temperature increases. The lower figure (b) indicates the contribution of different economic activities to total greenhouse gas emissions in 2010. Fossil fuel combustion in electricity generation, heat production, industry, and transportation is the largest source of emissions. AFOLU stands for Agriculture, Forestry, and Other Land Uses.

Source: IPCC (2014).

a byproduct of industrial human activity and the climatic feedbacks that this causes are the primary drivers (IPCC 2014).

Even the complete cessation of emissions would not prevent further anthropogenic (or human-caused) climate changes from occurring, given the duration that greenhouse gas molecules, particularly carbon dioxide, remain in the atmosphere, the prevalence of climatic and ecological feedbacks, and climatic and ecological momentum generally (Gillett et al. 2011). At this point, the issue is not whether anthropogenic global climate change will occur. It is how great its magnitude will be.

(cont.)

BOX 2.1 *(cont.)*

Why is global climate change regarded as such an important issue? Because the atmosphere and the climate impact almost all ecological processes and systems—precipitation patterns, wind velocities, storm intensities, species ranges and behaviors, plant growth rates and bloom dates, snow and glacial melt rates, air and water temperatures, sea levels, and ocean pH. As long as there has been climate, there has been climate change, and with it ecological change. And as long as there have been systems of living organisms, adaptation to ecological change has occurred. However, anthropogenic climate change involves a much higher *rate* and *magnitude* of climatic and ecological change than there has been in the recent historical past. This makes biological and cultural adaptation more difficult, for both us and other species. At the core of the concerns about global climate change is that species, ecological systems, and human societies will not be able to meet the **challenge of adaptation**, and that failure to do so will have high social, economic, ecological, and biodiversity costs. With respect to impacts on people, the Intergovernmental Panel on Climate Change (IPCC), which is charged by the United Nations with synthesizing the published science on climate change, reports:

> Projected climate change–related exposures are likely to affect the health status of millions of people, particularly those with low adaptive capacity, through: increases in malnutrition and consequent disorders, with implications for child growth and development; increased deaths, disease, and injury due to heat waves, floods, storms, fires, and droughts; the increased burden of diarrheal disease; the increased frequency of cardio-respiratory diseases due to higher concentrations of ground-level ozone related to climate change; and the altered spatial distribution of some infectious disease vectors. (IPCC 2007b, 12)

With respect to nonhuman species, one recent study found that 24 to 50 percent of bird species, 22 to 44 percent of amphibian species, and 15 to 32 percent of coral species have traits that make them "highly vulnerable" to climate change (Foden et al. 2013). Another found that up to 1 in 6 species will be threatened with extinction on the current emissions trajectory (Urban 2015). Earlier studies projected that 15 to 37 percent of species will be committed to extinction by 2050 on mid-level emissions scenarios (Thomas et al. 2004), with significantly increased rates of extinction even on very optimistic (or low) future emissions scenarios (IPCC 2007b).

(cont.)

BOX 2.1 *(cont.)*

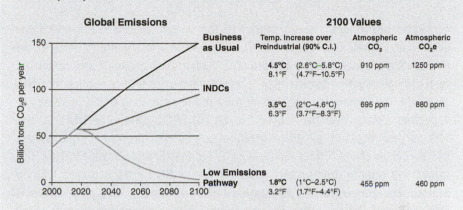

Figure 2.2   What the magnitude of global climate change will be depends in large part on the amount of future greenhouse gas emissions. Limiting the GMST increase to 2°C above preindustrial levels, as called for under the UNFCCC, requires dramatic reductions from current emissions levels (the business-as-usual scenario). Thus far, the emissions reduction commitments that countries have made—their INDCs or Intended Nationally Determined Contributions (see Box 16.3)—fall far short of what is necessary. Even if the current commitments were achieved, the atmospheric concentration of CO_2 is projected to reach around 695ppm, and all greenhouse gases taken together are projected to reach the equivalent (CO_2e) of 880 ppm of CO_2. This would likely cause increases in the GMST that far exceed 2°C.

Source: ©2016 Climate Interactive

In fact, the effects of global climate change are already occurring. Air temperatures are increasing (NASA 2015). Precipitation patterns are changing (IPCC 2014). Species ranges are shifting toward the poles (Chen et al. 2011). Plants are blooming earlier (Ellwood et al. 2013). Animals are migrating earlier (Gill et al. 2013). Snow pack, glaciers, and ice sheets are melting faster (IPCC 2014). The oceans are acidifying (NOAA 2015). Sea levels are rising and coastal flooding is becoming more frequent, severe, and persistent (Kopp et al. 2016). There are already **climate refugees**, people who have been displaced by the impacts of climate change, such as drought and sea level rise, and climate change already has been implicated in the extinction of some species (e.g., the golden toad).

The magnitude and rate of anthropogenic climate change depends upon the amount of future global greenhouse gas (GHG) emissions. The larger the amount of future emissions, the higher the concentrations of GHGs, the greater the anthropogenic forcing of the climate system, and the more severe the climatic and

(cont.)

BOX 2.1 *(cont.)*

ecological disruptions. The signatories of the United Nations Framework Convention on Climate Change (UNFCCC), which is the primary international effort for reducing global emissions and promoting adaptation capacity, are committed to pursuing reduction sufficient to "prevent dangerous anthropogenic interference with the climate system," which they define as limiting GMST increases to 2 degrees Celsius over preindustrial levels (UNFCCC 2009). The UNFCCC has 196 parties, including all major greenhouse gas emitters—the United States, the European Union, China, India, Russia, Indonesia, and Brazil. Meeting this target will require dramatically reducing future GHG emissions and limiting atmospheric concentrations of carbon dioxide to around 450 ppm, which is less than half the projected concentration on the current business-as-usual scenario (Climate Interactive 2015). There is tremendous potential for reducing the social and ecological challenges and losses associated with global climate change through mitigating future emissions. If a low emissions pathway could be accomplished (see Figure 2.2), the challenge of adaptation would be much less and there would be far fewer climate-change-driven species extinctions, economic and agricultural disruptions, refugees, and conflicts than on the current emissions pathway.

As indicated above, global climate change exacerbates numerous other environmental issues, from species conservation to food security. It is also raises questions about the sustainability of our current economic systems and lifestyles, as well as how we conceive our relationship with the natural world. There are myriad ethical considerations, such as rights, justice, and future generations, associated with how we ought to mitigate and adapt to climate change. It is in many respects the ultimate longitudinal collective action problem (Box 6.1, Box 8.6), and has been called a "wicked problem" and the "perfect moral storm" because it is global and intergenerational, may require structure changes to address, and the actors involved have competing perspectives and interests (Gardiner 2006). For all of these reasons, it will be frequently discussed throughout this textbook.

2.3 JUSTIFICATION IN ETHICS: THE PHILOSOPHICAL METHOD AND EVALUATING ARGUMENTS

Claims in environmental ethics need to be scientifically informed, but they cannot be settled by scientific methods alone. How then are claims in value theory and normative ethics evaluated? Over the course of this textbook we will study several different approaches to justification. What they have in common is that they aim to establish their conclusions by means of *rational (or reason-based), empirically informed inquiry.* This is sometimes referred to as the **philosophical method**, though it is by no means confined to the field of philosophy. At its core is the commitment that we ought to believe whatever has the best *arguments, reasons, justification,* and *evidence* in its favor, since these are *truth-favoring* or *truth-indicating.* If we want to know whether we should regard nonhuman animals as morally considerable, and one view has sound reasoning and true empirical claims in support of it, while the other has fallacious reasoning and false empirical claims, then we ought to believe the former. The one that is well justified and empirically informed is more likely to be true, and we are aiming for truth.

This last point, that in ethics we are aiming at truth, is important. There are other activities that make use of argumentation and evidence, but which do not aim at truth, but rather at persuasion. Political campaigning is often like this, as is advertising, and in some case lawyering. The goal in these activities is not to uncover what is true but to convince people to believe or do something, independent of truth—to acquit the defendant, vote for the candidate, or purchase the product. In the past this use of argumentation might have been referred to as rhetoric or sophistry, in order to distinguish it from science and philosophy, which aim at truth. Thus, the philosophical method is the use of arguments, reasons, justification, and evidence with the goal of gaining knowledge. Inquiry begins with a question or problem, and the aim is to reach the most justified answer. This requires approaching ethics with an open mind and an understanding that we are all fallible. What we believe at the start of an inquiry is not always what will be the most justified conclusion (and so what we should believe) at the end.

A conclusion is warranted to the extent that it is based on good information and good reasoning. This form of justification is standardly represented by the following argumentative form:

Premises
_____ [Inference]
Conclusion

What this form represents is that the premises of an argument are meant to justify the conclusion by means of an inference. The inference could be either *inductive* or *deductive.* A **deductive inference** is when it is intended that the conclusion must, by logical necessity, be true if the premises are true. An **inductive inference** is when it is intended that the conclusion is likely to be true if the premises are true. In both cases, the implication is that we ought to believe the conclusion because it is supported by strong reasons or considerations. (Inductive reasoning is not worse or weaker reasoning than deductive reasoning. In fact, the sort of reasoning commonly used in science, medicine, and everyday life is inductive. There are good and bad inductive inferences, just as there are good and bad deductive inferences, as we will see throughout this textbook.)

Here is an example of an argument represented in this way:

1. It is always wrong to cause unnecessary pain. [Premise 1]
2. Concentrated animal feed operations (CAFOs) cause pain unnecessarily. [Premise 2]
   _____ [Inference]
3. Therefore, people ought to be vegetarians. [Conclusion]

An advantage to representing arguments in this way is that it helps to clarify their elements and structure—what the premises are, what the conclusion is, and how the premises are supposed to justify the conclusion. Often arguments are incompletely presented or have vague or unclear elements. (Such arguments are sometimes called *enthymemes*.) Representing arguments formally requires filling in and clarifying the details. Another advantage is that it brings into focus two types of questions about the argument. First, *are the premises true?* Second, *is the reasoning in the inference valid?* That is to ask, *if* the premises are true, does the conclusion follow? There are two, and only two, ways for an argument to go bad: if the premises are false (or unsubstantiated) or the inference is invalid (or fallacious). If the premises of an argument are true and the reasoning is valid, then the argument is *sound*. Sound arguments have well justified conclusions. Thus, in applying the philosophical method to ethics, including environmental ethics, the aim is to gather good information and apply good reasoning to reach well-justified conclusions about value and how we ought to live.

In the case of the argument above, the inference is invalid. The conclusion does not follow from the premises. The reason for this is that there are lots of sources of meat besides meat produced from CAFOs—for example, hunting, ranging livestock, and small farming operations. Moreover, the premises do not actually have to do with eating meat, but with producing it in a particular way. Therefore, in order to make the inference valid, the conclusion needs to be modified into:

3'. CAFOs are wrong.

Now the reasoning in the argument is valid. If it is always wrong to cause unnecessary pain, and a particular activity or practice does so, then it is wrong to engage in that activity or practice. What about the premises? Are they true?

It is true that the standard practices of CAFOs, which are large agricultural enterprises where animals are raised in confined conditions, cause very large amounts of pain to animals due to the living conditions (e.g., crating and caging), the way the animals are treated (e.g., debeaking and castration), and how they are slaughtered. CAFOs are also unnecessary, in the sense that people's nutritional needs could be met without them. In fact, it would be easier to do so without them than it is with them, since they

make inefficient use of agricultural resources (Section 6.1). However, it would be diffi-
cult to meet current levels of meat demand in many affluent nations without CAFOs.
So, in evaluating the argument, the meaning of "necessary" must be clarified. Moreover,
Premise 1 is false. It is not always wrong to cause unnecessary pain. We do it to ourselves
all the time in acceptable ways—for example, getting tattoos and long distance running.
Given these considerations, Premise 1 needs to be revised to something like this:

1'. It is always wrong to cause significant amounts of pain *to others, without their consent, for the satisfaction of mere preferences.*

This is a much more plausible premise than 1. Not only does 1' clarify what is meant by
"unnecessary," it addresses the fact that causing unnecessary pain is not always wrong
by specifying conditions when it is. Moreover, Premise 2 can be revised in according
with it, since CAFOs cause significant pain to others (animals), without their consent,
in order to satisfy culinary preferences that involve large amounts of inexpensive meat.
The reasoning thereby remains valid. Here, then, is the revised argument:

1'. It is always wrong to cause significant amounts of pain to others, without their
consent, for the satisfaction of mere preferences. [Premise 1']
2'. CAFOs cause large amounts of pain to others, without their consent, for the
satisfaction of mere preferences. [Premise 2']
_____ [Inference]
3'. Therefore, CAFOs are wrong. [Conclusion]

This is a much more promising argument than the original. The premises are plausible and the conclusion follows from them—the reasoning is valid. There is, however,
one more issue that needs to be addressed before the soundness of the argument can
be determined: whether the pain of animals is morally relevant. That is, whether the
"others" in Premise 1' includes nonhuman animals.

Whether animals have moral status such that their suffering is morally considerable is discussed at length in Chapters 5 and 7. Here the point of the discussion has
been to illustrate the structure of argumentation, as well as emphasize the importance
of assessing the truth or plausibility of an argument's premises as well as the validity
of its reasoning when determining whether its conclusion is well justified. Moreover,
as was demonstrated above, this very often requires clarifying ambiguous or vague
elements of the premises and reformulating them into more plausible claims. It can
also involve modifying the argument so that the reasoning is valid. It is crucial to good
environmental ethics (indeed, to all forms of inquiry) to always try to interpret ideas
and arguments in their strongest or most promising form when evaluating them. This
is sometimes called the **principle of charity.** To fail to formulate ideas and arguments
in as plausible (or charitable) a way as possible is to commit the **straw man fallacy.**

It is a fallacy (or error in reasoning) because showing that a weak version of a view is mistaken does not warrant concluding that a more promising version is also mistaken.

It is also crucial to evaluate claims and principles on the basis of their consistency with other ethical beliefs. For example, many people argue that it is inconsistent to support animal welfare laws for pets and support the existence of CAFOs for food. *If* there is no difference between pet dogs and CAFO pigs that justifies differential moral consideration of them, then consistency requires that at least one of those views be modified.

Thus, the method for environmental ethics is to study, formulate, and evaluate arguments for different views on: how to understand the human relationship with the natural environment, what aspects of nature and the human-nature relationship have value, what principles or rules those values justify, and what those principles imply for how we ought to live. Therefore, quite a lot of this textbook involves presenting the arguments for and against different views in environmental ethics, as well as indicating the strengths and weaknesses of those arguments.

2.4 SKEPTICISM ABOUT ETHICS

Ethics is about how we ought to live. It is *prescriptive* and *normative*. We are supposed to avoid acting unethically and aim at acting ethically, regardless of whether we want to. It is wrong to lie, cheat, and steal even if we desire to do those things and do not care about ethics. In this way, ethics is different from the normativity of a game. When playing a game, such as football or chess, there are norms, rules that we have to follow, that make a claim on us. These rules can be formal (e.g., how the pieces move on the board) or informal (e.g., no getting help from observers). But they only apply when we are involved in the game. If we don't want to play that is fine, and then the behavioral guidelines simply don't apply.

In contrast, ethics is thought to be ineluctable. Its claim on us is not contingent on our desires or whether we agree to play. The ineluctable normativity (or prescriptivity) of ethics is distinctive of it. But it invites questions about where this normativity comes from, as well as about how ethics is possible or even whether it exists at all. **Ethical skepticism** is the view that it does not. There are two types of ethical skepticism. One is the view that there are no true claims about how we ought to live. This is sometimes called **ethical nihilism**. The other is that there are true ethical claims, but they do not have any special normativity. This is sometimes called **amoralism**.

The normativity of ethics—the claim that it is thought to make on us—rests in its justification. Prescriptive ethical claims are supposed to be normative because we have strong reasons to act in accordance with them. Their normativity is supposed to be ineluctable because those reasons apply independent of our attitudes or beliefs. Thus, ethical nihilism is really the view that no ethical claims are more rationally justified than any others. However, we have already seen that this is mistaken. Ethical beliefs and theories can be more or less justified based on the plausibility of the premises and the validity of the reasoning in support of them. For example, the view that people have different moral worth based on their ancestry or the color of their skin, and that it is permissible to treat those with certain ancestry or skin color like property, is an unjustified view. It is based on false beliefs about biology and violates the principle of treating like cases alike. The view that all people have equal worth because they are alike in all morally relevant respects, such as their self-awareness, ability to reason, and capacity to suffer, is more justified, and for this reason no one should be treated like property. Some ethical views are better justified than others.

What about amoralism? Amoralism is the view that we have no reason to behave ethically outside of our own wants and desires. However, if some ethical beliefs and theories are more justified than others then this view is mistaken. The reasons to act ethically just are the reasons that make some ethical claims more justified than others. Why is it wrong to steal money from vulnerable people? Because they have worth as individuals that is violated in doing so; they are not mere things to be used for the ends of others. If a person asks, "But why should I care that it is wrong?" they are, again, asking, "What reason do I have not to do this?" The answer, again, is that it violates the rights or disregards the worth of other people. Perhaps those who think that amoralism is plausible really mean to be asking something like, "Why is it in my interest to be ethical?" However, in asking this question they are restricting the kinds of reasons that can be justifying, and in excluding good reasons they are again being irrational. In some cases it might not be in a person's interest to act ethically, but that does not mean they do not have a good reason to do it. It only means they do not have a self-interested reason. Therefore, that some ethical beliefs are more justified than others implies that amoralism is mistaken.

If ethical skepticism is mistaken, why are some people drawn to it? One way people are drawn to it is by inferring from the fact that each person decides for herself what her ethical beliefs are to the conclusion that there are no more or less justified beliefs, just different opinions. On this view, each belief is just as good as another, and no ethical theory is more justified than any other.

It is true that each person is responsible for her own judgments (or entitled to her own beliefs), not only about ethics, but also about science and religion. However, it does not follow from this that there are no true or false beliefs. Some people believe that the earth is flat, and they are mistaken. They have an inaccurate belief about the world. Moreover, given the abundance of available evidence about the shape of the planet, their belief is unjustified. So the mere fact that people must choose what they believe (or are entitled to their beliefs) within a particular subject is not itself sufficient to establish that there are no more or less justified beliefs on the subject.

An ethical skeptic might claim that the response above works for scientific beliefs, but not for ethical beliefs. But why think that? That is, why think that because people must choose which ethical claims to believe no claims are more justified than others? The answer would have to be that with scientific beliefs, but not ethical beliefs, there is something to appeal to in order to adjudicate which beliefs are more justified. However, we have seen that there is a method for evaluating ethical beliefs. It is not the scientific method, but it is based on arguments, reasons, justification, and evidence. So the **everyone-must-choose-their-ethical-beliefs argument** (or the everyone-is-entitled-to-their-own-belief argument) for ethical skepticism appears unsound.

A second way in which people are led to ethical skepticism is that there is often deep and widespread disagreement on ethical issues. Some people believe that the reason for this is that there is not any fact of the matter about ethics—that is, people are able to disagree so widely and persistently because there is no correct view. This might be called the **argument from disagreement** for ethical skepticism.

People who offer this argument focus on the amount of ethical disagreement in the world. However, there is also quite a lot of agreement. It is rare to find someone who does not value human life, does not prefer pleasure to pain, or does not want meaningful relationships with other people. It is rare to find a culture that does not value cooperation among its members, does not advocate respect for ancestors, or does not encourage helping others. So while there is ethical disagreement, there are also considerable commonalities in ethical beliefs among individuals and across cultures. These commonalities might be starting points from which a justified ethical theory could be developed. Moreover, much of the apparent ethical divergence in the world is not due to differences in values, but differences in empirical beliefs. As these differences are resolved, ethical disagreement should diminish. The growing worldwide acceptance of universal human rights is an example of this.

However, the primary problem with the argument from disagreement is that it conflates *justification* with *consensus*. The extent to which there is disagreement on a view or belief is not a good proxy for whether there is good justification for it. For example, there is widespread disagreement about whether evolution by natural selection is the process by which biological complexity and diversity develops. A poll in the United States found that 65 percent of US adults believe that humans and other species evolved over time, while 31 percent believe that humans and other species have existed in their present form since the beginning of time. Moreover, among the majority that believes in evolution, 35 percent believe it occurs by natural processes alone, while 24 percent believe it involves natural processes guided by a supreme being (Pew Research Center 2014). Nevertheless, there is a fact of the matter, and the accumulated evidence in favor of evolution from fields such as genetics, evolutionary biology, experimental biology, developmental biology, ecology, and paleontology is overwhelming. (Among those who are most familiar with the evidence, the scientific community, the belief in evolution is much higher. For example, 98 percent of the members of the American Academy for the Advancement of Science believe biological diversity arises through evolution [Pew Research Center 2014].) Lack of consensus does not imply that there is no correct answer.

This is true for ethics as well. There is considerable disagreement globally regarding whether women should be afforded the same rights and opportunities as men.

However, the fact that there are divergent views does not imply that each position is equally well justified. The view that women ought not be afforded equal political, social, and legal standing is unjustified because it is based on false beliefs about the differences between men and women, mistakenly takes real differences between men and women to be ethically relevant, and/or involves a fallacious appeal to tradition. (The **fallacy of appeal to tradition** is to wrongly infer from the fact that some activity has been going on for a long time—in this case, that there is a tradition of disempowering women—to the conclusion that it is therefore not problematic.) As has repeatedly been emphasized, arguments, reasons, justification, and evidence can be used to adjudicate competing ethical views among people and between cultures. So the fact of disagreement does not imply that no ethical views are more justified than others.

A third way in which people are sometimes led to ethical skepticism is from the fact that there is never complete certainty about one's ethical beliefs. The reasoning behind this view is that since it is always possible that a person's ethical beliefs could be mistaken, no ethical beliefs can be proven to be the correct ones.

The difficulty with this **absence-of-certainty argument** for ethical skepticism is that it uses a standard of justification that is unreasonable and applied almost nowhere else. For example, it is possible that all of our scientific beliefs are false. After all, what we think of as the physical world could in reality be just an illusion or a computer simulation. It is possible that the laws of physics change every billion years, or that a super-being controls them with its mind and can change them at its whim. But, of course, these possibilities do not lead people to conclude that no scientific theory is more justified than any other or that there are no true scientific beliefs. What people rightly conclude is that there is a level of certainty that cannot be achieved, and if a person demands that much certainty she is bound to be disappointed. Consider, for example, the US judicial system. Proving that a person is guilty of committing a crime does not require absolute certainty. It need not be the case that it is impossible that one be mistaken about whether the offender is guilty. The standard of justification is "beyond reasonable doubt." If the skeptical criterion for proof were applied in the judicial system it would be impossible to prove that anyone is guilty (or innocent!) since it is always possible that our judgments are mistaken.

There are all sorts of standards for proof and justification. The level required by the proponent of this argument for ethical skepticism—that it be impossible for one to believe something and yet it be false—is extremely demanding. Indeed, there is very little that can be known with that sort of certainty. Moreover, it does not follow that everything that fails to meet this extremely stringent standard is equally unjustified or unproven. Some scientific theories are more justified than others. The theory that the sun is the center of our solar system is more justified than the theory that the earth is, even though neither can be proven with absolute certainty. Just so, some ethical beliefs are more justified than others even though none can be proven with the kind of certainty the skeptic demands.

We can see how inappropriate the skeptical criterion for proof is for ethics by con-sidering the human situation and the need for ethics in the first place. It is part of our situation that we are inescapably in the middle of things, making ethical decisions all the time—what to eat, how to dispose of our waste, whether to give to charity. We cannot withhold all ethical judgments until we have achieved a perfect level of proof and justification. We have no choice but to do the best we can with the arguments, reasons, justification, and evidence that we have at our disposal at the time when we must decide how to act. To insist on absolute certainty is to misunderstand the complexity, imme-diacy, and ineluctable nature of the human ethical situation. It is the wrong standard of justification for the field of inquiry, just as it is for science, medicine, and courts of law.

We should not be skeptical about ethics, including environmental ethics. Instead, we must be clear about what justification in ethics involves. To say that a value claim, prescription, or ethical theory is well justified is to say that it has arguments, reasons, and evidence in its favor, in comparison to the alternatives. The stronger the arguments, rea-sons, justification, and evidence for it, the more justified it is. It may turn out that more than one belief or theory is well-justified, and that there can be reasonable disagreement about them. But this is very different from the claim that no ethical theories are well justified or that all ethical beliefs have equal merit. They do not. As we have already seen (and will continue to see), some ethical views are more justified than others. The goal of environmental ethics is to determine which ethical theories and beliefs regarding ecological systems and nonhuman organisms are the more justified ones. This is not just a matter of opinion.

2.5 GOD AND ETHICS

An evidence- and reason-based approach to ethics is used in the field of environmental ethics and will be employed throughout this text book. It is not, however, the only approach to answering ethical questions. Another approach is to look to an authority for ethical guidance. Theological approaches to ethics look to religious authorities, often in the form of scripture or religious leaders. A full discussion of the relationship between religion and rationality is beyond the scope of what is possible here. However, I should like to make a brief case in favor of the view that theological and philosophi-cal approaches to environmental ethics ought to converge.

Let us assume that God exists—that there is something like an omniscient (all-knowing), omnipotent (all-powerful), omnibenevolent (purely good) being that created the world. If God exists and God created the world, then God is responsible for the creation of humans and for our possessing rational capacities. That is, God created us with the cognitive and creative abilities to try to understand not only how the world works, but also how we ought to live. If God is omnibenevolent, then these abilities should work. It would be deceptive to create us with the ability and drive to engage in rational inquiry but for it to be unreliable. It would be unjust to punish us for acting wrongly if our God-given reasoning capacities are misleading. So, if God exists, then God is something of a guarantor of our rationality. So long as we use it properly, it should help us understand how we ought to live.

The reliability of our rational capacities is also supported by the presumption that, if God exists, God is also rational. (If this is not the case—i.e., if God exists and is irrational or nonrational—then all theological claims would be undermined, since God's "plans" would be either nonexistent or unknowable.) If God is rational, then there should be a rational order, including an ethical system, embedded in the created world. In many theological traditions, one of the ways in which humans are thought to be in God's image is that we share in God's rationality. Thus, we should be able to use our rational capacities to understand that system. That is, we should be able to use reason and study of the world to learn how we ought to live. This, in fact, is at the core of the **natural law tradition** of religious ethics.

Either God exists or God does not exist. If God does not exist, then empirically informed rational inquiry is the best method for determining how we ought to live. If God does exist, then empirically informed rational inquiry should be a reliable method for determining how we ought to live. (This is, of course, compatible with the view that God also reveals ethics through scripture, prayer, and prophesy, for example.) Therefore, whether or not God exists, a reason-based approach to ethics should be an effective approach.

2.6 SUMMARY

The primary questions addressed in this chapter were:

- How can views in environmental ethics be rigorously assessed?
- What is the relationship between environmental ethics and environmental science?

The chapter demonstrated how to assess ethical beliefs and theories in a rigorous way by critically evaluating the justification, reasoning, and evidence offered in support of them. It explained the differences between descriptive, explanatory, predictive, evaluative, and prescriptive claims, including that the distinctive features of ethical claims are their evaluative and normative content. Ethics is about what is right and good (and wrong and bad), as well as about what we ought and ought not do. The chapter showed why the truth or falsity of ethical claims cannot be established by scientific methods alone, but that in order for ethical beliefs and theories to be well justified they must be empirically informed. It provided reasons why ethical skepticism is unwarranted, as well as why the primary arguments for ethical skepticism, such as the argument from disagreement and the everyone-must-choose-their-ethical-beliefs argument are unsound. It discussed why empirically informed, reason-based inquiry should be a reliable method for determining which ethical views are well justified and which are not.

Ethics is not just a matter of opinion or tradition. It is possible to critically evaluate ethical views, including those concerning the environment, by assessing the considerations offered in support of them, as well as the acceptability of their implications. Therefore, the chapters that follow focus on the reasons, justification, and evidence presented for different theories of environmental ethics and for different ethical beliefs on environmental issues. The topic of proof and justification in ethics will also be revisited throughout this textbook (see, in particular, Section 10.5).

KEY TERMS (SEE GLOSSARY FOR DEFINITIONS):

absence-of-certainty argument

amoralism

argument from disagreement

challenge of adaptation

climate refugees

deductive inference

descriptive claim

empirical claim

ethical evaluation (ethics)

ethical nihilism

ethical skepticism

ethical theory

evaluative claim

everyone-must-choose-their-ethical-beliefs argument

explanatory claim

fallacy of appeal to tradition

inductive inference

justifying claim

natural law tradition

philosophical method

predictive claim

prescriptive claim

principle of charity

straw man fallacy

REVIEW QUESTIONS

• What is the philosophical method and why is it thought to be an effective method for ethical investigation?

• What are the differences between description, explanation, prediction, evaluation, and prescription?

• In what ways does empirical information about ourselves and the world need to inform ethical beliefs and evaluations?

• What are the elements that make up an argument and what are the ways in which an argument can go wrong?

• What is the challenge of adaptation and why is anthropogenic climate change such an important environmental issue?

• What is skepticism about ethics and why is it thought to be unjustified?

DISCUSSION QUESTIONS

- Do you agree with the responses to the arguments for ethical skepticism discussed in this chapter? Why or why not?

- Is the argument presented in this chapter that religious ethics and reason-based ethics ought to converge sound?

FURTHER READING

There are many good introductory texts on logic, reasoning, and argumentation. Here are two of them:

Feldman, Michael. *Reason and Argument*, 2nd edition. Pearson, 1998.

Hurley, Patrick. *A Concise Introduction to Logic*, 12th edition. Wadsworth, 2014.

Two excellent introductions to the issue of justification and ethics, including how they relate to ethical skepticism, ethical realism, and the relationship between God and ethics are:

Shafer-Landau, Russ. *Whatever Happened to Good and Evil?* Oxford University Press, 2003.

Rachels, James, and Stuart Rachels. *The Elements of Moral Philosophy*, 8th edition. McGraw-Hill, 2014.

A number of insightful books and collections on the ethical dimensions of climate change have been published in recent years, including:

Arnold, Denis, ed. *The Ethics of Global Climate Change.* Cambridge University Press, 2014.

Broome, John. *Climate Matters: Ethics in a Warming World.* W. W. Norton and Company, 2012.

Di Paula, Marcello, and Gianfranco Pellegrino, eds. *Canned Heat: Ethics and Politics of Global Climate Change.* Routledge, 2014.

Gardiner, Stephen. *A Perfect Moral Storm: The Ethical Tragedy of Climate Change.* Oxford University Press, 2011.

Jamieson, Dale. *Reason in a Dark Time: Why the Struggle against Climate Change Failed—and What It Means for Our Future.* Oxford University Press, 2014.

PART II: NATURE AND NATURALNESS

CHAPTER THREE

THE NORMATIVITY OF NATURE

THE CONCEPTS OF "NATURE" and "naturalness" play a prominent role in environmental ethics. How, where, and to what extent natural systems ought to be protected from human activities is frequently contested. Novel biotechnologies are often objected to on the grounds that they are unnatural, while other practices, such as eating animals, are defended on the grounds that they are natural. There is even a growing discourse about whether human impacts on the environment are now so great that we have reached the "end of nature" and the dawn of a new geological age—the **Anthropocene** (the human age)—in which humans are the dominant planetary force (see Chapter 17). Therefore, clarifying the term "nature" and determining the extent to which naturalness is normative and/or valuable are a prominent part of environmental ethics. This chapter focuses on the definition and normativity of nature. The next chapter concerns the value of nature and naturalness.

3.1 WHAT IS NATURE?

The terms "nature" and "natural" are used in two distinct ways: descriptively and evaluatively/prescriptively. When someone says of a person, "That is his natural hair color," the term is being used descriptively. It is not an evaluation of whether his hair color is good or bad, right or wrong. It is an observation about its not being artificially colored, in just the same sense as the observation that he is 6 feet tall or has brown eyes. People frequently use "nature" in this descriptive way when they talk about the environment. For example, it is common to refer to "nature areas" or the "natural behaviors" of organisms.

However, when people talk about "natural foods" they often mean to not only describe, but also to evaluate. What is intended is not just that those foods are different from unnatural (or processed) foods, but they are superior. Similarly, when people say that genetically modified crops are "unnatural," they typically mean both that the plants contain genes from other species and that this is objectionable.

Thus, the first thing to notice about the term "natural" is that it is ambiguous. Sometimes it is used to merely describe and sometimes it is used to evaluate and prescribe. This section focuses on the descriptive sense of "natural", the next section discusses the prescriptive senses.

What is the descriptive meaning of "nature"? There are actually *a lot* of descriptive uses of the term. Here are three common ones (and you can probably think of others):

- Something is natural if it is subject to the "natural laws" that govern the material world, such as those of physics and chemistry. This sense of "nature" contrasts it with supernatural.
- Something is natural if it is part of the biological world. On this sense, the natural world is the living world. For example, a naturalist is a person who studies flora (plants) and fauna (animals).
- Something is natural if it is separate from humans and independent of human agency. This sense of "natural" contrasts it with artifactual.

Because there are many different definitions of "nature," whether something is natural depends upon which definition is being used. Consider, for example, human beings. The laws of nature apply to us, and we are evolved biological organisms, but we are not separate from human agency. That something can be part of nature on some definitions but not others seems to invite this question: What is the correct definition of "nature"? However, when it comes to definitions, there often are not right or wrong ones, but more or less useful ones, *and which definitions are useful depends upon context.* To see this, consider the term "family." If a person is at the doctor's office and is asked about her "family history" regarding heart disease, it would be counterproductive for her to give information about her adoptive parents. The reason for this is that, in that context, biological or genetic information is what is needed. But when the person she is dating asks to meet her "family," the person is asking to meet the people she loves, cares about, and depends upon—that is, her adoptive parents.

Similarly, the "right" definition of nature depends upon context. When practicing medicine and doing biomedical research human beings must be considered part of nature—in the sense that natural laws apply to us—because understanding the chemical and physical processes in the body are crucial to promoting health. However, when studying technology and engineering, it makes sense to distinguish what is human design from what is not. So the proper question for present purposes is not "Which definition of nature is correct?" but "Which definition of nature is most useful in the context of thinking about environmental issues and trying to understand our ethical relationships with the nonhuman world?"

Many environmental issues concern how people ought to value, impact, treat, modify, and protect nonhuman organisms and non-built environments. Therefore, it is extremely useful to have a term that picks out areas, entities, and processes that are independent from human beings. For this reason, it is common in environmental ethics to use the term "natural" in the following descriptive way:

> Something is **natural** to the extent that it is independent of human design, control, and impacts; and something is **artifactual** to the extent that it is the product of human design, control, and impacts.

Again, this is not to suggest that this is *the* correct definition of nature, only that it is a useful one for present purposes. On this definition, naturalness and artifactualness are a matter of degree. A wilderness area is more natural than a suburban park, which is more natural than a parking lot; a wild mouse is more natural than a genetically engineered mouse, which is more natural than a mechanical "mouse." As we will see in what follows, being clear about what is meant by "natural" is crucial when assessing whether (and in what ways) it ought to be used prescriptively.

✺ BOX 3.1 | TOPIC TO CONSIDER

WHAT IS WILDERNESS?

In an influential essay titled "The Trouble with Wilderness; or Getting Back to the Wrong Nature," William Cronon claimed that wilderness "is quite profoundly a human creation" (1995, 69). On its face, this seems an odd claim. After all, wilderness is distinguished by its separateness from people. "Wilderness" is the term used to refer to places untrammeled by humans, where the spontaneity and otherness of nature dominates. How could places like the Tongass Forest in Alaska or Congo Basin in west equatorial Africa be human creations?

However, Cronon did not mean to claim that the *places* and *processes* that we call "wilderness" are our creations. His claim was that the *idea of wilderness* dominant in North American environmentalism is a human creation: "For many Americans wilderness stands as the last remaining place where civilization, that

(cont.)

BOX 3.1 *(cont.)*

all-too-human disease, has not fully infected the earth. It is an island in the polluted sea of urban-industrial modernity, the one place we can turn to escape from our own too-muchness" (1995, 69). This romantic or sublime conception of wilderness rose in prominence following the Industrial Revolution, and is exemplified in the work of nature writers such as John Muir and Henry David Thoreau. Prior to its emergence, "To be a wilderness . . . was to be 'deserted,' 'savage,' 'desolate,' 'barren'—in short, a 'waste,' . . . Its connotations were anything but positive, and the emotion one was most likely to feel in its presence was 'bewilderment' or terror" (1995, 70). Cronon tracks these negative associations to biblical conceptions of wilderness, in which it "was a place to which one came only against one's will, and always in fear and trembling. Whatever value it might have arose solely from the possibility that it might be 'reclaimed' and turned toward human ends—planted as a garden, say, or a city upon a hill. In its raw state, it had little or nothing to offer civilized men and women" (1995, 71).

The romantic conception of wilderness helped to mobilize support for creating large national and international park and reserve systems where human activities are significantly limited. Approximately 15 percent of the terrestrial surface and inland waters of the earth and ~4 percent of the oceans are now officially protected in some way (~10 percent of the ocean area within national jurisdictions are protected) (UNEP-WCMC and IUCN 2016). Moreover, human too-muchness and too-manyness is what drives most of the world's environmental problems. Humans appropriate a disproportionate share of the planet's primary plant production. Humans consume resources faster than they can be replenished. Humans transform ecological spaces and systems to suit their purposes. Humans generate enormous amounts of pollution and waste. Furthermore, many people value nature for its spontaneity, otherness, and distinctiveness from humans. Why, then, do Cronon and others believe that we need to rethink the romantic conception of wilderness?

The underlying concern is that conceiving of wilderness in this way creates an oppositional binary between pure wilderness on the one hand and impure humans on the other hand. The implication then seems to be that any human presence in nature is inherently defiling. Some thinkers find this conceptually objectionable, as we will see during the discussion of the principle of noninterference (see Section 3.2.1). We are evolved biological organisms. How can it be that we are so radically separate and different from the rest of the biological and ecological world that our mere presence is problematic?

Critics of the wilderness ideal also worry about its practical implications. They are concerned that the human/wilderness binary results in an environmentalism

(cont.)

BOX 3.1 *(cont.)*

overly focused on how to make wilderness secure from us—sometimes called **fortress conservation** by its critics—rather than on how to live well with nature. But how people can flourish along with nature through responsible use is the more important issue, especially since there is so little pristine wilderness left. Cronon and others also argue that the separateness ideal can lead to unjust conservation policies, such as restricting indigenous peoples from engaging in traditional practices on their historical lands once they are designated for protection; and that it can foster marginalization of environmental issues that are not wilderness- and conservation-oriented, such as urban environmental justice issues involving the disproportionate exposure to environmental hazards faced by high-minority and low-income communities. In addition, Cronon in particular is concerned that the wilderness ideal blinds us from appreciating the wildness that is intertwined with the built environment, such as the organisms and ecosystems in our back yards and urban parks, which are also worthy of respect and wonder.

Nevertheless, wilderness protection has resolute defenders, such as conservation biologist Michael Soulé (2013) and environmental thinker Eileen Crist (2013). On their view, we need protected areas for wilderness and biological conservation now more than ever, precisely because there is so little left and so much at risk. When species are lost, they are irreplaceable. The evolutionary history encoded in them and the future evolutionary possibilities they provide are eliminated. Moreover, human activities, particularly when they are resource-intensive, disrupt what is wonderful about wilderness: its spontaneity and otherness. We have already appropriated so much of nature that fairness requires that we leave most of what is left for other species, on this view.

These thinkers recognize that we must also try to improve people's lives, reduce poverty, respect indigenous people's autonomy, and address environmental injustices. But they believe that we should do these things while also conserving as much remaining wilderness as possible, regardless of its usefulness to people. As a result, they are critical of what some call the "New Conservation," which instead of focusing primarily on wilderness and biodiversity conservation, advocates managing natural systems both to protect biodiversity and to promote ecosystem services for people, especially the poor.

What do you think about the wilderness debate? Does the wilderness ideal need to be rethought? Or is it important to highlight and protect places without (or with minimal) human impacts? Should wilderness protection and biological conservation be the primary goals in managing such places, or should greater consideration be given to human needs? The extent to which human wants and

(cont.)

BOX 3.1 *(cont.)*

needs should be considered in the context of ecosystem management, resource allocations, and biodiversity conservation is central to many environmental issues and will be discussed throughout this textbook: Should we take a more hands-on approach to ecosystem management and species conservation or expand the historically dominant park and reserve model (Sections 13.5–13.7)? Should we embrace the idea that humans have become such a dominant force on the planet that we are now in a new geological age—the Anthropocene—in which we need to take greater responsibility for designing and managing ecological processes (Chapter 17)? Does increasing food security and alleviating poverty take priority over species conservation (Section 16.3, Box 16.2)?

3.2 IS NATURE NORMATIVE?

As discussed above, the term "natural" is frequently used to not only describe, but to evaluate and prescribe—that is, to indicate what ought and ought not be done. There are actually several different ways in which naturalness is commonly used prescriptively: (1) that we ought not interfere with nature, (2) that we ought to follow nature, (3) that something is wrong when it is unnatural, and (4) that we ought to maintain the balance of nature.

3.2.1 Is It Wrong to Interfere with Nature?

Many people believe that it is wrong to interfere with natural ecosystems, even if it does not cause harm, unless there is a compelling reason for doing so. For example, we should not feed wild animals or introduce even benign nonnative species. This is frequently called the **principle of noninterference**. To be clear, the principle of noninterference does not claim that it is always wrong to interfere with natural systems and organisms. It claims that it is **prima facie wrong**. If something is prima facie wrong, then it ought not be done unless there are overriding considerations. For example, it would not be permissible to feed wild animals just because it is fun or to introduce nonnative species just because they are pretty. However, it would be permissible to alter or interfere with a system in order to produce food or to repair human-caused damage. Moreover, even when we have good reason to interfere, we ought to minimize our impacts. Thus, on this view, we ought to aim, so far as possible given our other ethical responsibilities, for a "hands-off" policy toward nature.

A number of objections have been made to the idea that we have even a *prima facie* duty not to interfere with nature. One is that it is incompatible with our form of life. Many people believe that what is distinctive about human beings is our robust cultural capacity. No other species innovates, accumulates, and disseminates ideas, social systems, and technologies at the rate or on the scale that we do. Moreover, our capacity for innovation and our ability to modify our environment is crucial to how we live. We could not survive or thrive without clothes, shelter, tools, agriculture, and medicines. We define the "ages" of human history—stone, bronze, iron—by the technologies in use; and the great "revolutions" in human history—agricultural, industrial, information—refer to major technological transitions. We are, on this view, *technological animals*. The idea that it is *prima facie* wrong for us to interfere with the natural world strikes many as being contrary to the human form of life, in which innovation, creation, and modification are central.

A second, related objection to the idea that interference with nature is *prima facie* problematic is that it would imply that all engineering and technology are as well. Everything from computers to yogurt involves modifying the natural world to some extent—for instance, cultivating organisms or transforming materials. If the mere fact of interfering is presumptively problematic, innovation and use of technology would only be acceptable if there were an overriding ethical reason in their favor. However, as we will see later (see Box 15.4), many people believe that the presumption should be the other way around. According to the **innovation presumption**, technological innovation and use are permissible unless they are shown to be ethically problematic, whereas a noninterference presumption would have them be problematic unless they are shown to be ethically necessary.

A third objection to the principle of noninterference is that it is not useful, since it is impossible for us to not interfere with the natural world. At the bare biological level, we must eat, breathe, radiate, and decompose, all of which involve exchanges with the natural environment and interactions with nonhuman organisms. We also must move through landscapes and procure food. We simply cannot be in the world and avoid interfering with nature. What we need is an ethic that helps us make distinctions between which forms or instances of interference are acceptable and which are not. A general "try not to interfere" principle fails to be helpful, because the issue is not whether or not to impact the natural world. It is when and in what ways we ought to do so.

Here is another way in which this point is sometimes made (Vogel 2002). On any descriptive definition of nature, either human beings are part of nature or we are not. If we are part of nature, then everything we do and create is natural—from styrofoam cups to football stadiums—and we cannot interfere with nature. If we are not part of nature, then everything we do is unnatural—from collecting food to using fire—and we always interfere with nature. Either way, the principle of noninterference fails to discriminate among human actions. Either everything is interference (and so *prima facie* wrong) or nothing is interference (and so unproblematic). Thus, the principle of noninterference is not useful in environmental ethics, where the whole point is to distinguish between what we ought and ought not do.

These objections to the idea of noninterference, if they are cogent, do not imply that it is permissible to do whatever we want to nature and nonhuman organisms. They just show that appeals to interference are not an appropriate basis for determining what we should and should not do, and that we must look elsewhere for guidance.

BOX 3.2   TOPIC TO CONSIDER

"HANDS OFF" NATURE?

When thinking about whether we should try to take a more "hands off" approach toward nature it can be useful to reflect on cases. Here are a few involving wild animals to consider:

1. *Bird Feeders*: Feeding wildlife is a common practice. In the United States, over 50 million people engage in wildlife feeding around their homes, principally bird feeding (USFW 2011). It is often problematic to feed birds. It can alter their behaviors and expose them to predators in ways that are detrimental to them. For example, it is estimated that domestic cats kill over a billion birds each year in the United States, often by stalking near feeders (Loss et al. 2013). But bird feeding can also be done conscientiously, with appropriate foods, at appropriate times of the year, at stations that are well maintained, and for species or in contexts that do not increase predation. Is it *prima facie* wrong to engage in conscientious bird feeding? If not, why not? If so, is the enjoyment people take in watching birds in their backyards sufficient justification to override the *prima facie* rule of noninterference?

2. *Wildlife Photography*: Observing and photographing wildlife is also a common practice. In the United States, over 70 million people engage in wildlife watching, which is more than angling (~33 million) and hunting (~13 million) combined. The majority of wildlife watchers do it around their homes. However, over 22 million take trips to do so (USFW 2011). Observing and photographing wildlife is thought to be a low-impact wilderness activity, in comparison to hunting and fishing. However, the presence and movement of people, particularly when they are trying to get close to wild animals to get good views and take good photographs, can startle animals and disturb nesting sites and other habitats. When observers are common in an area—for example, around frequently used hiking trails or heavily dived coral reefs—it can affect the movements and feeding patterns of wild animals in the area. But, as with bird feeding, it is possible to engage in responsible wildlife photography by not getting too close to animals, avoiding off-limit areas, and going with guides knowledgeable on how to avoid disrupting habitats. Is it *prima facie* wrong to participate in responsible wildlife photography in wilderness areas? Why or why not?

3. *Assisting Animals*: Animals are often injured by human activities and the built environment. They are hit by cars, attacked by pets, coated by oil from spills, or

(cont.)

BOX 3.2 *(cont.)*

Image 3.1a   A northern gannet, coated from the BP Deep Horizon oil spill in the Gulf of Mexico in 2010, being cleaned at a rescue center set up by the International Bird Research Center in Fort Jackson, Louisiana, USA.

Source: REUTERS / Alamy Stock Photo

Image 3.1b   Volunteers attempt to aid a pod of pilot whales that beached themselves at Farewell Spit, South Island, New Zealand in 2005.

Source: Ilan Adler/ Wikimedia Commons

(cont.)

BOX 3.2 *(cont.)*

they fly into windows. In those cases, assistance and rehabilitation are typically thought to be justified by a responsibility of restitutive justice (Section 9.2). However, wild animals also are often injured by other wild animals or by natural events and processes. For example, dolphins, porpoises, and whales sometimes beach themselves and get stranded on land. When this occurs, people and organizations frequently try to assist them by keeping them alive until the tide comes in or moving them closer to the water. Is it *prima facie* wrong to assist wildlife when the cause of their distress is not anthropogenic? Why or why not?

What do your reflections on these cases indicate, if anything, about whether there is a *prima facie* duty of noninterference? And, if there is a presumption in favor of noninterference, what do they indicate about the contexts in which it applies and the sorts of considerations that are sufficient for overriding it?

3.2.2 Should We Follow Nature?

Many people believe that what is natural for people and what occurs in nature should guide how we behave. For example, arguments in defense of eating animals often appeal to biological facts about us—for instance, humans are physiologically capable of eating meat and the capacity to eat meat evolved because it was advantageous for our ancestors to do so. Arguments also often appeal to facts about the nonhuman world—predators eat meat, lions eat gazelles and hawks eat chipmunks, so it is permissible for us to do so as well. The reasoning operative in these arguments is that if we are doing something *natural for us* or *common in nature*, then it is permissible for us to do it. We ought, in some sense, to follow or imitate nature.

However, the inference from (1) "Behavior X occurs in nature" to (2) "It is permissible to engage in behavior X" is widely recognized by ethicists as problematic for reasons famously articulated by John Stuart Mill:

In sober truth, nearly all the things which men are hanged or imprisoned for doing to one another are nature's every-day performances. Killing, the most criminal act recognized by human laws, Nature does once to every being that lives; and, in a large proportion of cases, after protracted tortures such as only the greatest monsters who we read of ever purposely inflicted on their living fellow creatures. If, by an arbitrary reservation, we refuse to account anything murder but what abridges a certain term supposed to be allotted to human life, Nature also does this to all but a small percentage of lives, and does it all in the modes, violent and insidious, in which the worst human beings take the lives of one another. Nature impales men, breaks them as if on the wheel, casts them to be devoured by wild beasts, burns them to death, crushes them with stones like the first Christian martyr, starves them with hunger, freezes them with cold, poisons them by the quick or slow venoms of her exhalations, and has hundreds of other hideous deaths in reserve. . . . Everything, in short, which the worst men commit either against life or property is perpetrated on a larger scale by natural agents" (Mill 1904, 17–18).

Nature is not an ethical guide for us, since so much that is common in nature—such as forced copulation and deception—is clearly wrong for us to do. Mill's argument uses a form of argumentation called **reductio ad absurdum** or reduction to absurdity. It aims to show that if you accept a principle—in this case, that if something occurs commonly in nature, then it is permissible for us to do—the implications are absurd and so unacceptable. Therefore, the principle should be rejected. *Reductio ad absurdum* is a common type of argument in applied ethics, including environmental ethics.

To see the practical implications of Mill's view, consider this formal representation of one of the arguments for meat eating mentioned earlier:

1. Eating other animals occurs in nature.
2. If something occurs in nature, then it is acceptable for us to do.

----

3. Therefore, it is acceptable for us to eat other animals.

If Mill's view is correct, then the second premise of this argument is false and the argument is unsound, since there are many things that occur in nature that are not acceptable for us to do. It is true that lions eat other animals. It is also true that male lions keep prides and sometimes kill their young. That male lions do these things does not mean that it is permissible for male humans to do them. This does not imply that eating meat is wrong. Whether and when it is depends upon many other considerations, including how we ought to value nonhuman animals (see Chapters 5 and 7). But it does imply that neither meat-eating nor any other practices can be justified by appeal to what occurs in nature or the behaviors of other species.

It is tempting to respond to Mill's argument with something like this: "When people say we should follow nature, they do not mean all of it, but only some aspects of it." However, for this sort of response to work there must be an independent basis or standard for determining which things in nature are appropriate for us to emulate and which things in nature are not. In which case, that standard or independent basis and not "nature" is doing all the normative or prescriptive work. Again, nature is not a guide to what we ought to do.

This is not to claim that it is wrong to look to nature for ideas in other domains. **Biomimicry** is based on the recognition that the natural world can be a source of inspiration, insight, and solutions in art and engineering. Sustainable architecture often draws from the structure of ecological systems and processes, and mobile robots frequently mimic the movement of living organisms, such as lobsters, bees, roaches, snakes, and dogs. The Millean claim is only that nature should not be taken as *ethically* guiding. Studying nature can provide suggestions on how to design low-waste systems, how to build stronger materials, or how to construct a high-mortality infectious disease. But there is nothing in nature to tell us which of those we ought to do. It takes a standard from outside the natural world to make those evaluations.

What about the idea that *human nature* should be our guide, that we should do what is *natural for us*—for example, that we should eat meat since we are biologically capable of it and evolved the capacity to do it because it was advantageous to our ancestors? This form of reasoning is thought to suffer from the same sorts of problems as the idea that we ought to imitate nature. We are capable of a great variety of things, some of which are wonderful, and some of which are horrible. There is a long human history of genocide, slavery, and oppression of women. The fact that people are capable of these things does not imply that it is permissible to do them. Similarly, the fact that something was advantageous in the past (or even the present) in terms of increasing an individual's biological fitness does not tell us that we ought to do it. If killing competitors and forcing copulation were fitness enhancing—that is, if they increased the probability of reproductive success—they would still be unethical. The principle that we ought to do what is natural for us— in the sense that we have done it in the past, it is evolutionarily advantageous, or we have the capacity to do it—has absurd and unacceptable implications. Therefore, this *reductio ad absurdum* concludes, we should reject the idea that human nature is normative.

It is important in ethics, including environmental ethics, to be alert for normative appeals to human nature. It is common to hear people try to justify behaviors, such as infidelity and selfishness, on the grounds that they are "human nature." Human nature does exist. We are different from other species, in terms of the form of our bodies, the structures of our brains, and our psychological and cognitive tendencies and capacities. There is a genetic ("nature") component to this and the sciences of human nature—for instance, neuroscience, genetics, and evolutionary biology—can teach us a good deal about the biological bases of our form of life. Moreover, our genetics circumscribes what is possible for us. For example, we cannot live without an oxygenated gaseous environment and we must care for our newborns in order for them to survive.

However, genetics is by no means destiny. All of our traits are the product of *both* our biology and our environment. Everything is nature *and* nurture, from how tall we are and our culinary preferences to our temperament and our intelligence. Furthermore, and crucially for present purposes, the sciences of human nature are *descriptive*. They can tell us something about how we are, how we came to be that way, what our tendencies are, and what is possible for us. But they do not tell us what we *ought* to do or how we *ought* to be. We have both cooperative and antisocial capacities and tendencies; we can forgive or we can take revenge; we can make peace or we can wage war; we can eat a meat-based diet or a plant-based diet; we can exploit natural resources for short-term gain or conserve them for future generations. Each of these is consistent with our biology, with our "nature." Therefore, appeals to human nature cannot justify one practice or policy over the other. To take human nature as normative is to confuse descriptive and explanatory accounts of the kind of creature we are with prescriptive accounts of what we should do (see Section 2.1).

For the reasons above, the idea that we should look to nature, including human nature and evolutionary history, as a guide for what we ought to do is widely rejected by ethicists. The form of reasoning "Events of type X occur in nature, therefore it is permissible for us to do X" is commonly referred to as the **fallacy of appeal to nature**. The form of reasoning "Behavior X has a biological or evolutionary basis (or we have a proclivity toward X), therefore we ought to do X" is an instance of this, and perhaps should be called the **fallacy of appeal to human nature**. As discussed earlier (Section 2.4), the form of reasoning "There is a history of people doing X, therefore it is permissible for us to X" is commonly referred to as the **fallacy of appeal to tradition**.

☀ BOX 3.3   TOPIC TO CONSIDER

POPULATION DYNAMICS AND THE BALANCE OF NATURE

In discussions about environmental issues, it is common to hear appeals to the *harmony of nature* or the *balance of nature*. However, what some people see as balance in nature others see as population dynamics. On the latter view, ecosystems are not organized systems. The appearance of "balance" is just the outcome of each individual expressing its own form of life, trying to survive and reproduce. Moreover, rather than being harmonious, nature is characterized by privation, predation, and death; it is "red in tooth and claw." The reason for this is that given the finitude of resources in any ecosystem—for example, food, mates, and habitat—most organisms die prior to reproducing. If this did not

(cont.)

BOX 3.3 *(cont.)*

occur, there would be exponential population growth. For example, a single pair of rabbits would result in thousands of rabbits in just a few generations.

The terms "balance" and "harmony" are clearly metaphorical when used to describe nature and ecosystems. What do you think they are supposed to mean and convey? Do you agree with the above critique of the "harmony of nature" and the "balance of nature"? Or do you think those ideas can hold up to critical scrutiny? If so, are they descriptive or normative? Do they accurately describe the way nature is? Do they tell us something about how things ought to be or what we ought to do? Or does appealing to them in a normative way commit a fallacy of appeal to nature?

3.2.3 Is a Behavior Wrong If It Is Unnatural?

Practices and behaviors are often criticized for being unnatural. For example, genetically modified organisms are frequently objected to because they involve altering genomes in ways that could not occur without human intervention—for instance, creating goats with spider genes, rice with daffodil genes, yeast with sweet wormwood genes, and corn with bacteria genes (see Box 3.4). In interpersonal ethics, in vitro fertilization, human cloning, and homosexuality have each been objected to on the grounds that they are unnatural.

However, unnaturalness objections are difficult to sustain. The problem is that they seem to either assume their conclusion or else equivocate on the meaning of "unnatural." Take for instance, the unnaturalness argument against genetically modified crops:

1. Genetically modified crops are unnatural.
2. Anything unnatural is wrong.

—————————

3. Therefore, genetically modified crops are wrong.

If by "unnatural" is meant "wrong" or "forbidden," then the argument does not justify its conclusion, it merely asserts it. Premise 1 would just be the claim that genetically modified crops are wrong. When a premise in an argument is also the conclusion of the argument it is a fallacy called **begging the question** or **assuming the conclusion**. But if "unnatural" does not mean "wrong," then for the argument to be sound there must be some meaning of the term "unnatural" that makes both Premise 1 and Premise 2 true. However, it is exceedingly difficult to see what that meaning could be. For example, the fact that something is uncommon in nature, does not occur at all in nature, could not have occurred without human intervention, or is not the evolved function of something does not make it problematic. If they did, then marathons, smartphones, hot air balloons, and chihuahuas would be unethical. Thus, in order to make the first premise true and the second premise plausible—that is, for it not to have absurd implications—the meaning of "unnatural" must change between the premises. But then the inference from the premises to the conclusion is not valid, since they concern different meanings of "unnatural." The argument would thereby commit what is called the **fallacy of equivocation** (or, sometimes, the **fallacy of ambiguity**).

There is a religious variant of the argument from unnaturalness, on which "unnatural" is identified with divinely proscribed or contrary to divine law. This type of argument can be valid. That is, it can avoid the fallacies of equivocation and question-begging. However, it would also undermine the normative significance of "naturalness" rather than salvage it, since the normativity would be grounded in the divine will and not nature. Thus, in the end, it is not really an argument from unnaturalness at all, and its soundness would depend upon whether God exists, whether God's will determines ethics, and whether God proscribes the practice at issue. Those are questions beyond the scope of this discussion (see Section 2.5). However, it should be noted that with respect to genetically modified crops, many religious ethicists and leaders have endorsed them. For example, the Vatican not only views them as acceptable, but believes that they should be promoted as part of the effort to achieve global food security (Vatican 2009).

If arguments from unnaturalness are unsound, it does not follow that GMOs and human cloning are permissible. All it means is that their being "unnatural" on some meaning of the term does not make them wrong or objectionable.

✳ BOX 3.4

GENETICALLY MODIFIED CROPS: INTRINSIC AND EXTRINSIC CONCERNS

People have been intentionally hybridizing organisms from different species for millennia by means of breeding and grafting. Wheat, grapefruit, tangelo, peppermint, and plumcot are examples of interspecific hybrid plants. There are a large number of intentionally created interspecific hybrid animals as well, such as the mule (donkey–horse) and beefalo (bison–domesticated cow). Although immensely successful in producing organisms with useful traits, hybridization through traditional breeding techniques has significant limitations. For instance, there is a lack of control over which traits offspring receive from each parent

(cont.)

BOX 3.4 *(cont.)*

(which is why back-breeding is needed) and there are constraints on possible genetic combinations (due to sexual compatibility and viability).

Beginning with the development of recombinant DNA techniques in the 1970s, these constraints have been increasingly loosened. The techniques enable isolation of genes that code for particular desired traits in individuals of one species and insertion of those genes into the genome of individuals of another species. This makes possible the creation of organisms with genomic material from species that could not have reproduced or combined in the absence of intentional gene level intervention—for example, rice with maize genes and salmon with ocean pout genes.

Hundreds of varieties of genetically modified (GM) crops have been created. However, only a small number of them are commercially cultivated. The most common GM crops are corn, cotton, soybeans, beets, and canola that have been engineered with bacteria genes to be resistant to general-use herbicides, particularly Monsanto's Roundup herbicide (Roundup Ready) and Bayer's Liberty herbicide (LibertyLink). These commodity crops have also been engineered to produce their own pesticide. These are called Bt crops, since the gene that confers the trait is from a bacterium called *Bacillus thuringiensis*. Crops engineered to be disease-resistant are also cultivated. The most prominent of these is papaya engineered to be resistant to a mosaic virus that had previously threatened yields in Hawaii. Some virus-resistant squash is also cultivated, and GM cassava resistant to a virus that has decimated yields in parts of Africa has been in development for some time. Genetic engineering of animals for agricultural purposes also occurs. For example, there are goats that have had golden orb spider genes inserted into their genome so that they produce protein precursors for silk in their milk, and salmon have been engineered with ocean pout genes so that they grow much more rapidly. In addition to agricultural applications, genetically engineered hybrids are also created for biomedical, scientific, conservation, and recreational purposes.

The mere existence of interspecific individuals is not out of the ordinary. Cross species hybridization is common among both plants and animals in the wild. Moreover, as mentioned above, it has long been employed in agriculture to engineer organisms with advantageous traits. Nevertheless, many people find genetic modification by intentional intervention at the genomic level objectionable, particularly when it involves combining genomic material from species that are not otherwise reproductively compatible. This is the source of the objection to them that they are *unnatural*.

(cont.)

BOX 3.4 *(cont.)*

It is common in the ethics of bioengineering (and in technology ethics generally) to distinguish between intrinsic objections and extrinsic objections. **Intrinsic objections** are based on the features of the technology itself, independent of whether its consequences are good or bad. The unnaturalness objection to GM organisms is an intrinsic objection. Like the objection that they involve "playing God," it is not about what will result from them, but about what sort of thing they are and how they came to be. In contrast, **extrinsic objections** to a technology are objections based on the expected or possible outcomes or consequences of it. With respect to GM crops, there are three different areas of extrinsic concern.

One area of extrinsic concern has to do with individual health and autonomy. The worry is that GM crops are not safe (or have not been adequately proven to be safe) for consumers. Moreover, this concern continues, people are being used as "guinea pigs" for GM crops, violating their right to informed consent, since products containing them often are not labeled and have not been adequately studied for human health effects.

A second area of extrinsic concern regarding GM crops has to do with their ecological and agricultural impacts. As indicated above, first-generation GM crops—those that are herbicide-resistant and produce their own pesticides—are intertwined with industrial commodity agriculture. Therefore, they are seen as helping to perpetuate intensive, agro-chemical monoculture and the ecological challenges associated with it—such as nutrient depletion, chemical pollution, overuse of water, topsoil loss, and evolution of "super" weeds and pests that are resistant to pesticides, herbicides, and traditional crop protection techniques. There are also concerns that genetic modifications will spread through unintended gene flow from GM plants to wild species, and that GM seeds will disperse into ecosystems where they could become ecologically problematic. The rapid expansion of GM crops, particularly in developing nations, is also thought to discourage genetic diversity within crops, as well as the diversity of crops, and thereby threaten food security.

A third area of extrinsic concern regarding GM crops is related to power, control, and justice. Here the concern is that, because GM crops are intertwined with industrial monoculture, they encourage a global commodity-based agricultural economy that advantages corporations and large farming operations, and disempower smallholding farmers and communities, particularly those who practice traditional subsistence polyculture. Moreover, because GM crops are patented and must be purchased (along with associated herbicides) each season rather than saved and shared, GM crops are thought to undermine cultural practices around seed-sharing

(cont.)

BOX 3.4 *(cont.)*

and enable a small number of powerful transnational seed corporations to have outsized control of global agriculture and food production. Critics of GM crops often refer to this as "corporate control of the food supply" (Shiva 2000). GM crops are thus seen as part of an undemocratic push for globalization and homogenization—in this case, with respect to agriculture—that threatens cultural difference, erodes national sovereignty, and undermines environmental and worker protections.

Given all of these concerns about GM crops, why have they become so prevalent and why do many people support their use and development? The first generation GM crops described above—those with herbicide resistance and pesticide production—do not provide a benefit to consumers. They are engineered for traits that are intended to be advantageous to farmers, principally by increasing the ease of pest and weed control and thereby yield per acre. For this reason, they have been readily adopted by commodity agricultural operations. Moreover, proponents of GM crops believe that the concerns raised regarding them are mistaken or overblown. GM crops have been part of the food supply for years now, and there is very little evidence that they are unhealthy for consumers (Nicolia et al. 2013). They also argue that GM crops do not pose serious environmental risks and can actually be ecologically beneficial—for example, by reducing the need to spray fields with chemical pesticides, alleviating the need to clear additional land for agriculture in order to increase production, and facilitating no-till farming (or conservation tillage).

That GM crops are intended to increase yields per acre is crucial to the primary positive argument offered in favor of them, which is that they are a necessary innovation for meeting rapidly increasing agricultural demands. There are already 795 million undernourished people in the world (FAO 2015a), and crop demand is projected to increase a further 60 to 120 percent over the coming decades due to changes in diet and population growth (Alexandratos and Bruinsma 2012; Cassidy et al. 2013). Given the finitude of agricultural resources, the only way to feed the world going forward—and to have any hope of doing so while leaving space and resources for other species—is to innovate and incorporate best practices and novel technologies to increase production, while also eliminating inefficiencies and losses throughout the agro-food system (see Section 6.1 and Box 16.1). Proponents of GM technologies see them as crucial for this. They allow researchers to more efficiently and precisely engineer desirable traits into agricultural plants, such as disease resistance, accelerated growth, nutritional enhancement, drought resistance, heat tolerance, and pest resistance. This is why the Vatican and the United Nations Food and Agricultural organization endorse them (FAO 2004).

(cont.)

BOX 3.4 *(cont.)*

Proponents also argue that people ought to be able to innovate and adopt technologies unless there is a compelling reason to prevent them from doing so, such as that they are harming others (this is sometimes referred to as the **harm principle**). The reason for this is that people are autonomous, independent, rational agents, and exercising and expressing their autonomy is part of living a good human life. Therefore, just as people ought to be able to associate with whomever they like (unless there is compelling reason to restrict them from doing so), they ought to be able to express their autonomy however they like (unless there is compelling reason to restrict them from doing so), including by technological innovation and adoption. Moreover, on this view, a presumption in favor of novel technologies has dramatically improved people's quality of life by encouraging technological innovation and dissemination.

Several of the extrinsic concerns regarding GM crops and the arguments for GM crops are discussed elsewhere in this textbook—for example, the feed-the-world argument (Box 16.1) and the innovation presumption (Box 15.4). Here I will make only a few general points regarding GM crops.

First, as indicated above, the science around GM crops is highly contested. But the research does favor one important conclusion: *different GM crops have different agricultural and ecological profiles.* For example, it appears that cultivation of herbicide-resistant GM crops often results in increased herbicide usage. However, the use of GM Bt crops often reduces the amount of pesticide on the field, as well as its spread to adjacent areas (because it is produced by the plants rather than sprayed on) (Fernandez-Cornejo and McBride 2000). The effects of GM crops on biodiversity also appear to vary. For some crops, insect and bird diversity is higher in conventional fields than in GM fields, for others it is not (DEFRA 2005). Variance is the theme with containment as well. Some GM crops have been documented to spread far afield, and some have characteristics that make them particularly likely to become ecologically problematic, such as high fecundity and herbicide resistance. This is the case with GM creeping bentgrass—an herbicide-resistant grass created for use on golf courses (Reichman et al. 2006). Other GM crops have not been documented as traveling very far and do not have high-risk characteristics.

Second, the majority of the extrinsic concerns regarding GM crops trade on the relationship between them, commodity-based monoculture, and global industrial food systems. Therefore, these concerns are legitimate only insofar as the criticisms of the global industrial food system and commodity monoculture

(cont.)

BOX 3.4 *(cont.)*

are valid and GM crops actually are intertwined with them. However, it is possible for GM crops to be developed independently from commodity monoculture. For example, golden rice is a rice genetically engineered to produce beta-carotene, the precursor to vitamin A, which is otherwise present in only trace amounts in rice. This is significant because vitamin A deficiency is a widespread and severe problem that results in hundreds of thousands of children going blind and dying each year, many of whom live in places where rice is a staple food. Golden rice is intended to address a serious global health problem and benefit the world's worst off (those who suffer from malnutrition). It was developed by researchers at the Swiss Federal Institute of Technology and has received humanitarian exemptions on the patents involved. It is being hybridized into locally favored seed varieties that will be given away freely (or at very low cost) to those in need.

Third, building off the two previous points, that a crop is genetically modified by means of recombinant DNA techniques or synthetic biology provides only one piece of information relevant to assessing its extrinsic ethical profile. *Differential assessment* of extrinsic ethical considerations is necessary because the fact that a plant has been genetically modified by particular techniques does not indicate very much about its potential benefits, costs, risks, cultural situatedness, control, oversight, or access. These are crucial to its impacts on well-being, rights, autonomy, power, and the environment, which in turn are central to determining whether it is compassionate, ecologically sensitive, just, and respectful. Unlike intrinsic objections, which concern the technology *as such*, extrinsic concerns must be evaluated on a case by case (or type by type) basis. As golden rice and GM creeping bentgrass indicate, not all genetically modified crops and organisms are likely to have the same impacts or outcomes. For this reason, unless the intrinsic concerns are cogent, it seems unlikely that either global endorsement or global opposition to GM plants and animals is justified. It is crucial to attend to the particulars of the technologies and their context, as well as to the design of regulatory systems and policies, so as to encourage development of and access to agricultural biotechnologies that promote human flourishing and are just, sustainable, efficient, and compassionate.

Do you agree with the argument above that neither universal endorsement nor universal rejection of GM crops is likely to be justified? Why or why not? Do you think there is an overriding ethical objection to them that justifies rejecting them altogether? If so, what is it and why does it favor comprehensive rejection? If not, what are the considerations that ought to be taken into account when evaluating whether to support or reject a particular GM crop?

3.3 EVOLUTION AND PRESCRIPTION

Drawing normative conclusions from components of evolutionary theory, such as "survival of the fittest," has a long and troubling history. Evolutionary theory has been appealed to in order to justify race and ethnicity based immigration policies, withholding aid to the poor, ethnic cleansing, eugenics, war, and unfettered capitalism. Most people now regard most of these as ethically repugnant. However, it is useful to understand why trying to justify prescriptions by appeal to evolutionary theory is problematic. One reason for this is that a basic understanding of evolutionary theory is important for doing environmental ethics. A second reason is that the misapplication of evolutionary theory to ethics sometimes occurs within environmental discourse.

Darwinism is the theory of evolution by natural selection. It is a theory that explains how biological complexity and diversity arose by natural processes from less biological diversity and less biological complexity. The evidence in favor of it is extremely strong and draws upon a diverse set of sources. Evolution by natural selection explains both the geographical distribution of fossils and the changes over time found in the fossil record. It is evidenced by the degree of genetic, morphological, and developmental similarities between species. It has been tested and documented in diverse contexts, from lab experiments involving microorganisms to ecological field research on predator/prey characteristics. It explains why pest and weed populations become resistant to pesticides and herbicides over time (i.e., individuals with greater resistance have more offspring so the trait spreads through the population). As mentioned last chapter, among those who are most familiar with the evidence, the scientific community, the belief in evolution is very high—it is 98 percent among members of the American Academy for the Advancement of Science. What follows is a rudimentary account of the theory, but one sufficient for discussing whether it has ethical implications.

Evolution by natural selection occurs under the following conditions: (1) when there are variations in fitness among individuals of a population, (2) when the variations in fitness are based on traits that are heritable, and (3) when there are competitive conditions. *Fitness* in this context refers to an individual's ability to reproduce. The more likely it is that an organism will succeed in getting its genes into the next generation, and the more copies of its genes that it is likely to pass on (particularly in comparison to other organisms in the population), the more fit it is. Differences in fitness are based on traits that are *heritable* if they have at least a partial genetic component. *Competitive conditions* obtain when there are factors that prevent individuals in the population from having an unlimited amount of offspring. Examples of competitive pressures are the existence of predators in the environment, a scarce food supply, and a limited number of mates. Under these conditions, the distribution of genes within the population will change over generations. Genes that confer greater fitness will increase in frequency and those that confer lesser fitness will decrease. Here is a simple idealized example to illustrate this.

Suppose there is a population of zebras whose members differ in speed and that this variation has a genetic basis. When lions hunt the herd the slower zebras are more likely to be caught, and so less likely to pass their genes on to the next generation. The faster zebras are more likely to survive, and so more likely to pass on their genes. Over generations, the genes that favor speed are going to become increasingly prevalent among the herd. That is microevolution, or a change in gene (or allele) frequency within a population. In addition to selection, changes in the gene frequency within a population can occur through such things as genetic mutations, gene flow (or exchange) with other populations, and genetic drift (or statistical randomness). Of course, in any actual case, selection and the other processes are acting simultaneously on all the traits within a population.

Speciation—the creation of new species or taxa—occurs when microevolution adds up over time within different populations. Suppose that some zebras in the herd are taller than the others such that they can reach the nutritious leaves of the trees that are native to the area, whereas the shorter zebras must eat grasses. The taller zebras are thus drawn toward one habitat—and tend therefore to interbreed with each other—whereas the shorter zebras are drawn toward another habitat— and tend to interbreed with each other. Over successive generations the traits that are advantageous for each habitat might be accentuated and new traits introduced through mutations to the point where the two populations become distinct species. One adapted to feeding from trees and avoiding predators in wooded areas and another adapted to feeding on grass and avoiding predators in open areas. That is speciation.

There are a couple common misunderstandings regarding evolutionary theory that are important for present purposes. First, evolution has no purpose or end. It is not trying to get anywhere or create any particular type of organism. Evolutionary explanations for why members of a species have a certain trait are always backward-looking. The explanation is that *in the past* individuals with those traits were successful in passing their genes on to subsequent generations. (Or they are a byproduct of an advantageous trait.) Whether the trait will be advantageous in the future is a different issue.

Second, fitness is always relative to some environment. A trait that is fitness-enhancing in one environment—for example, a thick layer of blubber in the Artic— might be detrimental in another—for example, a thick layer of blubber in a desert. An individual's fitness refers to how likely it is to survive and reproduce in the environment it is in, and an individual is more or less fit than another *relative to a given environment.* A classic example of this is the evolution of the peppered moth in early industrial England. Prior to industrialization, the vast majority of peppered moths were light colored (mostly white with some dark patterning) and black peppered moths were extremely rare. The reason for this was that light colored moths were better camouflaged on the foliage in the area, so predators more easily picked out black moths. However, industrialization resulted in the countryside being covered with dark soot from coal-burning factories. As a consequence, the dark moths were better camouflaged and the light moths stood out to predators. Over time, the peppered moth population evolved to being mostly black, since it had greater fitness in the changed environment.

We are now in position to see why it is problematic to appeal to "survival of the fittest" or "natural selection" as a guiding principle for policy or ethics. First, it mistakenly assumes that there is absolute fitness, when in fact there is no such thing as a simply superior species or individual. Fitness is always a function of an individual's traits set in a particular environment. So the idea that there is some "ideally fit" human being toward which the species could be made to progress is actually contrary to evolutionary theory. Moreover, members of one species might be better adapted to certain environmental conditions than members of another species—fish are better adapted to underwater environments than are humans—but that is all there is to it. This has implications for the commonly held belief that humans are evolutionarily superior to members of other species (see Sections 5.2 and 7.4).

Second, evolution does not function with any purpose or goal. It is not trying to make better individuals. It is not trying to accomplish or work toward anything. It merely describes how and why biological diversity and complexity arises through natural processes. So eugenicists err when they think that evolution has the purpose or goal of making a superior or perfect race of human beings; and people err when they think that human beings are the ultimate end or goal of evolution.

Third, the justification and evidence in favor of Darwinism is for it as a theory about how biological diversity and complexity arise by natural processes. Just because a theory is justified in one context does not mean it is appropriate in another. For example, that a theory is well justified in political science does not mean it is well justified as a football strategy. Employing "survival of the fittest" and other elements of evolutionary theory prescriptively makes just this sort of mistake. It takes a theory that is well justified in a descriptive domain (biology) and applies it to a prescriptive one (ethics) where it is not justified at all.

Fourth, it should now be clear that evolution by natural selection is an explanatory theory, not a prescriptive one. It *explains* why certain types of things occurred in the past and it can be used to make predictions about what might occur in the future. But it does not say anything at all about what *ought* to be the case (see Section 2.1). This is why using "survival of the fittest" as a prescriptive principle is an instance of the fallacy of appeal to nature.

As we will see in later chapters (7, 11, and 12), the fact that human beings are evolved biological organisms is considered by many environmental ethicists to be a crucial component of understanding the human-nature relationship. Therefore, we will revisit the issue of evolution's implications for environmental ethics. What this discussion has aimed to demonstrate is that the theory is not and should not *itself* be taken as an ethic. It is descriptive and explanatory, not evaluative or prescriptive.

3.4 SUMMARY

This chapter has focused on the concepts of "nature" and "naturalness." The primary questions addressed were:

- Is there a right definition of nature?
- Is nature normative?

With respect to the first question, there is no single correct definition of nature. Instead, there are several different ones, which are useful in different contexts. So it is crucial when doing environmental ethics to be clear about exactly what definition of nature is being used. Many environmental ethicists use a definition on which something is natural to the extent that it is independent of human control, design, and impacts. This definition is useful because so many environmental issues concern how and in what ways humans should interact with, treat, and modify the non-built environment and the organisms that comprise it.

With respect to the second question—whether nature is normative—several different ideas about how nature might be normative or prescriptive were discussed. In each case, there appears to be significant problems with appealing to naturalness (or unnaturalness) to explicate what is right and what is wrong for people to do. For this reason, claims about the normativity of nature are thought to commit the fallacy of appeal to nature.

If nature is not normative, then how ought environmental ethics be done? On what is it based? The alternative view, widely accepted among environmental ethicists, is that it should be oriented around what things have value and how we ought to care about and respond to their value. For this reason, which things have value and what sort of value they have are the focus of the next several chapters.

KEY TERMS (SEE GLOSSARY FOR DEFINITIONS):

Anthropocene	fallacy of ambiguity
artifactual	fallacy of appeal to human nature
biomimicry	fallacy of appeal to nature
Darwinism	fallacy of appeal to tradition
evolution	fallacy of assuming the conclusion
extrinsic objections	fallacy of begging the question

fallacy of equivocation

fortress conservation

harm principle

innovation presumption

intrinsic objections

natural

prima facie wrong

principle of noninterference

reductio ad absurdum

REVIEW QUESTIONS

- What are the different definitions of "nature" discussed in this chapter? Which one is most widely used in environmental ethics and why is it used?

- What are the ways in which the concept of "nature" is used prescriptively? And what are the objections to using it in those ways?

- What is the fallacy of appeal to nature?

- What are the concerns raised regarding the idea of "wilderness"? What are the responses to those concerns?

- What is the difference between an intrinsic ethical objection and an extrinsic ethical objection?

- What are the intrinsic and extrinsic objections to genetically modified crops? What are the responses to the objections?

- What are the difficulties with using concepts from evolutionary theory prescriptively?

DISCUSSION QUESTIONS

- Do you agree with the arguments in this chapter that it is best not to use "nature" as a prescriptive concept? Why or why not?

- Do you agree that there is a *prima facie* duty or responsibility of noninterference with nature? If so, what is the basis for it? If not, why not?

- Several examples of the fallacy of appeal to nature were discussed in this chapter. Can you think other issues or areas of ethics where fallacious appeals to nature (or human nature) are made?

FURTHER READING

John Stuart Mill's essay "On Nature" (in *Nature, The Utility of Religion, and Theism* [Watts and Co., 1904]) is by far the most widely read and influential work on the definition and normative use of "nature." An excellent recent work on the concept of "nature" and the normative roles it has played in environmental ethics is:

Vogel, Steven. *Thinking Like a Mall: Environmental Philosophy after the End of Nature.* MIT Press, 2015.

The issues raised in William Cronon's "The Trouble with Wilderness; or Getting Back to the Wrong Nature" (in W. Cronon, ed., *Uncommon Ground: Rethinking the Human Place in Nature* [W. W. Norton & Co. 1995]) continue to be widely discussed. A diverse set of perspectives on them, as well as on other ethical issues related to wilderness (the place and the idea), are collected here:

Callicott, J. Baird, and Michael Nelson, eds. *The Great New Wilderness Debate.* University of Georgia Press, 1998.

Callicott, J. Baird, and Michael Nelson, eds. *Wilderness Debate Rages On: Continuing the Great New Wilderness Debate.* University of Georgia Press, 2008.

An excellent introductory work on the relationship between evolution and ethics is:

Rachels, James. *Created from Animals: The Moral Implications of Darwinism.* Oxford University Press, 1990.

Two thought-provoking works on the relationship between human nature and ethics are:

Pinker, Steven. *The Blank Slate: The Modern Denial of Human Nature.* Penguin, 2003.

Radcliffe-Richards, Janet. *Human Nature after Darwin.* Routledge, 2001.

I discuss the ethical dimensions of genetically modified crops and agricultural biotechnology at greater length in *Food Ethics: The Basics* (Routledge, 2015). There are many other good books and informative collections that address the topic, including:

Ruse, Michael, and David Castle, eds. *Genetically Modified Foods: Debating Biotechnology.* Prometheus, 2002.

Bailey, Britt, and Marc Lappe, eds. *Engineering the Farm: Ethical and Social Aspects of Agricultural Biotechnology.* Island Press, 2002.

Thompson, Paul. *From Field to Fork: Food Ethics for Everyone.* Oxford University Press, 2015.

CHAPTER FOUR

NATURAL VALUE

IN THE PREVIOUS CHAPTER we saw that prescriptive uses of nature and natural-ness are problematic. A more promising way to approach environmental ethics is to orient it around the benefits that ecological systems provide and the ways in which nonhuman entities are valuable. Identifying the full range of environmental goods and values is central to this method of environmental ethics. We cannot effectively consider and protect environmental values if we are not cognizant of them. More-over, many ecological problems arise because people focus narrowly on short-term economic gains to the exclusion of broader and longer-term considerations.

This chapter begins by distinguishing several different types of value. The distinc-tions and terminology are a bit technical, but they are crucial within environmental ethics. The reason for this is that different types of value call for different sorts of responsiveness. For example, both people and natural resources are valuable, but they are valuable in different ways. Natural resources can be bought, sold, and utilized for our ends, whereas people should not be bought or sold, since they are not merely things for others to use. Therefore, it is important in ethics to determine not only who and what are valuable, but also the *type* and *basis* for their value. The second part of this chapter addresses whether naturalness is valuable and, if so, what sort of value it is. The idea that natural entities and processes are valuable in virtue of their naturalness has been an influential one in environmental ethics, and the issue has sig-nificant implications for ecosystem management, species conservation, and ecological restoration.

ENVIRONMENTAL VALUES PRIMER

Imagine a woodland or wetland ecosystem near a small town. How might the place be valuable? What valuable entities might be located there? How might it be beneficial to citizens of the town? List out all of the goods and values that you can think of. Do you see any interesting or useful ways to categorize them? Are there different kinds or types of values? Are some more important than others? If so, why?

4.1 INSTRUMENTAL VALUE

There are many different types of value or ways in which things are valuable. One type of value is **instrumental value**. Something is instrumentally valuable to the extent that it is an effective means to a desired or sought-after end. Instrumental value is, in short, usefulness value. The natural environment is immensely instrumentally valuable. We depend upon it for the atmosphere we breathe, the water we drink, the soil that grows our food, the energy that we use, the materials with which we build, and much more. These types of values are often referred to as **ecosystem services** and **natural resources**. Ecosystem services are processes from which we benefit—for example, water purification, storm surge buffering, food provision, soil regeneration, pollination, protection from harmful solar radiation, disease and pest regulation, carbon sequestration, waste disposal, and conversion of carbon dioxide to oxygen. Natural resources are things that we use for our purposes—for example, soil to grow crops, fossil fuels for energy, ore for steel, diamonds for jewelry, trees for lumber, water for drinks, fish for food, and minerals for electronics.

In addition to the basic and economic goods and services highlighted above, ecological systems provide an enormous range of opportunities for enjoyment, learning, personal growth, and well-being. People engage in myriad forms of outdoor recreation, such as hiking, wildlife viewing, fishing, and skiing. Many people find spiritual renewal, self-understanding and a sense of connection to things bigger than themselves through the natural world. Nature, from expansive landscapes to the structure of molecules, is beautiful and wonderful. Artists, writers, and poets are frequently inspired by it, and it is an object of study and source of knowledge to naturalists and scientists.

It is clear that ecosystems, landscapes, species, organisms, and other environmental entities possess a wide variety of instrumental values. Moreover, the natural world will be instrumentally valuable to us in the future in ways that we cannot now anticipate. No one knew a hundred years ago that rare earth minerals would be used in computers and cell phones. Thus, the natural world not only has present instrumental

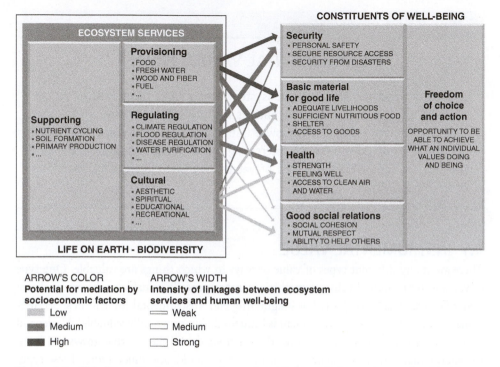

Figure 4.1 This figure illustrates several prominent linkages between types of ecosystem services and components of human well-being that were identified as part of the Millennium Ecosystem Assessment (2005), an extensive study on the relationship between human well-being and the environment.
Source: Millennium Ecosystem Assessment

value, it also has what is often called **option value**—that is, it is potentially useful in ways that we cannot currently predict. Option value is often used as a justification for preserving biodiversity. If we do not know where the next medical, agricultural, energy, or material innovation will come from, it seems prudent to try to preserve as many species (so as many options) as possible.

Most people agree that we ought to take care of the environment because we depend upon it for our survival and well-being. We need clean air to breathe, potable water to drink, nutritional food to eat, and materials with which to build. Most people also agree that nature provides a diverse array of enriching experiences and opportunities. So when people, corporations, or governments release toxic pollutants into the environment, over-exploit natural resources, cause species extinctions, or degrade ecological systems, it is harmful to people and diminishes the quality of people's lives in the long run.

However, many environmental thinkers worry about basing environmental policies only on nature's instrumental value. The reason for this is that instrumental value is *substitutable* and *replaceable*. If something is instrumentally valuable as a means to an end, it is possible to compare it to other potential means to the same end. If a means is lost, but some other equally adequate means exists, then there is no net value loss. This has led to what is sometimes called the **artificial alternatives concern**. If a stand of trees is instrumentally valuable for the carbon that it sequesters, the erosion that it prevents, and the materials that it provides, but we can engineer technologies that do these things as well or better than the trees, then the trees could be replaced without any loss of value. Moreover, if nature is *only* instrumentally valuable, then shouldn't we always be looking for ways in which to improve upon it or upgrade it? Shouldn't we modify ecological systems and use resources in ways that best accomplish our ends and serve our needs? Shouldn't we only worry about conserving those species that we need now (or might need in the future), not every last variety of minnow, beetle, or vine? Thus, one of the primary value issues in environmental ethics is whether the natural environment is merely a resource for us to use in whatever ways best serve human interests and goals, or if it (or some parts of it) matters or has value independent of us.

4.2 FINAL VALUE (OR INTRINSIC VALUE)

The contrasting type of value to instrumental value is **final value**, or what many environmental ethicists call **intrinsic value**. Final value is the value that something has for what it is, rather than what it does or provides. Something has final value if its value as a means to sought ends is not exhaustive of its value. (I prefer the term "final value" to "intrinsic value" because it better captures the contrast with instrumental value and because those who ascribe it to nature typically do so in part on the basis of relational properties, rather than only internal or intrinsic ones. However, what is important is being clear on the type, basis, and logic of the value, not the name used to refer to it. Similarly, the value categories that I employ in this chapter are not the only possible ones. There are other ways to break up the value terrain. I employ these categories and distinctions because they are useful and common within environmental ethics.)

A prominent value issue in environmental ethics concerns what, if anything, in the natural world possesses final value. The issue is thought to be crucial because, as discussed above, if the natural environment has only instrumental value to human beings, then it should be regarded and treated as a mere means to human ends. We should use it in whatever ways are best for us. However, if there are noninstrumental values in nature, if nature (or some parts of it) matters for what it is or in itself, then we ought to care for it and respect it *for its own sake*. The idea that nonhuman species ought to be preserved, wild animals ought to be left alone, or wilderness areas ought to be protected, *even if doing so does not serve the interests of people*, are only justified if they are a locus of value in themselves or for what they are—that is, only if they have final value.

There is an important distinction within final value, which concerns its basis. Something has **subjective final value** (hereafter just, **subjective value**) if it is valued by people for noninstrumental reasons—for instance, for its beauty, creativity, or symbolism. Something has **objective final value** (hereafter just, **objective value**) if its value is independent of anyone's particular evaluative attitudes. (In moral philosophy the view that there are objective values is often called **value realism**.) The reason why the distinction between subjective value and objective value is important is that if something is only subjectively valuable, if its value is based on people's particular attitudes or beliefs, then its value could change as attitudes and outlooks change. For example, so long as people regard wolves as amazing animals that are iconic of the wild and whose presence indicates intact and healthy ecological systems, then wolves would have positive subjective value. However, if they are instead regarded as symbolic of menace and of savage places, and as threats to valued ways of life, then they would have negative subjective value. Ultimately, when it comes to subjective value, the value depends or is contingent upon us (i.e., the valuers). We are the source of it, since it is created by our evaluative stances or attitudes. As Baird Callicott, a prominent proponent of the subjective final value of nature and species, has put it: "they may not be valuable *in* themselves but they certainly may be valued *for* themselves. According to this . . . account, value is, to be sure, humanly conferred, but not necessarily homocentric" (1989, 151).

Subjective final value is not unusual or mysterious. There are a wide variety of things that are valued noninstrumentally, such as personal mementos, cultural and religious artifacts, ceremonies, rituals, accomplishments, performances, and historical sites. The bases for approval of such things are diverse. For example, the valuing might be for what the thing represents, for what it embodies, for its rarity, for what it expresses, or for its beauty. In each case, the valuing is for noninstrumental reasons, rather than for what the entity can bring about. However, in each case the underlying evaluative attitudes could change. This is why subjective value is contingent upon people's attitudes, values, and outlooks.

Not all evaluative attitudes regarding nature are equally transient. Some are superficial, and can change easily based on such things as economic circumstances, recent experiences, and media portrayals. Others are more integral to people's worldviews, flow from their deeply held commitments, and express their ideals. This is often the case with respect to places and species that are central to cultural practices and narratives, such as Uluru to the Anangu people in central Australia and Chinook salmon to the Winnemem Tribe in the Northwestern United States. It also can be the case with respect to biodiversity and nature more generally, as seen with people who self-identify as environmentalist.

Nevertheless, so long as final value is based on evaluative attitudes, it is contingent upon those attitudes. It is always possible for individual and social attitudes to change over time, be it months, decades, or generations. Moreover, people have widely different perspectives on nature. This is exemplified in people's divergent attitudes toward wolves, sharks, and other large predators. It is also evident in how people value species and biodiversity generally. Many people value species and biodiversity for what they are, a multitude of unique and beautiful forms of life that evolved through human independent evolutionary processes stretching back through geological time. However, others care about species only insofar as they are useful to people and can contribute to human well-being.

BOX 4.2   TOPIC TO CONSIDER

CAN PEOPLE'S EVALUATIVE ATTITUDES BE WRONG?

An issue that arises regarding subjective value is whether people's attitudes can be, in some sense, mistaken. The reason this is important is that it bears on whether attitudes can be critically evaluated. If they can, then perhaps not all subjective values should be considered the same in decision-making processes.

On one hand, evaluative attitudes seem to be largely responsive or expressive, and not the sort of thing that could be mistaken or false, since they do not assert that anything is the case. Some people find the woods to be creepy and unsettling, others find them tranquil and comforting. Some people find genetic engineering to be repulsive, others find it amazing. People have contrary attitudes, but no attitudes are erroneous.

On the other hand, it seems like attitudes and responses can be unwarranted or unfitting. For example, they might be based on false beliefs. A person might be repulsed by bats, but only because he wrongly believes that they pose a threat to him. Or a person might find a colorful sunset beautiful, but only because he does not know it is caused by air pollution. Moreover, it seems like people can have inconsistent attitudes. For example, someone might be outraged by the practice of euthanizing unwanted animals, but delight in having bacon with every meal. If attitudes can be unwarranted, uninformed, inconsistent, or otherwise misguided, then perhaps they should not all be given the same consideration in decision-making contexts.

What do you think? Is it possible to critically evaluate people's attitudes and responses? Are some responses more appropriate or fitting to their object than others? It might be helpful to think of particular cases where people's evaluative attitudes differ—for example, regarding genetically modified organisms (GMOs) or snakes. It is possible to hold false beliefs about GMOs and snakes. But is it possible for a person's positive or negative attitudes about them to be inappropriate or unfitting? Do all evaluative attitudes need to be equally considered when determining environmental policies or ecosystem management plans, regardless of how misinformed they might be? Why or why not?

For these reasons, many environmental ethicists believe that the justification for such things as wilderness protection, species preservation, and compassion toward animals are only fully secure if these entities—ecological systems, species, and animals—have objective value or value that exists independent of anyone's actual evaluative attitudes. Only then does their value make a claim on all people to recognize it. The normative significance of objective value is perhaps best illustrated by the global human rights discourse. "Human rights" is an enormously powerful normative concept precisely because each person is claimed to have them, *regardless of what other people believe or what other people's attitudes toward them are*. The reason for this is that the rights are taken to be grounded in the value that each person has in themselves or for what they are. (See Section 9.4 for an extended discussion of environmental rights.) Here is how this is formulated within the United Nations *Universal Declaration of Human Rights* (1948):

> Article 1: All human beings are born free and equal in dignity and rights. They are endowed with reason and conscience and should act towards one another in a spirit of brotherhood.

> Article 2: Everyone is entitled to all the rights and freedoms set forth in this Declaration, without distinction of any kind, such as race, colour, sex, language, religion, political or other opinion, national or social origin, property, birth or other status. Furthermore, no distinction shall be made on the basis of the political, jurisdictional or international status of the country or territory to which a person belongs.

Because human rights are considered universal and unconditional, when women, indigenous peoples, or minority groups are denied basic rights a wrong is being done that needs to be corrected. The fact that their government or society does not believe that they should be afforded equal respect and rights is irrelevant, since human rights are not grounded in subjective or cultural attitudes. As the Declaration indicates, they are thought to be grounded in the value that each person has as a human being. Each person is due full respect and consideration for what they are, and other people's attitudes need to come in line with that.

If there are environmental entities that have value of this sort—objective value—it has tremendous significance for how we ought to treat them and what policies we ought to adopt regarding them. Their value would be due recognition and responsiveness, regardless of people's subjective attitudes. Therefore, there is quite a lot of discussion in environmental ethics concerning whether any environmental entities have objective value. Some environmental ethicists have argued that human-independent ecological systems and processes possess such value (see Section 4.4). Others have argued that plants and/or animals have such value (see Chapter 7). Still others have argued that species and ecosystems have such value (see Chapters 11–13).

☀ BOX 4.3   TOPIC TO CONSIDER

ENVIRONMENTAL AESTHETICS

Aesthetic value is the value that something possesses in virtue of its capacity to elicit emotional or attitudinal responses from people when experienced or contemplated. A perennial issue is whether, or to what extent, aesthetic value is subjective or objective. Do people's responses or judgments determine

Image 4.2a   Sunrise at Hunts Mesa, Monument Valley, AZ, USA
Source: Elena Suvorova/ Shutterstock.com

Image 4.2b   Flower pollination
Source:©iStock/Boris Katsman

(cont.)

BOX 4.2 *(cont.)*

a work of art's aesthetic value? Or does something possess aesthetic value in virtue of its formal (i.e., internal) and/or contextual (i.e., relational) properties? If beauty is truly in the eye of the beholder, then it would seem to be subjective. But if some creative works are more fitting or appropriate objects for appreciation than others, then it would seem not entirely subjective. What, if anything, do you think makes some works of art superior or more significant than others? What are the implications, if any, for whether aesthetic value is subjective or objective? What about environmental aesthetics? Are some aesthetic responses—for example, pleasure, awe, and wonder—to natural phenomena such as vistas, sunsets, storms, or organisms more appropriate than others? Are some environmental entities more fitting for aesthetic appreciation than others? Is the aesthetic value of the environment subjective or objective?

4.3 ECONOMIC VALUATION AND ENVIRONMENTAL VALUES

Environmental economists often aim to put an economic valuation on ecosystem services. The reason for this is that ecosystem services historically have been underconsidered and underappreciated in environmental decision-making and policy. Placing a monetary value on them increases their salience. The economic value of global ecosystem services is estimated to be ~$125 trillion per year (Costanza et al. 2014). This puts into perspective just how crucial well-functioning ecological systems are to human well-being as well as the extent to which human systems are intertwined with and dependent upon them. However, site- or system-specific economic valuations are often more important to environmental decision-making than is global or macro evaluation. Not all ecological systems and spaces have the same ecosystem services and natural resource value. For example, an average hectare of open ocean provides fewer services than does an average hectare of reef, and an average hectare of desert provides fewer than does an average hectare of tropical rainforest.

Many environmentalists have embraced economic valuation of ecosystem services because of how it makes them visible in decision-making processes. For example, suppose a golf resort has been proposed for a coastal area, but it will require clearing and draining a considerable amount of wetland. Putting an economic value on the full range of services that the wetland provides—for instance, recreation, tourism, food provision, storm protection, erosion control, carbon sequestration, and nurseries for fisheries—elucidates the losses involved. It can provide a basis for challenging the overall economic benefits claimed for the project. It can clarify who is benefited and who is harmed by it—for example, local fisherman as compared to corporate owners. It can inform design of the project to mitigate environmental impacts and distribute the costs and benefits more fairly. For these reasons, full and accurate economic valuation of ecosystem services and natural resources is widely regarded as a crucial component of good environmental decision-making with respect to policy (e.g., wetland, energy, conservation, pollution, and agricultural regulations), as well as local planning and project decisions (e.g., building a hydroelectric dam, developing an off-shore wind farm, permitting hydraulic fracturing for natural gas, or constructing a pipeline).

Very often, when rigorous and comprehensive economic assessments of ecosystem services are conducted, they favor decisions and policies that environmentalists prefer. For example, maintaining forests near tropical agriculture increases pollination rates and decreases pests for crops such as coffee and nuts. Conserving reefs, estuaries, and kelp forests are crucial to maintaining fisheries' productivity. Protecting urban bat populations often decreases mosquito density and associated disease transmission. Coastal forest protections prevent erosion and provide storm buffers. Wildlife parks frequently support ecotourism. Air quality regulations often reduce the negative human health and productivity impacts from pollution.

Nevertheless, many environmental ethicists have raised concerns about the economic valuation of ecological systems. One concern is that many values, particularly final or intrinsic values, cannot be meaningfully represented in economic terms. How do you place an economic valuation on the cultural and aesthetic significance of a place or phenomenon, or on a species or biodiversity? How much is having salmon run the Elwha River worth for the Lower Elwha Klallam Tribe? What is the economic value of Amazonian indigenous groups in the Xingu River basin maintaining their way of life? How much is the beauty and majesty of the Patagonia wilderness or Ngorongoro crater worth? What is the economic valuation of having panthers in the everglades, tigers in Sumatra, orangutans in Indonesia, gorillas in the Virunga Mountains, polar bears in the arctic, and delta smelt in the San Joaquin valley?

One aspect of this concern is that there is no market price for these things to indicate how much people are willing to pay for them and thereby assign an economic value to them. Economists often employ something called **contingent valuation method** to address this problem. They fix the economic value of a nonmarket good or service by determining how much people would be willing to pay to protect the good (e.g., an endangered species, beautiful vista, or cultural practice) or maintain or establish the service (e.g., access to outdoor recreation, noise buffering, or unrestricted water usage). The basic idea is that how much people say they would be willing to pay to create, maintain, or prevent something, given choices presented to them in hypothetical scenarios, is indicative of the strength of their preferences regarding it. Those preferences in turn indicate how much they value it, just as purchasing behaviors are indicative of how much people value market goods. How much people are willing to pay under contingent valuation scenarios sets the economic value of nonmarket environmental goods and services.

Many ethicists are critical of contingent valuation method on the grounds that it is not reliable or accurate. They argue that people's willingness to pay to establish, protect, or avoid something under constructed scenarios is not always a good proxy for their preferences or the values at issue. One reason for this is that people often have inadequate knowledge or appreciation of what is at stake, so their actual or stated preferences might not track well the cultural, aesthetic, social, or ecological values involved. People's valuations have also been found to be highly malleable based on how they are elicited and on factors such as economic status—for instance, wealthy people are willing to pay more to satisfy their weaker preferences. There also appears to be significant status quo bias. People are generally willing to pay more to maintain something that already exists (or that they already have access to) than to establish it or gain access to it. So one aspect of the concern about economic valuation of environmental values, particularly for nonmarket goods, is that it is not possible to get an accurate or reliable valuation of them. Environmental economists are, of course, aware of these difficulties and try to avoid and correct for them in their methods.

However, a second aspect of the valuation concern is that *no* economic valuation adequately represents such things as aesthetic value, cultural value, justice, and the value of species. They simply cannot be converted into economic units without remainder or distortion. Their market price (if they have one) and people's willingness to pay for them does not fully capture what is important about them. This is sometimes referred to as the **problem of incommensurability**, since the concern is that not all environmental values (particularly final values) are commensurate with economic valuation—that is, they cannot be represented by an economic value. On this view, there is no accurate economic value for panthers in the Everglades or the continuity of wild rice cultivation by the Ojibwe Tribe.

Another, related concern about the practice of placing economic values on ecosystem services and natural resources is that once an economic value is placed on a population, place, or process, the values that are not represented economically are marginalized in decision-making. Environmental economists often are clear that an economic valuation of ecosystem services and natural resources is not a comprehensive value assessment, but only represents the goods and services involved. Nevertheless, the economic value frequently becomes the focus of decision-makers. Considerations of justice, cultural significance, and species conservation are sidelined because they do not fit as neatly into the economic value discourse and cost-benefit form of reasoning that is often preferred by policy-makers.

Moreover, there is no guarantee that in a comprehensive economic analysis a full economic valuation of maintaining ecosystem services will outweigh the economic value of exploitation or development. For example, the economic value of a copper mine recently approved on appropriated lands that are sacred to the San Carlos Apache Tribe in Arizona is estimated to be over $60 billion. Mineral deposits in the Democratic Republic of Congo, much of it in environmentally sensitive areas of the Congo Basin that are home to many rare and endangered species, are estimated to be over $20 trillion. In cases like these, a strictly economic analysis could favor resource extraction, despite the significant cultural and ecological losses. Similarly, an economic analysis of water allocations in the Sacramento–San Joaquin delta may not favor allocations to conserve the delta smelt and other endemic (but not economically significant) fish species. Strictly economic analyses also often favor distributions of environmental hazards—such as pollutants, chemical waste, and industrial facilities—that disproportionately burden high-minority and low-income communities, which is widely regarded as unjust (see Section 15.1).

As a result of these concerns, environmentalists, indigenous communities, and environmental justice advocates are often in the position of doing two things at once: (1) arguing for the importance of a comprehensive economic valuation of the environmental goods and services at stake with a policy or project, and (2) arguing that a comprehensive economic evaluation, even when done well, does not fully capture all the values involved, such as justice, cultural integrity, and biodiversity.

How well economic valuations represent environmental values, including whether there are environmental values that cannot be represented economically, is thus a crucial issue in environmental ethics. Therefore, as different types of environmental values are introduced and discussed, it is important to consider the extent to which they are commensurable with economic valuation. Moreover, if they are not commensurable, it is important to determine how they should be considered in environmental decision-making. When, if ever, should noneconomic values be prioritized over economic ones? For example, when, if ever, should biodiversity and wilderness conservation take precedence over economic development and poverty reduction (see, e.g., Boxes 13.1 and 16.2)? How should consideration of distributive justice and economic efficiency inform public policies (see Sections 15.1–15.3)? The appropriate role of economic considerations in environmental decision-making is a topic that arises frequently, since almost all environmental issues have an economic component.

● BOX 4.4   THOUGHT EXPERIMENT

ECOLOGICAL REPLICATION

Imagine that a pristine natural landscape, such as an old-growth forest, is completely destroyed by human activities and then exactly replicated in the same place by human efforts. Would the replication have the same value as the original? Would it recreate everything that is valuable about the original? Why or why not? (For the purposes of the thought experiment, set aside concerns about whether this could be accomplished in practice; that is, assume the physical replication could be done.)

4.4 IS NATURALNESS VALUABLE?

As we have seen, the nonhuman environment is enormously instrumentally valuable. The issue addressed in this section is whether naturalness is itself valuable. That is, do entities, places, and processes have final value in virtue of their being independent of human design, control, and impacts? This question is relevant to a wide variety of ecosystem management issues. For example, if wilderness areas have value in virtue of their being independent of human impacts, then that favors policies that strongly limit human activities in them, such as snowmobiling, off-road vehicles, hunting, fishing, mining, logging, and road building. It would also favor prioritizing native species—species that are from or **endemic** to an area—over nonnative species, as well as assisted recoveries that aim to make ecosystems like they once were (or would have been) absent human intervention (see Box 4.5 and Section 13.5 for discussions of ecological restoration). In general, if ecosystems, species, and landscapes have value in virtue of their independence from humans, it supports limiting human influence on them. Any "improvements" or "developments" people might make to them would undermine their natural value.

The core idea behind **natural value** is that places or living things have value in virtue of their being independent from people. Another way of putting this is that naturalness is a *value-adding property*. If your response to the replication thought experiment (Box 4.4) is that the replica forest does not fully recreate the value of the old growth forest—even if it is physically identical—then you appear to believe that naturalness is a value-adding property. The reason for this is that the only difference between the original and the replica is their history, the way in which they were created. The original was created by human independent evolutionary, ecological, geological, and climatic processes, whereas the replica was created by human endeavors. They have the same plant and animal species, provide the same services, resources, and opportunities, and smell, look, and sound the same. The only difference is that one is more natural than the other. This is sometimes called the **replication argument** for natural value. Here is a formal representation of it:

1. A replica ecosystem is less valuable or lacks some of the values possessed by an original ecosystem.
2. The only difference between an original ecosystem and a replica ecosystem is that the original is natural, whereas the replica is artifactual.
3. Therefore, naturalness is value-adding for ecosystems.

It might seem odd that historical properties could be value-adding—that something's value could depend not only on what it is like, but also how it came about. However, this is actually quite common. Monuments are placed in particular places (and not in identical ones elsewhere) because important events occurred there in the past. Particular pieces of artwork or architecture are valuable in part because of the historical circumstances of their creation, and an identical replica is a forgery if it is passed off as the original. A simple object—a blanket, rock, or book—often has value to a person because of the role that it played in her history. The objects, in themselves, are mundane, but their histories make them valuable (or are value-adding). They cannot just be replaced.

In each of these cases—culturally significant sites, works of art, and mementos—historical properties add value. Therefore, there is nothing objectionable (or even unusual) in the idea that historical properties could be value-adding with respect to ecosystems or species. Moreover, many people value places, events, and species because of their naturalness or human independence. They support creating protected wilderness areas where human activities and impacts are minimized. They find naturally formed land-scapes and features, such as canyons and glacial lakes, amazing and awesome in large part because of the geological and climatic processes that created them. They wonder at the diversity of evolved biological life forms, as well as the uniqueness, beauty, and bizarreness of individual species. They marvel at natural phenomena, from mass migra-tions to the Northern Lights. There is no doubt that many people value naturalness in a broad range of entities and phenomena, and they regularly demonstrate this with their behaviors—for example, recreation, donations, activism, and career choices.

However, many other people do not value naturalness. Some people just do not care very much about such things as wilderness and keeping places and species free from human impacts. Others believe that it is the responsibility of people to try to control nature, to make use of its resources, to subdue its threats (e.g., diseases, predators, and natural disasters), and to generally have dominion over it and improve upon it. There is precedence for this attitude in the history of Western thought—both religious and secular—just as there is for the more romantic view that naturalness adds value (see, e.g., Boxes 3.1 and 5.4). Moreover, with respect to the replication thought experiment, some people's intuitions are that as long as the replica ecosystem provides the same resources, experiences, and services to us and to the species that inhabit it, then it is just as valuable as the original. This suggests that they do not believe that naturalness is value-adding.

If there are competing sets of attitudes and intuitions regarding whether natural historical properties are value-adding—some people and traditions value naturalness, whereas others do not—where does this leave us with respect to the question: Is natural-ness value-adding? Consider again monuments, rituals, and mementos. In those cases, what makes the item, place, or practice valuable is the fact that a person or group of people have a positive attitude toward it; it means or signifies something special to them. Their emotions, beliefs, and judgments—their *evaluative stances*—create the value. Without those stances, they are just mundane objects or places. Therefore, their value is *subjective*.

If a person or culture values a particular item, ritual, or place, it has subjective value (to them) even if others do not value it. For example, the Anangu people in central Australia value Uluru (Image 4.3), a large freestanding rock monolith, because it plays a prominent role in their cultural narratives, histories, and practices. The fact that tourists from North America, Europe, and Asia (who come to watch it change colors during sunset and climb it to view sunrise) do not value it in that way does not mean that it does not have that value. Moreover, visitors to Uluru ought to respect the value that it has to the Anangu. They should not defile or demean it with graffiti, trash, or other inappropriate behaviors. In this way, subjective value makes a claim on people, even if they do not share the stance or attitude that is the source of the value.

It seems clear that naturalness has subjective value in some environmental con-texts. It is valuable, at least in part, because many people care deeply about it, and this

Image 4.3   Uluru–Kata Tjuta National Park, Northern Territory, Australia
Source: Stanislav Fosenbauer/ Shutterstock.com

needs to be respected by others, even if they do not share the attitude. What is more controversial is whether naturalness has *objective value*. Objective value is final value that something has in itself, such that it is not dependent on people actually valuing it (i.e., it is not stance- or attitude-dependent). This idea is exemplified in Holmes Rolston's view regarding the natural historical value of species: "These things count, whether or not there is anybody to do the counting" (1982, 146). Does naturalness have objective value? Are those who do not value it in some way mistaken?

Consider again the replication thought experiment. For those who do not have the intuition that the replica is less valuable, is it possible to show that their attitude is somehow unwarranted? That it is not well informed by the ecological facts, based on misunderstanding, inconsistent with other beliefs that they hold, the product of a problematic inference or perspective, or imprudent? Can sound reasons be provided for why people ought to value naturalness, even if they do not? If they cannot be, then perhaps naturalness is not objectively valuable.

It might be beneficial for a person to cultivate an appreciation of naturalness, to value human-independent places and histories. Their engagement with the natural would be more pleasurable, rewarding, and meaningful. However, that it is beneficial for a person to care about and value nature does not imply that nature has objective value. After all, the same can be said about cultivating understanding of music and sport, for example. Appreciation of football can provide enjoyable and enriching experiences, but it does not follow that football has objective value. Thus, while it is clear that naturalness has subjective value, it is less clear whether it has objective value.

❋ BOX 4.5	TOPIC TO CONSIDER

ECOLOGICAL RESTORATION, NATURAL VALUE, AND THE "BIG LIE"

Ecological restoration is a variety of **assisted recovery** or intervening in a space in order to improve it from an ecological perspective. An assisted recovery is a restoration to the extent that *history* is incorporated into the project. Ecological restoration aims to improve the ecology of a place in the future by maintaining or reestablishing continuity with the past. (There is a broader use of the term "ecological restoration" on which it refers to ecological recovery generally.) Restoration projects occur all around the world. They are implemented by individuals, governments, and environmental organizations. They target small ecological spaces and large ecological systems. They involve remediating pollutants, culling nonnative species, reintroducing native species, and removing impediments to natural processes. Here are just a few examples:

- *Elwha and Glines Canyon Dam Removals*: The largest dam removal project in US history is on the Elwha River in Washington State. The goal is to reestablish the flow of the river, restore its native anadromous fish species, and rebuild near shore and river habitats, which involves planting hundreds of thousands of native plants.
- *Kissimmee River Restoration Project*: This project aims to restore more than 40 square miles of river floodplain, including tens of thousands of acres of wetlands, and help reestablish the flow of water through the South Florida Everglades, which has been reduced by channeling and diversion for agriculture.
- *Chesapeake Bay Restoration Project*: The Chesapeake Bay in Maryland and Virginia is the largest estuary in the contiguous United States, with nearly 4,000 square miles of surface area. Chemical and agricultural runoff from the bay's 64,000 square-mile watershed has led to its becoming one of the most degraded bodies of water in the country. This ongoing project aims to improve the water quality and ecological health of the bay through extensive pollution and sediment remediation, invasive species removal, reintroduction of native grasses and oyster reefs, and reestablishment of fish passages.
- *Private Prairie Restoration*: There were 170 million acres of tallgrass prairie in what is now the United States when European settlers arrived, of which less than 2 percent remains. Throughout the midwestern

(cont.)

BOX 4.5 *(cont.)*

United States individual landowners are engaging in micro-scale tall-grass prairie restorations. They are removing lawns and sowing native grasses and flowers intended to benefit native fauna, particularly migratory species such as butterflies and moths.

- *Costa Rican Forest Restoration*: La Reserva Forest Foundation in Tilaran, Costa Rica, has planted over 100,000 native trees to reestablish forest and pasture borders lost to agricultural clear-cutting. The reserve works with interested landowners and local indigenous peoples, and focuses on creating corridors between isolated forest patches to improve habitat connectivity for species such as howler monkeys, sloths, and manakins.
- *Eurasian Beaver Reintroduction*: Trial reintroductions of Eurasian beavers in Scotland, where they were extirpated centuries ago, have recently been completed. Eurasian beavers already have been reintroduced and are returning to former ranges in rivers throughout Europe. Key to the beaver's resurgence has been protections from hunting, as well as improved river health from dam removal and pollution remediation.
- *Golden Lion Tamarin Conservation*: In the Atlantic Coastal Forest of Brazil, the golden lion tamarin population has increased from just a few hundred individuals to over three thousand. This was accomplished through reintroductions as well as by identifying and restoring key wildlife corridors between fragmented habitats.
- *Kelp Forest Restoration*: Giant kelp forests provide crucial habitat for thousands of marine species and are among the most productive ecosystems on the planet. Kelp forests beds off the California coast have been reduced by as much as 80 percent over the past century due to the effects of pollution, sedimentation, and kelp-grazing sea urchins, whose density increased dramatically as predator populations, such as sea otters, declined (Image 4.4). Several governmental and non-profit organizations in California are engaged in kelp forest restoration programs that involve reducing runoff, as well as organizing divers to remove the overabundant sea urchins.

As mentioned earlier, many people believe that if naturalness has final value this favors protecting places from human impacts (i.e., creating parks and reserves), preserving species in their ecological contexts (i.e., *in situ* conservation), and returning degraded spaces to their pre-impact states or trajectories

(cont.)

BOX 4.5 *(cont.)*

Images 4.4 Otter abundance (a and b) is crucial to the health of kelp forests on the California coast (c) because they control the population of sea urchins that graze on the kelp (d).

Sources: (a) Reprinted from: Recovery of marine animal populations and ecosystems. Heike K. Lotze, Marta Coll, Anna M. Magera, Christine Ward-Paige, Laura Airoldi, with permission from Elsevier; (b) ©iStock/FRANKHILDEBRAND; (c) ©iStock/Alexander Sher; (d) National Park Service

(i.e., ecological restoration). However, in a much discussed article titled "The Big Lie: Human Restoration of Nature," Eric Katz (1992) argues that ecological restoration is actually inimical to naturalness and natural value.

Each of the ecological restorations described above is intended to benefit ecological systems, processes, and/or species. However, like all restorations, they are only necessary due to prior ecological degradation. One of Katz's concerns about ecological restoration is that it is a **technofix** for the widespread ecological harms caused by large human populations, high-impact lifestyles, and the socioeconomic systems that support them. Rather than changing behaviors or reforming ideologies and institutions, which are the sources of the

(cont.)

BOX 4.5 *(cont.)*

problems, restoration employs scientific and technology power to imperfectly and inadequately repair and recreate ecological systems. (See Box 12.3 for further discussion of technofix critiques). Another of Katz's concerns is that the products of restoration are not natural. They are "an artifact created to meet human satisfactions and interests" (2003, 391). On Katz's view, what distinguishes nature from artifacts is that nature is not intentionally designed and has no purpose, whereas artifacts "are essentially anthropocentric. They are created for human use, human purpose—they serve a function for human life. Their existence is centered on human life" (2003, 392). People choose to conduct ecological restorations. People design and implement them. Therefore, they express people's wants, interests, and desires for an ecological space. For this reason, they cannot produce nature or natural value, according to Katz. The big lie is that "technologically created 'nature' will be passed off as reality. . . . Depending on the adequacy of our technology, these restored and redesigned natural areas will appear more or less natural, but they will never be natural—they will be anthropocentrically designed human artifacts" (2003, 392).

Katz is not opposed to repairing ecological damage. He would agree that it is better for the Chesapeake Bay to not be polluted, for golden lion tamarin habitat to be connected, and for giant kelp forests to be reestablished. However, in his view, when we do these things "We are not restoring nature; we are not making it whole and healthy again" (2003, 396). Therefore, he believes that we must focus on preventing the causes of degradation, rather than promote the promise of ecological restoration. Moreover, we should not accept ecological degradation on the grounds that it can be undone and nature made as good as or better than before. Such claims are common in justifying extractive and industrial activities. For example, restoration to pre-impact conditions was promised as part of the approval processes for the Holcim cement plant in Sainte Genevieve, Missouri, which is one of the largest cement manufacturing facilities in the world. It can produce up to 4 million metric tons of cement each year (cement manufacturing is a significant source of greenhouse gas emissions), and includes 1,700 acres of quarry and plant operations. The promise of river and salmon run restoration is currently part of the justification for approval of the Chuitna strip coal mine in Alaska, which would be sited along a salmon spawning tributary to the Chuitna River. Katz's concern with these kinds of cases is not only that the restorations will not be successful in repairing the damage, but that even if they are the loss of naturalness will not be recovered.

(cont.)

BOX 4.5 *(cont.)*

For these reasons, Katz sees ecological restoration as a sort of **moral hazard**. He believes that the false promise of being able to return things to how they were prior to ecological degradation makes it more likely that people will permit ecologically harmful activities. Something is a moral hazard if it increases the probability of people engaging in risky behavior to the detriment of others. For example, federally subsidized coastal flood insurance in the United States is thought to be a moral hazard because it encourages people to build in places with a high likelihood of being damaged in storms, since they do not have to pay the full cost of the insurance. Research on geoengineering—intentionally manipulating climatic processes—to address global climate change is thought by some to be a moral hazard because it could reduce the urgency with which greenhouse gas mitigation is pursued.

What do you think of Katz's critiques of ecological restoration? Do you agree with him that restoration cannot recreate nature or natural value? Is Katz correct that all restorations are artifacts designed for human purposes and to satisfy human interests? Or can a restoration be nonanthropocentric, at least in the sense of being intended primarily to serve nonhuman interests? Do you think ecological restoration really is a moral hazard, such that the capacity for restoration ought not be used as part of the justification for ecologically degrading activities? Or is it reasonable to consider the capacity to repair ecological harms as part of the evaluation of and justification for industrial projects?

4.5 SUMMARY

The primary questions addressed in this chapter were:

- Do natural processes and systems have value in virtue of their being human independent—that is, is naturalness a value-adding property?
- If they do have value in virtue of their naturalness, what sort of value is it?

Over the course of discussing these questions several different types of value were distinguished. These included instrumental value and final (or intrinsic) value. Instrumental value is the value that something possesses as a means to an end. Final value is the value that something has in itself or for what it is. Within intrinsic value it is useful to distinguish between subjective and objective value. Subjective value is when something is valued for noninstrumental reasons. Objective value is when something's value is not dependent on the attitudes or stances of valuers. Objective value is thought to be important in environmental ethics because if something has objective value, then people need to recognize it as valuable, whether or not they currently do so. Therefore, if naturalness, species, ecosystems, or animals have objective value, that will make a claim on all people (or all valuers) to respond appropriately to them, regardless of their own personal views. It is clear that nature and naturalness often have subjective final value. Many people value places and species for the human-independent processes that created them and for their being free from human design, control, and impacts. It is less clear and more controversial whether naturalness has objective value. Consideration of natural value will arise throughout this textbook, and will be particularly salient during discussions regarding species conservation and ecosystem management (Sections 13.5–13.7).

KEY TERMS (SEE GLOSSARY FOR DEFINITIONS):

artificial alternatives concern	natural resources
assisted recovery	natural value
contingent valuation method	objective final value (objective value)
ecological restoration	option value
ecosystem services	problem of incommensurability
endemic species	replication argument
final value	subjective final value (subjective value)
instrumental value	technofix
intrinsic value	value realism
moral hazard	

REVIEW QUESTIONS

- What is the difference between instrumental and final (or intrinsic) value?
- What are the two types of final value discussed in this chapter and how do they differ?
- Why is the issue of whether anything in nature has final value, and especially objective value, thought to be so important to environmental ethics?

- What is the replication argument for the conclusion that naturalness is a value-adding property?
- Why is economic valuation of ecosystem services thought to be crucial to environmental decision-making?
- What are the concerns about economic valuations of environmental goods and values?

DISCUSSION QUESTIONS

- Do you agree that some values are incommensurable with economic valuation? If so, which sorts of values are they and why are they incommensurable?
- Do you think that naturalness is a value-adding property? If so, what sort of value is it—objective or subjective? Is it always value-adding, or only for some types of things or under some conditions?
- Do you agree that people's environmental responsibilities will be much stronger if nature, or some part of it, possesses final value, particularly objective final value? Why or why not?

FURTHER READING

Early and influential work on the intrinsic value of nature includes:

Rolston, Holmes, III. *Environmental Ethics: Duties to and Values in the Natural World.* Temple University Press, 1989.

Smith, Barry, ed. *The Intrinsic Value of Nature* (special issue). *The Monist* 75, no. 2 (1992).

O'Neill, John. *Ecology, Policy and Politics: Human Well-Being and the Natural World.* Routledge, 1993.

Excellent discussions on value realism and environmental values can be found in:

Jamieson, Dale. *Ethics and the Environment.* Cambridge University Press, 2008.

McShane, Katie. "Neosentimentalism and Environmental Ethics." *Environmental Ethics* 33, no. 1 (2011): 5–23.

O'Neill, John, Alan Holland, and Andrew Light. *Environmental Values.* Routledge, 2008.

Mark Sagoff's work on environmental values and environmental economics has been enormously influential in environmental ethics:

Sagoff, Mark. *The Economy of the Earth.* Cambridge University Press, 1988.

Sagoff, Mark. *Price, Principle, and the Environment.* Cambridge University Press, 2004.

Insightful discussions on nature, value, and ecological restoration can be found in:

Throop, William, ed. *Environmental Restoration.* Humanity Books, 2000.

Higgs, Eric. *Nature by Design: People, Natural Process, and Ecological Restoration.* MIT Press, 2003.

Thompson, Allen, and Jeremy Bendik-Keymer, eds. *Ethical Adaptation to Climate Change: Human Virtues of the Future.* MIT Press, 2012.

An influential accounting of ecosystem services can be found in:

Millennium Ecosystem Assessment. *Ecosystem and Human Well-Being: Synthesis.* Island Press, 2005.

PART III: MORAL CONSIDERABILITY: WHICH INDIVIDUALS MATTER?

CHAPTER FIVE

ANTHROPOCENTRISM, RATIOCENTRISM, AND INDIRECT DUTIES

ETHICS CONCERNS HOW WE ought to treat others. In interpersonal ethics, the focus is how we ought to treat other people. In environmental ethics, the focus is also on how we ought to treat nonhumans and the environment. Therefore, a central component of environmental ethics is determining which, if any, nonhumans we ought to care about and how we ought to care about them. These issues—*whom/what we ought to care about* and *how we ought to care about them*—are the focus of the next several chapters. They are crucial to how we should approach decisions regarding the environment. Should we aim to protect the rights of people? To maximize human welfare? Preserve every species? Prevent animal suffering? Promote ecological integrity? All of these things?

A large part of the "whom should we care about?" question concerns whether we should care primarily or even exclusively about people. The next two chapters focus on views that are **anthropocentric**. "Anthro" means "human" and "centric" means "centered," so these are views that argue for putting the interests of human beings at the center of environmental decision-making. Several later chapters (7, 11–13) focus on views that are **nonanthropocentric**, or that advocate considering the interests of nonhumans as well. This issue—anthropocentrism vs. nonanthropocentrism—is prominent within environmental ethics because what we ought to do is very different if the only goal is to promote human interests than if it also is to respect nonhuman organisms and species. For example, we ought to eat different foods if we need to concern ourselves with the suffering of animals than if we do not, and we ought to allocate water differently if the goal is to conserve species than if it is to promote economic activity.

This chapter begins with an overview of several terms and concepts that are prominent in the environmental ethics discourse regarding who and what we ought to care about. It then focuses on the arguments for and against anthropocentrism.

✳ BOX 5.1

CONSERVATION VERSUS PRESERVATION

Over 15 percent of the planet's terrestrial and inland water areas and ~10 percent of marine areas within national jurisdictions are officially protected (UNEP-WCMC and IUCN 2016). They are places that have been designated for management and maintenance of environmental goods and values. However, there are a wide variety of types of protected areas and goals for protected areas. Some protected areas are focused on *preserving* biodiversity and natural phenomena. Others focus on *conserving* natural resources and managing them for the long-term benefit of citizens. Very often, protected areas are intended to both preserve nature and provide goods and opportunities for people. For example, the legislation that created the National Park Service of the United States in 1916 states that it "shall promote and regulate the use of the Federal areas known as national parks, monuments and reservations. . . which purpose is to conserve the scenery and the natural and historical objects and the wild life therein and to provide for the enjoyment of the same in such manner and by such means as will leave them unimpaired for the enjoyment of future generations" (United States Congress, Sec. 1).

Because protected areas can involve conservation, preservation, or both, there is continuous debate regarding what sorts of activities should be allowed in them. **Conservationists**—those who believe that protections should be for the benefit of people—tend to push for greater access and use—for example, logging, off-road vehicles, increased development (such as roads and accommodations) in remote areas, grazing, mining, hunting and fishing. **Preservationists**—those who believe that management should be for the protection of nature—tend to oppose greater access and use. Therefore, administrating agencies are frequently faced with making highly contested determinations regarding what should be permitted. Here are just a few recent examples from

(cont.)

BOX 5.1 *(cont.)*

the United States: Should snowmobiles be allowed in Yellowstone National Park, and if so, how many? Should horizontal mining be allowed under national parks (i.e., a down shaft drilled outside the park and then a horizontal shaft to the

Image 5.1a Castle Geyser, Yellowstone National Park, USA
Source: ©iStock/Poul Riishede

Image 5.1b Palau National Marine Sanctuary, Republic of Palau
Source: robertharding / Alamy Stock Photo

(cont.)

BOX 5.1 *(cont.)*

Image 5.1c   Ngorongoro Conservation Area, Tanzania
Source: ©iStock/chuvipro

Image 5.1d   Lake Pehoe, Torres del Paine National Park, Patagonia, Chile
Source: ©iStock/padchas

(cont.)

BOX 5.1 *(cont.)*

minerals under the park)? Should hotel development be allowed on the rim of the Grand Canyon? Should new roads be prohibited in the Tongass National Forest? Should Breckenridge ski area in Colorado be allowed to expand onto an additional peak in a national forest? Should offshore oil drilling be expanded in the Gulf of Mexico or permitted in the Arctic National Wildlife Refuge?

Each of these cases has to do with what the goals for the protected area ought to be, which, in turn, depends upon the values that are operative. Conservationists often endorse anthropocentrism—the view that only people are directly morally considerable. Gifford Pinchot, the first chief of the US Forest Service, thought that "Forestry is the art of producing from the forest whatever it can yield for the service of man. . . . The central idea of the Forester, in handling the forest, is to promote and perpetuate its greatest use to men" (1914, 13, 23). Preservationists typically reject anthropocentrism and endorse human-independent values, such as the direct moral considerability of nonhuman plants and animals and the objective value of nature and biodiversity. John Muir, an influential naturalist, writer, and advocate of the preservation of wilderness once wrote, "The world, we are told, was made especially for man—a presumption not supported by all the facts" (1916, 160). Conservationists and preservationists are often on the same side of an issue. For example, conservationist hunters and anglers and ecologically-oriented preservationists both typically support protecting wetlands from pollution, draining, and logging. However, in many other cases preservationists staunchly oppose conservationist uses of protected areas.

One of the most prominent conservation-preservation debates in US history concerned a proposal in the early twentieth century to build a dam to flood the Hetch Hetchy valley in Yosemite National Park. Muir, who was instrumental in building public support for Yosemite and convincing President Theodore Roosevelt to incorporate the Yosemite Valley into the park, vigorously opposed the project: "Dam Hetch Hetchy! As well dam for water-tanks the people's cathedrals and churches, for no holier temple has ever been consecrated by the heart of man" (1916, para. 23). Pinchot strongly supported the dam on the grounds that the best use of the valley was as a drinking water reservoir for the city of San Francisco. In the end, Congress and President Woodrow Wilson authorized the project. In 1923 the O'Shaughnessy Dam was completed, damming the Tuolumne River. The resulting reservoir now provides drinking water to 2.6 million people in the San Francisco Bay area and generates 1.6 billion kilowatts of hydroelectric energy each year. However, the controversy has not ended. There is an ongoing movement to remove the dam, restore the flow of the Tuolumne, and "raise" the Hetch Hetchy Valley.

5.1 MORAL STATUS TERMINOLOGY

Something is **morally considerable** if it needs to be taken into account in deliberations regarding actions, practices, or policies that might affect it. Rocks generally are not regarded as morally considerable. If you and I are thinking about going down to the lake to skip some stones, we do not have to consider what the impacts will be on the stones. People generally are regarded as morally considerable. If you and I are thinking of going down to the lake to throw stones at people on the water, we do need to take into account how our actions will affect the people. Human beings are thought to have the sort of value that grounds, at a minimum, responsibilities not to harm them without good justification, and may even ground responsibilities to promote their good or interests. This is thought to hold independently of people's actual evaluative attitudes or stances regarding the worth of others. Even if we dislike the people on the lake, and believe that they are worthless, it would still be wrong to throw stones at them for our amusement. We ought to see them as morally considerable and take their interests into account, even if we currently do not. Thus, the **moral status** of people is different from that of stones.

But not all stones have the same moral status. Some stones are morally considerable. We saw this earlier with Uluru, the large rock monolith sacred to aboriginal peoples in Australia. It needs to be taken into account—it is considerable—because of its cultural significance. It also would not be permissible for you and me to take our friend's special rock collection without her permission in order to use it for stone skipping. In these cases, the rocks are **indirectly morally considerable**. We need to consider them, but not for their own sake. We only need to do so because they are the property of other people or valued by them. Their considerability is derivative on the respect we owe to people. It is the people that are **directly morally considerable**. We need to consider people's interests *for their own sake*. When something is directly considerable in this way—that is, when it has interests that we ought to care about for its own sake—it has **inherent worth**.

Anthropocentrism is the view that the criterion for having inherent worth is being a member of the species *Homo sapiens*, and that all and only human beings are directly morally considerable. **Nonanthropocentrism** is the view that at least some nonhumans have inherent worth. However, there are different versions of nonanthropocentrism based on what criteria they endorse for direct moral considerability and, therefore, which nonhumans they regard as directly morally considerable. **Ratiocentrism** is the view that all and only robustly rational beings are directly morally considerable. This includes cognitively developed humans, but would also encompass robustly rational artificial intelligences or members of other species, if there are any. **Sentientism** is the view that all and only organisms that have psychological states or mental experiences—such as birds and mammals—are directly morally considerable. **Biocentrism** is the view that all living things are directly morally considerable, since they all can be directly benefited or harmed.

Some environmental ethicists believe that collectives, such as ecosystems and species, also have inherent worth. **Individualism** is the view that only individual organisms are morally considerable. Anthropocentrism, ratiocentrism, sentientism, and biocentrism are individualist views. **Holism** is the view that some environmental collectives are also morally considerable.

This and the next chapter focus on anthropocentric and ratiocentric views. Chapter 7 focuses on nonanthropocentric individualist views. Chapters 11 through 13 focus on holistic views.

5.2 ARGUMENTS FOR ANTHROPOCENTRISM

Anthropocentrism is the view that all and only human beings have inherent worth. All other things—including the environment—are only valuable because we value them (subjective value) or because they are useful for accomplishing our goals or promoting our well-being (instrumental value). On this view, all value flows from us.

A number of arguments have been offered in support of anthropocentrism. Some of them are clearly unsound. For example, it is sometimes argued that anthropocentrism best corresponds to what most people really think about the environment; therefore, it is the one we ought to adopt. Even assuming that the empirical claim is true—that this is what most people think—it does not follow that we should adopt the view. The inference from "most people think this" to "this is true" is not reliable. There was a time when most people thought that women should not be able to own property or vote, and that the world was flat. To claim that something is true just because it is what most people believe is the **fallacy of appeal to the crowd**.

Another argument sometimes offered for anthropocentrism is the **argument from participatory decision-making**:

1. Decisions about how we should treat the environment are collective, participatory decisions.
2. Nonhuman beings lack the capacity to participate in collective decision-making processes.
3. If nonhumans cannot participate in these processes, it is not possible to know what their preferences/interests would be.
4. Therefore, only human preferences/interests can and should be included in decision-making processes.

This argument is unsound. Premise 3 is false. It is possible to infer what is in the interests of nonhuman organisms based on an understanding of what promotes their health and functioning, as well as by observing their responses to different situations and conditions. This is routinely done for animals in veterinarian offices and for plants in gardens, for example. It is no mystery that acid rain is bad for trees, heartworms are bad for dogs, and oxygen depletion is bad for fish. Those things are not in their interests. They impair their ability to thrive and cause them to suffer. Moreover, it is common to use proxies to represent the interests of others when they cannot do it for themselves. This is routinely done by parents for infants, for example. So there is no great difficulty in representing or considering the interests of whales in global whaling treaty deliberations or of trees in ecosystem management planning, even though whales and trees cannot participate in decision-making processes.

But there is also a deeper conceptual problem with the argument from participatory decision-making. According to anthropocentrism, whether something has inherent worth is determined by whether it is a member of a particular biological group. That is, it is a **biological group membership** approach to determining moral considerability. Whether something has inherent worth depends upon whether it is a member of the biological group *Homo sapiens*. However, the argument from participatory decision-making appeals to a capacity—the ability to participate in collective decision-making—in order to determine whether something's interests should be considered. But there is no reason to think that all and only members of the biological group (*Homo sapiens*) have the capacity at issue (the ability to participate in collective decision-making). In fact, there are many *Homo sapiens* who lack the capacity—for example, infants and severely mentally disabled people. Moreover, it is at least possible that there could be members of other species—alien species or future terrestrial species—that do have the capacity. Therefore, even if the capacity were necessary for possessing inherent worth, it would not support anthropocentrism, since some nonhumans might have the capacity and many humans lack it. Thus, there is a mismatch between the type of view that anthropocentrism is—biological group–based—and the criteria used in this argument to defend it—capacities-based.

BOX 5.2	THOUGHT EXPERIMENTS

MORAL STATUS

A. Imagine that it turns out that what we think of as *Homo sapiens* is actually two distinct species (*Homo mapiens* and *Home napiens*) that evolved independently to have the same physiological, psychological, and cognitive capacities. Do you think that upon this discovery the individuals of each species would be justified in ignoring the interests of the other species? Or justified in considering the interests of members of the other species less than those of their own species? For example, would it be permissible for members of *Homo mapiens* to try to exploit members of *Homo napiens*, and vice versa? Why or why not?

(cont.)

BOX 5.2 *(cont.)*

B. Imagine that you are stranded on a lifeboat with an orangutan, an adult human being with the same cognitive and psychological capacities as the orangutan, and an alien with cognitive and psychological capacities exceeding your own. The lifeboat can support only two of you, so two must be sacrificed. Who should it be and why?

C. Imagine that an orangutan is given a treatment to increase its general intelligence and range of psychological responses. As a result, its mental capacities are equivalent to (or even slightly exceed) those of healthy adult human beings. Is there any reason that its interests should not be afforded equal consideration to those of a human being?

Thinking about these hypothetical cases should help generate ideas related to whether moral considerability is properly based on biological group membership or on possession of capacities. Do the reasons on which you base your positions on the cases appeal to the capacities, relationships, or group membership of the individuals involved? Do the reasons hold up to critical evaluation?

One reason that people are attracted to anthropocentrism is that it is inclusive of all human beings, regardless of their stage of development or capacities. According to anthropocentrism, even if a human being has severe and permanent brain injuries, dementia, or mental disabilities, such that she is not able to engage in reciprocal cooperative schemes or cannot be held responsible for her actions, she still has the same worth as any other human being. She has human dignity and is entitled to respect, just as they are, because she, like them, is a human being.

But is a biological grouping approach to moral status defensible? Some have thought not. The reason is that unless some justification is provided for why a particular biological grouping should define the limits of inherent worth (or direct moral considerability), then the view commits the **fallacy of begging the question**. The answer to "why should only humans be regarded as having inherent worth" cannot be "because they are human." However, that is just what the species membership view seems to suggest. Peter Singer, a prominent animal welfare proponent (see Section 7.1), has influentially argued that moral status distinctions made on the basis of species membership are arbitrary in the same way as are moral status distinctions made on the basis of skin color or sex (Singer 1989). Differences in skin color and sex among human beings are **factual differences**. People really do have different colored skin and there really are different sexes. Moreover, these are explained (in part) by genetic differences between people. However, despite their being real biological differences, they are arbitrary and unjustified bases for attributing different worth to people. The reason for this is that the factual differences do not track anything ethically significant—for example, moral agency, autonomy, types (or range) of interests, or ability to participate in social relationships. As a result, skin color and sex are not **morally relevant properties**. To take them to be is racist and sexist.

Singer thinks the same is true of species membership. Members of *Homo sapiens* really are biologically different from those who are not members of the species, and there is a genetic explanation for this. But, like sex differences and skin colors, this fails to track anything morally significant. Some human beings are moral agents, highly autonomous, capable of reciprocal concern, and able to participate in complex cooperative arrangements, but not all are. Moreover, some individuals of some nonhuman species—for example, orangutans and dolphins—are more capable of these than some humans. Similarly, some nonhuman animals have equal or greater psychological capacities than do some human beings, and so have comparable or even more complex and diverse interests. Because membership in the species *Homo sapiens* seems to fail to track anything ethically significant, basing worth on it seems to those who offer this argument to be unjustified discrimination against nonhumans—that is, **speciesism**.

In response, proponents of anthropocentrism might argue that the fact that all healthy, fully biologically mature members of *Homo sapiens* have comparable interests and capacities justifies treating membership in the species as morally relevant. However, the question is asked, why should co-membership in a group confer the moral status associated with some members of the group to all members, even those that lack the relevant capacities? After all, there are a lot of possible biological groups—for example, vertebrates, eukaryotes, lactose-intolerant mammals. Why should we prioritize one grouping over another when determining direct moral considerability? To critics of biological grouping accounts of moral status it seems arbitrary and question-begging.

The alternative to a biological grouping account of moral considerability is a **capacities-based account**. According to capacities-based accounts, what matters to whether and how we should consider something's interests is what the individual is capable of, what its interests are, how it can be harmed and benefited, and the relationships that it can have. All the prominent individualist views on inherent worth other than anthropocentrism are capacities-based, although they differ with respect to *which* capacities are the basis for inherent worth. In fact, in response to the concerns raised above about biological group membership views of moral considerability, many proponents of "anthropocentrism" actually favor ratiocentrism, a capacities-based view on which being a robust rational agent is the basis for inherent worth.

※ BOX 5.3   TOPIC TO CONSIDER

CONSPECIFICITY AND MORAL STATUS

It is sometimes argued that we have a special responsibility or obligation to other members of *Homo sapiens* because we are members of the same species. Do you think that conspecificity—being a member of the same species—is a morally relevant property, such that it justifies prioritizing the interests of individuals of your own species? Or does this argument beg the question or assume its conclusion in the same way as those discussed above are thought to? Why or why not?

5.3 RATIOCENTRISM

Ratiocentrism is the view that only robust rational beings have inherent worth ("ratio" means "reason" in Latin). There are many different types of reason. There is creative reasoning, instrumental reasoning, inferential reasoning, formal reasoning, and strategic reasoning, for example. Many of these varieties of reason are exhibited throughout the animal kingdom. Birds, primates, cephalopods, and many other types of organisms have been shown to use creative problem-solving and to innovate tools to try to achieve their objectives. Some researchers have even suggested that plants and microbials exhibit a kind of collective intelligence in response to potential threats.

However, the variety of reason at issue with respect to ratiocentrism is that associated with being responsible for one's actions. A common view is that in order for someone to be held morally responsible—that is, to be praiseworthy or blameworthy for her actions—she needs, at a minimum, to understand moral concepts and principles. That is, she needs to have the capacity to understand that some things are right and some things are wrong. It is also commonly thought that moral responsibility requires the capacity to deliberate about what rules or principles should be adopted and what ought to be done in concrete situations, as well as to act on the basis of those deliberations. When these criteria are not met—for example, in toddlers, pets, and psychopaths—we do not ascribe responsibility in the same way as we do for those who possess the capacities (and are not under coercive conditions). We do not praise and blame them, though we might try to train them, rehabilitate them, or protect ourselves from them.

Because this type of rationality—often called **rational agency** or **moral agency**—is thought to be necessary for moral responsibility, it is often inferred that morality applies only to those who have it—that is, that all and only moral agents are directly morally considerable. Remove all the moral agents from the world and there is no ethics, just events that occur. Morality, and so direct moral considerability, only enters the world with moral agents. Therefore, only moral agents have the sort of value that is associated with inherent worth on this view.

A difficulty often raised against this argument for the moral agency criterion for inherent worth is that it conflates *moral worth* with *inherent worth*. Only moral agents can be morally good or morally bad (i.e., virtuous or vicious), and absent moral agents there is no moral action (i.e., actions that are right or wrong). However, it does not follow from this that when moral agents act they need to consider only the interests of other moral agents. It is true that there is no moral behavior in a world without moral agents, but this does not tell us what moral agents ought to value or care about when they are in the world. The fact that someone can be harmed by us, depends upon us, or can be benefited by us seems sufficient to make concern for their interests possible, and the question then becomes whether we ought to consider them. In some cases—such as infants—not caring for their interests for their own sake is commonly considered a failure of moral responsibility. Perhaps the same is true if we neglect the interests of nonhumans. At the very least, proponents of this criticism conclude, the fact that nonhumans are not moral agents does not settle the question of whether they have inherent worth. They might still be **moral patients** or **moral subjects**. Their interests might still be directly morally considerable.

The same problem applies to attempts to ground inherent worth in other capacities associated with rationality. For example, it has been argued that only rational beings have inherent worth because only they are capable of reciprocal concern and mutual obligation, representing themselves as objects of worth (or moral concern), or participating in collective decision-making. Even if it is correct that only sufficiently rational beings (or beings that are rational in certain ways) are capable of these things, it does not follow that they cannot be concerned for those who lack those capacities. This occurs all the time in parenting and end-of-life care, for example. The incapacity of nonrational living things to participate in the sort of activities and relationships that rational agents can does not itself imply that their good should not be considered by moral agents. If they can be harmed, why should their good not be taken into account? That nonhuman living things are not rational or moral agents does not settle the issue, according to this objection.

One commonly raised concern about ratiocentrism, which has already been alluded to, is that it excludes human beings who lack the requisite cognitive and psychological capacities for moral agency, such as infants and the severely mentally disabled. Since they are not moral agents, they lack inherent worth on this view. Yet, because of their vulnerability and dependence, it seems as if they are especially worthy of our concern and assistance. Thus, many people find the implications of ratiocentrism unacceptable. It seems to give up what is most attractive about anthropocentrism—that is, that all human beings have inherent worth, and they have it equally.

A concern frequently raised against both anthropocentrism and ratiocentrism is that they are not sufficiently "environmental" to function as an environmental ethic.

The core motivation for developing environmental ethics is that the predominant ethical views in Western thought, in which people are at the center of everything, are inadequate. Part of the reason that there are such deep and diverse environmental problems is that people have considered and treated the nonhuman environment as a boundless resource to be used to satisfy human needs and wants. People have viewed themselves as exceptional in the biological and ecological world, because of our elevated rational capacities and agency. But it is precisely our rationality and drive to innovate and consume without restraint, particularly in affluent countries since the Industrial Revolution, that have created the undesirable ecological situations that we face. We continue to consume resources faster than they can be replenished, degrade ecological systems, and produce enormous amounts of pollution and waste in order to satisfy our own desires. Therefore, this objection concludes, anthropocentrism and ratiocentrism are inadequate as environmental ethics. Far from being the solution, their elevation of and exclusive concern with humans and rational beings are part of the problem. Environmental ethics needs to get away from human-centeredness. In what follows, I refer to this as the **inadequacy objection.**

✳ BOX 5.4

CHRISTIANITY, ANTHROPOCENTRISM, AND THE HISTORICAL ROOTS OF THE ENVIRONMENTAL CRISIS

Environmental problems often have complex economic, technological, sociological, and ecological causes. However, there are also often attitudinal or ideological factors involved. How we treat the nonhuman world and use natural resources are influenced by how we conceptualize them and view our relationship to them. In an influential article title "The Historical Roots of Our Ecological Crisis," Lynn White Jr. argued that the crucial ideological contribution to environmental problems is the view that human beings are separate from nature and properly have dominion to use it in service of our ends. White also argued that this **dominion model** of the human-nature relationship has it roots in the Western Judeo-Christian tradition:

> Christianity inherited from Judaism not only a concept of time as nonrepetitive and linear but also a striking story of creation. By gradual stages a loving and all-powerful God had created light and darkness, the

(cont.)

BOX 5.4 *(cont.)*

heavenly bodies, the earth and all its plants, animals, birds, and fishes. Finally, God had created Adam and, as an afterthought, Eve to keep man from being lonely. Man named all the animals, thus establishing his dominance over them. God planned all of this explicitly for man's benefit and rule: No item in the physical creation had any purpose save to serve man's purposes. And, although man's body is made of clay, he is not simply part of nature: He is made in God's image.

Especially in its Western form, Christianity is the most anthropocentric religion the world has seen. . . . Christianity, in absolute contrast to ancient paganism and Asia's religions (except, perhaps, Zoroastrianism), not only established a dualism of man and nature but also insisted that it is God's will that man exploit nature for his proper ends.

. . . Hence we shall continue to have a worsening ecological crisis until we reject the Christian axiom that nature has not reason for existence save to serve man. (1967, 1205, 1207)

White then goes on to argue that the view that science and technology should be used to control and modify nature for human ends is intertwined with dominion theology.

Each of the key components of White's view has been widely discussed: (1) that anthropocentrism is a prominent contributing factor to ecological crises; (2) that the Judeo-Christian tradition is the historical source of anthropocentrism; (3) that the Western use of science and technology to master nature both expresses and reinforces the dominion theology; and (4) that the ultimate causes of our ecological crisis are as much spiritual or ideological as they are material (i.e., technological and economic). Many theologians and religion scholars have argued that the Western Judeo-Christian tradition is not ideologically tied to either anthropocentrism or the view that people have dominion over nature, even as they often acknowledge that the dominion view has been and remains prominent among Christians. After all, there is a diversity of Judeo-Christian traditions, each of which can have a plurality of conceptions of the human-nature relationship. White himself suggested that an alternative Christian conception of the human-nature relationship can be found in the example of the twelfth-century figure Saint Francis of Assisi, whom Pope John Paul II would later (in 1979) proclaim the patron saint of ecology. According to Saint Francis, all of creation needs to be recognized and respected as an expression of the

(cont.)

BOX 5.4 *(cont.)*

divine. When nature is viewed in this way, humans are not exceptional, but are "sisters" and "brothers" with all other creatures. We therefore ought to care for and protect both individual organisms and ecological systems as a whole with a sense of love, wonder, awe, and affection. This might be called the **care model**.

Another alternative to the dominion model of the human-nature relationship is often referred to as the **stewardship model**. On this view, God has entrusted humans, rational beings with conscience created in the divine image, with overseeing the rest of creation, which God also sees as good. Humans do have a unique and exceptional position on this view. But we do not have dominion over nature to use it for our ends. Instead, we have a special divinely prescribed responsibility to manage it in ways that do not diminish or disrespect its goodness, which includes not degrading ecological systems or reducing biological diversity. This view is sometimes described as theocentric, rather than anthropocentric, since nature is to be used and treated according to God's will rather than for human ends.

Elements of both the care model and the stewardship model can be found in Pope Francis's recent encyclical on the environment, *Laudato Si'* or *On Care for Our Common Home*. Pope Francis largely endorses White's view that "modern anthropocentrism" (or "distorted anthropocentrism" or "misguided anthropocentrism") in combination with "the technocratic paradigm" have been the enabling ideology for our ecological crisis (para. 101–136). "The technocratic paradigm" is the identification of increases in technological power to modify creation with "progress," as well as faith in technological innovation to solve all our problems and provide perpetual material growth (see Section 5.5 and Box 12.3). Moreover, Pope Francis agrees with White that "[s]ince the roots of our trouble are so largely religious, the remedy must also be essentially religious, whether we call it that or not" (White 1967, 1207). What is needed is "a change of humanity," or a change in our outlooks, attitudes, and values (Francis 2015, para. 9).

In *Laudato Si'*, Pope Francis "forcefully rejects" the dominion model and condemns the way in which "We have come to see ourselves as [Mother Earth's] lords and masters, entitled to plunder her at will" (para. 2):

We are not God. The earth was here before us and it has been given to us. This allows us to respond to the charge that Judeo-Christian thinking, on

(cont.)

BOX 5.4 *(cont.)*

the basis of the Genesis account which grants man "dominion" over the earth (cf. *Gen.* 1:28), has encouraged the unbridled exploitation of nature by painting him as domineering and destructive by nature. This is not a correct interpretation of the Bible as understood by the Church. Although it is true that we Christians have at times incorrectly interpreted the Scriptures, nowadays we must forcefully reject the notion that our being created in God's image and given dominion over the earth justifies absolute domination over other creatures. (para. 67) . . .

Clearly, the Bible has no place for a tyrannical anthropocentrism unconcerned for other creatures. (para. 68)

Pope Francis takes the example and teachings of Saint Francis of Assisi (who is the Pope's namesake) to demonstrate that "If we approach nature and the environment without [his] openness to awe and wonder, if we no longer speak the language of fraternity and beauty in our relationship with the world, our attitude will be that of masters, consumers, ruthless exploiters, unable to set limits on their immediate needs," (para. 11). In line with the stewardship view, he urges that "All of us can cooperate as instruments of God for the care of creation, each according to his or her own culture, experience, involvements and talents" (para. 14). He believes that "Each community can take from the bounty of the earth whatever it needs for subsistence, but it also has the duty to protect the earth and to ensure its fruitfulness for coming generations" (para. 67).

Each of these models—dominion, stewardship, and care—have close (albeit not perfect) analogs in nontheological environmental ethics. Like the dominion model, some versions of anthropocentrism hold that human beings are exceptional in ways that justify treating the environment in whatever ways best satisfy people's current wants and needs (see Section 5.4). Similar to the stewardship model, enlightened anthropocentrism holds that we ought to treat the environment in ways that are beneficial to all of humanity, now and in the future, even if that is different from what we currently would want to do (see Chapter 6). And like the care model, biocentrism, ecocentrism, and deep ecology argue that we should regard and treat the biological world with love and respect (see Chapters 7, 11, and 12). For reasons discussed earlier (Section 2.5), it is perhaps reasonable to believe that well-justified theological and nontheological environmental ethics should converge.

5.4 ACTUAL PREFERENCE ANTHROPOCENTRISM

As discussed above, many environmental thinkers have argued that far from being a solution to our environmental problems, anthropocentric and ratiocentric world-views and accounts of moral considerability are a contributing cause of them. This is why the field of environmental ethics has been dominated by the development of and discourse around nonanthropocentric and nonindividualistic (or holistic) ethics. Some environmental ethicists believe that an ethic cannot even be called "environ-mental" unless it in some way values nonhuman entities or human-independent pro-cesses for their own sake.

However, those who continue to endorse anthropocentrism (and ratiocentrism) often respond by arguing that the problem has not been anthropocentrism *per se*, but rather a particular type of anthropocentrism, which might be called **actual preference anthropocentrism**. According to actual preference anthropocentrism, we should treat the environment and manage natural resources in whatever ways best satisfy people's actual or current preferences. If people want inexpensive hamburgers, then the indus-trial farming practices and concentrated animal feed operations that provide them are justified. If people want to live low-cost high-energy lifestyles, then available natural resources—from fossil fuels to rivers—should be exploited to deliver it to them. If people want to build golf courses in nature reserves (as was done in Rio de Janeiro for the 2016 Olympics), then that is how the spaces ought to be utilized. If people want to eliminate wolves to increase the availability of game animals, then hunting programs should be established to do it. As William Baxter, a proponent of this view, has put it with respect to pollution:

> From the fact that there is no normative definition of the natural state, it
> follows that there is no normative definition of clean air or pure water—
> hence no definition of polluted air—or of pollution—except by reference
> to the needs of man. The "right" composition of the atmosphere is
> one which has some dust in it and some lead in it and some hydrogen
> sulfide in it—just those amounts that attend a sensibly organized
> society thoughtfully and knowledgeably pursuing the greatest possible
> satisfaction for its human members. (1975, 276)

On this view, the correct amount of pollution is whatever best satisfies people's prefer-ences overall. The same holds for protecting species and ecosystems:

> Damage to penguins, or sugar pines, or geological marvels is, without
> more, simply irrelevant. One must go further . . . and say: Penguins are
> important because people enjoy seeing them walk about rocks; and
> furthermore, the well-being of people would be less impaired by halting
> use of DDT than by giving up penguins. In short, my observations about

environmental problems will be people-oriented. . . . I have no interest in
preserving penguins for their own sake. (Baxter 1975, 275)

Actual preference satisfaction views are open to the inadequacy objection because people have treated and do treat the natural environment however they
need to in order to produce the goods and services that they want. Farmers have
pumped water out of underground aquifers to irrigate crops and increase their
yields, but now we face water shortages. Companies have industrialized their fishing fleets to increase catches, but now fisheries are depleted and aquatic ecosystems
are degraded. Manufacturers have produced huge amounts of inexpensive consumer goods—from personal electronics to plastic toys—but have released enormous amounts of pollution, waste, and greenhouse gases into the environment in
doing so. A narrow focus on satisfying human preferences seems to be what creates
environmental problems.

5.5 TECHNOLOGICAL OPTIMISM

A view that is often associated with actual preference anthropocentrism is **techno-
optimism**, or the idea that technological innovation rather than systemic and behavior
changes is the best way to address most of our significant environmental, health, and social
problems. The basis for technological optimism is that technological innovations have, in
general, dramatically increased the longevity, health, and opportunities in the lives of those
who have access to them. People in highly technologized nations live longer and more comfortably than have people at any time in human history. For instance, the life expectancy
for children born in the United States today is seventy-nine, whereas in 1900 it was forty-
seven (Arias 2011). In fact, life expectancy has increased dramatically in every country in
the world over that period, with global life expectancy at birth now over seventy-one, more
than double what it was in 1900, and healthy life expectancy at birth (the total number of
years a person is expected to live in full health) now over sixty-two (World Bank 2016a;
Murray et al. 2015). Technological innovation and dissemination in areas such as agriculture, food processing and storage, health care, energy, manufacturing, and building materials are widely regarded as among the main causes of longevity and quality-of-life increases.

Proponents of techno-optimism also argue that the rate of technological change
has historically been exponential. So while it is true that we face considerable ecological problems, our scientific understanding and technological capacity to address them
has never been greater; and so long as we continue to encourage innovation it will be
exponentially greater in the near future than it is now, as evidenced by rapid advances
in such things as information and computing technologies, nanomaterials, and synthetic genomics. They also highlight that there have long been warnings that we are
at the edge of social and ecological collapse from rapid growth in consumption and
population—for example, Thomas Malthus's *An Essay on the Principle of Population* in

1798 and Paul Ehrlich's *The Population Bomb* in 1968. But technological innovation has enabled us to dramatically increase the efficiency with which we produce goods. It has helped us to develop synthetic alternatives for scarce resources. It has allowed us to improve how we manage our waste and remediate our pollution. It is also what makes continued economic expansion possible, which is crucial to poverty alleviation.

Therefore, this view concludes, aggressively promoting future technological innovation and dissemination, with associated economic expansion, rather than limiting satisfaction of people's wants and needs and thereby reducing economic activity, is the best way to lift people out of poverty, improve the quality of lives generally, and address our ecological problems. Moreover, why would we make difficult and unwanted changes to our lifestyles and economic systems if we can develop easier to implement and less costly technological solutions to our problems? For example, if we can engineer a way to capture and store carbon dioxide, then we do not need to immediately and dramatically reduce fossil fuel use, which requires massive structural and behavioral changes and could make it more difficult to address energy poverty.

It is largely uncontested that technologies often improve people's lives and that technological innovation must be a crucial component of creating more just and sustainable societies. It is possible to reduce ecological impacts and improve human welfare by expanding low-emissions energy generation and access, designing environmentally benign manufacturing and end-of-life processes, and increasing efficiency in food production, for example. What is contested is how much technological innovation can accomplish in the absence of robust social, institutional, behavioral, and attitudinal changes. Strong technological optimism (or what Pope Francis calls the "technocratic paradigm") is in contrast with the views of Lynn White Jr. and Pope Francis (Box 5.4), as well as those of Aldo Leopold (Chapter 11), environmental virtue ethicists (Chapter 10), and deep ecologists (Chapter 12), each of whom argues that addressing our ecological challenges requires a change in outlook, attitudes, and values, not only technological innovation and dissemination. On their views, without these, increases in technological power are more likely to exacerbate social inequities and environmental challenges than they are to address them. After all, technological power has historically been a contributing cause of social and environmental wrongs and problems, from colonialism to global climate change. Moreover, even when technologies have turned out to be beneficial in the long run, they created very serious problems to which social institutions have had to respond. In the United States, for example, an environmental movement, a host of environmental laws, and federal and state governmental agencies have been needed to address the detrimental ecological and human health effects of industrialization. The United States is not exceptional in these respects; most highly technologized countries have had similar social movements and have institutions with similar responsibilities. Tremendous effort, sacrifice, and social innovation are often required to address the detrimental aspects of technologies.

The relationships between technological power, social justice, and ecological problems are a central component of many environmental issues. With respect to technological optimism, the issue is how much faith we ought to place in technology, as well as what social and attitudinal changes are required to ensure that technological innovation and dissemination—which are going to continue at a rapid pace—promote social justice and environmental sustainability. Moreover, in the context of specific environmental issues and cases—such as global climate change, fresh water shortages in California, air pollution in rapidly developing cities, biodiversity loss in Central America, deforestation in Indonesia, energy access in the developing world, and malnutrition in South Asia—what is the appropriate role for technology in addressing them in socially responsible and environmentally productive ways? Are some environmental problems more amenable to technologically oriented solutions than others? Are some technologies more conducive to improving social justice and environmental integrity than others? The ethics of technology is very much intertwined with environmental ethics.

5.6 INDIRECT DUTIES VIEWS

On anthropocentric accounts of moral status, nonhuman animals do not have inherent worth and are not directly morally considerable. We do not need to care about them for their own sake or in and of themselves. They have only instrumental and subjective value. However, many anthropocentrists emphasize that this does not imply that we can treat animals however we like. Even Immanuel Kant, who was an ardent ratiocentrist, thought that animals should not be harmed for sport, experimented on unnecessarily, killed painfully, or overworked. The reason for this is that nonhuman animals are indirectly morally considerable. We need to consider the interests of animals because of their relationship to people's interests; and we have responsibilities to animals that are derivative on our duties to other people. That is, we have **indirect duties** to them.

One basis for indirect duties to animals is that they are often owned by other people. It is wrong for me to visit your home and kick your television (without your permission) because it is your property, and part of my respecting you involves respecting your property. I do not have a duty to your television not to kick it. I have a duty to you regarding your television. Similarly, even if nonhuman animals do not have inherent worth, it is wrong for me to kick your dog. I have a duty to you not to harm your dog, since it is yours and not mine. My duty regarding your dog is indirect or derivative on the consideration that I owe you.

People also often have an interest in animals that they do not own. Many people care about animals generally and are opposed to their being harmed. Some animals, or animals of particular species, have symbolic, cultural, and economic value—for example, team mascots, California condors, and Chinook salmon. Some animals are valued because they are beautiful, cute, amazing, and unique—such as polar bears, leatherback turtles, and narwhals. Some are economically important or provide ecosystem services. When people care about the interests of animals, or are dependent upon them, that constitutes a reason for other people not to harm them. There is nothing special about the animals involved in this, since they do not have inherent worth on this view. It is just that when people (who do have inherent worth) value or derive benefits from something, other people have a reason to respect it—whether it is artwork, historical sites, ceremonies, or dolphins. These reasons are *pro tanto*. That is, there might be countervailing or overriding considerations that justify taking or harming animals, even when people care about them. But people's concerns for animals are, nonetheless, reasons to consider their interests.

Kant also famously argued that we need to be considerate of animals because cruelty toward them can foster cruelty toward people. On this view, we have a duty to be kind to animals because "tenderness [to them] is subsequently transferred to man" (1997, 212–13) and renders us more likely to fulfill our interpersonal duties. In support of this psychological claim, contemporary proponents of this argument frequently point out that perpetrators of violent crimes sometimes have a prior history of violence toward animals, and that butchers and slaughterhouse workers have at times been prohibited from serving on juries because they are regarded as being inured to suffering and death. (See Box 5.5 for discussion of this argument.)

Objections to indirect duties views typically do not challenge the claim that we have indirect duties to animals. After all, we have indirect duties to people. For example, we have duties to parents regarding their children. We have a responsibility not to interfere with a wide range of decisions that parents make regarding their children, even if we disagree with them. However, we do not have only indirect duties to children. We have responsibilities directly to them as well. We must respect and promote their interests; and this can outweigh our duties to respect parental decisions when those decisions endanger them. Similarly, critics of indirect duties views do not deny that we have indirect duties to animals. However, they believe that nonhuman animals also have inherent worth, their interests are directly morally considerable, and that this warrants protections and welfare laws that limit what people can do to them even if they are people's property and even if they do not foster cruelty toward people. (The core arguments for the inherent worth of nonhuman animals are discussed in Chapter 7.)

Critics also often emphasize the limitations of indirect duties views. If animals are only indirectly considerable, then it would seem to be permissible to treat your own animals however you like, even if it involves abuse or neglect, since it is permissible to harm or destroy your own property. It may be imprudent or irresponsible not to take good care of your car or to kick your television, but they are yours to do with as you will. Moreover, on indirect duties views different animals will be due very different consideration—for instance, industrial farm animals and household pets—since people care about them differently and they are owned for different purposes. These considerations are not arguments against indirect duties views, but they do indicate the limitations of indirect duties views' justificatory power. It is difficult for them to be critical of all cases of animal abuse, and they have what many consider to be an odd implication: If a person abuses animals or destroys their habitat, they wrong the animals' owners or the people who care about them, but not the animals themselves.

✳ BOX 5.5

CORRELATION AND CAUSATION

The claim that cruelty to animals fosters cruelty to people is an empirical claim. There is some quantitative evidence of a correlation between harming animals and harming people (McDonald 2011). However, even if there is a significant positive *correlation* between harming animals and harming people, it does not follow that harming animals *causes* perpetrators to be more likely to harm people (particularly in comparison to other causes of animal cruelty).

Many things that are positively correlated are not causally related. For example, there is a very strong correlation between where I live and who wins the Super Bowl. The NFL team of every city where I have lived has won the Super Bowl within two years of my moving there. However, we should not conclude from this that my moving to a city results in that city's football team winning the Super Bowl, since there is no causal mechanism involved. There is frequently *correlation without causation*. That is why it is a fallacy, the **causation-correlation fallacy**, to infer from the mere fact that two things are correlated, to the conclusion that one is caused by the other. Sometimes, as in the case above, they are not causally related at all. Other times there is a positive correlation between two things because they share a common cause. People carrying umbrellas and outdoor events being canceled are correlated. However, they do not cause each other. Instead, they are each independently caused by something else: rain. Therefore, even if it is shown that cruelty to animals and to humans is positively correlated, it is not justified to immediately conclude that the former causes the later. It might be that people who are cruel to animals are already disposed to be cruel generally—that is, there is a common cause.

It is important in environmental science, policy, and ethics to keep in mind that correlation does not itself imply causation. Conflating them can lead to mistaken conclusions about what causes environmental problems and what ought to be done to address them. For example, it is often claimed that affluence leads to improved air and water quality over time, so promoting economic growth is environmentally beneficial. The basis for this claim is that there is a negative correlation between some pollutants and per capita GDP—as per capita GDP has gone up, those pollutants have decreased (Grossman and Krueger 1991). However, the inference from this data to the conclusion that affluence *causes* pollution reduction is invalid in two ways. First, it commits the **fallacy of hasty generalization**. The fact that

(cont.)

BOX 5.5 *(cont.)*

the relationship obtains in a few cases is not enough to warrant the generalization. There are many other pollutants and places where increased per-capita GDP is not correlated with pollution reductions. Second, it commits the causation-correlation fallacy. In cases where there has been reduction in pollutants associated with economic growth it is often because people and governments in those societies have supported environmental regulations to address them. It is typically the regulations that cause the reduction in pollutants, not the economic growth, as evidenced by the fact that lower-income countries that adopt similar regulations also see the environment benefits (Stern 2004). Thus, when economic growth is pursued in ways that limit the capacity of societies to regulate pollution—as has been done with some trade agreements—it is a mistake to expect that growth will lead to a cleaner environment, since stronger regulations are a crucial part of the causal mechanism in cases where economic growth and pollution reduction are correlated (Cox 2007). Mistakenly or hastily asserting causal relationships will very often lead to misdiagnoses of environmental problems and misguided evaluation of possible responses to them.

5.7 SUMMARY

The primary question addressed in this chapter was:

• Is anthropocentrism (or ratiocentrism) a well-justified view on the question of who or what is directly morally considerable?

There is a sense in which all of ethics, environmental ethics included, is human-centered. It is about how we, humans, ought to live. Moreover, we, humans, are the ones engaged in the project of trying to figure it out. However, the type of human-centeredness at issue in the anthropocentrism versus nonanthropocentrism debate is different from this. It is not about who the moral agents are, but who is directly morally considerable. Therefore, to infer that only humans are directly morally considerable from the fact that ethics is about how humans ought to live commits the **fallacy of equivocation**. The meaning of the term "human-centered" changes during the course of the reasoning, thereby making it appear valid when in fact it is not.

This chapter has discussed the arguments for and the implications of anthropocentric and ratiocentric approaches to environmental ethics, the views that only human beings or rational beings are directly morally considerable (or have inherent worth).

On these views, nonhuman animals and the environment have only instrumental and subjective value. As a result, moral agents have only indirect duties to them—we have responsibilities regarding them that are grounded in our duties to other human beings.

One of the prominent concerns regarding actual preference anthropocentrism is that it is overly focused on satisfying people's immediate desires, and that this has helped to generate the environmental problems that we face. Therefore, most anthropocentric environmental ethicists reject actual preference anthropocentrism in favor of a view called enlightened anthropocentrism. Enlightened anthropocentrism is the focus of the next chapter.

KEY TERMS (SEE GLOSSARY FOR DEFINITIONS):

actual preference anthropocentrism

anthropocentrism

argument from participatory decision-making

biocentrism

biological group membership accounts of moral status

capacities-based accounts of moral status

care model

causation-correlation fallacy

conservationist

directly morally considerable

dominion model

factual difference

fallacy of appeal to the crowd

fallacy of begging the question

fallacy of equivocation

fallacy of hasty generalization (or fallacy of hasty conclusion)

holism

inadequacy objection

indirect duties

indirectly morally considerable

individualism

inherent worth

moral agency

moral patients

moral status

moral subjects

morally considerable

morally relevant properties

nonanthropocentrism

preservationist

ratiocentrism

rational agency (or moral agency)

sentientism

speciesism

stewardship model

techno-optimism

REVIEW QUESTIONS

•   What are anthropocentrism and nonanthropocentrism?
•   What is the difference between direct moral considerability and indirect moral considerability?

- What does it mean to say that anthropocentrism is a biological group membership account of moral status, whereas ratiocentrism is a capacities-based approach?
- What are the main arguments for anthropocentrism and ratiocentrism, and what are the primary responses to them?
- What is the difference between being a moral agent and being a moral patient?
- What is the indirect duties view regarding nonhuman animals?
- What is the inadequacy objection to anthropocentrism and ratiocentrism?
- What are the dominion, care, and stewardship models of the human relationship to creation?
- What is the correlation/causation fallacy and what are some examples of it?

DISCUSSION QUESTIONS

- Do you think that a biological group membership or a capacities-based approach to determining inherent worth is more justified, and why?
- Do you know of any arguments for favoring the interests of human beings over those of individuals of other species that were not discussed in this chapter? If so, would they be subject to any of the concerns raised against anthropocentrism?
- Do you think that the fact that robustly rational beings are moral agents implies that they have unique, greater or special inherent worth? Why or why not?
- Can you think of other bases for indirect duties to environmental entities in addition to those discussed in this chapter?
- Do you think strong technological optimism is warranted? If so, what are the implications for how we should address environmental problems? If not, why not? Do you think some types of environmental problems are more amenable to technology-oriented solutions than others? If so, which ones and why?

FURTHER READING

Defenses of anthropocentrism, ratiocentrism, and indirect duties views can be found in:

Baxter, William. *People or Penguins: The Case for Optimal Pollution*. Columbia University Press, 1974.

Kant, Immanuel. "Duties to Animals and Spirits." In *Lectures on Ethics*, edited by P. Heath and J. B. Schneedwind, 212–13. Cambridge University Press, 1997.

Svoboda, Toby. *Duties Regarding Nature: A Kantian Environmental Ethic*. Routledge, 2015.

I discuss group membership and capacities-based accounts of moral status at greater length in:

Sandler, Ronald. *The Ethics of Species*. Cambridge University Press, 2012.

Excellent discussions on the relationship between theology, religion, and environmental ethics can be found in:

Francis (Pope). *Laudato Si'* or *On Care for Our Common Home*, 2014, http://w2.vatican .va/content/francesco/en/encyclicals/documents/papa-francesco_20150524_ enciclica-laudato-si.html

Gottlieb, Robert, ed. *Oxford Handbook on Religion and Ecology.* Oxford University Press, 2006.

CHAPTER SIX

ENLIGHTENED ANTHROPOCENTRISM: EFFICIENCY, SUSTAINABILITY, AND FUTURE GENERATIONS

ONE OF THE PRIMARY arguments against anthropocentrism and ratiocentrism is that exclusive concern with the material wants and needs of people is not a credible basis for environmental ethics, since it has helped to create our environmental problems. In response to this inadequacy objection (Sections 5.3–5.4 and Box 5.4), anthropocentrists often argue that ecological problems are not the result of people being overly focused on human wants and needs, but of pursuing them in myopic and misguided ways. On this view, if people were ecologically informed and took everyone's interests into account—present and future, local and global—then anthropocentrism would not favor ecological exploitation and degradation. **Enlightened anthropocentrism**, unlike actual preference anthropocentrism, can be highly critical of current policies and practices. Therefore, according to its proponents, it can be the basis for an adequate environmental ethic. Moreover, even ethicists who advocate for nonanthropocentric environmental ethics recognize that wise use of environmental resources is an important component of environmental ethics. It is crucial to good environmental policy and practice, and is often necessary for enabling protection of human-independent environmental values.

The first part of this chapter elucidates enlightened resource utilization by high-lighting the ways in which ecological goods and services are frequently misused. The second part concerns what, if anything, we owe to future people.

6.1 THE ELEMENTS OF UNWISE RESOURCE USE

People misuse environmental resources in a variety of interrelated ways: inefficient use, underutilization, short-term use, exclusive use, and narrow use. Clear cases of each of these are found in agriculture and food production, which are the focus in this section for illustrative purposes. However, unwise use of environmental resources is certainly not restricted to food and agriculture. It occurs with respect to everything from species management and mining to energy generation and waste disposal.

Agriculture and food production are arguably the most environmentally impact-ful human activities. Approximately 38 percent of the terrestrial surface of the earth, and the vast majority of agriculturally favorable land, are used to produce food (FAO 2013a). There is an overall planetary limit to how much plant matter can grow in a year, crop or otherwise, based on such things as land availability, solar radiation, and precipi-tation (Running 2012), and humans already appropriate roughly 25 percent of the plan-et's net primary plant production (Haberl et al. 2007; Krausmann et al. 2013). People also have accessed a huge amount of aquatic resources for food. Ninety percent of the world's fisheries are fully exploited, overexploited, or recovering (FAO 2014). Globally, 69 percent of all freshwater usage is for agriculture (Aquastat 2016) (in the United States it is 80 percent [USDA 2015]), and many crucial freshwater sources—such as North America's Ogallala Aquifer—are being depleted faster than they can be replen-ished. The predominant causes of habitat destruction and thereby biodiversity loss are associated with agriculture and food production—for example, deforestation and trawl-ing. The agriculture and forestry sectors are responsible for 24 percent of greenhouse gas emissions, nearly two-thirds of which are from livestock (Edenhofer et al. 2014). In the United States alone, nearly 900 million pounds of pesticides and herbicides, and more than 12 million tons of fertilizer (nitrogen, phosphate, potash/potassium), are used each year, which has detrimental impacts on air, soil, and water quality (USDA 2015).

Despite the widespread and intensive use of planetary resources for agriculture, 795 million people are chronically undernourished. They lack access to the minimum amount of calories and nutrition needed for healthy development and functioning (FAO 2015a). Moreover, there is projected to be a 60 to 120 percent increase in global crop demand by 2050, due to such things as population growth, economic growth, and shifts in diets (Cassidy et al. 2013; Alexandratos and Bruinsma 2012). Given this, agriculture and food distribution are areas where the wise use of resources is crucial. It is also an area that is currently replete with waste, misuse, and detrimental unintended impacts.

6.1.1 Inefficient Use

Inefficient use of an environmental resource occurs when there are alternative uses for it that would better promote human welfare or when there are other ways of satisfying the relevant preferences that would require fewer resources. For example, over a third of the calories and half the protein produced by crop agriculture are fed to animals (Cassidy et al. 2013). However, feeding calories and protein to animals, which people then eat, is an enormously inefficient use of those resources, since the animals use them for all sorts of things other than muscle growth—for example, moving, breathing, and growing bones. For example, chicken has approximately a 12 percent caloric return on investment and a 40 percent protein return, while beef has approximately a 3 percent caloric return and a 5 percent protein return (the caloric and protein returns are higher for dairy and eggs) (Cassidy et al. 2013). Animal agriculture—particularly in its concentrated forms—is also inefficient with respect to water usage. Producing 500 calories of beef requires 5,000 liters of water, whereas producing 500 calories of poultry requires around 1,500 liters, and 500 calories of beans just over 400 liters. Similarly, the water used to produce 10 grams of protein from corn is only about 130 liters, whereas for 10 grams of protein from eggs it is nearly 250 liters and from beef it is 1,000 liters (Halweil et al. 2004; Steinfeld et al. 2006). Another inefficient use of crop calories is their conversion to biofuels. Approximately 4 percent of the human-edible calories produced from agriculture are used for fuel, frequently with limited energy return on investment—it often takes nearly as much energy to produce biofuels as the biofuels generate when combusted (Farrell et al. 2006).

One recent study found that utilizing agricultural resources more efficiently by shifting them from feed and fuel to direct consumption could increase the global food supply by up to 70 percent, enough to feed 4 billion people an adequate diet of 2,700 kcal/day (Cassidy et al. 2013). Even if only half of the crop calories fed to animals and used for fuel were to go to direct human consumption, 2 billion additional people could be fed at current levels of productivity. This would leave pasture available for animal agriculture, which uses 26 percent of the earth's land. The potential gains are particularly high in biofuel- and meat-intensive regions such as the United States, where only 27 percent of calories and 14 percent of protein produced by crops are directly consumed by people (Cassidy et al. 2013).

6.1.2 Underutilization

Underutilization of a resource occurs when it is possible for the resource to produce more goods and services than it does. Many agricultural resources are underutilized. Although food production per hectare has been increasing for decades, there remains a sizable gap between what many agricultural systems currently produce and what they could produce. How to close yield gaps and increase yield potentials effectively, sustainably, and in ways that decrease food insecurity are highly context-specific. What benefits smallholder subsistence polyculture in developing countries is different from what increases yields for conventional commodity agriculture in industrialized countries. However, in both cases yield increases by as much as 50 to 75 percent are frequently possible (Pretty et al. 2006; Foley et al. 2011; Mueller et al. 2012). For example, increasing nitrogen availability often can increase production in organic agriculture. Improving irrigation and fertilizer use often can increase production in polyculture. Implementing crop rotation and use of cover crops often can increase productivity in industrial agriculture. In general, improved capital availability, technology, seeds, soil conservation, pest control techniques, and market access can increase yields.

Underutilization of agricultural and food resources is also manifest in the enormous amount of food waste that occurs. The Food and Agriculture Organization (FAO) of the United Nations estimates that around a third of the food produced for human consumption is lost to wastage in both developed and developing countries. This amounts to 1.3 billion tons of food annually, with an economic cost of ~$750 billion (FAO 2013a). Wastage occurs at all points in the food life-cycle: agricultural production, postharvest handling and storage, processing, distribution, consumption, and disposal. However, the losses are differently distributed along the food supply chain in developed and developing nations. In less developed countries, the losses are predominantly at the production, transport, and processing stages, and are the result of spoilage and pests. This is primarily due to lack of infrastructure, such as harvesting technologies, storage capacity, efficient transportation, and refrigeration. There is very little wastage at the retail, preparation, and consumption stages in less developed countries, since there is not food abundance and the percentage of income spent on food is high. In affluent nations, where there is food abundance and robust infrastructure, food expenditure as a percentage of household income is much lower. As a result, the majority of food wastage occurs at the consumption and retail stages. In the UK, 15 percent of food and beverage purchases are wasted (DEFRA 2012). In the United States, ~25 percent of consumer's food and beverage purchases are ultimately discarded (Gunders 2012). Over the entire food supply-chain in the United States, 273 pounds of food per person, per year is lost (Buzby and Hyman 2012). There is thus an enormous amount of food to be "gained" by the food system through the elimination of food wastage. Not only are agricultural resources underutilized in the production of food, the food is itself underutilized. In fact, every region in the world (but not every country) produces enough calories to meet the dietary energy requirements of everyone in the region (FAOSTAT 2013; FAO 2013a). That is, even without increased food production, there is enough food for everyone in the world to have a nutritionally adequate diet, if it were utilized and distributed optimally. Instead, there are 795 million people who are chronically undernourished.

6.1.3 Short-Term Use

Short-term use of resources occurs when they are used to satisfy immediate interests in ways that are detrimental to people in the long-term. This happens often with wild capture fisheries. Approximate 90 million tons of fish have been captured each year for the past few decades (FAO 2012b). In addition, it is estimated that there is on average nearly 27 million tons of unintended bycatch each year—fish and other marine life that are not the commercial target but are incidentally caught and killed (FAO 1994). (Purse seining, gill-netting, and trawling are particularly conducive to by-catch.) As a result, 90 percent of fish stocks are fully or overexploited. Large predatory fish have been particularly hard hit, reduced to 10 percent of their preindustrial levels (Myers and Worm 2003). It is projected that on the current trajectory nearly all major commercial species populations will collapse by 2050 (Worm et al. 2006). This would constitute an ecological, social, and economic disaster. One in ten people depend upon fisheries for their livelihood and well-being, and 15 to 20 percent of animal protein consumed globally is from aquatic animals (FAO 2014). Moreover, harvest mortality and by-catch constitute a massive, constant biological depletion of aquatic systems, and the loss of large predatory fish reverberates throughout the food web to even non-fished species. The fishing process itself is also often ecologically destructive. Trawling and dredging—which involve towing nets behind boats—are particularly damaging to the ocean floor and release large plumes of sediment into the water. Industrial fishing impacts, combined with other stressors on aquatic systems, particularly pollution and global climate change (e.g., the impacts of increased temperature and ocean acidification on coral growth), have many people worried about the possible collapse of the ocean ecological systems on which we all depend. It seems as if long-term well-being and security is being traded for short-term economic gains.

Short-term use also often occurs with aquaculture. For example, intensive high-impact shrimp aquaculture in Southeast Asia has expanded dramatically in recent decades in order to meet rapidly increasing global shrimp demand. Its expansion has resulted in mangrove deforestation and decreased water quality from waste and antibiotics. It has significantly reduced the quality and number of other aquatic species that depend upon the mangroves as nurseries, increased exposure to storm surges, decreased a valuable source of wood for building, and detrimentally impacted coastal agriculture by increasing water salinity. Again, short-term gains are resulting in long-term ecological, social, and economic problems.

※ BOX 6.1

TRAGEDY OF THE COMMONS

Commercial fisheries are a paradigmatic case of a problem called the **tragedy of the commons**. A tragedy of the commons occurs when there is a shared or "common" (or "common-pool") resource to which multiple agents have access,

(cont.)

BOX 6.1 *(cont.)*

and each agent's acting in ways that are individually rationally self-interested would result in the depletion of the resource to everyone's detriment (often including their own). Deforestation is a tragedy of the commons; the accumulation of greenhouse gases in the atmosphere is a tragedy of the commons; fresh water depletion and eutrophication is a tragedy of the commons; and overfishing is a tragedy of the commons. They are tragedies of the commons because it is rational for people—in terms of their own economic self-interest, basic needs, or quality of life—to clear forest for agricultural land, to cut down trees for firewood, to pump more water to irrigate fields, to use large quantities of synthetic fertilizer, to catch more fish, or to live a high-emissions consumer lifestyle. However, if everyone does so, the cumulative impact is degradation or depletion of the resource base on which the activity depends and/or secondary effects that are detrimental to many more people in the long run. It results in biodiversity loss, polluted waterways, global climate change, reduced agricultural productivity, landslides, or fishery collapses. The **commons problem** is how to manage common-pool resources in ways that do not result in their degradation.

Commons problems are solvable (Ostrom 1990). Not all shared or common resources are used in ways that end in tragedies. In fact, several (nonexclusive) types of management strategies are used to forestall overuse. These include: privatization; management by a trustee (or holding the resource in public trust); the use of quotas, licensing, and take limits; increasing the cost to use the commons (e.g., through taxation or fee-for-use); prohibiting access; and ethical restraint (for example, out of obligation to future generations). National parks and forests, private land trusts, emissions allowances, pollution regulation, hunting permits (and seasons), carbon taxes, endangered species laws, and fishing licenses and take limits are all attempts to address commons problems, and they are frequently successful.

However, not all commons problems are equally easy to address. Successfully managing commons problems is more difficult the less socially and politically connected the users of a common resource, the less clear it is who has authority or jurisdiction to govern the commons, the less power the authority has, the less well-defined the common resource, the larger the number of agents involved, the less congruence there is between the users of the commons and those who suffer from its overuse, and the less congruence there is between those who shoulder the cost of management and those who gain from successful management. Global climate change is frequently described as the

(cont.)

BOX 6.1 *(cont.)*

ultimate commons problem because it has so many features that are inimical to organizing a solution: globalness, diffuse agents, lack of strong (or clear) authority, and spatial, temporal, and social incongruence between those most responsible for creating the problem and those who will be most affected by it (see, e.g., Boxes 2.1, 6.3, and 16.3).

With respect to fisheries, some have features that make them a relatively straightforward commons problem to manage. For example, Atlantic lobster fisheries in North America have a target species that does not migrate far, is comparatively easy to monitor, and about which quite a lot is known. The fishing communities are fairly small and well-defined, and the agents are familiar to each other. There are clear authorities, resources for enforcement, and established methods of conflict resolution. There is high congruence between those who must shoulder the burden of restraint and those who benefit from it in the long run. Overall in the United States, thirty-two fish stocks, such as coho salmon and Atlantic swordfish, have been rebuilt since 2000 (NOAA 2012).

However, in other cases fisheries pose challenging commons problems. This is particularly so for stocks within the exclusive economic zones (and so political jurisdiction) of countries with weak regulatory systems, as well as for species that cross many political boundaries or are found in international waters, such as sharks, rays, and tuna. In these places, illegal fishing is rampant. The agents involved are often diffuse, under different economic pressures, and fall under different political regimes. There are not easily-agreed-upon management goals. There is not a strong, clear authority. Fish populations are hard to measure and there is frequently limited knowledge of their behavior (e.g., migratory routes and reproductive cycles). Violations of agreements can be difficult to monitor and enforce.

As the examples above indicate, developing effective, just, and sustainable solutions to commons problems is a crucial component of achieving environmental sustainability, since so many environmental goods are common-pool resources and services.

6.1.4 Exclusive Use

Exclusive use of environmental resources occurs when not everyone's interests are fully taken into account. For example, globalization and industrialization of agriculture in order to satisfy the culinary preferences of people in affluent nations has been associated with the expansion of large commodity exporting and corporately controlled farms in developing nations and the displacement of small-holding sub-sistence farmers. The banana and pineapple industries in Central America histor-ically have been quintessential instances of this, and it frequently occurs in many areas through bulk land purchases, pumping down the water table level (combined with the capital costs of digging deeper wells), and pollution from synthetic chemical inputs. For example, between 2000 and 2010, approximately 70 million hectares were sold or leased in developing nations, over 56 million of which were in Africa, representing nearly 5 percent of its agricultural land (Worldwatch Institute 2012). The same phenomenon has occurred with fisheries. Industrial fishing fleets have dis-placed artisanal and subsistence fishing, thereby increasing food insecurity and dis-rupting communities, while also depleting fisheries. For example, in Tanzania's Lake Victoria, commercial fishing of Nile perch (an introduced species) has marginalized local fishermen, undermined social systems, and resulted in dramatic declines in food access and quality. The situation is similar for local fishing and coastal agricultural communities dependent upon the mangrove forests lost to shrimp aquaculture in Southeast Asia. In cases like these, satisfying some people's mere preferences—for example, the desire for abundant inexpensive seafood and year-round tropical fruits—has serious costs for others.

6.1.5 Narrow Use

Narrow use occurs when resource determinations do not consider the full range of goods and services provided by the environment. For example, wetlands are frequently drained or filled for a variety of purposes, such as expanding agriculture and building housing developments. However, they provide crucial breeding grounds for econom-ically and ecologically important aquatic species (e.g., shrimp, fish, and mollusks). They provide ecosystem services, such as protection against storm surge and water purification. They provide recreational opportunities for wildlife viewing, fishing, and hunting. They can be crucial to valued migrating species. Therefore, when a wetland is cleared for development, there often is a large net loss in overall ecosystem value. This is also frequently true of diverting water from rivers for irrigation. Doing so might be effective in maintaining crop yields, but it can be detrimental to riparian systems' capacity to maintain fisheries, provide drinking water, support recreation, and continue valued traditions and practices connected to them. When there is a full accounting of the value of the resource to people, it often turns out that the short-term agricultural benefits are significantly outweighed by the other services and goods that rivers provide.

Food and agriculture provide particularly clear examples of suboptimal uses of resources. However, they are by no means unique. Cases of inefficient use, narrow use, exclusive use, short-term use, and underutilization of environmental resources abound. Directly emitting pollution into the air and water may be the least expensive way for a company to dispose of its waste, but it can lead to large human health costs and depletion of environmental resources (e.g., forests, fisheries, and drinking water) over time. Selling rights for development and mining often provide smaller, shorter-term, and less local economic benefits with greater ecological impacts than does developing ecotourism. As discussed in Section 4.3, one of the aims of environmental economics is to elucidate the full range of services and goods provided by ecosystems and species so that they are not overlooked in environmental decision-making.

6.2 IDEAL PREFERENCE ANTHROPOCENTRISM

Enlightened anthropocentrism is the view that we ought to use resources and manage ecological systems in ways that are efficient, long-term, inclusive, and broadly considered. This often means not using them to satisfy people's actual preferences, since our actual preferences are frequently misguided.

For one thing, we often have preferences for things that would not make us better off, and might even make us worse off. For example, many people believe that owning more consumer goods will make them happier. However, there is an established body of research that shows that too great a focus on the accumulation of material goods tends to be detrimental to a person's well-being, particularly when it leads them to live in ways that undermine the quality of their relationships and ability to engage in meaningful activities (Kasser 2002; Kasser and Kanner 2004). People also have immediate preferences for things that are unhealthy for them. Perhaps the clearest example of this is excessive food consumption. In the United States, 35 percent of adults and 17 percent of children are obese (Ogden et al. 2012); and in the UK, 26 percent of adults are obese (Swinburn et al. 2011; Wang et al. 2011). Obesity is associated with elevated risk for heart disease, type 2 diabetes, depression, musculoskeletal problems, and some forms of cancer. Moreover, since everything we consume has an environmental footprint—for example, material extraction, energy use, and waste disposal—overconsumption can degrade the environment in ways that are harmful to other people.

People also often have mistaken beliefs about ecological risks and ecological services. For example, programs to eradicate bats around cities were once commonplace because they were thought to spread disease. However, we now know that the opposite is true. They only rarely bite people, and because they consume so many insects they actually reduce the spread of many diseases. In fact, there is a growing body of evidence that suggests that having large predators around population areas—from hawks to pumas—increases public health by controlling disease-carrying prey species such as deer, mice, and raccoons. If this is correct, then the desire to eliminate predators is contrary to what would best promote human welfare.

Many people do not know the ecological and social costs of the food that they eat, the trips that they take, or the goods that they consume. If people knew, they might revise their desires. Some people might not want to eat inexpensive wild-caught shrimp if they knew that industrial trawling degrades benthic ecosystems, reduces long-term productivity, displaces artisan fishing, and disrupts traditional fishing communities. They might not want inexpensive hardwood furniture if they knew that it is made possible by clearing old-growth forests in developing nations. They might not want the cheapest possible smartphone if they knew the rare minerals in them are mined by forced labor and used to fund violent conflicts. What is more, perhaps they *ought not* have those preferences. Some of our preferences might be *unendorseable* when the full costs and implications of satisfying them are understood.

The alternative to focusing on satisfying people's actual preferences (particularly the consumeristic desires of affluent people) is aiming to satisfy what their preferences would be if they were sufficiently informed, inclusive, and long-term—their **ideal preferences**. Once we appreciate how people now and in the future depend on reliable ecosystem services and sustainable supplies of natural resources, and understand how our own behaviors relate to their maintenance and production, we may see that many of our current preferences are deeply problematic. Unlike actual preference anthropocentrism, enlightened anthropocentrism can be highly revisionist. It does not accept that satisfying preferences is good merely because they are preferences. For this reason, its proponents believe that it has the normative capacity to challenge people's current lifestyles and practices, and that it can justify systematic change in order to reduce ecological impacts—that is, they believe that it is not susceptible to the inadequacy objection.

However, enlightened anthropocentrism is still anthropocentrism. Only people are directly morally considerable. Penguins do not matter in themselves, but only insofar as people care about them or they are important for providing ecosystem services now and in the future. For this reason, there are limits to what it can justify. It will not be necessary to conserve all species, since they do not all have value to us. Sometimes clearing wilderness for agriculture or development, damming rivers for electricity generation, and using animals for human purposes will be the enlightened thing to do because it will best serve people's interests. Therefore, there are two interrelated objections to enlightened anthropocentrism. The first is that enlightened anthropocentrism does not go far enough in protecting biodiversity and the nonhuman environment. The second is that it is based on a mistaken account of who is morally considerable. If species, ecosystems, nonhuman animals, and plants are directly morally considerable then enlightened anthropocentrism is itself far too narrow. It would have us make decisions about how to conserve and manage resources based only on human interests, when we ought to be considering nonhuman interests as well. What is best for people may not always be what is best for ecological systems or members of others species, particularly when it involves using them for our ends. (The question of whether species, ecosystems, and nonhuman organisms are directly morally considerable is discussed at length in Chapters 7 and 11–13. The extent to which enlightened anthropocentrism and nonanthropocentrism converge in practice is discussed in Section 14.4 and Box 14.4.)

* BOX 6.2

SUSTAINABLE DEVELOPMENT

A concept closely allied to enlightened anthropocentrism is that of **sustainable development.** The idea of sustainable development became prominent when it was used in a 1987 United Nations report titled *Our Common Future.* The report defined sustainable development as "development that meets the needs of the present without compromising the ability of future generations to meet their own needs" (WCED 1987, ch. 2). It emphasized the interconnections between society, the environment, and economics, and argued that long-term prosperity requires accomplishing sustainability in each. This would later be called the **"triple bottom line"** of people, planet, and profit (Figure 6.1).

The term "sustainable" has become commonplace: sustainable agriculture, sustainable architecture, sustainable forestry, sustainable energy, sustainable cities, sustainable dry cleaning, and so on. However, substantively specifying

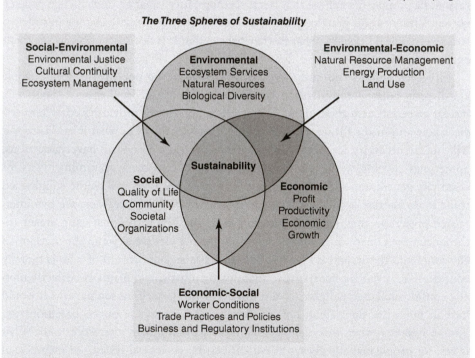

Figure 6.1   Comprehensive sustainability has environmental, social, and economic components intertwined. This is frequently referred to as the "triple bottom line" in economic development and business contexts.

(cont.)

BOX 6.2 *(cont.)*

and operationalizing the concept of "sustainability" has been difficult and con-troversial. For example, is sustainability primarily about meeting the economic needs of present and future people or maintaining the integrity of social and ecological systems? Does sustainability require ensuring that future people have access to the same resources that we currently do (sometimes called **strong sustainability**) or that they have the same capacity to meet their needs even with a diminished or different resource base (sometimes called **weak sustainability**)? Does economic sustainability require consistent eco-nomic growth or expansion, as is often supposed? Or does it require moving to a steady-state economy, since perpetual growth seems incompatible with a finite planetary resource base? What, in the end, is supposed to be sustained—cultural integrity, aggregate well-being, GDP, biodiversity?

The ambiguity and vagueness around "sustainability" and "sustainable de-velopment" have led some to conclude that it is no longer a useful concept. On this view, it has become muddled, vacuous, and co-opted by too many advertis-ing campaigns (commonly called "**greenwashing**") to be meaningful. However, many others—in business, academia, and nonprofit organizations—continue to do the difficult work of trying to make the concept of sustainability concrete and measurable in different domains. This has come to be known as **sustainability science**. It combines the physical and social sciences with public engagement in order to help define what sustainability means in particular contexts and de-termine how to assess and promote it. Sustainability science embraces the idea that human economic and social systems are not separate from or adjacent to biological and ecological systems, but are instead embedded within them and require **eco-social sustainability**.

6.3 THE PROBLEM OF FUTURE GENERATIONS

It is widely agreed that the interests of future generations need to be taken into account when evaluating environmental practices and policies. However, how much weight to put on their interests in comparison to those of present generations is contested. More-over, there are several features of future generations that complicate considering their interests in the same ways as those of present generations.

Some of the complications are practical. For example, the further we project into the future, the more difficult it is to predict what people's wants and needs will be. Some things that people used in the past are obsolete now (e.g., whale oil for lamp fuel), and some things that are crucial to people now were unused in the past (e.g., minerals for electronics). This is sometimes called the **unknown needs problem**.

Moreover, the further we project into the future, the more difficult it is to predict how current actions will impact the future. Thus, even if we knew future people's needs, it would be difficult for us to determine what to do now to ensure that they are satisfied later. This might be called the **unknown means problem**.

Furthermore, if we were to consider the interests of every future person the same as we do presently-existing people, then their wants and needs would completely outweigh ours, since there will be so many more of them over time. This is sometimes called the **swamping problem**. What is more, it seems unjustified for us to sacrifice our interests now if people in the future are likely to live better lives than we currently do, given the exponential (or, at least, very high) rate of technological change (see Section 5.5). This might be called the **they-will-be-gods problem**. The swamping and they-will-be-gods problems are part of the justification for discounting the interests of future people in comparison to those of currently existing people (see Box 6.3).

There are also some deep conceptual complications with considering the interests (or welfare) of future people in the same way as those of present people. The complications stem from the fact that future people do not currently exist and are highly contingent—that is, who comes to exist depends upon the decisions and actions of currently existing people. Here is why. Who will exist in the future is determined by which sperms fertilize which eggs. The odds of any particular sperm fertilizing any particular egg are incredibly small and dependent upon almost every action and decision people take—what to eat, whether to stay up late, where to go on vacation, and so on. So it is important not to think of future people as definite people—people with defined identities—who are just waiting somewhere to come onto the stage of existence. They are, before conception, nonexistent, indeterminate, and contingent.

The indeterminacy and contingency of future people has the following implication. It is not possible to make future people worse off than they would otherwise be. To see this, imagine that a country is considering whether to aggressively mitigate greenhouse gas emissions or continue with business as usual. If they decide to mitigate, fuel and electricity will become more expensive, which will change people's behaviors. As a result, different people would come into existence on the aggressive emissions scenario than on the business-as-usual scenario. Thus, aggressive mitigation would not make the people who would have existed on the business as usual scenario better off than they would otherwise have been. It would, instead, make them not exist.

Now suppose that the country opts for the business-as-usual scenario. The people who come into existence on that scenario would live in a more degraded environment than the people who would have come into existence had aggressive mitigation been pursued. However, their lives will not be any worse for it. The reason for this is that the other option for them is not existing. So, even if they come to exist under conditions of runaway climate change, they are not harmed or made worse off, since the alternative for them is not living under better environmental conditions, but nonexistence. This is commonly referred to as the **nonidentity problem** (Parfit 1984). The problem is that it is not possible to make sense of harm to future people in the same way as we commonly think about harm to existing people—that something occurs that makes them worse off than they would have been had it not occurred. If this is correct, then the implication seems to be that nothing we can do could benefit or harm people in future generations. All we can do is alter who constitutes them—that is, who exists. The nonidentity problem arises in any context in which decisions and policies impact which future people (or animals) exist and the conditions in which they live. Therefore, it is frequently discussed in reproductive ethics and animal ethics, in addition to environmental ethics.

Some responses to the nonidentity problem aim to provide an account of harm that does not require a person to be made worse off than they would otherwise be. Moreover, it does not immediately follow from the fact (if it is one) that it is not possible to *harm* future people that it is not possible to *wrong* them. The reason for this is that some things might be wrong, even if they are not bad for any particular person or people—that is, there may be *harmless wrongs*. These responses deny the **person-affecting principle** that an action can be wrong only if it makes someone worse off. What follows are several prominent responses to the nonidentity problem and the problem of future generations.

One common response, often associated with consequentialist ethical theories (see Chapter 8), is to claim that instead of focusing on the well-being of individuals, we ought to act in ways that bring about the greatest *aggregate* well-being of future people. Thus, the reason we ought to mitigate global climate change is that the total well-being of people who exist on that scenario will be greater than that of those who do so on the runaway climate change scenario. However, this response seems to be open to the swamping problem. Moreover, it appears to lead to what ethicists refer to as the **repugnant conclusion**, which is that it is better to have an enormous number of people whose lives are just barely worth living than a much smaller number of people with a very high quality of life (Parfit 1984). In response to the repugnant conclusion, it is tempting to claim that instead of maximizing *aggregate* well-being the right thing to do is to maximize *average* well-being. However, this implies that it is better to have a very small number of people living extremely well than it is to have many more people living slightly less well, which also strikes many as counterintuitive. Nevertheless, one response to the nonidentity problem is to try to identify a principled approach to comparing the well-being of different possible future people that does not lead to counterintuitive implications.

Another prominent response to the nonidentity problem and the problem of future generations is based on the idea of **intergenerational justice** or what each generation is entitled to receive from the prior one and is responsible for passing on to the next one. The most influential account of intergenerational justice was developed by a philosopher and political theorist named John Rawls (1971; 1993). According to Rawls, the equal worth and political standing of citizens implies that social, political, and economic institutions ought to be arranged as fairly and impartially as possible. Therefore, the basic principles of justice are those that reasonable and self-interested people would (hypothetically) agree to if they did not know anything particular about themselves that would enable biasing the principles in their favor—for example, their race, gender, class, ability, or generation. (This type of approach to specifying normative principles is often referred to as **social contract theory** or **contractarianism**.) With respect to intergenerational responsibilities, Rawls believed that reasonable, self-interested people behind a "veil of ignorance" about themselves, would endorse something like the following "just savings" requirements: (1) "to preserve the gains of our civilization"; (2) to maintain just and well-functioning institutions; and (3) to pass on resources—like capital and technology—to the next generation that are equivalent to if not greater than those received from prior generations (Rawls 1971, secs. 44–45). Thus, according to Rawls, each generation has responsibilities to the next that do not depend upon making any particular people better or worse off (which is why it is thought to avoid the nonidentity problem). These just saving responsibilities would presumably include ensuring that subsequent generations have as good or better access to natural resources and ecosystem services than do the current generation and/or that they receive the technological capacity to compensate for any resource or service diminishment.

A third type of response focuses on the characteristics of future generations, regardless of who constitutes them or the conditions in which they live. For example, although many of the details about future people's wants and needs are inscrutable, we can reasonably assume that they will have basic biological requirements for such things as clean air, potable water, and adequate nutrition. On a deontological normative framework (see Chapter 9), this means that future people, whoever they are, will have environmental rights to basic goods. Respecting these rights requires refraining from degrading the environment in ways that would undermine satisfaction of their basic needs, as well as providing them with adequate artificial alternatives and technological capacity to make up for any prior ecological degradation that threatens them. On a virtue ethics normative framework (see Chapter 10), there is value in human flourishing. Therefore, in addition to not undermining basic needs, we should not degrade the environment in ways that would make enriching engagement with the nonhuman environment more difficult—for example, by significantly diminishing biological diversity or reducing opportunities for communion with the nonhuman world. As with the intergenerational justice response, these responses to the problem of future generations are thought to not rely upon the possibility of making individual future people better or worse off than they would otherwise be. The idea is that it is better if people's rights are satisfied and people flourish than if people do not, regardless of who the people are. One concern about these responses is that it is difficult to define what "it is better" means, if it does not involve making determinate people better off, without being led back to aggregative or average well-being.

Yet another type of response to the problem of future generations is to focus on the ways in which the desires and projects of existing people connect to future people (O'Neill 1993; De-Shalit 1995). Perhaps the most straightforward case of this is familial relationships. Parents have an interest in the well-being of their children and grandchildren, and so in their living in ecological conditions in which they can flourish. Therefore, according to this view, we have a responsibility to consider the interests of (at least near) future generations that is grounded in the moral considerability of present people; future people are indirectly morally considerable. This ratcheting out cannot go on indefinitely. A person's flourishing cannot plausibly be tied up with that of their twentieth-generation descendants. However, it can expand to other worthwhile projects besides having children, such as building sustainable and just institutions, protecting biodiversity, and expanding knowledge. According to this view, we have a responsibility to those who engage in such projects to promote the ecological conditions for their continuation and success in the future.

There are thus several approaches to responding to the problem of future generations that seek to avoid the nonidentity problem. As indicated, many of them are tied to particular normative frameworks—for example, rights-based, consequentialist, or virtue ethics. Therefore, evaluation of them is connected to assessing the merits of the broader normative theories in which they are situated, which is the focus of several upcoming chapters (Chapters 8–10).

✳ BOX 6.3

DISCOUNTING THE FUTURE AND
GLOBAL CLIMATE CHANGE

Let us suppose that we ought to consider the impacts of our behaviors on future people (see Section 6.3). The next issue that arises is the extent to which we ought to do so. That is to ask: How much weight ought we put on the interests of future generations in comparison to the interests of present people? One place where this issue is particularly salient is in the ethics of climate change mitigation and adaptation. **Mitigation** refers to efforts to limit the magnitude of anthropogenic climate change by reducing greenhouse gas emissions and enhancing greenhouse gas sinks. **Adaptation** refers to efforts to moderate the harms and take advantage of the opportunities associated with global climate

(cont.)

BOX 6.3 *(cont.)*

change. A central policy issue regarding climate change concerns whether, and to what extent, mitigation or adaptation should be prioritized. Should we aggressively mitigate now so that adaptation challenges are lower later, or should we do less mitigation now and face larger adaptation challenges later?

One influential approach to addressing this question is **welfare economics,** which aims to identify the distribution of mitigation and adaptation that is socially and economically optimal—that would bring about the best balance of social and economic benefits over costs. Nicholas Stern (2006), for example, has argued in favor of aggressive mitigation on the grounds that it will cost much less socially and economically to mitigate now than it will to adapt later. William Nordhaus (2007a; 2007b), however, has argued that the socially and economically optimal approach would be to begin with some mitigation now (but not nearly so much as Stern advocates) and then increase the intensity of mitigation over time.

Among the reasons that welfare economic studies of global climate change produce divergent results regarding mitigation and adaptation is that they use different normative assumptions. For example, in order to make all social and economic costs comparable, welfare (e.g., pleasure, suffering, subjective well-being, and death) needs to be quantified in monetary metrics. There are no obvious or standard rates for converting, for example, malnutrition or being a refugee into monetary units, so there is often divergence with respect to value assignments. (For a discussion of the value assignment and commensurability challenges in environmental economics see Section 4.3.) However, the normative assumption that primarily drives welfare economics calculations apart concerns the relative weight placed on the present versus future generations.

It is common in economics to increasingly "discount" the future—to not count a dollar today the same as a dollar tomorrow, but rather to count a dollar today as worth more than a dollar in the future, and still more than a dollar in the further future. One reason for this is the expectation that a dollar today will be worth more than a dollar in the future in terms of purchasing power or goods acquisition. Purchasing power is used in economics as a proxy for the capacity to satisfy preferences. This, in turn, is taken as a measure of (or, in some cases, as being constitutive of) welfare or well-being, which is the ultimate concern of welfare economics. Thus, different economists will use a different **discount rate** if they have different views about future inflation and growth (or deflation and contraction)—about how much more (or less) goods or services will cost in the future. A second reason that economists discount the future is uncertainty

(cont.)

BOX 6.3 *(cont.)*

or risk—that sought outcomes are less assured to accrue the further one aims into the future. A third reason that economists discount the future is that if people in the future live increasingly better lives than do people in the present, then a determinate amount of purchasing power will have decreasing marginal utility in the future. That is to say, it will have less impact on future people's well-being, in the same way that gaining $1,000 has less impact on a wealthy person's well-being than it does on the well-being of someone in poverty. However, the main explanation for the divergence in discount rates used by welfare economists is that they adopt different **pure time preference** rates, in which goods in the future are discounted simply because they are in the future. The greater the pure time preference, the less the interests or welfare of future generations are considered (or counted) in comparison to the interests or welfare of the present generation. Pure time preference is the most ethically contested basis for discounting. The extent to which the welfare of future generations should be discounted against the welfare of present generations (if at all) is a normative question that cannot be addressed by economics or any descriptive or predictive science or social science alone. It has to do with how future generations ought to be valued.

Stern employs a near zero pure time preference. In his climate change cost calculations the welfare of individuals in future generations is counted virtually the same as the welfare of individuals in the present generation. Nordhaus employs a larger pure time preference. In his climate change cost calculations the significance of the welfare of individuals in future generations diminishes over time in comparison to that of individuals in the present generation. Therefore, future adaptation costs carry much more weight in Stern's calculations than they do in Nordhaus's. This makes taking on greater mitigation costs now much more justified on Stern's calculations than on Nordhaus's. The more that harms to individuals in future generations matter, the more it makes sense to take on costs now to avoid them. The harms associated with global climate change are back-loaded; they will be greater in the future than they are in the present. The reasons for this are that some greenhouse gases, including CO_2, remain in the atmosphere for many decades and the impacts of greenhouse gas increases on climatic and ecological processes can take considerable time to manifest. Therefore, calculations on whether to prioritize mitigation or adaption to global climate change, and at what time-points to do so, are particularly susceptible to variations in the discount rate.

(cont.)

BOX 6.3 *(cont.)*

One final note on welfare economics and environmental policy. A welfare economics calculation, even one that includes a thorough and critical examination of the discount rate, does not constitute a comprehensive ethical evaluation. For example, even if prioritization of adaptation over mitigation is justified on welfare economics grounds—if it would bring about the best balance of benefits and costs in the aggregate or overall—it might nevertheless be unjust. Wealthy people are disproportionately responsible for greenhouse gas emissions (per capita), since they consume more goods and energy than do those who are poor. They are also better resourced economically, technologically, and socially to adapt to the impacts of global climate change. Climate justice proponents believe that such considerations—regarding historical responsibility, present adaptive capability, and distribution of benefits and burdens more generally, for example—need to inform discussion of not only who should be responsible for mitigation and adaptation (see Box 16.3), but also whether to prioritize mitigation over adaptation. Mitigation reduces the magnitude of global climate change, and so has widely distributed benefits, whereas adaptation is more localized and targeted, based on who has access to resources. For this reason, environmental justice considerations seem to favor mitigation over adaptation. Other ethical considerations may also favor more intensive mitigation. For example, Simon Caney has argued that anthropogenic climate change violates human rights and that this consideration favors mitigation over compensation (see Section 9.4), while others argue that the final value of species that would be lost through anthropogenic climate change favors aggressive mitigation (see Section 13.8).

6.4 SUMMARY

The primary question addressed in this chapter has been:

- To what extent can an inclusive and environmentally informed anthropocentrism provide an adequate environmental ethic?

One of the main concerns about current practices regarding the environment is that they are short-sighted. People are too narrowly focused on satisfying their immediate wants and needs as easily as possible. This leads to externalizing environmental costs, profligate use of resources, and inadequate attention to the needs of others. Thus, a crucial component of environmental ethics—anthropocentric and nonanthropocentric—is promoting the efficient, long-term, inclusive, and broadly considered use of environmental goods and services. Once this is recognized, it becomes important to provide and operationalize well-justified conceptions of sustainability and sustainable development. It also becomes necessary to determine whether and to what extent future generations should be considered in environmental decision-making.

If environmental problems are primarily the result of non-optimal resource utilization and misguided preferences in pursuit of human well-being, then enlightened anthropocentrism can provide for an adequate environmental ethic. However, many environmental ethicists believe that nonhuman organisms, species, and ecosystem are directly morally considerable. If this is correct, then enlightened management of environmental goods and services is a crucial component of environmental ethics, but not the whole of it. We must also consider values in nature independent of us. Nonanthropocentric environmental ethics are discussed at length in the coming chapters (7, 11–13).

KEY TERMS (SEE GLOSSARY FOR DEFINITIONS):

adaptation

commons problem

discount rate

eco-social sustainability

enlightened anthropocentrism

exclusive use

greenwashing

ideal preferences

inefficient use

intergenerational justice

mitigation

narrow use

nonidentity problem

person-affecting principle

pure time preference

repugnant conclusion

short-term use

social contract theory
(or contractarianism)

strong sustainability

sustainable development

sustainability science

swamping problem

they-will-be-gods problem

tragedy of the commons

triple bottom line

underutilization

unknown means problem

unknown needs problem

weak sustainability

welfare economics

REVIEW QUESTIONS

• What are the ways in which environmental resources are used non-optimally?

• What is the difference between actual preference anthropocentrism and enlightened anthropocentrism?

- In what ways can people's preferences be misguided?
- What is the problem of future generations and how is the nonidentity problem related to it?
- What is the relationship between the problem of future generations and welfare economics?
- What are the prominent responses to the problem of future generations and the non-identity problem?
- What is a common-pool resource and what makes something a commons problem?
- What is sustainable development? In what respects is it a contested concept?

DISCUSSION QUESTIONS

- Did you find enlightened anthropocentrism to be a more justified view than actual preference anthropocentrism? Why or why not?
- Do you agree that enlightened anthropocentrism can be the basis for an adequate environmental ethic, one that can challenge ecologically detrimental practices and lifestyles? Why or why not?
- Did you find any of the responses to the problem of future generations and the nonidentity problem compelling? Why or why not?
- How much weight, if any, do you think should be put on the interests of future generations? To what extent should we be willing to forgo resources or change our lifestyles and socio-economic systems for the benefit of future generations?
- Can you think of common-pool resources other than those discussed in this chapter? Are they managed sustainably? If so, how is it accomplished? If not, why not?
- What do you think "sustainability" means? Does it correspond to any of the conceptions of sustainability discussed in this chapter?

FURTHER READING

Influential work on the adequacy of an enlightened anthropocentric approach to environmental ethics includes:

Norton, Bryan. *Toward Unity among Environmentalists*. Oxford, 1991.

Passmore, John. *Man's Responsibility for Nature: Ecological Problems and Western Traditions*. Charles Scribner's Sons, 1974.

Additional information on the ways in which agricultural practices and food systems use resources suboptimally, as well as on the ethics of food and agriculture more broadly, can be found in:

Sandler, Ronald. *Food Ethics: The Basics*. Routledge, 2015.

Thompson, Paul. *From Field to Fork: Food Ethics for Everyone*. Oxford University Press, 2015.

Two seminal works on common-pool resource problems are:

Ostrom, Elinor. *Governing the Commons: The Evolution of Institutions for Collective Action*. Cambridge University Press, 1990.

Hardin, Garrett. *Living within Limits: Ecology, Economics, and Population Taboos*. Oxford University Press, 1993.

Thoughtful discussions and analyses of the concept of sustainability can be found in:

Norton, Bryan. *Sustainability: A Philosophy of Adaptive Ecosystem Management*. University of Chicago Press, 2005.

Newton, Lisa. *Ethics and Sustainability: Sustainable Development and the Moral Life*. Prentice Hall, 2002.

Robertson, Margaret. *Sustainability: Principles and Practice*. Routledge, 2014.

Discussions of the problem of future generations and the nonidentity problem as they relate to environmental ethics can be found in:

De-Shalit, Avner. *Why Posterity Matters: Environmental Policies and Future Generations*. Routledge, 1995.

Parfit, Derek. *Reasons and Persons*. Oxford University Press, 2004.

Partridge, Ernest. "Future Generations." In *A Companion to Environmental Ethics*, edited by D. Jamieson, 377–89. Blackwell, 2001.

Discussion of the relationships between welfare economics, future generations, ethics, and global climate change can be found in:

Broome, John. *Climate Matters: Ethics in a Warming World*. W. W. Norton, 2012.

Gardiner, Stephen, Simon Caney, Dale Jamieson, and Henry Shue, eds. *Climate Ethics: Essential Readings*. Oxford University Press, 2010.

CHAPTER SEVEN

NONANTHROPOCENTRIC INDIVIDUALISM: THE MORAL CONSIDERABILITY OF PLANTS AND ANIMALS

A CENTRAL ISSUE IN environmental ethics is determining who or what is directly morally considerable or has inherent worth. When considering this issue, two core questions need to be addressed:

1. Which entities have interests (or a good of their own)?
2. Which entities with interests (or a good of their own) should moral agents care about?

These questions—what things have interests and what could justify not caring about them—are at the center of the arguments regarding anthropocentrism, ratiocentrism, sentientism, and biocentrism (see Section 5.1). For example, the primary objections to ratiocentrism and anthropocentrism are that not being a moral agent or a member of the species *Homo sapiens* are insufficient justifications for not taking an individual's interests into account (see Sections 5.2–5.3).

This chapter focuses on the positive arguments for the view that nonhuman animals (sentientism) and all living things (biocentrism) are directly morally considerable or have inherent worth. If they are, then we have responsibilities to them and not only regarding them, which has significant implications for everything from what we should eat to how we should allocate natural resources. (Holistic views on which ecosystems or species have directly considerable interests are discussed in Chapters 11–13.)

✳ BOX 7.1

LAST PERSON THOUGHT EXPERIMENT AND INTUITIONS IN ETHICS

Imagine that there is one person left on earth who has the capacity, just as she dies, to destroy all life on the planet. Would there be anything wrong with her doing so? If so, what makes it wrong? If not, why not?

Environmental ethicists often use this "last person" thought experiment to help identify people's intuitions on whether there is value in the biological world separate from humans. The idea is that if people think that destroying all living things is wrong—even if there would not be any people or moral agents around—then they are committed to the idea that there is something in the biological world that matters, or has value, independent of people.

Hypothetical thought experiments are frequently used in ethics, including environmental ethics. They are useful for helping to identify people's intuitions about cases, to get people to think about a topic in new ways, and to isolate certain aspects of an issue for discussion. I used the replication thought experiment (Box 4.4) and the thought experiments related to moral status (Box 5.2) for these purposes in earlier chapters.

Sometimes thought experiments are also used to help motivate or support a view. The last person thought experiment is frequently used in this way. Often, the fact that many people think that it would be wrong for the last person to destroy the biological world is taken as evidence that it is wrong, and that anthropocentrism must therefore be mistaken.

Using the outcomes of thought experiments in this way—as evidence for a view rather than as a tool to clarify issues, identify people's beliefs, and generate discussion and reflection—is more methodologically controversial in ethics. The reason is that it takes people's intuitions as being truth-indicating. But why should we think that people's responses to hypothetical cases are reliable indicators of what is true? As discussed earlier, people's ethical beliefs can be

(cont.)

BOX 7.1 *(cont.)*

biased and uninformed (Section 5.4). Moreover, to infer that something is true merely on the grounds that quite a lot of people believe it commits the fallacy of appeal to the crowd (Section 5.2).

Returning to the last person thought experiment, let us suppose that most people think that the last person would be wrong to destroy the biological world after his or her death (which is actually an empirical claim that would need to be tested). Should we take this as evidence for nonanthropocentrism? Probably not on its own. The reason is that we need some additional reasons or evidence for taking those intuitions as veridical or accurate. After all, at least some people have the opposite intuition that it would be permissible to do the destruction. Why should one set of intuitions take precedence over the other? One possible reason might be that the best explanation for why people have the intuition that it would be wrong to destroy all life is that living things (or at least some of them) have human independent or objective value. However, there are many other potential explanations for why people might have the intuition. They might be disposed against wanton destruction or they might not like the idea of a lifeless planet, for example. It is not warranted to infer from people's responses to the last person thought experiment to the conclusion that those people are nonanthropocentrists, let alone to the conclusion that nonanthropo-centrism is true.

Thought experiments have an important role to play in environmental ethics. They are useful tools for highlighting issues, generating discussion, and prompting critical reflection. Our responses to them can indicate ideas that we should consider and explore further—for example, nonanthropocentrism in the case of the last person scenario—and may be some evidence in support of a view in some cases. However, they should not be taken as establishing a view as correct. To do so seems to place too much authority on our intuitions. The most justified views are the ones that have the strongest reasons, justifications, and evidence in their favor, and our intuitions to hypothetical cases alone cannot tell us which those are.

7.1 ARGUMENTS FOR SENTIENTISM

Sentientism (also sometimes called **psychocentrism**) is the view that all and only sentient beings—those that have a mental life or are capable of experiencing pleasure and pain—have inherent worth. There are two complementary arguments frequently presented in support of this view.

The first is an **extensionist argument**, which is often associated with Peter Singer (1975; 1989), an influential moral philosopher and animal welfare advocate. The core idea of this argument is that human beings have interests that we ought to care about and there is no **morally relevant difference** between human beings and sentient non-human animals that would justify considering human interests and not the like interests of nonhumans—in particular, the interests in avoiding pain (and experiencing pleasure), having one's desires satisfied, and not dying. There are biological differences between human beings and individuals of other species. However, there are biological differences among human beings as well—for example, ancestry and sex. In both cases—inter-human and inter-species—these are merely **descriptive differences**, which do not justify differential consideration of interests or ascriptions of worth. To take them as such would be racism, sexism, and, on this view, speciesism. Here is a classic quotation from Jeremy Bentham that emphasizes this point:

> It may one day come to be recognized that the number of legs, the villosity of the skin, or the termination of the os sacrum are reasons equally insufficient for abandoning a sensitive being to the same fate. What else is it that should trace the insuperable line? Is it the faculty of reason, or perhaps the faculty of discourse? But a full-grown horse or dog is beyond comparison a more rational, as well as a more conversable animal, than an infant of a day or a week or even a month old. But suppose they were otherwise, what would it avail? The question is not, Can they reason? nor Can they talk? but, Can they suffer? (1823, 311)

Here is a formal rendering of this extensionist argument:

1. If something has the capacity to suffer, then it has an interest in avoiding suffering.
2. Nonhuman animals have the capacity to suffer.

———————

3. Therefore, nonhuman animals have an interest in avoiding suffering. (From 1 and 2)
4. The interest in avoiding suffering is morally considerable in all humans (regardless of the differences among them).
5. There is no difference between humans and nonhuman animals that justifies considering the suffering of humans but not that of nonhuman animal when evaluating actions, practices, and policies.

———————

6. Therefore, the interest of nonhuman animals in avoiding suffering needs to be considered when evaluating actions, practices, and policies. (From 3–5)

Singer uses a similar extensionist argument with respect to desire-satisfaction:

1. If something has desires, then it has an interest in having its desires satisfied.
2. Some nonhuman animals—for example, mammals and fowl—have desires (e.g., to survive and to engage in certain behaviors).

---

3. Therefore, these nonhuman animals have an interest in having their desires satisfied. (From 1 and 2)
4. The interest in having one's desires satisfied is morally considerable in all humans (regardless of the differences among them).
5. There is no factual difference between humans and nonhuman animals that justifies considering the desires of humans but not those of nonhuman animals when evaluating actions, practices, and policies.

---

6. Therefore, the interest of nonhuman animals in having their desires satisfied needs to be considered when evaluating actions, practices, and policies. (From 3–5)

Animal rights theorist Thomas Regan (1983) also uses an extensionist argument for the direct moral considerability of animals. (The difference between animal welfare and animal rights views is discussed in Section 8.1.) Regan's strategy is to identify what it is about human beings that makes us directly morally considerable and then ask if any nonhumans satisfy the criteria. He believes that what all humans have in common and grounds our inherent worth is that we are **experiencing subjects of a life**. That is, we have consciousness and, in some way and to some extent, how well our life goes matters to us—we have desires, goals, experiences, memories, and expectations. This "mattering" does not require cognizing oneself as being a subject of a life. It can be expressed through behaviors, such as infants crying in order to get their needs met. Here is a formal rendering of this argument:

1. All human beings are experiencing subjects of a life.
2. There is nothing else that all human beings have in common that could justify or explain their being directly morally considerable.

---

3. Therefore, being an experiencing subject of a life is sufficient for direct moral considerability.
4. Birds and mammals (and perhaps fish and reptiles) are also experiencing subjects of a life.

---

5. Therefore, birds and mammals (and perhaps fish and reptiles) are directly morally considerable.

Each of the arguments above aims to extend direct moral considerability from humans to nonhumans by showing that the basis for moral considerability in humans applies to (at least some) nonhuman animals. Therefore, consistency requires that we recognize them as directly morally considerable as well. The views are sentientist (or psychocentric) because in each case the criteria for direct moral considerability are tied to psychological capacities (or sentience).

A second type of argument for sentientism focuses on the badness of suffering. That suffering is bad for those experiencing it is evidenced by the fact that people typically try to avoid and alleviate it. Moreover, it seems part of the concept of suffering that it is undesirable. There are a wide variety of sensations that we count as suffering—for example, the felt experience of being left by one's partner is very different from that of breaking one's leg. What they have in common in virtue of which they are grouped together as "suffering" just is the level of undesirableness or unpleasantness involved.

To recognize suffering as bad is not to claim that it is always wrong to cause it *all things considered* or *under all circumstances*. If there are good enough reasons, then it can be permissible (or even obligatory) to cause suffering. Going to the dentist sometimes involves quite a lot of pain and suffering, yet we should still bring our children there, since it is beneficial for them in the long run. Nevertheless, according to this argument the unpleasantness and undesirableness of suffering implies that it should be taken into account in our deliberations. It constitutes a *pro tanto* reason not to cause it (and perhaps to alleviate it)—something that needs to be considered but that is not always decisive, since it can be outweighed by countervailing considerations. If this is correct, then the fact that nonhuman animals experience suffering requires that we take their suffering into account when evaluating actions, practices, and policies. The badness of suffering and pain is what explains why the other things about them—for instance, how many legs they have—are not morally relevant differences. The question is "Can they suffer?" Here is a formal rendering of this argument:

1. Pain and suffering are intrinsically bad—that is, part of what makes an experience suffering is its undesirableness and unpleasantness.
2. If something is intrinsically bad then that constitutes a *pro tanto* reason for moral agents not to cause it (and perhaps to alleviate it).
3. Some nonhuman animals have the capacity to suffer.

---

4. Therefore, there is a *pro tanto* reason not to cause animal suffering (and perhaps to alleviate it) with our actions, practices, and policies.

The next section discusses the primary responses to these arguments for sentientism.

❋ BOX 7.2   **TOPIC TO CONSIDER**

AN INTEREST IN NOT BEING KILLED?

Proponents of sentientism often assert that nonhuman animals have two primary interests: avoiding suffering and not being killed. As discussed above, several of the arguments for an interest in avoiding suffering draw on the nature of the experience. However, there is no experience of not being alive, since there is no consciousness associated with it. (There is the experience of the process of death or being killed, but that is something else than being dead.) What, then, are the arguments for an interest in not being killed? One common argument appeals to lost experiences. When an animal dies, the possibility of all future experiences is eliminated. If those experiences could have been overall positive had the animal not died, then it had an interest in not being killed, since it had an interest in having those (lost to death) experiences. Another argument is an extensionist argument from the badness of human death. If what makes the premature death (or killing) of a person bad is their lost experiences, that it frustrates their desires, or that they want (or strive for) their life to continue, then this should hold as well for nonhuman animals, so long as there is no morally relevant difference between them. Do you think these arguments are sound? What do you think makes premature death bad for people? Do those same considerations apply to nonhuman animals (or, at least, some of them)? If so, what does this imply for our use of animals for such things as food, leather, and experiments? If not, what are the psychological or cognitive differences between humans and nonhuman animals that make premature death worse for people than for nonhuman animals?

7.2 RESPONSES TO THE ARGUMENTS FOR SENTIENTISM

In each of the arguments for sentientism discussed above there is an empirical claim and an inference. The empirical claims concern whether nonhuman animals have certain psychological capacities or experiences, such as sentience, desires, or consciousness. The inference is to the conclusion that these capacities ground interests that matter for their own sake, either because of the nature of the interests or because they matter in humans. Both the empirical claims and the inferences have been challenged.

First, it is sometimes questioned whether animals really do experience pain or really are experiencing subjects of a life. What is the evidence for these empirical claims? The evidence offered is typically the same type of physiological and behavioral evidence that justifies the view that other people are sentient and conscious. You cannot experience the pain of other people firsthand. The belief that other people are sentient is nevertheless justified by the fact that they have the same underlying physiology as you do—for example, a neurological system—and exhibit the same behaviors that you do in situations that would cause you pain—for example, wincing and reporting discomfort. These same considerations hold for animals. Dogs, for instance, recoil and yelp when hit or burned. They also have a nervous system very similar to ours, with common evolutionary origins. It was once thought that animals were not sentient, on the grounds that they do not possess souls. However, that view has been discredited by the physiological and behavioral evidence, as well as by evolutionary biology, which explains the common origins of human and animal nervous systems and provides an evolutionary explanation for pain sensations. The same is thought to be true of animal consciousness. It seems reasonable to conclude that they are conscious in some way or to some extent, given the similarities in behavior, physiology, and evolutionary history between humans and many nonhuman animals. The evidence might not be as strong as with respect to other people—there are greater differences between humans and animals than between you and other people—but it is still quite strong analogical evidence. Sufficiently cognitively complex animals appear to be conscious and feel pain.

But do they suffer? Some philosophers and scientists have suggested that there is a distinction to be made between pain and suffering. The motivation for this is that the same sensation (or felt experience) can be desirable to some people, but not others. Some people enjoy the sensation of being tickled or eating spicy food, while others strongly dislike it. This suggests that the goodness and badness are not located in the bare sensations, but in the attitudes that people take toward them. If this is right, then the fact that animals feel pain and pleasure is not sufficient to establish that they have an interest in avoiding those sensations; they must also be capable of taking attitudes regarding them.

In response to this argument, it might be pointed out that "enjoyable pains" and "suffering pleasures" are exceptional. In general, people have a negative attitude toward pain and a positive attitude toward pleasure. This is particularly so when the pain is connected to physical injury, sickness, or death, which are what is at issue in the treatment of nonhuman animals as sources of food, clothing, and research subjects, for example. Moreover, the distinction between pain and suffering might only hold for very cognitively complex animals, such as humans. For nonhumans that undergo painful sensations and do not have the capacity to take differential attitudes toward them, the bare sensations might be what are bad. That is, the default for painful sensations might be that they are bad. Therefore, if a nonhuman feels pain, they have an interest in avoiding it, even if they are not capable of taking an evaluative attitude toward the pain.

Second, it is sometimes argued that even if animals feel pain and have interests we do not need to take them into account. One reason given for this is that it is simply

✳ BOX 7.3

SENTIENCE AND THE ANIMAL KINGDOM

There is tremendous variety in the capacities of nonhuman animals. Chimpanzees are psychologically and cognitively complex—they use tools, engage in

Image 7.1a   A brown Capuchin in Piauí State, Brazil, uses a rock to crack open nuts while a juvenile looks on.

Source: Luciano Candisani/ Getty Images

Image 7.1b   Pacific blue mussels in a tidal pool in California, USA.

Source: iStock/copyright Bruce Block.

(cont.)

BOX 7.3 *(cont.)*

social learning, and have complicated social systems—whereas sea sponges do not even have neurons. Moreover, there are greater psychological and cognitive differences between, for example, Capuchin monkeys and mussels than there are between us and Capuchins.

Therefore, even once it is recognized that *some* nonhuman animals are sentient, there is quite a lot of work to do determining which are and which are not. As discussed above, it is now widely accepted that mammals and fowl experience pain. It is currently contested whether fish and reptiles do. Insects and biologically simpler animals (such as sponges) typically are thought of as nonsentient, in that they do not experience pain, although they are capable of responding to external stimuli and those with neurological systems may experience the world in some sense. It is important to keep the diversity of the animal (and plant) kingdoms in mind, and not simply bifurcate the biological world into human and nonhuman. On a capacities-based account of moral considerability (see Section 5.2), different nonhuman animals will have different moral status and be morally considerable in different ways due to their differences in capacities.

ridiculous to suggest that we should treat animals like people. Are we going to send pigs to school and let chickens vote? This argument is intended to be a *reductio ad absurdum*. It aims to show that if we accept the view that nonhuman animals are directly morally considerable then it has absurd implications. Therefore, we ought not accept the view. However, the argument is unsound. It mistakenly conflates *consideration* with *treatment*. If sentient nonhumans are directly morally considerable, it does not follow that we must treat them the same way that we treat people. Both adult and infant humans are directly morally considerable, but we do not treat them the same and it would be wrong to do so. Similarly, if sentient nonhumans are directly considerable, we should not treat them the same as humans, or even the same as each other. It would be wrong to release cows into open water and graze dolphins in open pasture.

How something should be treated depends on both its moral status—for example, whether it has inherent worth—and the facts about what harms or serves its interests. The latter differs between organisms of different species. Sentientism asserts that the interests of sufficiently psychologically complex nonhumans need to be taken into account for their own sake. It does not claim or imply that nonhuman animals have the same interests as humans or that their interests can be promoted in the same way as humans. A good bovine life is different from a good human life, and healthy adult humans have a broader range of interests than cows due to our more robust psychological and cognitive capacities. This is so even if both humans and cows have a morally considerable interest in not suffering.

※ BOX 7.4   TOPIC TO CONSIDER

WILD-CAUGHT PETS

Tens of millions of wild reptiles, fish, birds, and mammals are caught each year to be sold as pets. Many of these animals die in the capture, transport, and transition processes. For many others, such as birds confined to cages, even if they survive the capture and transition processes their lives are likely to be much worse in captivity than they would have been in the wild. However, for some animals, such as some freshwater fish species, they may live longer and less stressfully in well-maintained captivity than they would in the wild, due to the lack of predators, reliable food supply, medical treatment, and consistent environment. In these cases, does sentientism imply that it is good for the individuals that they are captured? Do you think it is good for them? Why or why not? What, if anything, does thinking about this case reveal regarding the interests of wild animals? Do they have an interest in not being in captivity and in engaging in species-typical behaviors, even if that is worse for them in terms of longevity and comfort? If so, does this imply that how well their lives go is not exhausted by their psychological experiences?

7.3 DO PLANTS HAVE INTERESTS?

What about plants and trees? Do they have inherent worth? According to sentientism, they do not. Sentientism holds that having psychological capacities is *sufficient* for direct moral considerability. If a being can suffer or is an experiencing subject of a life, then its interests need to be taken into account. It also holds that psychological capacities are *necessary* for direct moral considerability. If a being cannot suffer or is not an experiencing subject of a life, then it does not have inherent worth. Biocentrism challenges this latter position. **Biocentrism** is the view that all living things—animals and plants—have interests that are directly morally considerable.

Some proponents of sentientism, like Singer, believe that nonconscious organisms (such as plants) do not have inherent worth because they do not even have interests. On this view, plant interests cannot be considered, because they do not exist:

> The capacity for suffering and enjoyment is a prerequisite for having interests at all, a condition that must be satisfied before we can speak of interests in a meaningful way. It would be nonsense to say that it was not in the interests of a stone to be kicked along the road by a schoolboy. A stone does not have interests because it cannot suffer.

> Nothing that we can do to it could possibly make any difference to its welfare. (Singer 1989, 172)

Several different lines of argument, many of them exemplified in this passage, have been offered for the conclusion that "suffering and enjoyment is a prerequisite for having interests at all." One is an argument from cases. It is nonsense to think that stones have interests, everyone agrees. What is the best explanation for their not having interests? In Singer's view, it is that stones cannot suffer. However, as arguments from cases go, this one is much too hasty. Stones are only one type of nonconscious (or nonsentient) entity. In order to build an argument from cases, one would need to get people's views about a variety of nonconscious things to see if they thought that all of them lack interests, and then show why those beliefs should be taken as veridical. But when this is done, the argument comes apart. The reason is that people widely believe that nonconscious living things—plants and trees—do have interests and can be harmed. People commonly speak about what is good or bad for the plants in their gardens; farmers work to create conditions that are good for their crop; and conservation biologists try to help threatened plant species recover and thrive. Therefore, Singer's argument from stones seems to commit the **fallacy of hasty conclusion**.

A second argument suggested in the passage above is that without sentience, nothing "could possibly make any difference to [a thing's] welfare." Why should this be? One reason that has been suggested is that it is part of the concept of "welfare" that its components are only psychological. However, it is a common view that a person's welfare depends on more than just her psychological states and experiences. It also depends upon such things as her bodily health, for example. If this is right—or even possibly right—then there seems no conceptual problem with the idea that plants could have a biologically-based, but not psychologically-based, welfare. (See Box 7.5 for discussion of different theories of welfare.)

❋ BOX 7.5

THEORIES OF WELFARE

A theory of welfare is an account of what constitutes someone's life going well or badly for them. There are several different types of theories of welfare.

- **Mentalistic:** According to mentalistic theories of welfare, how well or poorly someone's life is going depends entirely upon their mental states. Subjective well-being views, on which a person's life is going well to the extent that they feel that it is—for example, they are happy and

(cont.)

BOX 7.5 *(cont.)*

enjoying their life—are mentalistic. Classical hedonism, according to which happiness is identified with pleasure and the absence of pain, is also a mentalistic view.

- **Mind–World Correspondence:** According to mind-world correspondence views, how well or poorly someone's life is going depends upon the relationship between their mental states and the world. Desire-satisfaction views are mind-world correspondence views. According to desire satisfaction accounts of welfare, a person's life is going well to the extent that her desires are satisfied and not frustrated. This depends upon how the world actually is—for example, that a person actually has friends or is well thought of—and not just how they think it is or how they subjectively experience it (as would be the case with a mentalistic view).

- **Objectivist:** According to objectivist theories of welfare, how well or poorly someone's life is going depends at least in part on considerations that are not tied to their mental states. On most objectivist views, subjective well-being, experiencing pleasure (and the absence of pain) and desire-satisfaction are *part* of what makes a person's life go well. But so too are considerations such as health, autonomy, meaningfulness, strong relationships, and the richness of one's life, even when these are not tied to positive subjective experiences. For example, on an objectivist view, if a person's work improves the life of others, that counts in favor of their life going well, since it is meaningful and beneficial, even if they do not have a positive mental state or desire associated with it. And if a person spends all their time on trivial things, such as watching reality television, or they are not empowered to make decisions about their own life plans, then their life is going less well than it would be if it were richer and more meaningful or they had greater autonomy, even if they are satisfied with and desire their current life.

Which type of theory of welfare (and which particular theory of that type) is most justified is a perennial issue in moral philosophy. Aristotle (1985) was an objectivist about welfare, while John Stuart Mill (2001) was a mentalist, for example. The issue is important within environmental ethics because it bears on what sort of interests people and animals have, and so which environmental policies and practices will protect and promote their welfare. As discussed above, it is also relevant to whether nonconscious things, such as plants, have a welfare. If mentalistic or mind-world correspondence views are correct, then

(cont.)

BOX 7.5 *(cont.)*

plants do not, since those require mental states. Which view seems more plausible to you? Do you think that welfare is entirely to do with mental states, such as subjective well-being? Or do you think it also has components that are independent of mental states, such as whether there is meaning or importance in what you do?

Another reason often given for the view that nothing could make a difference to a nonconscious thing's welfare (or that it does not have a welfare at all) is that nothing could matter to it. Nonconscious things, because they are nonconscious, cannot care about what happens to them. That is, they cannot take an interest in anything, including what is done to them, precisely because they lack the capacity for intentions or desires. In response to this line of reasoning, defenders of biocentrism often argue that it commits the **fallacy of equivocation**. The fallacy of equivocation is when an argument appears to be sound, but only because one of the key terms in the argument changes meaning in the middle of it. In this case, the term changing meaning is "having an interest." "X has an interest in y" can mean either "x is interested in y" or "y is in x's interest." So, to say "oak trees have an interest in not contracting oak wilt fungal disease" can be understood either as "oak trees are interested in not contracting oak wilt" or "oak wilt is not in oak trees' interests." The first of these is absurd. Oak trees do not "take an interest" in anything, since they lack mental states. However, this is not the same as claiming that oak wilt is not in their interest. Once the ambiguity of "having an interest" is removed, proponents of biocentrism argue, it is clear that the fact that trees cannot take an interest in anything does not imply that they lack interests. It is not in the interests of an oak tree to have oak wilt, even if it does not care about it in a psychological sense.

Proponents of the view that plants lack a welfare sometimes respond by asking: If *they* (the plants) cannot take an interest in their welfare, why should their welfare matter to *us*? However, biocentrists point out that this response actually concedes that plants have interests, and changes the issue to whether we ought to care about them. Biocentrists also highlight that there actually is a sense in which plants take an interest in their welfare, albeit a nonconscious one. They act in ways that involve actively pursuing what is beneficial to them. They defend themselves against predators, repair damage, fight disease, and have phototropic leaves and skototropic roots, for example. Moreover, it is difficult to substantively specify "mattering to oneself how one's life goes" or "caring about one's own interests" in a way that is consistent with sentientism and excludes all nonconscious living things. If it requires having some sort of self-conception involving cognizance of oneself as a distinct individual with interests, then this would exclude most sentient nonhuman animals (and perhaps even some humans). Therefore, it must be understood in a way that does not require a self-conception or self-awareness. But then, biocentrists ask, why should nonconscious things be excluded? After all, they respond to stimuli and are active in protecting and promoting their own interests.

The discussion above concerns biocentrism's response to the view that consciousness is necessary for having interests. But for biocentrism to be justified, it is not enough to show that consciousness is not necessary for interests. It must also be demonstrated that all living things possess interests. If their interests are not based in psychological experiences and attitudes, where do they come from? The concept of interests is connected with that of benefit and harm. The general idea is that an individual has interests if we can talk meaningfully about benefiting and harming it directly, or without reference to anything else. It is bad or harmful for a coyote to have its leg caught in a steel jaw trap, quite apart from how it affects others or is regarded by them. Similarly, biocentrists believe, acid rain is bad for silver maples and oak wilt is bad for oak trees, regardless of how people or other organisms are affected or feel about it. Still, in order to establish that nonconscious living things have a good of their own, it is necessary to provide an account of what grounds their interests. That is, there must be an explanation for why Asian long-horned beetles boring into tree trunks is bad for the trees, whereas sunlight is good for them.

The most common explanation for what grounds the interests of nonconscious organisms (as well as the bare biological interests of conscious ones) is that they are **goal-directed systems** (Taylor 1986; Varner 1998). Their parts and processes are organized in ways and for reasons to do with accomplishing things such as resisting predators and reproducing. There are "in order that" explanations for why it is that they have the parts that they do, the processes that they do, and the life cycles that they do. Flowers produce nectar *in order to* attract pollinators; ivy has tendrils *in order that* it can climb; tree roots are skototropic *in order that* they grow deeper into the ground.

That nonconscious organisms are end- or goal-directed systems means that it is possible to affect them in ways that are conducive or detrimental to accomplishing their goals or ends—that is, to harm and benefit them. Asian long-horned beetle larvae, which bore into the bark of elm trees, are bad for the trees because they diminish the bark's capacity to distribute water and nutrients throughout the tree's living tissue, which is needed for the tree to accomplish its ends of survival and reproduction. Asian long-horned beetles are not bad for elm trees because they make them ugly to us, since the trees' parts and processes do not have the end of being attractive to us. The explanation for why the living tissue of elm trees has the function of nutrient distribution and not attractiveness to humans is that it was selected for because it performed this role in prior generations of elm trees. The trait has persisted—it exists in current elm trees—because it performs that function in the elm tree form of life. In the case of naturally evolved organisms, the selection etiology, or causal process by which the teleology of their parts and processes is determined, is natural selection (see Section 3.3). This is sometimes called an **etiological account** of the interests of nonconscious organisms. Its most influential proponent in environmental ethics is Paul Taylor (1986). Here is a summary of the **etiological argument** for the view that all living things having interests:

1. An entity has interests if it is possible to make sense of benefit and harm to it directly.
2. It is possible to make sense of benefit and harm to an entity directly if there is something it is striving for or aiming to accomplish (i.e., it is **teleologically organized**).
3. In nonconscious organisms, goal-directedness is accounted for by the "in order that" explanations for why their parts and processes persist in organisms of that type (i.e., it is etiologically explained).

---

4. Therefore, the interests of nonconscious organisms can be specified in terms of what resources, conditions, and treatments are conducive to, or detrimental to, the realization of their goals (e.g., survival and reproduction) in the ways characteristic of their life form.

This argument, if sound, establishes only that all living things have **biological interests**. It does not imply that they have the same interests as sentient nonhumans or as people, or that their biologically interests should be taken into account to the same extent or in the same way as the **psychological interests** of animals and people. In fact, the argument does not even establish that the biological interests of plants should be taken into account at all. That is, it does not show that they are morally considerable or have inherent worth. Is there any reason that we ought to care about the interests of plants for their own sake? This is the topic of the next section.

BOX 7.6 *(cont.)*

account of teleology—are what support the view that nonconscious living things have interests (see Section 7.3).

However, artifacts—the intentional creations of human agents—are also teleologically organized and there are also etiological explanations for their parts and processes. There is a reason that wheelbarrows have two handles set the width of a human body apart, a single front wheel and two rear feet. It makes it easier to load and move materials. The parts and processes were selected for (or designed) and persist in current wheelbarrows because they are conducive to accomplishing that end (moving materials). This is commonplace. Intentionally created functional artifacts are goal-directed systems whose parts and processes were selected for because of how they contribute to the purpose of the artifact. The temperature sensor in a thermostat is there *in order to* regulate temperature. The axles of a car are there *in order to* generate locomotion. The fan inside a computer is there *in order to* keep it from overheating. The sharp edge of a knife blade is there *in order to* cut effectively.

Does this mean that, in order to be consistent, acceptance of the argument in favor of nonconscious *organisms* having interests requires accepting that nonconscious *artifacts*, such as cars and wheelbarrows, have interests? And, if so, is this a reason to reject biocentrism? Is it a *reductio ad absurdum* of the etiological account of teleology and/or the teleological account of interests? Alternatively, should we accept the idea that artifacts can have interests if it is the only way to hold on to the widespread view that plants can be harmed and benefited (e.g., that weed killer is bad for weeds and humidity is good for orchids)? Or is there a difference between nonconscious biological organisms and artifacts that explains why the former but not the later should be regarded as having a good of their own? For example, Paul Taylor (1986) argues that the good of artifacts are derivative on their human designers' and users' goals or ends, so that while they have ends, they are not their own ends in the same sense as biological organisms. Is the fact that artifacts are (typically) not alive a relevant difference? Does it matter whether the selection etiology is natural or artificial (i.e., intentional)?

Here is a case to consider as you think about these questions: Imagine that researchers in a lab design and construct a microorganism that just happens to be identical to an already existing biologically evolved microorganism. Its parts and processes were selected for the same reasons and perform the same functions in support of survival and reproduction. Is there any reason to think that the biologically evolved organism has a good of its own, whereas the engineered

(cont.)

BOX 7.6 *(cont.)*

organism does not? Would the situation be any different if the engineered organism was identical to a conscious animal or a human being? And what about
partially engineered organisms, such as selectively bred, hybridized, and genetically modified plants? Is the fact that they are the product of both natural and
artificial selection relevant to whether they have a good of their own?

7.4 SHOULD WE CARE ABOUT THE INTERESTS OF PLANTS?

It is uncontroversial that we should care about nonconscious organisms for instrumental and other human-oriented reasons. For example, trees often provide ecosystem
services, are used as natural resources, are crucial to maintaining well-functioning
ecological systems, are people's property, and have subjective final value. As a result,
we often have indirect duties to them (see Section 5.6). But do trees, mussels, and
other nonconscious organisms have **inherent worth**? That is to ask, should we care
about their interests *for their own sake*, such that we have duties and responsibilities
directly to them and not only regarding them?

The most common approach used by biocentrists to argue that we ought to care
about the good of all living things is *extensionist*. It involves showing that there is no
adequate justification for caring about the interests of sentient (or conscious) organisms, but not the interests of nonconscious organisms. There are several interrelated
strategies for trying to motivate this conclusion. One is to apply the principle that
Singer uses when arguing for sentientism: *If something has interests, then the presumption is to consider them, unless a good justification is provided for why they ought not be
considered.* On this view, the absence of a good reason not to consider the interests of
nonconscious organisms is sufficient to establish that they are morally considerable
and have inherent worth.

A second extensionist strategy is to argue that if we ought to care about the biological interests of people and sentient nonhuman animals, independent of how it affects
their psychological experiences, then we ought to care about the biological interests
of nonconscious organisms (Varner 1998). Imagine that a person is being slowly poi-
soned. However, it is not causing her any psychological distress or pain, since the
damage is occurring at a very low rate and she has no knowledge of it. If the poisoning
is nevertheless contrary to her interests or welfare, this would seem to imply that bare
biological interests matter, independent of psychological impacts.

Another strategy for motivating extending direct consideration to nonconscious
organisms is *coherentist*. This is Paul Taylor's strategy (1986). Taylor argues that
consideration of the interests of all living things best coheres or fits with a proper

understanding of humanity's relationship with the natural world, which he calls the **biocentric outlook**. There are two main components of the biocentric outlook. The first is a set of empirical claims or beliefs that describe the many ways in which human beings are similar to organisms of other species. We, like them, are evolved biological organisms that have physical requirements for survival and well-being. We, like them, depend for our well-being on the natural world, which is itself a system of interdependence of which humans are a part. We, like them, are living things with a good of our own. The second component of the biocentric outlook is what Taylor calls the "**denial of human superiority**" (Taylor 1986, 134). Taylor believes that once a proper biological, ecological, and evolutionary understanding of *Homo sapiens* is accomplished we will:

> see ourselves as having a deep kinship with all other living things,
> sharing with them many common characteristics and being, like them,
> integral parts of one great whole encompassing the natural order of
> life on our planet. When we focus on the reality of their lives, we see
> each one to be in many ways like ourselves, responding in its particular
> manner to environmental circumstances and so pursuing the realization
> of its own good. It is within the framework of this conceptual system that
> the idea of human superiority is found to be unreasonable. (1986, 154–55)

Taylor takes the denial of human superiority to imply that there is no morally relevant difference between humans and nonhumans that would justify ascribing inherent worth to humans but not nonhumans. To assess this view it is necessary to ask:

1. What is distinctive about humans?
2. Does what is distinctive about humans justify superiority with respect to inherent worth?

Several historically common claims regarding unique human abilities have turned out to be mistaken. Human beings are not the only ones that communicate through language, use tools, teach their offspring, solve novel problems, are social, enforce group "rules," or are altruistic. For example, dolphins use sounds to communicate, crows use tools to extract food, cheetahs teach their young to hunt, octopuses are creative problem solvers, meerkats have complex social systems, orangutans enforce group rules, and vampire bats share food with others in their group. In an evolved biological world such as ours, differences between species tend to be matters of degree.

However, differences in degree can be important. So far as we know, no other species has such complex languages, social systems, or technologies as humans do. No other species innovates, disseminates, and accumulates knowledge, ideas, technologies, or social structures at the rate or on the scale that humans do. As a result, no other species exhibits such a broad range of ways of going about the world. Human societies have diverse foodways, social systems, approaches to raising children, and modes of production, for example. This sort of diversity is not found exclusively in humans. There is diversity in the food sources and tool use of different populations of chimpanzees and orcas, for example. Nevertheless, the extent of the diversity in human societies and the rate and magnitude of social and technological innovation, dissemination, and accumulation distinguish us from other species. There is no intentionally created tool or social arrangement in the nonhuman world that approaches the creativity and complexity involved with a sprinkler or a university, let alone the Internet or the Catholic Church. Human beings are, more than any other species, *cultural animals.*

Our cultural capacity distinguishes us from other species in many ways. For example, humans have been able to develop destructive power on a scale unlike other species—for instance, nuclear weapons and ocean floor trawling. Humans are able to adapt to more environments, and adapt more environments to us, than are individuals of other species. Humans also appropriate by far the largest share of planetary resources of any species. The complex psychological and cognitive capacities that make us cultural animals—which, of course, have a genetic basis—differentiate us in other ways as well. For example, we have a broader set of goods constitutive of our flourishing than do individuals of other species. Rich and complex relationships, long-term projects, and aesthetic/spiritual goods are open to us that are not to individuals of (most) other species. In addition, as discussed earlier, only human beings have the cognitive and psychological capabilities necessary for robust moral agency, which is why we can be held morally responsible for our actions, but lions and silver maples cannot (see Section 5.3).

There is thus quite a lot that is distinctive about human beings, even if we are in an ecological and evolutionary sense plain members of the biotic community. However, as Taylor (1986) emphasizes, being distinctive is nothing unique to us. Every species is distinctive; otherwise it would not be a separate species. We are excellent at mathematics, developing technology, and building complex social systems in comparison with individuals of other species, and our capacities are particularly important to our cultural form of life. However, other species' capacities are just as important to their forms of life. Buoyancy control is crucial for salmon; silk spinning is crucial for golden orb spiders; and photosynthesis is crucial for silver maples. This leads Taylor to ask: *Why should the traits that are crucial to the form of life of one species be the standard by which we judge the worth of the others?* He argues that it cannot be that cultural capacities or robust agency are the standard because they are crucial to us, since this assumes that we have special status in order to prove that we do. It commits the **fallacy of begging the question**, according to Taylor. He therefore concludes that there is no non-question-begging justification for asserting human superiority over other species. We do not hold a special, privileged, or unique place in earth's community of life; we are one unique species among many interdependent unique species. According to

Taylor, once human superiority is denied, we ought to accept the **principle of species impartiality**:

> [E]very species counts as having the same value in the sense that, regardless of what species a living thing belongs to, it is deemed to be prima facie deserving of equal concern and consideration on the part of moral agents. . . . Subscribing to the principle of species-impartiality, we now see, means regarding every entity that has a good of its own as possessing inherent worth. (155)

There are two key questions to ask when evaluating Taylor's argument for the inherent worth of all living things: (1) Is the biocentric outlook an accurate account of the relationship between humans and the rest of earth's community of life? (2) Is the view that all living things have inherent worth the most justified or reasonable one to adopt, given the biocentric outlook (or an appropriately revised version of it)? The first of these questions is a variation on the issue of whether any of the differences between members of *Homo sapiens* and members of other species are morally relevant differences, which was already discussed at several points in this chapter (see Sections 7.1, 7.2, and earlier in this section).

In response to the second question, some environmental ethicists have suggested that while the attitude of respect for nature might be a reasonable one to take in light of the biocentric outlook, it might not be the *only* reasonable one. It might be just as reasonable to take a holistic, ecocentric view as the individualist one endorsed by Taylor. In fact, Taylor's biocentric outlook is very similar to the worldview that Aldo Leopold uses to motivate his influential **land ethic**. Leopold (1968) believes that human beings are plain members and citizens of the biotic community, and that as a result we ought to act in ways that promote the integrity of ecological systems. (The land ethic is discussed at length in Chapter 11.)

Others have argued that even if the biocentric outlook justifies regarding all living things as possessing inherent worth, it does not justify the view that all living things have *equal* or *the same* inherent worth. Here is David Schmidtz on this point:

> It will not do to defend species egalitarianism by singling out a property that all living things possess, arguing that this property is morally important, then concluding that all living things are therefore of equal moral importance. The problem with this sort of argument is that, where there is one property that provides the basis for moral standing, there might be others. Other properties might provide bases for different kinds or degrees of moral standing. (1998, 59)

The idea that there are degrees of direct considerability, or else different forms or types of it, is often referred to as **pluralism**. It is the view discussed in the next section.

MEALS AND MICROBES

A common argument against biocentrism is that it is unlivable. It is simply not possible, or else too onerous, to live a human life without harming other living things. After all, we have to eat. Another, related criticism emphasizes that most living things are microorganisms. Biocentrism appears to imply that every bacteria has inherent worth and is due respect, which strikes many people as absurd (in addition to unlivable). We cannot avoid relentlessly killing microbes with our immune systems. Biocentrists standardly respond to these concerns by arguing that the claim that all living things have inherent worth is not equivalent to the claim that all living things have rights or that they should all be considered and treated in the same way. Biocentrism is the view that all living things have direct moral standing and therefore are not mere things (as rocks are) that can be treated thoughtlessly or without consideration. As a result, living things are due respect, even when we appropriately use them, as we must, for our own ends. Moreover, the response continues, what respect toward a plant amounts to is something quite different from respect toward a sentient animal, precisely because plants are not conscious. Furthermore, even if microbes have interests, we are not moral agents with respect to them, due to their scale and their multitude. It is not possible for us to consider their interests, so we do not need to do so. Do you think these responses are adequate? Why or why not? Are there other practical difficulties that you see arising from biocentrism?

7.5 PLURALISM

Each of the accounts of moral considerability that have been discussed thus far—anthropocentrism, ratiocentrism, sentientism, and biocentrism—are **individualist**. It is individual organisms, or some subset of them, that have inherent worth. They are also **monistic** and **egalitarian**. That is, they endorse a single standard for moral considerability (monism), and all organisms that meet the standard are equally considerable (egalitarian). If sentience is the standard, then all sentient beings are equally morally considerable (Singer 1989; Regan 1983). If being a teleological center of life is the standard, then all living things are equally morally considerable (Taylor 1986). If being a moral agent is the standard, then all robustly rational beings are equally morally considerable (Kant 1785; 1997).

Concerns have been raised regarding both monism and egalitarianism, as exemplified by the passage from Schmidtz at the end of the prior section. Norway maples, bottlenose dolphins, and human beings might all be teleological centers of life, and that may provide a basis for moral considerability. But dolphins are also sentient, intelligent, and sociable in ways that trees are not, and adult humans are moral agents on top of that. These capacities seem to many to be morally relevant, since they pertain to what sorts of relationships, interests, and responsibilities an individual can have. For this reason, some environmental ethicists argue that there are in fact a plurality of bases and degrees of moral considerability. Perhaps all living things have inherent worth and are due concern, but sentient beings are due additional consideration because they can suffer, and rational beings merit yet further consideration due to their autonomy and robust agency (VanDeVeer 1979). Similarly, **moderate anthropocentrism** is the view that while all living things (or sentient beings) have inherent worth, human beings have greater worth in virtue of their humanity. (**Absolute anthropocentrism** or **strong anthropocentrism** are the terms typically used for the view that all and only human beings have inherent worth.)

Alternatively, perhaps rather than *degrees* of moral considerability, there are different *forms*. Respect (for autonomy) might be appropriate to moral agents, compassion to sentient beings, and care for nonconscious organisms. If we were to encounter a species that had broader or more complex capacities and interests than ours, it would presumably be wrong to conclude that we have no worth or less worth than they do. Instead, on this view, we should recognize that the forms of responsiveness and consideration appropriate to them might be different or more diverse, just as ours is in comparison to magpies and bamboo. Another way to put this is that while all living things (or sentient things, depending upon the view) have inherent worth and are morally considerable, they might nevertheless have different **moral status**. How and to what degree the inherent worth of something ought to be considered could depend on its capacities and interests.

Some environmental ethicists also believe that moral status depends upon *relationships*. Consider, for example, a wild rabbit and a pet rabbit. They have the same psychological capacities, but it seems plausible that a person ought to consider the interests of her pet rabbit more or differently than those of a wild rabbit precisely because it is her pet. She ought to feed her pet and protect it from predators, but it would be absurd for her to try to feed and protect wild rabbits. It is not just that the costs and logistics would be unworkable—would she then also have to feed the hawks and coyotes that would eat the rabbits? The fact that they are wild seems to favor taking more of a hands-off approach. One argument sometimes raised against sentientism—particularly animal welfare views (see Section 8.5)—is that it reduces to absurdity because it would require us to actively try to reduce the suffering of wild animals (Sagoff 1984). However, if their wildness means that the way we ought to consider their interests does not include promoting them, but only not impairing them unnecessarily, then this objection does not hold. Some environmental ethicists, such as Taylor, have argued that for wild plants and animals their inherent worth calls for a presumption of restraint. Not only is it not required that we intervene to help them, it would be wrong to do so, except when redressing (or preventing) harms that we have done (or could do) to them (see Section 9.2). In this way, plants and animals could have differential moral status based on their histories, situatedness, and relationships, in addition to their capacities (Palmer 2010).

In response to these challenges to monism and egalitarianism, proponents of sentientism and biocentrism often argue that the criticisms are misplaced. It is not necessary to assert different levels of worth or different types of moral status in order to explain why sentient animals are due compassion, whereas trees are not. It is explained by the different sorts of interests that they have. Monism and egalitarianism do not imply that all interests need to be considered alike, but that *like interests need to be considered alike* (Singer 1975, 1989; Taylor 1986). Foxes are sentient, so have an interest in not experiencing pain. Fir trees are not sentient, so do not have an interest in avoiding pain. Of course we must be compassionate toward foxes but not fir trees. This follows from the types of capacities and interests that they have. Similarly, even if adult human beings and fir trees have equal inherent worth, people have a much more diverse range of interests than do trees. We have biological interests, as well as psychological interests in enjoyment, meaning, knowledge, and relationships. Therefore, on this view, what explains why human interests often ought to be considered differently or given greater weight than those of individuals of other species is not that human beings have greater worth or different moral status than they do, but that we have more diverse, complex, and longitudinal interests than they do.

※ BOX 7.8   TOPIC TO CONSIDER

PAMPERED PETS

People consider the interests of animals with similar capacities very differently. According to the American Pet Products Association, US citizens spent approximately $58 billion on their pets in 2014, on everything from food and medical care to toys and clothes. In contrast, animals in the industrial food system are treated as meat, milk, and egg factories, which results in a wide array of practices that cause them harm and suffering—such as confinement, debeaking, tail-docking, castration, overfeeding, and slaughtering. Moreover, people are often indifferent to the interests of wild animals or harvest them for human purposes.

Is there justification for this differential consideration of animals' interests—companion, livestock, and wild—if they have similar psychological capacities? For example, does the fact that livestock are created and raised for the purpose of providing food imply that it is permissible to treat them in whatever ways

(cont.)

BOX 7.8 *(cont.)*

Image 7.2a A nursing sow in a farrowing crate.

Source: ©iStock/Aumsama

Image 7.2b A golden retriever in a pet supply store. Pigs and dogs have comparable psychological complexity and capacities.

Source: ©iStock/choja

most efficiently produce it? Or does the fact that people are responsible for their existence imply that they have a responsibility to treat them well? Does wildness favor taking a "hands off" approach, such that while we should not

(cont.)

BOX 7.8 (cont.)

cause suffering needlessly, we also should not try to alleviate natural suffering (e.g., from disease, predation, or deprivation)? Do the relationships people have with their pets justify the enormous resource expenditures on them, even as they are indifferent to the interests of the animals that provide their (and their pets') food and clothing?

In thinking about whether relationships should matter to how we consider the interests of nonhumans, it can be useful to reflect on interpersonal ethics. It is a common view that we have different ethical responsibilities to people based on relationships and histories. (See Sections 8.5 and 14.2 for discussion of this view.) A parent has obligations to her children that she does not have to strangers, precisely because they are her children; and in practice we spend the bulk of our resources on those who are near and dear to us. Are we right to prioritize our friends and family (and pets) so much? If so, is the reason for this that moral considerability is sometimes dependent upon peoples' relationships or sentiments? If not, why not?

7.6 SUMMARY

This chapter focused on nonanthropocentric individualistic views regarding who/what is directly moral considerable: sentientism, biocentrism, and pluralism. The primary question addressed was:

- Are any nonhuman organisms directly morally considerable in the sense of having inherent worth—that is, do they have interests that we ought to care about for their own sake?

The chapter began by looking at the arguments in favor of extending direct moral considerability to all psychologically complex animals (sentientism). After considering some objections to sentientism, it then looked at the arguments for extending direct moral considerability to all living things (biocentrism). A significant part of that discussion concerned whether nonconscious entities have interests and, if so, what grounds them. This issue will also be salient when considering holistic views on direct moral considerability—whether species and ecosystems have interests that we should care about (see Sections 11.4.3 and 13.3.2). The discussion of biocentrism also involved identifying what is unique or distinctive about human beings—for example, our robust cognitive and psychological capacities and cultural form of life—as well as considering whether it is a basis for ascribing special or greater worth to us. Finally, pluralistic views on which there are different types or forms of direct moral considerability were discussed.

This and the previous two chapters concerned *who or what* is directly morally considerable. The next three chapters concern *how* the interests of morally considerable individuals should be considered.

KEY TERMS (SEE GLOSSARY FOR DEFINITIONS):

absolute anthropocentrism

biocentric outlook

denial of human superiority

egalitarianism
(regarding moral considerability)

etiological account of interests

etiological account of teleology

experiencing subject of a life

extensionist argument

fallacy of begging the question

fallacy of equivocation

fallacy of hasty generalization
(or fallacy of hasty conclusion)

factual difference (or descriptive
difference)

goal-directed system

individualism

inherent worth

land ethic

biocentrism

biological interests

mentalistic theories of welfare

mind-world correspondence views of
welfare

moderate anthropocentrism

monism (regarding moral considerability)

morally relevant difference (or morally
relevant property)

moral status

objectivist theories of welfare

pluralism (regarding moral
considerability)

principle of species impartiality

psychocentrism

psychological interests

sentientism

strong anthropocentrism

teleological account of interests

REVIEW QUESTIONS

- What makes an approach to environmental ethics "individualist"?
- What does it mean to say of something that it is directly morally considerable or has inherent worth?
- What is the difference between sentientism and biocentrism?
- What makes an argument "extensionist"?

- What is the difference between a descriptive difference and a morally relevant difference?
- What is the difference between equal consideration and same treatment?
- What is the basis for the denial of human superiority on Taylor's view? What is the principle of species impartiality?
- What is pluralism with respect to direct moral considerability?

DISCUSSION QUESTIONS

- What do you think is distinctive about human beings and does it imply that we have unique, special, or greater worth than individuals of other species?
- Do you agree that plants have interests even though they lack consciousness? Why or why not?
- Is the extension of direct moral considerability from human beings to animals warranted? What about the extension of direct moral considerability to plants? Why or why not?
- Is the principle that like interests should be considered alike without regard to the species membership of the individuals whose interest they are well-justified?
- Do you think that relational considerations, such as whether an animal is wild or one's pet, can be relevant to whether an individual is directly morally considerable (or how or in what ways they are considerable)?
- Which of the individualist views that have been discussed (anthropocentrism, ratiocentrism, sentientism, biocentrism, and pluralism) do you believe to be most justified and why?

FURTHER READING

There are many thoughtful books on the moral status of nonhuman animals. Here are several that are influential and insightful:

Gruen, Lori. *Ethics and Animals.* Cambridge University Press, 2011.

Midgley, Mary. *Animals and Why They Matter.* University of Georgia Press, 1983.

Palmer, Clare. *Animal Ethics in Context.* Columbia University Press, 2010.

Regan, Thomas. *The Case for Animal Rights.* University of California Press, 1983.

Rollin, Bernard. *Animal Rights and Human Morality.* Prometheus Books, 1980.

Singer, Peter. *Animal Liberation.* New York Review, 1975.

Among the influential and insightful works on the moral status of nonconscious organisms are:

Goodpaster, Kenneth. "On Being Morally Considerable." *Journal of Philosophy* 75 (1978): 308–25.

Taylor, Paul. *Respect for Nature: A Theory of Environmental Ethics*. Princeton University Press, 1986.

Varner, Gary. *In Nature's Interests? Interests, Animal Rights, and Environmental Ethics*. Oxford University Press, 1998.

PART IV: NORMATIVE THEORIES: HOW DO THINGS MATTER?

CHAPTER EIGHT

CONSEQUENTIALIST ENVIRONMENTAL ETHICS: ANIMAL WELFARE AND UTILITARIANISM

THE PRACTICAL AIM OF environmental ethics is to provide guidance on how we ought to interact with and treat the natural environment, including the nonhuman individuals that populate it. As discussed in prior chapters, two questions are central to this:

1. Who or what matters—that is, which things ought we to care about?
2. How do things matter—that is, how ought we take them into consideration?

The last several chapters primarily concerned the first of these questions—which individuals are directly morally considerable (Chapters 5–7), whether naturalness has final value (Section 4.4), and what sorts of goods and services ecological systems provide (Section 4.1). (We will return to the question of who or what matters when discussing holistic approaches to environmental ethics in Chapters 11–13.) The next three chapters concern the second question—how things matter. In particular, they are about how the interests of directly morally considerable individuals should be taken into account in decision-making. This is the purview of normative theory, the most predominant of which are deontology, consequentialism, and virtue ethics. As we will see, different normative theories advocate considering the interests of morally considerable individuals in different ways, and this leads to different conclusions regarding how we ought to interact with and treat nonhuman animals and the natural environment. Therefore, developing a well-justified environmental ethic requires evaluating the strengths and weakness of different normative theories, both in general and for their suitability for environmental ethics. This will be the most theoretical and conceptual portion of this textbook.

This chapter begins with a discussion of the dissimilarities between animal rights and animal welfare views in order to illustrate the importance of normative theory to environmental ethics. The rest of the chapter focuses on consequentialist approaches to environmental ethics. The next two chapters are on deontological and virtue-oriented approaches. In each chapter, the key normative concepts and structure of the theory are elucidated. The remainder of the chapter then focuses on the approach to environmental decision-making associated with the theory. Many of our most pressing environmental issues—such as allocations of scarce resources, land use decisions, and consumption patterns—involve determining which values or whose interests should take precedence in cases of conflict. Therefore, how the theories approach and adjudicate such situations is emphasized. Finally, each chapter includes discussion of challenges that have been raised against the normative theory.

8.1 DISTINGUISHING NORMATIVE THEORIES

As we saw last chapter (Section 7.1), both Peter Singer and Thomas Regan believe that sentient nonhuman animals are directly morally considerable. They agree that animals have interests and that we, moral agents, need to take their interests into consideration for their own sake. However, their views differ with respect to the *way* in which we ought to take animal interests into account. Regan believes that sentient beings should never be treated as a mere means to human ends. It is not permissible, in his view, to test medicines on them, use them for sport, or eat them. They have rights against those sorts of treatments. For this reason, Regan's view is an **animal rights view**. In contrast, Singer believes that sentient beings are entitled to equal consideration of their interests in determining which actions (or practices or policies) have the best outcomes overall. Therefore, it is not always or in principle wrong to use animals as a means to our ends. It is permissible, so long as doing so brings about the best overall outcomes or consequences of all the options available, taking into account the interests of everyone affected including sentient nonhumans. For this reason, Singer's view is not an animal rights view, it is an **animal welfare view**. We have to consider the interests of animals; their suffering and enjoyment are part of the determination of what we ought to do, but they are not always decisive. Here is an issue that illustrates the divergent practical implications of the views.

Animal welfare and animal rights views are both opposed to **concentrated animal feed operations** (CAFOs) because of the way they treat animals. Concentrated animal feed operations are agricultural operations in which animals are raised in enclosed areas and feed is brought to them, rather than their ranging or grazing for it (Images 8.1). The US Environmental Protection Agency (EPA) defines a large CAFO as one that has a minimum of 125,000 chickens, 82,000 laying hens, 10,000 swine, 1,000 cattle for consumption, or 700 dairy cattle. However, they are often much bigger than this. CAFOs are the product of the characteristic features of industrialization being applied to animal agriculture—for example, scale, efficiency, technologization, standardization, consolidation, and specialization. For this reason, they are sometimes referred to, particularly by their critics, as **factory farms**.

CAFOs are the predominant source of meat in the United States and are increasingly common around the world. In them, animals are considered and treated as part of an industrial process to produce as much meat (or eggs or milk) as possible at as low a cost as possible. Combined with the high concentration of animals, this results in practices that cause suffering. For example, egg-laying hens are typically kept in rows and stacks of small battery cages that do not allow them to stand or walk around. A large percentage of battery-caged birds have broken bones prior to slaughter. Chickens, turkeys, and other fowl are declawed and debeaked (without anesthesia) so that they do not harm each other and can be more easily handled. Swine are often housed in individual gestation crates that are so small they are not able to turn around. Breeding sows are often confined on their sides to make nursing more efficient (Image 7.2a). The tails of pigs are typically docked, and boars are castrated in order to improve the taste of pork. Dairy cows are typically given growth hormones and overfed in order to boost milk production. Reproduction is maximized through processes of artificial insemination, as soon as is viable. Beef and dairy cattle are often fed corn-based diets to which they are not well suited. Confinement of all animals prevents them from engaging in species-typical physical and social behaviors, and involves the use of large amounts of antibiotics to prevent the spread of diseases. All of these are standard practices in CAFOs. While they are not practiced in every case, they are considered industry norms. In addition to these treatment issues, there are also serious and widespread concerns about stress and improper implementation of slaughter processes, which can result in live animals being boiled or butchered.

Although both animal rights and animal welfare views oppose CAFOs, they do so on different grounds. On animal welfare views, it is primarily the suffering of the animals that makes them wrong. The suffering far exceeds the marginal enjoyment people take in eating inexpensive meat. (The marginal enjoyment is the enjoyment that people have beyond what they would have eating a non-CAFO diet.) On animal rights views, the primary problem with CAFOs is that they treat animals merely as a source of food for us. Animals have a right to not be treated as a mere means to our ends, so CAFOs are unethical.

The difference between the two views becomes salient when we start to think about what would make animal agriculture permissible. On an animal welfare view, the problem with CAFOs is the suffering involved. So if the suffering could be eliminated, or sufficiently reduced, then animal agriculture is permissible. For example, animal welfare concerns about gestation crates have led McDonald's and several other large purchasers of pork to require that their suppliers phase them out by 2020; and

Image 8.1a   A cattle feedlot near Lubbock, TX.

Source: Design Pics Inc / Alamy Stock Foto

Image 8.1b   A turkey house in Benton, AR.

Source: Jeff Vanuga, United States Department of Agriculture

animal welfare concerns about battery cages have led to restrictions on their use in the European Union and some US states. Perhaps it is possible to "clean up" industrial animal agriculture enough to make it acceptable. Moreover, alternative approaches to animal agriculture—for example, small-herd, free-range, and grass-fed—in which the animals live well and are killed with little stress or pain could be sufficiently humane to be ethically acceptable on an animal welfare view. However, on an animal rights view, none of these alternatives is acceptable, because they all involve treating animals as a mere means to our ends. There is another option—not eating farmed meat at all—which does not involve doing so. There are hundreds of millions of people who eat nutritious vegetarian diets. So not only does animal agriculture involve treating animals as a means, it does so for no necessary reason. The problem is the practice of producing animals for food (when there are ready alternatives), not only how they are treated in the process. The same goes with using animals in research and in entertainment. Here is how Regan puts the distinction between the two views:

> What's wrong—fundamentally wrong—with the way animals are treated isn't the details that vary from case to case. It's the whole system. The forlornness of the veal calf is pathetic, heart-wrenching; the pulsing pain of the chimp with electrodes planted deep in her brain is repulsive; the slow, tortuous death of the raccoon caught in the leg-hold trap is agonizing. But what is wrong isn't the pain, isn't the suffering, isn't the deprivation. These compound what's wrong. Sometimes—often—they make it much, much worse. But they are not the fundamental wrong.
>
> The fundamental wrong is the system that allows us to view animals as *our resources*, here for *us*—to be eaten, or surgically manipulated, or exploited for sport or money. . . .
>
> . . . [A] little straw, more space, and a few companions won't eliminate—won't even touch—the basic wrong that attaches to our viewing and treating these animals as our resources. A veal calf killed to be eaten after living in close confinement is viewed and treated in this way: but so, too, is another who is raised (as they say) "more humanely." To right the wrong of our treatment of farm animals requires more than making rearing methods "more humane"; it requires the total dissolution of commercial animal agriculture. (Regan 1985, 13–4)

Regan and Singer are both sentientists. They both regard all sentient beings as having direct moral considerability. So why does one hold an animal rights view and the other an animal welfare view? The reason is that they embed their sentientism within different **normative theories**. Normative theories provide approaches to evaluating actions, practices, and policies. Singer is a **consequentialist**. According to consequentialism, it is the outcomes or results of an action or policy that make it right or wrong.

☀ BOX 8.1	TOPIC TO CONSIDER

ZOOS AND AQUARIA

There are over 10,000 zoos and aquaria around the world, involving tens of millions of animals. How would animal welfare and animal rights views think differently about whether it is ethically acceptable to keep animals in zoos and aquaria? What sorts of questions would they ask in their evaluations of them? Under what type of conditions and circumstances, if any, would they be acceptable on an animal welfare view and on an animal rights view? Will the goals or aims of the zoo be relevant to the evaluation? Will the type of animals involved be relevant? Will the source of the animals be relevant?

Regan is a **deontologist**. According to deontology, an action is right or wrong to the extent that it conforms to the operative rules or duties. So on animal welfare views, such as Singer's, using animals is permissible so long as they are treated as well as reasonably possible and the outcomes are overall good in comparison to the alternatives. The rightness or wrongness depends upon the balance of the good and bad outcomes that result (or are expected to result) from the practice or action being evaluated. On animal rights views, such as Regan's, the direct moral considerability of animals implies a duty—to not use animals as a mere means for human ends—that must be followed, regardless of how the animals are treated or the outcomes involved. The rightness or wrongness of the practice or action being evaluated is determined largely by the features of it, whether it involves using animals as a mere means, and not by the outcomes.

As the case of animal agriculture demonstrates, understanding and evaluating theories of environmental ethics requires familiarity with and assessment of normative theories more generally. The point of ethical theory is to help provide guidance for choosing well regarding our actions, practices, and policies (see, e.g., Sections 1.2 and 10.5). One crucial part of ethical theory, discussed at length in previous chapters, is identifying which things have value (or matter), as well as what sort of value they have. Another crucial component is determining the relationship between value and what we ought to do. I have been talking about this in terms of "how things matter" in our deliberations. Another way to think about this is that ethical theories, in addition to specifying which things have value, must also describe how their value relates to right actions (or practices or policies). Normative theories—for example, consequentialism, deontology, and virtue ethics—are different accounts of the relationship between value and right action. Yet another way to think about this is in terms of approaches to ethical evaluation. Different normative theories provide different approaches for evaluating which actions (or practices or policies) are right and which are wrong.

A rough and simple way to distinguish among types of normative theories is to link them to different components of an action (or policy). For any intentional action, there is *the agent*—the individual, group, or institution—who performs the action or enacts the policy. There is *the action or policy itself*—what it involves doing or the principles that it embodies. And there are *the outcomes* of the action or policy—what results or comes about from it. It is possible to evaluate each of these. For example, consider a group of people who take their recreation by riding motorized off-road vehicles in wilderness areas, even when they have been designated for protection. We could evaluate the character of the people involved by asking, "What sort of person would enjoy and do this?" We could evaluate the principles on which they are acting, such as "I can violate legal restrictions for my own enjoyment." Or we could evaluate the outcomes of their activities, including the ecological impacts. Generally speaking:

- **Consequentialist normative theories** tie the rightness and wrongness of actions, practices, and policies to their outcomes.
- **Deontological normative theories** tie the rightness and wrongness of actions, practices, and policies to whether they conform to the operative duties or rules.
- **Virtue-oriented normative theories** tie the rightness and wrongness of actions, practices, and policies to the dispositions of the agent or the character traits expressed by them.

The remainder of this chapter focuses on consequentialist normative theory. The next two chapters focus on deontological and virtue-oriented theories respectively.

8.2 UTILITARIANISM

According to consequentialist normative theories what ought to be done is determined by comparing the outcomes (or expected outcomes) of the available options. The better the outcomes, the more justified the action, practice, or policy. There are many different versions of consequentialism. For example, **ethical egoism** is the view that an action is right if it promotes the best outcomes for the agent. Ethical egoism is not regarded as a viable environmental ethic. It is unlikely to generate the sort of guidance and restraint that is required to address ecological problems and so is subject to the inadequacy objection (see Sections 5.4 and 14.6). Moreover, sentientists, biocentrist, anthropocentrists, ratiocentrists, and holists all agree that there are sound arguments for considering interests other than one's own. They differ on which others are directly morally considerable, but they each reject egoism.

In contrast, **utilitarian** forms of consequentialism consider all morally considerable interests and call for performing the action (or enacting the policy) that has the best overall outcomes. The basic normative principle of utilitarianism is commonly referred to as the **principle of utility**:

> Something (e.g., an action or policy) is right to the extent that it brings about the greatest balance of good over bad among the options available to the agent, considering everyone and everything impacted.

All versions of utilitarianism accept some version of the principle of utility. It is what defines a view as utilitarian. But different versions of utilitarianism are generated by their incorporating different **value axiologies**, or accounts of what things are good and bad. For example, Singer is a utilitarian. He believes that something is right to the extent that it brings about the greatest balance of good over bad. He is also an egalitarian sentientist. He believes that all sentient beings are equally directly morally considerable, and that they have an interest in not suffering, not being killed, and not having their aims frustrated (Singer 1975; 1989). Thus, the value axiology that he endorses is that the suffering and interest frustration of all sentient beings are bad, while their enjoyment and interest satisfaction are good. Therefore, according to Singer's version of utilitarianism, an action (or policy) is right to the extent that it brings about the greatest balance of enjoyment (and interest satisfaction) over suffering (and interest frustration) among all sentient beings who are impacted by the action (or policy).

However, utilitarianism is flexible with respect to value axiology. For example, it is possible to be a biocentric utilitarian. On such a view, something is right to the extent that it brings about the greatest amount of flourishing for all living things affected. It is possible to be an anthropocentric utilitarian, as exemplified by Gifford Pinchot (see Box 5.1). It is possible to include natural value as part of a value axiology. Thus, any utilitarian theory of environmental ethics will: (1) accept some version of the principle of utility, and (2) endorse a particular value axiology. (Some moral philosophers reserve the label "utilitarianism" for views on which the value axiology is strictly welfarist—that is, on which the good is identified with welfare or well-being. On these views, if natural value or justice are part of the value axiology then the view is not utilitarianism, but pluralistic value consequentialism. However, here I follow the more inclusive usage of "utilitarianism" on which non-welfarist values can be part of a utilitarian value axiology.)

Utilitarianism has a number of appealing features. First and foremost, it seems intuitively plausible. The principle of utility in essence states that it is preferable to have more good and less bad. This strikes many people as being obviously and perhaps even conceptually true. "Good" is merely the term for things that are desirable, beneficial, or choice-worthy. Similarly, there are many things that people consider bad—for instance, pain, destruction, and exploitation. What they all have in common, which collects them under the umbrella of "badness," is that they are undesirable or things that we want to try to avoid. So it seems reasonable that the right thing to do is to promote as much good as possible and avoid as much bad as possible. That just seems to follow from the concepts of "good" and "bad."

A second appealing feature of utilitarianism is that it is impartial. It counts everyone's interests equally. No one is afforded extra consideration just because they are wealthy, a particular sex, a political leader, or a *Homo sapiens* (on nonanthropocentric versions). As we have seen, it is a common view within environmental ethics that everyone should be equally considered in deliberations about what to do, so long as there is no morally relevant difference between them (see, e.g., Sections 6.1, 7.1, and 7.4). Within utilitarian views, this idea is often expressed in the dictum "Everyone counts as one and only one."

A third appealing feature is that utilitarianism seems straightforward to apply to generate guidance on whatever action, practice, or policy one is considering—for example, how to allocate scarce water resources, whether to prioritize conserving endangered species over infrastructure development, how stringently to regulate carbon emissions, or what to eat for dinner. All one has to do is determine which candidate action (or policy) brings about the greatest balance of good over bad. Moreover, the process for determining this appears clear-cut, almost scientific. It involves identifying all the possible courses of action, identifying what the consequences for each of those actions will be (including probabilities), assigning appropriate values (good and bad) to those consequences, and then summing up each alternative to see which has the greatest balance of good over bad. This process is called a **utility calculus**.

The principle of utility is technically a principle of right action, not a method of decision-making. It is a statement of what is right, not instructions on how to figure out what is right. However, as indicated above, there is a decision-making approach implicit in it. If what is right is what has the best consequences, then what is needed is a way to determine the action or policy that has the best outcomes. Conducting a utility calculus is one possible way to do that. For example, imagine that there is a proposal to fill an urban wetland in order to build an athletic facility. Let us suppose for simplicity's sake that there are only two options, to build the facility in that location or to not build it at all and use the funding for other purposes. On an enlightened anthropocentric utilitarian view, determining which option to take involves identifying which better serves the interests of all the people impacted over the long run. If the facility is built, the benefits would include some job creation, recreational opportunities, a location for community events, and perhaps even improved health for those who use it. The costs would involve loss of ecosystem services and recreation opportunities for those who use the wetland, as well as the expense (and opportunity costs) of building the facility. If the goods associated with the facility outweigh the costs in comparison to not building the facility and using the funding for other purposes, then it ought to be built, according to utilitarianism. Of course, on a sentientist view, the impacts on the nonhuman animals that reside in the wetland or that use it as a stopover during migrations must also be considered. Most of the organisms impacted

---

✳ BOX 8.2   TOPIC TO CONSIDER

EFFECTIVE ALTRUISM AND ENVIRONMENTAL ACTIVISM

Many people engage in charitable giving, volunteering, and activism for environmental organizations and causes. Do you think that a person ought to aim to maximize the beneficial outcomes of her resources—sometimes called **effective altruism**—when thinking about where to give her money, where/how to volunteer, and what sorts of activism to engage in? Or are their other considerations—such as personal connections to an issue or organization—that are also relevant? For instance, is it permissible to give to a local environmental group, even if the resources would be more effectively used by a larger national organization? Is it permissible to be politically active in support of environmental legislation or campaigns that you care deeply about but have very little chance at success, and so are not likely to maximize the impact of your effort? Is it permissible to engage in activism that is illegal—such as breaking into labs to free research primates—if it is the most effective way to achieve beneficial ends? (Direct action environmental activism is discussed in Box 12.2.)

---

by the facility—fish, birds, reptiles, mammals—would likely be adversely impacted due to the habitat loss. Therefore, the benefits of the facility to people would need to sufficiently outweigh both the costs to people and the harms to sentient nonhumans in order for building it to be justified. As this example indicates, central to utilitarian decision-making is identifying and weighing interests. This is the focus of the next section.

8.3 IDENTIFYING AND WEIGHING INTERESTS

Utility calculi are straightforward in theory. All one has to do is identify which course of action, among those available, has the best overall outcomes. However, in practice, they can be exceedingly difficult to execute. One set of challenges associated with utility calculi is *epistemic*. It is difficult to identify in advance what all of the impacts are likely to be and how they will affect human and nonhuman well-being. Consider, for example, the athletic facility case discussed in the prior section. Will people be healthier because they have access to a new athletic facility, or would they simply find sources of athletic recreation elsewhere if it is not built? What ecosystem services does the wetland provide and what would be the costs of getting them in other ways? Do migrating birds that currently use the wetlands have ample alternative places for stopovers? If not, how will it impact the health of those populations?

What will be the ecological impacts of the fertilizer and herbicide/pesticide runoff from the athletic fields? Answering these sorts of questions will often require detailed and longitudinal study—for example, environmental impact assessments to determine what species are present and what services the wetland provides, economic analyses of the impacts on local businesses and jobs, and public surveys regarding how people currently use the wetlands and whether there is demand for the facility. Even with careful and patient study, the likely outcomes could remain uncertain or unclear, since basing decision-making on expected outcomes involves projecting into the future.

Another set of challenges associated with utility calculi is *evaluative*. In addition to the epistemic challenge of identifying the probable impacts on different scenarios, there is the challenge of how to aggregate and compare the interests of everyone and everything impacted. The hypothetical athletic facility case above is of moderate complexity. It is a one-off local land use decision. Nevertheless, it involves multiple competing values and affects many different types of entities, from local businesses to amphibians, in different ways. Do people's preferences for a convenient baseball diamond and football field outweigh the harms to the reptiles, fish, and amphibians that inhabit the wetland? Do the jobs and tax revenue created by the facility outweigh the ecosystems services—for instance, flood protection—and recreational opportunities—for instance, birding—provided by the wetlands? Inherent in utilitarian decision-making is choosing between competing sets of interests. It is therefore crucial to it that there be a way to make such adjudications. Many environmental ethicists advocate for some version of the **principle of equal consideration of interests**: Like interests are to be considered alike without respect to whose interests they are (see, e.g., Sections 6.1, 7.1, and 7.4). But even accepting this, we still need to know what count as like interests and how different interests are to be considered. And perhaps, contrary to the principle of equal consideration of interests, we ought to sometimes give more weight to the interests of some—such as friends and family—than others (see, e.g., Sections 7.5 and 14.2). The remainder of this section discusses the criteria used by utilitarian environmental ethicists when adjudicating among competing sets of interests or goods.

One widely used criterion is *strength of interests*. Not all interests are equally important to well-being. A person's interest in a nutritionally adequate diet is much stronger, in the sense of being more important to her welfare, than is her interest in eating gourmet cheese. It is therefore common among environmental ethicists to distinguish levels or types of interests:

- **Basic interests** are needs that must be met in order for a person (or nonhuman animal or nonconscious organism) to live and be healthy. People have a basic interest in access to nutritionally adequate food, potable water, and sufficient shelter and clothing. Without these sorts of things, they cannot survive at all.

- **Serious interests** are interests that, if not met, will substantially diminish the quality of a person's (or nonhuman animal's or nonconscious organism's) life or the range of her opportunities. People have a serious interest in a decent education, meaningful work, and strong friendships. It is possible to live without these, but, in general, they are strongly conducive to a better quality of life.
- **Significant interests** are interests that if met can improve a person's (or nonhuman animal's) life or opportunities. People have a significant interest in attending a high quality university, eating good-tasting food, and engaging in recreational activities about which they are passionate. Not having these sorts of things does not mean your life is not going well, but their presence can significantly improve it.
- **Peripheral interests** are mere wants. They are things that people (or nonhuman animals) desire to have, but do not materially impact the quality of their life. Many consumer preferences are like this—for example, wearing the current fashions, eating out at the hot restaurants, driving a luxury car, sleeping in high-thread-count sheets, and owning the latest electronics. Not having these preferences satisfied typically does not diminish the quality of a person's life, even when people think that it will (see Sections 6.2 and 15.4).

These terms—basic, serious, significant, and peripheral interests—do not delineate hard categories. There is a range of interests and preferences, from basic to trivial, and these terms pick out comparative levels of importance (to living well) along that continuum. Moreover, where something falls along the continuum can be contextual. For example, there are remote places where not having your own mode of transportation imperils your survival. People who live in these places arguably have a basic interest in possessing a car (or boat). In other places where things are very spread out and there is not adequate public transportation, not having a car might make it difficult to get to work or school, and so provide a challenge to maintaining employment or to education attainment. In such places, people arguably have a serious interest in owning a car. In yet other places, having a car might significantly increase convenience and reduce travel times, enabling space for important or meaningful activities, and so constitute a significant interest. But in some places, with extensive public transportation and a high density of walkable services, owning a car might be a mere preference. The importance of something can also be contextual to people's lives. Parents who depend upon participating in carpools to get their children to school and extracurricular activities might have a significant interest in a high-capacity car, whereas for those without children a large car may be a peripheral interest. Similarly, people whose work requires carrying tools and supplies might have a serious interest in owning a small truck, while doing so is a mere preference for many others.

That the type of interest something is can be contextual does not imply that it is subjective or wholly up to the person whose interest it is. The fact that someone thinks they have a serious interest in owning an oversized SUV or taking an exotic vacation does not mean that they do. It has to actually be the case that not having them would seriously diminish the quality of their life. Moreover, even if a person has a serious interest in reliable transportation or in having a respite from work to recharge and attend to personal matters, it does not follow that they have a serious interest in a luxury vehicle or vacation. How important something is to a person's quality of life is not just a matter of how they view it. As discussed earlier, people's judgments are often mistaken in these respects (Section 6.2).

It is a common view among environmental ethicists, including consequentialists, that, all other things being equal, *more basic interests should take precedence over less basic ones* (Taylor 1986; Singer 1975, 1989; VanDeVeer 1979). This has implications for resource allocations and consumption behaviors, for example. If there are people who need access to natural resources or ecological goods for their livelihood—for example, water for agriculture or reef access for subsistence fishing—then that should be prioritized over uses of those resources that are merely recreational or that benefit people who are already well off—for example, watering golf courses or sport fishing. It also has implications for policy-making. For instance, on this view, agricultural policies should aim to empower smallholding and subsistence farmers and promote local food security and autonomy, since these are conducive to raising people out of poverty and reducing malnutrition (FAO 2011, 2012a; Chapter 16).

Singer (1972) has suggested the following principle that embodies the idea that people ought to forgo peripheral and perhaps even significant interests, if doing so enables others to satisfy their serious and basic interests:

> **Principle of beneficence**: If you can prevent something very bad from happening with little cost to yourself, then you ought to do so.

Singer originally proposed this principle in the context of discussing people's responsibilities to actively help others—for instance, donating money to assistance programs and volunteering with charitable organizations. This is why it is a principle of beneficence. However, the principle applies as well to not impairing other people's ability to meet their basic and serious interests—that is, as a principle of nonmaleficence. For example, climate change makes it harder for many subsistence farmers to produce enough food to feed their families and has already contributed to creating millions of environmental refugees. According to this principle, people ought to change their consumption patterns, reduce population growth, and generally adopt lower-emissions lifestyles to minimize this, so long as doing so does not impair their basic or serious interests. And on sentientist value axiologies, this principle implies that we ought to eliminate CAFOs and other uses of animals that cause them suffering and/or premature death—that compromise their basic and serious interests—when it is done merely for our convenience and enjoyment.

The principle of beneficence/nonmaleficence (and others like it, see, e.g., Sections 9.2, 9.3, and 10.2) applies to cases where there are different strengths of interest at stake. It says that, all other things being equal, we ought to prioritize satisfying the more basic ones. Another widely accepted criterion for adjudication is that the *number of interests* matters. Since an action is right to the extent that it brings about the best consequences overall, we should prioritize satisfying more over fewer interests, when they are the same level of interest (Regan 1983; Taylor 1986).

Some environmental ethicists have suggested that when comparing or weighing up interests we ought to consider, in addition to the level of interests and number of interests, the *psychological complexity* of the individuals whose interests they are. Here is a version of a thought experiment that is sometimes thought to motivate this view. Imagine that you, me, a chimpanzee, and a chicken are adrift on a lifeboat with only enough water and food for three of the four of us. Either we will all die or one of us must be sacrificed. Clearly, according to utilitarianism, one of us should be sacrificed, since three surviving is a better outcome than none surviving. So how should we decide who to sacrifice? Level of interest will not differentiate, since the interest at stake for each of us is basic, our lives. Nor will number of interests differentiate, since no matter who we choose it will be three basic interests satisfied and one frustrated. Most people have the intuition that in such "lifeboat" cases the individual with the fewest or least robust psychological capacities should be sacrificed. It should be the chicken that goes, before the chimpanzee or one of us. Here is a formal rendering of this view by Donald VanDeVeer:

> When there is an interspecies conflict of interests between two beings, A and B, it is permissible, *ceteris parabis* (or all other things being equal):
>
> 1. to sacrifice the interest of A to promote a like interest of B if A lacks significant psychological capacities possessed by B,
> 2. to sacrifice a basic interest of A to promote a serious interest of B if A substantially lacks significant psychological capacities possessed by B,
> 3. to sacrifice the peripheral interest to promote the more basic interest if the beings are similar with respect to psychological capacity (regardless of who possesses the interest). (1979, 154)

VanDeVeer calls this view **two-factor egalitarianism**, since it weighs interests according to two factors: the levels of the interests and the psychological capacities of the individuals whose interests they are. He considers the view egalitarian because it is nonanthropocentric—that is, being a member of the species *Homo sapiens* is not one of the weighing factors. According to two-factor egalitarianism, not only is it justified to prioritize the like interests of more psychological complex individuals (Rule 1), it also is justified to prioritize the serious interests of psychologically complex individuals over the basic interests of significantly less complex ones (Rule 2).

As discussed earlier (Box 7.1), thought experiments are not arguments. Intuitions can be conditioned, uninformed, and biased, so they are not always truth-indicating and are not normatively decisive. But they can be setting off points for reflection and discussion. Most people agree that (at least in lifeboat cases) the interests of less-psychologically complex individuals should be given less weight than those of psychologically complex individuals. But what justifies this view? Are there any reasons for favoring the interests of more psychologically complex individuals?

One common idea is that doing so is justified because more psychologically complex individuals have a broader range of interests than less cognitively complex individuals. In general, if one of their interests is compromised, particularly a serious or basic one, it will lead to a greater amount of other interests being compromised. A chicken has an interest in not being killed, engaging in species-typical behaviors, and in not suffering in death. However, a person, in addition to these, has an interest in accomplishing her goals, fulfilling her life plans, and seeing her friends and family again. Chickens do not have these sorts of interests, since they do not have the psychological capacities requisite for them. Therefore, we ought to prioritize the interests of more psychologically complex individuals over those of less psychologically complex individuals, because of their broader range of interconnected interests.

Notice that on this way of understanding the prioritization—unlike two-factor egalitarianism—like interests are counted alike, without regard to whose interests they are. It is just that with psychologically complex individuals, their interests tend to be connected to more other interests. So psychological complexity is not itself what matters. It is a proxy for identifying when a greater amount or more complex interests are at stake, particularly over time. The implication of this is that, when like interests are considered, the interests of more psychologically complex individuals should be prioritized. For example, animal experimentation would be justified if it is in the service of curing life-threatening diseases in a large number of humans; and it would be permissible to eat animals when doing so is truly necessary for survival or good health.

However, on other views, psychological complexity is itself what matters. For example, it would be justified to favor the interests of more psychologically complex individuals if they have greater inherent worth than do individuals with less complexity. Similarly, a pluralistic account of moral considerability could support the view that the interests of psychologically complex individuals take priority because they are due more forms of consideration—such as care, compassion, and respect—than are significantly less psychologically complex individuals. Pluralistic and tiered views on direct moral considerability were discussed at length earlier (Section 7.5). Their relevance here is that, depending upon the details of the views, they could justify the commonly held position that psychological complexity is relevant to weighing and adjudicating interests—that is, they provide a possible explanation for why the chicken should be sacrificed.

| BOX 8.3 | THOUGHT EXPERIMENTS |

ADJUDICATING INTERESTS

Here are two additional thought experiments to generate ideas regarding how to weigh, compare, and adjudicate among competing interests:

1. *People in a Lifeboat*: Imagine that instead of two people, a chimpanzee and a chicken in the lifeboat, there are four people. If there are only enough resources for three to survive, what should be done? Should someone be sacrificed? If so, how should the decision regarding who to sacrifice be made? Should it be done by a random selection procedure? Or are there things that should be considered in deciding, such as health, future life expectancy, relationships, psychological complexity, or skill sets? Does thinking about this case suggest any considerations that would be applicable to adjudicating human-nonhuman interest conflicts? Why or why not?

2. *Experimenting on Chimpanzees and Humans*. Using psychological complexity as a criterion for prioritizing interests is not regarded as speciesist (or anthropocentric) because it is a capacities-based criterion, rather than a biological group membership criterion (Section 5.2). In the lifeboat case discussed earlier (Section 8.3), the chicken ought to be sacrificed, not because it is a chicken, but because it has lesser psychological capacities than do the other individuals on the lifeboat. But of course some human beings have lesser psychological capacities than do some animals. Severely mentally disabled infants have lesser capacities than healthy adult chimpanzees, for example. Imagine that researchers plan to test a new drug on chimpanzees, and they believe that it is warranted on utilitarian grounds because the drug has the potential to dramatically improve the health of tens of millions of people. If it is permissible to test on the chimpanzees, would it be permissible to test as well on people with equal or lesser psychological complexities, particularly since they are better test models (since they are *Homo sapiens*)? Does thinking about this case suggest any considerations that would be applicable to adjudicating human-nonhuman interest conflicts? Why or why not?

What about cases when the basic or serious interests of less psychologically complex individuals are in conflict with the peripheral interests of psychologically complex individuals? This is the situation with CAFOs, for example. People have a mere preference for large amounts of inexpensive meat, since they can get a nutritionally adequate diet in other ways, but animals have a basic interest in not being killed and a serious interest in not suffering. It is the situation as well with using animals for entertainment and fashionable clothing. Many people have a preference for seeing elephants in the circus, betting on cockfighting, and wearing fur-lined clothing, but the animals have a serious and basic interest not to be captive, treated badly, and killed.

Most nonanthropocentric utilitarians hold the view that the mere preferences of psychologically complex individuals—that is, people—do not justify causing serious and basic harms to nonhuman animals. The reason for this is that whether peripheral interests are satisfied has little if any impact on the overall quality of people's lives, and there are almost always alternative ways to get food, take recreation, produce clothing, and so on that do not cause as much pain, suffering, and death. Therefore, on a nonanthropocentric value axiology, preferences involving unnecessary harms to animals are not endorsable, and it is not good that they be satisfied. As discussed earlier (Section 6.2), it is possible to critically evaluate people's preferences, and in some cases to not put any weight on them.

To sum up, here is the general picture of the predominant view regarding how to approach adjudication of interests within utilitarian environmental decision-making:

1. Greater weight should be put on more basic interests than on less basic ones, when the individuals involved possess similar psychological capacities;
2. A greater number of interests should be prioritized over a smaller number, when they are of a similar level and the individuals involved possess similar psychological capacities;
3. The basic and serious interests of more psychologically complex individuals should be prioritized over those of significantly less psychologically complex individuals;
4. The peripheral interests of more psychologically complex individuals should not be prioritized over the basic and serious interests of much less psychologically complex individuals.

I have called this the predominant view, but it is by no means universally accepted. For example, some moderate anthropocentrists hold the view that all human preferences, even trivial ones, should take precedence over all nonhuman preferences. And some nonanthropocentrists reject the view that psychological complexity is at all morally relevant. Therefore, it is important to critically evaluate these criteria, particularly in light of the account of direct moral considerability that you believe is most justified, to determine whether they ought to be endorsed or revised. (How much weight to put on the interests of present generations in comparison to those of future generations was discussed at length in Section 6.3.)

✳ **BOX 8.4**   **TOPIC TO CONSIDER**

CULTURAL HUNTING

How much weight should be placed on a particular interest depends not only on how the person whose interest it is views its importance, but also on the extent to which its satisfaction would actually improve her life, as well as on whether it is endorsable. As a result, the level of interest something is and the normative significance it should have in decision-making is frequently contested. The issue of how to determine the level and weight of interests is highly salient in debates around cultural practices that involve killing or harming nonhuman animals—for example, dolphin drives, eating *foie gras*, and bullfighting. In these cases, the importance of the practice is often contested, as is whether it justifies killing or harming the animals involved. Cultural hunting is often this sort of case.

Some hunting is widely regarded as problematic. For example, the systematic hunting of elephants for ivory by organized groups is illegal and having a devastating impact on their populations. Commercial baby harp seal hunting done to satisfy people's peripheral fashion interests is viewed as cruel (it involves bludgeoning pups in the head) and unnecessary. Hunting endangered animals for the medicinal trade—for example, pangolins, gorillas, and tigers—is among the primary threats to their continued existence in the wild. Canned hunts conducted within enclosed areas or where animals are released or tracked prior to the hunt to ensure a kill are seen as unsporting, unskilled, and contrary to hunting ideals involving fair chase. Hunting wolves in Alaska (including by helicopter) to generate license revenue and increase the availability of moose and elk is regarded as ecologically problematic. In contrast, when hunting is crucial to survival and well-being—that is, necessary for **subsistence**—it is widely regarded as being ethically acceptable, since it serves basic and serious interests. For example, bushmeat in parts of central Africa and caribou hunting by the Inupiat in parts of the Arctic are often important sources of protein.

Nonsubsistence **cultural hunting,** in which the target animals are still eaten and used, is a more contested case. (Another contested case, hunting as part of ecosystem and species management plans is discussed in Box 9.3.) Cultural hunting includes hunting by indigenous peoples, such as the Makah who hunt gray whales on the Pacific Northwestern coast of the United States, as well as the Inupiat caribou hunts. It also includes hunting by nonindigenous people when it is viewed by them as part of their cultural identities—for example, ungulate, fowl, and bear hunting in many parts of the United States. It can also be tied to national identities, as with Icelandic, Norwegian, and Japanese whale

(cont.)

BOX 8.4 *(cont.)*

hunting. In each of these cases, those who engage in or support the hunts claim that the practice serves more than mere peripheral interests. The hunts are seen as a part of their heritage, as focal practices for their families and communities, and/or as a matter of tradition, cultural continuity, and pride. For these reasons, they believe that their interests in engaging in the practices justify the killing involved—that is, sacrificing the basic interests of the hunted animals.

Defenders of cultural hunting (as well as **sport hunting**—i.e., hunting for rec-reational purposes) also often emphasize that while hunting is not a basic inter-est, food is; and hunting can compare quite favorably from an ethical perspective to other sources of food. One reason for this is that all food production—crop and animal agricultural, commercial fishing, and hunting—involves killing animals. This is clear in the cases of hunting, fishing, and animal agriculture. However, crop agriculture (organic and conventional) causes animals to die from habitat loss, chemical inputs, and the use of heavy machinery for tilling, planting, and harvesting, which kills large numbers of reptiles, rodents, birds, and other field species. It is not possible to eliminate nonhuman death from the food supply, so hunting is not unique for involving killing. Furthermore, its proponents argue, hunting has several features that provide it with a positive ethical profile in comparison to agriculture, particularly industrial agriculture:

- Hunters take responsibility for the source of their food and the killing in-volved, rather than having the processes and costs concealed from them;
- Hunted animals live better quality lives than do livestock, whose time in industrial agricultural systems is short, full of suffering, and does not allow for species-typical behaviors;
- Hunting does not cause much suffering when done in accordance with hunting codes of ethics—which call for hunting only animals that you are skilled enough to take cleanly, taking only kill shots, and quickly tracking and putting down injured animals—in comparison with death from depri-vation, exposure, predation, or the forms of slaughter used in CAFOs;
- Hunting robust populations does not have the negative ecological im-pacts of agriculture and can be ecologically beneficial when the target species is over carry capacity and when fees from hunting and fishing licenses are used to fund conservation programs;
- Hunting done responsibly involves killing only animals that are used (and utilizing as much of them as possible), whereas animals killed through crop agriculture—for example, field animals and animals killed by habitat destruction—are byproduct and not used;

(cont.)

BOX 8.4 *(cont.)*

- Hunting can develop knowledge and character, since being a good hunter involves not only skills such as shooting, tracking, and concentration, but also engagement with and knowledge of the natural world, as well as traits such as patience, attentiveness, fortitude, responsibility, appreciation, and restraint;
- Hunting can foster environmental concern—for example, in North America, many local and national environmental organizations are "hook-and-bullet" in that they are constituted by hunters and anglers concerned about habitat loss, water and air pollution, road-building, and sustainable management;
- Hunting can be socially and culturally significant, since it can involve tradition, passing on knowledge, building cultural connection, and strengthening relationships.

Here is a summary of the core argument in favor of cultural hunting:

1. Cultural hunting is necessary for satisfying people's significant (and perhaps even serious) interests;
2. Hunting for food (including cultural hunting), when done responsibly, compares favorably from an ethical perspective with other forms of satisfying people's basic need for food;

3. Therefore, it is permissible to engage in cultural hunting.

Do you think that this argument is sound? Do you agree that cultural hunting—or at least some instances of it—is necessary for satisfying people's significant and serious interests—that is, is Premise (1) true? Or are there possible alternatives, such as symbolic "hunts" where no animals are taken? If satisfying these interests does require killing animals, are they endorsable? Are the considerations raised in support of hunting as an ethically acceptable method of food provision compelling—that is, is Premise (2) true? And assuming Premises (1) and (2) are true, does it follow that it is permissible to hunt animals for cultural purposes—that is, is the reasoning involved valid? Would an animal rights view endorse this inference, or does it follow only on an animal welfare or an anthropocentric view? Could a similar argument be made in support of sport or trophy hunting? Or in support of other cultural practices involving animals—for example, force-feeding fowl to produce *foie gras* which is traditionally eaten in France on Christmas Eve, or bullfighting in Spain, where many consider it the national sport?

8.4 SECONDARY PRINCIPLES AND INDIRECT CONSEQUENTIALISM

As discussed earlier, one of the attractive features of utilitarianism is that it can provide guidance on whatever action or policy one is considering. However, it is not practically feasible, with respect to time and resources, to do a complete and well-informed utility calculus for every decision. Moreover, it can be exceedingly difficult to project, with probability assignments, all the relevant consequences of actions and policies. It can also be difficult to assign values to many types of outcomes (see Sections 4.3, 8.2, and 15.2). For example, what is the correct disvalue of a bird species extinction or of a disturbed ceremonial site? How are values like justice, naturalness, and beauty to be included in the calculus? Furthermore, it is not always clear how much weight should be put on different interests—for instance, human, nonhuman, and future generations (see Section 8.3)? Thus, a long-standing objection to utilitarianism is that it is not practical for guiding actions and policies, since the calculi required are far too numerous and onerous.

The standard utilitarian response to these concerns was famously articulated by John Stuart Mill:

> It is truly a whimsical supposition that, if mankind were agreed in considering utility to be the test of morality, they would remain without any agreement as to what *is* useful, and would take no measures for having their notions on the subject taught to the young, and enforced by law and opinion. . . . Nobody argues that the art of navigation is not founded on astronomy, because sailors cannot wait to calculate the Nautical Almanack. Being rational creatures, they go to sea with it ready calculated; and all rational creatures go out upon the sea of life with their minds made up on the common questions of right and wrong, as well as on many of the far more difficult questions of wise and foolish. . . . *Whatever we adopt as the fundamental principle of morality, we require subordinate principles to apply it by.* (2001, 25–6, emphasis added)

Mill's point in this passage is that identifying the actions that best promote utility or good outcomes does not require conducting utilitarian calculi on every occasion. People can and do adopt **secondary principles** or guidelines, developed from experience and careful study, which in general and for the most part orient them toward right actions. We can teach them to our children, develop policies and practices based on them, and use them when it is infeasible to do a full calculus, which may be most of the time.

I have referred to secondary principles as *guidelines* because they are not absolute or inviolable, and they do not define right action. According to utilitarianism, what is right is what maximizes the balance of good over bad, not what conforms to the rules. Therefore, secondary principles should be violated when doing so would better promote utility, clearly and all things considered. Moreover, when they come into conflict, the principle of utility should be the arbiter: "If utility is the ultimate source of moral obligations, utility may be invoked to decide between [secondary principles] when their demands are incompatible" (Mill 2001, 27). On this view, we ought to aim at maximizing good over bad—promoting satisfaction of the interests of morally considerable individuals and protecting environmental and cultural values—and we should do so by following effective rules or guidelines most of the time (as well as cultivating utility promoting character traits) and performing more detailed utility calculations when appropriate or needed.

Thus, identifying the right secondary principles and developing the right character traits (see Section 10.2)—*ones that actually promote good social and environmental outcomes*—is crucial to consequentialist environmental ethics. As has been discussed several times, many environmental thinkers are critical of the predominant norms regarding the environment, particularly in affluent and highly industrialized nations, on the grounds that they have contributed to our environmental problems and are detrimental to people and nonhumans over the long run. Therefore, they advocate for new, environmentally informed norms. Several such norms have been (and will continue to be) introduced for you to consider—for example, "Reduce consumption associated with mere preferences" (Section 15.4), "Avoid eating food from concentrated animal feed operations" (Sections 2.3, 6.1, and 8.1), "Adopt policies that curb population growth" (Section 16.3), "Spend time experiencing and learning about the natural environment" (Section 11.3), "Ensure a full economic valuation of ecosystem services and resources in permitting and policy decisions" (Section 4.3), "Empower local communities regarding land use decisions in their neighborhoods" (Section 15.3), "Give precedence to basic interests in resource allocation" (Section 8.3), "Mitigate greenhouse gas emissions" (Sections 9.4 and 13.8; Boxes 2.1 and 6.3), and "Prioritize preventing environmental harms rather than relying on repairing environmental damage" (Boxes 4.5 and 12.3). As also has been discussed several times, which norms are well justified ultimately depends upon the correct account of environmental goods and value, as well as upon the relevant empirical information (see, e.g., Sections 2.2 and 2.3).

I have emphasized that secondary principles are guidelines in service of promoting utility or good outcomes, rather than hard rules. I have done this in order to ensure that utilitarianism is not confused with views on which right action is defined by acting in conformity with the rules. As discussed earlier this chapter (and at length next chapter), deontological views typically adopt rule conformity or duty based accounts of right action. So, too, does a form of consequentialism called **rule consequentialism**. According to rule consequentialism, an action is right if it conforms to the rules that if generally adopted would bring about the greatest balance of good over bad. On this view, rules are evaluated in terms of their consequences, and then actions are evaluated as right or wrong on the basis of whether they conform to outcome maximizing rules. This type of consequentialism is an example of what is called **indirect consequentialism**. It is indirect because actions (and practices and policies) are not

---

✳ BOX 8.5   EXERCISE

POP CULTURE AND SECONDARY PRINCIPLES

Identifying and adopting well-justified secondary principles or guidelines is crucial to good environmental decision-making and practice, particularly within
a consequentialist normative framework. Such rules are also often employed
within popular environmental discourse—for example, "Reduce, Reuse, Recycle"
and "Eat Local." What other environmentally-oriented guidelines have you heard
in popular discourse? Would you endorse them? What is the basis or evidence
that following them will generally produce good social and environmental outcomes? Are there any that you believe are not good guidelines despite their
being widely endorsed?

---

evaluated directly in terms of their consequences, but in terms of something else (in
this case rules) that are evaluated in terms of consequences.

8.5 CONCERNS ABOUT UTILITARIAN ENVIRONMENTAL ETHICS

In addition to the epistemic, evaluative, and practical concerns discussed above, several other worries have been raised regarding utilitarian normative theory, each of
which has a manifestation in the environmental ethics discourse.

One concern frequently raised regarding utilitarianism is that on it no action or
practice is in principle wrong. No matter how heinous or cruel something might seem,
if doing it would bring about the greatest balance of good over bad of the options
available, then it ought to be done. If utility would be best served by taking a person's
life, lying to put an innocent person in jail, mining in a pristine wilderness area, or
displacing people from their ancestral lands to build a dam, then according to utilitarianism it is the right thing to do. Those who believe that certain things are just
wrong—that the ends, no matter how good, do not always justify the means—often
find utilitarianism (and consequentialism more generally) objectionable and are drawn
to rights-oriented theories. For example, Regan's call for the total abolition of the use
of animals in research is based on the idea that it is always wrong to treat them as mere
means to our ends, no matter how beneficial the outcomes. This is sometimes called
the *no in-principle limits objection* to utilitarianism.

The no in-principle limits objection arises because according to utilitarianism the
rightness or wrongness of an action (or policy) is determined by the value of the outcomes of the action (or policy), not by the features of the act (or policy) itself. Other
objections to utilitarianism arise from its being a *maximizing* theory. It aims to bring

about the *best* outcomes. One concern frequently raised regarding maximizing theories is that they are inattentive to the importance of *distribution*. In some cases, it maximizes utility to treat a small number of people badly for the benefit of a much greater number of people. Distributive concerns often arise in the context of discussions about environmental justice (see Chapter 15). It might maximize overall utility to concentrate environmental hazards—such as waste treatment facilities, factories, and chemical plants—in one area, but then the communities in those areas have to shoulder the health and quality-of-life burdens for everyone else. If they do not consent to this, are not adequately compensated for it, and/or do not benefit sufficiently from it, then their exposure to the hazards appears not only to be unequal but also unjust. Thus, utilitarianism seems to many to be inadequately sensitive to considerations of distribution and justice.

Another concern about utilitarianism that arises from its being a maximizing view, in combination with everyone's interests being equally considerable, is that it is overly demanding. If we ought to bring about the *best* consequences for *everyone* overall, then we should always use our resources—time, expertise, and money—to benefit others, particularly those that are very badly off. We should enter professions that involve improving lives as much as possible; we should donate all of the money that we do not absolutely need; and we should not spend time on frivolous (i.e., non-utility-maximizing) things like sport, art, movies, and just hanging out with friends. For most of us, acting rightly according to utilitarianism would involve radical changes to almost all aspects of our lives. As mentioned earlier, objections have been made to sentientist utilitarianism on the grounds that, in order to maximize utility, we would have to constantly intervene in the natural world to assist animals in need and reduce suffering (Sagoff 1984). We would have to feed squirrels during lean times and provide lions with alternative diets so that they do not kill gazelles, for example. Not only is this overly demanding, it strikes many as being out of touch with the realities of nature—for example, predator-prey relationships—and to be too interventionist an attitude to take toward the natural world.

The *demandingness concern* about utilitarianism is related to another objection, which is commonly called the *near-and-dear problem*. The problem is that utilitarianism appears unable to countenance special consideration for one's friends and family. Imagine a situation where a person is in a position where she could save either her own child or another child. According to utilitarianism, if overall utility is better served by saving the other child, then she should save that child. It does not matter that one of the children in peril is her own, except insofar as the extra pain she feels for letting her own child die is included in the utility calculus. However, it is a common view that people should be particularly attentive to their friends and family, and that it is permissible to spend extra resources on them, simply because of the special relationships involved. The same is thought to hold with respect to people's relationships with their pets, in comparison to other animals (see Section 7.5 and Box 7.8), and with using resources in support of environmental causes or organizations that they have a history with or are passionate about, even if it is not the most effective and beneficial use of them (Box 8.2).

Advocates of utilitarianism are well aware of these concerns about the view. They often respond by trying to show that the concerns are spurious or that the view can be modified to avoid them—for example, by basing rightness on expected utility rather than actual consequences, adopting an indirect view (e.g., rule consequentialism), including distributional concerns as part of the value axiology, or weakening the connection between maximization and rightness so that an action is right if its outcomes are sufficiently good (sometimes called **satisficing consequentialism**). However, on any version of consequentialism, rightness of action is going to be closely tied, in one way or another, to outcomes. Those who believe that this is the fundamental problem with consequentialism, either in general or as an environmental ethic, are often drawn to deontological views, which prioritize such things as rules, rights, justice, and duty over consequences. Deontological environmental ethics is the focus of the next chapter.

✳ BOX 8.6 TOPIC TO CONSIDER

THE PROBLEM OF INCONSEQUENTIALISM

Many environmental problems are longitudinal collective action problems (see, e.g., Section 1.2 and Box 6.1). They arise from the cumulative unintended (and often unforeseen) effects of a vast amount of seemingly insignificant decisions and actions by individuals who often are unknown to each other and distant from each other (spatially, temporally, and socially). Global climate change is the paradigmatic longitudinal collective action environmental problem. However, many other environmental issues, such as pollution, fisheries depletion, population growth, and deforestation exhibit these features as well. It takes quite a lot of people, almost all of them acting without environmental malice (though often with environmental ignorance or indifference), to precipitate the problem.

Longitudinal collective action environmental problems are likely to be effectively addressed only by an enormous number of individuals each making a nearly insignificant contribution to resolving them. However, when a person's making such a contribution appears to have personal costs the **problem of inconsequentialism** arises: given that a person's contribution is nearly inconsequential to addressing the problem and may require some cost from the standpoint of her own life, why should she make the effort, particularly when it is uncertain (or even unlikely) whether others will do so?

(cont.)

BOX 8.6 *(cont.)*

For example, eating meat from CAFOs is an instance of the problem of inconsequentialism. One person giving up eating CAFO-produced meat is not going to reduce animals' suffering whatsoever. It is not as if there are particular animals assigned to particular people, such that if a person gives up eating meat their animal will be spared. Given this, why isn't the fact that a person enjoys eating large amounts of inexpensive meat sufficient reason for her doing it? Refraining from eating meat would decrease her pleasure, and it would not benefit any animals. It might be ethically better if there were not large amounts of animal suffering from CAFOs, and legislation to prevent or reduce it would be ethically good. However, a single person refraining from eating meat is also inconsequential to bringing about new policies or systemic change. Why should a person make an effort or take on the costs to change her behavior—for example, give up inexpensive CAFO meat, adopt a low-emissions lifestyle, or engage in environmental activism—when it will not make a difference to whether the problem is resolved?

The problem of inconsequentialism is familiar within environmental ethics, and several responses to it have been proposed. One is that inconsequential reasoning is self-defeating. If everyone applied it, then problems would not get resolved (and attempts to address them would not even be made), particularly since the problem of inconsequentialism arises in the context of political action as well. For example, inconsequential reasoning applied to voting would lead each person to conclude she should not cast a ballot. At a minimum, this response continues, everyone has to do their part to address collective action problems, since the only way to resolve them is through the cumulative effects of everyone's negligible contributions.

Another response appeals to complicity and integrity. Even though a single person cannot alone end animal suffering in CAFOs, or even save some number of animals, she can avoid benefiting from it and thereby being complicit with it. Similarly, even though one person cannot arrest global climate change, or even reduce its magnitude, she can avoid living the sort of lifestyle that she knows created and perpetuates the problem. This is a matter of integrity. If a person believes that child labor is ethically problematic, but nevertheless knowingly purchases cheap shoes that are made with child labor because he likes them, then he lacks integrity and is complicit with the exploitation. The same applies to eating meat produced in ethically problematic ways and using large amounts of energy from fossil fuels, according to this response.

(cont.)

BOX 8.6 *(cont.)*

Finally, the premises of the problem of inconsequentialism are often denied—that is, that each person's actions are inconsequential to addressing the issue and that there are costs for them to change their behavior. One common way of doing this is by appeal to the possibility of cascading effects. By embracing a nonmeat diet or a low-emission lifestyle a person can demonstrate that it is viable and beneficial, thereby encouraging others to do the same. They, in turn, can set an example for still more to follow, and so on. Moreover, when a person sees her behavior as something good and worthwhile, she will not consider it to be a sacrifice and will take enjoyment from doing it. This is sometimes referred to as the **integrating effect of virtue** (see Section 10.2).

What do you think about these responses to the problem of inconsequentialism? Are any of them sound? Do they justify making the effort or taking on costs to contribute to addressing longitudinal collective action problems? Why or why not? Can you think of other possible responses to the problem?

8.6 SUMMARY

The primary questions addressed in this chapter were:

- What are the distinctive features of consequentialist (particularly utilitarian) approaches to environmental ethics?
- What are the substantive views of the predominant utilitarian environmental ethics?

The chapter began by distinguishing the three primary types of normative theories: consequentialist theories, deontological theories, and virtue-oriented theories. The primary difference between the theories concerns how they believe things matter or should be considered in deliberations regarding actions, practices, and policies. The importance of these differences was illustrated by considering how animal welfare (consequentialist) and animal rights (deontological) views lead to different conclusions about when, if ever, it is permissible to use animals for such things as food, experimentation, and entertainment.

The remainder of the chapter focused on consequentialist normative theory and, in particular, on utilitarian approaches to environmental ethics. Utilitarianism involves aggregating and weighing interests (and other values) in order to identify the course of action that has the best outcomes overall. Therefore, after clarifying the general view, the focus turned to distinguishing different types of interests and the weight or priority they are given in utilitarian approaches to environmental ethics. These issues are crucial to environmental ethics (even nonconsequentialist theories), since many environmental issues involve competing interests, both among humans and between humans and individuals of others species.

Finally, several objections to utilitarian environmental ethics were discussed, as were several responses to them, including the use of secondary principles. Environmental ethicists who believe that consequentialist views cannot adequately address the concerns raised against them often embrace deontological or rights-based views, which are the topic of the next chapter.

KEY TERMS (SEE GLOSSARY FOR DEFINITIONS):

animal rights view

animal welfare view

basic interests

concentrated animal feed operations

consequentialist normative theories

cultural hunting

deontological normative theories

effective altruism

ethical egoism

factory farms

indirect consequentialism

integrating effect of virtue

normative theories

peripheral interests

principle of beneficence

principle of equal consideration of interests

principle of utility

problem of inconsequentialism

rule consequentialism

satisficing consequentialism

secondary principles

serious interests

significant interests

sport hunting

subsistence hunting

two-factor egalitarianism

utilitarianism

utility calculus

value axiology

virtue-oriented normative theories

REVIEW QUESTIONS

- What is the difference between animal rights views and animal welfare views?
- What distinguishes consequentialist, deontological, and virtue-oriented ethical theories?
- What are the two core components of utilitarianism?
- What is the difference between basic, serious, significant, and peripheral interests?
- What is the predominant view on how interests should be prioritized and conflicts of interests adjudicated within utilitarian environmental ethics?

- What are secondary principles and what is their role within consequentialist normative theory?
- What is the difference between direct and indirect consequentialism?

DISCUSSION QUESTIONS

- Do you agree with the predominant view on how to approach adjudication of competing interests? Why or why not?
- Do you think the principle of equal considerability of interests is well justified? Or is psychological complexity relevant to how much weight one's interest should be given in environmental decision-making?
- Would you endorse the principle of beneficence? What are some of its implications for how you should live?
- What environmentally oriented secondary principles would you endorse, and why?
- Do you find any of the concerns regarding utilitarianism compelling? If so, is it possible to modify the theory to avoid the concerns?
- Do you find consequentialism to be an attractive normative theory overall? Why or why not?

FURTHER READING

The classical statement of utilitarian ethical theory is:

Mill, John Stuart. *Utilitarianism.* Hackett, 2001.

Accessible introductions to the differences between consequentialist, deontological, and virtue-oriented ethical theories can be found in:

Rachels, James, and Stuart Rachels. *The Elements of Moral Philosophy*, 8th edition. McGraw Hill, 2014.

Hursthouse, Rosalind. *Ethics, Humans and Other Animals.* Routledge, 2000.

The most influential book on animal welfare, by far, is:

Singer, Peter. *Animal Liberation.* New York Review, 1975.

Other books that address animal welfare theories and their practical implications include:

Beauchamp, Tom, and R. G. Frey, eds. *The Oxford Handbook of Animal Ethics.* Oxford, 2011.

Gruen, Lori. *Ethics and Animals.* Cambridge University Press, 2011.

Jamieson, Dale. *Morality's Progress*. Oxford, 2003.

Singer, Peter. *In Defense of Animals: The Second Wave*. Wiley-Blackwell, 2005.

Additional discussion on consequentialist approaches to environmental ethics can be found in:

Attfield, Robin. *A Theory of Value and Obligation*. Croom Helm, 1987.

Hiller, Avram, Ramona Ilea, and Leonard Kahn, eds. *Consequentialism and Environmental Ethics*. Routledge, 2014.

CHAPTER NINE

DEONTOLOGICAL ENVIRONMENTAL ETHICS: RESPECT FOR NATURE, ANIMAL RIGHTS, AND ENVIRONMENTAL RIGHTS

THE FOCUS OF THIS chapter is deontological approaches to environmental ethics. **Deontological normative theory** is an alternative to consequentialism with respect to *how* moral agents ought to take directly considerable individuals into consideration. According to deontological theories, the rightness or wrongness of an action or policy is determined by its conformity to the relevant rules (or, as it is often put, the *moral law*). *Deont* means "being necessary" in Greek. So another way to think about deontology is that it is necessary, a duty, to act according to the correct moral rules or laws.

Immanuel Kant's ratiocentric ethic is deontological (see Section 5.3). Part of Kant's argument for ratiocentrism is that all and only robustly rational beings represent themselves as an end, as mattering in themselves or for what they are (Kant 1785). He then uses a generalization argument to reach the conclusion that all rational agents need to recognize and treat all and only other rational agents as an end and never merely as a means. The reason for this is that there is no morally relevant difference among rational agents that would justify the claim that some are valuable as an end and others are not. Thus, all rational agents need to respect each other as autonomous beings with their own aims and intentions. This is known as Kant's **categorical imperative**: Always treat rational beings as ends in themselves and never merely as a means. This principle implies that it is always wrong to use other moral agents for your own purposes without their consent. It is never permissible to harm an innocent person for your advantage, to buy and sell people, or to otherwise exploit them, *no matter how good the consequences that would result.*

Thomas Regan rejects Kant's ratiocentrism in favor of sentientism, since he argues that conscious experiences and intentionality, rather than robust rational agency, are the basis for direct moral considerability (Section 7.1). However, Regan, like Kant, embraces deontological normative theory (Regan 1985). That is, while he differs from Kant on *which* things are morally considerable, he concurs with him on *how* they are to be considered—as ends in themselves and not mere means to our ends. That is why, in his view, animal testing, animal agriculture, and animal sports are unacceptable even when the practices are "cleaned up." They are wrong, categorically (see Section 8.1).

Paul Taylor's biocentric view is also deontological (see Section 7.4). Taylor does not believe that all living things have rights. But he does believe that all living things are directly morally considerable, and that the primary way they ought to be considered involves treating them as ends by refraining from interfering with their pursuit of their good. He calls this type of moral consideration **respect for nature** (Taylor 1986). Kant, Regan, and Taylor have similar views on how directly morally considerable entities are to be considered—they are all deontologists—but they have very different views on which entities are directly morally considerable or have inherent worth.

This chapter begins by clarifying deontological normative theory. It then looks in detail at Taylor's biocentric and Regan's sentientist versions of it, before discussing human environmental rights. The chapter concludes with a discussion of the most prominent concerns regarding deontological theories.

9.1 THE MOTIVATIONS FOR DEONTOLOGY

Moral philosophers and environmental ethicists who advance deontological views often emphasize its normative resources. Deontology can account for rights, justice, and in principle limits much more readily than can consequentialism (see Sections 8.5 and 15.2). Many deontologists also argue that it best captures the character of ethical action (Kant 1785). Consider the following two scenarios:

1. A person is in a store and finds a pair of sunglasses that he likes. However, he does not have enough money with him to purchase the glasses. Therefore, he is considering whether to slip them into his pocket and walk out of the store without

paying. He is just about to do this when he catches a glimpse of a security guard. So he replaces the sunglasses on the rack and leaves the store.

2. A person is in a store and finds a pair of sunglasses that he likes. However, he does not have enough money with him to purchase the glasses. Therefore, he is considering whether to slip them into his pocket and walk out of the store without paying. After reflecting on it for a moment he concludes that people really should not take property that does not belong to them. So he replaces the sunglasses on the rack and leaves the store.

In these scenarios, the person does the exact same thing, with the exact same outcomes. However, it strikes many people that the second scenario has the tenor of moral or ethical action, whereas the first does not. What is the difference between the cases that could explain this?

According to deontologists, the difference is that in the first scenario, in which the person does the right thing out of fear of getting caught, it is just an accident that he does the right thing. It is a matter of luck or circumstances. If he did not catch sight of the guard, he would have acted wrongly. However, in the second scenario, because the person does the right thing because it is the right thing—or based on the right principle—it is not an accident that he acted rightly. His commitment to acting on proper principles ensures that he does what is right. If this analysis is correct, then the moral worth of actions is derived from the *principles* on which agents act, not on the consequences that result. Moral action is categorical—it is always wrong to shoplift, even when you can get away with it—and only an ethic based on principles (and not outcomes) can account for this.

Shoplifting might seem like an extreme scenario. After all, most of us are not inclined to do it. However, the phenomenon of people doing the right thing for reasons that are detached from what actually makes it right is widespread. People refrain from lying because they are afraid of being found out. People volunteer or recycle because it is required, expected, or makes them look good. Companies make their products more sustainable because it boosts sales. People consume less energy because it is economically expedient. In these kinds of cases, if the circumstances were different—for instance, if energy was less expensive or polluting was more cost-effective—then behaviors could change for the worse. Thus, deontologists conclude, what is crucial to ethical behavior is the commitment to act according to the right principles regardless of the circumstances.

On deontological views, an action is right if and only if it conforms to the moral law (or proper principles). Therefore, deontological views typically endorse a rule-oriented approach to decision-making. For example, on Kant's ratiocentrism, all rational agents have objective final value and are always to be treated as an end and never merely as a means. This overarching principle (the categorical imperative) generates moral rules or proscriptions against actions that involve treating people as mere means. It is always wrong to oppress people, to punish people for actions they did not do, and to steal people's property, even in cases where doing so would promote good outcomes. People have *rights* against being treated in these ways.

The particular rules, duties, and rights that a deontological environmental ethic endorses depends upon its account of who or what is directly morally considerable. However, in each case the approach to decision-making is the same. First one identifies the duties or rights that are operative. Then one determines whether the action (or practice or policy) under consideration conforms with or violates them. In what follows, I discuss the duties and rights associated with the predominant biocentric, sentientist, and anthropocentric/ratiocentric deontological environmental ethics. (There are also views that attribute moral rights and duties to species, rather than individuals. The view that there is a duty to conserve endangered species is discussed at length in Section 13.4.)

✳ BOX 9.1   TOPIC TO CONSIDER

LEGAL RIGHTS FOR TREES, RIVERS, AND SPECIES?

When Regan and other animal rights advocates claim that nonhuman animals have rights that moral agents need to respect, they do not mean that they have rights that are recognized within the framework of a legislative or legal system—that is, **legal rights**. After all, nonhuman animals often do not have legal rights. They mean that animals have *claims against things being done to them, no matter the current law of the land*—that is, that they have **moral rights**. On an animal rights view, nonhuman animals (with the requisite capacities) should be afforded legal rights because they have moral rights.

In the early 1970s, legal theorist Christopher Stone made the case that non-conscious natural objects—such as trees, species, ecosystems, rivers and "the natural environment as a whole" (1972, 456)—could and at least sometimes should be afforded legal rights. In his view, to hold legal rights involves three crucial components:

> They are, first, that the thing can institute legal action *at its behest*; second, that in determining the granting of legal relief, the court must take *injury to it* into account; and, third, that relief must run to the *benefit of it*. (1972, 458)

On this view, to hold legal rights is not merely to be the object of legislative protection. For example, the US Endangered Species Act (ESA) offers legal protections to individuals (plants and animals) of officially listed endangered and threatened species populations, and the ESA's citizen suit provision allows

(cont.)

BOX 9.1 *(cont.)*

citizens to file lawsuits in order to enforce the act. However, to bring a lawsuit under the ESA, citizens must demonstrate that they have standing to do so, which requires that they are or could potentially be injured (physically, materially, culturally, or aesthetically) by the lack of enforcement for a specific species or population. Thus, the ESA does not afford full rights to species in the sense articulated by Stone. The suits and listings are technically not on behalf of species for harms or wrongs they have suffered, even though management plans are for species' recovery and are in response to population depletions. If species were the *holders of legal rights*, then legal action could be taken on *their* behalf—that is, they would be the plaintiffs—for injuries done to *them*, in addition to the relief being for *their* benefit.

Image 9.1   The Whanganui River was recently granted legal rights by the New Zealand government.
Source: ©iStock/RnDmS

(cont.)

BOX 9.1 *(cont.)*

At the time he was writing, Stone described the idea of "natural objects" being afforded rights as almost "unthinkable." However, this is no longer the case. In 2008, Ecuador ratified by referendum a constitution that recognizes the rights of nature. In 2012, Bolivia adopted a "Law of the Rights of Mother Earth." In 2017, New Zealand granted legal rights to the Whanganui River. One justification for granting an entity legal rights is that doing so is crucial to helping protect its moral rights or standing. However, this is not the only justification. Legal rights can be justified by their bringing about socially or ecologically valuable ends. For example, granting legal rights to endangered species might be conducive to promoting ecological integrity. Granting legal rights to certain rivers or ecosystems might be conducive to protecting cultural traditions and practices.

Would you support legislation that affords some or all species, ecosystems, or nature as a whole legal rights? Why or why not? If you would, what sorts of rights would they be—what sorts of claims, protections, or entitlements would they involve? And who would be empowered with acting on the natural object's behalf? What are some concerns that might be raised about affording legal rights to natural objects?

9.2 RESPECT FOR NATURE

Paul Taylor defends a biocentric account of moral considerability, on which all living things have inherent worth (Sections 7.3 and 7.4). He also endorses a deontological theoretic framework. He therefore believes that all living things are due respect as ends in themselves, and advocates for rules and principles that are meant to express or embody that respect. There are two types of rules within his system, **prima facie duties** and **priority principles**. Prima facie duties are rules that ought to be followed unless there is a compelling reason to violate them—that is, unless they come into conflict with another, stronger duty. The priority principles indicate which prima facie duties take precedence, and under what conditions they do so, when they come into conflict.

Taylor defends four prima facie duties (1986):

- **Nonmaleficence.** "This is the duty not to do harm to any entity in the natural environment that has a good of its own" (172). It is a negative duty to not inflict harm on living things. It does not involve a positive duty to help prevent harm or alleviate suffering.
- **Noninterference.** "Under this rule fall two sorts of negative duties, one requiring us to refrain from placing restrictions on the freedom of individual organisms, the other requiring a general 'hands off' policy with regard to whole ecosystems and biotic communities, as well as to individual organisms" (173).

- **Fidelity.** "Under this rule fall the duties not to break a trust that a wild animal places in us (as shown by its behavior), not to deceive or mislead any animal capable of being deceived or misled, to uphold animal's expectations, which it has formed on the basis of one's past actions with it, and to be true to one's intentions as made known to an animal when it has come to rely on one" (179).
- **Restitutive Justice.** "In its most general terms this rule imposes the duty to restore the balance of justice between a moral agent and a moral subject when the subject has been wronged by the agent. . . . It requires that one make amends to the moral subject by some form of compensation or reparation" (186).

Taylor argues that the first of these duties—nonmaleficence—takes priority over the others. If all living things have inherent worth and should be considered ends in themselves, then the most important responsibility is to refrain from causing them harm so far as is reasonably possible. The second most important duty is restitutive justice. Respect for living things requires trying to make up for wrongful harms when possible, so long as doing so does not cause further harm. It is therefore permissible to interfere with natural systems and organisms, including deceiving animals and breaking their trust, in order to avoid future or remedy past harms—for instance, to restore habitat, rehabilitate injured animals, or study animal behaviors. However, it is best, in Taylor's view, to minimize our impacts on wild organisms and systems. After all, even when we intervene in ways that we believe are beneficial, we always are harming some living things—for example, those that compete with or are predators of the organisms that benefit. Since all living things are ends in themselves and equally considerable, there is no justification for trying to benefit some of them to the detriment of others. This is why Taylor's view is generally regarded as a "hands-off" environmental ethic.

A common objection to biocentric views, including Taylor's, is that they are unlivable. It is simply not possible to survive without harming large numbers of living things. We must eat, build homes, walk across grass, and swat mosquitos, for example. In response to this concern, Taylor defends additional priority principles that describe the conditions under which it is acceptable for people to interfere with and harm nonhuman living things. Taylor argues that it is permissible for people to harm wild organisms in order to meet their basic and serious interests (see Section 8.3), so long as they do so in ways that minimize the harms involved. Taylor also argues that it is permissible to harm nonhumans when pursuing significant interests, so long as they are interests that can be endorsed by a person who has adopted the attitude of respect for nature. For example, clearing land for an environmental science center is acceptable, but clearing land for a CAFO is not, since a person with respect for nature will value the former but not the latter. Moreover, when justified harms do occur, restitutive justice applies. Appropriate attempts must be made at reparation or compensation.

It is sometimes argued that although these principles address the livability problem, they are incongruent with the denial of human superiority and the equal considerability of all living things (see Section 7.4). That is, the principles Taylor endorses do not seem to cohere with the basic values they are supposed to express. If all living things, human and nonhuman, really have equal worth, how can it be that it is permissible for people to harm nonthreatening plants and animals to pursue their own interests?

The justification is supposed to come from values other than directly considerable interests—for instance, cultural values, aesthetic values, and social values. (Taylor's terminology is a bit different than what has been used throughout this textbook, but for consistency's sake I have converted it to the terminology used here.) This highlights a crucial point. Directly morally considerable individuals are not always the only consideration in ethical decision-making. Other values—such as natural value, aesthetic value, and historical value—can matter as well. So it is important for an ethic to provide an account of how to consider those values when they come into conflict with the interests of individuals. Taylor employs a *qualified agent approach* for adjudication. If the values are endorsable by a person who has the proper perspective—a person with the attitude of respect for nature—then they can take priority, so long as harms are minimized and redressed. Qualified agent approaches are commonly employed in ethics. People often look to moral exemplars—Ghandi, Martin Luther King Jr., Rachel Carson, Jesus—and try to take up their perspective or ask what they would do in order to help see what is right (see Section 10.3 and Box 10.2).

Taylor's view is biocentric. But the structure of his ethic is deontological. It involves basic duties as well as adjudication principles. It is possible to recast Taylor's principles to accommodate a sentientist account of moral considerability. The principles would simply be more restricted. They would apply to sentient animals, but not to plants. Therefore, when evaluating the rules and principles that Taylor proposes it is crucial to consider whether they cohere with and express the attitude of respect for nature, as well as whether they could be revised in ways that would express the account of moral considerability that you believe is most justified (if it is not biocentrism).

BOX 9.2   EXERCISE

APPLYING TAYLOR'S VIEW:
THE MUDDY RIVER RESTORATION PROJECT

Applying deontological decision-making to concrete cases involves: (1) identifying which rules apply to the case; (2) determining what the operative rules favor doing in that case; (3) adjudicating which rules take priority, if there is a conflict between them or they come into conflict with other values. Consider the following case.

(cont.)

BOX 9.2 *(cont.)*

The Muddy River runs through several communities in the greater Boston, Massachusetts area. It is a central piece of the Emerald Necklace, a 7-mile string of urban parks and green spaces that encompasses 1,200 acres and was designed by Frederick Law Olmsted (who also co-designed Central Park in New York City) in the late 1800s. The park is heavily used by residents, and the river functions as an urban wild, with fish, frogs, birds, turtles, snakes, coyotes, foxes, and many other small animals regularly seen. Over time, the flow of the Muddy River has been severely restricted. A dam on the Charles River, into which the Muddy empties, prevents tidal flushing, which causes sediment to accumulate. Parts of the river also have been filled and covered, with (too small) pipes installed to maintain flows, and the built environment has generally encroached upon it. During major storms the Muddy sometimes floods. Due to its urban location and condition, the flooding can cause expensive damage to property and transportation infrastructure along the river. Therefore, a project was proposed—the Muddy River Restoration Project—to reduce the prevalence and impact of future flooding. The restoration project involves diverting and draining parts of the river in order to make it possible to dredge the sediment, install larger culverts, and rebuild the river floor and shoreline. However, during the project, which has been approved and is ongoing, the organisms—including fish, plants and amphibians—and established ecology in those parts of the river are destroyed. After the project is completed and the sections are refilled, they will be repopulated by different organisms.

How do you think Taylor's ethical system would assess the Muddy River Restoration Project? Which rules apply and take precedence? Would they support or oppose the project? Do you agree with the assessment that Taylor's ethic generates? Would you support this project? Why or why not?

9.3 ANIMAL RIGHTS

Thomas Regan believes that all experiencing subjects of a life—all beings with consciousness or that can care about their own welfare—are directly morally considerable and ought to be treated as ends in themselves (see Sections 7.1 and 8.1). They have rights against being treated as mere means or resources for people. Therefore, the basic duties within his ethical system involve refraining from using animals as mere things in service of satisfying human interests and preferences. This includes, but is not limited to:

- the total abolition of the use of animals in science;
- the total dissolution of commercial animal agriculture;
- the total elimination of commercial and sport hunting and trapping (Regan 1985, 13)

However, rights can come into conflict. For example, people need to protect themselves against diseased or aggressive animals, and often need access to resources—such as water for agriculture or timber for building—that are also crucial to nonhuman animals. People should of course look first for solutions that do not involve any rights violations. But in cases where no such options are available, whose rights take precedence? What priority principles does Regan endorse?

Regan offers two primary principles of adjudication, the **miniride principle** and the **worse-off principle**. The miniride principle states that:

> [W]hen we must choose between overriding the rights of many who are innocent or the rights of few who are innocent, and when each affected individual will be harmed in a prima facie comparable way, then we ought to override the rights of the few in preferences of the many. (1983, 305)

According to the miniride principle, fewer rights violations are preferable to more rights violations, all other things being equal. The miniride principle helps to adjudicate in cases where the potential rights violations involve comparable harms. In cases where the conflicts involve non-comparable harms, the worse-off principle is operative. It states that:

> [W]hen we must decide to override the rights of the many or the rights of the few who are innocent, and when the harm faced by the few would make them worse off than any of the many would be if any other option were chosen, then we ought to override the rights of the many. (1983, 308)

The worse-off principle says to prioritize avoiding greater harms when adjudicating rights conflicts. Regan believes that rights violations of humans often involve greater harms than do rights violations of nonhumans, since humans have a broader range of interests and opportunities than do nonhumans. Therefore, in cases where we need to kill animals to protect people, or we need to use natural resources for basic human needs, then we ought to do so. This is why Regan would agree with utilitarians that in the lifeboat case discussed last chapter (Section 8.3), the chicken, rather than the orangutan or one of us, ought to be sacrificed.

Regan's view, like Taylor's, is sometimes criticized on the grounds that its adjudication principles do not cohere well with the theory's normative structure and account of moral considerability. If animals really do have equal worth and rights to people, how can it be that they should be sacrificed first in rights conflict cases? Regan might respond that it is not the species membership but the psychological capacities (or capacity to be harmed) of the individuals that is relevant, so his view is not speciesist. But this does not really satisfy the concern, since it does not explain why the rights of more psychologically complex individuals should be prioritized if every experiencing subject of a life has an equal right to be treated as an end and not merely as a means. Nevertheless, if rights violations must occur, the idea that it should involve the fewest violations and least harm possible strike many as reasonable.

✳ BOX 9.3   EXERCISE

APPLYING REGAN'S VIEW:
THERAPEUTIC HUNTING AND CAPTIVE BREEDING

(1) *Therapeutic Hunting*: The elimination of gray wolves and eastern cougars in many areas of the United States has contributed to an explosion in the white-tailed deer population, from approximately 500,000 in the early 1900s to tens of millions today. In addition to causing billions of dollars in economic losses—primarily through car accidents and agricultural damage—the overabundance of deer is detrimental to many other species, including the plant species that they eat, the bird species that nest in those plant species, and the animal species with which they have common diets. States and towns engage in what is sometimes called **therapeutic hunting** in order to manage deer populations—for instance, they hold public hunting seasons or hire private contractors. How would Regan's view assess therapeutic white-tailed deer hunting? Would it support it or oppose it? And why would it do so? (This case is taken from Varner 1998.)

  Therapeutic hunting is also frequently used to protect threatened and endangered species. For example, tens of thousands of wild goats have been killed on Galapagos islands in order to protect endemic plants and animals. Thousands of feral pigs have been killed in the Channel Islands off the coast of California to protect endangered island foxes. Thousands of nonnative lake trout are killed every year in Yellowstone Lake in order to protect the endemic cutthroat trout. Australia is piloting a program to cull feral cats (estimated to number over 10 million) to protect native species. Would Regan's view support these hunts? Would Taylor's views support them? Do you agree with these assessments? Why or why not?

(2) *Captive Breeding Programs*: Captive breeding programs are often used by conservation biologists to increase the population of an endangered species. They have been conducted for California condors, black-footed ferrets, Santa Cruz Island foxes, numbats, and pandas, for example. In these programs, members of the remnant wild population (and in some cases all of them) are captured. They are then kept in captivity, bred, and the young reared before being reintroduced into their prior locations or translocated to new ones. The programs are done for ecological ends—conserving endangered species—but they involve constraints and harms (e.g., stress, injury,

(cont.)

BOX 9.3 *(cont.)*

and sometimes death) to the individual animals involved. Would Taylor's ethical system support captive breeding programs for conserving endangered species? What about Regan's? What if the breeding programs were for other purposes, such as research, education, or commerce? Do you agree with the assessments their ethical theories generate? Why or why not?

Image 9.2   Island foxes in a captive breeding program to increase their population on Santa Cruz Island, CA (see Box 11.3).
Source: Stephen Francis Photography

9.4 HUMAN RIGHTS AND THE ENVIRONMENT

Deontological anthropocentric and ratiocentric environmental ethics prioritize the rights of people in environmental decision-making. The core idea is that there are extensive indirect duties regarding the environment that are based on the responsibility to protect people's rights and to satisfy the demands of justice (see, e.g., Sections 5.6, 15.2, and 16.4). On such views, what our environmental responsibilities are depends upon what rights and entitlements people have.

There is widespread agreement among rights theorists that people have **negative rights.** Negative rights are claims against things being done to a person. The rights to not be killed, not be exploited, not be discriminated against, and not be restricted in movement, association, or speech are examples of negative rights. Many rights theorists believe that basic negative rights follow from the worth or dignity of human beings, which is grounded in the capacities that they possess. This is Kant's view, for example, and it is expressed in Article 1 of the United Nation's *Universal Declaration of Human Rights* (UN 1948):

> All human beings are born free and equal in dignity and rights. They are endowed with reason and conscience and should act towards one another in a spirit of brotherhood.

Environmental rights are often considered to be prerequisites for and/or implications of basic human rights. Among the rights widely recognized as basic **human rights** are the right to life and the right to bodily integrity. The right to life involves a claim against being killed, as well as against being deprived of what is needed to survive. The right to bodily integrity involves a claim against things being done to your body without your consent. The environmental rights that are thought to follow from these basic rights include: the right to not have the air that one breathes contaminated; the right to not have one's agricultural lands degraded; the right to not be denied access to potable water; and the right to know about polluting activities in one's community and to participate in environmental decision-making processes. (Rights-oriented approaches to environmental justice are discussed in Section 15.3.)

As the examples above indicate, attending to the ways in which people's basic rights intersect with the environment can generate a strong set of responsibilities to refrain from polluting and ecologically degrading activities. For example, Simon Caney argues that human rights establish a responsibility to dramatically reduce greenhouse gas emissions. The impacts of global climate change are already impairing many people's ability to meet their basic needs and forcing them to migrate as environmental refugees—that is, it involves violations of their basic rights (Caney 2010). The greater the magnitude of global climate change, the more people will be put in this position and thereby have their rights compromised. Some small low-lying island nations—such as the Maldives, Kiribati, and Tuvalu—may even be submerged altogether by rising sea levels. Therefore, Caney believes people and countries have a duty, based on respect for the rights of others, to reduce their greenhouse gas emissions, even if it is costly to do so:

> A human rights approach . . . requires us to reconceive the way in which one thinks about the costs involved in mitigation and adaptation. Some have argued that it would be extremely expensive to prevent dangerous

climate change and hence that humanity should not do this. If, however, it is true that climate change violates human rights then this kind of reasoning is inappropriate. . . . If a person is violating human rights then he or she should desist even if it is costly. . . . The implications for mitigation and adaptation are clear. That mitigation and adaptation would be costly similarly does not in itself entail that they should not be adopted. If emitting greenhouse gases issues in rights violations it should stop, and the fact that it is expensive does not tell against that claim. (Caney 2010, 171)

If Caney is correct that activities that result in rights violations should cease, then people and communities have strong claims against any activities—forinstance, mining, industrial production, resource allocations, commercial fishing practices, and waste disposal—that displace them, reduce their food security, or pollute their air and water. They also have a claim against consumer behaviors that support such activities—for example, purchasing inexpensive farmed shrimp from Southeast Asia and electronics made with conflict minerals (see, e.g., Sections 6.1 and 6.2). (See Box 8.6 for a discussion of the problem of inconsequentialism, which is germane to this issue, and Section 15.4 for a discussion of the ethics of consumption.)

The *Universal Declaration of Human Rights* asserts that people also have a right to own property and to not have it seized or damaged by others:

1. Everyone has the right to own property alone as well as in association with others.
2. No one shall be arbitrarily deprived of his property. (UN 1948, Article 17)

On some views, particularly **libertarian** ones, this right is thought to flow from the fact that everyone owns their own lives and bodies. As a result, a person has rights over the products of her labor, as well as over anything that others freely trade with her or give to her. On other views, the right to own property is a secondary right, but one that is essential to accomplishing autonomy and security. In either case, the right generates a strong set of correlative environmental duties for people, corporations and governments, since land and water ownership must be respected and activities that degrade other's property without their consent are impermissible. For example, people ought not be forcibly relocated in order to build dams or create reserves; industrial discharge and agricultural runoff should not be allowed to contaminate water supplies; bulk water and land sales should not undermine the productivity of smallholding farms; governments should not claim and sell resource rights on indigenous lands; and unauthorized road-building, logging, farming, and poaching on public and private lands should be prevented.

✳ BOX 9.4

INTELLECTUAL PROPERTY AND BIOPIRACY

Property rights can apply to knowledge. For example, intellectual or cultural theft is thought to occur when cultural knowledge is used without appropriate consent or compensation, or when it is done in ways that are contrary to the culture's worldviews. This is the concern behind what Vandana Shiva (1997) has termed **biopiracy**—exploitative use of local or indigenous biological knowledge to create commercialized products. **Bioprospecting**, exploring for biological resources that could be developed into new products, is common in the agricultural and pharmaceutical industries, and it very often draws upon indigenous knowledge of plants and animals. Bioprospecting has been, and continues to be, a fruitful source for biotechnological innovation. However, because it makes use of cultural knowledge, it must be done in ways that are fair and culturally sensitive. When it is not—when it is done without consent of the community from which the knowledge is taken, does not benefit the community, or involves culturally offensive practices—then it is unjust. For example, several Ojibway tribes in North America have objected to the genetic modification and patenting of traditionally cultivated varieties of wild rice on the grounds that it will economically disadvantage them (by competing with their wild rice production, contaminating their rice beds, and opening them to patent infringement liability) and that genetic modification and patenting are contrary to their cultural practices and worldview regarding the integrity of wild rice, common heritage, and ownership (Streiffer 2005).

Rights over cultural traditions and knowledge, and against cultural appropriation and exploitation, are explicitly asserted in article 31 of the United Nations *Declaration on the Rights of Indigenous People*:

> Indigenous peoples have the right to maintain, control, protect, and develop their cultural heritage, traditional knowledge, and traditional cultural expressions, as well as the manifestations of their sciences, technologies, and cultures, including human and genetic resources, seeds, medicines, knowledge of the properties of fauna and flora, oral traditions, literatures, designs, sports and traditional games, and visual and performing arts. They also have the right to maintain, control, protect and develop their intellectual property over such cultural heritage, traditional knowledge, and traditional cultural expressions. (UN 2007)

People's negative rights—their rights against having certain things done to them—can generate considerable restrictions on ecologically harmful and exploitative activities. However, a negative human rights approach cannot ground entitlements (and, of course, restrictions on behaviors that harm only nonhumans). Some rights theorists believe that, in addition to negative rights, people also have **positive rights**. Positive rights are rights *to* something, rather than rights *against* something. Positive environmental rights involve claims on others to provide environmental goods or services. For example, if a person has a negative right to water, then they have a claim against others impairing their ability to secure clean water. But if a person has a positive right to water, then they have a claim to be provided access to clean water if they do not currently have it. Negative rights are not necessarily more morally significant than positive rights. Providing people with drinkable water is arguably just as important as is protecting their property.

Many international rights conventions and national constitutions recognize positive environmental rights. For example, the United Nations General Assembly has recognized the right to reliable access to safe drinking water and "the fundamental right of everyone to be free from hunger" (UN 2010; 1996), and numerous countries include a positive right to food and/or water in their constitution or laws—for example, South Africa, Nicaragua, Algeria, India, Sri Lanka, Belgium, and Uruguay. Nevertheless, 748 million people remain without access to an improved source of drinking water (i.e., one that is protected from contamination, particularly fecal matter) and "billions lack access to safe water that is reliably and continuously delivered in sufficient quantities" (WHO 2014, iv), while 795 million people are chronically undernourished. (Global food insecurity is discussed at length in Chapter 16; and a recent case in which the US government failed to ensure access to safe water is discussed in Box 15.1.)

There are significant distributive implications to positive rights. If people have unmet positive rights that require goods and services to satisfy, then those in a position to provide them have a duty to forgo some of their goods—such as wealth, resources, or property—to do so. For example, the United Nations resolution on a right to water calls upon

> states and international organizations to provide financial resources, capacity-building and technology transfer, through international assistance and cooperation, in particular to developing countries, in order to scale up efforts to provide safe, clean, accessible and affordable drinking water and sanitation for all. (UN 2010)

In order to satisfy a positive right to water (or other environmental goods, such as food or access to nature), either access to some amount of it needs to be publicly ensured or else everyone must be guaranteed a minimum amount of ownership of it or resources to produce or purchase it. For this reason, positive rights are often connected to theories of **distributive justice** according to which social policies and institutions should be designed to ensure that everyone has access to at least the minimal amount of resources, opportunities, or capabilities needed to live well or participate fully in society. However, it should be noted that negative rights also often have distributional implications. For example, enforcement of property rights can require an extensive and expensive legal system (e.g., policing and courts) that must be funded.

A negative human rights approach to environmental decision-making proceeds in the same way as does an animal rights approach. For any action or policy being considered, the impacts on the people involved must first be identified. Then it is evaluated in terms of whether those impacts violate or undermine anyone's rights. If it does, then it ought not be done (or it constitutes a strong reason against doing it). If high-emissions lifestyles contribute to violations of the rights of people living in low-lying areas, then people ought to reduce their emissions. If withholding information about local pollution and air quality violates people's right to informed consent, then that information should be fully disclosed. If prohibiting hunting within an indigenous group's ancestral lands violates their right to self-determination, then the prohibition should be removed.

If people have positive environmental rights, then those in position to do so should engage in practices and adopt policies that ensure that those rights are satisfied. If people have a right to potable water, then we ought to expand reliable clean water delivery infrastructure to everyone. If people have a right to experience wilderness, then we ought to protect appropriate areas and ensure that people have reasonable access to them. If people have a right to toxin-free homes, then we should compel landlords to remove lead paint from rental units and require furniture makers to replace hazardous flame-retardant chemicals (such as PBDEs) in their products with non-toxic alternatives.

This section has focused on the extent to which human rights justify environmental rights, duties, and responsibilities—that is, it has been discussing deontological anthropocentrism (or ratiocentrism). However, most environmental ethicists, anthropocentric and nonanthropocentric, deontological and consequentialist, believe that it is important to identify and respect people's environmental rights. Recognition of environmental rights is widely seen as crucial to justifying environmental laws, increasing citizen participation in environmental decision-making, reducing environmental injustice, drawing attention to environmental issues, promoting social and economic equality, empowering historically marginalized groups (e.g., smallholding women and indigenous peoples), and increasing people's well-being overall. Where theories differ is in whether people's rights ought to be the primary consideration in environmental decision-making or whether rights are one consideration among others that need to be taken into account but are defeasible, as well as in what they take to be the basis or the justification for rights (see Box 9.5).

✳ BOX 9.5

THE STATUS OF BASIC RIGHTS

Environmental rights are now widely recognized. According to one recent study:

> As of 2012, 177 of the world's 193 UN member nations recognize
> [the right to a healthy environment] through their constitution,
> environmental legislation, court decisions, or ratification of an
> international agreement. . . . The only remaining holdouts are
> the United States, Canada, Japan, Australia, New Zealand, China,
> Oman, Afghanistan, Kuwait, Brunei Darussalam, Lebanon, Laos,
> Myanmar, North Korea, Malaysia, and Cambodia. Even among
> these laggards, some subnational governments recognize the
> right to a healthy environment, including six American states
> [Hawaii, Illinois, Massachusetts, Montana, Pennsylvania, and
> Rhode Island], five Canadian provinces or territories [Ontario,
> Quebec, the Yukon, Nunavut, and the Northwest Territories], and
> a growing number of cities [e.g., Pittsburgh, Santa Monica, and
> Montreal]. (Boyd 2012)

Environmental rights are justified on the grounds that they are prerequisites for basic rights (e.g., life and health), implications of basic rights (e.g., property and bodily integrity), or themselves basic rights. But what is the basis or justification for basic rights? This is a perennial issue in social and political philosophy.

One view on the basis of basic rights is that people have them in virtue of their worth, autonomy, or value as human beings or as rational beings. This is Kant's view, as well as the view expressed in the United Nations' *Universal Declaration of Human Rights* and the United States' Declaration of Independence, according to which "all men" are "endowed" with "unalienable" rights to life, liberty, and the pursuit of happiness. This is sometimes referred to as a *status-based* or *natural rights* approach to grounding basic rights.

Another view is that basic rights are justified because establishment and recognition of them is an effective means to bringing about morally important ends, such as human flourishing, animal welfare, or social justice. This view is sometimes referred to as an *instrumentalist* approach. This is John Stuart Mill's view, for example. He believed that rights are claims that people should be

(cont.)

BOX 9.5 *(cont.)*

afforded because doing so increases utility or overall well-being (2001). Similarly, many animal welfare proponents advocate for the recognition of animal rights because they would be claims against treating animals in ways that cause suffering.

A third view is that the basis for basic rights is statutory. On this view, basic rights are created by their being recognized in legitimate international and national laws and upheld in legitimate judicial decisions. This view is sometimes referred to as a *conventionalist* approach. According to this view, there is a positive human right to water because the United Nations and myriad national governments have passed legislation and declarations asserting that people are entitled to reliable access to drinkable water. Prior to this, the right did not exist.

A fourth view on the basis for basic rights is that they are justified because reasonable people would affirm them. This is sometimes referred to as a *contractualist* approach. Its most prominent proponent is political philosopher John Rawls (1971). According to contractualist views, basic rights exist because people would seek them (or would assent to them, or could not reasonably reject them) in the context of rational deliberations about how societies and social institutions ought to be organized or structured.

Which of these is the proper basis for basic and environmental rights is closely tied to which normative theory is most justified. Deontology is frequently identified with a status-based approach. Consequentialism strongly favors an instrumental approach. Atheoretical views, such as pragmatism (see Sections 14.4 and 14.5), often favor a procedural or conventionalist approach. Social contract theories typically take a contractual approach.

A full discussion of these different bases for basic rights is beyond the scope of what can be covered here. However, it is important to recognize that this is not merely an academic matter. If basic rights are legislatively established, as part of ratification of a constitution or through international agreements among nations, the rights and their corresponding duties might not extend to all people, but be limited by political membership in jurisdictions in which they have been recognized. If basic rights are instrumentally justified, then what rights should be regarded as basic—and the strength of the claims they involve—will be contextual. Which rights claims maximize utility could differ by cultural and ecological context, for example. In contrast, on a status-based approach, all people have the same basic rights, regardless

(cont.)

BOX 9.5 *(cont.)*

of their political, legal, or cultural context. (Although how those rights are operationalized would be culturally sensitive.) Thus, the basis of basic rights is germane to their scope (i.e., to whom they apply), content (i.e., what claims they involve), stability (i.e., whether they change by context), and normativity (i.e., how strong a claim they make).

9.5 CONCERNS ABOUT DEONTOLOGICAL ENVIRONMENTAL ETHICS

Several concerns have been raised regarding deontological normative theory, each of which has manifestations within environmental ethics. One prominent concern is that the view is too unremitting. Many people feel that if the outcomes of an action or policy are good enough, then it should be done or enacted even if it involves violating an operative rule. For example, there is currently a highly infections fungal disease (chytridiomycosis) that is devastating populations of many frogs around the world. In response to this, herpetologists are capturing and harming large number of both healthy and unhealthy frogs in order to conduct research on why some species and populations are resistant to the fungus, while others are not. The goal is to devise methods to increase resistance and arrest the disease's transmission. This is not an exceptional case. Ecological research and conservation biology often involve capturing, monitoring, breeding and/or translocating animals, as well as manipulating parts of ecological systems, in ways that seem inconsistent with respecting them as ends in themselves with rights (in Regan's sense). Similarly, conducting medical research on animals is sometimes crucial to developing treatments that could save large number of human lives. Thus, a rights- or duty-based approach to environmental and animal ethics appears to rule out a wide variety of activities that are commonly recognized as not only acceptable but necessary. Sometimes—often, in fact—we ought to do things that harm or disrespect individuals for the greater good, according to this view.

Another concern often raised regarding deontological views is that they have no adequate way to adjudicate cases where different duties or rights come into conflict. For example, what do you do when it is necessary to violate people's legitimate property rights in order to protect an endangered species? If the duties that we ought to follow—for example, "forestall anthropogenic extinctions" and "protect property rights"—are universal and inviolable, then there is no in-principle way to determine which ought to take precedence, and it is not acceptable to violate either one in any case. It is, of course, always preferable to identify win-win solutions to environmental problems. For example, it is possible to reduce population growth by helping people to dramatically improve their lives (Section 16.3). Strong fisheries regulations can be beneficial to fishers, local communities, and ocean ecosystems and species. Aggressive development of alternative energies can mitigate climate change, create jobs, and increase consumer autonomy. Ecotourism can protect threatened species and help lift people out of poverty in sustainable ways. However, in many cases there are hard decisions to be made between competing goods and rights. Deciding how to allocate scarce resources— for example, water on which agriculture, towns, fisheries, and riparian systems all depend—frequently involves prioritizing some rights and claims over others. Expanding improved water and electricity access can require public works projects—for instance, wind farms and dams—that involve appropriating land and causing ecological impacts. Weakening intellectual property protections often can increase access to vital energy and medical technologies. Regulating practices on private property—such as disposing of waste, filling in wetlands, or drilling wells—is frequently necessary to forestall possible impacts downstream or downwind. If all an ethic provides is a set of inviolable rules or principles, it is not well positioned to reason through the complexity and contingencies involved in these sorts of hard cases, according to this concern.

What these concerns are taken to show is that deontology is too detached from the specifics of the actual world to function as an effective environmental ethic (and, in its critics view, an interpersonal ethic). The real world is complex and messy. Duties can come into tension with each other. Following the same rule can lead to very different outcomes in different circumstances. There sometimes are special or exceptional cases. Deontology's focus on principles that are unremitting and universal does not allow it to accommodate these important features of the ethical landscape. It is not adequately sensitive to the very important fact that outcomes matter when you are trying to decide what actions to take or policies to adopt, or that what you ought to do is often dependent upon what other people are doing—for example, how many resources they are using or what activities they are engaged in—and not only on the principles that your action embodies. Moreover, it seems to many that bringing things like well-being and sustainability about is crucial to ethically good behavior. On this view, merely refraining from committing wrongs is not enough.

In response to these concerns deontologists often endorse rules that describe when it is permissible to harm those with inherent worth. As discussed earlier, Regan defends the miniride and worse-off principles, which states that it is permissible to violate the rights of animals if doing so would prevent more rights violations or rights violations involving greater harms. Taylor endorses principles of self-defense and minimum wrong, which describe when it is permissible for people to harm wild animals and plants in pursuit of their own ends. These sorts of adjudication principles are meant to address the rigidity and rights/duties conflict concerns. Moreover, rights advocates sometimes moderate what counts as a rights violation or allow that rights are defeasible in some circumstances. For example, the right to control one's property may not be a claim against ever having it seized or used without consent, but against having it done without compelling cause or justification. Deontologists also often defend principles that call for promoting the good. Kant, for example, argues that moral agents have a duty to help others, and Regan suggests there is a responsibility to be active in the protection of animals. That is, they defend positive rights that require agents to promote the well-being of others, in addition to duties to avoid committing rights violations.

However, critics of deontology argue, the need for adjudication principles, allowing rights violations in exceptional cases, and establishing positive rights shows how important it is to consider outcomes when determining which actions to take and which policies to adopt. In the end, the overarching concern of critics of deontological normative theory is that it is misguided about what really matters. It is not respecting principles or rights that is the most important thing. It is the state of the world: how well people's lives are going, the integrity of ecological systems, and the protection of biodiversity. This is not to say that we should not care about the principles and motives on which people act. We should, on this view, since these are crucial to accomplishing desirable outcomes. For this reason, we need to advocate for environmental rights and encourage development of good environmental character. But we should not lose sight of what we ought to ultimately care most about: human and nonhuman flourishing.

9.6 SUMMARY

The primary questions addressed in this chapter were:

- What are the distinctive features of deontological approaches to environmental ethics?
- What are the substantive views of the predominant deontological environmental ethics?

The chapter began by clarifying what distinguishes deontological normative theory from other normative theories—that the rightness or wrongness of an action or policy is determined by its conformity to the operative rules (or principles, duties, or moral law). It then discussed what attracts people to deontology, which includes that it provides in principle limits and seems to captures the character of morally good actions, before focusing on the prominent deontological views in environmental ethics: Paul Taylor's respect for nature view; Thomas Regan's animals rights view; and human rights based views. In each case, the duties and principles that the view endorses and the approach to environmental decision-making that it advocates were emphasized. Finally, prominent concerns about deontological normative theories were presented. These include that it is too rigid or insensitive to the complexity of actual cases and that it cannot satisfactorily deal with situations in which duties (or principles or rights) conflict. However, the deeper disagreement between consequentialist and deontological normative theories lies in their conceptions of ethics. According to consequentialism, ethics is about bringing things about—for example, human and nonhuman flourishing—whereas according to deontology, ethics is about respecting entities with inherent worth as ends in themselves.

KEY TERMS (SEE GLOSSARY FOR DEFINITIONS):

biopiracy	miniride principle
bioprospecting	moral rights
categorical imperative	negative rights
deontological normative theories	positive rights
distributive justice	prima facie duties
duty of nonmaleficence	principle of noninterference
duty of restitutive justice	priority principles
environmental rights	respect for nature
human rights	therapeutic hunting
legal rights	worse-off principle
libertarian account of property rights	

REVIEW QUESTIONS

- What makes a normative theory deontological, rather than consequentialist?
- What is the proper approach to ethical evaluation and decision-making according to deontological theories? What are the roles of duties, rights and principles in it?
- What are the particular duties and principles endorsed by Taylor and by Regan?
- If Taylor, Regan, and Kant are all deontologists, why do they endorse such different duties and principles?
- What is the difference between positive and negative rights?
- What is the difference between moral and legal rights?
- What are environmental rights and what is their relationship to human rights?
- What are the prominent views on the basis or justification for human rights?
- What are the prominent concerns regarding deontological normative theories and how do the theories typically respond to them?

DISCUSSION QUESTIONS

- Do you agree with Taylor that respect for nature favors taking a "hands-off" approach to wild animals and ecosystems, so far as is reasonable possible? Why or why not?
- Do you agree with Regan that the fundamental problem with commercial animal agriculture and using animals in science is not how they are treated or the suffering that they undergo, but that they are used as a mere means to human ends? Would you support the complete abolition of them?
- What do you think is the basis for human rights? Do you think they are moral and not only legal rights?

- Do you think that human rights are only negative rights, or are there positive human rights as well?

- Do you agree with Caney that global climate change involves rights violations? If it does, are people morally required to immediately and dramatically reduce their greenhouse gas emissions? How does Caney's view on the relationship between environmental degradation and rights violations apply to other environmental issues and consumptive practices?

- Do you find the consequentialist or the deontological conception of ethics to be more compelling—that is, is ethics primarily about bringing things about or respecting entities with inherent worth as ends in themselves (or something else)?

FURTHER READING

The classical statement of deontological ethical theory is:

Kant, Immanuel. *Groundwork of the Metaphysics of Morals*, translated by M. Gregor. Cambridge University Press, 1785/1997.

The original sources for the deontological environmental ethics focused on in this chapter are:

Taylor, Paul. *Respect for Nature: A Theory of Environmental Ethics*. Princeton, 1986.

Regan, Tom. *The Case for Animal Rights*. University of California Press, 1983.

There are several accessible introductory texts on human rights, including:

Freeman, Michael. *Human Rights: An Interdisciplinary Approach*. Polity, 2011.

Nickel, James. *Making Sense of Human Rights*. Wiley-Blackwell, 2007.

Books that address animal rights and their practical implications include:

Beauchamp, Tom, and R. G. Frey, eds. *The Oxford Handbook of Animal Ethics*. Oxford, 2011.

Gruen, Lori. *Ethics and Animals*. Cambridge University Press, 2011.

Rollins, Bernard. *Animal Rights and Human Morality*. Prometheus Books, 1980.

Sunstein, Cass, and Martha Nussbaum, eds. *Animal Rights: Current Debates and New Directions*. Oxford University Press, 2005.

Interdisciplinary research related to environmental rights (or human rights and the environment) can be found in:

Boyd, David. *The Environmental Rights Revolution*. UBC Press, 2011.

Bullard, Robert, ed. *The Quest for Environmental Justice: Human Rights and the Politics of Pollution*. Counterpoint, 2005.

Lennox, Corinne, and Damien Short, eds. *Handbook of Indigenous People's Rights*. Routledge, 2015.

CHAPTER TEN

CHARACTER ETHICS: VIRTUE, VICE, AND THE ENVIRONMENT

THE PREVIOUS CHAPTERS FOCUSED on normative theories that connect rightness to outcomes (consequentialism) and normative theories that connect rightness to fulfilling duties and respecting rights (deontology). In this chapter, the focus is on the attitudes, outlooks, and dispositions of the people who perform actions and enact policies. In moral philosophy, this area of ethical theory is called **virtue ethics**, since it concerns what sorts of character traits we ought and ought not have—that is, virtues and vices.

Reflections on character are prominent in the work of historically influential environmental thinkers. For example, according to Henry David Thoreau, temperance and simplicity are conducive to happiness because they foster an uncluttered life and mind, which enable focusing more readily on things that have real and lasting value, such as beauty, nature, justice, and friendship:

> Most of the luxuries, and many of the so-called comforts of life, are not only not indispensable, but positive hindrances to the elevation of mankind. . . .
> To be a philosopher is not merely to have subtle thoughts, nor even to found a school, but so to love wisdom as to live according to its dictates, a life of simplicity, independence, magnanimity, and trust. (Thoreau 1906, 15–16)

Aldo Leopold (whose land ethic is discussed at length in Chapter 11) frequently emphasizes the link between character and activity. On his view, proper treatment of the environment is only possible when we gain an appropriate perspective on it and cultivate love and respect toward it:

> We abuse land because we regard it as a commodity belonging to us. When we see land as a community to which we belong, we may begin to use it with love and respect. . . . That land is a community is the basic concept of ecology, but that land is to be loved and respected is an extension of ethics. (Leopold 1949/1968, viii–ix)

Like Leopold, Rachel Carson (the author of *Silent Spring*) believed that cultivating virtue is central to appreciating the value and beauty of the natural world. On her view, wonder is a preeminent environmental virtue, since "Wonder and humility are wholesome emotions, and they do not exist side by side with a lust for destruction" (Carson 1999, 94). Moreover, like Thoreau, Carson believed that wonder opens a person up to nature and enriches her life:

> It is our misfortune that for most of us that clear-eyed vision, that true instinct for what is beautiful and awe-inspiring, is dimmed and even lost before we reach adulthood. . . . I should ask that . . . each child in the world be [given] a sense of wonder so indestructible that it would last throughout life, as an unfailing antidote against the boredom and disenchantments of later years, the sterile preoccupation with things that are artificial, and alienation from the sources of our strength. (Carson 1956, 42–43)

Virtue language and concepts are ubiquitous within contemporary environmental discourse. After conducting an extensive survey of the ethical terminology employed by environmental thinkers, both secular and religious, Louke van Wensveen reported that she did not "come across of piece of ecologically sensitive philosophy, theology, or ethics that does not in some way incorporate virtue language" (1999, 5). She concludes that virtue language is integral and indispensable to environmental ethics, since virtue terms provide a powerful set of evaluative concepts and perspectives that can enhance our capacity to understand and respond to environmental issues. Thomas Hill (1983) also advocates for the indispensability of environmental **character ethics** on the grounds that environmentally problematic activities often have features that are not fully captured by consequentialist or deontological evaluation. Consider, for example, a person who chooses to cut down and pave over an entire wooded lot so as to avoid the hassle of maintaining it. Hill believes that neither the language and concept of utility nor the language and concept of rights fully expresses what is disturbing about such behavior. In his view, there is something troubling that goes beyond the action and outcomes, and is captured by the question, "What sort of person would do that?" This is a question about the motives, values, intentions, and perspectives of the agent; it is about her character.

Providing substantive accounts of environmental virtues and vices, as well as articulating the relationships between environmental virtue and right action are thus widely regarded as important projects within environmental ethics. However, there is a split between those who regard environmental virtue ethics as a *complement* to the predominant theoretical approaches to environmental ethics (e.g., consequentialist and deontological), and those that regard it is an *alternative* approach. After clarifying what virtues and vices are, these views are discussed in turn.

10.1 WHAT ARE ENVIRONMENTAL VIRTUES AND VICES?

Imagine that you and I are walking in the deep woods and come across a hiker with a leg injury. You immediately begin to help the injured person and start developing plans for how we can safely get medical assistance to him. However, I insist that we must keep going if we are going to bag the peak for which we are aiming, and that we can see about helping him on our way out if no one else has come along to aid him. Suppose that this happens regularly. I am generally moved neither emotionally nor to action by the plight of others, whereas you generally are empathetic and try to alleviate their suffering (when in appropriate position to do so). We are disposed regarding the same thing—the suffering of others—but we are differently disposed. I am *insensitive* and you are *compassionate*. We have different **character traits** or dispositions to take certain types of considerations as reasons (or as motivational) for action or emotion under certain types of circumstances. Different people have different character traits if they are disposed to respond differently toward the same types of considerations.

A **character virtue** (hereafter just "virtue") is a well-justified character trait. It is a disposition to respond to considerations in the world in excellent ways. If the suffering of others is bad, and a person is indifferent to it (or aims to cause it) then she fails to respond well to a morally salient fact about the world. Therefore, *cruelty* and *insensitivity* toward the suffering of others are vices, and *compassion* toward others is a virtue. To paraphrase Aristotle (1985), a virtuous person is disposed to respond to the right thing, for the right reason, and in the right way, while also having the right desires and feelings about it. Specifying what counts as "right" for each of these is the primary project of **virtue theory**.

There are several competing virtue theories, but the most prominent ones share this crucial feature: What constitutes right responsiveness is largely determined by the goods and values in the world (and the nature of those values), as well as by the relevant facts about the agent (and her situation). When a character trait is justified as a virtue at least in part by environmental goods and values—be they instrumental goods (e.g., natural resources or ecosystem services) or final values (e.g., natural value or inherent worth)—it is an *environmentally justified virtue*. When a character trait involves responsiveness to an environmental entity—such as ecosystems, organisms or landscapes—it is an *environmentally responsive virtue*. When a character trait is conducive to accomplishing environmental ends or goals—for instance, promoting sustainability or protecting valued species—it is an *environmentally productive virtue*. Thus, there are several, not mutually exclusive, ways in which a character virtue can be an **environmental virtue**.

✳ BOX 10.1

KEY ENVIRONMENTAL VIRTUES AND VICES

The table on the following page organizes a typology of environmental virtues and vices. It is intended to demonstrate the diversity of virtue and vice terms that have appeared in the environmental ethics literature and how they relate to environmental values, behaviors, and practices. A particular environmental virtue or vice need not be exclusive to one variety. This is *a* typology of environmental virtue not *the* typology, since there are many other possible categories and ways in which virtue and vice terms might be divided. Moreover, while the virtue and vice terms in this table are among the more prominent ones in environmental ethics, they are only a sample of those that appear in environmental discourse. Louke van Wensveen (1999) identified 189 distinct virtue terms and 174 distinct vice terms in the environmental ethics literature.

Some of the character traits listed on the table are thought to be conducive to engaging well directly with nature and nonhuman animals (i.e., *virtues of communion with nature*) or to responding well to the value of nature and non-humans animals (i.e., *virtues of respect for nature/animals*). Some are character traits that are thought to be conducive to promoting environmental sustainability (i.e., *virtues of sustainability*). Some are thought to be conducive to acting to protect environmental goods and values on behalf of others (i.e., *virtues of environmental stewardship*) or to success in securing them in social and political domains (i.e., *virtues of environmental activism*). Would you agree that the character traits listed are virtues and vices? Or are there some that you believe should not be regarded as virtues or vices? Why or why not? Are there any that you believe are particularly vital for responding well to environmental issues and challenges? If so, why? Are there additional character traits to the ones listed above that you believe are important for environmental ethics? What are they and why are they important?

(cont.)

BOX 10.1 *(cont.)*

An Illustrative Typology of Environmental Virtues and Vices				
Virtues of Sustainability	**Virtues of Communion with Nature**	**Virtues of Respect for Nature/Animals**	**Virtues of Environmental Activism**	**Virtues of Environmental Stewardship**
temperance	wonder	care	perseverance	benevolence
frugality	openness	compassion	cooperativeness	loyalty
far-sightedness	appreciation	restitutive justice	commitment	justice
attunement	attentiveness	considerateness	optimism	honesty
humility	love	ecological sensitivity	creativity	diligence
Corresponding Vices				
materialism	indifference	cruelty	apathy	carelessness
intemperance	laziness	intolerance	complacency	untrustworthiness
greed	hubris	negligence	misanthropy	light-mindedness
short-sightedness	close-mindedness	callousness	pessimism	uncooperativeness
profligacy	inattentiveness	maleficence	cowardice	selfishness

Table 10.1

10.2 CHARACTER AND ENVIRONMENTAL ETHICS

Character ethics is considered an essential component of environmental ethics even when it is seen as a complement, rather than an alternative, to deontological and consequentialist approaches to environmental ethics. One reason for this is that the language of virtue and vice is far more diverse and nuanced than the languages of duty and consequences. There are hundreds of virtue and vice terms—honest/dishonest, compassionate/cruel, generous/miserly, optimistic/pessimistic, courageous/cowardly, temperate/intemperate, grateful/ungrateful, tolerant/intolerant, and so on. This allows for more subtle evaluations of both character and conduct than the standard deontological and consequentialist categories—wrong, right, permissible, obligatory, and supererogatory. This diversity and richness is crucial for environmental ethics because of the complexity of the human relationship with the natural environment. Nature is a source of basic resources, knowledge, recreation, renewal, and spiritual experience. It is also a threat, indifferent to us, and a locus of human-independent values (on nonanthropocentric views). Environmental ethics needs the resources to accommodate this complexity, and the language of virtue and vice provides them. This is a large part of why it is so integral and pervasive in environmental discourse.

Moreover, as Thoreau and Carson emphasize, environmental virtue is beneficial to its possessor. On Carson's view, this is because it opens a person to positive experiences and relationships with nature. The natural environment provides aesthetic and recreational goods, as well as opportunities to develop physically, intellectually, morally, and spiritually. However, these goods are more available to some people than to others. Those who possess traits like wonder, humility, and love experience nature and relate to it differently than a person who is arrogant, lazy, and indifferent to the natural world. For the former, nature often is a source of nurturing, renewal, knowledge, and joy; for the latter it is less likely to be so, since they are less likely to go into nature and explore, study, reflect, and appreciate it.

Environmental virtue is also thought to benefit its possessor by focusing her on what is truly valuable in life. This is largely the basis of Thoreau's advocacy for simplicity and temperance. For people with these traits, foregoing unnecessary material things is not likely to be regarded as a sacrifice. They will be pleased to be without the burden of them, since they are distractions that do not add to the quality of their lives. Environmentally virtuous people also are likely to find the conspicuous and disposable consumption patterns that characterize materialistic society unappealing due to their ecological impacts. (The ethics of consumption is discussed at greater length in Section 15.4). This is an instance of what might be called the **integrating effect of virtue**. Environmentally considerate behaviors often appear to require sacrifice from the perspective of a person who does not possess the relevant virtues, but from the perspective of the virtuous person they are not sacrifices at all. Many people who are environmentally committed take pleasure in the activities that it involves—for example, composting, reducing energy use, or biking to work—even as those who do not share their values or commitments (i.e., their virtues) would consider these activities to be burdensome. By emphasizing how ecological sensitivity, care and concern (and other environmental virtues) can benefit their possessor, environmental virtue ethics contributes to a positive vision for the human-nature relationship, one in which human and environmental flourishing not only coincide but are intertwined with each other (Cafaro 2001).

Another role of character ethics within environmental ethics is related to the fact that character is relevant to how a person behaves. As Leopold and Carson emphasize, how people act depends in part upon what of the world they are attentive to and how they perceive it (see Section 11.3). A person who loves and respects nature does not see a particular landscape or run of river as merely a resource for satisfying human wants and needs. She sees it as well as a place of beauty, the product of complex ecological processes, where nonhuman organisms strive to flourish. As a result she is more likely to want to maintain and protect it. An environmentally virtuous person—precisely because of her virtue—is disposed both to recognize environmental values and to respond to them appropriately. Thus, environmental virtue disposes its possessor to act according to the rules, principles, or norms of action of the corresponding environmental ethic.

Good character also is crucial to the correct application of an environmental ethic's rules and principles. In order to determine what to do in a particular case, the relevant rules need to be properly applied to that case. This requires sensitivity to the relevant contextual details to determine which rules or principles are applicable to which situations, as well as for determining what courses of action they recommend in those situations. This awareness is just what virtuous character involves. So not only does virtue dispose a person to do the right thing, it also can be crucial to identifying what is the right thing.

Although there is general agreement that character ethics is a crucial component of environmental ethics, different theories prioritize different character traits. The reason for this is that which character traits an environmental ethic recognizes or emphasizes as environmental virtues and vices depends upon the environmental values that it endorses, as well as upon the normative framework that it employs. For a utilitarian environmental ethic such as Peter Singer's (Section 8.2), on which the criterion for direct considerability is the capacity to experience pleasure and pain (Section 7.1), the virtue of compassion and the vice of cruelty are central, and a character trait is a virtue to the extent that it is conducive to promoting pleasure and the absence of pain (or interest satisfaction)—for example, considerateness and benevolence. For a deontological biocentric ethic such as Paul Taylor's (Sections 7.4 and 9.2), on which all living things are regarded as having inherent worth, the virtue of respect for nature and the vice of maleficence toward living things are central, and a character trait is a virtue to the extent that it is conducive to allowing living things to pursue their goods unconstrained by human activity—for example, restraint and wonder. On a communitarian environmental ethic such as Aldo Leopold's (Chapter 11), on which the biological community is of primary importance, the virtue of ecological sensitivity and the vice of thoughtlessness are central, and a character trait is a virtue to the extent that it promotes the health, integrity, or flourishing of the biotic community—for example, love and gratitude.

However, there are some norms of character on which theories of environmental ethics tend to converge. For example, most theories recognize hubris, indifference, apathy, greed, wastefulness, materialism, and laziness as environmental vices, and most theories recognize humility, courage, benevolence, temperance, perseverance, integrity, and wonder as virtues. The reason for this convergence is that ecological degradation tends to compromise a wide range of environmental goods and values: human health, nonhuman flourishing, ecosystem services, natural resources, recreational opportunities, biodiversity, and natural beauty. Therefore, there tends to be agreement among different types of environmental ethics—anthropocentric/nonanthropocentric, individualist/holist, and consequentialist/deontological—in support of character traits that promote ecological sustainability and against traits that foster ecological degradation. (See Box 14.4 for a discussion of convergence in environmental ethics.)

10.3 ENVIRONMENTAL VIRTUE ETHICS

Some environmental ethics consider virtue ethics to be an alternative (rather than a supplement) to utilitarian and deontological normative frameworks. The distinctive feature of a virtue ethics framework is that *how things matter* is explicated through the virtues, rather than through the enumeration of duties (deontology) or the consideration of interests (consequentialism). That is to say, the core normative content within a distinctively virtue ethics framework is provided by substantive accounts of the virtues—that is, specifying what constitutes compassion, respect, honesty, loyalty, tolerance, humility, appreciation, and so on. Right action is then determined through the virtues. Therefore, within a virtue ethics framework, virtue is not only conducive to doing the right thing or bringing about good consequences; what is appropriate responsiveness and what is right are articulated through the virtues. An action is right if it is virtuous, hits the target of virtue, or is what a virtuous person would do. Here is an example of a *virtue ethical principle of right action*:

> An action is right to the extent that it is more virtuous—that is, it better expresses or hits the targets of the operative virtues in the situation— than the other courses of action available to the agent.

Thus, the distinctive feature of a virtue ethics approach to environmental ethics is that the normative force of action-guiding prescriptions is drawn from the substance of the virtues. And a virtue ethics approach to environmental evaluation and decision-making proceeds by (1) determining which virtues are operative or applicable in the situation; and (2) determining which of the available actions or policies best expresses or accomplishes the target of the virtues taken together. On a virtue ethics approach, if a person ought not pave over her yard in order to avoid having to take care of it, the reason is not that doing so would not produce the best consequences or that it violates the moral law. The reason is that it fails to express or misses the targets of care, compassion, and ecological sensitivity, and instead expresses indifference and laziness. An action or policy is more or less justified depending upon how virtuous or vicious it is.

Consider, for example, the use of off-road vehicles (ORVs) in ecologically sensitive wilderness areas. If an ORV driver treats wilderness as a playground to be run over and through, she fails to see the natural environment and the individuals that constitute it as mattering, as well as the ways in which they are a shared common good. She may be having fun, but she is indifferent and selfish, since her activity destroys habitat, disrupts migratory patterns, and degrades alternative forms of outdoor recreation. Because there are other ways to experience and enjoy the natural world that do not diminish or degrade it, and that do not interfere with the recreation of others, the pleasure of the ORV driver is unendorsable. It is a lack of respect, ecological sensitivity, and considerateness that allows her to take pleasure in the activity. On a virtue-oriented approach to evaluation, her actions are wrong because they miss the target of virtue, hitting instead the "targets" of vice.

A common criticism of virtue ethical theories is that they are insufficiently action-guiding. Particularized to environmental ethics, the concern is that specification of environmental virtues will provide an account of what sort of dispositions one should have regarding the natural environment, and perhaps indicate the general sort of environmental behavior one should engage in, but will not provide specific guidance in concrete situations or on concrete issues. To claim that people should act in ways that express environmental virtue is not to direct them regarding what those ways are, nor is it to provide a decision-making mechanism by which agents who are not environmentally virtuous can identify them. Knowing that we should be compassionate, respectful, appreciative, and just, for example, does not tell us how to allocate a scarce environmental resource or design an ecosystem management plan.

In response to this concern, virtue ethics approaches to decision-making aim to provide resources for determining the extent to which actions or policies express or hit the target of virtue. The types of resources virtue ethicists typically appeal to include: virtue-rules (v-rules) drawn from the substantive content of the virtues; the use of mentors, models, case studies, and collaborative discourse; and moral wisdom (Hursthourse 2001).

V-rules follow from concrete specifications of particular virtues. For example, if a disposition to help alleviate the suffering of others when there is little cost to oneself is constitutive of compassion, there is a corresponding v-rule: "help alleviate the suffering of others when there is little cost to oneself." If respect for the worth of all living things is constitutive of virtue, there is a corresponding v-rule: "do not prevent living things from pursuing their good." V-rules can be taught, learned, and applied to provide action guidance by those who do not have the corresponding (i.e., virtuous) dispositions. If people can eliminate suffering by giving up meat from concentrated animal feed operations, then the compassion v-rule above indicates that they should do so (assuming that nonhuman animals are directly morally considerable, see Section 7.1). V-rules are as accessible and action-guiding within virtue ethics as rights or rules are within deontological theories and secondary principles are within utilitarian theories, according to virtue ethicists.

Virtue ethical decision-making in concrete situations therefore involves identifying which virtues are operative (or which v-rules apply), and determining what actions the applicable virtues (or v-rules) recommend. It additionally involves determining what to do in the event that different operative virtues (or v-rules) favor different courses of action. The challenges involved in these tasks are not confined to virtue theoretics.

✹ BOX 10.2	TOPIC TO CONSIDER

WHO ARE THE ENVIRONMENTAL EXEMPLARS?

Moral wisdom, as the term is used by virtue ethicists, refers to the fact that a virtuous person with experience in an area often sees things differently and better than a nonvirtuous person. She may be attentive to different details, feel differently about them, take them as having different normative force, conceptualize them differently, and orient them within different outlooks. This is why people look to the teachings and lives of ethical exemplars for guidance—Martin Luther King Jr. and Jesus, for example. They are thought to have ethical expertise from which we can learn.

Many environmental thinkers and activists are regarded as inspirational and heroic by people in the environmental and environmental justice movements—for example, Aldo Leopold, Cesar Chavez, Ken Saro-Wiwa, Wangari Maathai, Rachel Carson, Wendell Berry, Wes Jackson, and Henry David Thoreau. Do you agree that these people are environmental exemplars? If so, what is it about them and their lives that makes them worthy of our admiration? Are there character traits that they possess that help to make them exemplary?

Are there other people that you regard as environmentally virtuous or that you look to for examples or guidance? Why do you look at them in that way—what is it about them that is exemplary? These need not be famous or iconic figures. They could be people from your community, from the organizations in which you work, or from your personal life. As important as iconic figures and leaders may be, it is also important for there to be exemplars in everyday life that provide viable examples of how we can do better.

As we have seen, every normative theory's approach to decision-making must include a process for identifying which of the theory's norms are applicable, as well as for determining what the applicable norms favor both independently and all things considered (i.e., when they conflict). These are the roles of secondary principles and utility calculi within utilitarian decision-making, for example. No normative theory can eliminate the need for good situational judgment in the application of the rules and principles it endorses; and no theory can avoid the need for adjudicating complex cases. "Act virtuously" is no more difficult to operationalize and apply than is "maximize utility" or "treat everyone always as an end and never merely as a means," according to proponents of virtue ethics (Hursthouse 2001).

What resources are available within a virtue-oriented approach to assist in decision-making processes? In cases where it is difficult to identify the operative virtues (or applicable v-rules), it is unclear what they call for, or there are conflicting v-rules, many virtue ethicists advocate making use of role models, advisors, case studies, and collaborators for assistance. It is here that virtue-oriented decision-making deviates significantly from the structure of deontological and utilitarian decision-making. On a virtue-oriented approach, there is no strict hierarchy of virtues or definitive procedure that provides adjudication in each and every case—no priority principles (deontology) or utility calculus (utilitarianism). In some cases, discerning which virtues are operative and how their targets are best hit requires *moral wisdom* or sensitivity regarding the application of the virtues in particular contexts. This is not something that all people possess to the same degree, since it is developed over time through attentive experience. It does not, however, follow that those who lack moral wisdom are without resources for guidance in difficult situations. They can look to those who are morally wise as advisors, mentors, or models, and they can make use of case studies that provide information on how decisions on similar cases have worked out in the past. This is in fact something that many people often do. When unsure of what to do, they seek guidance from those whom they recognize as possessing moral wisdom in the relevant area. They ask thoughtful and experienced people that they trust for advice. They consult their own and others' past experience. They talk things through with their friends and family.

Overall, then, action guidance on a virtue ethics approach is accomplished through the application of the relevant virtues and v-rules to a concrete situation, informed by moral wisdom, the counsel of mentors, the study of models, and collaboration with others. As indicated above, virtue ethicists believe that this process reflects quite well how ethical deliberations actually proceed. It is common for people to think about what would be the honest, compassionate, or loyal thing to do in a particular situation, and to explain their actions in those or other virtue terms. It is also common for people to seek advice, talk things through with others, and pattern their behavior on those they recognize as models of ethical excellence or insight. Both religious and secular ethical traditions exhibit these features. They provide exemplars, authorities, forums, and dialogical resources to assist in deliberations on difficult cases.

✳ BOX 10.3   **EXERCISE**

APPLYING VIRTUE ETHICS

We have seen that normative theories support different approaches to decision-making. Utilitarian views focus on the outcomes of the available options. Deontological views focus on the rights and duties involved. Virtue-oriented views focus on which virtues are operative and what they call for. How would the

(cont.)

BOX 10.3 *(cont.)*

three approaches differ with respect to how they work through the following cases discussed earlier (assuming whichever account of direct moral considerability that you believe is most justified)? (1) Whether to proceed with the Muddy River Restoration Project (Box 9.2); (2) Whether to support cultural and/ or therapeutic hunting (Boxes 8.4 and 9.3); (3) Whether to engage in captive breeding programs for endangered animal species (Box 9.3); and (4) Whether to allow wild caught pets (Box 7.4).

10.4 CONCERNS REGARDING ENVIRONMENTAL VIRTUE ETHICS

While environmental ethicists and moral philosophers generally agree that character ethics is a crucial component of ethical theory and environmental practice, several prominent concerns have been raised about adopting a virtue ethics approach to environmental ethics. One concern, already considered in the prior section (10.3), is that virtue ethics decision-making resources are not robust enough to generate specific guidance in concrete cases. Virtue ethics can tell us what sort of person we ought to be in general, but not what to do in particular, according to this concern.

A second prominent concern about virtue ethics is that there is no way to provide the detailed substantive specifications of the virtues that the theory requires. As discussed earlier (Section 10.3), what is distinctive about virtue ethics is that the normative content is provided by the virtues and vices. It is through articulating what the virtues and vices are that the theory generates an account of what sort of people we ought to be and what we ought to do in concrete situations. So virtue and vice specifications are absolutely critical. However, it is often pointed out, different cultures (not to mention different people) have very different ideas about what character traits are virtues, both historically and contemporaneously. The character traits that have been valorized vary considerably among, for example, ancient Greeks, Victorians, medieval Catholics, Mahayana Buddhists, and Australian aboriginal peoples. This is an instance of the challenge from ethical disagreement—that because there is so much disagreement on ethical matters, there is no correct view on ethics. The typical responses to these concerns from proponents of virtue ethics are the same as were discussed earlier (Section 2.4): (1) it is a fallacy to infer from the fact of disagreement to the conclusion that no view is more justified than another; (2) it is possible to evaluate different specifications of virtue based on the quality of the empirical information and reasoning in support of them, as well as their consistency with other ethical beliefs. For example, Victorian accounts of feminine virtuousness—piousness, purity, submissiveness, and domesticity—are unjustified because they are based in false beliefs about women's abilities and worth, as well as on fallacious appeals to tradition, authority, and nature.

A third concern about virtue ethics is that it misplaces evaluation. Suppose that a well-off contractor is dumping hazardous substances directly into a storm drain rather than having them properly disposed of in order to save time and money. According to a virtue ethics approach to environmental ethics, what is wrong with this is that his actions are vicious; they are ecologically insensitive, reckless, lazy, and greedy. However, it strikes many that the primary problem with the action is not the character of the agent, but the consequences of his behavior or the nature of the act itself. He might lack virtue, and this in part explains why he does it, but it is still the consequences or principle violation that makes the action wrong. In response to this concern, virtue ethicists often point out that virtue involves sensitivity to context. The reason why his actions are ecologically insensitive and reckless is, in part, because of their potential ecological and human health consequences. If it were not ecologically problematic, it would not be ecologically insensitive. Moreover, his actions violate v-rules against acting in ecologically insensitive and reckless ways.

Finally, virtue ethics has been criticized by some environmental ethicists for being anthropocentric or even egoistic (Rolston 2005). The reason for this is that it is thought to prioritize virtue—and thereby the agent's own flourishing—over other people and nature. This concern typically arises in response to a particular type of virtue ethics, **eudaimonistic virtue ethics**. According to eudaimonistic virtue ethics, the virtues are character traits that *a person needs to flourish or live well*. Given this account of what makes a character trait a virtue, it seems as if what matters, ultimately, is the agent's own flourishing. Everything else is secondary, including nature and other people. In response to this concern, many proponents of eudaimonism argue that genuine concern for other people (or even members of other species) is part of living well or flourishing. That is to say, it might be part of the good human life that one *not* be egoistic or anthropocentric, and that one promote the good of others for their own sake. Moreover, other virtue ethicists have argued that virtue ethics does not need to be eudaimonistic. If all living things have inherent worth, then a character trait is a virtue to the extent that it contributes to *human and nonhuman flourishing*, not just to the agent's own flourishing (Sandler and Cafaro 2005).

10.5 EVALUATING ETHICAL THEORIES

A comprehensive theory in environmental ethic involves both a theory of value (i.e., an account of which things matter) and a normative theory (i.e., an account of how things matter). These are the basis for deriving the principles, rules, and norms that provide guidance on how we should interact with and treat the nonhuman environment. Here are a few examples. **Hedonistic utilitarianism** is the view that pleasure is good and pain is bad (both human and nonhuman), and that an action is right to the extent that it brings about the greatest balance of pleasure over pain. **Ratiocentric deontology** is the view that all and only rational beings have objective final (noninstrumental) value, therefore they should never be treated as a mere means to the ends of others. **Biocentric virtue ethics** is the view that all living things have equal inherent worth, therefore they should all be treated with care and respect. **Ecocentric communitarianism** is the view that we ought to be responsible members of the biotic community, therefore we should act in ways that protect and promote its ecological integrity and stability (Chapter 11).

Given the diversity of views on environmental values and normative frameworks, a reasonable question is: *How do you go about determining which of them is correct?* Here is a brief overview of the sorts of considerations that are appealed to in order to justify theories in environmental ethics. Each of them has already been discussed (though some will be addressed at greater length in later chapters):

1. *Quality of the reasoning in support of the view.* Environmental ethicists do not merely assert their value theories and normative theories. They give arguments, reasons, justification, and evidence in support of them. It is possible to evaluate these by assessing the quality of the premises and the reasoning or inferences involved (see Section 2.3).
2. *Internal consistency and coherence.* Ethical theories that are internally (or self-) contradictory are to be rejected; and a view that is more internally coherent is preferable to one that is less internally coherent. For example, one objection to biocentric egalitarian (and animal rights) views is that the principles the views endorse—which typically allow human beings to use living things (or animals) for their own ends if the interests at stake are serious enough—are not compatible with the biocentric egalitarian (or animal rights) value system on which all living things (or animals) have equal inherent worth (see Sections 9.2 and 9.3).
3. *Compatibility with what we know about ourselves and our world.* An ethical theory should be compatible with our best science and nonmoral philosophy. For example, many proponents of biocentrism, ecocentrism, and deep ecology argue against anthropocentric environmental ethics on the grounds that it does not cohere with an ecologically and evolutionarily informed understanding of our relationship to the biological world (see, e.g., Sections 7.4, 11.1, and 12.2).
4. *Acceptability of implications.* An ethical theory is preferable, all other things being equal, if its prescriptions in particular cases can be reconciled with (unbiased, unmanipulated, and undistorted) views regarding them. For example, one objection to hedonistic utilitarian approaches to environmental ethics is that they seem to imply that we should intervene in wild systems in order to reduce the suffering of animals—for example, feed starving animals and reduce predation—and this strikes many people as absurd (Section 8.5). One of the primary arguments against actual preference anthropocentrism is that it is inadequately critical of the practices that give rise to our most pressing environmental problems (Section 5.4).

5. *Ability to capture the human experience.* An ethical theory is preferable, all other things being equal, the better that it captures the texture of ethical discourse and practice. For example, we will see an argument next chapter for a communitarian approach to ethics on the grounds that questions about how to live emerge from the challenges associated with communal interactions (Section 11.1).

6. *Resources for providing action guidance in concrete situations.* A theory of environmental ethics is inadequate if it does not provide resources and decision-making processes that offer situational action-guidance. As discussed earlier (Sections 10.3 and 10.4), one of the primary objections to virtue ethics approaches to environmental ethics is that they do not provide adequate resources for making decisions on actions and policies.

7. *Compatibility with generally accepted deliberative principles.* An ethical theory is preferable, all other things being equal, the more compatible it is with well-established deliberative principles, such as "Like cases should be treated alike" or the law of non-contradiction. For example, extensionist arguments for the moral considerability of nonhuman animals are based on the grounds that they are like humans in all relevant respects (e.g., they are sentient or experiencing-subjects-of-a-life) so rational consistency requires extending consideration to them (Section 7.1).

8. *Explanatory power.* An ethical theory needs to explain what makes things right or wrong. For example, an objection to virtue ethics is that it inverts the proper explanatory order. An environmentally virtuous person consumes less than others because it is the right thing to do (see Sections 10.2 and 15.4), and her virtue enables her to see that and disposes her to do it. So, on this view, while it is true that a virtuous person will reliably do the right thing (i.e., virtue tracks right action), it is not the fact that a virtuous person would do something (or that it is virtuous) that makes it right. It is the fact that the action is right that explains why the virtuous person does it—that is, virtuous behavior is correlated with right action but does not explain it (see Box 5.5).

These considerations arise repeatedly in the discourse on which theories of environmental ethics are and are not well justified. How much weight to put on each of them, as well as the extent to which different theories satisfy them, will continue to be discussed in coming chapters.

How to evaluate competing ethical theories is among the most important methodological issues in moral philosophy. The process of developing a well-justified ethical theory using the sorts of considerations enumerated above is sometimes referred to as the method of **wide reflective equilibrium**. The general strategy behind this approach to ethical theorizing is to continually improve a view by adjusting it in response to considerations as they arise. For example, many consequentialists have attempted to develop views that avoid the common concerns associated with utilitarianism—for example, the near and dear, distribution, and demandingness problems—by adjusting the structure of the theory (e.g., moving to indirect consequentialism), the principle of right action (e.g., adopting satisficing consequentialism), or the value axiology (e.g., incorporating distribution as a value) to avoid them (Sections 8.4 and 8.5). Similarly, deontological environmental ethics often try to refine the rules and principles they endorse in order to avoid irresolvable conflicts and counterintuitive implications.

The basic idea behind wide reflective equilibrium is to try to always be moving toward a more sound, justified, informed, and useful ethical theory and environmental ethic. The goal is to make progress in our understanding of the ethical landscape, our ethical responsibilities and obligations, and the ways in which we ought to live and make decisions. There might be several different approaches to doing this. That is to say, there might not be *the one* singularly and absolutely correct ethical theory. Perhaps there is more than one reasonable environmental ethic, even if there are many that are unjustified and unreasonable. Perhaps the "right" deontological view, consequentialist view, and virtue ethics view will converge on similar values, rules, and principles as they are continually revised and improved in response to new information and challenges from each other.

Taking a progress-based approach to theorizing is common and does not imply skepticism or relativism. After all, it is operative in the sciences. Scientists do not believe they have a complete and perfect understanding of physics or evolution. They have a better understanding of these than they once did, but scientific theories are continually being revised and improved in light of new data, insights, models, and experiments. It would be mistaken to conclude from this that science is all subjective or a matter of opinion. The more reasonable view is that there is a lot about the physical world to try to understand, it is difficult to do, people have not been working on it very long, and our tools are limited. Nevertheless, scientists are making progress. The same may well be true with respect to ethics, ethical theory, and ethical theorists. It is difficult terrain to characterize, and people have not been working it very long—particularly with respect to environmental ethics—but progress is being made (Jamieson 2002).

10.6 SUMMARY

The primary questions addressed in this chapter were:

- What are environmental virtues and vices?
- What are the roles of character ethics in environmental ethics?
- What are the distinctive features of a virtue ethics approach to environmental ethics?
- What are the core considerations when evaluating ethical theories?

The chapter began by emphasizing the importance of virtue/vice language and concepts within environmental ethics. It then explicated what it means to say of a character trait that it is a virtue or vice and distinguished several different types of environmental virtue. The particular character traits that a theory recognizes and emphasizes as virtues depends upon its account of value and normative framework. For example, compassion is a prominent virtue within animal welfare views, while respect for nature is a prominent virtue within biocentric deontological views. Nevertheless, there are some character traits that are recognized as virtues by a wide variety of environmental ethics, since they favor sustainability and ecological integrity generally— traits like ecological sensitivity, attentiveness, humility, wonder, and simplicity.

Most environmental ethicists consider character ethics to be a crucial component of environmental ethics, since virtue disposes people toward right action and benefits its possessor. However, some environmental ethicists consider environmental virtue ethics to be an alternative to consequentialist and deontological normative theories. On these views, normative content is generated through substantive specifications of virtues and vices, and right action is defined in terms of hitting the target of virtue (or being what a virtuous person would do). Thus, on a virtue ethics view what makes something right is not that it satisfies the relevant duties or has good consequences, but that it is virtuous—compassionate, honest, courageous, or respectful. Virtue-ethical decision-making therefore involves identifying which virtues (or v-rules) are operative and determining what they call for in a particular situation, informed by moral wisdom, the counsel of mentors, the study of models, and collaboration with others. Objections to virtue ethics normative theory, as well as virtue ethicists' responses to them, were then discussed. Finally, the chapter compiled the types of considerations that are frequently appealed to when assessing theories of environmental ethics.

An environmental ethic has several components: a conception of the human-nature relationship, a value system, a normative framework, and an approach to decision-making. Each of these has now been discussed for the most prominent *individualist* approaches to environmental ethics. As we have seen, normative frameworks and moral considerability can vary independently. For example, a consequentialist normative framework can be paired with either an anthropocentric or nonanthropocentric account of whose interests matter; and a nonanthropocentric account of moral considerability can be paired with a deontological or virtue ethics normative framework. Therefore, when thinking about which environmental ethics are well justified, it is important to evaluate both competing normative theories and competing value theories. Moreover, evaluating normative theories and value axiologies can include considering the acceptability of their implications and whether they provide adequate decision-making guidance. Thus, it is not merely that the right methods of decision-making, principles, and rules follow from the most justified normative and value theories. Instead, all of them must be evaluated together. What is crucial is that, in the end, a theory of environmental ethics is theoretically sound, practically adequate, and internally coherent. Some environmental ethicists argue that an individualist theory of environmental ethics cannot accomplish these. They believe that a *holistic* or *ecocentric* approach is necessary for environmental ethics. The next several chapters focus on such theories.

KEY TERMS (SEE GLOSSARY FOR DEFINITIONS):

character ethics	moral wisdom
character traits	virtue
character virtue	virtue ethics
environmental virtue	virtue-oriented normative theories
eudaimonistic virtue ethics	virtue theory
hedonistic utilitarianism	wide reflective equilibrium
integrating effect of virtue	

REVIEW QUESTIONS

- What is a character trait? What makes a character trait a virtue?
- What are the different ways in which environmental considerations relate to virtue—that is, what are the different types of environmental virtues?
- Why is character ethics considered to be important to environmental ethics?
- Why is being environmentally virtuous thought to be beneficial to a person?
- What is the virtue ethics approach to environmental decision-making, and how does it differ from the approaches associated with consequentialism and deontology?
- Why are substantive specifications of virtues and vices so crucial to a virtue ethics normative theory?
- What are the criteria for evaluating competing ethical theories?

DISCUSSION QUESTIONS

- Do you agree that character ethics is crucial for environmental ethics and that environmental virtue benefits its possessor?
- What character traits do you believe are particularly vital environmental virtues? What traits do you believe are particularly problematic environmental vices?
- Do you think that the virtue ethics approach to decision-making is sufficient for providing action guidance?
- Do you think that any of the criteria for evaluating ethical theories are more important than others? Are any less important?
- Which of consequentialism, deontology, and virtue ethics do you believe to be the more justified normative theory? What are your reasons?

FURTHER READING

Recent work on environmental virtues and vices, as well as the role of character ethics within environmental ethics includes:

Cafaro, Philip. *Thoreau's Living Ethics: Walden and Pursuit of Virtue.* University of Georgia Press, 2006.

Cafaro, Philip, and Ronald Sandler, eds. *Virtue Ethics and the Environment.* Springer, 2011. (Also available in the *Journal of Agricultural and Environmental Ethics* 23, no. 3 [2010].)

Sandler, Ronald, and Philip Cafaro, eds. *Environmental Virtue Ethics.* Rowman and Littlefield, 2005.

Sandler, Ronald. *Character and Environment: A Virtue-Oriented Approach to Environmental Ethics.* Columbia University Press, 2007.

Thompson, Allen, and Jeremy Bendik-Keymer, eds. *Ethical Adaptation to Climate Change: Human Virtues of the Future.* MIT Press, 2012.

Treanor, Brian. *Emplotting Virtue: A Narrative Approach to Environmental Virtue Ethics.* SUNY Press, 2014.

Van Wensveen, Louke. *Dirty Virtues: The Emergence of Ecological Virtue Ethics.* Humanity, 1999.

Influential work on virtue ethical theory generally includes:

Aristotle. *Nicomachean Ethics.* Harvard University Press, 1985.

Hursthouse, Rosalind. *On Virtue Ethics.* Oxford University Press, 1999.

Swanton, Christine. *Virtue Ethics: A Pluralistic View.* Oxford University Press, 2003.

PART V: HOLISTIC ENVIRONMENTAL ETHICS

CHAPTER ELEVEN

ECOCENTRISM

IN 1973, RICHARD SYLVAN delivered an influential paper at the World Congress of Philosophy titled "Is There a Need for a New, an Environmental, Ethic?" The paper begins from the premise that ethical thinking about the environment, particularly within affluent industrialized societies, is inadequate. The evidence for this is the wide range of very serious environmental problems that humanity faces. Western ethical traditions simply had not provided sufficient guidance on how to conserve resources, limit pollution, maintain ecosystems, preserve species, and protect people from environmental hazards in the industrial age. The question that Sylvan's paper poses is whether it is possible to develop an adequate environmental ethic, one that could provide effective guidance, from ethical theories in the Western tradition, or whether a new theory is needed.

In thinking about this question, Sylvan considers the predominant view to be that the nonhuman environment is a resource to be used for human ends (see, e.g., Section 5.4 and Box 5.4). As we have seen, some environmental ethicists argue that it is possible to develop an adequate ethic with this basic structure, so long as all the ways in which people depend upon the environment are fully considered and the interests and rights of all people (present and future) are taken into account. According to this **enlightened anthropocentrism** view, the problem is not the theory, but its implementation, particularly since the Industrial Revolution (Chapter 6). We are too narrowly focused, short-sighted, and misinformed about how we need to treat the nonhuman environment in order to advance human flourishing and protect human rights and values given the power of modern technology, rapid population growth, and globalization.

242

Other environmental ethicists argue that the problem is not only that we fail to use resources and treat the environment in the ways that would best protect human rights, satisfy human interests, and promote human values. We also fail to appreciate the claims of nonhuman interests and human-independent values. According to this view, part of the problem is what Sylvan calls "basic (human) chauvinism . . . [that] humans, or people, come first and everything else a bad last" (1973, 207). Those who hold this view defend **nonanthropocentric** environmental ethics—accounts of direct moral considerability that extend to nonhuman animals and plants and/or the objectivity of natural and aesthetic values. They believe that only by articulating and responding to these values can we recognize and fulfill our full range of duties and responsibilities regarding the environment (Chapter 7).

Still other environmental ethicists argue that the problem is not only that we are using resources inefficiently and that we are not adequately considering the worth of nonhuman plants and animals, but that our ethics are overly individualistic. We are too concerned with satisfying individual preferences and interests, rather than protecting and promoting the communal good. We are too concerned about the welfare of individual animals, rather than the condition of their populations or species. According to this view, when it comes to environmental ethics, we need to prioritize what is best for the biotic community as a whole. What is important is that species persist and that ecosystems are healthy, which sometimes requires compromising the good of individuals—for instance, culling overpopulated animals and capturing endangered ones for breeding programs. Moreover, the value of individuals should be understood as derivative on their relationship to the health of the system. For example, we should reintroduce native predators because they are crucial to population regulation, but we should eliminate invasive ones because they diminish native biodiversity. This view, which is typically referred to as **ecocentrism** or **holism**, is the focus of the next three chapters. In this and the next chapter I discuss the two most prominent holistic theories: the **land ethic** and **deep ecology**. In the subsequent chapter, I discuss the view that species and biodiversity have value or are morally considerable above and beyond the individuals that constitute them.

11.1 THE ARGUMENT FOR THE LAND ETHIC

Aldo Leopold is the most historically influential advocate of ecocentrism. Leopold was born in the United States in the late 1880s, earned a degree in forestry, and then joined the newly established US Forest Service, which managed the national forests primarily in order to ensure a reliable supply of timber for expansion and development. The first chief of the forest service was Gifford Pinchot (see Box 5.1), who believed that "[t]he central idea of a Forester, in handling the forest, is to promote its greatest use to men. His purpose is to make it serve the greatest good of the greatest number for the longest time" (1914, 23).

When Leopold began working in the forest service he shared Pinchot's anthropocentric utilitarianism. He specialized in managing wildlife, and at that time managing wildlife for "its greatest use to men" meant eliminating predators so that they did not harass livestock, threaten people, or take game away from hunters. However, Leopold's experiences would lead him to change his perspective, not only about predators but also about how to approach ecosystem management:

> My own conviction on this score dates from the day I saw a wolf die. We were eating lunch on a high rimrock, at the foot of which a turbulent river elbowed its way. We saw what we thought was a doe fording the torrent, her breast awash in white water. When she climbed the bank toward us and shook out her tail, we realized our error: It was a wolf. A half-dozen others, evidently grown pups, sprang from the willows and all joined in a welcoming melee of wagging tails and playful maulings. What was literally a pile of wolves writhed and tumbled in the center of an open flat at the foot of our rimrock.
>
> In those days we had never heard of passing up a chance to kill a wolf. In a second we were pumping lead into the pack, but with more excitement than accuracy: how to aim a steep downhill shot is always confusing. When our rifles were empty, the old wolf was down, and a pup was dragging a leg into impassable slide-rocks.
>
> We reached the old wolf in time to watch a fierce green fire dying in her eyes. I realized then, and have known ever since, that there was something new to me in those eyes—something known only to her and to the mountain. I was young then, and full of trigger-itch; I thought that because fewer wolves meant more deer, that no wolves would mean hunters' paradise. But after seeing the green fire die, I sensed that neither the wolf nor the mountain agreed with such a view.
>
> Since then I have lived to see state after state extirpate its wolves. I have watched the face of many a newly wolfless mountain, and seen the south-facing slopes wrinkle with a maze of new deer trails. I have seen every edible bush and seedling browsed, first to anemic desuetude, and then to death. I have seen every edible tree defoliated to the height of a saddlehorn. . . .
>
> I now suspect that just as a deer herd lives in mortal fear of its wolves, so does a mountain live in mortal fear of its deer. And perhaps with better cause, for while a buck pulled down by wolves can be replaced in two or three years, a range pulled down by too many deer may fail of replacement in as many decades. (1949/1968, 129–32)

In this passage Leopold is not moved to revise his view about extirpating predators by the suffering of the individual animals, but by the way in which their absence has complex, cascading, and detrimental effects throughout the rest of the system. His realization is that these mountain ecosystems require wolves to be healthy.

At the same time that Leopold was working in the forest service, and later as the first professor of game management in the country, the field of ecology was developing into a scientifically rigorous discipline. Leopold documented, through his professional and public writings, the impact that his experiences and growing ecological understanding had on his thinking about ecosystem management. He came to see the relationship between people and the land as not only an economic one but also a moral one; and he came to view the health of the system as a whole as being prior in importance to that of its individual parts. This is the basis for what would come to be known as his **land ethic**: "A thing is right when it tends to preserve the integrity, stability, and beauty of the biotic community. It is wrong if it tends otherwise" (1949/1968, 224–25).

⚘ BOX 11.1   **TOPIC TO CONSIDER**

THE STATE OF WOLVES

There are three species of wolves in the world, the red wolf, Ethiopian wolf, and gray wolf. (There is currently some scientific debate about whether the gray wolf population in the United States is actually two distinct species, the gray wolf and the eastern wolf.)

Red wolves are listed as "critically endangered" by the International Union for the Conservation of Nature (IUCN). They once ranged throughout the southeastern and mideastern United States, and perhaps into eastern Canada. However, by 1980 they were extinct in the wild due largely to hunting, habitat loss, and hybridization with coyotes (though it is possible that there is a remnant population in far eastern Canada). There is now a reintroduced population of red wolves of a few hundred individuals in North Carolina, as well as a captive population of similar size. Human-induced mortality (e.g., hunting and car collisions), disease, predation, and hybridization are the greatest threats to the wild population.

Ethiopian wolves, which are endemic to the Ethiopian highlands, are listed as "Endangered" by the IUCN. There are currently less than five hundred individuals remaining in isolated populations in the wild, at least one of which is functionally extinct. Ethiopian wolf numbers continue to decline, largely due to habitat encroachment for herding and diseases, such as rabies and distemper, which were transferred into their populations from free-ranging dogs.

Gray wolves once ranged nearly the entirety of the northern hemisphere and were "the world's most widely distributed mammal" (IUCN 2016). They remain widespread, particularly in northern North America, eastern Europe, and Asia, although their range has been reduced by about a third. The species is

(cont.)

BOX 11.1 *(cont.)*

Image 11.1   The Leopold wolf pack hunting two elk in Yellowstone National Park, USA. The pack was one of the first to form after wolves were reintroduced into the park.
Source : National Park Service

listed as "least concern" for extinction by the IUCN. This is a change in status from the early 1970s when it was classified as "vulnerable" because its population was shrinking due primarily to habitat loss and deliberate targeting by humans. Legal protections, land use changes, and rural-to-urban migration contributed to arresting its population declines. There have been a few gray wolf reintroductions—in Yellowstone National Park, USA, for instance—but most of the gray wolf recovery has been through recolonization.

Although the species as a whole is not endangered, many local populations are at risk. For example, in the United States, the gray wolf is protected under the Endangered Species Act (ESA) in the Northeast (where there is no confirmed breeding population), California, Arizona, and New Mexico, where there is a Mexican gray wolf population of ~100 individuals. However, it has been federally delisted, due to increased numbers, in Montana, Idaho, and parts of Washington, Oregon, and Utah. At the time of writing the gray wolf's status in Wyoming and the western Great Lakes region (Wisconsin, Minnesota, and Michigan) is being contested. It had been delisted, but was then relisted by court order. The US Fish and Wildlife Service estimates that there are now at least 5,500 wolves in the contiguous United States. Gray wolves never have been protected under the

(cont.)

BOX 11.1 *(cont.)*

ESA in Alaska, where the population is estimated to be ~7,000–11,000. Human impacts—from, for example, hunting, car collisions, and habitat fragmentation—remain the greatest threat to gray wolves in the United States. Several states now have permitted wolf hunting—including Alaska, Idaho, and Montana.

Do you believe that protections for wolves should be lifted if their populations are sufficiently robust? Or should they be kept in place to ensure that they remain stable? Is it permissible to hunt wolves? If so, for what reasons and under what circumstances? If not, why not?

Leopold did not so much argue for the land ethic as try to motivate it through narratives, case studies, examples, and ecological science. However, it is possible to formalize his reasoning in support of it. Here is the core argumentative structure:

1. Morality (or ethics) concerns how we ought to act as members of the communities of which we are part.
2. Human beings are "plain members and citizens" of the biotic community (i.e., the land).
3. The biotic community can and should be regarded as a moral (or ethical) community.
   _____
4. Therefore, we ought to behave as good members of the biotic community. (From 1–3)
5. Being a good member of a community involves not disrupting, degrading, or destroying it.
   _____
6. Therefore, we ought to act in ways that "preserve the integrity, stability, and beauty of the biotic community." (From 4–5)

In what follows, I present Leopold's thinking behind each of these premises, drawing heavily on passages from his seminal work, *A Sand County Almanac*.

The first premise of the argument expresses a **communitarian conception of ethics**. On Leopold's view, questions about ethics, about how to behave, only arise in a community context. It is when people realize they are part of a community that they must begin to think about whether and how to moderate pursuit of their own desires and self-interest out of respect for the community and others in it:

An ethic, ecologically, is a limitation on freedom of action in the struggle for existence. An ethic, philosophically, is a differentiation of social from antisocial conduct. These are two definitions of one thing. The thing has its origin in the tendency of interdependent individuals or groups to evolve modes of cooperation. The ecologist calls these symbioses. Politics and economics are advanced symbioses in which the original free-for-all competition has been replaced, in part, by cooperative mechanisms with an ethical content. . . .

All ethics so far evolved rest upon a single premise: that the individual is a member of a community of interdependent parts. His instincts prompt him to compete for his place in that community, but his ethics prompt him also to cooperate (perhaps in order that there may be a place to compete for) (1949/1968, 202–204).

On this view, an individual who is not part of a community is not confronted with questions of right and wrong. They can pursue their self-interest without restraint. It is only when they come into a community, into relationships with others, that questions about how to cooperate and how to moderate their actions even make sense. Ethics concerns how to act as a member of a community, because questions about how we ought to behave only arise in a community context.

Leopold believes that the second premise—that human beings are members of the biotic community—follows from a scientifically informed worldview. The considerations that he appeals to in support of it are largely the same as those that Taylor emphasized in his defense of the biocentric outlook (Section 7.4): that human beings, like all other species, are interconnected with and interdependent upon ecological systems; that we cannot survive or thrive without the many goods (soil, water, energy, protection, materials) that ecological systems provide; that our activities significantly impact ecological systems and the organisms that constitute them; and that human systems (e.g., agricultural and economic) are in constant energy, material, and nutrient exchanges with ecological systems. Because of this, it is contrary to the ecological facts to regard ourselves, and human practices and institutions, as distinct from or outside of ecological systems. We are part of the biotic community.

Leopold believes that the second premise is also supported by the role that ecological considerations and events play in human history:

That man is, in fact, only a member of a biotic team is shown by an ecological interpretation of history. Many historical events, hitherto explained solely in terms of human enterprise, were actually biotic interactions between people and land. The characteristics of the land determined the facts quite as potently as the characteristics of the men who lived on it. (1949/1968, 205)

There are myriad examples of what Leopold is referring to here. Human migrations have been driven by food scarcity associated with droughts and climatic change, as well as by extreme weather and geological events. Societies have grown wealthy or expanded due to the natural resources at their disposal—from trees for ships to soil for agriculture—and they have fallen due to overexploitation of resources. Moreover, most cultural practices are explained, in part, by the ecological contexts in which they developed. The reason that small island peoples developed fishing- and ocean-oriented foodways, while grassland peoples developed herding- and hunting-oriented ones is so obvious that it almost goes without saying: their ecological contexts. The same holds for their technologies, rituals, stories, and social organization. Cultural practices and cultural differences are explained, in large part, by ecological considerations. Culture and environment are intertwined.

Leopold considers the third premise—that we can and should regard the biotic community as a moral community—to be an "evolutionary possibility and an ecological necessity" (1949/1968, 203). He views the history of ethics as involving expansion of the ethical community over time. People have come to realize that everyone—regardless of their sex, race, or wealth—is part of the moral community and worthy of respect. It is for this reason that we cannot treat other people as mere property to be bought, used, sold, and disposed of in whatever way is most expedient. This was not always the case. Slavery has been (and too often still is) widely practiced. Women have been (and too often still are) politically disempowered, unable to own property, and "given" for dowry. Wealth and land-ownership have been (and too often still are) qualifications for political participation. However, in more and more places, these exclusions are recognized as unacceptable, both legally and in practice. The ethical community has been and continues to be expanding.

Leopold argues that expansion of the ethical community can and should be extended to the land. "The land ethic simply enlarges the boundaries of the community to include soils, waters, plants, and animals, or collectively: the land" (1949/1968, 204). That the land can be recognized as part of the ethical community is established, in Leopold's view, by the fact that we are capable of conceiving of our relationship to it as a moral one and not only an economic one. We can value the integrity, stability, and beauty of the biotic community, and not only the natural resources and ecosystem services that it provides. We can regard ourselves as having responsibilities to the land, and not only to the people who make use of it. Given that it is possible to recognize the land as part of the ethical community, the question becomes whether we ought to regard it this way. Leopold believes that we should, that it is an "ecological necessity," because economically-oriented conservation has not effectively arrested the exploitation and despoliation of ecological systems or the unsustainable depletion of environmental goods. In his view, the only thing that can is coming to see the land as part of our community:

> Conservation is getting nowhere because it is incompatible with our Abrahamic concept of land. We abuse land because we regard it as a commodity belonging to us. When we see land as a community to which we belong, we may begin to use it with love and respect. There is no

other way for the land to survive the impact of mechanized man, nor
for us to reap from it the esthetic harvest it is capable, under science, of
contributing to culture.

That land is a community is the basic concept of ecology, but that
land is to be loved and respected is an extension of ethics. (1949/1968,
viii-ix)

Thus, in Leopold's view, the key to environmental ethics is to take up a proper
ecologically-informed perspective, revise the way in which we conceive of our relationship to the land, and thereby develop an "ecological conscience" (1949/1968, 207–10).
When we do this, we will see ourselves, as we should, not as masters of the biotic
community, but as members of it with responsibilities to it. This is Premise 4 of the
argument:

In short, a land ethic changes the role of *Homo sapiens* from conqueror
of the land-community to plain member and citizen of it. It implies
respect for his fellow members, and also respect for the community as
such. (1949/1968, 204)

Once we conceptualize ourselves as ethically responsible members of the biotic
community, the question becomes how to be a good member of the community. Leopold
holds the view that being a good member of a community involves, at a minimum,
not disrupting or destroying it (Premise 5). After all, this is how we distinguish social
from antisocial conduct in human communities. For ecosystems, not being disruptive
means not undermining its health and good-functioning, understood in ecological
terms—for example, refraining from engaging in activities that decrease its resistance
and resilience to stressors, and not modifying its structure or the energy flows through
the system. This, then, is the land ethic:

A thing is right when it tends to preserve the integrity, stability, and
beauty of the biotic community. It is wrong when it tends otherwise.
(1949/1968, 224–25)

Pollution, habitat destruction, anthropogenic climate change, biological depletion, and invasive species disrupt the processes, populations, and relationships that
comprise ecosystems. Therefore, they are wrong according to the land ethic. In contrast, pollution mitigation, ecological restoration, and creation of land and marine
reserves protect and promote ecological stability and integrity, and for this reason are
right. This holistic way of thinking about environmental problems and approaching
environmental decision-making differs significantly from an individualist one. Rather
than trying to determine how a prospective action or policy would affect morally

considerable individuals and then making a decision on that basis, Leopold believes we should focus instead on how it will affect the *biotic community as a whole*. This is why the land ethic is regarded as *ecocentric*. We should care more about whether there is a healthy wolf population to prevent the deer population from overrunning the ecosystem, than about the well-being of individual wolves and deer.

Although ostensibly a "land ethic," the considerations and reasoning Leopold appeals to in support of the ethic apply as much to marine systems as to terrestrial ones. Human systems are interconnected and interdependent with aquatic ecosystems. For example, 15 percent to 20 percent of the animal protein consumed globally is from aquatic animals and a tenth of the world's population depends upon fisheries for their livelihood or well-being (FAO 2014). Oceans and aquatic ecosystems perform numerous services on which human beings and virtually all other species depend, such as carbon absorption, temperature regulation, hydrological balancing, resource provision, and nutrient cycling. Moreover, the combination of industrialization, commodification, narrow economic self-interest, and population and consumption growth that Leopold believes drives the degradation of the land is doing so as well to the oceans. Ninety percent of the world's fisheries are fully or overexploited. Plastic waste is accumulating at both astonishing large and astonishingly small scales (e.g., the great Pacific garbage patch and microplastics). Industrial fishing practices destroy aquatic habitats and cause massive biological depletion of both target and nontarget species. Large hypoxic dead zones are created by nutrient overloading from agriculture. The oceans are acidifying from the buildup of carbon dioxide in climatic systems, which could result in the collapse of crucial coral ecosystems. Therefore, in what follows, the "land ethic" is also taken to be a "sea ethic."

✳ BOX 11.2

AN ALTERNATIVE INTERPRETATION: PRAGMATIC HOLISM

The standard interpretation of the land ethic is the communitarian one presented above. However, there is an alternative on which it is understood as a form of enlightened anthropocentrism (Norton 1991). According to this reading, the land ethic is anthropocentric in the sense that human beings are ultimately important. However, the best way to promote human interests and protect what people value about the environment overall and in the long run—not just with respect to immediate economic interests—is by ensuring that the integrity and stability of the biotic community is maintained.

(cont.)

BOX 11.2 *(cont.)*

On this interpretation, the land ethic is an instance of **pragmatic holism**. According to pragmatic holism, we should approach environmental issues from a holistic or ecocentric perspective, but only because that is the best way to serve the interests of morally considerable individuals. Pragmatic holism takes the moral considerability of individuals to be the basis for environmental ethics—that is, it is individualist at the value level—but advocates holistic thinking at the decision-making level. Paul Taylor, for example, advocates pragmatic holism in situations where it is not possible to account for the interests of all living things individually. He is a biocentrically justified pragmatic holist in those cases. According to this interpretation of the land ethic, Leopold is an enlightened anthropocentric pragmatic holist. We should follow the land ethic and act in ways that promote the integrity and stability of the biotic community, because doing so best protects the land's aesthetic, cultural, spiritual, and economic value. The land ethic is a secondary principle for enlightened anthropocentrism, on this view.

Whereas proponents of the standard interpretation emphasize the passages in which Leopold reflects on the communal nature of ethics and our relationship with the land, proponents of the alternative interpretation emphasize those in which Leopold connects ecological integrity with the preservation of cultural, aesthetic, spiritual, moral, recreational, economic, and other human-oriented values. It is possible that Leopold did not prioritize one or the other. He might have believed that we should promote the integrity, stability, and beauty of the biotic community because we have a responsibility to the biotic community as plain members and citizens of it *and* because doing so best serves human interests overall and in the long run.

11.2 IMPLICATIONS OF THE LAND ETHIC

It is possible to apply the land ethic to evaluate projects, policies, and practices by asking whether they will promote or undermine ecological integrity and stability in comparison with the alternatives. For example, based on their ecological impacts, the land ethic would oppose industrial trawling (Section 6.1.3), permitting pet cats from roaming outside (Box 3.2), and concentrated cattle feed operations (Section 6.1.1). It would favor the Elwha river dam removal (Box 4.5), Chesapeake Bay restoration project (Box 4.5), water allocations to sustain riparian systems (Box 1.1), and aggressive mitigation of greenhouse gas emissions (Section 2.3).

The land ethic is thought to favor species conservation and native species prioritization on the grounds that biodiversity contributes to the integrity of ecological systems.

It may not be entirely clear to us why a particular species of plant or insect is ecologically significant, and it may be that a species of vine or beetle taken in isolation is not. Nevertheless, when too many species are lost from a system it becomes less stable and robust. There is not enough ecological redundancy (i.e., multiple species that can play a particular functional role), role adaptability (i.e., capacity for species to develop into new roles), or evolutionary rapidity (i.e., capacity for new species to quickly evolve to fill empty roles) to compensate for sustained species losses significantly above normal historical rates. Therefore, the land ethic is associated with aggressive efforts in support of native species conservation, as well as against nonnative species that are or might become invasive. (Biodiversity and species conservation are discussed at length in Chapter 13.)

The land ethic's support for species conservation includes maintaining healthy populations of apex predators, since eliminating them from an ecological system often has cascading effects through the system. For example, wolves were extirpated in Yellowstone National Park in the 1920s. Their absence resulted in larger elk populations that were able to graze undisturbed for long periods. This led to extremely low survival rates for sprouts of aspen trees, cottonwoods, and willows, which over time significantly reduced nesting habitat for songbirds. It also led to a decrease in the beaver population, which in turn reduced fish and waterfowl populations in some areas. The absence of wolves also enabled a larger coyote population, which was detrimental to the red fox population because it reduced the availability of small prey. Since the reintroduction of wolves in the 1990s, elk and coyote populations have declined, while aspen, cottonwood, willow, songbird, beaver and red fox populations have recovered. Similarly, a decline in sea otter populations on the Pacific Coast of the United States has contributed to an overpopulation of sea urchins that has decimated kelp forest ecosystems and reduced the abundance of species who depend upon them (see Images 4.4). Large herbivores—such as elephants, tapirs, gorillas, deer, bovine, and rhinoceros—are similarly ecologically important. As with predators, a high percentage of them (~60 percent) are threatened or endangered, and their loss often impacts not only other species in the system but also "processes involving vegetation, hydrology, nutrient cycling, and fire regimes" (Ripple et al. 2015, para. 1). Therefore, the land ethic justifies prioritizing their conservation as well.

The land ethic generally supports the creation of parks, reserves, marine sanctuaries, no-take zones, and wildlife corridors, since these are conducive to protecting ecological integrity by restricting anthropogenic activities and impacts. Protecting large intact areas is also often crucial for maintaining healthy populations of apex predators and large herbivores. Moreover, many animals—such as pronghorn sheep, wildebeest, monarch butterflies, warblers, humpback whales, and great white sharks—migrate over both short and long distances, and their entire range (or all of their stopovers and breeding and feeding grounds) needs to be accessible to them. Therefore, the land ethic favors avoiding fragmentation of habitats through development, agriculture, industry, and road-building. It also requires coordinated management across political jurisdictions, since ecological systems and nonhuman populations do not map onto or adhere to human created political boundaries.

The land ethic is also strongly antipollution. Air, water, and soil are part of the land, and they are crucial to the health of organisms and the functioning of ecological systems. Therefore, the land ethic favors restricting industrial emissions, particularly when they are untreated; reducing the runoff of synthetic fertilizers, pesticides, and herbicides in agriculture; eliminating waste disposal in the oceans; and remediating pollutants that are already in the environment. It also favors reducing the risks associated with industrial activities, such as oil, gas, and mineral extraction, particularly when they are in ecologically sensitive areas.

An implication of the considerations above is that the land ethic calls for moderating individual consumption (among affluent people) and slowing population growth, since these are what drive increases in greenhouse gas emissions, habitat destruction, generation of industrial waste, and unsustainable use of resources:

> [O]ur bigger-and-better society is now like a hypochondriac, so obsessed with its own economic health as to have lost the capacity to remain healthy. The whole world is so greedy for more bathtubs that it has lost the stability necessary to build them, or even to turn off the tap. Nothing could be more salutary at this stage than a little healthy contempt for a plethora of material blessings. (1949/1968, ix)

Leopold, like many environmental ethicists, has two concerns. One is that economic expansion and population growth results in inadequate space are resources for other species and intact ecological systems. The second is that it is not possible to continue to increase human population and per capita consumption without undermining the resource base required to support societal "health" and human well-being.

✳ BOX 11.3   EXERCISE

APPLYING THE LAND ETHIC

(1) *Santa Cruz Island*: Santa Cruz Island is an island roughly the size of Manhattan in Channel Island National Park off the coast of California. Santa Cruz Island has the largest population of the island fox, which is found only on the channel islands and is one of the smallest canid species in the world (see Image 9.2). In the 1990s, the population of island fox plummeted from several thousand (spread over the islands) to a few hundred. The primary cause of the decline was predation from golden eagles. Golden eagles historically had been deterred from settling on the islands by a resident bald eagle population. However, the bald eagle population was decimated by

(cont.)

BOX 11.3 *(cont.)*

DDT exposure. (DDT is a synthetic pesticide used in agriculture and to control mosquitos. It was banned in the United States in 1972. When ingested in sufficient quantities by birds it causes them to produce eggshells that are thin and brittle, which results in cracking and reproductive failure.) Golden eagles were attracted to settle on the islands by the presence of the foxes as well as a large feral pig population. Pigs, along with sheep, had been introduced onto the islands in the mid-1800s. Golden eagles preyed on piglets as well as foxes (particularly after the pigs had been eliminated on some of the other islands). Thus, by the early 2000s, the situation on Santa Cruz Island was this: An introduced feral pig population (which was detrimentally impacting endemic plant species), was the largest remaining food source for a golden eagle population (whose presence was enabled by the anthropogenic demise of a bald eagle population), which was the prime threat to an endangered fox population. In response, the Nature Conservancy, US Fish and Wildlife Service, and California Department of Fish and Game proposed the following: (1) capturing, breeding, and reintroducing island foxes; (2) capturing and relocating golden eagles; (3) reintroducing bald eagles; (4) exterminating over five thousand feral pigs (the feral goat population had been culled previously to protect the native vegetation).

Would the land ethic support this plan? Why or why not? What about some of the other views that have been discussed—for example, Taylor's biocentric individualism and Regan's deontological sentientism? Do you believe that the plan—both its goals and its means—was well justified? This is a complex case because there are so many potentially relevant considerations involved—disturbance by humans, ecological integrity, restoration, endangered species, animal welfare, and therapeutic hunting. Therefore, sorting out what should have been done requires determining which values are most salient in this context, as well as applying the principles that those values support.

(2) *Ecology Field Experiments.* Ecologists frequently conduct controlled field experiments. In some cases, the experiments involve intentionally damaging small systems or populations in order to study how they respond. Here are three examples:

- Island biogeography theory hypothesizes that the number of species (**species richness**) on an island reaches an equilibrium based largely on the size of the island and its distance from the mainland (or the

(cont.)

BOX 11.3 *(cont.)*

source from which species immigrate to the island). In the 1960s, E. O. Wilson and David Simberloff conducted an experiment to test this hypothesis as well as to study colonization processes. They covered six small mangrove islands off the coast of Florida in plastic sheeting and fumigated them with methyl bromide to kill all the terrestrial arthropod species (insects). They then monitored colonization of the island at regular intervals over the following year and documented the colonization process. Their findings largely confirmed the dynamic equilibrium hypothesis and substantially contributed to understanding the underlying processes that generate it (Simberloff and Wilson 1969).

- In Ontario, Canada, there is an experimental lakes area in which fifty-eight formerly pristine freshwater lakes and their watersheds are used to study how different stressors affect aquatic systems. For example, in the 1970s researchers added sulfuric acid to the lakes in order to test the hypothesis that acid rain caused by sulfur dioxide and nitrogen emissions from coal-burning power plants could cause fish populations to decline. The added sulfuric acid resulted in the collapse of fish populations in the lake, thereby confirming the hypothesis. The lakes have also been used to study the relationship between phosphorous, nitrogen, and algal blooms; the impact of endocrine disruptors on fish reproduction; and the effects of aquaculture and pollutants (e.g., mercury and nanosilver) on lake ecosystems (IISD 2015).

- In order to study the population regulation mechanisms of migrating birds, researchers reduced nesting density by culling (killing) ~60 black-throated blue warblers within a healthy population. In response to lower population densities, the warblers fledged a greater number of young and maintained significantly larger territories. The researchers concluded that crowding functions as a regulatory mechanism for the population (Rodenhouse et al. 2003).

Would the land ethic endorse these ecological experiments? Why or why not? How would some of the other views that we have studied evaluate them—for example, Singer's utilitarian sentientism and Taylor's biocentrism individualism? What sorts of considerations do you believe are relevant to evaluating when, if ever, it is permissible to conduct ecological field research that harms individuals, populations, or ecosystems? Given those considerations, would you support these research projects? In what respects, if any, are the experiments ethically different from each other?

11.3 MORAL DEVELOPMENT AND OUTDOOR RECREATION

A consistent theme throughout *A Sand County Almanac* is the need for people to develop proper perspective on the human-nature relationship. In Leopold's view, the "key-log" to beginning to treat the land with "love and respect" is to see it as a moral community to which we belong. Like Carson, Leopold believed that learning about the natural world and experiencing it firsthand are crucial to the development of an "ecological conscience." People must get out into the woods and onto the water. But they must do so in ways that improve their awareness and understanding.

> To promote perception is the only truly creative part of recreational engineering. . . . The only true development in American recreational resources is the development of the perceptive faculty in Americans. (1949/1968, 173–74)

Leopold was particularly worried about people approaching outdoor experiences as consumers. For example, driving (or being guided) into wildlife parks and "wilderness" areas to collect a trophy—a photograph, fish, deer, or peak; using whatever techno-gadgets make it easiest—GPS, fish-finders, bird identifiers, and off-road vehicles; then returning to lodges and campsites with all the amenities to which they are accustomed—toilets, running water, and wifi. In his view, this approach to outdoor recreation undermines what is particularly distinctive and valuable about being in wilderness. The experience of being away from civilization and the patient (and often unsuccessful) process of accomplishing your aims in ways that involve knowledge of the natural world and skill developed through practice.

> The pleasure . . . is, or should be, in the seeking as well as in the getting. The trophy, whether it be a bird's egg, a mess of trout, a basket of mushrooms, the photograph of a bear, the pressed specimen of a wild flower, or a note tucked into the cairn on a mount peak, is a *certificate*. It attests that its owner has been somewhere and done something—that he has exercised skill, persistence, or discrimination in the age-old feat of overcoming, outwitting, or reducing-to-possession. (1948/1969, 168–69)

Leopold is also concerned about the ways in which consumer-oriented outdoor recreation degrades ecological systems and experiences. If roads and tour guides make it easier for more and more "trophy-recreationists" to access an area, the ecological integrity and recreational value will be diminished. The fish stocks will be reduced, the flora and fauna will be disturbed and become scare, the garbage and waste will accumulate, there will be less quiet solitude and communion with nature, and there will be fewer opportunities to develop knowledge, skill, appreciation, and character.

It would appear, in short, that the rudimentary grades of outdoor recreation consume their resource-base; the higher grades, at least to a degree, create their own satisfactions with little or no attrition on the land or life. It is the expansion of transport without a corresponding growth of perception that threatens us with qualitative bankruptcy of the recreational process. Recreational development is a job not of building roads into lovely country, but of building receptivity into the still unlovely human mind. (1949/1968, 176–77)

Leopold is not opposed to people visiting wilderness areas. He does not subscribe to a strong human/nature dichotomy or hold the view that any human presence defiles the purity of nature (Box 3.1). He believes that people should interact with nature, but that it ought to be done in ways that foster rather than undermine ecological integrity and appreciation of the natural world. It should promote environmental knowledge and virtues, such as ecological sensitivity, sportsmanship, love, and respect. Off-road vehicle tours, wildlife cruises, luxury "wilderness" accommodations, killing predators to increase game, outdoor gadgetry, and paved roads do not do this, in his view. Instead, they commodify nature and reduce nature experiences to a variety of commercial transaction. They undermine their own resource base and are detrimental to ecosystem health. They also diminish the experiences of others: "Mechanized recreation already has seized nine-tenths of the woods and mountains; a decent respect for minorities should dedicate the other tenth to wilderness" (1949/1968, 194).

A Sand County Almanac was published in 1949, but Leopold's concerns ring true to many today. Leopold would be appalled by the Alaska Department of Fish and Game hunting wolves from helicopters to increase the populations of game species, the waste buildup at base camp of Mount Everest, the rate of road-building in the Amazonia and Central Africa, the use of fish finders (with integrated lure recommendations) among anglers, the proliferation of fishing and hunting competitions (and canned trophy hunts), the pollution and wilderness disruption from snow machines in national parks, the proposed luxury resort on the edge of Grand Canyon National Park, and the general idea that increasing the ease of access and "success" in wilderness areas constitutes developing them and increasing their value.

BOX 11.4   TOPIC TO CONSIDER

THE DEVICE PARADIGM

Leopold's concern about the proliferation of gadgetry in outdoor recreation is an instance of what Albert Borgmann (1984) would later call the **device paradigm**. Borgmann believes that the tendency of modern technology and technological

(cont.)

BOX 11.4 *(cont.)*

systems is to provide goods and service as efficiently as possible, while hiding the means of production. Those of us in affluent industrialized societies do not need to understand how our home heating systems work, how electricity is generated and distributed, how the Internet functions or who maintains it, how or where our food is produced, or where our waste goes after we set it on the curb. We simply pay for the good or service and it is provided. Increased ease and accessibility for goods and services is very often beneficial. However, Borgmann, like Leopold, believes that it can also be problematic. As Leopold famously put it: "There are two spiritual dangers in not owning a farm. One is the danger of supposing that breakfast comes from the grocery, and the other that heat comes from the furnace" (1949/1968, 6).

One worry about the device paradigm is that because the means of production are invisible, consumers are not required to confront its problematic aspects, which enables them to continue. This concern is increasingly raised regarding personal electronic devices, such as smartphones and computers, for example. When people purchase and use them, they do not need to consider the human rights violations that are often involved in mining minerals for them, the ways in which the profits from those minerals encourage and support violent conflicts, the mistreatment and exploitation of the workers who manufacture the product, or the ways in which the product's hazardous elements are disposed (which often involves high levels of exposure by workers, sometimes children, in developing countries). This concern is also frequently raised regarding agriculture and food manufacturing. When people purchase food from a retailer or restaurant, they do not confront the suffering of the animals involved, the habitat destruction to expand production, or the exploitation of immigrant laborers, for example. It is also raised with respect to electricity. When people turn on the lights and start their computers they do not have to consider the conditions under which miners work, the ecological impacts of extraction (e.g., fracking for natural gas and mountaintop removal to access coal), the health impacts of power plant pollution, or the contribution to global climate change.

A second worry is that increasing the ease of production and eliminating participation in the means of production can undermine important personal and cultural goods related to the activity. This is Leopold's concern about gadgetry in outdoor recreation. It diminishes what is valuable about engaging in the activity in the first place. If you hire a fishing guide who uses a fish finder to locate and identify fish, and then tells you what lure to use and at

(cont.)

BOX 11.4 *(cont.)*

what depth, then your catching a fish is not much of an accomplishment. It does not require or increase your knowledge, skill, or appreciation of the biotic community. It is just another commercial transaction. Borgmann raises a similar concern about food. Eating diets high in prepared and processed foods that are purchased from chain stores marginalizes valuable practices and relationships around food preparation and consumption. These include developing skill and creativity in cooking, learning about culinary traditions and practices, cultivating relationships with those who grow, process, and distribute food, and socializing with friends and family around food. The slow food and local food movements are based in part on the idea that maximizing the convenience and minimizing the cost of food, particularly through industrialization, often comes at the expense of personal, social, and cultural goods and values (Box 12.1).

Borgmann argues that when we embrace too much gadgetry or too many devices we displace **focal things and practices.** These are the things that enrich our lives and that often provide meaning and orientation. In Borgmann's view, what is characteristic of focal activities is that they involve a desire to develop skills and knowledge. How the goods or outcomes are produced and the experiences involved in producing them are as important as the product. Food preparation and consumption can be a focal activity. Running can be a focal activity. Music can be a focal activity. Hunting can be a focal activity. When a practice or activity is focal, it impacts a person's perspectives and value. For example, focal hunters are not primarily concerned about bagging the biggest buck or hitting their limit of waterfowl. They care about hunting with the proper ethos, improving their knowledge of game, restoring and protecting habitat, and teaching their children the skills and perspectives for becoming successful and responsible hunters. Similarly, focal foodies are not primarily concerned with eating at the hottest restaurant or food touring the most exotic places. Instead, they care about improving their own culinary abilities, learning about how different foods are grown and prepared, ensuring that the animals they eat are treated humanely, studying the ways in which traditions and preparations have changed over time, and promoting access to healthy, culturally appropriate foods.

Do you believe that Borgmann is correct about the way in which modern technologies tend to increase efficiency and hide the means of production? Do you see this tendency in areas other than those discussed above? Do you agree that this is problematic in the ways suggested by Leopold and Borgmann?

11.4 CONCERNS REGARDING ECOCENTRISM

The land ethic is enormously influential, not only among environmental ethicists but also among environmentalists, scientists, and land managers. However, a number of concerns have been raised regarding it. These concerns can be categorized into three general types: problematic implications, lack of conceptual clarity, and misapplication of moral concepts.

11.4.1 Problematic Implications: Ecofascism and Misanthropy

Critics of the land ethic have argued that its subordination of the individual to the communal good leads to unacceptable implications. For example, animal rights theorist Thomas Regan (1983) refers to the view as **environmental fascism**, since it countenances killing large numbers of animals for the benefit of the greater ecological community—for example, feral cats in Australia and feral pigs on the Channel Islands. It also seems to permit hunting for sport, capturing wild animals for amusement (e.g., aquaria), and other practices detrimental to individual animals, so long as they do not impair the integrity or stability of ecological systems. If the value of individuals is determined by their relationship to the ecosystem, and they are either detrimental or incidental to it, then they have negative or no value. They can be, and in some cases should be, destroyed.

What is more, this appears to extend to people. Nothing is more detrimental to the integrity of ecological systems than human beings. We are the ones that pollute, overexploit, and generally degrade them. There would be much greater ecological integrity and stability in a world without industrialized human activities or large numbers of *Homo sapiens*. Therefore, the land ethic appears to require that we reduce our population and our impacts, and that we put ecological integrity before the interests of people. For this reason, the land ethic seems to some to be **misanthropic**. (When, if ever, it is permissible to prioritize protecting nature over meeting the basic needs of people is discussed in Section 16.3 and Box 16.2.)

In response to the charges of fascism and misanthropy, proponents of the land ethic point out that the value of ecological integrity and stability is not the only thing to which we must attend when evaluating what we should do; and the land ethic is not the only principle that is operative in human-environment interactions (Callicott 2001). It is possible to be a compassionate and/or respectful ecocentrist. Perhaps we ought to promote the integrity and stability of the biotic community, but do so in ways that do not cause unnecessary suffering for animals or compromise the rights and autonomy of people. Proponents of the land ethic might also argue that these criticisms focus too narrowly on the land ethic principle and disregard the love, respect, and ecological sensitivity that it involves. The land ethic is as much about the attitudes, perspectives, and dispositions that people ought to have toward the land, which include "respect for fellow members" (Leopold 1949, 204), as it is about the principle.

11.4.2 Conceptual Clarity: Defining Ecosystems and Ecological Integrity

The land ethic claims that we ought to promote the integrity, stability, and beauty of the biotic community. Adhering to it therefore requires having a clear idea of what the biotic community and its integrity, stability, and beauty are. Some critics of the land ethic argue that we do not have this. The biotic community is generally regarded as being an ecosystem, an assemblage of organisms located within a geographic space or abiotic environment. But it is possible to divide up the ecological world in enumerable ways. Is the Pacific Ocean an ecosystem? What about a particular coral reef? Is the watershed in which you live an ecosystem? What about your backyard? What about you? Most of the cells within your body are actually not yours, but a collection of microbials. Is your body their environment, such that you constitute a distinctive ecosystem? If it is our responsibility to promote the integrity of ecosystems—if they are the primary unit of concern—then it is crucial to define their limits. If each deer is an ecosystem our responsibilities are going to be very different than if each micro-habitat, each mountain, or each mountainous region is the unit of concern. Thus, one concern about the land ethic is that it is difficult to define and delineate ecosystems in a principled and clear way.

Some critics have pushed the concern about defining ecosystems still further, wondering whether ecosystems exist at all, above and beyond the particular organisms, processes, and abiotic features that comprise them. On this view, which might be called **ecosystem nominalism**, ecosystems are just overlapping convergences of different species populations in an area. They are unplanned and accidental assemblages, the product of myriad individual organisms expressing their form of life among other organisms and abiotic conditions and processes. They are unlike individual organisms, which have what is sometimes called **organic unity**. The organs in your body are there because of what they do *for you*. Your heart is there because it pumps blood and your liver is there because it removes toxins. The parts and processes in your body have organic unity, on this view, since the explanation for why they are there and do what they do depends on their interdependent relationships to other parts of the system (your body), which together make up a whole that is more than the sum of its parts. Just as the individual brushstrokes of a painting combine to make something more than a collection of color streaks, the cells of organisms combine to make something more than just a collection of cells. You have experiences, plans, and desires, but your individual cells do not.

However, according to this objection, this is not the case with respect to the organisms that comprise ecosystems. Organisms, or even populations of them, are not found in a place because they perform a role or function for some greater entity—the biotic community or ecological whole. Oysters filter water and thereby benefit individuals of other species that thrive in less silty water, but they are not there because they do that. It is just what oysters do. Wolves hunt deer and elk, and this has cascading effects on other organisms and populations. But they do it because that is what wolves eat, not because they have a role to play in managing the deer population for the good of the ecosystem. It is not their function within the ecosystem, since there is not any end or goal or organization of the ecosystem. Ecosystems, unlike individual organisms, lack organic unity. They are not really anything above and beyond their individual parts. If this is correct, then, according to this view, there are no ecosystems for us to consider (Cahen 1988).

A consideration sometimes offered in support of the view that ecosystems lack organic unity is that they do not migrate or shift intact or as wholes. The current ecosystems of New England are not, as a result of global climate change, going to be found largely intact in mideastern Canada in a hundred years. Rather the New England ecosystems are going to disassemble—some species will disappear, others will become more prevalent, new ones will arrive—and the abiotic features of the place will be changed. This will be the case as well for the ecosystems in mideastern Canada. There are evolved dependencies and interactions between species populations—for example, mutualisms and parasitisms—that sometimes have an effect of holding some species combinations together under changing conditions. As birds migrate they will bring with them the seeds of the foods they eat, as well as the parasites in their bodies, for example. However, these too are just the result of each organism doing what that type of organisms does. They are not explained by appeal to any greater entity—ecosystem or biotic community— beyond the individual organism interactions, according to ecosystem nominalism.

Suppose, contrary to the concerns described above, that it is possible to adequately delineate ecosystems and that they are real entities above and beyond their constituent parts. Some ethicists and philosophers of science have wondered whether it is possible to specify what constitutes their stability and integrity in a definite way. Ecological systems are highly dynamic. Species ranges shift, climate patterns change, and transformative events occur. So whatever integrity and stability are, they must accommodate the fact that ecological spaces are always in flux. But once this is recognized it becomes difficult to define ecological integrity and stability in terms of such things as consistent patterns of energy flows through a system, maintaining types and abundance of species populations, or capacity to respond to stressors and return to recent prior states (e.g., resistance and resilience). In order to accommodate the dynamism of ecological systems, Baird Callicott, an influential exponent of the land ethic, has proposed reformulating its core principle to this:

> A thing is right when it tends to disturb the biotic community *only at normal spatial and temporal scales*. It is wrong when it tends otherwise.
> (2001, 216, italics added)

But even this does not satisfy some critics who wonder how we are to define "normal" rates of climatic and ecological change. For example, from a geological perspective, comparatively large and abrupt ecological changes are not abnormal. They regularly occur given a long enough time scale. There have been five prior mass extinctions, numerous minor extinction events, and continents have been breaking apart and reforming for billions of years, for example. So no matter how ecosystems are delineated—in terms of organic unity or energy patterns, such as food webs, for example—there remains the additional difficulty of defining what constitutes integrity and stability in a way that does not conceptualize ecological systems as overly static.

In response to these conceptual concerns, proponents of the land ethic typically defer to ecological science. These are technical concepts, and our best ecological science will elucidate what standards we should use for defining ecosystems, as well as the measures of their integrity and stability. As Leopold notes when discussing the effects of deer overpopulation, some ecological systems are healthier than others. It is one of the projects of ecology to develop assessments of ecosystem health. To the extent that ecologists are successful in doing so, this concern will be addressed. Moreover, proponents of the land ethic emphasize that we should not demand too much. There will of course be no hard line at the edge of a biotic community. There are transitional areas and hybrid zones. But this does not imply that we cannot distinguish between ecological communities any more than the vagary of species boundaries implies that different species do not exist (see Section 13.1). There will be some indeterminacy and hard cases. However, this is a product of the complexity, gradation, and general messiness of the biological and ecological world. As Aristotle (1985) emphasized, we should expect only as much clarity as the subject matter will allow. Ecology is a real science, and ecological concepts are capturing real phenomena, even if it is not as precise and universal as geometry and physics, on this view.

✸ BOX 11.5   TOPIC TO CONSIDER

WHAT MAKES ONE INTEGRITY BETTER THAN ANOTHER?

Ecological systems are dynamic, and species ranges and populations are always changing. Given this, what makes one ecological state better than another? Consider the case of wolves in Yellowstone (Section 11.2). In the absence of wolves, the density and distribution of species was different. There were more coyotes and elk, and fewer beavers and red foxes, for example. But what, if anything, made Yellowstone superior rather than just different, from an ecological perspective, *after* wolves were reintroduced, compared with *before*? In both cases—with and without wolves—there was a functioning ecological system with predation, mating, migration, and foraging. Why is one integrity better than the other, or why does one have more integrity than the other? (The same

(cont.)

BOX 11.5 *(cont.)*

questions can be asked regarding Santa Cruz Island before and after the interventions to conserve the island fox.)

Suppose wolves had been absent from Yellowstone for four hundred years.
In that case, wouldn't reintroduction be disruptive of the ecological integrity
that had developed over that time? How long must ecological relationships,
introduced species, or novel assemblages be in place before they are considered part of the true or proper integrity for a place? Why should we count any
particular state of an ecological system, or time period, as the "true" integrity
and stability at which we should aim in ecosystem management and ecological
restoration? Isn't this an ethical, rather than a scientific determination? If so,
what are the relevant ethical considerations?

11.4.3 Misapplication of Moral Concepts

A third set of criticisms regarding the land ethic concerns the way in which it applies
moral concepts to ecosystems and our relationships with them. (The criticisms in this
subsection apply to the standard interpretation of the land ethic, but not to the alternative pragmatic holism interpretation [Box 11.2].)

One common criticism is that Leopold mistakenly transitions from the fact that
we are part of the biotic community in an *ecological* sense to the conclusion that we
should regard the biotic community as a *moral* community. Many people believe
that a moral community is characterized by mutual care and concern. Our churches,
schools, families, and towns are moral communities not only because we are part of
them and depend upon them, but because we have reciprocal responsibilities with
other members of the community. On this view, a moral community is more than just
a set of interdependencies. It is one in which members of the community recognize
each other as co-members and have duties to them and the community as a whole.
We do not have that sort of relationship with the land. Ecological systems and the
organisms that constitute them do not care about us or have responsibilities to us.
They are not capable of such things, since they are not moral agents. For this reason,
they are more like our houses than our family members. We are dependent upon both
for aspects of our well-being. We need shelter and physical security, as well as love
and support. However, our house is not part of our moral community. We do not
have obligations to it and we do not need to treat it with love and respect. We need to
maintain it. It is our friends, family, and co-citizens that we need to love and respect
and from which we can expect the same. Similarly, this criticism continues, we need
to maintain ecological systems because of the goods and services that they provide
for us, but it is a mistake to conceptualize them as a moral community to which we

belong. The ecological community is not characterized by mutual recognition, concern, concern, cooperation, and coordination, as our moral communities are, but by struggle and conflict—for instance, competition for resources and predator-prey interactions.

In response to this criticism, proponents of the land ethic might point out that not all our ethical relationships require mutual concern and obligations. We have responsibilities to infants. We have responsibilities to severely mentally disabled people. We have responsibilities to future generations. None of these are moral agents capable of reciprocal recognition and duties. So, this response continues, we should not think that all moral communities must fit the mutual concern and recognition paradigm. We can see the biotic community as a moral community worthy of love and respect, and doing so is an "ecological necessity." That is what matters, not whether bristlecone pines and praying mantises can also see it that way.

A second criticism of the land ethic's use of concepts concerns its treatment of integrity and stability as *normative* and not merely *descriptive*. Let us suppose, contrary to the criticisms discussed earlier, that it is possible to substantively specify an ecosystem's integrity and stability. Why think that these should be protected and promoted? According to the standard interpretation of the land ethic, it is because it is good for the biotic community. But some critics have wondered if the biotic community has a good of its own, or interests of its own. Can ecosystems or biotic communities really be harmed and benefited? Is increasing ecological integrity really good *for them* and disrupting it bad *for them*? The biotic community does not have a mind. It does not have psychological experiences or mental states. (Some of the individuals in them do—for example, birds and mammals—but the system itself does not.) As a result, what is good or bad for it cannot be grounded in intentions, desires, or experiences. It must have a nonmentalistic good, if it has a good or interests at all.

When discussing biocentrism—the view that all living things have inherent worth—an analogous issue arose (Section 7.3). Trees and mushrooms do not have minds. Therefore, if they have a good *of their own* it must be grounded in something nonmentalistic. The most plausible account of what grounds the good of nonconscious living things is that they are goal-directed systems—their parts and processes are organized in order to accomplish things like survival, growth, and reproduction. It is possible to make sense of harming and benefiting a tree by looking at whether its ability to pursue its ends are impaired or enhanced. Asian long-horned beetles are bad for a tree because they reduce the capacity of the tree's tissue to distribute water and nutrients, thereby impairing its ability to grow and survive. Moreover, the explanation for why organisms are teleologically organized is etiological—their parts or processes were selected for in prior generations, and persist in current generations, because of the contribution that they make to their ends. Thus, it seems possible to make sense of harm, benefit, and health with respect to plants, even though they are not conscious. (This is discussed in greater detail in Section 7.3.)

However, some critics of the land ethic have argued that it is not possible to do this for ecosystems or the biotic community. The reason is that they are not goal-directed systems. They were not selected for *as a system* and there is no internal organization—they lack organic unity. According to this view, when ecosystems appear to be goal-directed systems that maintain or repair themselves, or that tend toward some stability and equilibrium, this is only a byproduct of the behavior of the individuals pursuing their own good and the natural features that comprise the system. As a result, it is not possible to ground claims about the good of ecosystems either in terms of mental states or goal orientation. Therefore, according to this criticism, when people refer to the "health," "good," or "benefit" of ecosystems, they are really using the terms to indicate something like the aggregate good of the organisms in the system or the capacity of the system to maintain ecological processes and produce ecological services.

This is not to deny that there are general patterns or regularities in ecological process that can be described and modeled—for instance, population dynamics or vegetation succession. Ecology is a legitimate science. But this does not establish that ecosystems have interests or a good of their own. We can characterize all sorts of physical processes, from erosion to oxidation, but it does not follow that hillsides or scrap metal have interests. Integrity and stability may be measures of what is going on in an ecological space, but they are not constitutive of ecosystem welfare, well-being, interests, or good, according to this criticism.

Finally, critics of the land ethic have challenged its communitarian conception of ethics. The land ethic holds that questions about ethics arise in a community context and that we ought to be responsible members of the communities of which we are part, which involves promoting their good functioning. But critics argue that the reason why we should care about the well-functioning of human communities tracks back to the well-being of the individuals that comprise them. Well-functioning communities should be supported when and because they are conducive to human flourishing. Suppose there was a society in which a small number of people lived lavishly as a result of their exploiting large numbers of other people. We would not want to promote the integrity and stability of that community. We would want it to break down and a more just and broadly beneficial social arrangement to replace it. If this is correct, then individual flourishing is the primary object of moral concern, not the community; and we should be individualists, not communitarians about ethics.

In response to this concern, proponents of the land ethic might agree that we ought to prioritize individual welfare when ethically evaluating communities within interpersonal ethics, due the worth of rational beings. However, they might argue that we ought not do so within environmental ethics, since there are not such strong individual claims. Other possible responses are to move toward pragmatic holism or else adopt a pluralistic view on which both individuals and the system are regarded as having worth. Perhaps we ought to promote well-functioning communities both because they are valuable in themselves and because they are conducive to individual flourishing. This pluralistic view is embraced by deep ecology, which is the topic of the next chapter.

WHAT ABOUT BEAUTY?

Many readers of *A Sand County Almanac* wonder why Leopold includes "beauty" among the characteristics of ecosystems that we ought to protect and promote. Even people who argue that it is possible to rigorously define "integrity" and "stability" often have doubts about "beauty." If, as is commonly said, beauty is in the eye of the beholder, then the "beauty" component of the land ethic would seem to countenance whatever people believe will make an ecospace more aesthetically pleasing, even if it involves introducing new species, eliminating native ones, and altering landscapes, which are precisely the sorts of things that Leopold opposed. There is an influential tradition in Western thought and practice which sees wildness as unruly and ugly, and in need of being tamed, controlled, civilized, and cultivated by people (see, e.g., Boxes 3.1 and 5.4). People's aesthetic tastes do not always run toward integrity and stability, and they do not always favor large intact ecosystems with minimal human impact. Some people prefer orderly hedgerows and manicured lawns. So what is "beauty" doing in the land ethic?

   Here is a possible answer. On Leopold's view, not all perspectives are equally valid. The creative part of ecosystem management is helping people develop an ecologically informed perspective that involves seeing the natural world as not only an economic resource but also a community to which they belong and should relate to with love and respect. It is what is beautiful, wonderful, and amazing from that perspective that we ought to protect and promote—the diversity of life forms, the complexity of ecological interactions, astounding migrations, and awesome landscapes. A colorful sunset or glittering mountain may look pretty to some, but it will not be seen as beautiful by a person who loves the land and knows that they are the product of synthetic chemicals in the atmosphere and toxic waste from mining operations. This is what might be called a *qualified observer* account of aesthetics. The beauty that we ought to promote is not whatever anyone thinks is pretty. It is what a well-informed person who loves and respects the land finds beautiful.

   What do you think about this conception of environmental aesthetics? Do you believe that beauty understood in this way should be included in the land ethic? Or would it be better to not involve aesthetics in the land ethic at all?

11.5 SUMMARY

The primary questions addressed in this chapter were:

- What are ecocentric environmental ethics in general and Aldo Leopold's land ethic in particular?
- What are the primary arguments for and the practical implications of the land ethic?
- What are the most prominent concerns regarding the land ethic (and ecocentrism)?

The chapter began by providing some background on why some ethicists are drawn to holistic approaches to environmental ethics. It then reviewed the core argument for the land ethic, on its standard communitarian interpretation, drawing heavily from Leopold's writings. The focus then turned to the practical implications of the land ethic, with respect to both ecosystem management and moral development. Finally, three types of concerns about the land ethic were discussed—problematic implications, lack of conceptual clarity, and misapplication of moral concepts—as were responses to them.

Over the course of the chapter several questions about the role the land ethic should play within environmental ethics arose: Should we adopt an individualist or communitarian approach to ethics? Should the land ethic be seen as a pragmatic principle or as a basic principle? Should the land ethic be supplemented with other principles and considerations to generate a compassionate, just, or pluralistic holism? The prominence of these questions suggests that the land ethic perhaps ought not be regarded as a comprehensive environmental ethic (and it may be that Leopold did not see it as one). Moreover, even if it is well justified, the land ethic does not seem to provide guidance on issues such as the treatment of animals in captivity or environmental justice, for example. The next chapter focuses on another holistic view: deep ecology. Proponents of deep ecology often see the adoption of holism as part of a broader effort to address the underlying conceptual and structural causes of ecological degradation and social injustice.

KEY TERMS (SEE GLOSSARY FOR DEFINITIONS):

communitarian conception of ethics	enlightened anthropocentrism
deep ecology	environmental fascism
device paradigm	focal things and practices
ecocentrism	holism
ecosystem nominalism	land ethic

misanthropic   pragmatic holism

nonanthropocentrism   species richness

organic unity

REVIEW QUESTIONS

- What distinguishes a holistic approach to environmental ethics from an individualist approach?

- What is the core principle of the land ethic?

- What is Leopold's reasoning in support of the land ethic?

- Why is the land ethic thought to favor native species prioritization, species conservation, and creation of ecological reserves?

- What does Leopold mean by "ecological conscience" and why does he think perspective and perception are so crucial to ecological ethics?

- What is the device paradigm?

- What is the alternative (noncommunitarian) interpretation of the land ethic?

- What are the three types of concerns regarding ecocentrism and what are some examples of them?

DISCUSSION QUESTIONS

- Do you agree with Leopold's communitarian conception of ethics? Is ethics primarily about our responsibilities as members of a community?

- Do you agree with Leopold that we ought to regard the biotic community as a moral community? Why or why not?

- Do you think the use of "integrity" and "stability" in the land ethic commits a fallacy of appeal to nature? Are they being used as normative concepts when they should not be?

- Is it reasonable to think that the value of nonhuman organisms is tied to their ecological relationships, but the value of human beings is not?

- Do you think that ecosystems have a good of their own or welfare distinct from that of the individual organisms that comprise and populate them? Why or why not?

- Do you think that individual organisms or collectives (ecosystems, populations, and species) should be prioritized in environmental ethics?

- Do you agree with Leopold's critique of trophy-oriented outdoor recreation? Can you think of other activities that people engage in that are subject to similar problems—that is, that focus too much on the end product rather than the process and experiences involved?

- Do you agree that the land ethic needs to be complemented by other environmental values or principles in order to avoid the misanthropy and fascism concerns? If so, what other values or principles would you endorse?

FURTHER READING

There are several thoughtful reflections on and explications of the land ethic (including, of course, Leopold's own):

Callicott, Baird. *In Defense of the Land Ethic*. SUNY Press, 1989.

Callicott, Baird, ed. *A Companion to A Sand County Almanac*. University of Wisconsin Press, 1987.

Leopold, Aldo. *A Sand County Almanac*. Oxford University Press, 1968.

Norton, Bryan. "The Constancy of Leopold's Land Ethic." *Conservation Biology* 2, no. 1 (1988): 93–102.

Other ecocentric environmental ethics include:

Callicott, Baird. *Thinking Like a Planet*. Oxford University Press, 2014.

Johnson, Lawrence. *A Morally Deep World*. Cambridge University Press, 1993.

Westra, Laura. *An Environmental Proposal for Ethics: The Principle of Integrity*. Rowman and Littlefield, 1994.

CHAPTER TWELVE

DEEP ECOLOGY

THE LAND ETHIC IS not the only holistic approach to environmental ethics. The other prominent environmental philosophy associated with ecological holism is **deep ecology**. The term "deep ecology" was popularized by Norwegian philosopher Arne Naess in the 1970s. Naess wanted to distinguish two strands of environmental movements and philosophies, what he called the **shallow ecology** movement and the **deep ecology** movement. Both movements are interested in addressing environmental issues. However, on his view, the shallow ecology movement is oriented around treating the problematic effects of industrial activities and promoting sustainable practices, particularly insofar as they impact "the health and affluence of people in the developed countries" (Naess 1973, 95). In contrast, the deep ecology movement aims to address the underlying causes of ecological degradation. As a result, deep ecologists often emphasize the systemic, structural, and ideological dimensions of ecological problems.

This chapter begins by explicating the value commitments and practical implications of deep ecology. It then focuses on the most prominent account of its philosophical underpinnings, before considering concerns regarding deep ecology.

12.1 PRINCIPLES OF DEEP ECOLOGY

Here are some examples to illustrate the differences, as Naess conceived them, between deep and shallow approaches to environmental problems. Shallow ecologists aim to restrict discharges from manufacturing facilities that pollute the air and water; deep ecologists aims to do this and challenge the power structures that enable

272

externalizing ecological costs onto the environment and the public. Shallow ecologists promote fishing regulations and sustainable management in order to maintain fishery productivity over time; deep ecologists challenge the view that aquatic ecosystems are "fisheries" to be managed for human ends, rather than independently valuable ecological systems. Shallow ecologists aim to ensure that agricultural resources are used and distributed efficiently so as to maximally satisfy people's dietary needs and preferences; deep ecologists insist that we must reduce our population and alter our food preferences so that they are compatible with all species and systems having the capacity to survive and thrive. Overall, shallow ecology aims to "clean up" the unintended impacts, excesses, and inefficiencies of our current practices—to treat the symptoms—whereas deep ecology also aims to challenge the economic, ideological, and political systems that are seen as the root causes of our ecological and social problems. As Naess puts it, what deep ecology calls for "is not a slight reform of our present society, but a *substantial reorientation of our whole civilization*" (1989, 45).

✳ BOX 12.1

REFORM OR REPLACE: THE FOOD SYSTEM DEBATE

Whether addressing environmental and social problems can be accomplished by reforming current practices or it requires restructuring social arrangements and institutions is at the heart of the food system debates. **Food systems** are the complex network of processes, infrastructures, and actors that produce the food we eat and deliver it to where we eat it. Every food system involves agricultural production or capture, processing, preparation, consumption, and waste disposal. They all involve transportation, distribution, technology, and exchange (or trade). What is distinctive about the increasingly predominant **global food system** is that food production and delivery networks are *transnational* and *industrial*. The transnational and industrial character of the system, which prioritizes efficiency, cost minimization, and market success, favors the following features, which are common across global industrial production and delivery systems: global sourcing, economies of scale, large actors (e.g., corporations), mechanization and innovation, standardization, commodification, cost externalization, and high input needs. Advocates of the global food system argue that embracing these forms of efficiency is the most (and only) effective way to meet the food demands of a population of over 7.3 billion people and growing. No other system has the ability to produce as much of the foods that people want, when they want them, at a price they are willing to pay. (Food security is discussed at length in Chapter 16.)

(cont.)

BOX 12.1 *(cont.)*

The global food system has received a barrage of criticism in recent years, including that it displaces smallholding farmers, exploits workers, undermines cultural practices, disrupts rural communities, degrades the environment, promotes unhealthy eating, empowers corporations over individuals, causes animal suffering, diminishes food autonomy and security, and reduces the aesthetic quality of food. Critics of the global food system argue that we ought to reject the system in favor of shorter food supply chains and more local and regional food systems, which engender responsibility and empower smaller producers, workers, communities, families, and individuals. The *alternative food movement*—promoting slow foods, local foods, organic foods, and food justice—is constituted by individuals, families, food cooperatives, farmers, community organizations, student groups, restaurant owners, chefs, NGOs, activists, and others trying to eat independently of the global food system, develop alternative agro-food networks, and address the problematic features of the global food system. However, the alternative food movement has itself been subject to large amounts of criticism on the grounds that its food system vision would actually reduce food security, diminish diet quality, decrease food access, and make our diets less aesthetically interesting. Moreover, the movement has been charged with being classist, valorizing elitist ideas about "good food," and promoting a false nostalgia about preindustrial food conditions and practices (Sandler 2015).

Thoughtful proponents of the industrial food system and the alternative food movement frequently agree that food production and delivery are too often associated with ecological degradation, unsustainable practices, animal suffering, and social injustices. They disagree on why this is and what can and should be done to address it. Many critics of the global food system argue that the problems associated with it are due to its industrial and global character, and so are inherent to it. For example, the drive to reduce price and increase profits incentivizes externalizing environmental and health costs and compensating workers as little as possible. Standardization and global sourcing favor top-down control, disempowering growers, and reducing crop and breed diversity. Commodification favors conceptualizing and treating animals as meat, dairy, and egg production units, rather than as sentient beings that can suffer.

In response, those who defend the system argue that improved policies and practices could reduce or eliminate most of the problems. On this view, if there were living wage laws, enforcement of worker protections, compassionate animal handling standards, internalization of ecological costs, fair trade, and better consumer information, for example, we could have the advantages of a global food system—reliable access to low cost, convenient, and diverse foods—without the

(cont.)

BOX 12.1 *(cont.)*

current problems with the system. In support of this position, proponents high-light that there already are successes in this respect—for example, food workers are paid a living wage in some countries and many large retailers are requiring that their suppliers eliminate the use of gestation crates for pigs.

However, critics of the global food system argue that even if this is true in prin-ciple, the political realities and entrenched interests and power structures make it practically impossible. The more promising and preferable option is to build an alternative model. Moreover, they point out that if all the changes to the industrial food system needed to "clean it up" were actually made, the result would be some-thing very much like the systems advocated by the alternative food movement.

The food system debate exemplifies that when assessing environmental and social problems and evaluating possible responses to them, it is important to clarify the extent to which their causes are the product of policies, incentives, or practices that can be revised within existing social and institutional frameworks or if they flow from features of the underlying social, political, and economic structures.

Naess and fellow deep ecologist George Sessions proposed eight principles that they believe express the values and practical commitments associated with deep ecology (Devall and Sessions 1985). The principles have been widely accepted by the diverse movements, philosophies, and organizations that identify as deep ecology. They are also shared by others who do not consider themselves deep ecologists, including many who have never even heard of deep ecology. Proponents of deep ecology embrace the fact that people could come to these principles from a wide variety of traditions and experiences, as well as disparate theological and philosophical worldviews. Here are the principles:

1. The well-being and flourishing of human and nonhuman life on earth have value in themselves (synonyms: inherent worth, intrinsic value, inherent value). These values are independent of the usefulness of the nonhuman world for human purposes.
2. Richness and diversity of life forms contribute to the realization of these values and are also values in themselves.
3. Humans have no right to reduce this richness and diversity except to satisfy vital needs.
4. Present human interference with the nonhuman world is excessive and the situation is rapidly worsening.
5. The flourishing of human life and cultures is compatible with a substantial decrease of the human population. The flourishing of nonhuman life requires such a decrease.

6. Policies must therefore be changed. The changes in policies affect basic economic, technological, and ideological structures. The resulting state of affairs will be deeply different from the present.

7. The ideological change is mainly that of appreciating life quality (dwelling in situations of inherent worth) rather than adhering to an increasingly higher standard of living. There will be a profound awareness of the difference between big and great.

8. Those who subscribe to the foregoing points have an obligation directly or indirectly to participate in the attempt to implement the necessary changes.

These principles explicitly reject anthropocentrism and human chauvinism, and embrace **biocentric egalitarianism**, the view that all forms of life have equal value. They are also standardly interpreted as holding that species and ecological systems—the "richness and diversity of life forms"—have value above and beyond that of individual organisms. That is, they involve embracing holism. Thus, with respect to its value commitments, deep ecology might more accurately be called **biocentric pluralism**: It values both individual living organisms and the species/systems that they constitute and populate.

The practical implications that deep ecologists associate with the value system are also explicit in the principles. Supporters of deep ecology are committed to dramatically reducing the human footprint on the Earth. This means decreasing overall levels of consumption and population, as well as eliminating exploitative practices and transforming the worldviews, structures, and institutions that support them.

What the principles do not provide is the justification or basis for the value commitments. The considerations that many deep ecologists offer in support of biocentric pluralism are the focus of the next section. As with most of the other ethics that have been discussed, the value system is thought to be supported by a proper understanding of the human-nature relationship.

✸ BOX 12.2   TOPIC TO CONSIDER

DIRECT ACTION ENVIRONMENTAL ACTIVISM

The eighth principle of deep ecology asserts that there is an obligation to engage in activities to help realize the goals expressed in the other principles. This could include political activities (e.g., protesting, community organizing, and lobbying policy makers), volunteer activities (e.g., assisting at nonprofits, participating in

(cont.)

BOX 12.2 *(cont.)*

restorations, and engaging in citizen science), or economic activities (e.g., opening environmentally sustainable businesses, donating to charities, and reducing
consumption). Some environmentalists believe that environmental activism also
should involve direct action against those who engage in ecologically problematic activities. Direct action can be nonviolent—for example, tree-sits to prevent
old growth forests from being logged, civil disobedience to draw attention to
issues, and disrupting public events to shame corporate actors. It can also involve destruction of property—for example, breaking into labs to free research
animals, spiking trees to prevent logging, or engaging in arson.

Not surprisingly, direct environmental action that involves destroying property or disrupting economic activities is the most controversial form of environmental activism. (No environmental groups advocate intentionally harming
people.) Those who support it often refer to it as **radical environmentalism**,
ecotage, or **monkey wrenching**, a term that was popularized by Edward Abbey's
1975 book *The Monkey Wrench Gang*. Critics of destructive direct action call it

Image 12.1a   A Sea Shepherd ship engages a Japanese whaling vessel in the Southern
Ocean in 2008 -2009 in an attempt to disrupt their hunt for minke and fin whales and
raise public awareness about the whaling industry.
Source: Sea Shepherd / Adam Lau

(cont.)

BOX 12.2 *(cont.)*

Image 12.1b   Julia Butterfly Hill lived in a 1,000-year-old, 180-foot-tall California redwood for 738 days in order to prevent it from being cut down by the Pacific Lumber Company and to draw attention to the logging of old-growth redwood forests.
Source: ©Stuart Franklin/Magnum Photos

ecoterrorism, and the US Federal Bureau of Investigation (FBI) recognizes it a form of domestic terrorism. The FBI considers groups such as Earth First!, the Animal Liberation Front (ALF), the Earth Liberation Front (ELF), and Sea Shepherds to be terrorist organizations (FBI 2002). Examples of destructive direct intervention include cutting trawling nets, arson (e.g., SUVs, condominiums, fur companies, and a ski lodge), disabling construction and logging equipment, and vandalizing animal research facilities. Nondestructive but often still economically damaging activities include such things as blocking roads and bridges, harassing whaling vessels, and disrupting oil rig activities.

Radical environmentalists justify their actions by arguing that trying to protect animals and the environment by legal, nondestructive means alone is frequently ineffective. Once an old-growth forest is logged or a whale is hunted, it is gone forever. Therefore, to protect them, direct intervention is necessary. Of course, in the long term there must be systemic changes. But immediate

(cont.)

BOX 12.2 *(cont.)*

protection is also crucial, and this often requires damaging property. Proponents of radical environmentalism also argue that it can draw attention to issues and make less radical environmentalism more effective. Critics of radical environmentalism believe that it is unethical because of the property rights violations involved and the risks that it poses to people. They also challenge the idea that it is effective in the long run, on the grounds that it makes environmentalism as a whole seem radical and can invite public and policy backlash. They further argue that if every group that cared passionately about a social or environmental issue turned to destructive means to achieve their goals it would undermine the ability of social institutions to function.

Do you believe that direct environmental action is ever permissible? Why or why not? If you believe it is justified, when or under what conditions is it justified? Which forms are acceptable and which are not? Is civil disobedience or direct action for environmental ends ever ethically required, rather than just permissible? That is, do people ever have an obligation to engage in civil disobedience and direct forms of activism for environmental ends? What does your view regarding direct environmental action imply for activism on other, nonenvironmental, issues? What sorts of reasoning are you employing to justify your views—consequential, deontological, or virtue-oriented?

12.2 METAPHYSICAL HOLISM AND SELF-REALIZATION

As mentioned above, proponents of deep ecology emphasize that a person can come to support its core principles from any number of different experiences, perspectives, and traditions. (Naess famously referred to his particular ecological philosophy—or ecosophy—as "ecosophy T," which he described as drawing from Mahayana Buddhism, Spinozistic pantheism, and Gandhian philosophy. The "T" in ecosophy T refers to Naess's mountain hut in Norway, Tvergastein.) However, with respect to the principles' justification, the most prominent view—embraced by influential deep ecology philosophers such as Naess, George Sessions, Bill Devall, and Warwick Fox—is that it is connected to attaining a proper understanding of ourselves and our relationship to others. This understanding is not merely social or ecological, as it is for Leopold and advocates of the land ethic, but **metaphysical**. It involves understanding the deeper reality—sometimes called *ontology*—of the world. The idea is that once people achieve a higher level of awareness, they will embrace the core value commitments expressed in the principles: "The foundations of deep ecology are the basic intuitions and experiencing of ourselves and Nature which comprise ecological consciousness. Certain outlooks on politics and public policy flow naturally from this consciousness" (Devall and Sessions 1985, 65).

These deep ecologists believe that the metaphysical aspect of the view is crucial, since it challenges the underlying ideologies supporting the currently predominant, and ecologically destructive, industrial capitalistic economic system and hierarchical authoritarian political system. The problematic ideologies are that human beings are distinctive in (or from) nature and that people are isolated individuals or "egos." According to deep ecologists, these views foster prioritizing the individual over the whole and the human over the nonhuman. They also favor a materialistic and consumptive conception of human flourishing. **Ecological consciousness** involves coming to see them as illusory. Instead of conceiving of human beings as distinct and exceptional individuals, an ecologically conscious person will embrace **ontological holism and egalitarianism**: every entity, human and nonhuman, biotic and abiotic, is fundamentally relational, an equally significant node in the interconnected fabric that constitutes reality. When we see ourselves as only one interconnected part of the whole—just like insects, wombats, cacti, and rainfall—we will identify with the other components of the natural world. We will not aim to elevate ourselves over them or master them, and we will not oppress, exploit, or degrade them.

Deep ecologists refer to coming to this deeper awareness as **self-realization**. Here are several key passages from Naess's influential description of it:

> What I am going to say more or less in my own way and that of my friends, may roughly be condensed into the following six points:
> 1. We under-estimate ourself. I emphasize "self." We tend to confuse it with the narrow ego.
> 2. Human nature is such that with sufficient allsided maturity we cannot avoid "identifying" ourself with all living beings, beautiful or ugly, big or small, sentient or not. I need of course to elucidate my concept of identifying. I'll come back to that. . . .
> 3. Traditionally the *maturity of the self* has been considered to develop through three stages, from ego to social self, comprising the ego, and from there to metaphysical self, comprising the social self. But nature is then largely left out in the conception of this process. Our home, our immediate environment, where we belong as children, and the identification with human living beings, are largely ignored. I therefore tentatively introduce, perhaps for the first time ever, a concept of *ecological self*. We may be said to be in, of, and for nature from our very beginning. Society and human relations are important, but our self is richer in its constitutive relations. These relations are not only relations we have to other humans and the human community. . . .
> 4. Joy of life and meaning of life is increased through increased self-realization. That is, through the fulfilment of potentials each

has, but which never are exactly the same for any pair of living beings. Whatever the differences increased self-realization implies broadening and deepening of self.

5. Because of an inescapable process of identification with others, with growing maturity, the self is widened and deepened. We "see ourself in others." Self-realization is hindered if the self-realization of others, with whom we identify, is hindered. Love of ourself will fight this obstacle by assisting in the self-realization of others according to the formula "Live and let live!" Thus, all that can be achieved by altruism—the *dutiful, moral* consideration of others—can be achieved—and much more—through widening and deepening ourself. . . .

6. A great challenge of today is to save the planet from further devastation that violates both the enlightened self-interest of humans and nonhumans, and decreases the potential of joyful existence for all. . . .

I shall only offer one single sentence resembling a definition of the ecological self. The ecological self of a person is that with which this person identifies.

This key sentence (rather than definition) about the self, shifts the burden of clarification from the term "self" to that of identification, or rather "process of identification." . . .

What would be a paradigm situation of identification? It is a situation in which identification elicits intense empathy. My standard example has to do with a nonhuman being I met forty years ago. I looked through an old-fashioned microscope at the dramatic meeting of two drops of different chemicals. A flea jumped from a lemming strolling along the table and landed in the middle of the acid chemicals. To save it was impossible. It took many minutes for the flea to die. Its movements were dreadfully expressive. What I felt was, naturally, a painful compassion and empathy. But the empathy was *not* basic, it was the process of identification, that "I see myself in the flea." If I was alienated from the flea, not seeing intuitively anything even resembling myself, the death struggle would have left me indifferent. So there must be identification in order for there to be compassion and, among humans, solidarity. (Naess 1987, 35–36)

Naess believes that rather than being isolated egos, our metaphysical self encompasses all of our relations—social and ecological. We extend out through these relations, and "allsided maturity" involves seeing oneself in this way. It is this metaphysical identification—seeing oneself in the other—that enables compassion and empathy. Thus, this deeper metaphysical understanding is crucial to ethical awareness.

Deep ecology's metaphysical outlook (which is sometimes referred to as **metaphysical holism**) is contrary to most Western philosophical views of the individual, which emphasize distinctiveness, independence, and consciousness (or what Naess refers to as the "ego"). It is particularly antithetical to **Cartesian dualism**, the view that there is a strong divide between the mental and the physical, and that what is essential to a person's identity is that she is a distinct thinking thing. However, deep ecologists often point out that metaphysical holism and the extended or ecological self view is common in other traditions, such as Buddhism, some forms of Hinduism, and some indigenous people's worldviews. In many varieties of Buddhism, enlightenment is achieved with the realization that the egoistic self is illusory. Deep ecologists also see the self-in-Self metaphysic in the philosophy of Baruch de Spinoza, a seventeenth-century Dutch philosopher famous for arguing that there exists only one fundamental substance—nature or God—of which everything else is a finite mode or expression.

Naess, like many deep ecologists, believed that self-realization cannot be accomplished by accepting a line of reasoning, since it is not merely a rational belief. It is a deep perspective, a way of "being in the world." As a result, it can only be accomplished through a meditative, deep-questioning process, which brings about a perspectival or gestalt shift. Here is Devall and Session's formulation of this view:

> For deep ecology, the study of our place in the Earth household includes the study of ourselves as part of the organic whole. Going beyond a narrowly materialist scientific understanding of reality, the spiritual and the material aspects of reality fuse together. While the leading intellectuals of the dominant worldview have tended to view religion as "just superstition," and have looked upon ancient spiritual practice and enlightenment, such as found in Zen Buddhism, as essentially subjective, the search for deep ecological consciousness is the search for a more objective consciousness and state of being through an active deep questioning and meditative process and way of life. . . .
>
> In keeping with the spiritual traditions of many of the world's religions, the deep ecology norm of self-realization goes beyond the modern Western *self* which is defined as an isolated ego striving primarily for hedonistic gratification or for a narrow sense of individual salvation in this life or the next. . . . Spiritual growth, or unfolding, begins when we cease to understand or see ourselves as isolated and narrow competing egos. . . . We must see beyond our narrow contemporary cultural assumptions and values, and the conventional wisdom of our time and place, and this is best achieved by the meditative deep questioning process. Only in this way can we hope to attain full mature personhood and uniqueness.
>
> A nurturing nondominating society can help in the "real work" of becoming a whole person. The "real work" can be summarized symbolically as the realization of "self-in-Self" where "Self" stands for organic wholeness. This process of the full unfolding of the self can be

also summarized by the phrase, "No one is saved until we are all saved,"
where the phrase "one" includes not only me, an individual human,
but all humans, whales, grizzly bears, whole rain forest ecosystems,
mountains and rivers, the tiniest microbes in the soil, and so on. (Devall
and Sessions 1985, 66–67)

Both deep ecology and the land ethic hold that we can improve our perspective
through experience and understanding, and that when we do we will see our relationship to the land differently, more holistically and, ultimately, more ethically. However,
deep ecology differs from the land ethic in its form of justification for a more holistic
approach to environmental ethics, as well as the type of perspectival change that it
advocates. The justification for the land ethic is primarily ecological/scientific, whereas
the justification for deep ecology is much more metaphysical/spiritual.

12.3 THE "DEEP" IN DEEP ECOLOGY

We have now seen several respects in which proponents of deep ecology believe it to be
"deeper" than mainstream environmentalism. According to deep ecology:

- We must not only clean up environmental problems, but also address their
  underlying causes.
- The underlying causes of environmental problems are fundamental features of
  our current philosophical, cultural, and economic systems, including human
  chauvinism, individualism, and industrial capitalism.
- We must not only attempt to avoid participating in and perpetuating these
  systems and worldviews, we must also actively try to disrupt and dismantle them.
- We must recognize that all living things, forms of life (i.e., species), ecological
  systems, and diversity have final (or intrinsic or inherent) value.
- We must fit ourselves—our lifestyles and practices—within the limits of ecological systems, rather than dominating, manipulating, and engineering the systems
  and other organisms to better serve our wants and ends, and this requires
  significantly reducing fertility rates as well as consumption by affluent people.
- We must reconceptualize human flourishing, away from material accomplishment and possession and toward fulfilling and meaningful activities,
  relationships, and engagement.
- We must reject the view that humans are separate from the ecological world and/
  or hold a unique or privileged place within it, and instead see ourselves as one
  part of a greater ecological whole.
- Our interconnectedness and interdependence with nature is not merely ecological
  or social, but also metaphysical, such that we are fundamentally relational and
  the view that we are each a distinct, isolatable individual is mistaken.

- Accomplishing a relational, nonegoistic conception of ourselves cannot be achieved through rational argumentation and thought alone, but requires a radical shift in perspective that can be accomplished through such things as direct experience, deep questioning, and meditation.
- We should reject the strictly materialist ontology that currently dominates Western thought, and embrace instead the material-spiritual interconnectedness found in traditions such as Taoism, Buddhism, and many indigenous people's worldviews.

Many deep ecologists believe that these commitments support and cohere well with each other. However, as discussed earlier, there is considerable diversity in views among those who self-identify as deep ecologists. Some accept the practical principles, but not all of the value commitments. Others accept the value commitments, but not the spiritualism or metaphysical commitments. Moreover, many other environmental ethics accept several of the "deep" views enumerated above. Almost all of the theories we have studied support reducing fertility rates and reject overly materialistic conceptions of human flourishing. Many of them favor systemic reforms over technological fixes for environmental problems. All nonanthropocentric ethics reject human chauvinism and the strict commoditization or monetization of nature (i.e., valuing it only economically or instrumentally). Biocentrism accepts the view that all living things have final value. Leopold's land ethic embraces holism. Thus, there are quite a lot of views that fall between the fully deep and the fully shallow.

✳ BOX 12.3   TOPIC TO CONSIDER

THE TECHNOFIX

Deep ecology is often associated with rejecting technological fixes for environmental and social problems. The term **technofix** refers to using technology to address the problematic effects of practices, activities, or institutions, rather than addressing the underlying causes of the problems—the practices, activities or institutions themselves. For example, Eric Katz considers ecological restoration to be a technofix, since it does not address the causes of ecological degradation and instead tries to undo it after it occurs (Box 4.5). Moreover, he worries that the promise of restoration makes it less likely that people will be motivated to prevent ecological degradation, thereby enabling the underlying problematic activities.

(cont.)

BOX 12.3 *(cont.)*

Technofix concerns are common in environmental ethics. An objection to genetically modified crops is that they are a technofix for agricultural problems generated by industrial commodity monoculture (Box 3.4). An objection to deextinction and conservation cloning is that they are technofixes for anthropogenic species extinctions (Box 13.4). An objection to fish stocking is that it is a technofix for overfishing and habitat destruction. And a prominent objection to **geoengineering** (or **climate engineering**) is that it is a technofix for climate change. Geoengineering involves large-scale intentional intervention in climatic and ecological processes to counteract the effects of climate change. For example, some researchers have proposed introducing sulphate aerosols into the stratosphere or spraying seawater into the atmosphere in order to reduce the amount of solar radiation that reaches the planet. The technofix concern about such *solar radiation management* proposals is that they do not address the underlying causes of anthropogenic climate change—such as population growth and high-emissions lifestyles—and that the prospect of them could be a disincentive for people to alter their consumption practices and for governments to adopt policies to mitigate greenhouse gas emissions.

Those who use the term "technofix" intend it to be pejorative. They find technofixes objectionable because they do not prevent ecological problems and can help perpetuate the practices that give rise to them. Moreover, technofixes depend for their success upon the ability to predict and control the impacts of technological interventions in complex systems, as well as on the capacity to find new technological solutions for whatever undesirable side effects the previous technological fix might have. They also are seen as crowding out or displacing alternatives that, although less technologically sophisticated, may be more immediate, more likely to succeed, and less susceptible to unintended side effects. (To be clear, those who oppose technofixes are not necessarily opposed to novel technologies generally. The technofix objection concerns employing technology in a particular way. It is consistent to oppose technofixes while supporting technological innovation and dissemination to prevent environmental problems and promote sustainability—for example, to oppose geoengineering but support alternative energy innovation, or to oppose herbicide-resistant crops but support developing improved water recapture systems.)

Given these concerns, why are technofix approaches to environmental problems so often embraced and pursued? One reason is **technological optimism** (Section 5.5). People have faith, based on prior experience, in the capacity for technological innovations to improve lives and solve problems. Another is that

(cont.)

BOX 12.3 *(cont.)*

technological fixes generally do not require significant behavioral and institutional changes. Geoengineering does not require people to reduce their energy usage or countries to transition to a low-emissions energy portfolio, for example. So if a technological fix works, it appears to eliminate the need to make demands on people or to pursue difficult to accomplish and potentially expensive policy and structural changes.

Can you think of additional cases (environmental, health, or social) in which technology is employed as a technofix? Do you think that it is always problematic to pursue a technofix? If so, why? If not, under what conditions is it justified? Can you provide examples of well-justified technofixes? Do you agree that there is an important ethical distinction between technologies that are developed to remediate problematic unintended effects and those that are developed to prevent problems from arising in the first place? Is prevention always preferable to treatment or remediation? Why or why not?

12.4 CONCERNS REGARDING DEEP ECOLOGY

Several of the concerns commonly raised regarding deep ecology are similar to those that arise with biocentrism and ecocentrism. The reason for this is that it shares value commitments with them—that all living things have intrinsic (or final) value and that we should be concerned about ecosystems and species as a whole.

Deep ecology's commitment to biocentric egalitarianism is sometimes criticized on the grounds that it is not plausible that all living things could be equally valuable and considerable, given their divergent capacities and interests. Eating carrots cannot be ethically equivalent to eating elk, let alone people. It is also sometimes argued that an ethic that regards all living things as having equal intrinsic value, and that this value implies a claim against being harmed for the ends of others, is unlivable, since we must kill living things to survive. The responses that deep ecologists offer to these types of concerns are largely the same as those provided when they are raised with respect to other theories, such as deontological biocentrism (Section 9.2). For example, although Naess insisted on nonhierarchical accounts of value, some deep ecologists have endorsed value differentiation among living things, while other deep ecologists have argued that equal value does not imply the same consideration or treatment. Moreover, many deep ecologists, including Naess, are explicit that respecting the intrinsic value of all life cannot require living without any ecological impacts and taking of nonhuman life (as Principle 3 of the deep ecology principles indicates).

Deep ecology, like the land ethic, is sometimes criticized on the grounds that it is ecofascist and that ecosystems do not have interests distinct from the individuals that comprise them. Again, deep ecologists' responses to these concerns are similar to those that defend ecocentrism. The view is not fascist, deep ecologists argue, since individuals are also recognized as valuable, and their flourishing needs to be promoted. It therefore favors respectful or compassionate holism. Moreover, in practice, what is good for species and ecosystems is generally good for the individual organisms that comprise them, and vice versa. The idea that ecosystems and species have interests is defended by appeal to our ordinary use of language, which involves describing them as healthy or unhealthy, as well as by the practices and concepts used in ecology and conservation biology. (These objections and responses were discussed at some length in Section 11.4, and will be revisited in Section 13.3).

Other concerns regarding deep ecology are particular to its distinctive metaphysical and epistemological commitments. Deep ecology asserts that rather than being discreet individuals, people are primarily relational and a part of a greater whole, not just ecologically or socially, but metaphysically. However, many people believe that this relational (self-in-Self) conception of identity is mistaken. We are in fact distinct, isolatable individuals with clearly distinguishable consciousnesses. This is not an illusion; it is the way things are. If you go bird watching while I stay home to study, I am not in any sense out walking in the woods experiencing the pleasure of a good sighting. If I die while you are gone, you (and the trees and birds in the park) continue to be as alive as before. So while it is true that we are connected to each other in social, political, and ecological ways, we are truly metaphysically distinct. If we were not, then my ceasing to exist would imply that at least some aspect of you also ceases to exist.

It is here, in response to this conception of the self, that deep ecologists appeal to self-realization. On the deep ecology view, self-realization cannot be intellectualized; it is experiential awareness. Once a person gains higher consciousness, she will see that the above objection to the "ecological self" or "allsided self" is mistaken. However, critics of deep ecology often argue that this epistemology or form of "knowing" is problematic. How could a person know if such self-realization is veridical or accurately depicts the way the world is? It might very well be deceptive, or merely a physiological phenomenon that is induced by certain parts of the brain becoming engaged or disengaged through "deep meditative practices." After all, it is possible to induce a feeling of oneness or connectedness with others by using some types of drugs. Why should we regard the sense of self that some deep ecologists experience as metaphysically authoritative?

Deep ecologists sometimes suggest that the self-realization experience verifies itself. The idea is that once a person has the experience or takes up the perspective, she is aware of its veracity. It is justified from the inside, so to speak. However, this is unlikely to satisfy critics of the deep ecology epistemology. They might ask, how can an experience be self-verifying in that way? Of course it seems like that is the way things "really are" when a person is having the experience. Experience is just like that. Dreams often feel real when one has them, but that they feel real or true does not make them so. Metaphysical beliefs must be justified by reasoning or conceptual analysis, for example. They cannot be justified by their experiential or qualitative character, on this view.

Moreover, many people do not have the self-realization experience, even when they are meditating or communing with nature. Some people experience nature as radically other, alien, or separate. Why should the deep ecology experience of self-awareness be privileged over the experiences of those who have a contrary one? Deep ecology would seem to not be justified for them. Indeed, a person who has not had the experience of self-realization has no reason to support deep ecology's metaphysic, and may have experiential reasons to reject it (if such experiences can be justifying). Thus, this criticism concludes, the experience of self-realization does not provide a basis for privileging the ecological self view. A deep ecologist might appeal to the experience as verifying itself, but so could an advocate of an alternative. What is more, the internal characteristics of an experience are not sufficient for accepting either a metaphysical view or an environmental ethic.

Another epistemological criticism regarding deep ecology is that its conception of "identification" is problematic. A person cannot identify with nonconscious living things or ecological systems and processes in the way that deep ecologists advocate, since nonconscious beings lack subjectivity. There is no "what it is like" to be an elm tree or a river, and perhaps not even a flea. So not only can we not see ourselves in them, and identify with them in that way, we also cannot know what it is like to be them, and so empathize with them. If, as Naess argues, identification is prior to moral concern, then it is difficult to see how moral concern could properly be extended to nonconscious entities. In response to this objection, deep ecologists might appeal to the same sorts of considerations as other biocentrists and holists. For example, we have much in common with living things and we can understand what is good and bad for them, even when imagining what it is like to be them is impossible.

Some critics of deep ecology have also puzzled over generating ecological consideration by means of expansion of the self. One concern is that there is an inherent tension in this strategy: Deep ecology advocates nonanthropocentrism even while the basis for the ethic is an extended conception of oneself (i.e., the ecological self). Another concern is that people are generally permitted to harm or modify themselves in all kinds of ways if they like. They can kill brain cells by drinking whiskey, get tattoos and piercings, and eat unhealthy foods. Some of these things might not be prudent, but they are permissible. So if all of nature and all living things are part of oneself, perhaps it is permissible to harm and modify them as well.

In response to these types of concerns, deep ecologists might emphasize that on their view the natural world and the living individuals that populate it are part of our extended selves, but they are not only that. They are also selves-in-Self. They are distinct modes or parts of the greater interconnected whole. This is why when one individual dies the others do not; and why it is not permissible to harm others on the grounds that they are part of your extended self. However, critics of deep ecology might argue, with this sort of response deep ecologists seem to want to have things both ways. One the one hand, we are so metaphysically intertwined with nature that when we harm others we harm ourselves and no one is saved until we are all saved. On the other hand, we are sufficiently metaphysically distinct that we are not justified in harming others on the grounds that they are part of ourselves and our existence is independent of the existence of others.

Finally, some critics of deep ecology have raised concerns about the transition be-tween the deep ecology metaphysic and its value system. Even supposing the deep ecol-ogy metaphysic, it seems doubtful that when one harms other living things one also harms oneself. Moreover, ontological equality or connectedness does not seem to imply equal moral status or value. Boulders and babies might be equally ontologically real and interconnected components of ecological systems and processes, but that seems insuf-ficient to establish any value claims regarding them. Moreover, if everything has value and has it equally in virtue of their ontology, then value claims do not distinguish. But part of what ethical theory needs to do is indicate which things we should care about and how we should care about them. If everything has value of the same sort and in the same way, then there is no differentiation, no helpful guidance, according to this concern.

As this section has demonstrated, there are myriad concerns about deep ecology's metaphysic and epistemology. Again, deep ecologists often emphasize that you can be a supporter of deep ecology—you can accept its value orientation and its prac-tical implications—without being committed to the metaphysical underpinnings. However, when the distinctive metaphysic and epistemology are cut loose, and the justification shifts to a focus on social and ecological interconnectedness, then deep ecology begins to resemble a pluralistic ecocentrism—for example, a respectful or compassionate land ethic (see Section 11.4.1).

12.5 SPIRITUAL EXPERIENCE AND ENVIRONMENTAL ETHICS

Even if spiritual and meditative experiences are not an adequate justificatory basis for environmental ethics, the fact that many people have a spiritual relationship with the natural environment is relevant to environmental ethics. For many people, such as Naess, Muir, Carson, and Leopold, the natural environment is a source of inspiration, renewal, nurturing, insight, religious communion, and ecstatic experience. That people experience the natural environment in these and related ways, and that they feel con-nected through it to processes and purposes greater than themselves is a significant di-mension of the human-nature relationship. The question, then, is how this feature of the human-nature relationship should inform or be incorporated into environmental ethics.

The arguments against deep ecology are primarily arguments against *basing* an environmental ethic on spiritual or metaphysical experience. The primary concern is that there must be a way to evaluate or justify which experiences are veridical and which are not. *Contra* deep ecology, the experiences themselves cannot provide this.

It requires measuring them (or comparing them) to the world, especially since many contrary experiences seem veridical to those who have them. So we must use reasons, arguments, justification, and evidence in order to adjudicate between competing environmental ethics, not the qualitative nature of spiritual and metaphysical experiences.

However, there are other, non-basic, roles that the spiritual dimension of the human-nature relationship might play in environmental ethics. First, those who experience spiritual connections with nature report that they find them beneficial. That is to say, they are standardly considered by those who have them to be desirable, either because of the quality of the experiences themselves or the consequences resulting from them. Given that they are beneficial, a person is better off having them than not. This justifies both cultivating an openness or receptivity to such experiences and promoting opportunities for them. This argument is analogous in many ways to Leopold's argument that we should preserve wilderness because it provides recreational opportunities (of the right sort), and that we should cultivate the kind of dispositions that enable us to fully benefit from those opportunities (see Sections 10.2 and 11.3).

Second, the spiritual dimension of the human-nature relationship might help promote environmentally considerate behavior. A large number of people report being concerned about environmental issues, even while they do little about them. For example, in the United States 42 percent of people described themselves as *sympathetic but inactive* regarding the environmental movement (Dunlap 2010). People often agree that they ought to consume less, not support CAFOs, buy more efficient cars, recycle, and generally engage in environmentally friendly behaviors, but then fail to act in accordance with their own ethical evaluations. Perhaps promoting a spiritual connection between people and nature is one way—in addition to behavioral, economic, and educational approaches—to help reduce the dissonance between some people's evaluations and their behaviors regarding the environment. Thus, even if appeals to spiritual and experiential considerations are tenuous foundations or justifications for an environmental ethic, there are important roles for them within environmental ethics.

12.6 SUMMARY

The primary questions addressed in this chapter were:

- What are the core values, principles, and practical commitments associated with deep ecology?
- In virtue of what do proponents of deep ecology consider it to be "deep" in comparison to other environmental ethics and movements?
- What are the distinctive metaphysics and epistemology often associated with deep ecology?
- What are the most prominent concerns regarding deep ecology?

Deep ecology is an influential view within environmental ethics. It involves crucial critical perspectives on environmental problems and what is required to address them. It poses challenging questions regarding predominant ideologies, power relationships, and social, political, and economic institutions. It emphasizes the responsibilities that we have—individually and collectively—to address ecological problems and the factors that give rise to them. Therefore, even for those who do not embrace deep ecology in total, it provides valuable resources for analyzing and evaluating environmental issues and problems.

Deep ecology has much in common with biocentrism and ecocentrism, particularly with respect to their value and practical commitments. The more philosophical versions of deep ecology are distinguished by their metaphysical underpinnings, their epistemologies, and thereby their justifications for biocentric pluralism. Thus, quite a lot of the discussion regarding deep ecology concerns the viability of its distinctive metaphysical and epistemological commitments. However, even if they are ultimately not tenable, many of the principles of deep ecology may nevertheless be justified, since they are supported by several other approaches to environmental ethics.

KEY TERMS (SEE GLOSSARY FOR DEFINITIONS):

biocentric egalitarianism

biocentric pluralism

Cartesian dualism

deep ecology

ecological consciousness

ecotage (or monkey wrenching)

ecoterrorism

food system

geoengineering
(or climate engineering)

global food system

ontological holism and egalitarianism (or metaphysical holism)

metaphysics

radical environmentalism

self-realization

shallow ecology (or shallow environmentalism)

technofix

technological optimism

REVIEW QUESTIONS

• How does Naess conceive of the difference between deep and shallow environmentalism?

• What does it mean to describe something as a technofix?

• What are the core value commitments associated with deep ecology? What principles and practical commitments are they thought to support?

- Why is deep ecology often associated with direct action environmentalism and supportive of social justice activism?
- What is self-realization and how does it relate to deep ecology?
- What are some of the respects in which deep ecology is considered by its proponents to be "deeper" than other environmental ethics?
- What are the primary criticisms against the distinctive metaphysics and epistemology proposed by some deep ecologists?

DISCUSSION QUESTIONS

- Do you agree that environmental movements should focus on addressing the underlying causes of environmental problems, rather than merely addressing them after they arise? If so, do you agree with Naess that this requires substantial reorientation in perspectives and ideologies, as well as structural and systemic changes to economic, social, and political systems? Why or why not?
- Which of the eight principles of deep ecology would you endorse? Why would you endorse them? Why would you not endorse the others?
- Do you think that the self-in-Self metaphysical holism view is more justified than the view that individuals are metaphysically isolated or distinct? Why or why not?
- Do you agree that spiritual experiences and connections with nature cannot play a basic justificatory role for a theory of environmental ethics? Why or why not?
- Which of the "deep" aspects of deep ecology do you believe ought to be part of a theory of environmental ethics? Which of the theories that have been discussed so far incorporate them?
- Why do you think deep ecology is often considered to be a more radical environmental ethic than the other theories that have been discussed?

FURTHER READING

Influential foundational statements on deep ecology can be found in:

Devall, Bill, and George Sessions, *Deep Ecology: Living as if Nature Mattered*. Gibbs Smith, 1985.

Naess, Arne. "The Shallow and the Deep, Long-Range Ecology Movement." *Inquiry* 16 (1973): 95–100.

Naess, Arne. "The Deep Ecology Movement: Some Philosophical Aspects." *Philosophical Inquiry* 8 (1986): 10–31.

Naess, Arne. "Self-Realization: An Ecological Approach to Being in the World." *The Trumpeter* 4, no. 3 (1987): 35–42.

Naess, Arne. *Ecology, Community and Lifestyle.* Cambridge University Press, 1989.

Work that clarifies, defends, extends, and/or critiques deep ecology includes:

Barnhill, David Landis, and Roger S. Gottlieb, *Deep Ecology and World Religions.* SUNY Press, 2001.

Bookchin, Murray. "Social Ecology versus Deep Ecology." *Socialist Review* 18, no. 3 (1988): 11–29.

Curry, Patrick. *Ecological Ethics.* Polity, 2011.

Drengson, Alan, and Yuichi Inoue, *The Deep Ecology Movement.* North Atlantic Books, 1995.

Grey, William. "Anthropocentrism and Deep Ecology." *Australasian Journal of Philosophy* 71, no. 4 (1992): 463–75.

Katz, Eric, Andrew Light, and David Rothenberg, eds. *Beneath the Surface: Critical Essays in the Philosophy of Deep Ecology.* M.I.T. Press, 2000.

Keller, David. "Gleaning Lessons from Deep Ecology." *Ethics and the Environment* 2, no. 2 (1997): 139–48.

Salleh, Ariel Kay. "Deeper than Deep Ecology: The EcoFeminist Connection." *Environmental Ethics* 6 (Winter 1984): 339–45.

Sessions, George, ed. *Deep Ecology for the Twenty-First Century: Readings on the Philosophy and Practice of the New Environmentalism.* Shambhala, 1995.

Zimmerman, Michael. *Contesting Earth's Future: Radical Ecology and Postmodernity.* University of California Press, 1994.

CHAPTER THIRTEEN

SPECIES AND BIODIVERSITY

AT THE CORE OF conservation biology, as well as many forms of environmentalism, is the value commitment that the "[d]iversity of organisms is good . . . [and] the untimely extinction of populations and species is bad" (Soulé 1985, 729–32). These values are reflected in policies and practices around the world. The United Nations Convention on Biological Diversity, which has over 150 signatories, calls upon nations to protect biodiversity within their borders. Many countries have legislation that requires identifying species at risk of extinction and taking steps to preserve them—for example, the United States' Endangered Species Act and Canada's Species at Risk Act. National and international nongovernmental organizations (NGOs), such as the International Union for the Conservation of Nature (IUCN), Nature Conservancy, and World Wildlife Fund, are committed to raising awareness about at-risk species and mobilizing efforts to protect them. Among the approaches commonly employed to conserve species are creation of parks and reserves, ecological restoration, setting take limits, captive breeding programs, and species translocations and reintroductions. Conservationists are also increasingly pursuing novel strategies, such assisted colonization, rewilding, cloning, and deextinction.

Although there is widespread agreement that preserving biodiversity is important, there are divergent views about why species and biodiversity are valuable. Some advocate managing biodiversity and particular species to maximally satisfy people's economic, medical, material, and recreational needs and wants—on the basis of their **instrumental value**. Others advocate preserving biodiversity on the grounds that some species might prove useful to us in the future in ways that we cannot now

294

anticipate—on the basis of their **option value**. Still others argue that species and biodiversity have **subjective final value** in virtue of people's valuing of them and preferences for preserving them. Yet others argue that species have **objective final value** either in the form of **inherent worth** (i.e., they have interests or a good of their own that we ought to care about) or **natural value** (i.e., in virtue of being wondrous forms of life arising from natural historical processes). (These types of value are discussed at length in Chapter 4.)

In many cases, these views about the importance of species and biodiversity converge in practice. For example, there is a correlation between positive socioeconomic outcomes and positive conservation outcomes for parks and reserves (Oldekop et al. 2015). Protecting biologically diverse areas in ways that empower local communities and involve them in management often maintains ecosystem services, has economic benefits, and protects aesthetic and cultural values, in addition to helping to conserve species. However, there are also cases where different views on the value of species and biodiversity have divergent practical implications. For example, if species and biodiversity are only instrumentally valuable, then they might justifiably be traded off for other things that are more instrumentally valuable. Perhaps we ought not put conserving a rare and endemic species of fish, spider, or bird ahead of economic development, job creation, property rights, or infrastructure expansion. Or if species only have subjective final value, then perhaps we need not put resources toward conserving species that people do not care about and that are not useful to us. In contrast, if species have final objective value—if they matter in themselves or for what they are—then perhaps we have duties to try to conserve all species, or at least as many as possible, even if that means placing limits on what people can do with their land or restricting industry and development in some places. There are thus a number of conservation issues whose resolution depends upon gaining clarity on how and why species and biodiversity are valuable, such as:

- Should resources be put toward protecting species that are not ecologically or economically significant?
- Can species protection justify restricting people from accessing resources or using their property in ways they would like?
- Is it permissible to kill large numbers of a common or nonnative species in order to protect a smaller number of a rare or endemic species?
- How intensively should people intervene into ecological systems in order to preserve threatened species or populations?
- Is it permissible to capture wild animals and keep them in captivity in order to use them in species conservation efforts such as breeding programs and translocations?
- Should bioengineering-oriented species conservation strategies be adopted, such as conservation cloning, deextinction, and gene drives?

This chapter focuses on different views about the value of species and biodiversity, as well as the practical implications of those views. However, it is first necessary to clarify what species and biodiversity are.

13.1 WHAT ARE SPECIES AND BIODIVERSITY?

Earlier I suggested that with contested or ambiguous terms such as "nature" there often is not a uniquely correct definition (Section 3.1). Therefore, the focus should be on clarifying which definition is most useful in a particular context. For example, the conception of "family" that is useful depends upon whether the topic is a person's medical history or who she should invite to a special occasion; and which conception of "nature" should be employed depends upon whether a person is doing physics or planning a hike. The same holds with respect to "species" and "biodiversity." There is no single widely agreed upon definition of "species" or "biodiversity." Instead, there are several (sometimes related) species and biodiversity concepts that are usefully employed in different contexts.

In general, the term "species" is used to refer to a taxonomic category that differentiates within a *genus*. For example, the bear family (*Ursidae*) includes the genus *Ursus*, which includes the polar bear (*Ursus maritimus*), brown bear (*Ursus arctos*), and black bear (*Ursus americanus*), among other species. So species concepts are used to group organisms together (and differentiate them from other groups of organisms) based upon their having similar, biologically important characteristics. However, there are a lot of biologically important features of organisms, and different species concepts focus on different ones. For example, species are sometimes conceived of in terms of reproductive isolation—as interbreeding (or potentially interbreeding) populations. On this view, two organisms are **conspecific** (i.e., the same species) if they are capable of having offspring together. Species are sometimes conceived of phylogenetically or evolutionarily—as a lineage of ancestral-descendant populations. On this view, organisms are conspecific if they are on the same "branch" of the evolutionary tree. Species are sometimes conceived of ecologically—as populations that occupy an ecological niche different from that of any other lineage in its range. On this view, whether organisms are conspecific depends in part on the similarity of their fit within their ecosystems. Species are also sometimes conceived of genetically—in terms of overall genotypic similarity distinct from that of other organisms—or morphologically—in terms of shared anatomical features different from those of other groups of organisms.

Part of the explanation for why there are myriad conceptions of species is that biologists with different concerns and research projects refer to different kinds of groups as "species." For instance, the ecological species concept is more useful for ecologists formulating and studying questions about ecological relationships and functions than is the phylogenetic species concept; whereas the phylogenetic species concept is better suited to the work of evolutionary biologists interested in ancestral relationships than is the ecological species concept. And while reproductive isolation is a useful approach to categorization when trying to distinguish groups of sexually reproducing organisms whose ranges overlap, it is less useful where populations do not overlap geographically and it is not at all useful when studying populations of asexually reproducing organisms. That there are multiple species concepts that are used productively to study and explain the biological world provides support for a view called **species pluralism**—the view that there is a plurality of legitimate species concepts. The idea that there is a single best way to divide organisms into species—**species monism**—seems belied by productive biological practice. Organisms have phylogenies (evolutionary histories), ecological niches, genotypes, and reproductive communities. These are all explanatorily important, and no one of them seems to be more basic or to pick out the fundamental causal structure of the biological world. So, again, the issue is not which species concept is uniquely correct, but which concept is useful in which contexts.

In what follows, I employ a conception of species that many environmental ethicists believe captures what is crucial to the value of species. Here is Holmes Rolston III, the most prominent advocate of the objective value of species, describing the concept:

> It is admittedly difficult to pinpoint precisely what a species is, and there may be no single, quintessential way to define species. . . . All we need for this discussion, however, is that species be objectively there as living processes in the evolutionary ecosystem; the varied criteria for defining them (descent, reproductive isolation, morphology, gene pool) come together at least in providing evidence that species are really there . . .
> *A species is a coherent, ongoing form of life expressed in organisms, encoded in gene flow, and shaped by the environment.* (Rolston 1989, 210, italics added)

On this view, species are groups of biologically related organisms that are distinguished from other groups of organisms in virtue of their shared **form of life**. A species' form of life refers to how individuals of the biological group typically strive to make their way in the world. It concerns what sorts of things they consume, how they reproduce, how (and when and whether) they move, how they avoid predators, and how they repair themselves when damaged. It is straightforward to distinguish and group organisms on this basis. The form of life of a cottonmouth snake is clearly different from that of a silver maple, a black swallowtail butterfly, and an arctic fox. It is also quite different from that of eastern garter snakes and timber rattlers. These species have distinct life cycles, behaviors, habitats, predators, prey, and protections. Of course, they do so largely because of differences in their biological parts and processes—their phenotypes. These, in turn, are largely (though not entirely) explained by their genetic differences—their genotypes. Thus, species are forms of life "encoded in gene flow, and shaped by the environment."

The **form of life conception of species** is a familiar one. It is operative in zoology and botany when work in those fields involves describing what biologically related individuals do and how they go about doing it. It is the conception around which nature programs about species are organized when they focus on how species migrate, hunt, reproduce, survive the winter, and generally get on in the world. Moreover, it is the conception of species that picks out what troubles many people when it comes to anthropogenic species extinctions: beautiful, amazing, and unique forms of life will cease to be instantiated. It is not the genotype that they primarily want to see preserved, or even the phenotype as it might be in a zoo or farm, but organisms going about the world in their distinctive ways—migrating wildebeest, soaring Andean condors, roaming polar bears, spawning Chinook salmon, towering torreya, leafcutter ants, dancing honeybees, and breaching humpbacks. Therefore, I employ this conception of species (unless otherwise noted), not because it is the uniquely correct way to "carve up" the biological world and classify organisms, but because it is what many environmental ethicists and environmentalists find crucial to the value of species.

As with "species," there is no single, universally employed conception of "biodiversity." There is instead a plurality of important varieties of biodiversity, and different conceptions of biodiversity are useful for different purposes. For example, intraspecific genetic diversity is useful when studying the viability of species populations and their capacity to respond to stressors. Generally, the less genetically diverse a population, the less robust and adaptable it is in comparison to a more genetically variable (and comparably sized) population of the species. This is true for both wild populations and cultivated species (i.e., crops). However, intraspecific genetic diversity does not provide information regarding the importance of organism or population traits to the systems in which they are located. For this reason, functional diversity often is more useful when studying the integrity and stability of systems, since it concerns the role of organisms and populations in ecosystem processes. Because it concerns ecosystem processes, functional diversity is also crucial to the capacity of ecosystems to reliably provide ecosystems services. Another type of biodiversity, beta diversity, concerns the diversity between areas or ecosystems. The greater the beta diversity between two or more systems, the more species that are found in one but not the other system. Beta diversity is therefore useful for studying why species are distributed as they are, and it is crucial to decision-making regarding protected area designations and management planning. Overall, biological diversity encompasses variability "within species [i.e., genetic], between species, and of ecosystems" (UN 1992, Article 2), and it includes differences with respect to composition, structure, and function. Each of these dimensions of biological diversity captures something biologically and ecologically significant. But, again, some conceptions of biodiversity are more useful in particular contexts than are others.

Because the focus of this chapter is on issues related to species conservation, "biodiversity" will be used to refer to species-level diversity understood through the form of life conception of species, and not genetic diversity or phylogenetic diversity, for example. More specifically, biodiversity will be understood in terms of **species richness**—the number of species in a geographic area or system (or what is referred to as alpha diversity)—informed by their relative abundance and uniqueness. Biodiversity is thus a property of places and systems. One area or system is more biodiverse than another if it has a greater variety of species, less common species, or larger populations of species than the other.

13.2 THE INSTRUMENTAL VALUE OF SPECIES AND BIODIVERSITY

It is widely recognized that species and biodiversity are useful for people (see, e.g., Sections 4.1, 4.3, 5.6, and 9.4). They provide ecosystem services. For example, bees pollinate crops and mangrove forests provide storm surge protection. They are economically value. For example, they provide natural resources (e.g., lumber and food) and support ecotourism. They are recreationally valuable. For example, people enjoy fishing and wildlife viewing. They are medically significant. For example, they are a source for medicinal herbs and drug discovery.

Preserving species and maintaining biodiversity are also thought to be essential to maintaining ecological integrity—they have **ecological value**. On some theories, such as the land ethic and deep ecology, ecological integrity is important because ecosystems have value or worth that we ought to care about for its own sake. On other accounts, ecological integrity is valuable because ecosystems provide us with a broad array of natural resources, ecosystem services, and self-realization goods (e.g., educational, developmental, and spiritual opportunities). Whether biodiversity promotes ecosystem integrity and associated instrumental goods is an empirical question. Evidence suggests that in many cases it does. For example, plant species richness has been found to enhance ecosystem multifunctionality (Maestre et al. 2012); restoration of biodiversity has been found to increase ecosystem services and productivity (Benayas et al. 2009; Worm et al. 2006); and maintaining biodiversity appears to be associated with a lower prevalence of infectious disease transmission (Keesing 2010). In addition, all species have at least some instrumental value for other organisms. Even when they are not beneficial for us, they are for the organisms that predate on them, live in them, or otherwise make use of them.

Moreover, species that have little instrumental value now may turn out to be valuable in the future, either because we discover something useful about them or because they (or species descended from them) become more ecologically significant over time.

For example, an enzyme discovered in a bacterium that survives in hot springs at Yellowstone National Park is central to the process of polymerase chain reaction (PCR). PCR is a technique that rapidly and accurately duplicates fragments of DNA, which is crucial to genetic research and applied biotechnology—in drug discovery, genomic sequencing, and cloning, for example. In 1993, Kary Mullis won the Nobel Prize in chemistry for its discovery. Since we do not know where the next discovery or ecologically important species will come from, biological diversity has significant option value.

The myriad ways in which species and biodiversity are valuable to us is often highlighted in conservation policies. For example, the US Endangered Species Act begins as follows:

> The Congress finds and declares that—(1) various species of fish, wildlife, and plants in the United States have been rendered extinct as a consequence of economic growth and development untempered by adequate concern and conservation; (2) other species of fish, wildlife, and plants have been so depleted in numbers that they are in danger of or threatened with extinction; (3) *these species of fish, wildlife, and plants are of esthetic, ecological, educational, historical, recreational, and scientific value to the Nation and its people.* (United States Congress 1973, italics added)

The preamble of the United Nations Convention on Biological Diversity (CBD) also recognizes the variety of goods and services provided by biodiversity, in addition to asserting its intrinsic value, stating that the signatories are:

> *Conscious* of the intrinsic value of biological diversity and of the ecological, genetic, social, economic, scientific, educational, cultural, recreational, and aesthetic values of biological diversity and its components,
>
> *Conscious also* of the importance of biological diversity for evolution and for maintaining life sustaining systems of the biosphere, . . .
>
> *Aware* that conservation and sustainable use of biological diversity is of critical importance for meeting the food, health, and other needs of the growing world population, . . .
>
> *Determined* to conserve and sustainably use biological diversity for the benefit of present and future generations. (UN 1992, Preamble)

These statements reiterate what has been highlighted many times throughout this textbook: Human well-being is tied to ecological processes that involve living organisms and ecosystems. However, inferring from the fact that *biodiversity* has significant instrumental value (including option value) and the fact that each species contributes to biodiversity to the conclusion that *each species* has significant instrumental (or option) value commits the **fallacy of decomposition**. Just because the whole has some property—for instance, you are conscious or biodiversity has significant option value—it does not follow that each of its parts has the same property—for instance, your organs are conscious or each species has significant option value. In fact, species differ widely in the types and amounts of instrumental value they possess. Some species are keystone species (e.g., eastern hemlock and African elephants); some are recreationally valuable (e.g., rainbow trout and sequoia redwoods); some are medicinally significant (e.g., horseshoe crabs and sweet wormwood); some are economically significant (e.g., honeybees and mahogany); some are culturally valuable (e.g., Chinook salmon and wild rice); and some are scientifically valuable (e.g., platypuses and chimpanzees). However, many species are none of these. In fact, only a small portion of species are keystone or dominant species, economically significant, scientifically crucial, or medicinally useful (Maclaurin and Sterelny 2008). Therefore, case-by-case assessment of the instrumental value of species is needed.

Moreover, instrumental values can be substituted, replaced, and traded off. A species might be extremely valuable as a food or medicinal source, until technological development and dissemination makes other foods or medicines more easily and cheaply available. For example, an anticancer drug that was developed from a compound found in the bark of the Pacific Yew tree is now more cheaply and easily produced synthetically than from harvested trees. Or a charismatic species might draw some wildlife tourism, and so provide some economic value, but its habitat might have much greater natural resource value. This is the case, for example, with many sea turtle nesting beaches in the Caribbean and Central America. They generate some ecotourism, but it would be far more economically valuable to develop them into resorts.

For these reasons, instrumental value alone is insufficient to justify the view that there is a duty to try to conserve all anthropogenically threatened species, even those that are ecologically insignificant, narrowly distributed, economically unimportant, and not of much interest. This is especially so when conserving them has substantial opportunity costs—that is, when it requires significant expenditures, limiting agriculture, leaving natural resources unaccessed, or slowing development. Therefore, if there is a duty to conserve all endangered species, it must be grounded in their having final value, which is why the issue of whether species and biodiversity have final value, and unconditional or objective final value in particular, is so practically significant.

SPECIES CONSERVATION AND DEVELOPMENT: THE BRAKEN BAT CAVE MESHWEAVER VERSUS SAN ANTONIO COMMUTERS

The Endangered Species Act (ESA) is the United States' most powerful piece of conservation legislation. A large part of the reason for this is that protection of species, as it is operationalized within the ESA, involves not only keeping species in existence, but doing so in their historical range (i.e., *in situ*). The provisions of the act are not met if a listed species is kept in existence only in a zoo or collection (i.e., *ex situ*). Therefore, when a species or population is listed as threatened or endangered, the individuals of the species are protected from being "taken" (i.e., killed or harvested) *and* their "critical habitat" (i.e., the geographical areas and ecological processes crucial to their conservation) is protected from being destroyed or adversely modified. Protecting the critical habitat of species often requires restricting economic activities and infrastructure expansion, including on private property. This is the primary reason why the ESA remains controversial and is regularly politically contested.

We have already seen cases in which species conservation comes into tension with economic interests and development. For example, protecting the delta smelt's critical habitat requires allocating scarce water resources to its conservation that might otherwise go to agriculture, industry, or cities (Box 1.1). Protecting the gray wolf requires restricting what ranchers can do to protect their herds from depredation (Section 11.1 and Box 11.1). A past high-profile case is the northern spotted owl's ESA listing in 1990, which requires timber companies to leave intact at least 40 percent of old-growth forests within 1.3 miles of any owl nest or activity center. Another is the controversy around whether protecting the snail darter (a species of perch) required maintaining water flows of the Little Tennessee River, on which the Tellico Dam was built in the 1970s. The snail darter case went all the way to the US Supreme Court in 1978, which ruled that the ESA afforded species conservation the highest priority, which meant that protecting the fish took precedence over the economic and development benefits of the dam. However, following the ruling Congress passed an amendment to the ESA that authorized assessing the economic impacts of a listing and taking them into account when developing management plans or "rules." Congress also passed an amendment to a different act that specifically exempted the Tellico Dam area from the ESA. This enabled the gates of the dam to be closed and led to the snail darter being lost in that area (although several other small populations have since been found elsewhere).

(cont.)

BOX 13.1 *(cont.)*

Here is a more recent case to consider. In early 2012, work began on a project in San Antonio, Texas, to build an underpass to improve traffic flows at a congested highway intersection through which nearly 100,000 commuters pass daily. A few months into construction, a biologist consulting on the project spotted a dime-sized spider that appeared to be a Braken Bat Cave meshweaver, a local endemic that had only been seen once before (approximately 5 miles from the construction site) and was placed on the endangered species list in 2000. When dissection of the spider confirmed that it was in fact a Braken Bat Cave meshweaver, the project was immediately and indefinitely halted to determine if it was feasible to continue without further disturbance of the meshweaver habitat. After two years, the Texas Department of Transportation and the Fish and Wildlife Service developed a plan that would allow construction to move forward, but with an overpass rather than an underpass. (The spiders live in caves, and an overpass involves much less excavation and ground disturbance than an underpass.) However, the cost of the project nearly tripled from $15.1 million to $44 million. The Department of Transportation is also required to conduct an extensive survey of the area for other occurrences of the spider, as well as other endangered endemics, so that they can be protected in the future.

Image 13.1   A Braken Bat Cave meshweaver.
Source: Dr. Jean K. Krejca, Zara Environmental LLC   *(cont.)*

BOX 13.1 *(cont.)*

Do you believe that protecting the Braken Bat Cave meshweaver's habitat justified putting the highway project on hold for over two years and tripling its costs? Why or why not? Do you think the solution reached was a reasonable compromise between protecting the spider and improving the highway for commuters? Suppose that it was not possible to continue the project without doing significant harm to the meshweaver's critical habitat. Would you support abandoning the highway improvement project altogether or allowing it to go forward?

13.3 THE FINAL VALUE OF SPECIES

Many conservationists and environmental ethicists recognize that while instrumental considerations justify preventing large-scale species extinctions and conserving many particular species, they do not justify the view that there is a responsibility to try to conserve each and every species. Therefore, those who advocate for a duty to prevent all species from anthropogenic extinction—and consider all anthropogenic species extinctions wrong—typically do so on the grounds that each species has final (or intrinsic) value. Here is a general formulation of the core argument that there is a duty to conserve all anthropogenically threatened species (hereafter, the **argument to preserve all species**):

1. Each species has unique and/or irreplaceable final value.
2. If something has unique and/or irreplaceable final value, then there is a duty to not destroy it (and to prevent others from doing so).

   _____

3. Therefore, there is a duty not to destroy species (and to prevent their extinction when their endangerment is anthropogenic).

The reasoning in this argument is valid. *If* the premises are true, then the conclusion follows. So let us focus on the premises. Why do proponents of this view believe that each species has unique or irreplaceable final value? There are two types of reasons offered. One is that each species has natural-historical value. The other is that each species has inherent worth. These are discussed in turn below.

BOX 13.2   THOUGHT EXPERIMENT

BIODIVERSITY, RARITY, AND WELFARISM

Imagine that you are faced with a choice between two options, A and B, both of which will result in the death of one hundred organisms with similar

(cont.)

BOX 13.2 *(cont.)*

psychological complexity and similar instrumental value. The only difference is that in option A the organisms are part of a populous species, whereas in option B the organisms are the last remaining members of their species. Would you choose option A, option B, or use a random choice procedure (e.g., flip a coin)?

This thought experiment is used to motivate the idea that individualistic approaches to environmental ethics are inadequate. Most people believe that option B is worse than option A—that it is worse to destroy the last members of a species than the same number of a more numerous species. But if all that matters—all that has value—is the welfare of the individuals involved (a view sometimes called **welfarism**), then A and B would seem equally bad, since they involve the same sorts of harms to the same number of organisms. Therefore, the fact that people find B worse than A seems to suggest that there must be more at stake, more that has value, than just individual welfare. What could this be?

Several different (not mutually exclusive) views have been offered. The most common view, discussed at length in this chapter, is that species have intrinsic or final value—typically natural-historical value or inherent worth—distinct from that of the organisms that comprise them, and this is what makes causing extinction bad above and beyond the organism killing involved. Another common view is that scarcity and/or specialization is a value-adding property when it comes to species: "[S]omething about the rarity of endangered species heightens the element of respect and accompanying duty" (Rolston 1989, 526). A third view is that species have value because they comprise biodiversity, which is valuable. On this view, species have *contributory value*, which is when "something has value in virtue of its part-whole relations" (Bradley 2001, 49).

What do you think about this thought experiment? Does it favor the view that it is worse to kill (or let die) individuals of an endangered species than a numerous one, all other things being equal? If so, what explains this? Is it one of the reasons discussed above or something else? How might an individualist respond to this thought experiment? Is there a way to account for the fact that most people believe option B is worse that is consistent with individualism—for example, by appealing to option value or subjective values?

Moreover, what do you think about the idea that rarity in this context is a value-adding property? In what other contexts does rarity add to value? Is there any reason that rarity at the species level should be value-adding, rather than rarity at the subspecies or variety level, for example? Are there good reasons for prioritizing concern for diversity at the species level, rather than at the subspecies (or genus or variant) levels?

13.3.1 The Natural Historical Value of Species

Natural value refers to the value that something has in virtue of its independence from human design, control, and impacts (Section 4.4). Many environmental philosophers and conservationists believe that species have such value. Holmes Rolston III is a prominent proponent of this view. He argues that each species has final (or intrinsic) value because it is a distinctive historical form of life that is the product and instrument of creative and generative evolutionary processes:

> A naturalistic account values species and speciation intrinsically, not as resources or as a means to human excellence. Humans ought to respect these dynamic life forms preserved in historical lines, vital informational processes that persist genetically over millions of years, overleaping short-lived individuals. It is not form (species) as mere morphology, but the formative (speciating) process that humans ought to preserve, although the process cannot be preserved without some of its products, and the products (species) are valuable as results of the creative process. An ethic about species sees that the species is a bigger event than the individual organism, although species are always exemplified in individual organisms. (1995, 522)

In this passage, Rolston affirms the view that concern for species (the form of life) should take precedence over concern for the individual organisms that instantiate it. (The priority of the species over the individual is why the view is regarded as holistic.) One reason for this is that individual organisms are replaced with each generation. Another is that their deaths are crucial components of ecological and evolutionary processes. In contrast, species are not replicable. Extinction ends all generations. It terminates all future evolutionary possibilities:

> Death of a token is radically different from death of a type; death of an individual, different from death of an entire lineage . . .
>   Extinction shuts down the generative processes, a kind of superkilling. This kills the forms (*species*)—not just the individuals. This kills "essences" beyond "existences," the "soul" as well as the "body." This kills collectively, not just distributively. To kill a particular plant is to stop a life of a few years, while other lives of such kind continue unabated, and the possibilities for the future are unaffected; to superkill a particular species is to shut down a story of many millennia and leave no future possibilities. (1995, 523)

Given the priority of species over individuals, if it is necessary to cull nonnative species, capture and translocate individuals, or conduct captive breeding programs in order to preserve at-risk species, then these ought to be done. Moreover, on Rolston's view it is not enough to merely keep individuals of a species in existence in zoos or aquaria. What is valuable is their form of life. Therefore, in order to preserve the value of species it is necessary to preserve the habitat in which the form of life is expressed:

> It is not preservation of *species* that we wish, but the preservation of *species in the system*. It is not merely *what* they are, but *where* they are that we must value correctly . . . The species *can* only be preserved *in situ*; the species *ought* to be preserved *in situ*. (1995, 524)

The CBD (like the ESA) seconds this view:

> the fundamental requirement for the conservation of biological diversity is the *in-situ* conservation of ecosystems and natural habitats and the maintenance and recovery of viable populations of species in their natural surroundings. (UN 1992, Preamble)

On this view, "species conservation" means "maintaining viable independent populations that express the species' form of life in its historical range." Therefore, the natural historical value of species favors creating large areas of protected land and sea that enable species to roam, hunt, migrate, disperse, reproduce, and generally go about the world in their distinctive ways.

But do species and biodiversity actually possess natural-historical value? It is clear that many people value species for what they are and for their connection to historical evolutionary processes. This is evidenced by the CBD assertion that biodiversity and its components possess "intrinsic value," widespread membership in and contributions to environmental organizations, and social science research on people's attitudes regarding species, biodiversity, and naturalness (Kempton et al. 1995; Bosso 2005; Bruskotter et al. 2015). Therefore, species and biodiversity have subjective final value.

However, subjective final value, like instrumental value, is not sufficient for generating a duty to preserve all species. There might be some species that are not highly valued by people, or people might value some other things more than conserving species. If the value of species depends upon people valuing them or their continued existence (sometimes called **existence value**), then their value is contingent and will not ground a duty to preserve each and every anthropocentric threatened species. (See Section 4.2 for discussion of this point regarding subjective value generally).

Therefore, many proponents of the argument to preserve all species argue that species possess objective value. According to Rolston, "endangered species are objectively valuable kinds, good in themselves" (1995, 526). As discussed earlier (Section 4.2), objective value is not based on people's evaluative attitudes. Instead, valuers need to recognize it, discover it. Thus, if species possess objective natural-historical value, it must be that everyone ought to recognize their final value, even if they currently do not. That is, there must be reasons for valuing them that are not dependent upon people's actual beliefs and judgments. Those who advocate for the objective value of species and biodiversity generally believe that a rational, fully informed person who understands the ecological and evolutionary significance of species and biodiversity will value them as unique and wondrous achievements of nonhuman nature. Species and biodiversity are thought to *merit* our valuing them for their being expressions of the creativity and exuberance of nature, repositories of millions of years of evolutionary history, and the loci of future evolutionary possibilities.

Critics of the objectivity of the natural historical value of species and biodiversity believe that the reasoning offered in support of it is fallacious. Proponents seem to infer that species and biodiversity possess objective value because they generate and are generated from other species, which possess the value. But this commits the **fallacy of begging the question**, since the issue just is whether species are objectively valuable in virtue of their natural historical properties. Moreover, it cannot be that they are objectively valuable because evolutionary processes or ecosystems, which depend crucially on species, have objective value. This reasoning commits a version of the **genetic fallacy**. One cannot conclude that something has a certain value because it is produced by something that has that value. For example, human beings have inherent worth, but it does not follow that the furniture people build does. Critics also believe that the claim that species are objectively valuable in virtue of their being unique achievements of evolution commits the **fallacy of asserting the conclusion**. It merely states the view that species are valuable because of how they are evolutionarily situated or produced. It does not explain why these properties are valuable or confer value. Finally, critics of the objectivity of the natural historical value of species challenge the view that rational, ecologically informed people would value all species and biodiversity. It seems possible for a person, even if they are reasonable and informed, to not value conserving ecologically and instrumentally unimportant species, or to value other worthwhile things more than species conservation. It is true that many people find species valuable in virtue of their ecological and evolutionary properties. They have subjective final value for this reason. But a person who does not value them in this way, despite understanding well the ecological and evolutionary facts, does not appear to be irrational or unreasonable, on this view.

Thus, the claim that species and biodiversity have objective natural historical value is a contested one, even while it is widely recognized that they can and often do have substantial instrumental and subjective final value.

DOES BIODIVERSITY HAVE FINAL (OR INTRINSIC) VALUE?

Imagine two ecosystems, equal in ecological integrity, which contain the same amount of organisms with the same worth and instrumental value. The only difference between the two ecosystems is that one of them consists of only a handful of species, whereas the other involves a multitude of species. Do you think that the more diverse ecosystem is more valuable? If so, why is that? Is it in virtue of its diversity? If so, what makes biodiversity value-adding?

Suppose that biodiversity is valuable, such that a more biodiverse system has more final (or intrinsic) value than does a less biodiverse one (all other things being equal). Does this imply that we ought to translocate species and engineer novel species in order to increase biodiversity and thereby the value of ecosystems (so long as the species are not disruptive)? Should we try to make species-poor areas, such as deserts, richer in biodiversity? Why or why not?

Now suppose that biodiversity is not value-adding to ecological systems. Does this imply that it would be permissible to reduce biological diversity, including causing species extinctions, if doing so was not ecologically destabilizing and increased the overall welfare of the individuals in the system either in aggregate or on average? If so, should we try to continue to increase human numbers and welfare, even if some species are sacrificed in the process?

Is there a way to consistently hold the view that (1) it would not be value-adding to engineer increases in species richness, and (2) it would be value-reducing to cause species extinctions? (On such a view, the source of diversity, its origins or context, might need to be value relevant and/or it might involve a nonconsequentialist [or, at least, non-act utilitarian] normative framework.)

13.3.2 Do Species Have Inherent Worth?

The second type of objective final value that some environmental ethicists ascribe to species is inherent worth. Inherent worth is the type of value that something possesses if it has interests that moral agents ought to care about (Section 5.1). It is the sort of value that is typically thought to ground human rights and, on sentientist views, the direct moral considerability of nonhuman animals (see, e.g., Sections 7.1 and Box 9.5). So to claim that species have inherent worth is to claim that: (1) species have interests or a welfare, distinct from that of the organisms that comprise them; and (2) there are nonsubjective reasons that we ought to care about their welfare for their own sake. James Sterba is among those who believes these are the case:

> Species are unlike abstract classes in that they evolve, split, bud off new species, become endangered, go extinct, and have interests distinct from the interests of their members. For example, a particular species of deer, but not individual members of that species, can have an interest in being preyed upon. Hence, species can be benefited and harmed and have a good of their own. (1998, 30)

Rolston also believes that species "have their own welfare" (1995, 526) and that we ought to prioritize it over that of individuals:

> The species line is the more fundamental living system, the whole, of which individual organisms are the essential parts. The species too has its integrity, its individuality; and it is more important to protect this than to protect individual integrity. The appropriate survival unit is the appropriate level of moral concern. (Rolston 1995, 524)

Critics of the view that species have inherent worth typically argue that species do not have a welfare distinct from that of the individual organisms that comprise them—they deny condition (1) above. This might seem an implausible view, given the common parlance of some activity or policy being beneficial (or harmful) to a species. Nevertheless, many environmental ethicists believe that this language is merely metaphorical or else just a convenient way to talk about the aggregate well-being of the individual organisms comprising a species or population. What leads them to this view?

Species are not sentient or conscious. People and wolves have mental states and psychological experiences, but *Homo sapiens* and *Canis lupus* do not. Species do not feel, care, desire, or aspire to anything. Therefore, species cannot have interests or a welfare that is cognitively or psychologically based.

That species lack psychological interests does not imply that species do not have interests at all. It implies only that if they have interests, those interests must be non-conscious. As discussed at length earlier (Section 7.3), biocentrists believe that plants, which are nonconscious organisms, have interests. What is thought to ground their interests is that they are teleological centers of life and goal-directed systems. Their parts and processes were selected for and are arranged in order to bring about such things as survival, growth, repair, and reproduction. Therefore, plant interests are specified in terms of what resources, conditions, and treatments are conducive to or detrimental to the realization of those ends. Damaging the roots of an oak tree is bad for the tree because it diminishes its stability and its capacity to draw up water and nutrients, which are necessary for the tree to survive and reproduce.

However, species, unlike individual organisms, are not teleological centers of life. One reason for this is that they are not living things. Individual people and wolves are alive, but *Homo sapiens* and *Canis lupus* are not. Therefore, they do not have biological interests. They cannot be killed, become diseased, or be unhealthy. Moreover, according to proponents of this view, species are not teleologically organized. They do not have ends or goals. Perhaps the most promising candidates for the ends or goals of species are such things as persisting over time, maintaining (or increasing) population size, and adapting to changing environmental conditions (or being pliable). However, while these might be measures of the robustness of a species, they are really byproducts of the organisms that comprise species pursuing their own individual ends. The reason for this is that species are not themselves a unit of selection. There is not competition between species as such, but between organisms and, in some cases, highly internally organized and cohesive collectives of organisms, such as ant colonies and beehives. What is more, the individual organisms that comprise species are not organized or coordinated to bring anything about. In fact, conspecifics very often are in competition with each other for such things as mates, food, and habitat. For these reasons, proponents of this view believe that although individual wolves, human beings, silver maples, and some internally organized collectives (such as ant colonies) have interests, *Canis lupus*, *Homo sapiens*, and *Acer saccharinum* do not. They are not conscious, are not alive, and are not teleologically organized. Therefore, they do not have psychological, biological, or teleological interests or inherent worth. Thus, just as the claim that species have objective natural historical value is contested, so too is the claim that species have inherent worth.

Anthropogenic species extinctions are sometimes referred to as "superkillings," since they eliminate not just individual organisms but entire lineages or forms of life. However, if species are not alive, they cannot be killed, and such language must be understood metaphorically. Moreover, a form of life does not cease to exist upon a species extinction. It ceases to be instantiated. There is still the form of life of the passenger pigeon. There is a way in which passenger pigeons, when they exist, go about the world, even though there are no current instantiations of the passenger pigeon (see Box 13.4). That humans caused the passenger pigeon to go extinct is tragic, for reasons to do with the deaths of the individual organisms, the value of the species, and the callousness and thoughtlessness that their extinction involved. However, if species do not have interests distinct from individual passenger pigeons, it was not a wrong to *Ectopistes migratorius*, since it does not have inherent worth and cannot be harmed or wronged directly. On this view, it is bad that *Ectopistes migratorius* went extinct, but not because it was bad for *Ectopistes migratorius*.

BOX 13.4   TOPIC TO CONSIDER

PASSENGER PIGEON DEEXTINCTION

Passenger pigeons were the most numerous bird species in North America when European settlers arrived. It is estimated that there were between 3 billion and 5 billion passenger pigeons and that they constituted 25 to 40 percent of the total bird population in what is now the United States. There were reports of nesting areas that covered over 850 square miles and that contained over 100,000,000 birds. However, habitat destruction and commercial hunting enabled by technological innovation and dissemination in the nineteenth century (e.g., guns, railroads, and the telegraph) resulted in a rapid decline in their numbers. The last passenger pigeon, Martha, died in the Cincinnati Zoological Garden one hundred years ago, alone and encaged.

There is interest in "reviving" the passenger pigeon, bringing it back from extinction. This is **deextinction**, and it may be possible by means of synthetic genomics and interspecific surrogacy. The plan is to reconstruct a passenger pigeon genome so far as possible using DNA fragments from existing specimens; fill in missing segments using genetic information from the closely related

Image 13.2   Martha, the last known passenger pigeon
Source: AP Photo/Susan Walsh

(cont.)

BOX 13.4 *(cont.)*

band tailed pigeon; synthesize the genome; insert it into enucleated band tailed pigeon stem cells that differentiate into germ cells, which would then be injected into developing band-tailed pigeons. If the band tailed pigeons then mate successfully, the result would be offspring with a high level of genetic similarity to formerly existing passenger pigeons. Repeating this enough times with sufficient genetic variation could, it is hoped, produce a founder population, from which a larger population could be rebuilt.

Proponents of passenger pigeon deextinction believe that it would help to make up for the wrong done in causing the species to go extinct, as well as provide a boost to conservation generally. It would be an act of species recovery, rather than loss, which could galvanize public support for conservation. Extinction would no longer be forever. As long as a species' genetic information and an appropriate surrogate persist, it could be recovered. In fact, scientists already are "banking" the tissue from endangered species in "frozen zoos" for possible reconstitution in the future.

However, many conservation biologists doubt that it would be viable or advisable to introduce passenger pigeons into ecological systems in order to create independent populations, even if they could be reconstituted. One reason for this is that the form of life of the passenger pigeon—the way in which it made its way through the world—involved enormous flocks. It may not be possible to have a small flock of passenger pigeons that successfully breeds and resists predators. Another reason is that the ecological systems in North America have "moved on," such that many of the pigeon's food sources are no longer prevalent, for example. Moreover, accomplishing adequate genetic diversity and learned behaviors without existing birds as models (and without significant hybridization) are seen as enormously challenging. For these reasons, it is perhaps more likely that scientists recreate a small numbers of human-dependent birds, rather than flocks of passenger pigeons migrating throughout North America.

Suppose that it is technically possible to bring back passenger pigeons in this way. Would you support deextinction of the passenger pigeon? Why or why not? Do you think that it would help to make up for the wrongs involved in its extinction? Would it be a symbol of conservation hope, or a reminder of the wrongs that we have done and continue to do?

The passenger pigeon is not the only species that has been proposed for deextinction. Others include the mammoth, thylacine (Tasmanian tiger), gastric brooding frog, Caribbean monk seal, and heath hen. In fact, there already has

(cont.)

BOX 13.4 (cont.)

been a "successful" deextinction. The bucardo, an Ibex subspecies that went extinct in 2000, was cloned by researchers in 2009 using genetic material from preserved tissue samples and a domestic goat surrogate. Most of the embryos created in the effort failed, but one was born alive. It survived for several minutes before dying from lung abnormalities. The bucardo has now gone extinct twice.

What do you think about deextinction more generally—beyond just the passenger pigeon? If it were done successfully would the organisms created be the same species as the one that went extinct (Section 13.1)? If so, would it constitute conserving the species (Section 13.4)? Is deextinction a problematic technofix (Box 12.3)? Does it pose a moral hazard that would undermine the urgency of addressing the causes of extinction (Box 4.5)? Or is it an amazing techno-scientific accomplishment that should be celebrated? One that has an important role to play in species conservation? After all, what other options are there for species that have already gone extinct or that are in an extinction vortex below their minimum viable population? Does your view on deextinction depend upon whether the individuals created are used for scientific purposes, kept in a zoo/wildlife park, or released into the environment? Do you have any ecological or animal welfare concerns about deextinction? If so, do you think that they could be adequately addressed?

13.4 IS THERE A DUTY TO PRESERVE SPECIES?

The second premise of the argument for preserving all species is that if something has unique and/or irreplaceable final value, then there is a duty to not destroy it (and to prevent others from doing so). Is this premise true? Is it the case that if something has unique or irreplaceable value then there is a duty to conserve it? (For the purposes of assessing this premise, let us assume that species have final value.)

Whether something's possessing irreplaceable final value establishes a duty to preserve it depends in part on the type of normative theory employed. On a consequentialist framework—for example, utilitarianism—it does not. All it implies is that the value needs to be considered in outcome assessments. Its value might be outweighed in a particular case by other values. For example, even if species have irreplaceable final value it might be justified to compromise a rare species' habitat or allocate resources away from conservation in order to build a hospital, expand energy access, or provide water for irrigation. Final value is not inviolable value or absolute value within a consequentialist normative framework, and nothing is in principle wrong according to utilitarianism (Section 8.5).

The type of final value that species have is also relevant to whether there is a duty to conserve them. If species have only subjective final value (and not objective value) then there might be only indirect duties to them (Section 5.6). This is often thought to be the case with such things as historical sites, religious artifacts, important works of art, and personal memorabilia. We do not have duties to sculptures, battlefields, or treasured letters. We have a duty to protect and preserve them, out of respect for the people who care about them, were connected to them, or will inherit them in the future. However, these duties are often regarded as secondary to direct duties. Few people would advocate putting protection of historical artifacts ahead of protecting people in emergency situations, even when they are irreplaceable. Moreover, it is not always wrong to price and sell an important piece of art or a family heirloom. Other considerations, such as financial need, can take precedence. Therefore, if species have only subjective final value, our duties to preserve them might be weaker and more contingent than the argument for preserving all species suggests.

The case for a duty to try to preserve all anthropogenically threatened species is strongest when it is premised on species possessing objective final value and is situated within a deontological framework. But even then, some might argue that there are situations in which it is permissible to let a species go extinct. That is to say, even on a deontological view, the duty to preserve endangered species could be *prima facie* (Section 9.2). It might be a duty that we ought to fulfill generally, but that can sometimes be overridden when it comes into conflict with other duties, such as protecting human basic and cultural rights (see, e.g., Section 9.4 and Box 16.2). Moreover, with respect to people, many hold the view that in certain situations—for example, when a person is terminal and suffering significantly—the respectful thing to do is to let her die. This can even be the case in a tragic situation, such as a car accident, when another person is responsible for her condition. If this is right, then on a human rights–based view (a deontological view on which people have objective final value), there is not a duty to try to save all people all the time. Circumstances can be such that other considerations, such as compassion and dignity, take precedence, or the means of doing so are not acceptable. Perhaps it is similar with species. Even if species have objective final value, in some cases what is required to save a very rare or threatened species—for instance, capturing or harming the remaining individuals or shifting resources away from other more promising species recovery programs—may not be acceptable or warranted. In such cases, the reasonable, albeit tragic, thing to do might be to let them go extinct or maintain them only ex situ (see Box 13.5 for further discussion of this issue).

Advocates of a duty to conserve species will point out that many of the situations discussed above are exceptional and preventable. They arise out of prior problematic human activities, which reduce populations and habitats to a point where recovery requires heroic efforts. Therefore, even if they concede that we do not have a duty to conserve each and every species in each and every case, they are likely to insist that in the vast majority of cases for the vast majority of species we do *and* that we have a further duty to try to avoid the cases where we do not. The remainder of this chapter looks at how widespread anthropogenic impacts, and global climate change in particular, raise interesting and challenging questions about how exceptional these cases are likely to be in the future and what methods of species conservation are justifiable.

❋ BOX 13.5 | TOPIC TO CONSIDER

CONSERVATION TRIAGE

The view that under some circumstances it can be permissible to let an endangered species go extinct rather than try to save it is sometimes referred to as **conservation triage**. Those who defend conservation triage argue that we have no choice but to prioritize some species and let others go extinct, since there are not enough resources available to save every species, some species are not savable without large costs (or risks or harms), and some species are not savable at all *in situ*. They see triage as crucial to the efficient use of resources to achieve conservation goals. Not only must we choose which species to save, but rational use of resources requires that we prioritize species that can be saved efficiently, are ecologically (or scientifically) important, and/or are highly valued by people (e.g., for cultural or economic reasons). This is why it is reasonable to focus on charismatic, keystone, and umbrella species, for example. Critics of conservation triage sometimes call it "defeatist conservation." They argue that it accepts the status quo and, thereby, the inevitability of extinction when instead conservationists ought to be advocating for additional resources and developing new conservation programs and strategies.

What is your view regarding conservation triage? Can it be justified, or even right, to let a species go extinct, or just maintain it *ex situ*, rather than try to preserve it *in situ*? Why or why not? Under what, if any, conditions is it justified? Or do you think that to embrace triage is to acquiesce to a problematic status quo and fail to attempt to fulfill our ethical responsibilities?

13.5 CLIMATE CHANGE AND THE CONSERVATION DILEMMA

The historically predominant and preferred approach to species conservation is place-based or *in situ* conservation. The primary place-based conservation strategies are:

- **Establishing Parks and Reserves:** Designating ecological spaces where external stressors, such as pollution, extraction, and recreational use, on nonhuman species populations and their habitats are eliminated or reduced.

- **Ecological Restoration**: Actively assisting in the recovery of degraded spaces, including their species compositions, to some approximation of what they were or would have been absent anthropogenic impacts.

Most theories of environmental ethics are supportive of these management strategies to at least some extent, since they protect and promote a diverse range of environmental values—for example, natural-historical value, the worth of nonhuman organisms, ecosystem services, cultural value, ecological integrity, and aesthetic value. However, macroscale anthropogenic change, and climate change in particular, can pose serious challenges to the effectiveness of and justification for place-based conservation. To illustrate why this is, consider the case of polar bears.

Polar bears are in trouble. Sea ice is a crucial component of polar bear habitat. The bears depend upon it as a platform for hunting seals and other marine mammals, which are their primary food sources. As the climate has warmed, arctic sea ice has begun breaking up earlier in the year, so bears have less time to build up the fat reserves that they need during the period of food scarcity until the sea ice reforms. They also must swim longer distances between ice platforms, further depleting their energy reserves. The result has been decreases in the average body weight of the bears in some populations. This has, in turn, led to higher mortality rates, lower percentages of bears having litters, and smaller litter sizes. Consequently, bear numbers are declining in those populations (Molnár et al. 2011; Regehr et al. 2010). Because climatic change and not just local factors, such as hunting or mining, are driving the decreases in population sizes, local management plans alone are inadequate for protecting them. Designating and protecting critical habitat areas will not itself preserve the bears in their current locations, since it will not limit increases in surface air temperature.

The polar bear is a charismatic and high-profile case, as well as a particularly difficult and stark one given its habitat. But it is not atypical. The distinctive features of anthropogenic climate change are the increased magnitude, rate, and uncertainty of climatic and ecological change in comparison to the recent geological past (Box 2.1). There has always been ecological change, and species populations have always had to adapt or else go extinct. However, the greater the rate and magnitude of change the more difficult is adaptation. Many species populations are dependent upon environmental conditions that may no longer obtain in their current and historic ranges. This means that the traditional place-based conservation strategies—creating protected parks, designating critical habitats, and engaging in ecological restorations—are not going to be as effective as they have in the past. It is not possible to preserve coral reefs and the species that depend upon them by designating their locations marine sanctuaries when increases in ocean temperatures due to climate change and ocean acidification due to elevated atmospheric levels of carbon dioxide are the causes of coral declines. It is not possible to preserve American pika populations in the western United States or cloud forest orchid populations in Costa Rica by protecting the mountain tops where they live, when climactically altered temperature and precipitation patterns and not local land uses are the threat to them. It is not possible to preserve Canada lynx and wolverine populations in greater Yellowstone through local management plans when it is increases in air temperature that are reducing their crucial snow pack habitat. Place-based preservation strategies depend upon the relative stability of background climatic and ecological conditions. Global climate change disrupts that stability. To the extent that it does so in a particular location, place-based preservation strategies for the at-risk species that are there are less viable.

How widespread and large is this effect likely to be? It of course depends upon the magnitude and rate of anthropogenic change. The background or historical rate of extinction is thought to be less than one species per million per year or 0.000001 percent annually (Baillie et al. 2004; Vos et al. 2015; Ceballos et al. 2015). On most estimates, there are 10 million to 20 million eukaryotic (plant and animal) species. Thus, a "normal" number of extinctions would be less than twenty extinctions per year. However, the current extinction rate is already hundreds or perhaps even thousands of times higher than the background rate due to human-related activities, such as habitat destruction, extraction, pollution, and introduced species (Vos et al. 2015;

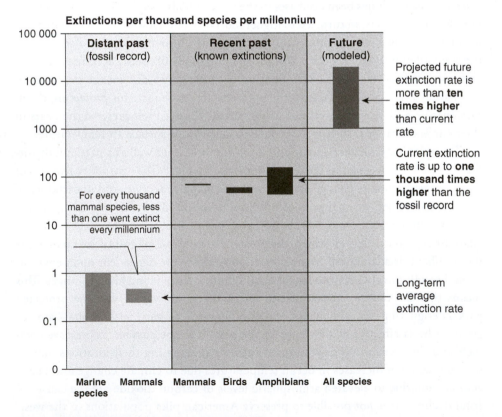

Figure 13.3   Past and projected species extinction rates

Source: Millennium Ecosystem Assessment

Ceballos et al. 2015). Moreover, global climate change is expected to dramatically increase extinction rates still further (Figure 13.3). As discussed earlier (Box 2.1), one study found that 24 to 50 percent of bird species, 22 to 44 percent of amphibian species, and 15 to 32 percent of coral species have traits that make them "highly vulnerable" to climate change. Other studies have projected that 15 to 37 percent of species will be committed to extinction by 2050 on mid-level climate change scenarios, with significantly increased extinction rates even on optimistic future emissions scenarios. These studies have led some researchers to argue that the earth is on the cusp of what could be the *sixth mass extinction* of the past half billion years, the last of which, 66 million years ago, involved the dinosaurs. Whether we are entering an extinction event of that magnitude is uncertain and contested. Nevertheless, there is general agreement that global climate change will dramatically increase species extinctions and that if it is not aggressively mitigated it will result in a very large and widespread (and perhaps even mass) extinction event, which could precipitate ecological collapses and disruptions of the ecosystem processes on which people depend.

Which species are most at risk? Species that only gradually change their geographical ranges (e.g., that disperse seed only locally or migrate slowly) are less likely to meet the challenge of adaptation than are those that are more mobile. For them, suitable habitat might contract, shift, or otherwise disappear more quickly than they are able to adjust. Mountain, small island, and other geographically constrained populations are also highly vulnerable, given the limits on their capacity to migrate as their environments change. Small and non-diverse populations (phenotypically and genetically) are also more vulnerable, as are populations of species that depend on very particular environmental conditions (or on particular other species). In addition, populations of species that have fewer offspring and longer developmental periods (e.g., large mammals) are less likely to be able to biologically adapt to changing ecological conditions than are populations of species that reproduce rapidly and abundantly (e.g., weedy plants).

This, then, is the **conservation dilemma**. On the one hand, macroscale ecological change, particularly when driven by global climate change, will dramatically increase the number of species that are at risk of extinction. On the other hand, macroscale ecological change, particularly when driven by global climate change, appears to undermine the effectiveness of and justifications for place-based conservation. In response to this situation, many conservation biologists have begun to argue for novel, more "hands on," approaches to species conservation and ecosystem management, such as assisted colonization, rewilding, ecosystem engineering, conservation cloning, gene drives, and deextinction.

13.6 NOVEL SPECIES CONSERVATION STRATEGIES

Rapid anthropogenic change poses challenges to traditional place-based conservation strategies, particularly when species are **climate-threatened**—they are at risk because of ecological changes associated with shifting climatic background conditions. For them, local management strategies and protections may not be sufficient to preserve them. Many conservation biologists and environmental ethicists have argued that if the standard species conservation strategies are less effective for climate-threatened species, and we want to try to preserve them outside of zoos or captive breeding programs, then new, more *interventionist* strategies are needed. Several novel strategies have been proposed.

Assisted Colonization is intentionally moving species beyond their historical range and establishing an independent population of them in order to prevent them from going extinct. The idea is that there may be suitable habitat for them in the future, but they cannot reach it without our assistance. Assisted colonization is gaining proponents and, in some cases, practitioners. In the United Kingdom, two butterfly species have been successfully translocated northward to sites that climate-species models suggest will be more conducive to their long-term survival than their prior ranges. In Canada, scientists have relocated dozens of tree species to locations beyond their recent historical range. In the United States, an environmental group called the Torreya Guardians has translocated specimens of *Torreya taxifolia,* a threatened conifer, from its present range in Florida to a more northerly location in North Carolina. Assisted colonization has been proposed for a wide variety of other species, from lobster to lynx.

Rewilding involves assisted colonization and reintroduction of multiple species in order to "rewild" human-impacted habitats. Advocates of **Pleistocene rewilding** propose translocating wild (or de-domesticating nonwild) tortoises, camels, cheetahs, horses, elephants, and lions from Asia and Africa, among other places, to expansive parks in the Great Plains and western United States. (It has been proposed for Australia as well.) They believe that the species are appropriate ecological proxies for large vertebrates that went extinct in North America 13,000 years ago, in part due to overhunting by humans. Moreover, many of the proxy species are at risk in their current habitats, so this would contribute to species conservation by providing an intercontinental refuge. There are other, more modest, rewilding projects. For example, in the Netherlands, Konic Ponies, Heck Cattle, and Galloway Cattle have been introduced as proxies for extinct herbivores in two comparatively small and lightly managed reserves. Several similar efforts are being planned throughout Europe.

Rewilding is an instance of **ecosystem engineering** in that it involves designing ecosystems as we believe they ought to be, or need to be, in the future for reasons related to species conservation or ecological function. Traditionally, ecosystem engineering for conservation reasons (as opposed to economic or agricultural ones) has been largely restorationist. It has aimed at replicating species and processes that obtained in a space in the past—for example, removing invasive species, reintroducing native ones, and remediating contaminants. It was reasonable to believe that species assemblages that obtained in a place in the past would be well suited to it and conducive to ecological integrity in the future. However, with global climate change, the ecological futures of many places are going to be very different from their recent ecological past. Moreover, there are a growing amount of **novel** or **no-analog systems**. A novel system is one in which anthropogenic activities have resulted in a system in which the biotic features (e.g., species distributions) and abiotic characteristics (e.g., soil composition) significantly depart from those of the pre-impacted system. The more novel the system, the more difficult is restoration, particularly under conditions of rapid climatic change. Therefore, ecosystem engineering for conservation purposes has begun to take on a more forward-looking rather than historical outlook. For example, researchers have begun to study and develop processes for cultivating coral species that are tolerant to higher temperatures and lower pH (more acidic) conditions, with an eye on engineering climate-change-resilient reef systems.

Cloning, or creating an organism that is genetically nearly identical to its "parent" organism, was first accomplished using genomic material from an adult animal in 1996 with the birth of Dolly, a domestic sheep. Cloning is now performed regularly with agricultural and companion animals. Meat from cloned animals has even been approved for human consumption by the US Food and Drug Administration. **Conservation cloning** refers to cloning animals for conservationist reasons, such as increasing the genetic diversity or population size of a threatened species. It often involves using interspecific surrogates, and has been done successfully with the guar (a bovine species) and African wildcat, as well as proposed for black-footed ferrets, for example. **Deextinction** involves cloning organisms with high levels of genetic similarity to species that have already gone extinct (see Box 13.4).

Gene drives are genomic modifications that cause a genetic trait to spread rapidly through a sexually reproducing population. They work by increasing the rate or frequency at which a gene sequence gets passed on to offspring (Figure 13.4). Sexually reproducing organisms receive one set of chromosomes from each of their parents, and pass only one on to their offspring. The predominant gene drive approach uses a system (called CRISPR/Cas9) that cuts the chromosome inherited from the non-modified parent and inserts the desired genetic trait and drive system. Thus, when the desired trait and drive system is engineered into an organism it ensures that both sets of its offspring's chromosomes (even the one inherited from the other parent) will contain the trait and drive system. This, in turn, ensures that all of its offspring will pass on the trait and drive system to all of its offspring, and that all of its offspring's offspring will pass it on to all of its offspring, and so on. Therefore, by engineering a strain of organism with a desired trait and gene drive, mass-rearing them, and releasing them into the field, it may be possible to genetically modify entire wild populations. The most prominently discussed conservation application of the technology is to use it to drive deleterious traits, such as distorted sex ratios or chemical vulnerability, through invasive species populations and disease vectors—for example, cane toads in Australia, black and Norway rats on Pacific islands, avian-malaria-carrying mosquitoes in Hawaii, and Asian carp in the central United States. However, researchers are also considering the possibility of using it to drive beneficial traits through populations of at risk species, such as resistance against the chytrid fungus in frogs and white-nose

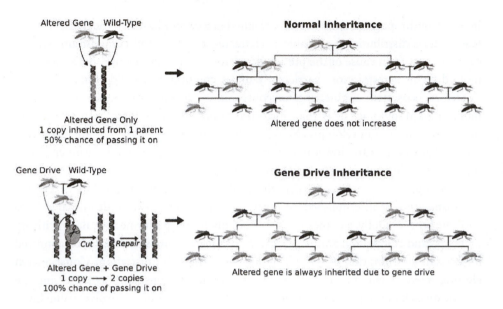

Figure 13.4 Gene drives increase the frequency with which the target gene is passed on to the offspring of sexually reproducing organisms, thereby "driving" the gene through the population. *Source: Esvelt et al. (2014)*

syndrome in bats. (Research is also being done on driving deleterious traits through wild populations of human disease vectors, such as malaria-transmitting mosquitoes.)

What these strategies have in common is that they involve designing and engineering organisms and ecological systems. Therefore, they seem antithetical to commitments, such as native species prioritization and historical fidelity, that have traditionally characterized conservation biology and preservation-oriented ecosystem management. Rather than deferring to where species are now or have been in the past (or even what species exist now), they involve putting species where we think they ought to be in the future. The primary justifications offered for this shift in outlook and approach are that: (1) traditional approaches to species conservation are no longer feasible for some species; (2) the biotic and abiotic features of ecological systems are already so impacted by human activities that there is little "naturalness" or independence-from-humans left to preserve in most places; and (3) we must do these things to make up for the harms that we have done to species and ecosystems. On this view, we have so altered the planet that we must now take responsibility for its management.

13.7 INTERVENTION OR RESTRAINT?

Three types of concerns frequently arise regarding more interventionist species conservation strategies. One is that human interventions into ecological systems are the cause of ecological degradation and the species extinction crisis in the first place.

Global climate change is not intentional. But it illustrates that our actions very often have significant and detrimental unintended consequences. Moreover, many of our other ecological interventions, such as introducing species and clearing forest for agriculture, have been both intentional and ecologically destructive. Proponents of interventionism might respond that these novel interventions will be done for the good of nonhuman species and the biotic community, rather than for human interests. However, even granting this, challenges remain. After all, people will be choosing which species and functions to prioritize, and well-intentioned interventions often have unintended impacts. On this view, the interventionist outlook is **hubristic**. It involves an overestimation of our ability to predict and control the consequences of our alterations of complex ecological and biological systems.

Consider, for example, assisted colonization and rewilding. The species most commonly proposed for translocation are those that we care about—charismatic or economically significant ones—and not necessarily those that are most ecologically important. Moreover, assisted colonization and rewilding involve establishing independent nonnative populations. Nonnative species are usually benign, but in some cases become invasive and highly ecologically (and economically) disruptive. Furthermore, the translocations would occur in the context of rapid and uncertain ecological change, which increases the difficulty of both predicting where suitable habitats will be in the future and ensuring that the target species do not become ecologically problematic in the recipient systems. (It may also require moving them again in several decades, since elevated rates of change will continue and candidate species often have lower adaptive capacity.) So one concern about interventionism is that, particularly under conditions of global climate change, it will often not be successful or else will further stress ecological systems.

A second concern is that even if the interventions are successful—for instance, if species are translocated and established without becoming ecologically problematic—what is most important about them is not preserved. Many of the types of value that species possess are tied to their ecological and evolutionary relationships. Moving species outside their historical ranges, engineering new systems, and reintroducing long extinct species do not maintain or reestablish those relationships. Therefore, when value is tied to ecological and historical properties, such as ecosystem function and independence from human design, interventionist approaches to species conservation might preserve the species without preserving their value. Cheetahs and lions in Kansas, although exciting, may not have the same ecological or final value as cheetahs and lions on the Serengeti.

The third concern is that interventionist conservation strategies are something of a distraction. On some projections, there will be tens of thousands of species extinctions per year within a few decades. However, these strategies typically focus on only one or a few species at a time. They cannot scale to the magnitude of the problem that we face. At most, they might enable us to forestall the extinction of some of the species that people care most about. But we should be concerned about the extinction crises as a whole and the ecological collapse that it might precipitate.

What is needed are conservation strategies that capture large numbers of species, in the way that parks and reserves have. Furthermore, most interventionist conservation strategies do not address the causes of species extinctions—such as climate change, habitat destruction, and overextraction. They are reactive. What is more, they might perpetuate the false view that there are ways to deal effectively with the extinction crisis, thereby functioning as a moral hazard that fosters inaction on the causes of extinction (Box 4.5). On this view, conservation cloning, gene drives, and deextinction are amazing techno-scientific achievements, but they are not the sort of "solutions" that we need for the crisis we face.

But what, if anything, is the alternative to taking a more hands-on approach? Proponents of interventionism are critical of the traditional park and reserve model of ecosystem management on the grounds that its effectiveness for accomplishing species conservation is undermined by global climate change—it is "mismatched to a world that is increasingly dynamic" (Camacho et al. 2010, 21). However, critics of interventionism find this conclusion too hasty. Although anthropogenic climate change diminishes the effectiveness of parks and reserves for preserving particular species, species assemblages, and ecosystems, they are likely to maintain *comparatively high* ecological (including species preservation) value when measured against nonprotected areas. Protected areas and corridors provide some adaptive space and more adaptive possibilities for populations and systems. Moreover, more biodiverse places, often the target of protection, are likely to have more species with sufficient behavioral and evolutionary adaptive potential to meet the adaptation challenge of global climate change. Therefore, identifying and protecting biologically diverse and rich habitats (including diverse physical environments), crucial or productive wildlife corridors and ecological gradients and promoting landscape permeability continue to be well justified under conditions of global climate change on this view. In addition, familiar stressors of ecosystems and species—such as pollution, extraction, and habitat fragmentation—decrease their robustness (e.g., resistance and resilience). Reducing or managing such factors can increase the adaptive potential of species and ecosystems, again by removing anthropogenic impediments, rather than by more interventionist activities. Thus, traditional managing for resilience and protection of biodiverse (and physically diverse) places and corridors increases the adaptive capacity of populations and systems to global climate change. Along with aggressive mitigation, it can lessen the magnitude of the conservation dilemma.

Another reason offered for not giving up on parks and reserves is that, under conditions of rapid ecological change, they are often conducive to accomplishing goals other than species conservation. For example, protecting and lightly managing areas often is an effective approach to maintaining ecosystem services (e.g., clean water, storm surge protection, and carbon sequestration), particularly when measured against nonprotected areas. Moreover, lightly managed spaces will continue to have value as places where ecological and evolutionary processes play out comparatively independent of human intention, design, and manipulation. Therefore, natural value, natural historical value, and the worth of wild organisms continue to be supportive of park and reserve–based management. Under conditions of rapid ecological change, place-based protection, rather than being valuable for maintaining a space largely as it is, may be valuable for the processes of change that occur—for example, human-independent adaptation and reconfiguration. This requires changing expectations for what these approaches can accomplish. It may also require shifting management practices appropriately—for instance, deemphasizing historicity in assisted recovery, placing less priority on nativeness, and refraining from intensive efforts to prop up dwindling populations or communities (when it is associated with climate change–driven ecosystem change).

In addition to revising management goals, expectations, and practices for protected places, proponents of restraintful ecosystem management argue that we also need to adapt our attitudes toward those places and to ecological change more broadly. Openness toward the ecological future, accommodation of human-independent processes in determining that future, appreciation of new ecosystem arrangements (even if they are partly anthropogenic and not what we would have preferred) and patience as ecological transitions and reconfiguration occur are seen as crucial to place-based management, as well as to good ecological engagement more generally, under conditions of rapid ecological change. The ecological and evolutionary processes that produced what is valued now will continue, and over time will generate new species populations, communities, and systems. (The issue of whether a more restraintful or interventionist approach to species conservation and ecosystem management is justified under conditions of rapid ecological change is revisited in Chapter 17.)

13.8 SUMMARY

The primary questions addressed in this chapter were:

- What are species and biodiversity?
- How are species and biodiversity valuable?
- Is there an ethical obligation to conserve biodiversity?
- Is there a duty to try to prevent all anthropogenically threatened species from going extinct?
- How does climate change, and macroscale ecological change generally, complicate traditional approaches to species conservation?
- Should we embrace novel species conservation strategies, such as assisted colonization and deextinction?

When it comes to forestalling species extinctions we are often choosing among undesirable options. *Ex situ* conservation does not preserve what many people value most about species—expression of their distinctive form of life in their ecological context.

In situ conservation is often costly and difficult to accomplish, particularly for highly endangered species and when endangerment is the result of habitat loss and macro-scale ecological change. The case is even worse with respect to large-scale extinctions. On the one hand, interventionist strategies do not begin to scale, often do not preserve value, could pose a moral hazard, and could cause further ecological disruption. On the other hand, restraintful strategies require reconciling ourselves to letting many amazing species go extinct, even though we are the cause.

Given this, perhaps the most important point to take away from this discussion is that there is no good strategy for preserving highly endangered species or responding to the large-scale species extinctions associated with climate change. In the political discourse about how to respond to global climate change, the following question is often posed: Should mitigation or adaptation be prioritized (see, e.g., Box 6.3)? When it comes to species and biodiversity conservation, the answer to this question is clear. There is no scalable, value-conserving adaptation option. Therefore, in order to avoid climate change-driven species extinctions, we need to try to reduce the scale of the problem by preventing population sizes from becoming so small that conservation plans are desperate efforts and we need to get on a low emissions trajectory to reduce the number of species populations that are climate change–threatened. The only way to do that is by consuming a smaller share of planetary resources by changing our consumption patterns, reducing our population, and/or innovating technologies (see, e.g., Sections 5.5, 15.4, and 16.3).

KEY TERMS (SEE GLOSSARY FOR DEFINITIONS):

argument to preserve all species	fallacy of asserting the conclusion
assisted colonization	fallacy of begging the question
climate-threatened	fallacy of decomposition
cloning	form of life
conservation cloning	form of life conception of species
conservation dilemma	gene drives
conservation triage	genetic fallacy
conspecific	hubris (environmental)
deextinction	inherent worth
ecological restoration	*in situ* conservation
ecological value	instrumental value
ecosystem engineering	natural value
existence value	novel (or no-analog) system
ex situ conservation	objective final value

option value

Pleistocene rewilding

rewilding

species monism

species pluralism

species richness

subjective final value

welfarism

REVIEW QUESTIONS

- What are some of the different conceptions of species and biodiversity? What is the "form of life" conception of species employed by Rolston?

- What are some of the ways in which species and biodiversity are instrumentally valuable?

- What is the argument to preserve all species?

- What is the difference between natural-historical value and inherent worth?

- What is the difference between psychological interests, biological interests, and teleological interests? What is the argument against the view that species have interests distinct from those of the individuals that comprise them?

- Why do many environmental ethicists and conservation biologists believe that *in situ* preservation is the only true preservation?

- What is the conservation dilemma generated by rapid anthropogenic change?

- What are deextinction, conservation cloning, gene drives, assisted colonization, and rewilding?

- What is the difference between interventionist and restraintful ecosystem management? What is the core reasoning in support of each of them?

DISCUSSION QUESTIONS

- Do you think that Rolston's "form of life" definition of species is a useful one for environmental ethics? Do you agree that it captures what most people value and want to conserve regarding species?

- Do you think that the instrumental value of species is sufficient justification for a responsibility to conserve biodiversity and prevent anthropogenic species extinctions? Why or why not?

- Do you think that species have final value, above and beyond the value of the individuals that comprise them? Why or why not? If so, is the value objective or subjective final value? Is it inherent worth or natural value?

- Do you believe that there is a duty to try to conserve every anthropogenically threatened species? Or is it sometimes permissible to let a species go extinct? If so, what kinds of considerations justify letting a species go?

- Are there any conditions under which it would be permissible to intentionally cause a species to go extinct? Why or why not?

- Would you support the use of gene drives to genetically engineer a wild population for conservation purposes? If so, under what conditions would you support it? What sorts of concerns would you have about the use of gene drives in wild populations?

- Do you favor a more interventionist or more restraintful approach to species conservation and ecosystem management? What are your reasons for doing so? What do your views imply for conservation strategies such as assisted colonization, rewilding, and ecosystem engineering?

FURTHER READING

Accessible discussions of the "species problem" or the problems associated with defining what species and biodiversity are can be found in:

Clarke, Ellen, and Samir Okasha. "Species and Organisms: What Are the Problems?" In *From Groups to Individuals*, edited by Philippe Huneman and Frederic Bouchard. MIT Press, 2013.

Ereshefsky, Marc. "Species." *Stanford Encyclopedia of Philosophy*. Center for the Study of Language and Information (CSLI), Stanford University, 2010.

Maclaurin, James, and Kim Sterelny, *What Is Biodiversity?* University of Chicago Press, 2008.

Early and influential views on the value of species and the duty to try to preserve them can be found in:

Norton, Bryan, ed. *The Preservation of Species*. Princeton University Press, 1986.

Rolston, Holmes, III. "Duties to Endangered Species." *BioScience* 35 (1985): 718–26.

Sober, Elliott. "Philosophical Problems for Environmentalism." In *The Preservation of Species*, edited by B. Norton, 173–94. Princeton University Press, 1986.

More recent discussions of the value and moral status of species and biodiversity can be found in:

Maier, Donald. *What's So Good about Biodiversity?* Springer, 2013.

Sandler, Ronald. *The Ethics of Species*. Cambridge University Press, 2012.

Sarkar, Sahotra. *Biodiversity and Environmental Philosophy*. Cambridge University Press, 2005.

Smith, Ian. *The Intrinsic Value of Endangered Species*. Routledge, 2016.

PART VI: SOCIAL JUSTICE AND THE ENVIRONMENT

CHAPTER FOURTEEN

ECOFEMINISM AND ENVIRONMENTAL PRAGMATISM

CONSEQUENTIALISM, DEONTOLOGY, AND VIRTUE ethics are the three most prominent types of ethical theory and each has proponents among environmental ethicists (see Chapters 8–10). However, other environmental ethicists are critical of them, not just individually but taken together. One prominent concern is that they tend to be individualistic, prioritizing the well-being or moral status of individuals rather than that of collectives. Advocates of holism argue that in environmental ethics the focus must instead be on the good or value of ecosystems and species (Chapters 11–13). On this view, the primary concern should not be the welfare or rights of antelopes or mangrove trees, but the health of antelope populations and mangrove ecosystems.

This chapter focuses on two other critical perspectives on the dominant ethical theories: **ecofeminism** and **environmental pragmatism**. Ecofeminism is a family of views that identify and challenge myopic, gendered, and patriarchal features of Western philosophical thought regarding nonhuman nature and animals. It also emphasizes the connections between the ways in which women and nonhuman nature are conceptualized, characterized, (mis)valued, and (mal)treated. Environmental pragmatism is a family of views that deemphasize ethical theorizing in favor of more procedural or situational approaches to characterizing environmental problems and engaging in environmental decision-making. The first half of this chapter discusses ecofeminism; the second half discusses environmental pragmatism.

14.1 ECOFEMINISM: BACKGROUND AND CONTEXT

Ecofeminism (or ecological feminism or feminist environmental philosophy) is associated with a number of critical perspectives within environmental ethics, as well as with positive views on our ethical relationships with other people, animals, and nature. In what follows I provide some background to help situate ecofeminism within environmental ethics before characterizing some of its more influential aspects.

The history of Western thought, both religious and philosophical, is filled with dichotomous (and hierarchical) thinking in which the world is divided into two (or more) categories and one is set as superior to the other: human vs. nature; reason vs. emotion; male vs. female. This is found in ancient Greek philosophy, Judeo-Christian worldviews, and enlightenment thinking (see, e.g., Boxes 3.1 and 5.4). Not only is there a value orientation of human/reason/male over nature/emotion/female, but the former have historically been enjoined to control the latter. One of the functions of reason is to moderate our passions and emotions. Nature and animals are resources to be subdued and used by people as needed. Men are head of the household and women are to submit to them. In many places only men have been able to serve as religious or political leaders, permitted to own land, or have the right to vote, while women are treated as property (like land and animals), the rights over which can be given, sold, or exchanged.

We might wish to think that so problematic a patriarchal cultural orientation is a thing of the past. However, a frank look at contemporary cultural practices reveals that this is not the case. For one thing, many of the "historical" examples cited above persist. In many religions women are excluded from high leadership still today. In many places in the world women cannot hold property, and they can be given or purchased (or, more precisely, access to the sexual use of their bodies can be). Women also are not permitted to participate in governance or civic life in many places, are required to wear (or prohibited from wearing) particular clothing, are not permitted to drive, cannot reveal their skin or hair in public, are prohibited from going into public spaces unattended, and are excluded from certain educations and professions. These are all ways in which women are disempowered and treated in ways that limit their autonomy and maintain male control and dominance.

Even in nations when there are no longer legal exclusions and restrictions, problematic power relationships persist. Men are still widely regarded as authoritative decision-makers, whereas women are considered more emotional and nurturing. Women are disproportionately responsible for maintaining the home and raising children (even when they are in the workforce). Women are underrepresented in leadership positions in government, business, and high-status, high-earning professions, and dramatically overrepresented in lower-paying, lower-status, caregiving professions. Sexism, sexual harassment, sexual assault, and sex trafficking remain all too common. There are lingering perceptions that girls are less capable at the "rational" subjects of math, engineering, and science than are boys. Being called "girly" is an insult to a boy because it is meant to call out lack of strength, confidence, and power. Moreover, women are routinely objectified. This occurs through everything from beauty pageants to music videos, advertisements, and pornography. The message presented to girls by Western popular culture is often that the most important thing is how they look and that they are attractive to men, not whether they excel at academics, athletics, or creativity. Misogyny is rampant, and it is casually accepted and encouraged in popular culture, including sports, video games, advertising, fashion, politics, and reality television. That patriarchy, sexism, gender discrimination, problematic gender roles and ideals, exploitation, and misogyny persist and are perpetuated in these and other ways underlies the importance of critical feminist, including ecofeminist, perspectives.

✳ BOX 14.1

GENDER INEQUALITY BY THE NUMBERS

Here are quantitative illustrations of the differential social, political, and economic status of men and women.

- Women held only 19 percent of the seats in the US Congress, 29 percent of the seats in the UK Parliament, and 14 percent of the seats in the Turkish Parliament in 2015 (World Bank 2016b)
- Only 4 percent of CEOs, 19.2 percent of board members, and 25.1 percent of executive officers/senior-level managers at S&P 500 companies are women (Catalyst 2015)
- Only 31.5 percent of the computer systems and programming workforce in the United States is women (Department of Labor 2016)
- 93.8 percent of the paid childcare workforce in the United States is women (US Bureau of Labor Statistics 2016)
- One-third of women workers surveyed in the UK reported experiencing gender-related barriers to advancement during their careers (Robert Half 2014)
- 82.4 percent of the over 27,000 sex-based discrimination and 7,000 sexual harassment charges in the United States in 2013 were filed by women (EEOC 2014a; 2014b)
- Women earn on average only 78 to 84 cents for every dollar that men earn in the United States, both due to their disproportionately working in lower-paying fields and due to their being paid less than their male counterparts in many occupations (Pew 2013; White House 2015; Department of Labor 2014)

(cont.)

BOX 14.1 *(cont.)*

- It is estimated that at least 20 million people are victims of human trafficking and forced labor each year, the majority of whom are women and girls, and women and girls are estimated to make up as much as 98 percent of the 4.5 million victims of forced sexual exploitation (ILO 2012)

14.2 THE LOGIC OF DOMINATION AND THE ETHICS OF CARE

One of the contributions of ecofeminism to environmental ethics is to draw out connections between the commoditization and exploitation of nature and the objectification and oppression of women. Karen Warren (1990) influentially argued that they both exhibit the **logic of domination** described above—dichotomous (or hierarchical) conceptualizations in which one side of the dichotomy is identified as superior and therefore justified in dominating or subordinating the other. Men and masculinity are valorized and set over women and femininity, just as human and civilization are valorized and set over nature and wildness (Boxes 3.1 and 5.4). Women, like animals and nature, are objectified and treated as mere things to be used, consumed, and "hunted" as trophies and conquests by men. Particularly when objectified or demeaned, women are often referred to by animal terms—"vixens," "birds," "chicks" and "bitches." They are dehumanized. In much the same way, animals are de-individualized and de-animalized when they are for human use—"broilers," "layers," "livestock," and "game." Components of natural systems are similarly claimed for human use by reconceptualizing and renaming them—"timber," "stocks," "resources," and "services" (Crist 2013).

As we have seen, many environmental ethics seek to expand the scope of what is recognized as having inherent worth. The grounds for this often involve rejecting the view that humans have a special or unique place within nature or else are separate from and superior to it (Sections 7.1, 7.4, 11.1, and 12.2). That is, it involves rejecting the standard dichotomies and hierarchies. However, in highlighting the logic of domination, ecofeminism suggests that the problem is not only that too much is traditionally excluded from having worth and treated as a mere resource, but that the project of trying to clearly demarcate what is "in" and what is "out" is problematic. On this view, the dichotomous conceptualization between what has final value and what are mere things (and only instrumentally valuable) is the deeper conceptual problem, and it needs to be jettisoned (Plumwood 2002).

An alternative approach to thinking about value and worth, often associated with ecofeminist ethics, is that it is established relationally. The core idea of **relational accounts of value** is that the capacities or properties of individuals—for example, that they are sentient or alive—do not tell the whole story about their moral considerability. We must also look at their relationships with others. Aspects of this view are incorporated into the idea that how we ought to consider the interests of wild animals can be different from how we should consider those of our companion animals, due to the different histories and relationships involved (Section 7.5). This idea is also manifest in holistic views, such as deep ecology, where the interconnectedness and interdependence of components of ecological systems—animals, plants, rivers, and rocks—are the basis of value for both the whole and its constituent parts (Sections 12.1 and 12.2). The view is expressed as well in virtue-oriented ethics in which appropriate responsiveness is informed by relationships, such as friendship, shared history, and connection to place (Sections 10.1 and 10.2).

Some ecofeminist thinkers also argue that relationships themselves often have value. It is not only that a parent and their child have worth, but there is value to be found in the relationship between parents and children. It is not only that sea otters and kelp forests have value, but so too do sea otters in kelp forests. In this way, value is often organic and interwoven such that it cannot be broken up conceptually or practically into distinct components attached to discrete organisms or entities. This conception of value informs many holistic environmental ethics as well, including deep ecology's biocentric pluralism (Section 12.1) and the view that species can only truly be preserved *in situ* (Sections 13.3 and 13.4).

Recognition of the significance of relationships to the analysis of value and ethical responsiveness foregrounds the question of how we ought to relate to others. Prioritization of this question is often associated with a view in moral philosophy called **care ethics**. Care ethics emphasizes the role of such things as attachment, emotion, connection, partiality, trust, dependence, openness, and empathy in good ethical engagement and reasoning. These are the sorts of traits that have historically been associated with women in dichotomous thinking, and that have been marginalized in Western philosophical ethics in favor of impartiality, duty, rules, rights, efficiency, and universality. Emotion, passion, and particularity have at times even been characterized as impediments to acting morally because they undermine the rational impartiality that is thought to be central to recognizing and doing one's duty or maximizing good outcomes overall. Thus, in the view of many feminist ethicists, the dominant ethical traditions have, at best, only been addressing some ethical perspectives and some parts of the ethical landscape—those involving cool impartiality—while overlooking or devaluing others—those involving emotion and partiality (Gilligan 1982; Noddings 1984).

Moreover, many care ethicists emphasize that when we think about our daily lives, the most important interactions and relationships are generally not with those with whom there is equality of power or for whom impartiality is appropriate. It is with our neighbors, friends, family, and co-workers. It is with people with whom we are and should be emotionally connected. It is with people for which there is, and sometimes should be, differential power or authority. It is in situations where trust and empathy are crucial to understanding what is at stake and responding well. Annette Baier (1986) has argued that trust is in fact crucial to almost every human interaction. Without it relationships would become untenable and social systems would break down. Everything from schooling and banking to driving and medicine depend upon social cooperation and presumptions about good intentions, which in turn depend upon trust. Other ethicists have argued much the same for empathy and care. Rather than being antithetical to justice, duty, obligation, and ethical reasoning and conduct generally, proper emotion (sometimes called **moral emotion**) is a necessary condition for it, on this view.

Many environmental ethicists hold similar views with respect to our relationships with animals and nonhuman nature. For example, both Leopold and Carson emphasize that love for the land and wonder toward nature are crucial not only to proper action but also to proper understanding of our environmental problems and responsibilities; and that to cultivate these traits we must build a relationship with nature by engaging with it (Sections 10.2 and 11.3). Lori Gruen (2015) argues that empathy is central to developing appropriate relationships and forms of engagement with nonhuman animals, and thereby to fulfilling our responsibilities to them. Environmental virtue ethicists emphasize the significance of emotion to proper perspectives, dispositions, and conduct regarding the environment generally (Sections 10.1 and 10.2). Even environmental ethicists who endorse traditional or mainstream normative theories—such as Kantian and consequentialist—often now aim to show that they can incorporate moral emotions, character, partiality, and difference into their theories in appropriate ways.

14.3 THE IMPORTANCE OF DIVERSE PERSPECTIVES

Given the growing acceptance of the importance of care, empathy, love, trust, and other emotions in good moral reasoning and engagement, a reasonable question is why they have been marginalized in moral philosophy in the first place. A common view is that it is the product of a narrowness of perspectives:

> The great moral theorists in our tradition not only are all men, they are mostly men who had minimal adult dealings with (and so were then minimally influenced by) women. . . . It should not surprise us, then, that particularly in the modern period they managed to relegate to the mental background the web of trust tying most moral agents to one another, and to focus their philosophical attention so single-mindedly on cool, distanced relations between more or less free and equal adult strangers. . . . Explicitly assumed or recognized obligations toward others with the same obligations and the same power to see justice done to rule breakers then are seen as the moral norm. . . .
>
> Relations between equals and nonintimates will *be* the moral norm for adult males whose dealings with others are mainly business or restrained social dealings with similarly placed males. But for

lovers, husbands, fathers, the ill, the very young, and the elderly, other
relationships with their moral potential and perils will loom larger. . . .
Philosophers who remember what it was like to be a dependent child, or
to know what it is like to be a parent, or to have a dependent parent, an
old or handicapped relative, friend, or neighbor will find it implausible to
treat such relations as simply cases of comembership in a kingdom
of ends. . . .

[A] complete moral philosophy would tell us how and why we
should act and feel toward others in relationships of shifting and
varying power asymmetry and shifting and varying intimacy. (Baier
1986, 247–8, 252)

Another contribution of feminist ethics to environmental ethics has been to
emphasize the importance of avoiding myopia—of not conceptualizing and approaching environmental problems from too limited a perspective. Accomplishing
this requires being attentive to diverse voices and points of view, both on particular
issues and regarding our relationship to the natural world more generally. For this
reason, many environmental philosophers advocate attending to and incorporating
insights from indigenous worldviews and Eastern philosophies into environmental
ethics, while others argue for inclusivity in environmental deliberations and decision-
making, for example.

Attending to difference requires not presuming that one's own perspective or situation is the norm. This is particularly important for those of us living comfortably
and with privilege in wealthy nations. For example, global climate change is a different type of problem for people of affluence with high levels of adaptive capacity than
it is for subsistence farmers whose livelihood depends upon local rainfall patterns.
Effective ecosystem management of a park or reserve is a different type of problem for
an international environmental organization than it is for an indigenous community
whose history and cultural practices are connected to the place. Many ecofeminists
emphasize that avoiding myopia requires listening to the narratives, stories, knowledge and perspectives of all affected peoples when trying to characterize and address
ecological problems, especially those who are too often marginalized or disempowered in social and political contexts—for example, immigrants, minority groups, indigenous peoples, people with disabilities, the elderly, the poor, and women. What is
considered to be an environmental problem—as well as what problems we prioritize
and put resources toward resolving—often depend upon our perspectives. Providing
potable water for one's family, maintaining plants for traditional foods and medicines, and ensuring a safe place for children to play are problems that many people
around the world, particularly women, contend with on a daily basis. These are as
much environmental issues as are species conservation and natural resource management (Section 1.1).

BOX 14.2

TRADITIONAL ECOLOGICAL KNOWLEDGE

Indigenous peoples possess an enormous amount of knowledge about the biological world, ecological processes, and local systems. This knowledge is frequently referred to as **traditional ecological knowledge** (TEK) or **indigenous knowledge** (IK). The Convention on Biological Diversity describes traditional knowledge as:

> [T]he knowledge, innovations, and practices of indigenous and local communities around the world. Developed from experience gained over the centuries and adapted to the local culture and environment, traditional knowledge is transmitted orally from generation to generation. It tends to be collectively owned and takes the form of stories, songs, folklore, proverbs, cultural values, beliefs, rituals, community laws, local language, and agricultural practices, including the development of plant species and animal breeds. Traditional knowledge is mainly of a practical nature, particularly in such fields as agriculture, fisheries, health, horticulture, and forestry. (UN 1992a, Article 8)

Most characterizations of TEK emphasize features similar to those highlighted above: it is generated within an indigenous community over time; it is detailed and largely location- and culture-specific; it is spiritual but also practically focused and concerns topics critical to human life and survival, such as food production, resource management, and environmental change; it is dynamic, adaptive, and based on observation, experience, and experimentation; it is primarily orally transmitted and not systematically documented; it is shared among the community but the content and extent of knowledge varies from individual to individual (depending upon age, status, role, gender, profession, etc.).

TEK has historically been marginalized by "modern" science, which has viewed it as unsystematic and unreliable, or even superstition and myth. Scientists often have been more inclined to treat indigenous peoples as an object of their studies, rather than as studiers or knowledge bearers from whom they might learn and with whom they might collaborate. What is worse, traditional knowledge has frequently been actively denigrated, suppressed, and erased by colonizers through such things as language prohibitions, relocations, imposed educational systems, assimilation, and forcible removal of children for "re-education." TEK was neither valued nor respected, and traditional languages, social structures, and practices that maintained it were discouraged or destroyed.

(cont.)

BOX 14.2 *(cont.)*

However, the social and political rights of indigenous peoples, including with respect to TEK, have been increasingly recognized in recent years. For example, the United Nations Declaration on the Rights of Indigenous Peoples, which enshrines protection of TEK, was adopted in 2007. Respect for TEK and the crucial role that indigenous peoples can and must play in addressing environmental issues and challenges also has been growing. Many conservation biologists, ecosystem managers, resource managers, and climate scientists now recognize that indigenous peoples are highly knowledgeable about their environments, are enormously sensitive to ecological variation, and have generations of experience managing resources and responding to ecological change. TEK involves tremendous local expertise and longitudinal environmental study. Therefore, it can provide invaluable ecological baseline data, as well as insights on possible management and adaptation strategies. Here is an example of this recognition from the Intergovernmental Panel on Climate Change's (IPCC) Fourth Assessment Report:

> Among Arctic peoples, the selection pressures for the evolution of an effective knowledge base have been exceptionally strong, driven by the need to survive off highly variable natural resources in the remote, harsh Arctic environment. In response, they have developed a strong knowledge base concerning weather, snow, and ice conditions as they relate to hunting and travel, and natural resource availability. These systems of knowledge, belief, and practice have been developed through experience and culturally transmitted among members and across generations. This Arctic indigenous knowledge offers detailed information that adds to conventional science and environmental observations, as well as to a holistic understanding of environment, natural resources, and culture. There is an increasing awareness of the value of Arctic indigenous knowledge and a growing collaborative effort to document it. In addition, this knowledge is an invaluable basis for developing adaptation and natural resource management strategies in response to environmental and other forms of change. Finally, local knowledge is essential for understanding the effects of climate change on indigenous communities and how, for example, some communities have absorbed change through flexibility in traditional hunting, fishing, and gathering practices. (IPCC 2007a)

Although the validity and value of TEK is more widely recognized by the scientific community than it has been in the past, challenges remain regarding how to effectively and respectfully integrate scientific knowledge with TEK.

(cont.)

BOX 14.2 *(cont.)*

For example, while the IPCC explicitly recognizes the value of TEK to climate science and climate adaptation, it has been slow to incorporate it into its assessments
and reports, in part because it does not appear within the peer-reviewed research
literature that defines the scope of the IPCC purview. The Alaska Native Science
Commission (N.d) identifies a number of differences between traditional and scientific knowledge, many of which can pose challenges to synthesis and collaboration:

Comparisons between Traditional and Scientific Knowledge	
Comparison between Knowledge *Styles*	
Indigenous knowledge	**Scientific Knowledge**
assumed to be the truth	assumed to be a best approximation
sacred and secular together	secular only
teaching through story telling	didactic
learning by doing and experiencing	learning by formal education
oral or visual	written
intuitive	model-or hypothesis-based
holistic	reductionist
subjective	objective
Comparison between Knowledge *In Use*	
Indigenous Knowledge	**Scientific Knowledge**
lengthy acquisition	rapid acquisition
long-term wisdom	short-term prediction
powerful prediction in local areas	powerful predictability in natural principles
weak in predictive principles in distant areas	weak in local areas of knowledge
explanations based on examples, anecdotes, parables	explanations bases on hypotheses, theories, laws

Table 14.1

Source: Patricia Longley Cochran, http://www.nativescience.org

(cont.)

BOX 14.2 *(cont.)*

In addition to these formal, methodological, and stylistic differences, cultural differences as well as mistrust arising from a history of domination, colonization, and exploitation can be barriers to successful collaboration. Moreover, indigenous peoples and scientists can have very different perspectives or conceptualizations of what environmental problems are, what needs protecting, how decision-making should proceed, what methods are appropriate, and who are the relevant stakeholders and authorities (Whyte 2013; Latulippe 2015). However, these challenges notwithstanding, efforts exist all around the world in which traditional knowledge–holders and scientists are trying to work together to characterize, study, and respond to environmental issues, such as climate change, species conservation, fire management, and resource stewardship (Mason et al. 2012; UNESCO 2013). As the issue of bioprospecting (Box 9.4) makes clear, it is critical in these efforts that traditional knowledge–holders are respected, tribal sovereignty is protected, TEK is not exploited, and everyone shares in any benefits that result (CTKW 2014).

Another reason that TEK is crucial to addressing environmental issues is that there are over 350 million indigenous people in the world, and indigenous groups live in and have political jurisdiction over some of the most biodiverse and ecologically important places on earth. Native American landholdings in North America contain more wild lands than do national parks, for example. In addition, many indigenous communities, particularly those that engage in traditional farming, hunting, and fishing, are among those most at risk from ecological degradation and global climate change. When indigenous peoples are empowered over their land and water, and their political and environmental rights are upheld, they are often responsible stewards and strong protectors of them. For example, reserves managed by indigenous groups in Brazilian Amazonia and other tropical forests have lower rates of deforestation than do other managements systems (Lewis et al. 2015). Therefore, strengthening the legal control of indigenous peoples over their lands is frequently a win-win. It promotes human rights and often addresses historical injustices, while also reducing ecological degradation.

The importance of attending to marginalized and less visible perspectives connects with the concern that the challenge many people face is not how to behave as an empowered individual among likewise empowered individuals, but how to respond to conditions of disempowerment, marginalization, and oppression (see, e.g., Sections 14.2, 15.1, and 15.3). These are the more pressing problems in interpersonal ethics. Moreover, these features characterize our relationship with the nonhuman environment, where the core problem is exploitation and domination, and the subject of exploitation lacks agential capacity. The human relationship with nature and animals is inescapably asymmetrical. We are moral agents, they are not. We have power over them—to control, manipulate, and destroy—in ways that they do not have over us. For these reasons, the environment cannot be conceived of and interacted with as an equal. Ecosystems, species, and plants are simply not the sorts of things that could care about us or with which we could engage in reciprocal concern and cooperative decision-making. Therefore, environmental ethics cannot only be about how to behave as an equal among equals. It must consider as well what we owe to those that are different from us and over which we are empowered, according to this view.

This chapter has so far focused on several of the major contributions that feminist ethics has made to environmental ethics. The views discussed are associated with ecofeminism, but are not an ecofeminist doctrine. Many thinkers embrace some of them, but not others. While I have tried to highlight ways in which ecofeminist perspectives have informed and been incorporated into theories of environmental ethics, I do not mean to suggest that ecofeminism has been fully "mainstreamed" by the field of environmental ethics, such that its critical perspectives are no longer needed. There remain concerns that the perspectives of privileged people in affluent nations are overly influential; that forms of knowledge and inquiry that deviate from the scientific and analytic model are not fully appreciated; that wilderness and species conservation issues are prioritized over the environmental challenges that face the global poor; that not nearly enough consideration is given to the concerns and perspectives of disempowered peoples in framing and addressing environmental problems; and that dichotomous "in" or "out" thinking remains prevalent.

Several of the views discussed above are thought to favor the conclusion that there is no single or uniquely correct ethical perspective or theory. Perhaps, rather than a single most justified ethic, there is instead a diversity of valid perspectives, which emerge out of the specific contexts of people's lives and experiences. This sort of ethical pluralism, relativism, or contextualism is often associated with a "theory" of environmental ethics called **environmental pragmatism**, which is the focus of the remainder of this chapter.

✳ BOX 14.3   TOPIC TO CONSIDER

AN ECOFEMINIST PERSPECTIVE ON AGRICULTURE

Vandana Shiva is a prominent proponent of traditional smallholding agriculture and critic of industrial agriculture—that is, large monocultural commodity farming that uses synthetic inputs (e.g., chemical fertilizers, pesticides, and

(cont.)

BOX 14.3 *(cont.)*

herbicides) (see, e.g., Box 3.4 and Section 6.1). In the passage below, Shiva provides an ecofeminist analysis of industrial agriculture.

> There is a conceptual inability of statisticians and researchers to define women's work inside the house and outside the house (and farming is usually part of both). This recognition of what is and is not labor is exacerbated both by the great volume of work that women do and the fact that they do many chores at the same time. It is also related to the fact that although women work to sustain their families and communities, most of their work is not measured in wages.
>
> Science and technology have rendered women's knowledge and productivity invisible by ignoring the dimension of diversity in agricultural production. As the Food and Agriculture Organisation (FAO) report on Women Feed the World mentions, women use more plant diversity, both cultivated and uncultivated, than agricultural scientists know about. In Nigerian home gardens, women plant 18 to 57 plant species. In Sub-Saharan Africa women cultivate as many as 120 different plants in the spaces left alongside the cash crops managed by men. In Guatemala, home gardens of less than 0.1 half acre have more than ten tree and crop species.
>
> In a single African home garden more than 60 species of food-producing trees were counted. In Thailand, researchers found 230 plant species in home gardens. In Indian agriculture women use 150 different species of plants for vegetables, fodder, and health care. In West Bengal, 124 "weed" species collected from rice fields have economic importance for farmers. In the Expana region of Veracruz, Mexico, peasants utilize about 435 wild plant and animal species of which 229 are eaten. Women are the biodiversity experts of the world. Unfortunately, girls are being denied their potential as food producers and biodiversity experts under the dual pressure of invisibility and domination of industrial agriculture.
>
> While women manage and produce diversity, the dominant paradigm of agriculture promotes monoculture on the false assumption that monocultures produce more . . .
>
> Feeding the world requires producing more food and nutrition with fewer resources—producing more with less. In this, women are experts and their expertise needs to filter into our institutions of agricultural research and development.

(cont.)

BOX 14.3 *(cont.)*

However, instead of building on women's expertise in feeding the world through diversity, the dominant system is rushing headlong into destroying diversity and women's food-producing capacities, then pirating the results of centuries of innovating and breeding through patenting.

Lack of women's property rights are a major constraint on women's capacity to feed the world. These property rights include rights to land, and common property rights to common resources like water and biodiversity . . .

While women are being denied their rights to resources and we are seeing the feminization of subsistence agriculture, the dominant agriculture is showing increasing signs of masculinization as it appropriates resources and rights from women in subsistence agriculture and presents itself as the only alternative for feeding the world . . .

Our food security is too vital an issue to be left in the hands of a few transnational corporations with their profit motives or to be left up to national governments that increasingly lose control over food security decisions, or to a few, mostly male national delegates at UN conferences, who make decisions affecting all our lives. (Shiva 2009, 19–21, 31)

What are Shiva's core concerns in this passage? In what ways do they illustrate the ecofeminist perspectives discussed above? Did this passage get you to think of the problem of food security and hunger in different ways than you had previously? Did it encourage you to make new connections among different agricultural, social, and environmental issues? If so, in what ways?

14.4 THE MOTIVATION FOR PRAGMATISM

Interest in environmental ethics developed from the view that the standard ways of conceiving of the human-nature relationship and the standard norms applied to our interactions with nonhuman nature, particularly in highly industrialized countries, were (and continue to be) problematic. The worry is that so long as the nonhuman world is seen as a boundless resource to be used for human benefit, people will treat it in ways that are destructive and unsustainable. Thus, both *theoretical* and *practical* concerns motivate environmental ethics. The theoretical concern is that we are mis-conceiving our relationship with nature and not recognizing and responding well to the full range of values present in it. The practical concern is that we need an ethic that will provide a basis for promoting sustainable practices and policies.

Most environmental ethics aim to address the practical concern via addressing the theoretical concern. The basic idea is that developing a well-justified theory of environmental ethics will provide the platform needed to demonstrate why unsustainable practices and policies should be rejected. As such, the ethics are in the form of a theory. They provide a background account of the human-nature relationship, defend a set of environmental values informed by that relationship, situate the account of value within a normative theory, and thereby generate a set of norms, rules, and principles that can be used to evaluate actions, policies, and practices (Chapter 1). However, some environmental ethics do not fit the theory model. The most prominent and influential nontheoretic approach to environmental ethics is environmental pragmatism.

Views are generally regarded as pragmatic either because they draw from the American pragmatic philosophical tradition and/or because they discount the importance of ethical theorizing in favor of more pragmatic (i.e., contextual and procedural) approaches to characterizing environmental problems and engaging in environmental decision-making. It is useful to distinguish between two different motivations for environmental pragmatism. Some ethicists are led to environmental pragmatism because they believe that it is not possible to build a well-justified unified theory of environmental ethics. Others accept that ethical theorizing can be successful in principle, but believe that under the current circumstances developing a unified theory of environmental ethics is unnecessary and possibly a distraction. We urgently need solutions to environmental problems, and according to this view it is clear enough what the problems are and what has to be done in response to them. Therefore, we do not need to get sidetracked into arguments about basic values and theoretical structures. Instead, we need to make use of whatever arguments and decision-making approaches best move people and institutions toward ecological sustainability. Another way to put this is that we can and should address the practical concerns of environmental ethics, without worrying too much about the theoretical concerns.

As with ecofeminism, there is not an environmental pragmatism dogma or manifesto. Instead, there are a number of commitments or positions that views that identify as pragmatist tend to accept and that are thought to reinforce each other. These "themes" of environmental pragmatism are discussed in the next section.

✳ BOX 14.4   TOPIC TO CONSIDER

THE CONVERGENCE THESIS

In support of the view that it is not necessary to settle theoretical disagreements in order to act on environmental issues, many environmental pragmatists appeal to some version of the **convergence thesis** proposed by Bryan Norton. According to the convergence thesis, "if one takes the full range of human

(cont.)

BOX 14.4 *(cont.)*

values—present and future—into account, one will choose a set of policies that can also be accepted by an advocate of a consistent and reasonable nonanthropocentrism" (Norton 1997, 87). The basic claim behind the convergence thesis is that what is good for human beings overall and in the long run will typically *converge* with what is good for nonhuman nature.

The convergence thesis is actually a hypothesis, which can be tested by looking at different environmental issues from the perspective of enlightened anthropocentrism and nonanthropocentric theories. If the theories largely converge in what they would recommend across a wide range of cases, then that supports the convergence thesis and, thereby, environmental pragmatism's contention that theoretical environmental ethics is not needed. If they diverge in what they recommend in many instances, then that is evidence against the thesis and supports the need for theoretical environmental ethics.

Reflect on the environmental issues and cases that have been discussed throughout this textbook—such as pollution mitigation, endangered species conservation, global climate change, animal agriculture, fisheries management, water resource allocations, captive breeding programs, wild-caught pets, cultural hunting, and ecological restoration—as well as on other issues that you are familiar with and care about. In these cases and on these issues, do enlightened anthropocentrism and nonanthropocentrism (individualist and/or holist) converge or diverge? Are there some types of issues on which they tend to converge, others on which they diverge? Do they tend to converge more on general goals and positions or on specific policies and practices (or neither)? What are the implications for the convergence thesis and the need for theorizing in environmental ethics?

14.5 THEMES OF ENVIRONMENTAL PRAGMATISM

Many environmental pragmatists emphasize that environmental ethics, like all ethics, is always done from one's own perspective. We cannot take up an unattached or impartial standpoint, since we only have access to our own consciousness. Moreover, we are historically located. We live in a particular time and place, under particular circumstances. We can try to imagine how things look to others or what it would be like to view things objectively. But that is always us trying, in our particular and historically located way, to do so. There is simply no escaping our particularity. Each of us has only an individual, finite, and partial perspective on the world. This is an ineliminable feature of being human, and we must not pretend to be able to transcend to an "objective" or "impartial" point of view free from any individual contingencies, idiosyncrasies, or biases.

This perspectival theme is often thought to cohere with a set of "theoretical" and methodological themes. Since there is no objective perspective, only particular, partial, and in-the-middle-of-things ones, we ought to reject claims about objective value and unified theories of ethics. Many pragmatists also believe that such ethics depend upon problematic metaphysical and epistemological commitments, such as that there could be moral facts or values in the world independent of valuers and that we can somehow intuit them. Thus, pragmatists conclude, we either ought to reject ethical theorizing altogether or else recognize the legitimacy of a diversity of theories and avail ourselves to whichever one is best suited to the environmental issue or situation at hand. (The latter view is sometimes referred to as **theoretical pluralism**.) In either case, environmental ethics ought not aim for a single most justified theory, overarching principle, or set of values and rules that everyone ought to accept and that should be applied across all contexts when making decisions.

The pragmatic alternative to a theory-oriented approach to ethical decision-making is a procedural and situationalist one. On a **procedural approach to ethics**, ethical decisions and policies are not justified by their conforming to, expressing, or fulfilling certain norms or principles, but by the process by which they are reached. Environmental pragmatism is generally proceduralist in this way. We are inextricably located in personal, social, and historical contexts. Therefore, the only way for change to occur is for it to proceed from this position through critical, creative, and communal reflection on both our current practices and future possibilities. Moreover, the greater the diversity of perspectives and points of view represented in the process, the more informed and inclusive it is, and the less biased and more legitimate are the outcomes. As a result, environmental issues are best addressed through public and democratic decision-making mechanisms. It is the appropriateness of the decision-making process that legitimates or justifies the outcome, on this view. "While a pragmatist might endorse a policy framed in the language of rights or utility, the philosophical justification for this endorsement will be procedural, and hence not an endorsement of rights or utility theory" (Thompson 1996, 187).

Given a procedural approach to environmental ethics, it is crucial to avoid clinging to foundational or immovable value commitments. Therefore, environmental pragmatists often criticize what they see as dogmatism in environmental ethics. One ought not believe from the outset that only one sort of environmental ethic—for example, nonanthropocentric, holistic, or intrinsic-value-based—can be adequate. Moreover, the traditional distinction between instrumental value and intrinsic (or final) value ought to be given up. If appeals are made to "intrinsic value," it must be a conception of it that is not metaphysical or universal. Instead, it must be "contextualized" and "justified in terms of [its] ability to contribute to the resolution of specific environmental problems" (Minteer 2001, 70).

Again, not all environmental pragmatists accept all of these positions. But most environmental ethics that are self-described as philosophical pragmatism endorse some combination of a significant number of them.

I referred to the family of views above as **philosophical pragmatism** in order to distinguish them from **strategic pragmatism**. According to philosophical pragmatism, we ought to be environmental pragmatists because we ought to reject (or put to the side) the project of building a unified ethical theory and instead embrace contextualist and procedural approaches to ethics. This is a philosophical view. Strategic pragmatism is the view that, when it comes to public discourse about environmental issues, we ought to embrace whatever justifications or arguments are most effective in promoting environmentally acceptable policies and practices. Which types of values and principles are most persuasive in practice and policy domains is situational. In some cases, intrinsic value arguments might be effective in building support for preserving species or protecting landscapes, while in other cases economic or future generations arguments might be more impactful. Philosophical pragmatists are almost always strategic pragmatists. However, theory-oriented environmental ethicists also can be, and almost always are, strategic pragmatists. This is possible because there is a distinction between engaging in ethical theorizing and engaging in public decision-making processes. A theory of environmental ethics aims to provide an approach for determining what we ought to do, but does not provide a strategy for getting people to do it. Moreover, it is not meant to displace legitimate social and political processes for developing environmental policies and making environmental decisions. Therefore, theoretical environmental ethicists and philosophical pragmatists can agree that in the public sphere adequately addressing environmental problems should be prioritized over settling theoretical disputes. They can both be strategically pragmatic.

☼ BOX 14.5   TOPIC TO CONSIDER

OVERLAPPING CONSENSUS: ENERGY, ECONOMICS, AND CLIMATE CHANGE

The evidence establishing that global climate change is already occurring and that it is caused in large part by human activities is very strong (Box 2.1). In the United States, which historically has been one of the countries most skeptical of climate change, recent surveys have found that 63 to 70 percent of people now believe that climate change is real (Borick et al. 2015; Howe et al. 2015). However, only 48 to 65 percent of Americans believe that climate change is mostly caused by human activities (Saad and Jones 2016; Howe et al. 2015). Moreover, only 37 percent of Americans worry a great deal about climate change (Saad and Jones 2016). This makes federal legislation focused on addressing climate change very difficult to accomplish.

Does this mean that it is fruitless to advocate for federal policies to reduce greenhouse gas emissions in the United States? Many people believe that it does

(cont.)

BOX 14.5 *(cont.)*

not. What it means is that instead of arguing over areas of deep disagreement, such as whether climate change is anthropogenic, it is more promising to look for areas of **overlapping consensus**—that is, policies or initiatives that can be supported by people who do not agree that climate change is occurring or that do not find it to be an urgent issue. For example, there is widespread support among Americans for research into renewable energies (77 percent) and for regulating CO_2 as a pollutant (74 percent) (Howe et al. 2015). There has also been long-standing support for federal rebates to consumers for purchasing fuel-efficient vehicles, improving home energy efficiency, and installing alternative energy systems (e.g., solar). People may hold these views for a number of different reasons—for example, public health, economic development, economic self-interest, national security, or environmental. But it is not necessary for people to agree on the justification for these policies or initiatives in order to move them forward; nor does it matter whether their reasons are anthropocentric/nonanthropocentric, individualist/holist, or consequentialist/deontological. What matters is that people support them and that they appeal to a wide range of considerations, which makes them realistic policy goals that can be achieved through legitimate governance processes.

Many environmental pragmatists believe that there are numerous areas of overlapping consensus on environmentally related issues, and that environmental sustainability would be better promoted if more effort were spent identifying these collaborative opportunities rather than on fighting entrenched battles about science and values (Norton 2005). Both anglers and conservationists care about keeping rivers unpolluted. Both public health advocates and climate activists oppose coal-burning power plants. Both birders and environmental justice advocates support maintaining urban green spaces. Both grocery stores and environmentalists want to prevent food from going to landfills.

Can you think of other environmental issues on which diverse interests or concerns support similar goals or policies? Can you think of any environmental issues on which there are intractable disagreements regarding desirable outcomes and/or acceptable means, such that achieving overlapping consensus on a path forward is very unlikely?

14.6 PRACTICAL EFFICACY IN ENVIRONMENTAL ETHICS

There are two strands to environmental pragmatism, one critical and one positive. The critical strand is that theoretical approaches to environmental ethics are problematic. The positive strand is that a procedural and contextual approach to environmental ethics is both philosophically and practically justified.

In response to the critical strand, theory-oriented environmental ethicists reject the view that individual particularity undermines the legitimacy of ethical theorizing. It is true that we are always and inescapably in the middle of things, and that we cannot step outside of our own perspectives. But it does not follow from this that we cannot understand the perspectives of others or use reasoning and evidence to build well-justified theories. It can be difficult to overcome our unreflective assumptions and individual biases, as well as to understand how things look to others, but it can be done. Moreover, many theories of environmental ethics endorse value pluralism and emphasize the importance of sensitivity to context (see, e.g., Sections 7.5, 10.2, 11.4.1, and 12.1). If some accounts of environmental values or normative frameworks are more justified than are others, then the pragmatist critique would seem to be mistaken. (See, also, the discussions of ethical skepticism [Section 2.4], final value [Section 4.2], and justifying normative theories [Sections 2.3 and 10.5].)

Some theory-oriented environmental ethicists have also challenged the view that a procedural approach to environmental ethics is practically superior to a theory-oriented one. As discussed earlier, there is general agreement among environmental ethicists that an adequate environmental ethic will provide a basis for advocating and promoting environmentally sustainable practices, policies, and lifestyles (e.g., Sections 5.4 and 6.2). I referred to this as the **practical adequacy condition**. However, there is considerable disagreement regarding what is required to satisfy the practical adequacy condition.

Some environmental ethicists, particularly those who emphasize the importance of intrinsic or final values to environmental ethics, stress the practical adequacy condition's normative dimensions. An environmental ethic, they argue, must not be susceptible to pressures that could result in its endorsing environmentally unsustainable practices, policies, or lifestyles. Many advocates of intrinsic value theories have insisted that in order to satisfy this condition an environmental ethic must involve a commitment to the objective final value of nature (or individual organisms). After all, if nature is valuable only instrumentally or subjectively, and people's preferences and desires are for goods, activities, or landscapes that require exploitive treatment of the natural environment, then there is nothing wrong (and everything right) with treating nature in just that way.

Many intrinsic value theorists therefore believe that a pragmatic approach to environmental ethics can, under not uncommon circumstances, pander to human preferences and desires that favor unsustainable environmental policies. They argue that the procedural constraints that some pragmatists advocate for determining public policy—public and democratic decision-making, for example—are not sufficient to ensure that the preferences and desires of the people involved will not produce problematic environmental outcomes. Holmes Rolston III has been particularly critical of the pragmatic approach. Responding to Ben Minteer, an environmental pragmatist, Rolston writes: "Minteer will reply that he wants to take account of a pluralism of values in human experiences. He wants a democratic debate among contesting parties. I think he is left in a muddle. Talk about a debate that is a 'non-starter'! In this one there are no grounds (aka 'foundations') for argument; the outcome will be only the result of a power struggle, which may be disguised as 'pragmatic'" (1998, 356).

For their part, many environmental pragmatists stress the efficacy aspect of the adequacy condition. They argue that an environmental ethic must be effective in promoting solutions to real-world environmental problems. It must help bring about, not merely justify, environmentally sustainable practices, policies, and lifestyles. This requires the capacity to successfully engage social and political discourse in ways that advance real-world environmental solutions. They are critical of intrinsic value-oriented environmental ethics on the grounds that such theories are often insensitive to the political and social facts that are part of most environmental issues, and for that reason often are resented by the people whose lives are affected by the issues. It is not acceptable to dictate to ranchers that wolves have inherent worth or *canis lupus* has natural value so they must accept wolves being reestablished in the area, for example. Instead, there must be a robust and open discourse among all stakeholders regarding how best to manage wolves in order to address economic, ecological, ethical, and social concerns.

Environmental pragmatism has influenced nonpragmatic environmental ethics. One way in which it has done so is by emphasizing the importance of effectively engaging public discourse. As discussed above, many environmental ethicists who reject philosophical pragmatism accept strategic pragmatism. The importance of practical efficacy is also manifest in the growing interest in environmental virtue ethics due to the connection between character, motivation, and action.

As mentioned above, many environmental ethicists also share the pragmatic conception of the human ethical situation: ethics begins with the problem of what to do in our concrete circumstances; we are inextricably in the middle of things; and we cannot get outside our own finite perspective. Where the approaches diverge is on what can be accomplished from this position. Pragmatic views are skeptical about the prospects of establishing an objective foundation for ethics. In contrast, theory-oriented approaches argue that it is possible to establish nonrelativistic values, rules, and principles from this position by means of accurate empirical information and sound reasoning. Because of this, identifying proper environmental practice and policy is not reducible to the product of public deliberations or appropriately democratic decision-making—it is not strictly procedural. Some such procedures might be dominated by uninformed or distorted preferences or might not attend adequately to the ethically salient features of the situation. Environmental pragmatists are certainly correct that dogmatism in ethical thought must be avoided. There is always the possibility that the available information could change or errors in reasoning might be revealed. But theorists emphasize that openness to reconsidering and testing one's commitments in light of new evidence, perspectives, or challenges implies that there are standards of evidence and reasoning that can be used to evaluate people's views and determine whether moral progress is being made.

Finally, as with ecofeminism, environmental pragmatism's advocacy for inclusiveness, respect for diverse perspectives, and value pluralism is now widely seen as crucial to reducing biases and myopia, and so for doing environmental ethics well, both in theory and in practice. Moreover, in moral philosophy generally there has been a move away from thinking that an ethical theory ought to provide a single clear answer for what one ought to do in every situation. Particularly in ethically complex cases, where there are multiple important values in play, as there often are with environmental issues, there may be more than one reasonable decision or outcome.

Thus, even if one does not accept environmental pragmatism as a comprehensive ethic, there are important insights in it that should inform any environmental ethic.

14.7 SUMMARY

This chapter has focused on two critical perspectives regarding theory-oriented environmental ethics, ecofeminism and environmental pragmatism. The central questions addressed were:

- What motivates ecofeminism and environmental pragmatism?
- What positions or themes are associated with them?
- What critical perspectives do they bring to bear on theories of environmental ethics?
- What positive views do they offer environmental ethics?
- How have their views influenced theories of environmental ethics?

Both ecofeminism and environmental pragmatism provide crucial perspectival and methodological insights on ethics that have influenced the field of environmental ethics and that ought to inform the development of any theory of environmental ethics. These include avoiding cultural myopia, considering environmental problems from diverse perspectives, being open to the possibility that more than one theory or view might be well justified (while at the same time accepting that not every view is), being wary of dichotomous thinking, and recognizing the need for environmental ethics to be practically efficacious. Moreover, both ecofeminism and environmental pragmatism defend positive views that are influential in environmental ethics, such as relational accounts of value and procedural approaches to ethical justification and decision-making.

KEY TERMS (SEE GLOSSARY FOR DEFINITIONS):

care ethics

convergence thesis

ecofeminism (or ecological feminism or feminist environmental philosophy)

environmental pragmatism (or philosophical pragmatism)

logic of domination

philosophical pragmatism

practical adequacy condition   strategic pragmatism

procedural approach to ethics   theoretical pluralism

relational accounts of value   traditional ecological knowledge (or in-
                                             digenous knowledge)

REVIEW QUESTIONS

- What are "dichotomous thinking" and the "logic of domination"?
- What is thought to be the connection between the exploitation of nature and the oppression of women?
- What distinguishes relational accounts of value?
- What is care ethics and what distinguishes it from other approaches to ethics?
- Why is it so important to be inclusive of different perspectives when character- izing and responding to environmental problems, as well as when doing ethical theory?
- What are the critical and positive themes of environmental pragmatism?
- What distinguishes procedural approaches to justification in ethics?
- What is the difference between philosophical pragmatism and strategic pragmatism?
- What are the normative and efficacy dimensions of the practical adequacy condition?

DISCUSSION QUESTIONS

- Do you agree that there are similarities between the exploitation and domination of nature and the oppression and domination of women? Why or why not?
- Do you think that the theories of environmental ethics studied thus far, partic- ularly the ones that you believe to be well justified, adequately incorporate rela- tional considerations and emotions in their value theories and accounts of good ethical engagement? If not, could they be modified to do so?
- Can you think of examples of environmental issues or cases in which not attend- ing to all of the perspectives involved has led (or could lead) to ethically problem- atic ecological and/or social results?
- Do you believe that a proceduralist approach or a theory-oriented approach to ethical evaluation and justification is more justified?
- What if the outcome of an inclusive deliberative process involves unsustainable use of resources, environmental degradation, or unequal distribution of environ- mental impacts? Would they then be justified? Why or why not?

- Does the theory (or theories) of environmental ethics that you believe to be well justified meet the practical efficacy condition? Why or why not?

FURTHER READING

Influential foundational work on feminist ethics include:

Baier, Annette. *Moral Prejudices.* Harvard University Press, 1995.

Gilligan, Carol. *In a Different Voice: Psychological Theory and Women's Development.* Harvard University Press, 1982.

Noddings, Nel. *Caring: A Feminine Approach to Ethics and Moral Education.* University of California Press, 1984.

Prominent work on the relationship between feminist ethics and environmental ethics in general, as well as on some of the particular ecofeminist themes discussed in this chapter include:

Adams, Carol. *The Sexual Politics of Meat: A Feminist-Vegetarian Critical Theory.* Continuum, 1991.

Cuomo, Chris. *Feminism and Ecological Communities: An Ethic of Flourishing.* Routledge, 1998.

Gruen, Lori. *Entangled Empathy: An Alternative Ethic for Our Relationship with Animals.* Lantern Books, 2015.

Plumwood, Val. *Feminism and the Mastery of Nature.* Routledge, 1993.

Plumwood, Val. *Environmental Culture: The Ecological Crisis of Reason.* Routledge, 2002.

Salleh, Ariel. *Ecofeminism as Politics: Nature, Marx, and the Postmodern.* Zed Books, 1997.

Warren, Karen. "The Power and Promise of Ecological Feminism." *Environmental Ethics* 12 (1990): 125–46.

Warren, Karen, ed. *Ecofeminism: Women, Culture, Nature.* Indiana University Press, 1997.

Influential and insightful works on environmental pragmatism include:

Katz, Eric, and Andrew Light, eds. *Environmental Pragmatism.* Routledge, 1996.

McKenna, Erin, and Andrew Light, eds. *Animal Pragmatism: Rethinking Human-Nonhuman Relationships.* Indiana University Press, 2004.

Minteer, Ben. *Refounding Environmental Ethics: Pragmatism, Principle and Practice.* Temple University Press, 2011.

Norton, Bryan. *Sustainability: A Philosophy of Adaptive Ecosystem Management.* University of Chicago Press, 2005.

Norton, Bryan. *Toward Unity among Environmentalists.* Oxford University Press, 1994.

CHAPTER FIFTEEN

ENVIRONMENTAL JUSTICE

QUITE A LOT OF environmental ethics concerns our ethical relationships to the environment: our vulnerabilities and dependencies on it, our duties and responsibilities to it, and how to flourish with it. However, there is another aspect of environmental ethics that concerns our ethical relationships and responsibilities to other people, but involving the environment. We saw this in the discussions about environmental economics (Section 4.3), instrumental values (Sections 4.1 and 13.2), enlightened anthropocentrism (Chapter 6), indirect duties (Section 5.6), and environmental rights (Section 9.4). This dimension of environmental ethics might be called **interpersonal environmental ethics**. One important area of interpersonal environmental ethics is **distributive justice**, or what people owe to each other with respect to the distribution of environmental benefits and burdens. For example, **intergenerational justice** concerns what each generation owes to those that come after it (Section 6.3).

This chapter focuses on the allocation of environmental burdens and benefits among communities within and between societies, an issue commonly referred to as **environmental justice**. Many environmental burdens are the byproducts of the production, use, and disposal of consumer goods—such as food, energy, transportation, clothing, and electronics. Therefore, the chapter concludes with a discussion of the ethics of consumption.

15.1 UNEQUAL EXPOSURE AND ENVIRONMENTAL INJUSTICE

Distributive environmental justice concerns the allocation of environmental burdens and benefits among peoples or communities. **Environmental burdens** are hazards, land uses, facilities, or activities that diminish the quality of the environment—for example, agricultural waste streams, air pollution, toxic waste sites, incinerators, waste transfer

354

stations, refineries, transportation depots, mine tailings, and sewage treatment facilities. They are the negative externalities of industrial activities. **Environmental benefits** are the commodities, experiences, and wealth whose production generates the burdens.

Not all communities are equally exposed to environmental burdens. In the United States, low-income communities and high-minority communities are disproportionately exposed to environmental hazards:

> For 2000, neighborhoods within three kilometers of commercial hazardous waste facilities are 56 percent people of color whereas non-host areas are 30 percent people of color. Thus, percentages of people of color as a whole are 1.9 times greater in host neighborhoods than in non-host areas. . . . Poverty rates in the host neighborhoods are 1.5 times greater than non-host areas and mean annual household incomes and mean owner-occupied housing values in host neighborhoods are 15 percent lower. (Bullard et al. 2007, 52)

The situation is starker in some places than in others. For example, in Massachusetts, low-income communities (median income less than $39,525) face a cumulative exposure rate to hazardous facilities and sites that is *2.5 to 4 times greater* than higher income communities; and communities with high-minority populations (greater than 25 percent) face a cumulative exposure rate that is *over 20 times greater* than communities with low-minority populations (less than 5 percent) (Faber and Kreig 2005). In Massachusetts, as in the nation, race is significant above and beyond class when it comes to exposure to environmental burdens.

✳ BOX 15.1

LEAD CONTAMINATION OF FLINT, MICHIGAN'S WATER SUPPLY

Unequal exposure to environmental hazards is not only correlated with lower economic status and social disempowerment, it is often partly explained by them. Flint, Michigan, is a city of just under 100,000 people approximately 70 miles outside of Detroit, Michigan. It is 57 percent black or African American. In the last few decades, Flint has experienced significant declines in population, incomes, and tax base as a result of manufacturing plant closings and job losses associated with contraction of the area's automobile industry, to which Flint's economy has long been tied. Flint's median household income is just $24,800, and 41.5 percent of residents live below the federal poverty line. The city's

(cont.)

BOX 15.1 *(cont.)*

fiscal situation had grown so difficult that in 2011 the governor of Michigan, Rick Snyder, began appointing emergency managers for the city charged with addressing its budgetary problems. Over the next four years, four different managers were appointed to oversee the city's operations.

Michigan law confers ultimate governing authority to emergency managers for the municipality to which they are appointed (State of Michigan 2012). They determine what powers elected officials are permitted to exercise. They are responsible for the city's financial and operating plans. They control the city's budgets. Moreover, they have the power to break and renegotiate city contracts and collective bargaining agreements, sell city assets, fire employees, reduce benefits and salaries, and eliminate city ordinances. Managers also have very strong liability protection.

It was in this economic and governance context that the city of Flint made the decision in 2013, supported by the city council 7–1, to switch the source of its water supply from the city of Detroit's water authority to a new, less expensive regional water authority. The new Karegnondi Water Authority would, like Detroit's system, draw water from Lake Huron. However, the new system would not be in place until 2016 at the earliest. Therefore, to cut costs in the interim, the decision was made at the direction of the emergency manager to draw water from the Flint River beginning in 2014.

Residents worried about using water from the Flint River at the time the decision was made, given the history of industrial pollutants in the area and the river's reputation as a dumping ground. Nevertheless, the switch was made in April 2014. Problems began almost immediately. The water was often brown, it tasted and smelled bad, there were *E. coli* contaminations, and it contained unsafe levels of carcinogenic chemicals. Residents reported experiencing myriad health problems, such as headaches, nausea, and skin rashes. However, the largest public health crisis would not emerge until the following year, when it was discovered that a growing number of Flint's children had elevated levels of lead in their blood. The number of children found to have excessive lead levels jumped from 2.1 percent in 2013 to 4 percent in 2015, with rates over 6 percent in some neighborhoods. Lead is a neurotoxin that crosses the blood-brain barrier and is particularly hazardous to children. High exposure can cause cognitive, mental health, and behavioral control problems over a person's lifetime, and the damage it does to the brain is thought to be irreversible. It was quickly determined, largely through testing done by citizens working with university researchers, that the change in water was the source of the problem. The Flint

(cont.)

BOX 15.1 *(cont.)*

River water is highly corrosive (five times more so than Detroit's), and Flint is estimated to have ~15,000 water service lines made of lead.

That the Flint River water is highly corrosive and that Flint's water infrastructure contains large amounts of lead pipes were known prior to the decision to draw from the river. Moreover, there are regulations that require corrosion monitoring and corrosion control plans for cities the size of Flint. How then was this able to occur? Three public agencies (in addition to the governor's office) had oversight responsibilities and authority: the Flint Utilities Department, the Michigan Department of Environmental Quality (MDEQ), and the US Environmental Protection Agency (EPA). In each case, they failed to act to protect the citizens of Flint when they could have.

The Flint Utilities Department was required to do household testing to ensure that the new water source did not result in hazardous levels of lead. This included testing the water in homes known to be serviced by lead pipes to check for corrosive effects. However, their testing practices were inadequate (and possibly negligent) since they often claimed that homes had lead pipes servicing them when they did not know whether it was the case. As a result, their conclusion that there was not a corrosion problem was unwarranted and mistaken.

The MDEQ, which is charged with ensuring the safety of Flint's water supply, allowed the city to use the water from the Flint River without any corrosion control, including chemical treatments that had been used with the less corrosive water from Detroit's system. Moreover, MDEQ and the governor's office continued to insist (until September 2015), wrongly and on the basis of inadequate testing, that the water was safe, even after significant concerns had been raised and the Flint city council had voted (in March 2015) to return to Detroit's system. The emergency manager at the time prevented the switch, echoing the MDEQ claim that the Flint River water was safe by all EPA and MDEQ standards.

When the EPA learned (in early 2015) that the MDEQ was not requiring Flint to implement a corrosion control system and had not performed adequate monitoring—something about which EPA officials expressed significant concerns— the EPA could have exercised its power to compel it do so, but it did not. There was thus regulatory failure by multiple agencies—local, state, and federal—and at multiple levels—prevention, monitoring, enforcement, and oversight.

It was only after a study (released in September 2015) by independent researchers from Virginia Tech on lead in Flint residents' water and another study (also released in September 2015) by a Flint-area physician that established the elevated lead levels in children that the emergency manager, MDEQ, and

(cont.)

BOX 15.1 *(cont.)*

Governor Snyder acknowledged the water was not safe, that monitoring had been inadequate, and that inappropriate corrosion control protocols had been used. Flint was then allowed (in October 2015) to reconnect to the Detroit water system and residents were advised not to use unfiltered water for drinking, cooking, or bathing. Nevertheless, corrosion from the use of the Flint River water continues and the levels of lead in the water system remain very high. Immediate assistance to Flint residents (e.g., bottled water and filters) was also slow in coming. It was not until January 2016 that the state of Michigan and the US federal government declared a state of emergency in Flint and promised significant amounts of short-term assistance. Addressing the problem in the long term (e.g., remediating the lead and replacing the problematic infrastructure) may cost hundreds of millions of dollars, much more than the state or federal governments have pledged in aid, let alone made available.

    This case exhibits many features that are associated with environmental injustice and that are discussed in what follows: lack of public accountability, inadequate data on hazards, absence of meaningful public participation in decision-making, poor environmental monitoring, insufficient compliance, inadequate oversight and enforcement, prioritizing lowering costs over public health, decision-makers disconnected from the communities affected, slow and inadequate remediation, and lack of consideration of citizens' rights. It also clearly demonstrates how a community's being lower income and politically disempowered can lead to high exposures to environmental hazards. It was in part because of Flint's economic problems that it was looking to reduce costs wherever possible; and it was because the city was in receivership that the decision to switch to (and later to continue to use) the Flint River lacked due process, oversight, and public participation.

    Many children in Flint will have learning disabilities and behavioral problems because of the decision to use the river as a water source and the near abdication of regulatory responsibility. Children in the lowest income households, which are more likely to have lead service lines and for whom acquiring bottled water and filters was (and continues to be) a hardship, will likely be most affected. Flint's school system and social services will have an additional long-term burden. The economic costs to Flint will be enormous, much greater than the few millions of dollars that was projected to be saved by switching water sources. There will be long-term health care, education, infrastructure, remediation, and social costs, in addition to legal expenses (lawsuits have been filed and an FBI investigation has been opened). Thus, this case clearly demonstrates how environmental injustices compound beyond the immediate health impacts.

(cont.)

> BOX 15.1 *(cont.)*
>
> It is not only that the affected citizens of Flint are "unhealthy." Many of the children, families, and communities affected by this face longitudinal education, economic, and social challenges as a result of it, and they do so without robust economic and public resources to assist them.

Unequal exposure to environmental hazards is not limited to the United States. All over the world, minority, poor and disempowered peoples are disproportionately exposed to environmental hazards. They also are less likely to enjoy the benefits of environmental resources and industrial activities, and are slower to receive compensation or remediation for environmental harms. For example, victims of the 1984 Bhopal chemical disaster in India—in which a gas leak from a pesticide production facility run by Union Carbide is estimated to have sickened hundreds of thousands of people, killing between 3,000 and 15,000 and permanently disabling tens of thousands of others—received minimal compensation only after years of litigation and activism toward the Indian government and Union Carbide. Ogoni communities in the Niger Delta have been campaigning for decades against the Nigerian government and Shell Petroleum Company for greater autonomy and local benefits sharing with respect to the oil fields in their lands, as well as for redress for the environmental degradation caused by the oil industry. Indigenous communities in the eastern Ecuadorian rainforest have been litigating since 2003 for compensation from Texaco and Chevron (which took over Texaco in 2001) for environmental degradation and contamination associated with improper waste disposal of the byproducts from oil extraction in the region.

The unequal distribution of environmental burdens and benefits is widely considered to be *unjust*. There are many different theories of justice—for example, libertarian, liberal, utilitarian, communitarian, and Marxist. Most of them allow for there to be social and economic inequalities within a society. However, all those that permit inequalities require that they be justified. That is, they accept something like the following principle of justice:

> **Principle of Social Cooperation:** "Justice increases when the benefits and burdens of social cooperation are born more equally, except when moral considerations or other values justify greater inequality." (Wenz 2007, 58)

Theories of justice differ with respect to what counts as acceptable justification for inequality. For example, libertarian theories of justice require that they be earned noncoercively or acquired through free and fair exchange, while a prominent liberal theory of justice requires that they are reasonably expected to be to everyone's advantage (even those who are the worst off in society). However, *no* theory of justice endorses race, ethnicity, or class as a basis for unequal consideration or treatment. The reason for this is that doing so would violate the basic value commitment that all people have equal worth and should enjoy equal standing within social, economic, and political institutions.

When researchers have looked at the causes of unequal exposure in the United States, they have found that cases differ substantially. The economic, social, legal, and procedural causes of high exposures to agricultural chemicals among immigrant farm worker communities are different from those of mining-related hazards on Native American tribal lands and from elevated levels of air pollutants in urban high-minority communities. However, in almost all cases, the explanations involved include some element of social and political disempowerment or marginalization—for example, NIMBY (Not In My Back Yard) effects, differential political influence, redlining in insurance and lending practices, discriminatory use of restrictive covenants, zoning and land planning legacies from segregation, racism in job hiring and advancement, lack of legal standing to seek redress, language barriers, inadequate information disclosures, closed decision-making processes, rubber-stamp permitting, and corporate influence and the marginalization of local communities in land use decisions (Bullard 1990; Westra and Lawson 2001). Again, these are illustrative of the factors that are often involved in the production of unequal exposure. They are not operative in all cases, and many other factors play a role. For example, there are frequently economic explanations involved. People with lower incomes often live closer to industrial facilities because housing costs are lower, and low-income communities are sometimes more willing to accept undesirable land uses if they are expected bring jobs and economic development to the community (Sandler and Pezzullo 2007).

The fact that unequal exposure to environmental hazards very often is caused, at least in part, by problematic social and political factors is one of the primary reasons why it is considered to be **environmental injustice**. The other reason is that the benefits associated with environmental hazards are often not substantially shared by the communities that shoulder the burden of the hazards. Low-income communities are more exposed to hazards than are affluent communities, but it is affluent people who enjoy a greater proportion of the wealth and goods that generate them. This seems to violate another widely accepted principle of justice:

> **Principle of commensurate burdens and benefits:** Those who enjoy the benefits of some activity should also shoulder the associated burdens, and vice versa, unless there is good justification for them not doing so. (Wenz 2001)

The principle of commensurate burdens and benefits embodies the idea that people should get what they deserve and deserve what they get. As with the principle of social cooperation, this need not always be the case. There might be good reasons for exceptions or deviations from the principle—for instance, to promote well-being, ensure equal opportunity, or protect basic rights. But the deviations are not justified in cases of unequal exposure to environmental hazards caused by problematic social and political factors.

Here, then, is a summary of the basic argument that unequal exposure (in the United States) is unjust:

1. The principles of social cooperation and commensurate burdens and benefits would be endorsed by a wide range of theories of justice, since they are premised on all people having equal worth and political standing.
2. Unequal exposure to environmental hazards in the United States violates one or both these principles, both systematically and in particular cases.

_____

3. Therefore, unequal exposure in the United States is unjust, both systematically and in particular cases.

An analogous argument can often be made for systematic inequalities and cases of unequal exposure in countries other than the United States, including those mentioned earlier, as well as for global distributions of environmental burdens and benefits. For instance, at the core of concerns about **climate justice** is the fact that those who are most responsible for causing global climate change—affluent people with high-emissions lifestyles—are least exposed to its hazard, since they have comparatively large adaptive capacity due to their wealth and mobility. In contrast, those who are least responsible for causing it—the global poor with low-emissions lifestyles—are most exposed to its hazards because they often depend more directly on ecological stability and have fewer resources for adaptation.

BOX 15.2   TOPIC TO CONSIDER

ENVIRONMENTAL JUSTICE AND ENVIRONMENTAL RACISM

In the United States, environmental injustice is sometimes also referred to as **environmental racism**. Part of the reason for this is that high-minority communities are exposed to greater levels of hazards than are low-minority communities, and that the explanation for this in many cases involves social and political disempowerment and economic discrimination. That is to say, the causes are in part related to structural disadvantages faced by people of color and communities of color.

Another reason environmental injustice is sometimes called environmental racism is that the struggle for environmental justice is frequently situated within

(cont.)

BOX 15.2 *(cont.)*

the framework of the civil rights movement. The environmental justice movement is seen by many activists in it as part of the effort to secure, maintain, and enforce the rights and equal political standing of people of color—for example, the rights to clean air, clean water, safe living spaces and working conditions, and meaningful political participation. Moreover, many of the actors in the movement have historical ties to the civil rights movement or are organizations that advocate and organize for social justice including and beyond environmental justice. Thus, the environmental justice movement is not only about environmental inequalities, but is often seen as part of the continuing struggle against race-based exclusion, discrimination, and exploitation, or, in the case of Native Americans, appropriation and colonization. The movement for environmental justice is part of a broader effort to secure respect for civil rights and community empowerment and uplift.

A third reason that many environmental justice advocates see the disproportionate burdens placed on high-minority communities as a form of racism is that it seems to betray a conception of those communities as themselves marginal or polluted. On this view, they are treated as the sorts of places onto which it is acceptable to displace environmental hazards—"sacrifice zones"—because they and the people who live in them are disvalued. As with substandard education and a lack of public safety, exposure to environmental hazards is seen or treated as not mattering as much when it occurs in high-minority or low-income communities. For example, many environmental justice leaders have questioned whether the lead contamination in Flint, Michigan (Box 15.1) would have been allowed to occur and remain unaddressed for so long, and public concerns so readily and summarily dismissed, if Flint were a largely white, affluent suburb.

This last reason is related to a point touched upon earlier (Sections 1.1 and 14.3) regarding what is considered to be an environmental issue. Many environmental justice advocates emphasize that the environment encompasses "where we live, work, and play." When conceptualized this way, lead paint, substandard housing, workplace safety, potable water, degraded parks, and asbestos in schools are environmental issues. The environmental justice movement has at times been critical of environmentalism and environmental organizations for not only failing to see these as important environmental problems, but also for pursuing environmental goals in ways that are detrimental to poor and disempowered people—such as fortress conservation and restricting economic development (see, e.g., Boxes 3.1 and 16.2) (Sandler and Pezzullo 2007).

The term "environmental racism" is more controversial than "environmental injustice." One reason for this is that not all environmental justice communities

(cont.)

BOX 15.2 *(cont.)*

are high-minority communities, and not all cases of unequal exposure involve communities that are systematically disadvantaged. Another reason is that it appears to imply that the people involved in siting and remediating hazardous facilities, or that are inattentive to environmental justice issues, are racist, when often they are not. Siting decisions typically are not intended to be discriminatory and are not overtly made based on racial considerations. They are very often made on the basis of economic or efficiency analysis (see, for example, the discussions of cost-benefit analysis [Section 15.2] and the Flint, Michigan, water contamination case [Box 15.1]). This is not a situation unique to environmental hazards and environmental injustice. When disadvantage and disempowerment are structural, injustice does not always track to particular people making particular decisions with discriminatory intent. It is for this reason that many environmental justice advocates emphasize that discriminatory intent is not a necessary condition for wrongful discrimination; what matters is that there are disparate impacts.

Do you think that environmental injustice should, at least in some cases, be considered a form of racism? Why or why not? What does your view imply for other social justice issues, such as racial disparities in educational outcomes, incarceration rates, and employment? Do you agree that something is unjust and violates the equal political standing and worth of people if it has disparate impacts on minority groups, even if there is no discriminatory or race-based intent? Why or why not?

15.2 ENVIRONMENTAL JUSTICE AND COST–BENEFIT ANALYSIS

The sources of environmental injustice include social and political inequalities and disempowerment. Therefore, it might seem reasonable that it could be addressed by adopting an impartial decision-making process regarding the siting and remediation of environmental hazards. One such process is **cost-benefit analysis** (CBA). According to cost-benefit decision-making, environmental (and other) policies and decisions should be made on the basis of what maximizes the social benefits over social costs—that is, they should aim at what is best for society overall. Moreover, in the context of assessing the costs and benefits of different options everyone should be considered equally. CBA is thus an impartial efficiency maximization approach to analyzing options and making decisions.

However, CBA is widely regarded as being a contributing cause of unequal exposure to environmental hazards, rather than an effective approach to addressing it. Here is why. Imagine that a city or company is doing an impartial economic analysis of where to site a locally undesirable land use, such as a transportation depot, waste management plant, or manufacturing facility. Among the relevant economic considerations are the cost of procuring the land for the facility, the effects on nearby property values, the cost and length of the permitting and approval processes, the loss of productivity from any environmental health impacts, and the economic benefits to the community. These considerations, and others like them, are going to favor siting the facility in a lower-income, lower-employment, less socially and politically empowered community. Thus, the concern is that CBA does not correct for political and economic inequalities and injustices. Instead, it locks them in as background features of an "impartial" economic analysis, such that the analysis reflects the inequalities.

Moreover, this concern continues, CBA will tend to favor siting hazardous facilities in close proximity to each other. The reason for this is that once one facility is sited in a location, the costs of siting another one there will be reduced—for example, local property values will be lower, the necessary zoning will be in place, and the supporting infrastructure will be built. Therefore, when a CBA is conducted for the next facility, the location or community where the previous one was sited will appear even more favorable than it did the last time. As a result, hazardous facilities often are clustered. Some high-profile cases of this in the United States are "cancer alley" between Baton Rouge and New Orleans, an 85-mile stretch along the Mississippi River with over one hundred petrochemical plants (Image 15.1), and the "toxic doughnut" around Altgeld Gardens on the South Side of Chicago, which includes over fifty hazardous waste landfills and over one hundred factories and industrial facilities. This concern regarding CBA is similar to one discussed earlier regarding utilitarianism (Section 8.5), another impartial maximization approach to evaluation. In both cases, the worry is that aggregate maximization cannot adequately accommodate concerns about distribution or rights.

Another concern about CBA is that in order to sum and compare the outcomes of the different options being considered, the outcomes must all be represented in a common unit of value—economic value. As discussed in the section on economic valuation and environmental values (Section 4.3), many environmental ethicists argue that not all values can be accurately represented in monetary units. In this case, the worry is that social justice and individual rights will be either marginalized or misrepresented.

Finally, CBA is criticized on the grounds that not all social decisions or policies should aim at aggregate maximization of either welfare or economic value. The concern is not just that it cannot accommodate all social or environmental values, but that other values should sometimes take priority. For example, in some cases it may be more important to avoid compounding historical injustices than it is to maximize social utility.

None of this is to claim that economic analyses of available options should not be conducted or that they should not inform social policies and public decision-making. They very often should. For example, *cost-effectiveness analysis* is crucial to identifying the most efficient way of realizing a policy goal, such as improving education or delivering basic environmental goods. Moreover, CBA often illuminates when a policy or project is going to do more harm than good. (See the discussion on economic valuation [Section 4.3] for examples of this.) Economic considerations also often are vital to deciding among policy goals. For example, in setting pollution policy it is important to know the costs and

Image 15.1   A stretch of "Cancer Alley" along the lower Mississippi River in Louisiana, USA.
Source: ©Jeffrey Dubinsky Photography

benefits associated with different possible standards and forms of regulation. For these reasons, most critics of CBA do not believe that it should play no role in social and environmental decision-making. Their view is that it should not always be determinative. In some cases, maximizing efficiency is not an appropriate goal or a strictly economic analysis fails to capture all of the values or considerations relevant to the decision. Furthermore, decision-making should very often be inclusive and collaborative. Thus, even when CBA should be used to inform decision-making processes, it often ought not be decisive.

15.3 ADDRESSING ENVIRONMENTAL INJUSTICE

Distributive injustices involving environmental goods and hazards are often the product of procedural and recognition injustices. Unequal exposure frequently comes about because high-minority and low-income communities are systematically disempowered, marginalized, and/or are not afforded full and equal participation or standing in environmental decision-making processes. Therefore, accomplishing environmental justice requires not only addressing unequal exposure, but doing so in ways that empower communities and address the social, economic, and political factors that have enabled it. This view is evident in the ***Principles of Environmental Justice*** adopted at the First National People of Color Environmental Leadership Summit in 1991. The summit was a gathering of activists from across the United States, as well as Canada, Central America, and the Marshall Islands. On the final day of the summit, the delegates adopted seventeen principles, which have since served as the defining document for much of the environmental justice movement (see Box 15.3). The principles embody an expansive conception of environmental issues, and locate them within an encompassing social, political, and ethical outlook and agenda that includes securing universal protection, meaningful political participation, and self-determination for all peoples.

✳ BOX 15.3

PRINCIPLES OF ENVIRONMENTAL JUSTICE

The following principles of environmental justice were adopted by the delegates to the First National People of Color Environmental Leadership Summit, October 24–27, 1991, in Washington DC:

> We, the people of color, gathered together at this multinational People of Color Environmental Leadership Summit, to begin to build a national and international movement of all peoples of color to fight the destruction and taking of our lands and communities, do hereby reestablish our spiritual interdependence to the sacredness of our Mother Earth; to respect and celebrate each of our cultures, languages, and beliefs about the natural world and our roles in healing ourselves; to ensure environmental justice; to promote economic alternatives which would contribute to the development of environmentally safe livelihoods; and, to secure our political, economic, and cultural liberation that has been denied for over five hundred years of colonization and oppression, resulting in the poisoning of our communities and land and the genocide of our peoples, do affirm and adopt these Principles of Environmental Justice:

1. Environmental Justice affirms the sacredness of Mother Earth, ecological unity and the interdependence of all species, and the right to be free from ecological destruction.
2. Environmental Justice demands that public policy be based on mutual respect and justice for all peoples, free from any form of discrimination or bias.
3. Environmental Justice mandates the right to ethical, balanced, and responsible uses of land and renewable resources in the interest of a sustainable planet for humans and other living things.
4. Environmental Justice calls for universal protection from nuclear testing, extraction, production, and disposal of toxic/hazardous wastes and poisons

(cont.)

BOX 15.3 *(cont.)*

and nuclear testing that threaten the fundamental right to clean air, land, water, and food.

5. Environmental Justice affirms the fundamental right to political, economic, cultural, and environmental self-determination of all peoples.

6. Environmental Justice demands the cessation of the production of all toxins, hazardous wastes, and radioactive materials, and that all past and current producers be held strictly accountable to the people for detoxification and the containment at the point of production.

7. Environmental Justice demands the right to participate as equal partners at every level of decision-making, including needs assessment, planning, implementation, enforcement, and evaluation.

8. Environmental Justice affirms the right of all workers to a safe and healthy work environment without being forced to choose between an unsafe livelihood and unemployment. It also affirms the right of those who work at home to be free from environmental hazards.

9. Environmental Justice protects the right of victims of environmental injustice to receive full compensation and reparations for damages as well as quality health care.

10. Environmental Justice considers governmental acts of environmental injustice a violation of international law, the Universal Declaration On Human Rights, and the United Nations Convention on Genocide.

11. Environmental Justice must recognize a special legal and natural relationship of Native Peoples to the U.S. government through treaties, agreements, compacts, and covenants affirming sovereignty and self-determination.

12. Environmental Justice affirms the need for urban and rural ecological policies to clean up and rebuild our cities and rural areas in balance with nature, honoring the cultural integrity of all our communities, and providing fair access for all to the full range of resources.

13. Environmental Justice calls for the strict enforcement of principles of informed consent, and a halt to the testing of experimental reproductive and medical procedures and vaccinations on people of color.

14. Environmental Justice opposes the destructive operations of multinational corporations.

15. Environmental Justice opposes military occupation, repression and exploitation of lands, peoples and cultures, and other life forms.

16. Environmental Justice calls for the education of present and future generations which emphasizes social and environmental issues, based on our experience and an appreciation of our diverse cultural perspectives.

(cont.)

BOX 15.3 *(cont.)*

17. Environmental Justice requires that we, as individuals, make personal and consumer choices to consume as little of Mother Earth's resources and to produce as little waste as possible; and make the conscious decision to challenge and reprioritize our lifestyles to ensure the health of the natural world for present and future generations.

Many environmental justice advocates also emphasize that the goal of environmental justice efforts cannot only be to empower environmental justice communities so that they can succeed in their own attempts to resist unwanted land uses and hazards in their communities. Unless there are fewer hazards overall, they will simply be displaced into someone else's community—that is, the aim cannot just be NIMBY, but must be NIABY (Not In Anyone's Back Yard). Thus, addressing environmental injustice requires accomplishing several interconnected goals, each of which is operative in the *Principles of Environmental Justice* (Box 15.3):

1. Reduce the disproportionate exposure to environmental hazards experienced by high-minority and low-income communities.
2. Address the structural features, policies, and processes of social, political, and economic institutions that enable unequal exposure to environmental hazards.
3. Empower environmental justice communities, and the people in them, with respect to environmental decision-making impacting their communities, as well as with respect to seeking redress for environmental harms that they, their families, and their communities have experienced.
4. Reduce the overall amount of hazardous facilities and undesirable land uses in society.

Two interrelated ethical considerations are widely regarded as core to pursuing these aims: **environmental rights** and **free informed consent.**

Environmental rights are central to the work of influential environmental justice researcher and advocate Robert Bullard (1990; 2001). According to Bullard, "every individual has a right to be protected from environmental degradation" (2001, 10). This right is often considered to be a fundamental or human right (see Section 9.4 and Box 9.5). However, environmental justice activists and researchers emphasize that it is also a civil right that governments have an obligation to ensure for their citizens. All citizens, regardless of race, ethnicity, class, or location are due equal protection from environmental hazards, equal participation in environmental decision-making, equal treatment in environmental remediation, and equal standing in seeking redress for environmental harms. Every citizen has a right to nondiscrimination regarding environmental protection, just as they do nondiscrimination in housing, education, voting, and employment. This follows directly from the equal worth and political standing of all people. Therefore, if governments do not already have legislation that guarantees these environmental protections and that addresses persistent inequalities in them, then they have a responsibility to create and enforce them. For example, in the United States, former president Bill Clinton issued Executive Order 12898, *Federal Actions to Address Environmental Justice in Minority Populations and Low-Income Populations* (1994). It directs federal agencies to "make achieving environmental justice part of its mission by identifying and addressing as appropriate, disproportionately high and adverse human health or environmental effects of its programs, policies, and activities on minority populations and low-income populations in the United States and its territories and possessions." Several states such as Massachusetts and California also have legislation and orders that address disparate environmental impacts. However, implementation of many of these laws and directives has so far been slow and incomplete.

Free informed consent refers to the fact that citizens and communities are entitled to due process in environmental decision-making. Realizing free informed consent requires such things as ensuring that affected communities have access to all the relevant information, that there are opportunities for citizens to play a meaningful role in deliberations, that decision-makers are accountable to affected communities in appropriate ways, and that communities and individuals receive reasonable and negotiated compensation for hazards or risks to which they are exposed (Shrader-Frechette 2002). Free informed consent is thought to be justified by the worth and autonomy of individuals, and it is often conceived of as a right. That is, people have a right to be consulted about what sorts of facilities are located in their communities or on their lands, in appropriately open and participatory ways. Moreover, if they do not agree to them, then compensation must be offered in order to gain agreement. A community might be willing to accept a facility if adequate protections are put into place, liability for harms is clearly established, and the community receives some ancillary benefits—for example, tax revenue, guarantee of jobs, or health centers. In the absence of free informed consent obtained through appropriately democratic or participatory processes, exposing people to environmental hazards is unjustified, on this view.

Taken together, ensuring civil environmental rights and establishing norms of free informed consent would empower individuals and environmental justice communities. It would ensure procedural and standing justice. It would address structural impediments to equal environmental protection and redress, as well as make "environmental discrimination illegal and costly" (Bullard 2001, 23). Therefore, it would likely decrease unequal exposure over time. It would also increase the costs and difficulties associated with siting environmental hazards in general, and so incentive reducing the number of facilities to be sited as well as minimizing the hazards associated with them. Thus, promoting environmental rights and informed consent would be conducive to accomplishing each of the environmental justice goals.

Activists and researchers have proposed numerous policies and practices that if implemented would help promote environmental rights, free informed consent, and environmental justice. Below is an illustrative sample, several of which were touched upon earlier. These are derived largely from the environmental justice discourse in the United States, but in many cases could be adapted for other countries:

- Pass environmental justice legislation at the state and federal level that is modeled on non-discrimination legislation in employment, education, and voting (e.g., the Civil Rights Act, Fair Housing Act and the Voting Rights Act in the United States).
- In the United States, fully fund and implement all aspects of Executive Order 12898, such as the Environmental Protection Agency's "Environmental Justice Plan" and "Policy for Environmental Justice for Working with Federally Recognized Tribes and Indigenous Peoples."
- Adopt a precautionary approach with respect to chemicals and industrial processes that places the burden of proof on industry to establish that they are safe before they are used, as opposed to assuming they are safe and placing the burden of proof on communities or consumers to demonstrate that they are hazardous. (The European Union has begun to implement a strict premarket approval process, sometimes referred to as "no data, no market" for new chemicals, whereas the United States has a premarket approval process for some chemicals, such as pesticides, but not others. See Box 15.4 for discussion of the precautionary principle.)
- Adopt policies that encourage pollution reduction, such as: implement strict pollution limits, develop comprehensive toxics substitution programs, provide government funding, tax benefits, and regulatory incentives for sustainable production processes, foster cost internalization (e.g., establish pollution taxes that require industry to price in the health and ecosystem services costs associated with production and use of their products), increase liability for environmental discrimination and harms, require polluters to pay for the full costs of remediation, and require manufacturers to be responsible for the end-of-life-disposal of the goods that they produce.
- Collect and make accessible better data about pollutants that are released into communities—for example, require more detailed and comprehensive Toxics Release Inventory reporting and expand citizen science and monitoring programs.
- Encourage participation and increase the influence of local communities in zoning and industrial permitting processes—for example, by curbing the power of corporations associated with their personhood status in the United States.
- Make systematic disparate impacts sufficient to establish unlawful discrimination, rather than requiring proof of discriminatory intent.
- Redress past environmental injustices through such things as government- and industry-funded remediation of brownfields and abandoned sites, as well as

incentivizing community-oriented redevelopment through public programs and public-private partnerships aimed at local ownership, job creation, and economic development.

- Require communities to take direct responsibility for the wastes and hazards that they generate, rather than collecting and transferring them elsewhere.

The foregoing is intended to indicate the kind of policies that have been proposed to protect environmental rights and promote free informed consent, and thereby be conducive to environmental justice. They are, for the most part, policies that would address problematic aspects of current political, legal, and economic systems and institutions. That is, they are reformative. However, on many views, the underlying cause of environmental problems are the dominant ideological, technological, economic, and political structures that encourage marginalizing people, treating the environment as a mere resource (including for waste disposal), and focusing on personal material gain (see, e.g., deep ecology [Section 12.3] and Pope Francis's *Laudato Sí* [Box 5.4]). On this view, social injustice, including environmental injustice, is not likely to be accomplished merely by cleaning up the current system. It will require radical political, economic, and ideological change—for example, economic systems in which environmental hazards are not acceptable (regardless of expediency), conceptions of human flourishing that are not tied to material accumulation, and decentralized political structures that empower local communities over large economic actors (e.g., transnational corporations).

☀ BOX 15.4   TOPIC TO CONSIDER

PRESUMPTION IN ETHICS: THE PRECAUTIONARY PRINCIPLE AND THE INNOVATION PRESUMPTION

Where the burden of justification (or proof) lies is crucial to many issues in ethics. For example, as discussed in Sections 7.1 and 7.4, a presumption in favor of considering something's interests as being morally considerable, unless there is a compelling justification not to, pulls toward more inclusive views such as sentientism and biocentrism. In technology ethics, it is often claimed that there is an **innovation presumption**. People should be allowed to create and adopt novel technologies—from new materials to artificial intelligences—unless good reasons are provided against their doing so. The **harm principle** is a more generally applicable presumption. It asserts that people ought to be able to engage in an activity—for instance, same-sex marriage, gun ownership, urban beekeeping,

(cont.)

BOX 15.4 *(cont.)*

and riding motorcycles without helmets—so long as it does not harm anyone or anything else. According to both the harm principle and the innovation presumption, the default is to allow the activity, and the burden of justification is on those who propose to restrict it. These presumptions are not merely asserted, but argued for. The harm principle is thought to be justified by respect for people as autonomous agents and by the value of liberty. The innovation presumption it is thought to be justified by autonomy and liberty, and that favoring technological innovation promotes well-being overall in the long run.

There are alternative views. For example, discourse theory, which has been developed prominently by Jürgen Habermas, holds that in order for an action or policy to be justified it must be the case that it could be accepted by all those affected by it in a reasonable discourse. On such a view, novel technologies or practices are not presumed justified. They have to be shown to be, based on their being justifiable to all reasonable persons impacted by them.

In environmental ethics and policy, the issue of presumption is prominent in discussions about how to respond to uncertainty about hazards and risks. **Risk** is a quantitative measure of the frequency and magnitude of a hazard. For example, the risk of lead poisoning from drinking a water source refers to the frequency with which it occurs—the number of incidents relative to exposures—as well as how bad it is when it occurs—the probabilistic range of outcomes. **Safety** is *acceptable risk*, not zero risk. The quantity of risk itself does not determine whether something is safe, since people accept different amounts of risk for different things. This can be seen easily in the case of food. People do not aim for a diet as low in food-borne illness risk as possible, which would involve not eating out, not eating raw fish or rare meats, cooking all vegetables thoroughly, and generally eating very highly processed, pasteurized, and irradiated foods. The reason for this is that eating is about aesthetics, experiences, convenience, social interactions, and cultural practices, in addition to health and nutrition. People are willing to trade these off against risk of illness, and it is reasonable to do so. Eating raw fish sushi is safe, the risks of doing it are acceptable, even though the quantitative risk of food-borne illness is higher than when eating granola bars. So not only is safety acceptable risk, what level of risk is acceptable is frequently contextual.

Many environmental justice activists and environmentalists advocate for applying the **precautionary principle** in response to unknown risks, particularly with respect to new technologies. According to the precautionary principle,

(cont.)

BOX 15.4 *(cont.)*

when there is scientific uncertainty about risk—when we do not adequately understand the ecological and health risks of a new technology (e.g., a chemical or genetically modified crop)—rather than presuming that it is acceptable, we should restrict it until it is demonstrated to be safe. Whereas the innovation presumption puts the burden of justification on those who would like to restrict the technology, the precautionary principle places the burden of justification on those who would like to employ it.

There are myriad formulations of the precautionary principle, but when applied to environmental issues, a formulation known as the Wingspread Statement (1998) is often invoked:

> Where an activity raises threats of harm to the environment or human health, precautionary measures should be taken even if some cause and effect relationships are not fully established scientifically.

The implication of this principle for novel chemicals and genetically modified organisms, for example, is that they should be restricted until safety to human health and the environment is established. The Wingspread formulation of the precautionary principle is conservative. It does not just say that it is permissible to take precautionary measures if there are possible threats. It says that such measures *should* be taken. Other formulations do not require taking precautionary measures (they only permit it), specify that measures should only be taken if the risks are quite serious, and/or allow countervailing considerations against taking measures. One formulation along these lines is from the UN Rio Declaration on the Environment (1992b):

> In order to protect the environment, the precautionary approach shall be widely applied by States according to their capabilities. Where there are threats of serious or irreversible damage, lack of full scientific certainty shall not be used as a reason for postponing cost-effective measures to prevent environmental degradation.

The standard for restricting new chemicals or genetically modified organisms based on the Rio formulation is much higher than that on the Wingspread formulation. The threats must be serious and the measures must be cost-effective, for example. These two formulations of the precautionary principle illustrate

(cont.)

BOX 15.4 *(cont.)*

that there is no such thing as the precautionary principle as such. Instead, there are a range of views—from the conservative Wingspread precautionary principle to the technological optimism of the innovation presumption—on how much caution and how much confidence we should have with respect to the environmental and human health risks of new technologies.

All policy-making and all technological innovation and implementation take place under at least some level of uncertainty, since information is never perfect and they aim to impact the future. Thus, a perennial issue in both environmental ethics and the ethics of technology is determining, in particular contexts and for particular issues, how much precaution and risk-reduction is appropriate. Do you believe that a precautionary approach should be taken for new technologies? If so, how precautionary should it be? And does it differ depending upon the technology—for example, chemicals, genetically modified crops, alternative energy technologies, hydraulic fracturing, or geoengineering? Why or why not? What about the risks and uncertainties of not developing and implementing these technologies? Could they be greater than the risks and uncertainties of doing so? If so, what does this imply for the view that we ought to take a precautionary approach regarding novel technologies?

15.4 THE ETHICAL DIMENSIONS OF CONSUMPTION

Environmental burdens are undesirable. Waste and pollution are expensive for companies to manage. They are hazardous to workers. They are costly for governments to remediate. They are detrimental to communities. They make people unhealthy. They harm the environment. Environmental burdens only exist because they are the unintended byproducts of the industrial production of things that people need and want—such as energy, electronics, cars, food, and travel. They are generated over the life-cycle of consumer goods: resource extraction, refining, manufacturing, transportation, use, and disposal. Therefore, the more consumption there is, the more environmental burdens there are, all other things being equal. The same is true of resource depletion. People do not desire to overuse resources or undermine their capacity to be replenished. These are the byproduct of excessive demand. The more consumption there is—of fish, water, forests, energy, soil, and pangolins—the more finite resources are depleted, all other things being equal. This is why many environmental thinkers believe that the overarching environmental problems are

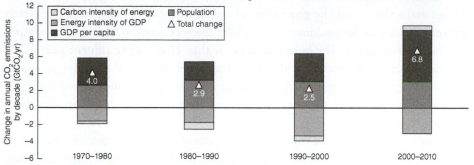

Figure 15.2   Growth in population and per capita GDP (or consumption) have been the primary drivers of carbon dioxide emissions increases since 1970. Reductions in energy intensity and carbon intensity (prior to 2000) have decreased emissions from what they otherwise would have been.
Source: IPCC (2014)

overpopulation and overconsumption: there are too many people, consuming too many resources, and producing too much waste. Several of the views that have been discussed—including biocentrism (Chapter 7), deep ecology (Chapter 12), and the land ethic (Chapter 11)—call for significant reductions in population and consumption by affluent people.

Population and per capita consumption are not the only factors that are relevant to ecological degradation. How efficiently and in what ways products are produced also matter. Take energy, for example (Figure 15.2). Increased economic activity results in greater energy use only if it outstrips the pace of efficiency gains. The **energy intensity** of the economy refers to how much energy is used per unit of economic activity. If energy intensity improves fast enough (i.e., if economic activity becomes more energy efficient) then it is possible for energy use to be stable (or even decrease) while economic activity increases. It is also possible for the **carbon intensity** of the energy supply to improve. Carbon intensity refers to the amount of carbon that is emitted per unit of energy production. If carbon intensity improves fast enough, by shifting from fossil fuels to alternative energy sources, then it is possible for economic activity and energy usage to increase without carbon emissions doing so. This example illustrates that while population and per capita consumption are crucial to environmental impacts, so too are efficiency and methods of production. This was highlighted earlier during the discussions of sustainability (Box 6.2) and wise use (Section 6.1).

As we have seen, there is widespread agreement among environmental ethics that the current consumption patterns of affluent people and nations are environmentally and socially problematic. They drive resource depletion, ecological degradation, species extinctions, and the generation of environmental hazards, which adversely impact subsistence, low-income, and socially disempowered people and communities disproportionately. The question, then, is this: How ought affluent people and societies change the ways in which they consume? There are several interrelated considerations that ethicists focus on when addressing this question: quantity of consumption; quality of consumption; systems of consumption; and attitudes about consumption.

Some ethicists emphasize that the sheer *volume of consumption* that affluent people engage in is problematic. In the United States, for example, the average household now has more televisions than it does people and more cars than it does drivers. Not only does such overconsumption harm the environment for reasons discussed above. It does so with no significant benefits to the overconsumer. People are not benefited by having closets full of clothes that they never wear and rooms full of toys that are not played with. This type of excessive consumption does not satisfy any basic needs or serious interests. In fact, it can often be detrimental to the consumer. People eat more food than is healthy for them, as evidenced by the very high obesity rates in affluent countries. People spend less meaningful time directly engaging their friends and family when everyone has several personal electronic devices at hand. Therefore, the volume of consumption that affluent people engage in involves harms and wrongs to other people and to nature, without any adequate justification. It ought to be reduced, according to this view, in order to decrease the burdens it creates and to make more resources available for other people and nature.

A concern sometimes raised regarding the claim that affluent people ought to significantly reduce the quantity of their consumption is that large reductions could actually be detrimental to other people, since consumer spending maintains national and global economies within a capitalist economic system and decreased economic activity often results in job and income losses. This concern favors the position that changes in consumption patterns should prioritize the *quality of consumption*. On this view, the problem is that people currently consume massive amounts of low-quality, disposal goods that are made artificially inexpensive by the externalization of ecological and social costs. If people consumed higher quality, sustainably produced, and more durable goods in which the ecological and social impacts are priced in, then there could be as high a level of consumption (with respect to economic activity, if not volume) with much lower impacts. Moreover, consumer demand for such goods would spur organizational and technological innovations to increase efficiency and reduce polluting production methods. This approach is manifest in policy efforts to make the price of consumer goods reflect their true production costs—for instance, carbon taxes and living wage laws—as well as in a wide variety of environmentally and socially responsible certification programs—for instance, fair trade, organic, humanely raised, and sustainable forestry and fisheries. It is also possible to consume experiences and services that do not involve material goods acquisitions—for example, music lessons and education. Prioritizing these goods could be another way to maintain economic activity while reducing ecological and social costs.

The two approaches above—reducing consumption and improving the quality of consumption—fall within what deep ecologists would consider shallow environmentalism. They aim to clean up and improve upon currently problematic practices. They do not challenge the underlying structural and ideological features that give rise to them—that is, capitalist economic systems, conceptions of human flourishing tied to personal material acquisition, and techno-optimism (Section 12.3). According to many "deep green" political and economic theorists, problematic consumption will continue unless these are addressed. On this view, it is simply not possible to build a sustainable and just society in a materially finite world when the underlying economic and political philosophies are premised on continually expansion and growth. Therefore, there needs to be radical revision in the ways in which affluent people conceive of human flourishing and the ways in which societies promote it. People should aim for enjoyable, rich, and meaningful experiences and relationships that do not involve overappropriating for themselves. Consumption of material goods beyond what is needed for health, security, and well-being needs to be seen as not only gratuitous, but unjust. Economic activity, policies, and institutions need to be reordered so they are in the service of human well-being, rather than economic expansion. Social and political power must not be concentrated with those who most benefit from an overly materialist society (e.g., corporations). On this view, it is obtaining *systems of consumption* and *attitudes about consumption* that are the deeper problems in need of addressing.

Many environmental ethicists agree with the view that *consumeristic dispositions* are ethically problematic. One reason for this is that they favor overconsumption in ways that are detrimental to the environment and to other people. However, another reason is that research on the psychology of consumption has found that those with materialistic value orientations report lower levels of well-being than those with more social and self-realization value orientations:

> People who are highly focused on materialistic values have lower
> personal well-being and psychological health than those who believe
> that materialistic pursuits are relatively unimportant. . . . The studies
> document that strong materialistic values are associated with a pervasive
> undermining of people's well-being, from low life satisfaction and
> happiness, to depression and anxiety, to physical problems such as
> headaches, and to personality disorders, narcissism, and antisocial
> behavior. (Kasser 2002, 22)

The research indicates that part of the explanation for why people with material-istic value orientations have lower levels of well-being is that "needs for security and safety, competence and self-esteem, connectedness to others, and autonomy and au-thenticity are relatively unsatisfied when materialistic values are prominent in people's value systems" (Kasser 2002, 97). It also suggests that the causal relationship between materialism and need frustration runs both ways:

> Materialistic values become prominent in the lives of some individuals
> who have a history of not having their needs well met. . . . But materialistic
> values are not just expressions of unhappiness. Instead, they lead people
> to organize their lives in ways that do a poor job of satisfying their needs,
> and thus contribute even more to people's misery. (Kasser 2002, 28)

Thus, materialistic dispositions are not conducive to living well. Greed is not good. Character traits such as simplicity, frugality, and temperance are more conducive to a person flourishing, in addition to being conducive to promoting ecological sustain-ability. For this reason, they are often considered to be important environmental vir-tues, while character traits such as profligacy, wastefulness, and intemperance are rec-ognized as environmental vices (Wenz 2005; Cafaro 2005; Thoreau 1906).

As indicated by the discussion above, the four dimensions of consumption—volume, quality, systems, and attitudes—are interconnected. Reducing the volume of consump-tion is more likely to occur if attitudes about consumption change, and improving the quality of consumption is more likely to occur if changes are made in the systems of con-sumption. Therefore, moving toward more ethical consumption may require addressing each of them to at least some extent. However, different theories of environmental ethics tend to prioritize different aspects of consumption. For example, enlightened anthropo-centric theories tend to emphasize the quality and quantity of consumption, while deep ecology views tend to stress the need for systemic and ideological changes.

BOX 15.5   TOPIC TO CONSIDER

THE PRINCIPLE OF ANTICIPATORY COOPERATION

The environmental problems associated with overconsumption are collective action problems. Global climate change, fisheries depletion, CAFOs, pollution, and deforestation are not problems that any single person can solve on their own by changing their consumption patterns. Therefore, the ethics of consump-tion must address the problem of inconsequentialism (Box 8.6). Why should a

(cont.)

BOX 15.5 *(cont.)*

person make the effort or sacrifices to reduce her own consumption, if doing so will not make any significant difference to solving the problem?

Peter Wenz (2005) has argued that the problem of inconsequentialism has two implications for the ethics of consumption: (1) a person should not be ethically required to alter her consumption in ways that undermine her prospects for flourishing—it should not require "heroic sacrifice"; (2) whatever changes a person is required to make in her consumption behaviors should encourage others to follow suit—it should set a reasonable example for others to follow. In light of these considerations, Wenz suggests the principle of anticipatory cooperation (PAC), which calls for actions, behaviors, and practices that "deviate from the social norm in the direction of the ideal . . . but which do not deviate so much that [it] impairs instead of fosters flourishing" (Wenz 2005, 211). Here is Wenz's description of the practical implications of PAC with respect to car use, for example:

> If life without a car is nearly crippling, the PAC does not require that . . . people abjure car ownership and use. It requires only that they try to arrange their lives so that their car use and its adverse impacts are substantially less than is common in that society at that time. . . . She will also use public transportation and carpool more than is common when she can do so without bending her life out of shape. Her behavior anticipates more widespread participation in such practices and therefore helps to move society in a desirable direction. (Wenz 2005, 211)

Do you agree with Wenz that PAC describes well the extent to which affluent people should change their consumption practices, behaviors, and lifestyles? What would its implications be for other areas of consumption, such as food, clothing, electronics, or travel? Do you believe that PAC is too demanding? Or not demanding enough? How do you think a proponent of deep ecology would assess PAC? Is it a problem or a positive of PAC that it uses the societal norm as a baseline for evaluating a person's behavior?

15.5 SUMMARY

The primary questions addressed in this chapter were:

- What are the causes of unequal exposure to environmental hazards faced by high-minority and low-income communities in the United States, as well as by politically disempowered and marginalized communities around the world?

- Is unequal exposure to environmental hazards unjust?
- What ethical considerations are relevant to realizing environmental justice and how might they be promoted in practice?
- What are the aspects of consumption that need to be addressed to reduce the hazards generated by high levels of consumption?

The unequal distribution of environmental burdens and benefits are unjust according to several widely endorsed principles of justice. Moreover, responding to the injustices associated with unequal exposure requires more than merely reducing the inequalities. It requires addressing the underlying social, political, and economic factors that give rise to them. Many theories of environmental justice argue that crucial to doing so is respecting environmental rights and ensuring robust informed consent to undesirable land uses and exposure to ecological hazards. This in turn requires that people have appropriate judicial redress for environmental rights violations, that communities are provided with accurate and timely information about environmental impacts in their communities, and that there is due process and meaningful public input on zoning, siting, and land use decisions, among many other things.

Many proponents of environmental justice also believe that it requires reducing the overall amount of environmental hazards and degradation generated by industrial, agricultural, and extractive activities. Accomplishing this requires more efficient and less destructive and polluting production processes, as well as significant changes in the consumption practices of affluent people and countries. There are several different dimensions of consumption that need to be considered when thinking about the ethics of consumption: the quantity of consumption; the quality of the goods consumed; the systemic context of consumption; and the character traits of consumers. Though different views emphasize different dimensions, they are intertwined with each other and most ethics converge in the view that consumeristic dispositions are ethically problematic.

KEY TERMS (SEE GLOSSARY FOR DEFINITIONS):

carbon intensity

climate justice

cost-benefit analysis

distributive justice

energy intensity

environmental benefits

environmental burdens

environmental injustice

environmental justice

environmental racism

environmental rights

harm principle

innovation presumption

intergenerational justice

interpersonal environmental ethics

precautionary principle

principle of commensurate burdens and benefits

Principles of Environmental Justice   safety

principle of social cooperation   unequal exposure

risk

REVIEW QUESTIONS

- What are environmental burdens and benefits?

- Why is unequal exposure to environmental hazards considered to be unjust?

- What does addressing environmental injustice require (i.e., what are the goals involved in doing so)?

- What are free informed consent and environmental rights, and what is their relationship to environmental justice?

- What is cost-benefit analysis?

- What is the relationship between consumption and environmental justice?

- What are the ethically relevant dimensions of consumption?

- Why are consumeristic value orientations thought to be bad for the environment and bad for people?

- What are the precautionary principle and the innovation presumption?

DISCUSSION QUESTIONS

- Do you agree that unequal exposure to environmental hazards is unjust even in cases where there is no discriminatory intent? That is to ask, are disparate impacts sufficient to establish something as unjust?

- Would you endorse the principles of social cooperation and commensurate burdens and benefits? Why or why not? What are their implications for issues beyond the environment, such as education and taxation?

- Do you agree that cost-benefit analysis should not be determinative in setting public policies or making particular decisions? If not, what role should it play?

- Do you agree that people have a right to not have chemicals or pollutants enter their body without their consent? If not, why not? If so, does this mean that air and water pollution involve rights violations? What are the implications for pollution regulation and enforcement?

- Do you agree that the consumption behaviors of affluent people ought to change? If so, in what ways and to what extent?

- Do you think that the problem of environmental injustice can be addressed within existing political and economic frameworks or does it require fundamental changes to them? What are the reasons for your view?

FURTHER READING

There has been a large amount of excellent work in recent years that documents environmental injustice, the factors that give rise to it, and efforts to resist and address it, both systematically and in particular cases, including:

Adamson, Joni, Mei Mei Evans, and Rachel Stein, eds. *The Environmental Justice Reader.* University of Arizona Press, 2002.

Agyeman, Julian, Robert Bullard, and Bob Evans, eds. *Just Sustainabilities: Development in an Unequal World.* MIT Press, 2003.

Alkon, Alison Hope, and Julian Agyeman, eds. *Cultivating Food Justice: Race, Class, and Sustainability.* MIT Press, 2011.

Bullard, Robert, ed. *The Quest for Environmental Justice: Human Rights and the Politics of Pollution.* Counterpoint, 2005.

Bullard, Robert. *Dumping in Dixie: Race, Class, and Environmental Quality*, 3rd edition. Westview Press, 2000.

Pellow, David Naguib. *Resisting Global Toxics: Transnational Movements for Environmental Justice.* MIT Press, 2007.

Sandler, Ronald, and Phaedra Pezzullo, eds., *Environmental Justice and Environmentalism: The Social Justice Challenge to the Environmental movement.* MIT Press, 2007.

Stein, Rachel, ed. *New Perspectives on Environmental Justice: Gender, Sexuality, and Activism.* Rutgers University Press, 2004.

Westra, Laura, and Bill Lawson. *Faces of Environmental Racism: Confronting Issues of Global Justice.* Rowman and Littlefield, 2001.

Influential work on the relationship between theories of justice, principles of justice, and environmental justice include:

Schlosberg, David. *Defining Environmental Justice: Theories, Movements, and Nature.* Oxford, 2009.

Shrader-Frechette, Kristin. *Environmental Justice: Creating Equality, Reclaiming Democracy.* Oxford, 2005.

Wenz, Peter. *Environmental Justice.* SUNY Press, 1988.

Popular and academics books on the ethics of consumption and consumerism include:

Crocker, David, and Toby Linden, eds. *Ethics of Consumption: The Good Life, Justice, and Global Stewardship.* Rowman and Littlefield, 1997.

de Graaf, John, and David Wann. *Affluenza: The All-Consuming Epidemic.* Berrett-Koehler, 2005.

Heinberg, Richard. *The End of Growth: Adapting to Our New Economic Reality.* New Society Publishers, 2011.

Jackson, Tim. *Prosperity without Growth: Economics for a Finite Planet.* Routledge, 2011.

Kasser, Tim. *The High Price of Materialism.* Bradford Books, 2002.

Lewis, Tania, and Emily Potter. *Ethical Consumption: A Critical Introduction.* Routledge, 2011.

Putnam, Robert. *Bowling Alone: The Collapse and Revival of American Community.* Touchstone, 2001.

Schwartz, David. *Consuming Choices: Ethics in a Global Consumer Age.* Rowman and Littlefield, 2010.

Singer, Peter, and Jim Mason. *The Ethics of What We Eat: Why Our Food Choices Matter.* Rodale Books, 2007.

CHAPTER SIXTEEN

GLOBAL JUSTICE: POPULATION, POVERTY, AND THE ENVIRONMENT

THERE ARE OVER 7.3 BILLION people in the world, 1.2 billion of whom live in extreme poverty and 795 million of whom are chronically undernourished. Agriculture and food production are among the most ecologically impactful human activities, and there is projected to be a 60 to 120 percent increase in agricultural demand by 2050 due to population growth and changing consumption patterns associated with increased affluence (Section 6.1). There is thus an enormous challenge at the intersection of population, food security, poverty, and the environment: How can everyone have reliable access to a nutritionally adequate, culturally appropriate, and ecologically sustainable diet, while also leaving sufficient space and resources for other species?

In environmental ethics, the discussion of this question has focused on the following issues:

- Is it possible to both feed over 7 billion people and protect (noninstrumental) environmental values?
- Is it ever necessary and permissible to put protecting environmental values (i.e., saving nature) ahead of feeding people (i.e., saving people)?
- Should affluent people and nations transfer resources to assist people in extreme poverty and suffering from chronic malnourishment?

384

These questions are the focus of this chapter, which begins with a brief overview of some of the primary factors that give rise to global malnutrition.

16.1 THE EXTENT AND SOURCES OF MALNUTRITION

Two billion people suffer from micronutrient deficiency, and 795 million people are chronically undernourished, which means they cannot meet their minimum daily energy and nutritional requirements (UN 2013; Olinto et al. 2013; FAO 2012a). The vast majority of undernourished people are in developing regions, particularly sub-Saharan Africa, eastern Asia, and southern Asia. In sub-Saharan Africa a quarter of the population is undernourished (FAO 2013b).

The impacts of caloric and nutrient malnourishment include stunting, wasting, chronic health problems, and increased susceptibility to diseases. Over 2.5 million children die from malnutrition each year (FAO 2012a). For example, the WHO estimates that 250 million children suffer from vitamin A deficiency, which results in 250,000 children going blind annually, half of whom die within a year of doing so. In several countries in sub-Saharan Africa and southern Asia the stunting rates for children under five exceed 30 percent (FAO 2013b). Stunting has developmental impacts with long-term effects on educational achievement and economic productivity. Thus, pervasive malnourishment has immediate impacts on people's welfare and presents longitudinal societal challenges.

Several of the factors that contribute to chronic malnourishment involve *suboptimal use of resources*—for example, wastage, spoilage, underproduction, inefficient use,

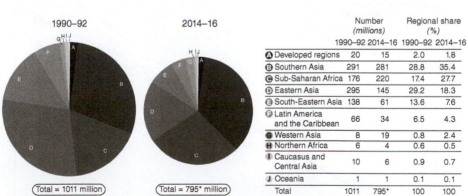

The Changing Distribution of Hunger in the World: Numbers and Shares of Undernourished People by Region 1990–92 and 2014–16

	Number (millions)		Regional share (%)	
	1990–92	2014–16	1990–92	2014–16
Ⓐ Developed regions	20	15	2.0	1.8
Ⓑ Southern Asia	291	281	28.8	35.4
Ⓒ Sub-Saharan Africa	176	220	17.4	27.7
Ⓓ Eastern Asia	295	145	29.2	18.3
Ⓔ South-Eastern Asia	138	61	13.6	7.6
Ⓕ Latin America and the Caribbean	66	34	6.5	4.3
Ⓖ Western Asia	8	19	0.8	2.4
Ⓗ Northern Africa	6	4	0.6	0.5
Ⓘ Caucasus and Central Asia	10	6	0.9	0.7
Ⓙ Oceania	1	1	0.1	0.1
Total	1011	795*	100	100

1990–92   Total = 1011 million

2014–16   Total = 795* million

Figure 16.1   The vast majority of undernourished people in the world are in Southern and Eastern Asia, as well as sub-Saharan Africa. Eastern Asia, South-Eastern Asia, Latin America, and the Caribbean have had significant declines in the number of malnourished people since 1990–92, while sub-Saharan Africa has had significant increases.

Source: FAO (2015a)

and underutilization. These factors were discussed at length in Section 6.1. Another factor relevant to global food insecurity is *population*. There are ecological and planetary limits to food production. There is a finite amount of cultivatable land, fresh water, and solar radiation, for example. Already, over a third of the terrestrial surface of the earth, and the vast majority of agriculturally favorable land, is employed for food production. Humans use ~25 percent of the planet's net primary plant production, and over 90 percent of the world's fisheries are fully exploited, overexploited, or recovering. The more people there are, the more food needs to be produced from planetary resources in order to feed everyone a nutritionally adequate diet.

There are over 7.3 billion people on earth. How many people there will be in the future depends upon **fertility rates**, which is the number of children born per woman. It is not possible to know precisely what those rates will be, so future population is discussed in terms of scenarios. The current global fertility rate is approximately 2.5 children per woman. According to United Nations projections (Figure 16.2), if by the middle of this century the fertility rate drops to 2.25 children per woman (the median projection), global population will be approximately 9.7 billion in 2050 and 11.2 billion by 2100. If fertility rates are 2.75 children/woman (the +.5 projection), the projected population is 10.8 billion in 2050 and 16.6 billion in 2100. If the rate plummets to 1.75 children/women (the −.5 projection), the population is projected to be only 8.7 billion by mid-century and 7.3 billion by 2100 (UN 2015b).

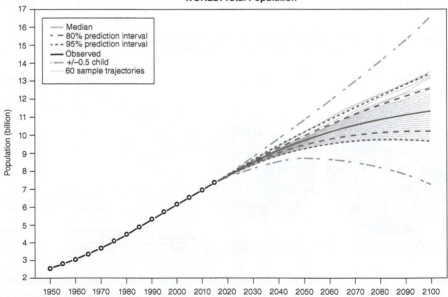

Figure 16.2   Past and projected total global population on high, low and median fertility scenarios

Source: United Nations (2015b)

There *currently* is enough food for everyone to have sufficient calories and nutrition (FAOSTAT 2013; FAO 2013b). This is true globally, as well as for *every developing region*—including sub-Saharan Africa and southern Asia—though not every nation (FAOSTAT 2013). In some countries, such as Egypt, Kazakhstan, Nicaragua, and Malawi, there is widespread malnutrition, and high rates of stunting of young children (20–45 percent), despite their having dietary supplies well above requirements (FAOSTAT 2013). If there are enough calories and nutrition in the food supply for everyone, and some countries have high rates of malnutrition despite having adequate dietary energy supplies, then food insecurity is not always, or even usually, due to limitations in food production or food availability. It is often a matter of food *access*. It results from people not having the social, material, or physical resources or *capabilities* to secure food for themselves and their families (Sen 1992; 2001). Limits on these capabilities are very often economic. Not surprisingly, food insecurity is positively related to *poverty*.

About 1.2 billion people live below the extremely low poverty line of $1.25 US ppp/day. That is, they try to live on less than the equivalent of what $1.25 would purchase in the United States in 2005 (Olinto et al. 2013). In a great many places, this (or even double it) is not enough to afford a nutritionally adequate diet. Poverty, like food access, is not only, or even primarily, due to insufficient resource availability. It is often the result of *distribution*. In 2007, 20 percent of people earned nearly 83 percent of total global income, while the poorest 20 percent earned only 1 percent and the poorest 60 percent only 7.3 percent. The top 1 percent of earners (61 million people) had the same total income as the bottom 56 percent (3.5 billion people) (Ortiz and Cummins 2011). Global wealth inequality is just as extreme as global income inequality. In 2012, the wealthiest 0.7 percent of adults in the world (those with net worth over 1 million USD) held 41 percent of the world's wealth, while the top 8.4 percent (the 393 million adults with net worth over $100,000 USD) held 83 percent and the lowest 68.7 percent (the 3.2 billion adults with less than $10,000 USD) held only 3 percent (O'Sullivan and Kearsley 2012). There is, again not surprisingly, a strong correlation between income/wealth and food consumption (Ortiz and Cummins 2011). Per capita food consumption is over four times greater in high-income countries than in low-income countries, and per capita consumption of animal products is as much as twenty times greater in high-income countries than in very low income countries.

Global malnutrition is thus the product of resource finitude, suboptimal resource use, resource distributions, population, and poverty, as well as the myriad social, political, and economic institutions, practices, and policies that impact these.

16.2 THE LIFEBOAT ETHIC

In an influential article on the ethics of food insecurity, population, and the environment, Garrett Hardin (1974) argued that affluent nations should not send food aid to low-income nations. Hardin suggested that we think of each country as a lifeboat, with a limited amount of space (or carrying capacity) defined by its resource base. Countries with high rates of poverty and malnutrition have more people than they are able to support; they are over capacity. This is a terrible situation, and it is understandable that some nations and people might want to send aid or let people into their own country via immigration. However, in Hardin's view doing so would only make matters worse. For one thing, it would enable further population growth, increasing the number of people in already over-capacity countries, and thereby the number of people suffering. It would also deplete the capacity of countries currently not overpopulated to provide for their own citizens and protect resources for nonhuman species. Moreover, it would function as a disincentive for countries to take steps to address the causes of their resource and population problems. The end result of direct food assistance, on his view, would be unabated growth in population and depletion of resources and biodiversity until there is, finally, a dramatic ecological and population collapse. Therefore, although not sending aid may seem callous, it is the lesser of two bad scenarios. Providing aid would only make matters much worse in the long run for both people and nature.

Here is a formal summary of Hardin's core reasoning:

1. Providing direct assistance provides a disincentive for countries to make reforms to address population and resource problems.
2. Providing direct assistance enables continued population growth in regions where there already are resource shortages.
3. Providing direct assistance diminishes the capacity of donor countries to conserve resources for other species and reduces their resource margin for possible emergencies in the future.

_____

4. Therefore, affluent nations ought not provide direct assistance to countries with high rates of malnutrition and population growth.

Some aspects of Hardin's view are widely regarded as having merit. For example, his view is sensitive to the fact that international institutions and policies are relevant to population, poverty, and malnutrition, and that they frequently impact national policies (see Section 16.3 below). It recognizes the need to reserve resources for the protection and maintenance of biodiversity and ecological integrity. And, of course, population is a significant factor in global poverty and malnutrition. Nevertheless, critics argue, the lifeboat ethic is a misrepresentation of the international situation, makes false assumptions about how to effectively reduce population, poverty, malnutrition, and resource depletion, and is unethical.

Regarding the lifeboat analogy, nations are not independent entities with discrete resources that define their carrying capacity. They are interconnected. This is the distinctive feature of globalization, and it is operative in many environmental issues. Affluent nations make use of the goods and services in other countries, such as agricultural land, labor, oil, and minerals. Air and water pollution cross political jurisdictions and solid waste is often shipped internationally. Greenhouse gas emissions contribute to climatic change that affects weather patterns, ocean acidity, and sea levels all over the world.

Another difficulty with the lifeboat analogy is that countries do not have fixed carrying capacities. How many people a defined resource base can support depends upon how efficiently the resources are used, their distribution, and the level of individual and societal consumption. In addition, technological innovations can increase a resource base by enabling access to additional resources, supplying artificial alternatives to natural resources, or even creating new types of resources. Consider energy, for example. Over 1.3 billion people (18 percent of the global population) do not have regular access to electricity. There is a positive relationship between energy poverty, economic poverty, and food insecurity, since modern energy services are crucial to lighting, health care, transportation, refrigeration, and information technologies. How much economic activity can be supported by a country's energy supply depends not only on the size of the supply but also on the amount of energy used per unit of economic activity (i.e., efficiency); and how many people the energy supply and economic activity can support depends upon how they are distributed and per capita consumption. Moreover, an energy supply can be expanded through technologies that reach previously inaccessible resources (e.g., deep water drilling and hydraulic fracturing), produce familiar types of energy in novel ways (e.g., engineering algae to produce biofuels), and create new energy sources (e.g., nuclear energy). Thus, the question, "How many people can have economic security, food security, and reliable energy given a particular country's natural resources?" does not have a fixed answer. It can vary widely based on available technology, infrastructure, utilization, per capita usage, and distribution.

However, the deeper problems with the lifeboat ethic, according to its critics, are that it is ethically problematic and based on a mistaken analysis of how to effectively reduce population growth. The next section focuses on the best evidence regarding how to reduce fertility rates. The section after that focuses on the ethical argument for assistance.

☀ BOX 16.1   TOPIC TO CONSIDER

THE ARGUMENT FOR TECHNO-INTENSIFICATION

One of the primary arguments in favor of genetically modified crops is that they are necessary in order to feed the world a nutritionally adequate diet under increasingly challenging agricultural conditions, such as global climate change and soil depletion, particularly if resources and space are to be reserved for other species (Box 3.4). This is an instance of the **ecological argument for techno-intensification**,

(cont.)

BOX 16.1 *(cont.)*

which is frequently used not only for crop agriculture, but also agroforestry, aquaculture, and ecosystem services (such as carbon sequestration):

1. The more productivity that can be gotten from the areas and resources that have been appropriated for human use, the less pressure there will be to expand into additional areas and appropriate additional resources.
2. Technological innovations—such as genetically engineered organisms, nano-technologies, drones, sensors, fertilizers, and nutritional enhancements—are crucial to increasing efficiency and productivity.

_____

3. Therefore, proponents of biodiversity and wilderness protection ought to support techno-intensification of production.

Do you believe that the argument for techno-intensification is sound? Should production of environmental goods and services be intensified in at least some cases? If so, for what sorts of goods or under what circumstances? If not, why not? How might some of the perspectives discussed in earlier chapters, such as deep ecology, respond to this argument?

16.3 FEEDING PEOPLE AND SAVING NATURE

The global fertility rate has been declining for decades (Figure 16.3). In 1960, it was 5 births per woman; in 2013, it was 2.5. It has dropped in both highly industrialized nations and in less developed nations. Nearly half the world's population now lives in nations with fertility levels below replacement rates (UN 2015b).

It is of course possible to dramatically reduce fertility rates by placing strict restrictions on the number of children women can have, as was done in China, where the fertility rate dropped from 5.8 in 1960 to 1.7 in 2013 (UNdata 2016). However, there are also several highly effective and noncoercive approaches.

*   **Economic Development.** Fertility rates are inversely related to national per capita incomes. Many industrialized nations, including Japan, several European countries, the United States, Australia, Taiwan, and Singapore have fertility rates below replacement levels (CIA 2015). Raising incomes, particularly for those in lower deciles, not only increases the capability of people to purchase food now, it reduces the number of people in the future (Myrskylä et al. 2009).
*   **Opportunities for Women.** There is a strong correlation between educational attainment for women and fertility rates. The longer women stay in school, the

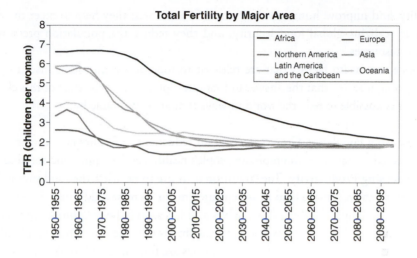

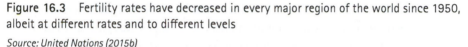

Figure 16.3 Fertility rates have decreased in every major region of the world since 1950, albeit at different rates and to different levels

Source: United Nations (2015b)

fewer children they tend to have over the course of their lifetime. As the percent of girls enrolled in secondary school begins to exceed 80 percent, national average fertility rates tend to decrease to below replacement rates. Similarly, the more workforce, professional, and civic opportunities that women have, the lower are fertility rates (World Bank 2011; Reading 2011).

- **Access to Health Care.** There is a strong relationship between access to health care and lower fertility rates, particularly when health care access results in a decreased infant mortality. When infant mortality rates (the number of children who die before one year of age per 1,000 live births) decrease to ~30, fertility rates tend to decrease to around replacement levels (World Bank 2011).

- **Access to Family Planning.** There is a strong relationship between access to contraception and fertility rates. In developing nations, this has been demonstrated by both natural and controlled experiments. For example, the fertility rate in Pakistan is over a child more (3.3) than in Bangladesh (2.2), where contraception is more widely available; and an intervention in which contraception was made available in part of Bangladesh in the 1970s and 1980s resulted in a drop in fertility rates of nearly two children per women (Ezeh et al. 2012; Cleland et al. 2006).

Overall, there is a strong record of significant reductions in fertility rates, across cultural and sociopolitical contexts, when women have improved access to health care, family planning, education, employment outside the home, and economic opportunity. Pursuing these goals (which needs to be done in context-specific and culturally sensitive ways) is a win-win-win: they increase women's autonomy, promote equality, and improve human welfare and life outcomes; they help to meet the challenge of realizing global food security; and they reduce the population pressure on natural resources.

Once the macro factors that are relevant to food access and food insecurity are understood, it seems that the answer to first question posed at the start of this chapter is that it is possible to feed the world in ways that are sustainable by:

- **Reducing Population Growth.** Significant reductions in fertility rates can be achieved in ways that also promote people's health, gender equity, and social justice.
- **Increasing Productivity.** The "traditional" route to growing the food supply has been to convert more land to agriculture and to increase wild catch. However, this is no longer feasible. Most usable land has already been appropriated and to bring in what remains would have enormous detrimental impacts on biodiversity. Moreover, almost all global fisheries are fully accessed (or overaccessed). However, significant productivity increases can be accomplished by closing yield gaps in ways that also reduce pollution and water usage through improved irrigation, technology access, seeds, soil conservation, and pest control techniques, for example (Section 6.1.2). Moreover, innovations in technology and farming practices can increase what is considered "maximum yield."
- **Changing Utilization Patterns.** In India, 89 percent of crop calories are directly consumed by people, in China and Brazil it is ~45 percent, while in the United States only 27 percent of calories (and 14 percent of protein) produced by crops are directly consumed by people (Cassidy et al. 2013). A large part of this divergence is explained by the different amount of crop calories that are used for fuel and feed (Section 6.1.1). Thus, it is possible to dramatically increase food availability by increasing direct human consumption of calories and nutrition in meat and biofuel intensive regions, as well as by forestalling the shift toward biofuel and CAFOs that is occurring in many parts of Asia and Africa.
- **Reducing Wastage.** The FAO estimates that a third of the food produced for human consumption is lost to wastage globally. There is thus an enormous amount of food to be "gained" by the food system through its elimination. In many less-developed countries, improving technology access, storage capacity, transportation, financing availability, and electricity are crucial to reducing spoilage and loss to pests. In affluent nations with food abundance, retail and consumer waste could be decreased by reducing portion sizes, eliminating subsidies (thereby increasing the cost of food), and improving the accuracy of expiration dates, for example (Section 6.1.2).
- **Reducing Poverty.** One of the primarily barriers to food access is economic. Many malnourished people live in places where adequate food and nutrition are available, but they cannot afford it. Thus, it is possible to reduce food insecurity by improving poor people's economic condition or decreasing the cost of food to them.

- **Decreasing Inequality.** Economic growth alone does not ensure that poverty rates decline. Growth needs to reach those at the lower end of the economic distribution. When it does, malnutrition rates generally decline. Moreover, there are regions with comparatively low per capita economic activity that also have low food insecurity. One of the most prominently cited examples of this is Kerala, India, where there have been large increases in quality of life outcomes—improved educational achievement, more widespread civic participation, decreased infant mortality rates, and significant poverty reduction—despite limited economic growth. This is attributed largely to efforts to reduce social and political inequality, both gender- and class-based, as well as to more equitable distributions of resources, particularly with respect to education and health care. Thus, programs and policies that address economic inequality or promote a decent minimum standard of living for everyone can increase people's ability to secure adequate calories and nutrition (in addition to reducing fertility rates).

Taken together, the foregoing indicates the tremendous potential for achieving sustainable food security globally. This is not to suggest that it is easily accomplished. It would require an enormous amount of people and organizations doing the hard work of developing, implementing, and evaluating context-appropriate strategies, technologies, and programs for realizing these goals. Moreover, it would require addressing the broader social, political, and economic institutions and policies that affect productivity, waste, utilization, poverty, inequality, population, and access. These include such things as agricultural subsidies, land policies, international trade/investment agreements, wage and compensation laws, welfare and food assistance policies, loan/aid agreements, biofuel mandates, immigration and visiting worker laws, and environmental, agricultural, and labor regulations. Thus, realizing sustainable food security requires social and political changes that extend well beyond agriculture and food systems.

BOX 16.2   TOPIC TO CONSIDER

FEEDING PEOPLE VERSUS SAVING NATURE

As discussed above, it appears that *in general and in the long run* environmental sustainability requires reducing global poverty and malnutrition, and vice versa (Carter 2004). Moreover, cases of apparent conflict between protecting environmental values and respecting human rights (or promoting human welfare) often "arise" from not considering the full range of alternatives, not taking a broad and long enough view of the situation, or not acting proactively to prevent conflicts from occurring.

(cont.)

BOX 16.2 *(cont.)*

However, there can be immediate situations in which the serious or even basic interests of people come into tension with species conservation or other significant environmental values. For example, people who have been displaced for economic, political, or ecological reasons might try to access land in protected areas to live and farm. Or people living in poverty might turn to poaching protected animals for food or trade, or to cutting down protected forests for firewood or to sell. In these sorts of cases, is it permissible to put protection of species and nature ahead of letting people use them to meet their material needs? Holmes Rolston III (1996) has argued that in some cases it is permissible—that we ought not always put feeding people ahead of saving nature. Here is his summary of his reasoning:

> Ought we to feed people first, and save nature last? We never face so simple a question. The practical question is more complex.
>
> If persons widely demonstrate that they value many other worthwhile things over feeding the hungry (Christmas gifts, college educations, symphony concerts),
>
> and if developed countries, to protect what they value, post national boundaries across which the poor may not pass (immigration laws),
>
> and if there is unequal and unjust distribution of wealth, and if just redistribution to alleviate poverty is refused,
>
> and if charitable redistribution of justified unequal distribution of wealth is refused,
>
> and if one-fifth of the world continues to consume four-fifths of the production of goods and four-fifths consumes one-fifth,
>
> and if escalating birth rates continue so that there are no real gains in alleviating poverty, only larger numbers of poor in the next generation,
>
> and if low productivity on domesticated lands continues, and if the natural lands to be sacrificed are likely to be low in productivity,
>
> and if significant natural values are at stake, including extinctions of species, then one ought not always to feed people first, but rather one ought sometimes to save nature. (1996, 265)

Rolston is aware that the idea that we ought to sometimes put nature before people is controversial. But he points out that we very often put other things ahead of saving people, some of them worthwhile and some trivial. Countries could lower the speed limit, which would reduce car fatalities, but they do not. People could

(cont.)

BOX 16.2 *(cont.)*

give money to charity rather than spend it on holiday gifts and eating out, but they do not. Affluent countries could let more refugees immigrate to them, but they do not. So, Rolston challenges, why wouldn't it be permissible to put something very important, such as preventing species extinctions, ahead of helping people?

Do you agree with Rolston that in some cases it is permissible to put conserving species and protecting nature ahead of helping people? Why or why not? Some people have argued that Rolston is setting up a false choice—that it is always possible to both feed people and save nature. Do you agree with this? Or are there some situations where there is a legitimate conflict between them? Do you know of any actual cases that appear to involve this sort of tragic dilemma—that seem to require choosing between nature and people? If so, what would you recommend in those cases?

16.4 AN OBLIGATION TO ASSIST?

The third question posed at the start of this chapter was whether affluent people and nations should transfer resources to assist people in extreme poverty and suffering from chronic malnourishment. Here is what many ethicists regard as the **core argument for assistance:**

1. There is an ethical responsibility to assist people in deep poverty and suffering from chronic malnourishment if in a position to do so effectively and the costs of doing so are not overly onerous.
2. Affluent nations (and affluent individuals) can contribute to assisting people in deep poverty and suffering from chronic malnourishment in ways that are effective (e.g., long-term, sustainable, and empowering).
3. The costs to affluent nations (and affluent individuals) to assist people in deep poverty and suffering from chronic malnourishment are not overly onerous.

_____

4. Therefore, affluent nations (and affluent individuals) have an ethical responsibility to assist people in deep poverty.

The reasoning in this argument is valid. The conclusion follows from the premises. The question, then, is whether the premises are true. Premise 2 was discussed above in the context of the lifeboat ethic. Providing effective assistance is not a matter of just sending food, and aid often has been provided in ways that exacerbate problematic power structures, undermine local producers, and foster forms of dependence. However, when done properly, assistance can support sustainable development, empower local people, promote autonomy, and encourage reforms. This is why rigorous, context-sensitive economic, ecological, political, and ethical evaluation of assistance programs and policies is needed. It is crucial that assistance addresses the factors that give rise to poverty and malnutrition, and that it do so efficiently, sustainably, and in ways that are not ethically problematic. There are many agricultural, financial, educational, health care, and other types of organizations and programs that satisfy these conditions. (Precisely where to provide resources, which types of efforts and organizations to support and in what locations, is beyond the scope of this discussion.) Thus, Premise 2 is true. Affluent nations and individuals can assist in effective ways. The remainder of this section focuses on Premise 1; the next section focuses on Premise 3.

The first premise of the argument for assistance—that there is an ethical responsibility to help people suffering from poverty and malnutrition—is the normative premise. There are several values and ethical considerations, emphasized by different normative theories, which are taken to support it: the equal worth of people, compassion, human/environmental rights, historical justice, structural justice, and moral luck. I discuss these in turn.

Many consequentialist normative theories emphasize the equal worth of people and the importance of human (and nonhuman) well-being (Section 8.2). Deep poverty and chronic malnourishment are clearly detrimental to people's well-being. They prevent people from thriving, cause large amounts of suffering, and have socially deleterious effects. Thus, they are very bad and (all other things equal) it is better if there are less of them overall. To be *compassionate* is to be moved by the suffering of others to act in ways that acknowledge and alleviate it. Therefore, the compassionate thing to do is to provide assistance to those suffering from deep poverty and malnutrition (Singer 2009).

Deontological normative theories often appeal to human rights as the basis for an ethical responsibility to assist people who are chronically malnourished. International statements on human rights are clear that people have a right to basic sustenance and the minimum resources needed to be healthy (Section 9.4). For example, the Universal Declaration of Human Rights asserts that:

> Everyone has the right to a standard of living adequate for the health and well-being of himself and of his family, including food, clothing, housing, and medical care and necessary social services, and the right to security in the event of unemployment, sickness, disability, widowhood, old age or other lack of livelihood in circumstances beyond his control. (UN 1948, Article 25)

Moreover, many other internationally recognized rights, from self-determination to access to the benefits of science and technology (UN 1966), presuppose food security. It is difficult for people to exercise their rights, or to advocate for them, when they are suffering from chronic malnutrition and occupied with trying to feed their family. National statements of individual rights also often include rights to basic resources for life and health, and the constitutions of many countries, such as Brazil, Guatemala, Cuba, Iran, and South Africa, explicitly include a right to food. Many deontologists believe that these international and national *legal rights* are legislative expressions of **moral rights** that are grounded in the worth of individuals (Box 9.5).

Another ethical consideration offered in support of national assistance is *justice*. There are several different but interrelated bases for the claim that affluent nations (and their affluent citizens) should address global poverty and malnutrition as a matter of justice. The **historical argument** points out that in many places where there is significant poverty and food insecurity affluent nations contributed to creating the situation through their past activities, such as engaging in colonialism, forcibly appropriating resources, perpetrating a slave trade, establishing national boundaries, participating in armed conflict, and installing governments. The claim is not that all global poverty and food insecurity are the result of the past actions of affluent nations or that, where it is a cause, it is the primary or sole one. The claim is that in parts of Africa, Asia, Latin America, the Caribbean and the Middle East the exercise of external military, economic, and political power were a significant contributing factor to the ecological, social, and economic conditions that give rise to the problem of poverty and food insecurity in those places.

The **international order argument** for assistance is based on the fact that international institutions are largely set up and dominated by powerful affluent nations, which frequently promote policies that serve their own economic and geopolitical interests to the disadvantage of less developed nations. This charge is commonly made regarding economic institutions such as the World Bank, the International Monetary Fund, and the World Trade Organization, whose policies and agreements have significant impacts on trade, economic development, property ownership, agriculture, and debt in the developing world. According to this argument, since international organizations, agreements, and arrangements (regarding things as diverse as arms sales and intellectual property protections) benefit countries (and their citizens) that are already well off to the disadvantage of those that are worse off, affluent nations (and their affluent citizens) owe a debt of justice to less developed nations. This responsibility can be discharged, at least in part, by helping to address deep poverty and food insecurity in less developed countries.

The **shared benefits argument** for a responsibility of assistance is based on the claim that affluent nations benefit from the economic position of less developed nations in numerous ways—for example, by having access to inexpensive labor, purchasing their natural resources, buying their land, externalizing environmental costs onto them, and coercing them to open their markets and commodify their agriculture (e.g., through the terms of loans and aid). If affluent nations benefit from poverty in less developed nations, then justice requires that they share the benefits with them, according to this argument. Contributing to the alleviation of poverty and malnutrition is a crucial aspect of doing so. Thus, there are thought to be historical, structural, and benefits-sharing bases for the claim that justice requires affluent nations to address global poverty and malnutrition.

✳ BOX 16.3

CLIMATE CHANGE: DIFFERENTIAL RESPONSIBILITY AND THE PARIS AGREEMENT

There is a significant justice dimension to global climate change. People in affluent nations are disproportionately responsible for greenhouse gas emissions on a per capita basis and are the beneficiaries of the high levels of past emissions by their countries, while poor people in low-income countries are least responsible for global climate change on a per capita basis, but generally are more exposed to the hazards of global climate change and have lower levels of adaptive capacity. It is a common view among developing nations, as well as many climate ethicists, that remediating this injustice requires affluent nations to take on greater responsibility than less developed nations in addressing global climate change. In the United Nations Framework Convention on Climate Change (UNFCCC), this is referred to as **common but differential responsibility**. It is the common responsibility of all nations to respond to global climate change, but how much and in what ways countries are required to contribute is differential. One of the primary points of contention in international climate negotiations has been concretely specifying the bases for and extent of differential responsibilities.

The most widely recognized bases for responsibility differentiation are historical emissions and capacity to mitigate and adapt. The basic idea behind past emissions-based differentiation is that those who are most responsible for causing an environmental problem have the most responsibility to address it. This is sometimes called the "polluter pays" or "you broke it, you fix it" principle (Singer 2002), and it is commonly accepted with respect to environmental remediation. On this view, the United States, Western Europe, and other historically high emitters have a disproportionate responsibility to mitigate future emissions, help other countries adapt to climate change, and compensate for climate change–related damages. The basic idea behind capacity-based differentiation is that affluent nations have more emissions to mitigate, greater technological and economic resources with which to do so, and more inessential emissions—emissions that are associated with satisfying peripheral interests (sometimes called "luxury emissions") rather than serious or basic interests (sometimes called "subsistence emissions") (Shue 1993). Therefore, it is easier, less costly, and less demanding for affluent nations to mitigate and adapt.

(cont.)

BOX 16.3 *(cont.)*

The foregoing does not imply that low-income countries do not have any responsibility to address climate change. Most of the projected future emissions growth is in less affluent countries, and many countries with low per capita emissions are among the world's largest aggregate emitters of greenhouse gases—for example, Brazil, India, and China. Sufficient mitigation simply cannot be accomplished without their contributions (Box 2.1). Of course, many low-income countries also need to achieve food security and alleviate poverty. Accomplishing both of these—poverty alleviation and climate change mitigation—requires low-emission sustainable development (Box 6.2). Therefore, one area where there is near universal agreement on differential responsibility is that affluent nations have a responsibility to provide assistance to low-income countries so that they can develop low-emission energy sources and infrastructures, as well as expand agricultural and economic opportunities that do not involve deforestation and land degradation. The most recent agreement under the UNFCCC, the Paris Agreement, sets a minimum goal of $100 billion USD of assistance per year from developed countries to low-income countries to finance mitigation, adaptation, and low-emissions development.

With respect to allocation of mitigation responsibilities, the Paris Agreement does not include legally binding reduction commitments. Instead, it continues an approach adopted with the Copenhagen Accord in 2009, which requires each party (or country) of the agreement to submit their intended nationally determined commitments (INDCs). These commitments will be revisited and increased every five years until sufficient mitigation to meet the target of the UNFCCC is accomplished—"Holding the increase in the global average temperature to well below 2°C above pre-industrial levels" (UNFCCC 2015, Article 2).

The Paris Agreement will be the framework for the UNFCCC process going forward. Both practical and ethical concerns have been raised regarding it. The core practical concern is whether the non-legally-binding "nationally determined contribution" approach to ratcheting up mitigation commitments can produce sufficient mitigation to keep the global average temperature below 2°C above preindustrial levels. The core ethical concern is whether the agreement is a just way to operationalize "common but differential responsibilities" with respect to mitigation and adaptation assistance or whether it is too generous (i.e., not demanding enough) to already affluent nations.

Yet another ethical consideration offered in support of a responsibility of assistance is moral luck. The **moral luck argument** is based on the idea that no one deserves the situation that they are born into. The reason for this is that prior to conception people do not exist, and if they do not exist they cannot have done anything to deserve anything. So it is just a matter of luck (and not desert) that some people are born into a situation of affluence while other people are born into a situation of extreme poverty. Moreover, among the greatest predictors of people's economic outcomes over the course of their lives are the socioeconomic situation into which they are born and whether they are male or female (something else people generally have no control over). There are several commonly accepted normative principles, based on the equal worth of people, on which this situation is problematic: A person should get what they deserve and deserve what they get; All people should have an equal opportunity at social and economic success; People should be socially and economically equal unless there is a good reason for inequality (see, e.g., Section 15.1). None of these principles implies that there must be equality of outcome—that people should end up with roughly the same social and economic results. They allow for inequalities on the condition that there is justification for them—for example, that they are earned or beneficial even to those who are less well off. Because the undeserved starting positions involved in the "natural lottery" of birth do not satisfy these conditions, there is a responsibility to address them, according to this argument. At a minimum, this requires those who are born into affluence assisting those who are born into extreme poverty to achieve the amount of nutrition required for normal development and health.

Taken together, these considerations—justice, rights, compassion, and moral luck—provide a diverse set of ethical considerations in support of affluent nations (and affluent individuals) having a responsibility to assist people in extreme poverty and suffering from malnutrition (i.e., Premise 1 of the argument for assistance). Not all normative theories will endorse each of them; but most theories will endorse at least some of them.

16.5 HOW MUCH TO ASSIST?

Premise 3 of the argument for assistance is that affluent people and nations can assist in ways that are not too onerous for them. Part of this premise is empirical—for example, it concerns the extent of people's and nations' resources. However part is also normative—what counts as "too onerous."

It is a common view that people have a responsibility to help others in dire situations when they are in position to do so and the costs of helping are not too high. If you are walking past a park and there is a child who is drowning in a pond, you have an obligation to assist her, even if it will cost you some resources—for example, it will ruin your new clothes or make you late for work. Not helping a drowning child on the grounds that it will cost you $150 in pay or clothing would be wrong, most people would agree. In an influential article on the ethics of assistance, Peter Singer (1972) argues that the same considerations that hold in the drowning child scenario also apply to donating money (or time and effort) to famine relief and international assistance organizations: You can help to prevent the suffering or death of a child and (for most of us in affluent nations) the cost of doing so is not very high. So if the loss of $150 is not too onerous to save a drowning child, then it is not too onerous to save a chronically malnourished one. Estimates differ, but it appears that for most children living in extreme poverty $150 USD is enough to deliver vaccinations, provide basic health care, and close the nutrition gap between the crucial ages of two and five; and 6.6 million children died before the age of five in 2012 (UNICEF 2015). Therefore, even modestly affluent people can prevent some child poverty and malnutrition, and potentially help to save a child's life, with little cost to themselves by donating a relatively small amount of money (or time and effort) to reputable and effective aid organizations.

Thus, one way to understand "not too onerous" is that *one should assist so long as it does not significantly impact one's own welfare.* This means foregoing things that are trivial, mere preferences and luxuries, but it does not require diverting resources from things that are relevant to one's quality of life, such as health care and education. Singer (1972) has at times suggested that an even stronger standard might be justified, that *one should give so long as the benefits of the assistance to others outweigh the costs to oneself.* This would mean that a person should give just up to the point of becoming economically insecure herself, which strikes many as far too demanding. Moreover, it depends on the implausible idea that a person should not put any more weight on her own welfare (or that of her family and friends) than on that of a stranger's. In between these two principles, with respect to level of demandingness, is that people should forego their significant, but not serious or basic, interests to assist others (Section 8.3).

Another, more deontological (and less consequentialist) principle that has been proposed to describe the extent of the obligation of assistance is that people with more than adequate resources have *an obligation to do their fair share* to address global poverty and malnutrition. One way a fair share is sometimes defined is as an *equal share*, or the amount that each person with adequate means would have to give to achieve global food security (or eliminate global poverty) if everyone gave the same amount. A World Bank analysis estimated the global aggregate poverty gap—the amount of money that would be required to bring everyone up to the very low poverty line of $1.25 ppp/day— to be $169 billion USD (Olinto et al. 2013), while one by the Brookings Institution put it at only $66 billion USD (Chandy and Gertz 2011). Closing the global poverty gap would cost more than this, since it is not possible to perfectly target the resources at zero cost and accomplishing food security will often require that people have more than $1.25ppp/day on which to live. So let us suppose that $400 billion USD per year is required. On this assumption, and taking the top 1 percent of global earners as those with adequate means—that is, households with incomes above ~$34,000 USD per person after taxes or $136,000 for a family of four (Milanovic 2012)—this would amount to ~$5,500/year/per person. A fair share is also sometimes defined a *proportional share*—a share relative to a person's overall income or wealth. On an income- or wealth-relative share, the demand on most of the world's affluent people drops significantly, since the income and wealth of the super-rich are so great. The 2012 income of the one hundred wealthiest people in the world was $240 billion, and the total net worth of the world's billionaires is estimated to be $6.4 trillion (Kroll 2014).

At present, donations from affluent individuals to international aid organizations fall far short of what is needed to address global malnutrition and close the global poverty gap. In the United States, for example, only ~$19 billion was given to international aid organizations by individual donors in 2012, less than was spent on phone apps and cosmetic surgery. (United States citizens and foundations made over $300 billion in charitable contributions in 2012, ~$100b of which went to religious organizations and ~$80b of which went to domestic health and human services organizations.) By far the largest source of contributions by individuals to "international aid" is the over $400 billion dollars in remittances that migrant workers from developing countries send home each year to their families, which is over three times the amount of official development assistance (World Bank 2013; FAO 2013b).

Let us now consider affluent nations. Could they help to address global poverty and malnutrition without it being too onerous for them and their citizens? The answer

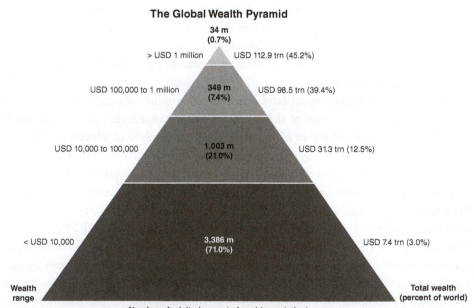

The Global Wealth Pyramid

> USD 1 million	34 m (0.7%)	USD 112.9 trn (45.2%)
USD 100,000 to 1 million	349 m (7.4%)	USD 98.5 trn (39.4%)
USD 10,000 to 100,000	1,003 m (21.0%)	USD 31.3 trn (12.5%)
< USD 10,000	3,386 m (71.0%)	USD 7.4 trn (3.0%)

Wealth range

Total wealth (percent of world)

Number of adults (percent of world population)

Figure 16.4   This pyramid illustrates the unequal distribution of wealth globally. Over 45% of the world's wealth is held by the 34 million individuals (0.7 percent of the adult population) with over $1 million USD. Those with less than $10,000 USD—nearly 3.4 billion people or 71 percent of the adult population—have only 3 percent of the world's wealth combined.

Source: Davies et al. (2015)

here appears to be a clear "yes." The global poverty gap is only a few hundred billion dollars per year. This is a very small fraction of the gross domestic income of affluent nations. Global economic activity (total GDP for all nations) in 2012 was ~$72 trillion (World Bank 2014). The European Union's GDP was ~$17 trillion, and the United States' was ~$16 trillion. In 2012, the official development assistance of the member countries of the OECD (Organisation for Economic Cooperation and Development) was only 0.29 percent of gross national incomes (GNI), ~$125 billion. For the United States it was 0.19 percent and for the UK it was 0.56 percent. In fact, only five countries met the United Nations goal of 0.7 percent—Denmark, Luxembourg, Norway, Netherlands, and Sweden (OECD 2013). In comparison, global military expenditures in 2012 were ~$1.6 trillion, 39 percent (~$625 billion) of which was by the United States. Thus, the resources exist to address global food insecurity and poverty, and the costs to developed nations would in fact be quite low (probably under 1 percent of GNI). Moreover, it would likely have ancillary benefits to them, with respect to national security and ecological sustainability, for example.

There appear to be ample resources in affluent nations to help address global poverty and malnutrition in sustainable ways, without serious or even significant costs to them or their citizens. Moreover, several of the ethical considerations discussed above—for instance, historical justice and human rights—pull toward the conclusion that the costs to affluent nations and people should not be regarded as too onerous even if they were significant. That is, satisfying justice, promoting human rights, or maximizing well-being might sometimes require compromising one's own significant interests.

BOX 16.4   TOPIC TO CONSIDER

IMMIGRATION AND THE ENVIRONMENT

Another way that affluent nations could assist people suffering from poverty and malnutrition in developing countries is to allow higher levels of immigration. However, some environmental advocates have argued against doing so on the grounds that it would decrease affluent nations' ability to accomplish sustainability and protect environmental values domestically. This was one of Hardin's justifications for the lifeboat ethic, for example. More recently, Philip Cafaro and Winthrop Staples III have offered an **environmental argument for reducing immigration** (Cafaro and Staples 2009; Cafaro 2015). Sovereign nations have a legal right to control their borders and a responsibility to their own citizens to do so in ways that protect and promote important public goods, such as social justice and security. Cafaro and Staples believe that environmental values, such as conserving endangered species, protecting wilderness, and ecological

(cont.)

BOX 16.4 *(cont.)*

sustainability, should be among the public goods considerations that determine immigration policies. In the United States, immigration is the source of pop-ulation growth (fertility rates are slightly below replacement), and population growth is one of the primary drivers of resource depletion, habitat loss, pollu-tion, greenhouse gas emissions, and ecological degradation generally. Therefore, environmental considerations favor lower immigration rates, in their view. Their argument is focused on the United States, but if sound, would apply *mutatis mutandis* to many other affluent nations as well. Here is their summary of it:

1. Immigration levels are at a historic high and immigration is now the main driver of US population growth.
2. Population growth contributes significantly to a host of environmental problems within our borders.
3. A growing population increases America's large environmental footprint beyond our borders and our disproportionate role in stressing global environmental systems.
4. In order to seriously address environmental problems at home and become good global environmental citizens, we must stop US population growth.
5. We are morally obligated to address our environmental problems and become good global environmental citizens.

_____

6. Therefore, we should limit immigration to the United States to the extent needed to stop US population growth. (2009, 5–6)

Do you think this argument is sound? Should environmental considerations be included in determining immigration policy? If not, why not? If so, how much weight do you think should be put on environmental considerations in com-parison to other considerations—for example, security, economic sustainability, human rights, and social justice? Do you agree that environmental values, if considered, favor greater limitations on immigration to the United States (or other affluent nations)? Why or why not?

Quite a few responses have been offered to the argument for assistance. For the most part they do not aim to show that there is no responsibility at all, but that it is qualified. For example, a consideration sometimes raised against a responsibility of assistance is that international aid will be ineffective due to the dysfunction of governments in devel-oping nations, or that it empowers despotic leaders and regimes by providing them lever-age (food provision) over their people and by forestalling public opposition to them. But while this may be true in some cases—that is, some regimes might be so dysfunctional or corrupt, or the situation so unstable, that aid would be ineffective or even problematic—it is not true of all cases. Thus, this objection applies only to assistance in some cases.

Another response to the argument is that the problem is simply too big for any one nation, let alone person, to address. However, the argument for assistance does not claim that each country or person has a responsibility to *end* malnutrition. It only claims that there is a responsibility to help to the point of its being overly onerous. Moreover, the fact that a person cannot help everyone does not imply that she should not try to help anyone. To accept that would be to commit the **perfectionist fallacy**, that is, to mistakenly infer from the fact that it is not possible to do something perfectly to the conclusion that it is not worth doing it at all. Furthermore, as discussed above, it may be that some affluent nations, such as the United States, actually do have sufficient resources to address the problem.

A related response to the argument is that there are always more people who are in desperate need. So if a person sends aid one time, she will be repeatedly asked to provide aid thereafter, and over time the accumulated impacts of helping others could compromise her own significant or serious interests. However, if this becomes the case, then there is no longer a responsibility to assist, since at that point it has become too onerous. Similarly, $150 is significant to some people in affluent nations, particularly those in or near poverty. But, according to the argument for assistance, the responsibility to assist is conditional on its not being a hardship. Therefore, it does not apply to people in that situation—they do not have a responsibility to assist (at least in that way).

Yet another response sometimes offered is that affluent nations should prioritize helping their own in need citizens. However, this is as much an acceptance of the argument as it is a response to it. It assumes that affluent people and nations have a responsibility to help those in serious need. The question, then, is which people in serious need to help. Should it be those with whom we stand in political relationships? Or those for whom we can maximize the impact of our aid (Box 8.2)? It may well be that affluent nations have the resources to do both without it being too onerous. (In fact, affluent nations do prioritize their own citizens. Even the United States, which has a large number of people [~50 million] who are food insecure, spends much more on domestic food assistance programs [~$75 billion] than on international food aid [~$2.3 billion].)

Finally, it is sometimes argued that while it would be ethically good for affluent people and nations to help address global poverty and malnutrition, they do not have an *obligation* to do so. This is how many people think about charity. It is good to volunteer to help others and make donations to charitable organizations. It is ethically better to do these things than to spend time playing video games and spend money on designer shoes. However, it is not *wrong* to refrain from doing them. After all, people have a right to use their time and resources how they like. Perhaps this is how we ought to think about international assistance. It is ethically preferable for countries to shift resources from their militaries to addressing global malnutrition, and it is ethically preferable for affluent people to shift resources from luxuries for themselves to helping those in deep poverty, but it is not wrong if they don't.

Whether something is ethically required or merely ethically good depends upon the justification for doing it, as well as the costs involved. If the justification is very strong—for example, if there are extremely important things at stake or the justification appeals to one's own role in creating an ethically problematic situation—it pulls toward obligation. With respect to food insecurity, the welfare of 795 million people is at stake, and several of the arguments for assistance appeal to the role of affluent nations and people in creating, perpetuating, and benefiting from this situation. Therefore, it may be that the types of ethical considerations that support the Argument for Assistance justify the conclusion that not only would it be ethically good to provide assistance, but also ethically wrong not to do so.

16.6 SUMMARY

The focus of this chapter has been poverty, food security, population, and the environment. The overarching challenge at the confluence of these is how to enable everyone in the world to have food security and a decent quality of life, while also protecting environmental values. This chapter has focused on the following questions related to this challenge:

- Is it possible to both feed over 7 billion people and protect (noninstrumental) environmental values?
- Is it ever necessary and permissible to put protecting environmental values (i.e., saving nature) ahead of feeding people (i.e., saving people)?
- Should affluent people and nations transfer resources to assist people in extreme poverty and suffering from chronic malnourishment?

Reducing population growth would significantly contribute to realizing sustainable food security. However, it is by no means the only relevant factor. Efficiency, resource utilization, economic distributions, technology, and consumption patterns are also highly relevant. It appears possible to sustainably produce enough food for everyone to have a nutritionally adequate diet. However, widespread social, ecological, agricultural, and economic changes are required to accomplish it. In addition, while it appears that in the long run poverty alleviation and food security require sustainability, and vice versa, there may be immediate situations where the interests of people and significant environmental values conflict. In those cases, it may be necessary to choose between feeding people and saving nature.

With respect to the ethics of assistance, it appears that the lifeboat ethic is neither an effective nor an ethically acceptable approach to reducing population and protecting environmental resources, but neither is merely sending food aid. Instead, context-specific programs that empower people and promote sustainable development need to be implemented, rigorously evaluated, and continually improved upon. Many such programs, including those that focus on health care, education, and opportunities for women, are win-wins. They improve people's lives and reduce fertility rates, thereby decreasing resource demands in the future. There are a number of ethical considerations, grounded in different ethical theories, which support an ethical responsibility to assist people in deep poverty. More vexing is determining the extent of that responsibility and whether it is obligatory or merely good to do.

KEY TERMS (SEE GLOSSARY FOR DEFINITIONS):

common but differential responsibility

core argument for assistance

ecological argument for techno-intensification

environmental argument for reducing immigration

fertility rate

historical argument

international order argument

lifeboat ethic

moral luck argument

moral rights

perfectionist fallacy

shared benefits argument

REVIEW QUESTIONS

- What are some of the prominent contributing factors to food insecurity and malnutrition?
- What is the lifeboat ethic?
- What are thought to be some of the difficulties with the lifeboat analogy?
- What are the historically effective ways of reducing fertility rates?
- What are some of the macroscale strategies for reducing food insecurity and malnutrition?
- What ethical considerations are thought to justify the view that affluent nations and people have a responsibility to address global poverty?
- What are some of the different views on the extent of the responsibility to assist?

DISCUSSION QUESTIONS

- Do you agree with the critiques of the lifeboat ethic presented in this chapter? Why or why not? What, if anything, do you believe the lifeboat ethic gets right?
- Which of the strategies for addressing global malnutrition would you prioritize? Are any preferable to others? Do some have greater ancillary benefits? Are there different levels of difficulty involved? Can some be pursued more quickly than others? Are some more scalable? Are some more sustainable, ecologically or socially?
- Do you agree that affluent nations and people have a responsibility to help address global poverty? If so, do you believe that it is an ethical obligation or just a good thing to do?

- Which, if any, of the principles describing the extent of the responsibility to assist would you endorse, and why?

- Do you think that it is justified to prioritize addressing hunger and food insecurity in one's own country or city, even if the resources involved could be used to help many more people suffering from malnutrition in less developed countries? Why or why not?

- What forms should international aid take in your view—for example, direct wealth transfer, technology transfer, development assistance, direct food aid, health and family planning programs, education-based, agricultural? Do you know of any types of aid that have been found to be problematic in the past? Any that have been shown to be particularly effective? Are some more conducive than others in promoting autonomy or sustainability?

FURTHER READING

Influential and thoughtful reflections on food insecurity, environmental values, population, and the ethics of assistance can be found in:

Attfield, Robin. "Saving Nature, Feeding People, and Ethics." *Environmental Values* 7, no. 3 (1998): 291–304.

Cafaro, Philip, and Eileen Crist, eds. *Life on the Brink: Environmentalists Confront Overpopulation*. University of Georgia Press, 2012.

Carter, Alan. "Saving Nature and Feeding People." *Environmental Ethics* 26, no. 4 (2004): 339–60.

Nussbaum, Martha. *Creating Capabilities: The Human Development Approach*. Harvard University Press, 2011.

Pogge, Thomas. *World Poverty and Human Rights*, 2nd edition. Polity, 2008.

Rolston, Holmes, III. "Feeding People versus Saving Nature." In *World Hunger and Morality*, edited by W. Aiken and H. LaFollette, 248–67. Prentice Hall, 1996.

Sen, Amartya. *Poverty and Famines: An Essay on Entitlement and Deprivation*. Oxford University Press, 1983.

Sen, Amartya. *Development as Freedom*. Anchor, 2000.

Shiva, Vandana. "Women and the Gendered Politics of Food." *Philosophical Topics* 37, no. 2 (2009): 17–32.

Singer, Peter. *The Life You Can Save: How to Do Your Part to End World Poverty*. Random House, 2010.

Singer, Peter. "Famine, Affluence, and Morality." *Philosophy and Public Affairs* 1, no. 3 (1972): 229–43.

Unger, Peter. *Living High & Letting Die: Our Illusion of Innocence*. Oxford University Press, 1996.

PART VII: FINAL THOUGHTS

CHAPTER SEVENTEEN

THE ANTHROPOCENE AND ENVIRONMENTAL ETHICS

OVER THE COURSE OF this textbook, we have seen that a well-informed and comprehensive understanding of the human-nature relationship is crucial to developing a well-justified theory of environmental ethics. It is vital to identifying the full range of environmental goods and values, as well as to defining the extent of our environmental impacts and agency. These, in turn, inform our environmental responsibilities and accounts of how we can flourish along with nature. Because of this, *if* the human-nature relationship were to radically change, then the perspective from which we ought to think about environmental values, principles, and responsibilities *might* need to be revised as well.

Some environmental thinkers believe that such changes are already occurring and that they do justify reconsidering our environmental responsibilities and how we approach environmental problems. Their view is that human impacts on the earth are now so pervasive and long-lasting that we must revise our understanding of the "natural" world and our relationships to it. We must recognize that human beings are now (and for the foreseeable future) the dominant planetary force, whether we like it or not. We need to acknowledge the roles that we fill in ecological and climatic systems and embrace the responsibility of managing them, from the flow of rivers to the composition of the atmosphere. We must reconceive the ecological world as a "rambunctious garden" (Marris 2011) to be tended by people, rather than as a wilderness to be protected from them (see, e.g., Section 13.6).

Other environmental thinkers believe that this is a mistake. On their view, the fact that we have such large and detrimental impacts on the natural world is confirmation of human too-manyness and too-muchness. It is the scale of our influence on the natural world that is the problem that needs to be addressed. The way to do this is not by taking more control, but by pulling ourselves back. We must decrease our population and consumption. We must reduce our efforts to design and manage ecological systems and processes as we think they should be. We must ensure that we leave enough resources for other species and spaces for human-independent ecological and evolutionary processes. Extensive intervention into ecological systems is what created our environmental problems. Increasing them further, no matter how good intentioned, is apt to cause more problems and further undermine environmental values.

This disagreement about whether to respond to anthropogenic change with greater intervention or greater restraint is at the heart of the exploding discourse regarding the **Anthropocene**, the idea that we have entered a new age in natural history dominated by human activities. In this brief closing chapter, I raise some questions to consider when thinking about whether we are in the Anthropocene and, if we are, its ethical significance.

✳ BOX 17.1

EXAMPLES OF PLANETARY SCALE ANTHROPOGENIC IMPACTS

Biological and Ecological

- Human beings appropriate approximately 25 percent of the earth's primary plant production (Krausmann et al. 2013)
- Over a third of the terrestrial surface of the earth is used for agriculture (FAOSTAT 2015)
- Over 90 percent of global fish stocks are fully or overexploited and large predatory fish populations have been reduced by as much as 90 percent, which have cascading effects through ocean ecosystems (FAO 2014; Myers and Worm 2005)
- Humans are responsible for more habitat destruction and ecosystem transitions than any other planetary force due to, for example, deforestation, filling wetlands, damming rivers, conversion to crop agriculture, and building out cities (Millennium Ecosystem Assessment 2005)
- Species extinction rates are several orders of magnitude above baseline historical rates due primarily to human activities such as species introductions, capture, and habitat loss and degradation (Vos et al. 2015; Ceballos et al. 2015)

(cont.)

BOX 17.1 *(cont.)*

- Vertebrate populations—mammals, birds, reptiles, amphibians, and fish—are estimated to have been reduced by half on average in the past forty years due to human activities (WWF 2014)
- Humans are responsible, either directly or indirectly, for the most movement of species beyond their historical ranges—for example, the United States is estimated to contain over 50,000 introduced species (US Fish and Wildlife 2012)
- Among the most widely occurring plants on the planet are those cultivated by humans (e.g., rice, wheat, and maize) and the most populous large animal species are humans (over 7.3 billion) and those raised by humans (e.g., 1.5 billion cattle and 1.2 billion sheep) (FAO 2015b)

Chemical and Geophysical

- Human activities generate more reactive nitrogen than do all other planetary processes (Galloway et al. 2004)
- Human activities, particularly agriculture, mining, and building, move more earth than do all other planetary processes (Wilkinson and McElroy 2007)
- The atmospheric concentration of carbon dioxide is higher than it has been in millions of years due primarily to fossil fuel use, and this is causing the oceans to acidify as they absorb greater amounts of carbon dioxide (NOAA 2015; Tripati et al. 2009)
- Damming, irrigation, channeling, pumping, and floodplain engineering now control or influence the movement of most freshwater and sediment (Syvitski and Kettner 2011)
- Synthetic chemicals and waste from human industrial activities permeate terrestrial and aquatic systems and organisms—for example, plastics (micro and macro), agricultural runoff (e.g., phosphorus, pesticides, and herbicides), and air pollutants (e.g., particulates and chemicals)
- Sea level rise in the twentieth century was ~5.5 inches, faster than the previous twenty-seven centuries, largely due to global climate change (e.g., glacial loss and thermal expansion) (Kopp et al. 2016), and it is rapidly accelerating with twenty-first-century increases projected to reach up to four feet (Mengel et al. 2016)
- Human beings possess destructive capabilities (e.g., nuclear weapons) as great as anything biological (e.g., disease) or geophysical (e.g., earthquakes and volcanoes)

17.1 ARE WE IN THE ANTHROPOCENE?

Human impacts on the planet are immense. This is not contested. Box 17.1 contains a sample of those often highlighted in the Anthropocene discourse. When considered together, it is clear that human impacts on the environmental are pervasive, trans-formative, and long-lasting. The term "Anthropocene" is often used by scientists and environmental thinkers to highlight the scale of human impacts and power. Referring to our current time period as the "human age" draws attention to the enormous role that human activities now play in ecological systems and processes.

Some scientists have proposed that the human influence on the environment is so deep and permanent that it actually constitutes a geological transition. They be-lieve that we have entered a new geological period of the earth's natural history—the Anthropocene—which is defined by human power and impacts (Zalasiewicz et al. 2011; Waters et al. 2016). At the time I am writing, a working group of the Interna-tional Commission on Stratigraphy, comprised largely of geologists, ecologists, and climate scientists, has been convened to make a recommendation to the next Inter-national Geological Congress on whether we are in a new epoch, a new age within the Holocene (the epoch that began approximately 11,700 years ago following the Pleistocene), or no new geological period at all (Subcommission on Quaternary Stratigraphy 2016).

There are thus two different descriptive senses of the "Anthropocene," one that involves a formal scientific designation and one that does not. So when the question is posed, "Are we in the Anthropocene?" the answer depends on the descriptive sense being used. It is undoubtedly the case that human beings have enormous influence on the nonhuman environment and are leaving a mark on earth's natural history as a result. However, it is (at the time of writing) an open question to be settled in large part by the scientific facts whether this is sufficient for designating a new geological time period—"[T]he 'geological signal' currently being produced in strata now forming must be sufficiently large, clear, and distinctive" (Subcommission on Quaternary Stratigraphy 2016).

17.2 WHY THIS DEFINITION AND THIS NAME?

Whether we are in the "Anthropocene" in the descriptive senses discussed above is largely an empirical question *once the definition is fixed*. However, decisions about which concepts and terms to use is not a strictly scientific or empirical determina-tion. We saw this earlier with "species" (Section 13.1) and "nature" (Section 3.1), as well as during the discussion of claiming by naming (Section 14.2). Concepts, terms, and definitions are often employed because they are thought to be *useful*, pick out something thought to be *significant*, or convey something thought to be *important*.

There is a value-laden component to asking whether we are in a new geological epoch defined by humans. Just as there is no uniquely correct way to break up the

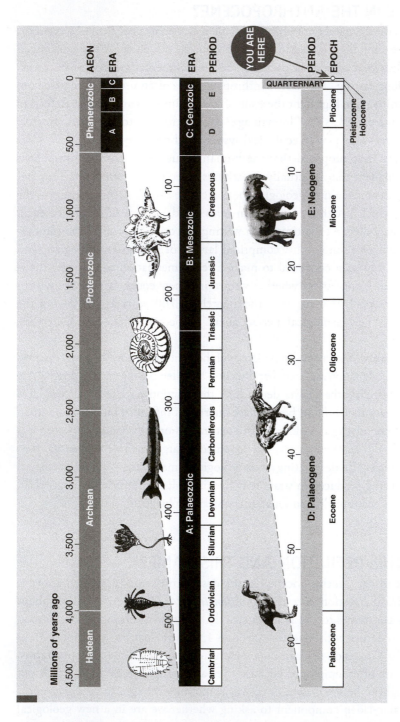

Figure 17.1 The Geological Time Scale
Source: The Economist Newspaper Limited

biological world into groups of organisms (Section 13.1), there is no uniquely correct way to break up the geological history of the earth. Researchers choose to mark
differences based not only on empirical facts but also on what is useful for research
purposes and what they believe merits highlighting. The reasons for focusing on the
descriptive question of whether we are in a new human-dominated geological period
are thus partly evaluative and programmatic. After all, this is the first time researchers
have tried to determine a geological transition *at the time it is occurring*. Therefore,
the evidence to substantiate it cannot be found by studying the geological strata laid
down in the past, but by projecting what will be geologically significant in the future.
The value-ladenness of the science is also evident in the discourse around determining the starting point of the Anthropocene (if it is a new geological age). Among
the events researchers have argued for are the agricultural revolution, North-South
colonization, the Industrial Revolution, the post-WWII "Great Acceleration," and
the advent and testing of nuclear technologies (Steffen et al. 2011; Lewis and Maslin
2015; Waters et al. 2016). Different starting points focus on different dimensions of
human activities—for example, destructive power, technological progress, and social
change—and are in part expressions of what researchers believe should be emphasized.

There is also a value-laden aspect to the term "Anthropocene." The name that is
given to something can influence how people think about it and respond to it. This
is why they are often politically contested. Calling the largest mountain in North
America "Denali" conveys different meanings, invokes different histories, and expresses different values than if it is called "Mount McKinley." Use of "Anthropocene"
has rapidly gained momentum in part because people who study, think, and talk
about global ecological change find it to be a convenient way to refer to and emphasize
the extent of human influences. But it does more than this. It conveys that the scale of
anthropogenic impacts mark an important transition to a different state of the planet,
a new "age of humans." It is thus a *loaded* term, meant to both describe and suggest
(Moore 2013). The term is a confirmation of human power, influence, and dominance
within ecological, climatic, and geological systems. It claims this period of natural
history for us; and a formal designation would make it our time of influence, officially.
How could we not take control of ecological and climatic systems in that case, when,
after all, we already will have been? Is it not better that we design them rationally
than destroy them thoughtlessly? The name itself seems to favor the interventionist
view that we need to take a more hands-on and active approach toward managing the
nonhuman environment.

That "Anthropocene" is normatively loaded in this way is one reason that critics are
wary of the term. A robust discussion about whether the human-nature relationship
has changed and, if it has, what it means for our policies and practices in the future is
needed. Instead, the term is another instance of claiming by naming. But rather than
claiming some part of the natural world, it seems to be claiming all of it as the era of
human domination (Crist 2013).

Another normative worry about "Anthropocene" is that it is problematically in-clusive. Not all of humanity has contributed equally to generating planetary scale changes. Affluent people and nations are disproportionately responsible. Moreover, this is not the age of human domination and control in general, since many people are themselves marginalized, oppressed, and dominated (Chapters 14–16). Referring to this period as the "Anthropocene" is therefore misleading, on this view. It obscures the social, political, economic, and ecological differences among people that bear on their relationships to each other and to anthropogenic change.

"Anthropocene" suggests that all people are similarly situated with respect to the eco-logical future. But if a more interventionist attitude and approach toward the natural envi-ronment is adopted, those with access to technological, economic, and political power will be the ones deciding upon and engineering ecological systems. This raises procedural and distributive justice–oriented concerns about "embracing the Anthropocene." These con-cerns are manifest in discussions regarding geoengineering, for example: Who is going to make the decision whether to intentionally intervene into climatic systems to try to adjust the climate? Who will set the goals for the intervention? Who will control the process and have oversight over it? For many who raise these questions the worry is that affluent nations with the capacity to develop and deploy geoengineering technologies will control the pro-cess and will aim to further their own economic and geopolitical advantages.

For these reasons, some environmental ethicists are critical of designating (formally or informally) a new geological period based on human influence and are opposed to naming it the "Anthropocene." They do not deny the enormous anthropogenic impacts on the earth or the need to consider their significance for how we ought to engage the ecological world. However, they find the Anthropocene discourse problematic because of how it biases those inquiries and obscures important social and ethical considerations.

17.3 ENVIRONMENTAL ETHICS WITH OR WITHOUT THE "ANTHROPOCENE"

Having a concept that picks out the accumulation of anthropogenic changes and influ-ences on climatic and ecological systems is useful to scientists who study global change. Having a term that highlights the scale of human impacts on the nonhuman environment is rhetorically powerful and evocative. But is "Anthropocene" a useful concept or term for *ethical* analysis and evaluation? The worries raised in the prior section suggest that it may not be. For example, it may obscure, rather than illuminate important ethical consider-ations related to anthropogenic change, responsibility, and social justice. It also appears to endorse the dominant control-oriented technoscience paradigm that many ethicists see as a source of social and ecological problems (see, e.g., Box 5.4 and Sections 12.1 and 14.2).

Another difficulty with utilizing "Anthropocene" in ethical analysis and evalu-ation is that it designates the entire earth. If we are in the Anthropocene, then all ecological and climatic systems are anthropocenic. Therefore, if the discussion of how we ought to respond to macroscale anthropogenic change is tied to the debate about the "Anthropocene" (the name or the geological period), it seems all or nothing. If this is the Anthropocene, and that implies that we need to take greater responsibility and control of ecological systems to make up for past harms and ensure future goods and values, then we are licensed to do that everywhere and all the time. After all, it would be the Anthropocene everywhere and all the time.

But the extent of human impacts and control is not the same everywhere and all the time. Many ecological spaces are now novel, no-analog, or hybrid systems (Section 13.6). However, others retain relatively high levels of historical continuity and human independence. Fifteen percent of the terrestrial surface of the earth is protected and a much larger percentage is ecologically intact and lightly touched by people (UNEP-WCMC 2016). This suggests that an all-or-nothing ethical response to the "Anthropocene" is not justified. Or, to put this another way, the ethical challenge is not determining how people ought to respond to the "Anthropocene." The challenge is determining how people ought to respond to a wide variety of issues and cases involving anthropogenic change, from species conservation to environmental justice. Settling the question of whether or not we are in the Anthropocene does not provide guidance on geoengineering, assisted colonization, ecological restoration, gene drives, scarce resource allocations, or genetically modified crops, either in general or in particular cases.

Here is a more formal way to put this point (Vucetich, Nelson, and Batavia 2015). It is problematic to infer from this:

1. We are in the Anthropocene

To this:

2. Therefore, we ought to X (where X is any general behavior type)

It is problematic because either "Anthropocene" is a strictly descriptive concept, in which case it is invalid to infer from the fact that we are in the Anthropocene (if it is a fact) to a prescriptive conclusion without any additional normative or value premise (Sections 2.1–2.3), or "Anthropocene" is a normatively loaded concept that smuggles in normativity without sufficient argument for it, in which case the inference commits the **fallacy of asserting the conclusion**. In either case, the inference is fallacious and the conclusion is not warranted.

Here is yet one more way to think about this. The "Anthropocene" is consistent with either of the general responses discussed at the start of this chapter: greater restraint or greater intervention. Merely being in the Anthropocene does not itself tell us which response is warranted. Other considerations need to be provided to settle the issue. Moreover, as just discussed, a blanket position is not likely to be justified. There is too much divergence in types of systems, social contexts, and operative values. In some cases highly interventionist species conservation strategies might be justified, in other cases more restraintful approaches may be. In some cases highly controlled resource management might be justified, in other cases it might be better to defer to human-independent ecological processes.

If this is correct, then the "Anthropocene" may be a distraction when it comes to environmental ethics. Anthropogenic impacts on the planet are enormous. We need to determine how to respond to them, from global climate change to microplastic pollution. Moreover, we need to be more attentive to how technological power and population growth have changed our relationships to the natural world, as well as our ethical responsibilities to the environment and to other people. However, as we have seen over the course of this textbook, these are precisely the sorts of issues with which environmental ethics is already engaged. Designating the current epoch "Anthropocene" does not change the facts about the ecological problems that we face, the types of ethical questions that we must ask, or the values that are operative. Nor does it help make decisions on a case-specific basis.

Imagine that a team of conservationists is trying to decide whether they ought to engage in an assisted colonization for a climate-threatened alpine mammal species, such as the American pika. To determine whether it is feasible and well-justified, they would need a great deal of information about the species, the recipient system, and climate change. They would also need to engage in extensive discussions with local stakeholders and conduct a comprehensive value analysis. But at no point during these processes would the fact that we are in the Anthropocene (if it is a fact) add scientifically relevant information or enhance the ethical analysis or public engagement. If anything, introducing the Anthropocene discourse would distract from what is germane to making an informed, well-reasoned decision about the case: the empirical facts, people's views, the values at stake, and the normative principles that are operative.

It is possible to consider the ethical significance of macroscale anthropogenic change both in theory and in practice without invoking the term "Anthropocene." This has been done throughout the history of environmental ethics (and this textbook) with respect to the human-nature relationship, ecosystem management, species conservation, global climate change, ecological restoration, technology adoption, artificial alternatives, natural value, restitutive justice, natural resource management, pollution, genetic technologies, and many other issues. Moreover, it may well be preferable to leave the Anthropocene discourse aside when doing environmental ethics. Even if it is a useful concept in the natural sciences and has rhetorical power in public discourse, it might be more trouble than it is worth in ethical analysis of anthropogenic environmental issues and evaluation of what practices, policies, and attitudes we ought to adopt in response to them.

17.4 CONCLUSION

I suggested earlier that we ought to think about ethics in terms of making progress (Section 10.5). We are never going to have an ethically perfect world. We are never going to be ethically perfect people. We are never going to construct a perfect ethical theory.

Moreover, technological innovation, improved scientific understanding, and changing ecological and social circumstances can cause the justification for ethical norms to shift and change. What is important is that we strive to improve individually and collectively both in our understanding of our ethical responsibilities and the extent to which we meet them.

When it comes to our consideration and treatment of the nonhuman world, there is massive room for improvement. Crucial to making progress is clarifying which things matter, how they matter, and the implications for how we should live. The overarching aim of this textbook has been to introduce you to the most prominent value and normative theories in environmental ethics and encourage you to critically assess them on both their theoretical and practical merits. If it has been successful, you should now be in possession of the following:

- An informed and reasoned view of the human-nature relationship, including any ways in which human beings are distinctive or special.
- An informed and reasoned view on the full range and types of environmental goods and values.
- An informed and reasoned view on which normative frameworks are and are not well justified.
- An appreciation of the many ways in which environmental issues are intertwined with social justice issues.
- A diverse set of tools and perspectives for analyzing and evaluating ideas, arguments, and issues.
- An understanding of the practical implications of the values, norms, and principles that you endorse across a broad range of issues and cases.
- Recognition that the sources of environmental problems are complex and multifarious, and that addressing them may involve ideological, behavioral, social, political, economic, and technological innovation and change.

Of course, we can, all of us, continually improve our ethics in both theory and in practice.

KEY TERMS (SEE GLOSSARY FOR DEFINITIONS):

Anthropocene   fallacy of asserting the conclusion

REVIEW QUESTIONS

- What are the two descriptive uses of the term "Anthropocene"?
- Why is "Anthropocene" thought to be a useful term or concept?
- In what ways is "Anthropocene" a loaded term?
- What are the concerns about using "Anthropocene" in ethical analysis and evaluation?

DISCUSSION QUESTIONS

- Do you believe that "Anthropocene" is a useful term for picking out the scale of human impacts and influences on the earth? Why or why not?
- Do you agree that "Anthropocene" is a loaded term? If so, in what ways? If not, why not?
- Do you believe that the "Anthropocene" concept is useful for environmental ethics? Why or why not?

FURTHER READING

Work by environmental ethicists and scholars that addresses the "Anthropocene" and the ethical significance of high-magnitude and long-lasting anthropogenic change includes:

Crist, Eileen. "On the Poverty of Our Nomenclature." *Environmental Humanities* 3 (2013): 129–47.

Heise, Ursula, Jon Christensen, and Michelle Niemann, eds. *Routledge Companion to the Environmental Humanities.* Routledge, 2016.

Sandler, Ronald. *The Ethics of Species.* Cambridge University Press, 2012.

Thompson, Allen, and Jeremy Bendik-Keymer, eds. *Ethical Adaptation to Climate Change: Human Virtues of the Future.* MIT Press, 2012.

Vogel, Steven. *Thinking Like a Mall: Environmental Philosophy after the End of Nature.* MIT Press, 2015.

Williston, Byron. *The Anthropocene Project.* Oxford University Press, 2015.

There has been a rapid proliferation of popular books on or related to the "Anthropocene." Here are a few of the more widely discussed and thoughtful ones:

Ackerman, Diane. *The Human Age: The World Shaped by Us.* Norton, 2014.

Kolbert, Elizabeth. *The Sixth Extinction: An Unnatural History.* Henry Holt, 2014.

Marris, Emma. *Rambunctious Garden: Saving Nature in a Post-Wild World.* Bloomsbury, 2011.

Pearce, Fred. *The New Wild: Why Invasive Species Will Be Nature's Salvation.* Beacon Press, 2015.

Purdy, Jedediah. *After Nature: A Politics for the Anthropocene.* Harvard University Press, 2015.

Wapner, Paul. *Living through the End of Nature: The Future of Environmentalism.* MIT Press, 2013.

Wuerthner, George, Eileen Crist, and Tom Butler, eds. *Keeping the Wild: Against the Domestication of Earth.* Island Press, 2014.

REFERENCES

Abbey, E. 1975. *The Monkey Wrench Gang*. Philadelphia, PA: J. B. Lippincott & Co.

Alaska Native Science Commision. N.d. *Comparisons between Traditional and Scientific Knowledge*. Retrieved from http://www.nativescience.org/html/traditional_and_scientific.html

Alexandratos, N., and J. Bruinsma. 2012. *World Agriculture towards 2030/2050: The 2012 Revision*. Rome, Italy: FAO.

American Pet Products Association. 2016. *Pet Industry Market Size and Ownership Statistics*. Retrieved from http://www.americanpetproducts.org/press_industrytrends.asp

AQUASTAT. 2016. *Information System on Water and Agriculture*. Retrieved from http://www.fao.org/nr/water/aquastat/water_use/index.stm

Arias, E. 2011. "United States Life Tables, 2011." *National Vital Statistics Report 2011,* 64 (11). Washington, DC: U.S. Department of Health and Human Services. Retrieved from http://www.cdc.gov/nchs/data/nvsr/nvsr64/nvsr64_11.pdf

Aristotle. 1985. *The Nicomachean Ethics*. Translated by T. Irwin. Indianapolis, IN: Hackett.

Baier, A. 1986. "Trust and Antitrust." *Ethics* 96 (2): 231–60.

Baillie, J. E. M., L. A. Bennun, T. M. Brooks, S. H, M. Butchart, S. C. Janice, . . . S. N. Stuart. 2004. *2004 IUCN Red List of Threatened Species: A Global Species Assessment*. Cambridge, UK: IUCN. Retrieved from http://data.iucn.org/dbtw-wpd/html/Red%20List%202004/completed/cover.html

Baxter, W. F. 1975. *People or Penguins: The Case for Optimal Pollution*. New York, NY: Columbia University Press.

Benayas, J. M., A. C. Newton, A. Diaz, and J. M. Bullock. 2009. "Enhancement of Biodiversity and Ecosystem Services by Ecological Restoration: A Meta-Analysis." *Science* 325 (5944): 1121–24.

Bentham, J. 1823. *An Introduction to the Principles of Morals and Legislation*. London, UK: William Pickering.

Borgmann, A. 1984. *Technology and the Character of Contemporary Life: A Philosophical Inquiry*. Chicago, IL: University of Chicago Press.

Borick, C., B. G. Rabe, and S. B. Mills. 2015. *Acceptance of Global Warming among Americans Reached Highest Levels since 2006*. Retrieved from http://closup.umich.edu/files/ieep-nsee-2015-fall-climate-belief.pdf

Bosso, C. J. 2005. *Environment Inc. from Grassroots to Beltway.* Lawrence, KS: University Press of Kansas.

Boyd, D. R. 2012. "The Constitutional Right to a Healthy Environment." *Environment,* July/August. Retrieved from http://www.environmentmagazine.org/Archives/Back%20Issues/2012/July-August%202012/constitutional-rights-full.html

Bradley, B. 2001. "The Value of Endangered Species." *The Journal of Value Inquiry* 35: 43–58.

Bruskotter, J. T., M. P. Nelson, and J. A. Vucetich. 2015. *Does Nature Possess Intrinsic Value? An Empirical Assessment on America's Belief.* Retrieved from http://www.michaelpnelson.com/Publications_files/Bruskotter%20et%20al.%20%282015%29%20IV%20Report.pdf

Bullard, R. D. 1990. *Dumping in Dixie: Race, Class, and Environmental Quality.* Boulder, CO: Westview Press.

Bullard, R. D. 2001. "Decision-Making." In *Faces of Environmental Racism,* edited by L. Westra and R. Bullard, 3–28. Lanham, MD: Rowman and Littlefield.

Bullard, R. D., P. Mohai, R. Saha, and B. Wright. 2007. *Toxic Wastes and Race at Twenty—1987–2007.* Cleveland, OH: United Church of Christ. Retrieved from https://www.nrdc.org/sites/default/files/toxic-wastes-and-race-at-twenty-1987-2007.pdf

Bureau of Labor Statistics. 2015. *Occupational Employment Statistics: Occupational Employment and Wages, May 2015: Combined Food Preparation and Serving Workers, Including Fast Food.* Retrieved from http://www.bls.gov/oes/current/oes353021.htm

Buzby, J. C., and J. Hyman. 2012. "Total and Per Capita Value of Food Loss in the United States." *Food Policy* 37 (5): 561–70.

Cafaro, P. 2001. "Thoreau, Leopold, and Carson." *Environmental Ethics* 23 (1): 3–17.

Cafaro, P. 2005. "Gluttony, Arrogance, Greed, and Apathy: An Exploration of Environmental Vice." In *Environmental Virtue Ethics,* edited by R. Sandler and P. Cafaro, 135–58. Lanham, MD: Rowman and Littlefield.

Cafaro, P. 2015. *How Many Is Too Many? The Progressive Argument for Reducing Immigration into the United States.* Chicago, IL: Chicago University Press.

Cafaro, P., and W. Staples III. 2009. "The Environmental Argument for Reducing Immigration into the United States." *Environmental Ethics* 31 (1): 5–30.

Cahen, H. 1988. "Against the Moral Considerability of Ecosystems." *Environmental Ethics* 10 (3): 196–216.

Callicott, J. B. 1989. *In Defense of the Land Ethic: Essays in Environmental Philosophy.* Albany, NY: State University of New York Press.

Callicott, J. B. 2001. "The Land Ethic." In *A Companion to Environmental Philosophy,* edited by D. Jamieson, 204–17. Malden, MA: Blackwell Publishers.

Camacho, A. E., H. Doremus, J. S. McLachlan, and B. A. Minteer. 2010. "Reassessing Conservation Goals in a Changing Climate." *Issues in Science Technology* 26 (4): 21–26.

Caney, S. 2010. "Climate Change, Human Rights, and Moral Thresholds." In *Climate Ethics*, edited by S. Gardiner, S. Caney, D. Jamieson, and H. Shue, 163–77. Oxford, UK: Oxford University Press.

Carson, R. 1956. *The Sense of Wonder*. New York, NY: Harper and Row.

Carson, R. 1999. *Silent Spring*. Boston, MA: Houghton Mifflin.

Carter, A. 2004. "Saving Nature and Feeding People." *Environmental Ethics* 26 (4): 339–60.

Cassidy, E. S., P. C. West, J. S. Gerber, and J. A Foley. 2013. "Redefining Agricultural Yields: From Tonnes to People Nourished per Hectare." *Environmental Research Letters* 8 (3).

Catalyst. 2015. *Knowledge Center: Women in S&P 500 Companies*. Retrieved from http://www.catalyst.org/knowledge/women-sp-500-companies

Ceballos, G., P. R. Ehrlich, A. D. Barnosky, A. Garcia, R. M. Pringle, and T. M. Palmer. 2015. "Accelerated Modern Human-Induced Species Losses: Entering the Sixth Mass Extinction." *Science Advances* 1 (5).

Chandy, L., and G. Gertz. 2011. *Poverty in Numbers: The Changing State of Global Poverty from 2005 to 2015*. Washington, DC: The Brookings Institution.

Chen, I., J. K. Hill, R. Ohlemuller, D. B. Roy, and C. D. Thomas. 2011. "Rapid Range Shifts of Species Associated with High Levels of Climate Warming." *Science* 333 (6045): 1024–26.

CIA. 2015. *The World Factbook. Country Comparison: Total Fertility Rate*. Retrieved from https://www.cia.gov/library/publications/the-world-factbook/rankorder/2127rank .html

Cleland, J., S. Bernstein, A. Ezeh, A. Faundes, A. Glasier, and J. Innis. 2006. "Family Planning: The Unfinished Agenda." *The Lancet* 368 (9549): 1810–27.

Climate Interactive. 2015. *Scoreboard Science and Data*. Retrieved December 10, 2015, from https://www.climateinteractive.org/tools/scoreboard/scoreboard-science-and-data/

Cohen, H. 1988. "Against the Moral Considerability of Ecosystems." *Environmental Ethics* 10 (3): 195–216.

Costanza, R., R. D. Groot, P. Sutton, S. V. Ploeg, S. J. Anderson, I. Kubiszewski, . . . R. K. Turner. 2014. "Changes in the Global Value of Ecosystem Services." *Global Environmental Change* 26: 152–58.

Cox, J. R. 2007. "Golden Tropes and Democratic Betrayals: Prospects for Environmental Justice in 'Neoliberal' Free Trade Agreements." In *Environmental Justice and Environmentalism: The Social Justice Challenge to the Environmental Movement*, edited by R. Sandler and P. Pezzullo, 225–80. Cambridge, MA: MIT Press.

Crist, E. 2013. "On the Poverty of Our Nomenclature." *Environmental Humanities* 3: 129–47.

Cronon, W. 1995. *Uncommon Ground: Rethinking the Human Place in Nature*. New York, NY: W.W. Norton and Company.

CTKW. 2014. *Guidelines for Considering Traditional Knowledges in Climate Change Initiatives*. Retrieved from https://climatetkw.wordpress.com/guidelines/

Davies, J., R. Lluberas, and A. Shorrocks. 2015. *Credit Suisse Global Wealth Databook*. Credit Suisse.

DEFRA. 2005. *Managing GM Crops with Herbicides: Effects on Farmland Wildlife*. London, UK: DEFRA. Retrieved from http://webarchive.nationalarchives.gov.uk/20080306073937/http://www.defra.gov.uk/environment/gm/fse/results/fse-summary-05.pdf

DEFRA. 2012. *Food Statistics Pocketbook 2012*. London, UK: DEFRA. Retrieved from https://www.gov.uk/government/uploads/system/uploads/attachment_data/file/183302/foodpocketbook-2012edition-09apr2013.pdf

Department of Labor. 2014. *Data and Statistics*. Retrieved from http://www.dol.gov/wb/stats/stats_data.htm

De-Shalit, A. 1995. *Why Posterity Matters: Environmental Policies and Future Generations*. London, UK: Routledge.

Devall, B., and G. Sessions. 1985. *Deep Ecology*. Salt Lake City, UT: G.M. Smith.

Dunlap, R. E. 2010. *At 40, Environmental Movement Endures, with Less Consensus*. Retrieved from http://www.gallup.com/poll/127487/Environmental-Movement-Endures-Less-Consensus.aspx?g_source=orientation%20toward%20environmental%20movement&g_medium=search&g_campaign=tiles

Edenhofer, O., R. Y. Pichs-Madruga, E. Sokona, S. Farahani, K. Kadner, I. Seyboth, . . . J. C. Minx. 2014. *Climate Change 2014: Mitigation of Climate Change. Contribution of Working Group III to the Fifth Assessment Report of the Intergovernmental Panel on Climate Change*. Cambridge, UK and New York, NY: Cambridge University Press.

EEOC. 2014a. *Enforcement and Litigation Statistics*. Retrieved from http://www.eeoc.gov/eeoc/statistics/enforcement/index.cfm

EEOC. 2014b. *Sexual Harassment Charges EEOC and FEPAs Combined: FY 1997–FY 2011*. Retrieved from http://www.eeoc.gov/eeoc/statistics/enforcement/sexual_harassment.cfm

Ehrlich, P. R. 1968. *The Population Bomb*. New York, NY: Ballantine Books.

Ellwood, E. R., S. A. Temple, R. B. Primack, N. L. Bradley, and C. C. Davis. 2013. "Record-Breaking Early Flowering in the Eastern United States." *PLoS ONE* 8 (1).

Estes, J. A., J. Terbough, J. S. Brashares, M. E. Power, J. Berger, W. J. Bond, . . . D. A. Wardle. 2011. "Trophic Downgrading of Planet Earth." *Science* 333 (6040): 301–306.

Esvelt, K., G. Church, and J. Lunshof. 2014. "'Gene Drives' and CRISPR Could Revolutionize Ecosystem Management." *Scientific American*. Retrieved from https://blogs.scientificamerican.com/guest-blog/gene-drives-and-crispr-could-revolutionize-ecosystem-management/

Ezeh, A. C., J. Bongaarts, and B. Mberu. 2012. "Global Population Trends and Policy Options." *The Lancet* 380 (9837): 142–48.

Faber, D. R., and E. J. Krieg. 2005. *Unequal Exposure to Ecological Hazards 2005: Environmental Injustices in the Commonwealth of Massachusetts*. Boston, MA: Northeastern University. Retrieved from http://www.northeastern.edu/nejrc/wp-content/uploads/Final-Unequal-Exposure-Report-2005-10-12-05.pdf

FAO. 1994. *A Global Assessment of Fisheries Bycatch and Discards*. Rome, Italy: FAO.

FAO. 2004. *Agricultural Biotechnology: Meeting the Needs of the Poor?* Rome, Italy: FAO.

FAO. 2011. *The State of Food Insecurity in the World: How Does International Price Volatility Affect Domestic Economies and Food Security?* Rome, Italy: FAO.

FAO. 2012a. *The State of Food Insecurity in the World: Economic Growth Is Necessary but Not Sufficient to Accelerate Reduction of Hunger and Malnutrition*. Rome, Italy: FAO.

FAO. 2012b. *World Review of Fisheries and Aquaculture*. Rome, Italy: FAO.

FAO. 2013a. *Food Wastage Footprint: Impacts on Natural Resources—Summary Report*. Rome, Italy: FAO.

FAO. 2013b. *The State of Food Insecurity in the World: The Multiple Dimensions of Food Security*. Rome, Italy: FAO.

FAO. 2014. *The State of the World Fisheries and Aquaculture 2014*. Rome, Italy: FAO.

FAO. 2015a. *The State of Food Insecurity in the World 2015. Meeting the 2015 International Hunger Targets: Taking Stock of Uneven Progress*. Rome, Italy: FAO.

FAO. 2015b. *FAO Statistical Pocketbook 2015*. Rome, Italy: FAO.

FAOSTAT. 2013. *FAO Statistical Yearbook: 2013: World Food and Agriculture*. Rome, Italy: FAO.

FAOSTAT. 2015. *Food and Agricultural Organization of the United Nations Statistics Division*. Retrieved from http://faostat.fao.org

Farrell, A. E., R. J. Plevin, B. T. Turner, A. D. Jones, M. O'Hare, and D. M. Kammen. 2006. "Ethanol Can Contribute to Energy and Environmental Goals." *Science* 311 (5760): 506-508.

FBI (Federal Bureau of Investigation). 2002. "The Threat of Eco-Terrorism: Hearings before the House Resources Committee, Subcommittee on Forests and Forests Health." Testimony of James. F. Jarboe. Retrieved from https://www.fbi.gov/news/testimony/the-threat-of-eco-terrorism

Fernandez-Cornejo, J., and W. D. McBride. 2000. *Genetically Engineered Crops for Pest Management in U.S. Agriculture: Farm-Level Effects*. Washington, DC: US Department of Agriculture.

Foden, W. B., S. H. Butchart, S. N. Stuart, J. Vié, H. R. Akçakaya, A. Angulo, . . . G. M. Mace. 2013. "Identifying the World's Most Climate Change Vulnerable Species: A Systematic Trait-Based Assessment of All Birds, Amphibians, and Corals." *PLoS ONE* 8 (6).

Foley, J. A., N. Ramankutty, K. A. Brauman, E. S. Cassidy, J. S. Gerber, M. Johnston,. . . D. P. Zaks. 2011. "Solutions for a Cultivated Planet." *Nature* 478 (7369): 337–42.

Francis (Pope). 2015. *Laudato Si': On Care for Our Common Home* [Encyclical]. Retrieved from http://w2.vatican.va/content/francesco/en/encyclicals/documents/papa-francesco_20150524_enciclica-laudato-si.html

Galloway, J. N., F. J. Dentener, D. G. Capone, E. W. Boyer, R. W. Howarth, S. P. Seitzinger, . . . C. J. Vorosmarty. 2004. "Nitrogen Cycles: Past, Present, and Future." *Biogeochemistry* 70 (2): 153–226.

Gardiner, S. M. 2006. "A Perfect Moral Storm: Climate Change, Intergenerational Ethics, and the Problem of Moral Corruption." *Environmental Values* 15 (3): 397–413.

Gill, J. A., J. A. Alves, W. J. Sutherland, G. F. Appleton, P. M. Potts, and T. G. Gunnarsson. 2013. "Why Is Timing of Bird Migration Advancing When Individuals Are Not?" *Proceedings of the Royal Society B: Biological Sciences* 281 (1774).

Gillett, N. P., V. K. Arora, K. Zickfeld, S. J. Marshall, and W. J. Merryfield. 2011. "Ongoing Climate Change following a Complete Cessation of Carbon Dioxide Emissions." *Nature Geoscience* 4 (2): 83–87.

Gilligan, C. 1982. *In A Different Voice: Psychological Theory and Women's Development.* Cambridge, MA: Harvard University Press.

Grossman, G. M., and A. B. Krueger. 1991. *Environmental Impacts of a North American Free Trade Agreement.* Cambridge, MA: National Bureau of Economic Research.

Gruen, L. 2015. *Entangled Empathy: An Alternative Ethic for Our Relationships with Animals.* Brooklyn, NY: Lantern Books.

Gunders, D. 2012. *Wasted: How America Is Losing up to 40 Percent of Its Food from Farm to Fork to Landfill.* Natural Resources Defense Council. Retrieved from http://www.nrdc.org/food/files/wasted-food-ip.pdf

Haberl, H., K. H. Erb, F. Krausmann, V. Gaube, A. Bondeau, C. Plutzar, . . . M. Fischer-Kowalski. 2007. "Quantifying and Mapping the Human Appropriation of Net Primary Production in Earth's Terrestrial Ecosystems." *Proceedings of the National Academy of Sciences* 104 (31): 12942–47.

Halweil, B., L. Mastny, E. Assadourian, and L. Stark. 2004. *State of the World 2004: Special Focus: The Consumer Society.* New York, NY: W.W. Norton and WorldWatch Institute.

Hansen, J., R. Ruedy, M. Sato, and K. Lo. 2010. "Global Surface Temperature Change." *Reviews of Geophysics* 48 (4).

Hardin, G. 1974. "Lifeboat Ethics: The Case against Helping the Poor." *Psychology Today,* September, 800–12.

Hill, T. E. 1983. "Ideals of Human Excellence and Preserving Natural Environments." *Environmental Ethics* 5 (3): 211–24.

Howe, P. D., M. Mildenberger, J. R. Marlon, and A. Leiserowitz. 2015. "Geographic Variation in Opinions on Climate Change at State and Local Scales in the USA." *Nature Climate Change* 5 (6): 596–603.

Hursthouse, R. 2001. *On Virtue Ethics.* Oxford, UK: Oxford University Press.

IEA (International Energy Agency). 2016. "Energy Poverty." Retrieved from http://www.iea.org/topics/energypoverty/

IISD (International Institute for Sustainable Development). 2015. "About." Retrieved from http://www.iisd.org/

ILO. 2012. "21 Million People Are Now Victims of Forced Labour." Retrieved from http://www.ilo.org/global/about-the-ilo/newsroom/news/WCMS_181961/lang—en/index.htm

IPCC. 2007a. *Climate Change 2007: Working Group 2: Impacts, Adaptation and Vulnerability. Case Study: Traditional Knowledge for Adaptation.* Geneva, Switzerland: IPCC. Retrieved from https://www.ipcc.ch/publications_and_data/ar4/wg2/en/ch15s15-6.html

IPCC. 2007b. *Summary for Policymakers. Climate Change 2007: Impacts, Adaptation and Vulnerability.* Geneva, Switzerland: IPCC. Retrieved from https://www.ipcc.ch/pdf/assessment-report/ar4/wg2/ar4-wg2-spm.pdf

IPCC. 2014. *Climate Change 2014 Synthesis Report Summary for Policymakers.* Geneva, Switzerland: IPCC. Retrieved from https://www.ipcc.ch/pdf/assessment-report/ar5/syr/AR5_SYR_FINAL_SPM.pdf

IUCN SSC Wolf Specialist Group. 2010. *"Canis Lupus."* Retrieved from http://www.iucnredlist.org/details/3746/0

Jamieson, D. 2002. *Morality's Progress: Essays on Humans, Other Animals, and the Rest of Nature.* Oxford, UK: Clarendon Press.

Kant, I. 1785. *Groundwork for the Metaphysic of Morals.* Edited by M. Gregor. Cambridge, UK: Cambridge University Press.

Kant, I. 1997. "Duties to Animals and Spirits." In *Lectures on Ethics,* edited by P. Health and J. B. Schneewind, 212–13. Cambridge, UK: Cambridge University Press.

Kasser, T. 2002. *The High Price of Materialism.* Cambridge, MA: MIT Press.

Kasser, T., and A. D. Kanner. 2004. *Psychology and Consumer Culture: The Struggle for a Good Life in a Materialistic World.* Washington, DC: American Psychological Association.

Katz, E. 1992. "The Big Lie: Human Restoration of Nature." *Research in Philosophy and Technology* 12: 231–41. Reprinted in *Environmental Ethics: An Anthology*, edited by A. Light and H. Rolston, 390-397, Cambridge, UK: Blackwell Publishers, 2003.

Keesing, F., L. K. Belden, P. Daszak, A. Dobson, C. D. Harvell, R. D. Holt, . . . R. S. Ostfeld. 2010. "Impacts of Biodiversity on the Emergence and Transmission of Infectious Diseases." *Nature* 468 (7324): 647–52.

Kempton, W., J. S. Boster, and J. A. Hartley. 1995. *Environmental Values in American Culture*. Cambridge, MA: MIT Press.

Kopp, R. E., A. C. Kemp, K. Bittermann, B. P. Horton, J. P. Donnelly, W. R. Gehrels, . . . S. Rahmstorf. 2016. "Temperature-Driven Global Sea-Level Variability in the Common Era." *Proceedings of the National Academy of Sciences* 113 (11).

Krausmann, F., K. Erb, S. Gingrich, H. Haberl, A. Bondeau, V. Gaube, . . . T. D. Searchinger. 2013. "Global Human Appropriation of Net Primary Production Doubled in the 20th Century." *Proceedings of the National Academy of Sciences* 110 (25): 10324–29.

Kroll, L. 2014. *Inside the 2014 Forbes Billionaires List: Facts and Figures*. Retrieved from http://www.forbes.com/sites/luisakroll/2014/03/03/inside-the-2014 -forbes-billionaires-list-facts-and-figures/#eb9f36b7a997

Latulippe, N. 2015. "Situating the Work: A Typology of Traditional Knowledge Literature." *AlterNative: An International Journal of Indigenous Peoples* 11 (2): 118–31.

Leopold, A. 1949/1968. *A Sand County Almanac, and Sketches Here and There*. New York, NY: Oxford University Press.

Lewis, S. L., D. P. Edwards, and D. Galbraith. 2015. "Increasing Human Dominance of Tropical Forests." *Science* 349 (6250): 827–32.

Lewis, S. L., and M. A. Maslin. 2015. "Defining the Anthropocene." *Nature* 519 (7542): 171–80.

Loss, S. R., T. Will, and P. P. Marra. 2013. "The Impact of Free-Ranging Domestic Cats on Wildlife of the United States." *Nature Communications* 4: 1396.

Lotze, H. K., M. Coll, A. M. Magera, C. Ward-Paige, and L. Airoldi. 2011. "Recovery of Marine Animal Populations and Ecosystems." *Trends in Ecology and Evolution* 26 (11): 595–605. Reprinted from: Recovery of marine animal populations and ecosystems. Heike K. Lotze, Marta Coll, Anna M. Magera, Christine Ward-Paige, Laura Airoldi

Maclaurin, J., and K. Sterelny. 2008. *What is Biodiversity?* Chicago, IL: University of Chicago Press.

Maestre, F. T., J. L. Quero, N. J. Gotelli, A. Escudero, V. Ochoa, M. Delgado-Baquerizo, . . . E. Zaady. 2012. "Plant Species Richness and Ecosystem Multifunctionality in Global Drylands." *Science* 335 (6065): 214–18.

Malthus, T. 1798. "An Essay on the Principle of Population." *Electronic Scholarly Publishing*. Retrieved from http://www.esp.org/books/malthus/population/malthus.pdf

Marris, E. 2011. *Rambunctious Garden: Saving Nature in a Post-Wild World*. New York, NY: Bloomsbury.

Mason, L., G. White, G. Morishima, E. Alvarado, L. Andrew, F. Clark, . . . S. Wilder. 2012. "Listening and Learning from Traditional Knowledge and Western Science: A Dialogue on Contemporary Challenges of Forest Health and Wildfire." *Journal of Forestry* 110 (4): 187–93.

McDonald, S. 2011. *Childhood Animal Abuse and Violent Criminal Behavior: A Brief Review of the Literature*. Retrieved from http://www.mass.gov/eopss/docs/doc/research-reports/briefs-stats-bulletins/summaryofanimalabuseliteraturefinal.pdf

Mengel, M., A. Levermann, K. Frieler, A. Robinson, B. Marzeion, and R. Winkelmann. 2016. "Future Sea Level Rise Constrained by Observations and Long-Term Commitment." *Proceedings of the National Academy of Sciences* 113 (10): 2597–602.

Milanovic, B. 2012. *The Haves and the Have-Nots: A Brief and Idiosyncratic History of Global Inequality*. New York, NY: Basic Books.

Mill, J. S. 1904. On Nature. *Nature, The Utility of Religion and Theism*, 7–33. London, UK: Watts and Co.

Mill, J. S. 2001. *Utilitarianism*. Indianapolis, IN: Hackett.

Millennium Ecosystem Assessment. 2005. *Ecosystems and Human Well-Being: Biodiversity Synthesis*. Washington, DC: World Resources Institute.

Minteer, B. A. 2001. "Intrinsic Value for Pragmatists?" *Environmental Ethics* 23 (1): 57–75.

Molnár, P. K., A. E. Derocher, T. Klanjscek, and M. A. Lewis. 2011. "Predicting Climate Change Impacts on Polar Bear Litter Size." *Nature Communications* 2: 186.

Moore, K. D. 2013. "Anthropocene Is the Wrong Word." *Earth Island Journal*, Spring. Retrieved from http://www.earthisland.org/journal/index.php/eij/article/anthropocene_is_the_wrong_word/

Mueller, N. D., J. S. Gerber, M. Johnston, D. K. Ray, N. Ramankutty, and J. A. Foley. 2012. "Closing Yield Gaps through Nutrient and Water Management." *Nature* 490 (7419): 254–57.

Muir, J. 1912. "The Hetch-Hetchy Valley." *The Yosemite*. New York, NY: The Century Co.

Muir, J. 1916. *A Thousand-Mile Walk to the Gulf*. Boston, MA: Houghton Mifflin.

Murray, C. J. L., R. M. Barber, K. J. Foreman, A. A. Ozgoren, S. F. Abera, . . . T. Vos. 2015. "Global, Regional, and National Disability-Adjusted Life Years (DALYs) for 306 Diseases and Injuries and Healthy Life Expectancy (HALE) for 188 Countries, 1990–2013: Quantifying the Epidemiological Transition." *The Lancet* 386 (1009): 2145–91.

Myers, R. A., and B. Worm. 2003. "Rapid Worldwide Depletion of Predatory Fish Communities." *Nature* 423 (6937): 280–83.

Myers, R. A., and B. Worm. 2005. "Extinction, Survival or Recovery of Large Predatory Fishes." *Philosophical Transactions of the Royal Society B: Biological Sciences* 360 (1453): 13–20.

Myrskylä, M., H. Kohler, and F. C. Billari. 2009. "Advances in Development Reverse Fertility Declines." *Nature* 460 (7256): 741–43.

Naess, A. 1973. "The Shallow and the Deep: Long-Range Ecology Movement." *Inquiry* 16 (1–4): 95–100.

Naess, A. 1987. "Self-Realization: An Ecological Approach to Being in the World." *The Trumpeter* 4 (3): 35–42.

Naess, A. 1989. *Ecology, Community, and Lifestyle: Outline of an Ecosophy.* Translated by D. Rothenberg. Cambridge, UK: Cambridge University Press.

NASA. 2015. *Climate Change: Vital Signs of the Planet.* Retrieved from http://climate.nasa.gov/vital-signs/global-temperature/

NDMC. 2016. "California Drought, April 2016." Retrieved from http://drought monitor.unl.edu/

Nicolia, A., A. Manzo, F. Veronesi, and D. Rosellini. 2013. "An Overview of the Last 10 Years of Genetically Engineered Crop Safety Research." *Critical Reviews in Biotechnology* 34 (1): 77–88.

NOAA. 2012. *Status of Stocks 2012: Annual Report to Congress on the Status of U.S. Fisheries.* Retrieved from http://www.nmfs.noaa.gov/stories/2013/05/docs/2012_sos_rtc.pdf

NOAA. 2015. *What Is Ocean Acidification?* Retrieved from http://www.pmel.noaa.gov/co2/story/What+is+Ocean+Acidification%3F

Noddings, N. 1984. *Caring: A Feminine Approach to Ethics and Moral Education.* Berkeley, CA: University of California Press.

Nordhaus, W. 2007a. "Economics: Critical Assumptions in the Stern Review on Climate Change." *Science* 317 (5835): 201–202.

Nordhaus, W. 2007b. "A Review of the *Stern Review* on the Economics of Climate Change." *Journal of Economic Literature* XLV (September): 686–702.

Norton, B. G. 1991. *Toward Unity among Environmentalists.* New York, NY: Oxford University Press.

Norton, B. G. 1997. "Convergence and Contextualism." *Environmental Ethics* 19 (1): 87–100.

Norton, B. G. 2005. *Sustainability: A Philosophy of Adaptive Ecosystem Management.* Chicago, IL: University of Chicago Press.

OECD. 2013. *Aid to Poor Countries Slips Further As Governments Tighten Budgets.* Retrieved from http://www.oecd.org/newsroom/aidtopoorcountriesslipsfurther asgovernmentstightenbudgets.htm

Ogden, C. L., M. D. Carroll, B. K. Kit, and K. M. Flegal. 2012. "Prevalence of Obesity and Trends in Body Mass Index among US Children and Adolescents, 1999–2010." *Journal of American Medical Association* 307 (5): 483.

Oldekop, J. A., G. Holmes, W. E. Harris, and K. L. Evans. 2015. "A Global Assessment of the Social and Conservation Outcomes of Protected Areas." *Conservation Biology* 30 (1): 133–41.

Olinto, P., K. Beegle, C. Sobrado, and H. Uematsu. 2013. *The State of the Poor: Where Are the Poor, Where Is Extreme Poverty Harder to End, and What Is the Current Profile of the World's Poor?* World Bank. Retrieved from http://siteresources.worldbank.org/EXTPREMNET/Resources/EP125.pdf

O'Neill, J. 1993. *Ecology, Policy, and Politics: Human Well-Being and the Natural World.* London, UK: Routledge.

Ortiz, I., and M. Cummins. 2011. *Global Inequality: Beyond the Bottom Billion—A Rapid Review of Income Distribution in 141 Countries.* UNICEF. Retrieved from http://www.unicef.org/socialpolicy/files/Global_Inequality.pdf

Ostrom, E. 1990. *Governing the Commons: The Evolution of Institutions for Collective Action.* Cambridge, MA: Cambridge University Press.

O'Sullivan, M., and R. Kearsley. 2012. *The Global Wealth Pyramid.* Credit Suisse. Retrieved from https://www.credit-suisse.com/us/en/about-us/research/research-institute/news-and-videos/articles/news-and-expertise/2012/10/en/the-global-wealth-pyramid.html

Palmer, C. 2010. *Animal Ethics in Context.* New York, NY: Columbia University Press.

Palmer, C. 2011. "Does Nature Matter? The Place of the Non-Human in the Ethics of Climate Change." In *The Ethics of Global Climate Change*, edited by D. G. Arnold, 272–91. Cambridge, UK: Cambridge University Press.

Parfit, D. 1984. *Reasons and Persons.* Oxford, UK: Clarendon Press.

Pew Research Center. 2013. *How Pew Research Measured the Gender Pay Gap.* Retrieved from http://www.pewresearch.org/fact-tank/2013/12/11/how-pew-research-measured-the-gender-pay-gap/

Pew Research Center. 2014. "Trend on Beliefs about Evolution." Retrieved from http://www.pewinternet.org/2015/01/29/chapter-3-attitudes-and-beliefs-on-science-and-technology-topics/

Pinchot, G. 1914. *The Training of a Forester.* Philadelphia, PA: J. B. Lippincott & Company.

Plumwood, V. 2002. *Environmental Culture and the Ecological Crisis of Reason.* London, UK: Routledge.

Pretty, J. N., A. D. Noble, D. Bossio, J. Dixon, R. E. Hine, F. W. T. Penning De Vries, and J. I. Morison. 2006. "Resource-Conserving Agriculture Increases Yields in Developing Countries." *Environmental Science and Technology* 40 (4): 1114–19.

Rawls, J. 1971. *A Theory of Justice.* Cambridge, MA: Harvard University Press.

Rawls, J. 1993. *Political Liberalism.* New York, NY: Columbia University Press.

Reading, B. F. 2011. *Education Leads to Lower Fertility and Increased Prosperity. Data Highlights.* Earth Policy Institute. Retrieved from http://www.earth-policy.org/data_highlights/2011/highlights13

Regan, Tom. 1983. *The Case for Animal Rights.* Berkeley, CA: University of California Press.

Regan, Tom. 1985. "The Case for Animal Rights." In *In Defense of Animals*, edited by Peter Singer, 13–26. New York, NY: Basil Blackwell.

Regehr, E. V., C. M. Hunter, H. Caswell, S. C. Amstrup, and I. Stirling. 2010. "Survival and Breeding of Polar Bears in the Southern Beaufort Sea in Relation to Sea Ice." *Journal of Animal Ecology* 79 (1): 117–27.

Reichman, J. R., L. S. Watrud, E. H. Lee, C. A. Burdick, M. A. Bollman, M. J. Storm, . . . C. Mallory-Smith. 2006. "Establishment of Transgenic Herbicide-Resistant Creeping Bentgrass (*Agrostis stolonifera L.*) in Nonagronomic Habitats." *Molecular Ecology* 15 (13): 4243–55.

Ripple, W. J., T. M. Newsome, C. Wolf, R. Dirzo, K. T. Everatt, M. Galetti, . . . B. V. Valkenburgh. 2015. "Collapse of the World's Largest Herbivores." *Science Advances* 1 (4).

Robert Half. 2015. *More Than a Third of UK Female Employees Have Faced Barriers during Their Career.* Retrieved from https://www.roberthalf.co.uk/press/more-third -uk-female-employees-have-faced-barriers-during-their-career-while-nearly-half-hr

Rodenhouse, N. L., T. S. Sillett, P. J. Doran, and R. T. Holmes. 2003. "Multiple Density-Dependence Mechanisms Regulate a Migratory Bird Population during the Breeding Season." *Proceedings of the Royal Society: Biological Sciences* 270 (1529): 2105–10.

Rolston, H., III. 1982. "Are Values in Nature Subjective or Objective?" *Environmental Ethics* 4 (2): 125–51.

Rolston, H., III. 1989. *Philosophy Gone Wild.* Amherst, NY: Prometheus.

Rolston, H., III. 1995. "Duties to Endangered Species." *Encyclopedia of Environmental Biology* 1: 517–28.

Rolston, H., III. 1996. "Feeding People versus Saving Nature." In *World Hunger and Morality*, edited by W. Aiken and H. LaFollette, 248–67. Upper Saddle River, NJ: Prentice Hall.

Rolston, H., III. 1998. "Saving Nature, Feeding People, and the Foundations of Ethics." *Environmental Values* 7 (3): 349–57.

Rolston, H., III. 2005. "Environmental Virtue Ethics: Half the Truth but Dangerous as a Whole." In *Environmental Virtue Ethics*, edited by R. Sandler and P. Cafaro, 61–78. Lanham, MD: Rowman and Littlefield.

Running, S. W. 2012. "A Measurable Planetary Boundary for the Biosphere." *Science* 337 (6101): 1458–59.

Saad, L., and J. M. Jones. 2016. *U.S. Concern about the Global Warming at Eight-Year High.* Gallup. Retrieved from http://www.gallup.com/poll/190010/concern -global-warming-eight-year-high.aspx?g_source=Politics&g_medium=newsfeed& g_campaign=tiles

Sagoff, M. 1984. "Animal Liberation and Environmental Ethics: Bad Marriage, Quick Divorce." *Osgoode Hall Law Journal* 22: 297–307.

Sandler, R. 2015. *Food Ethics: The Basics.* London, UK: Routledge.

Sandler, R., and P. Cafaro, eds. 2005. *Environmental Virtue Ethics.* Lanham, MD: Rowman and Littlefield.

Sandler, R. L., and P. C. Pezzullo, eds. 2007. *Environmental Justice and Environmentalism: The Social Justice Challenge to the Environmental Movement.* Cambridge, MA: MIT Press.

Schmidtz, D. 1998. "Are All Species Equal?" *Journal of Applied Philosophy* 15 (1): 57–67.

Sen, A. 1992. *Inequality Reexamined.* New York, NY: Russell Sage Foundation.

Sen, A. 2001. *Development as Freedom.* Oxford, UK: Oxford University Press.

Shiva, V. 1997. *Biopiracy: The Plunder of Nature and Knowledge.* Boston, MA: South End Press.

Shiva, V. 2000. *Stolen Harvest: The Hijacking of the Global Food Supply.* Cambridge, MA: South End Press.

Shiva, V. 2009. "Women and the Gendered Politics of Food." *Philosophical Topics* 37 (2): 17–32.

Shrader-Frechette, K. S. 2002. *Environmental Justice: Creating Equality, Reclaiming Democracy.* Oxford, UK: Oxford University Press.

Shue, H. 1993. "Subsistence Emissions and Luxury Emissions." *Law and Policy* 15 (1): 39–60.

Simberloff, D. S., and E. O. Wilson. 1969. "Experimental Zoogeography of Islands: The Colonization of Empty Islands." *Ecology* 50 (2): 278–96.

Singer, P. 1972. "Famine, Affluence, and Morality." *Philosophy and Public Affairs* 1 (1): 229–43.

Singer, P. 1975. *Animal Liberation: A New Ethics for Our Treatment of Animals.* New York, NY: New York Review.

Singer, P. 1989. "All Animals Are Equal." In *Animal Rights and Human Obligations,* edited by T. Regan and P. Singer, 148–62. Upper Saddle River, NJ: Prentice Hall.

Singer, P. 2002. *One World: The Ethics of Globalization*. New Haven, CT: Yale University Press.

Singer, P. 2009. *The Life You Can Save: Acting Now to End World Poverty*. New York, NY: Random House.

Soulé, M. 1985. "What Is Conservation Biology?" *BioScience* 35 (11): 727–34.

Soulé, M. 2013. "The 'New Conservation.'" *Conservation Biology* 27 (5): 895–97.

State of Michigan. 2012. *Local Financial Stability and Choice Act 436 of 2012*. 11 USC 901 to 946.

Steffen, W., J. Grinevald, P. Crutzen, and J. Mcneill. 2011. "The Anthropocene: Conceptual and Historical Perspectives." *Philosophical Transactions of the Royal Society A: Mathematical, Physical and Engineering Sciences* 369 (1938): 842–67.

Steinfeld, H., G. Pierre, T. Wassenaar, V. Castel, M. Rosales, and C. de Haan. 2006. *Livestock's Long Shadow: Environmental Issues and Options*. Rome, Italy: FAO.

Sterba, J. P. 1998. "A Biocentrist Strikes Back." *Environmental Ethics* 20 (4): 361–76.

Stern, D. I. 2004. "The Rise and Fall of the Environmental Kuznets Curve." *World Development* 32 (8): 1419–39.

Stern, N. H. 2006. *The Economics of Climate Change: The Stern Review*. Cambridge, UK: Cambridge University Press.

Stone, C. 1972. "Should Trees Have Standing?" *Southern California Law Review* 45: 450–501.

Streiffer, R. 2005. "An Ethical Analysis of Ojibway Objections to Genomics and Genetics Research on Wild Rice." *Philosophy in the Contemporary World* 12 (2): 37–45.

Subcommission on Quaternary Stratigraphy. 2016. *Working Group on the "Anthropocene."* Retrieved from http://quaternary.stratigraphy.org/workinggroups/anthropocene/

Swinburn, B. A., G. Sacks, K. D. Hall, K. Mcpherson, D. T. Finegood, M. L. Moodie, and S. L. Gortmaker. 2011. "The Global Obesity Pandemic: Shaped by Global Drivers and Local Environments." *The Lancet* 378 (9793): 804–14.

Sylvan, R. 1973. "Is There a Need for a New, an Environmental, Ethic?" *Proceedings of the XVth World Congress of Philosophy* 1: 205–10.

Syvitski, J. P., and A. Kettner. 2011. "Sediment Flux and the Anthropocene." *Philosophical Transactions of the Royal Society A: Mathematical, Physical and Engineering Sciences* 369 (1938): 957–75.

Taylor, P. W. 1986. *Respect for Nature: A Theory of Environmental Ethics*. Princeton, NJ: Princeton University Press.

Thomas, C. D., A. Cameron, R. E. Green, M. Bakkenes, L. J. Beaumont, Y. C. Collingham, . . . S. E. Williams. 2004. "Extinction Risk from Climate Change." *Nature* 427: 145–48.

Thompson, P. B. 1996. "Pragmatism and Policy: The Case of Water." In *Environmental Pragmatism*, edited by A. Light and E. Katz, 187–208. London, UK: Routledge.

Thoreau, H. D. 1906. *Walden*. Boston, MA: Houghton Mifflin.

Tripati, A. K., C. D. Roberts, and R. A. Eagle. 2009. "Coupling of CO_2 and Ice Sheet Stability over Major Climate Transitions of the Last 20 Million Years." *Science* 326 (5958): 1394–97.

United States Congress. 1916. *National Park Service Organic Act*, (16 USC 1 2 3, and 4).

United States Congress. 1973. *Endangered Species Act of 1973*, 16 USC 1531–44.

UN. 1948. *Universal Declaration of Human Rights*. Retrieved from http://www.ohchr .org/en/udhr/pages/introduction.aspx

UN. 1966. *International Covenant on Economic, Social and Cultural Rights*. Retrieved from http://www.ohchr.org/EN/ProfessionalInterest/Pages/CESCR.aspx

UN. 1992a. *Convention on Biological Diversity*. Retrieved from http://www.cbd.int/ doc/legal/cbd-en.pdf

UN. 1992b. *Report of the United Nations Conference on Environment and Development*. Retrieved from http://www.un.org/documents/ga/conf151/aconf15126-1annex1.htm

UN. 1996. *Rome Declaration on World Food Security*. Retrieved from http://www.fao .org/docrep/003/w3613e/w3613e00.HTM

UN. 2007. *United Nations Declaration on the Rights of Indigenous Peoples*. Retrieved from http://www.un.org/esa/socdev/unpfii/documents/DRIPS_en.pdf

UN. 2010. *Resolution on The Human Right to Water and Sanitation*. Retrieved from http://www.un.org/es/comun/docs/?symbol=A/RES/64/292&lang=E

UN. 2013. *Millennium Development Goals Report 2013*. New York, NY: UN.

UN. 2015a. *World Fertility Patterns 2015*. New York, NY: UN, Department of Economic and Social Affairs.

UN. 2015b. *World Population Prospects: The 2015 Revision, Key Findings and Advance Tables*. New York, NY: UN, Department of Economic and Social Affairs.

UN data. 2016. *World Development Indicators*. Retrieved from http://data.un.org/ Data.aspx?d=WDI&f=Indicator_Code:SP.DYN.TFRT.IN

UNEP-WCMC and IUCN. 2016. *Protected Planet Report 2016*. Cambridge, UK: UNEP-WCMC. Retrieved from: https://wdpa.s3.amazonaws.com/Protected_ Planet_Reports/2445%20Global%20Protected%20Planet%202016_WEB.pdf

UNESCO. 2013. *Best Practices and Available Tools for the Use of Indigenous and Traditional Knowledge and Practices for Adaptation, and the Application of Gender-Sensitive Approaches and Tools for Understanding and Assessing Impacts, Vulnerability and Adaptation to Climate Change*. Retrieved from http://www.unesco.org/new/fileadmin/ MULTIMEDIA/HQ/SC/pdf/UNFCCC-TP-2013-11.pdf

UNFCCC. 2009. *Report on the Conference of Parties on its Fifteenth Session, Held in Copenhagen from 7 to 19 December 2009.* Retrieved from http://unfccc.int/resource/docs/2009/cop15/eng/11a01.pdf

UNFCCC. 2015. *Adoption of the Paris Agreement.* Retrieved from https://unfccc.int/resource/docs/2015/cop21/eng/l09.pdf

UNICEF Statistics. 2015. "Child Nutrition Interactive Dashboard." Retrieved from http://data.unicef.org/resources/child-nutrition-interactive-dashboard-2015-edition.html

Urban, M. C. 2015. "Accelerating Extinction Risk from Climate Change." *Science* 348 (6234): 571–73.

US Bureau of Labor Statistics. 2016. "Establishment Data: Table B-5a. Employment of Women on Nonfarm Payrolls by Industry Sector, Seasonally Adjusted." Retrieved from http://www.bls.gov/opub/ee/2016/ces/table5a_201603.pdf

USDA. 2015. "Irrigation and Water Use." Retrieved from http://www.ers.usda.gov/topics/farm-practices-management/irrigation-water-use.aspx

US Fish and Wildlife Service. 2012. *Frequently Asked Questions about Invasive Species.* Retrieved from http://www.fws.gov/invasives/faq.html

US Fish and Wildlife Service. 2011. *2011 National Survey of Fishing, Hunting, and Wildlife-Associated Recreation. Revised.* Washington, DC: U.S. Government Printing Office. Retrieved from http://www.census.gov/prod/2012pubs/fhw11-nat.pdf

Van Wensveen, L. 1999. *Dirty Virtues.* New York, NY: Humanity Books.

VanDeVeer, D. 1979. "Interspecific Justice." *Inquiry* 22 (1–4): 55–79.

Varner, G. E. 1998. *In Nature's Interests? Interests, Animal Rights, and Environmental Ethics.* New York, NY: Oxford University Press.

Vatican. 2009. "Transgenic Plants for Food Security in the Context of Development." Vatican City: *PAS Study Week.* Retrieved from http://www.ask-force.org/web/Vatican-PAS-Statement-FPT-PDF/PAS-Statement-English-FPT.pdf

Vié, J., Hilton-Taylor, C., and S. N. Stuart. 2009. "Species Susceptibility to Climate Change Impacts." In *Wildlife in a Changing World: An Analysis of the 2008 IUCN Red List of Threatened Species*, edited by J-C. Vie, C. Hilton-Taylor, and S. N. Stuart, 77–88. Gland, Switzerland: IUCN. Retrieved from https://portals.iucn.org/library/efiles/documents/RL-2009-001.pdf

Vogel, S. 2002. "Environmental Philosophy after the End of Nature." *Environmental Ethics* 24 (1): 23–39.

Vos, J. M., L. N. Joppa, J. L. Gittleman, P. R. Stephens, and S. L. Pimm. 2015. "Estimating the Normal Background Rate of Species Extinction." *Conservation Biology* 29 (2): 452–62.

Vucetich, J. A., M. P. Nelson, and C. K. Batavia. 2015. "The Anthropocene: Disturbing Name, Limited Insight." In *After Preservation: Saving American Nature in the Age of Humans*, edited by B. A. Minteer and S. J. Pyne, 66–73. Chicago, IL: University of Chicago Press.

Wang, Y. C., K. Mcpherson, T. Marsh, S. L. Gortmaker, and M. Brown. 2011. "Health and Economic Burden of the Projected Obesity Trends in the USA and the UK." *The Lancet* 378 (9793): 815–25.

Warren, K. J. 1990. "The Power and the Promise of Ecological Feminism." *Environmental Ethics* 12 (2): 125–46.

Waters, C. N., J. Zalasiewicz, C. Summerhayes, A. D. Barnosky, C. Poirier, A. Galuszka, . . . A. Wolfe. 2016. "The Anthropocene Is Functionally and Stratigraphically Distinct from the Holocene." *Science* 451 (6269).

WCED. 1987. *Report of the World Commission on Environment and Development: Our Common Future*. Retrieved from http://www.un-documents.net/our-common-future.pdf

Wenz, P. 2001. "Just Garbage." In *Faces of Environmental Racism*, edited by L. Westra and B. Lawson, 57–72. Lanham, MD: Rowman and Littlefield.

Wenz, P. 2005. "Synergistic Environmental Virtues: Consumerism and Human Flourishing." In *Environmental Virtue Ethics*, edited by R. Sandler and P. Cafaro, 197–214. Lanham, MD: Rowman and Littlefield.

Wenz, P. 2007. "Does Environmentalism Promote Injustice for the Poor?" In *Environmental Justice and Environmentalism: The Social Justice Challenge to the Environmental Movement*, edited by R. Sandler and P. C. Pezzullo. Cambridge, MA: MIT Press.

Westra, L., and B. E. Lawson. 2001. *Faces of Environmental Racism: Confronting Issues of Global Justice*. Lanham, MD: Rowman and Littlefield.

Westra, L., and P. S. Wenz. 1995. *Faces of Environmental Racism: Confronting Issues of Global Justice*. Lanham, MD: Rowman and Littlefield.

White, L. 1967. "The Historical Roots of Our Ecologic Crisis." *Science* 155 (3767): 1203–207.

White House. 1994. *Federal Actions to Address Environmental Injustice in Minority Populations and Low-Income Populations*. Executive Order 12898, 59 FR 7629.

White House. 2015. *Gender Pay Gap: Recent Trends and Explanations*. Retrieved from https://www.whitehouse.gov/sites/default/files/docs/equal_pay_issue_brief_final.pdf

WHO. 2014. *Investing in Water and Sanitation: Increasing Access, Reducing Inequalities. UN-Water Global Analysis and Assessment of Sanitation and Drinking-Water GLAAS 2014 Report*. Geneva, Switzerland: WHO. Retrieved from http://www.who.int/water_sanitation_health/glaas/en/

Whyte, K. P. 2013. "On the Role of Traditional Ecological Knowledge as a Collaborative Concept: A Philosophical Study." *Ecological Processes* 2 (1): 1–12.

Wilkinson, B. H., and B. J. McElroy. 2007. "The Impact of Humans on Continental Erosion and Sedimentation." *Geological Society of America Bulletin* 119 (1–2): 140–56.

Wingspread Statement on the Precautionary Principle. 1998. Retrieved from http://www.gdrc.org/u-gov/precaution-3.html

World Bank. 2011. *World Development Report 2012: Gender Equality and Development, The International Bank for Reconstruction and Development.* Washington, DC: World Bank.

World Bank. 2013. *Migrants from Developing Countries to Send Home $414 Billion in Earning in 2013.* Retrieved from http://www.worldbank.org/en/news/feature/2013/10/02/Migrants-from-developing-countries-to-send-home-414-billion-in-earnings-in-2013

World Bank. 2014. *Data: GDP Ranking.* Retrieved from http://data.worldbank.org/data-catalog/GDP-ranking-table

World Bank. 2016a. *Indicators.* Retrieved from http://data.worldbank.org/indicator

World Bank. 2016b. *Proportion of Seats Held by Women in National Parliaments (%).* Retrieved from http://data.worldbank.org/indicator/SG.GEN.PARL.ZS

Worldwatch Institute. 2012. *Despite Drop from 2009 Peak, Agricultural Land Grabs Still Remain above Pre-2005 Levels.* Retrieved from http://www.worldwatch.org/despite-drop-2009-peak-agricultural-land-grabs-still-remain-above-pre-2005-levels

Worm, B., E. B. Barbier, N. Beaumont, J. E. Duffy, C. Folke, B. S. Halpern, . . . R. Watson. 2006. "Impacts of Biodiversity Loss on Ocean Ecosystem Services." *Science* 314 (5800): 787–90.

WWF. 2014. *Living Planet Report 2014.* Gland, Switzerland: WWF. Retrieved from http://wwf.panda.org/about_our_earth/all_publications/living_planet_report/

WWF. 2016. *Farmed Shrimp.* Retrieved from http://www.worldwildlife.org/industries/farmed-shrimp

Zalasiewicz, J., M. Williams, A. Haywood, and M. Ellis. 2011. "The Anthropocene: A New Epoch of Geological Time?" *Philosophical Transactions of the Royal Society A: Mathematical, Physical and Engineering Sciences* 369 (1938): 835–41.

GLOSSARY

absence-of-certainty argument   The argument that ethical skepticism is justified by the fact that there is never complete certainty about one's ethical beliefs.

absolute anthropocentrism   The view that all and only human beings have inherent worth. See also **strong anthropocentrism**.

actual preference anthropocentrism   The view that people should treat the environment and manage natural resources in whatever ways best satisfy people's actual or current preferences.

adaptation   Efforts to moderate the harms and take advantage of the opportunities associated with global climate change.

aesthetic value   The value that something possesses in virtue of its capacity to elicit emotional or attitudinal responses from people when experienced or contemplated.

alpha diversity   Species richness or the number of species in a geographic area or system.

amoralism   The view that ethics does not have any special prescriptivity or claim on what a person ought to do.

animal rights view   The view that sentient beings should never be treated as a mere means to human ends.

animal welfare view   The view that the interests of sentient beings should be considered when determining which actions (or practices or policies) have the best outcomes overall.

Anthropocene   The term or concept used to refer to the idea that the earth has entered a new geological age in natural history dominated by human activities.

anthropocentrism   The view that the criterion for direct moral considerability (or having inherent worth) is being a member of the species *Homo sapiens*.

argument from disagreement   The argument that ethical skepticism is justified because there is often deep and widespread disagreement on ethical issues.

argument from participatory decision-making   The argument that the interests of nonhuman individuals ought not be taken into account because they cannot participate in collective decision-making processes.

argument to preserve all species   1. Each species has unique and/or irreplaceable final value. 2. If something has unique and/or irreplaceable final value, then we have a duty to not destroy it (and to prevent others from doing so). 3. Therefore, we have a duty not to destroy species (and to prevent their extinction when their endangerment is anthropogenic).

artifact   Something that is the product of human design, control, and agency.

artificial alternatives concern   If something in nature is only instrumentally valuable for the resources or services it provides, then it could be replaced without any loss of value if technologies are engineered that provide the resources or services as well or better than the natural entity.

assisted colonization   Intentionally moving individuals of a species beyond its historical range and establishing an independent population of them in order to prevent the species from going extinct.

assisted recovery   Actively and intentionally intervening in a space in order to help improve it from an ecological perspective.

attitude of respect for nature   The evaluative, emotional, conative, and practical outlook, advocated for by Paul Taylor, that all living things have inherent worth and are deserving of moral consideration for their own sake.

basic interests   Needs that must be met in order for a person (or other living thing) to live and be healthy.

beta diversity   The diversity between areas or ecosystems; the greater the beta diversity between two or more systems, the more species that are found in one but not the other system.

biocentric egalitarianism   The view that all life forms have equal intrinsic or final value.

biocentric outlook   The belief system Paul Taylor defends to help justify the attitude of respect for nature. It emphasizes the interconnectedness and interdependence of ecological systems, as well as the ecological and evolutionary similarities between human beings and members of other species.

biocentric pluralism   The view that both individual living organisms and the species/systems that they constitute and populate have intrinsic or final value.

biocentrism   The view that all living things—animals and plants—have interests that are directly morally considerable and therefore possess inherent worth.

biological diversity   The variability within species, between species, and of ecosystems, including differences with respect to composition, structure, and function.

biological group membership accounts of moral status   Accounts on which something's moral status is determined by whether it is a member of a particular biological group—e.g., anthropocentrism.

biological interests   The interests that something has in virtue of being a living thing (or teleological center of life), such as those connected to survival, growth, and reproduction.

biomimicry   Looking to the natural world as a source of inspiration, insight, and solutions in art and engineering.

biopiracy   The term used by Vandana Shiva to refer to the exploitative use of local or indigenous biological knowledge to create commercialized products.

bioprospecting   Exploring for biological resources that could be developed into new agricultural and pharmaceutical products.

capacities-based accounts of moral status   Accounts on which something's moral status is determined by its capacities—e.g., what the individual is capable of, what its interests are, how it can be harmed and benefited, and the relationships that it can have.

carbon intensity   The amount of carbon that is emitted per unit of energy production.

care ethics   An approach to ethics that emphasizes the role of attachment, emotion, connection, partiality, trust, dependence, openness, and empathy in good ethical engagement and reasoning; care ethics contrasts with approaches to ethics that emphasize impartiality and pure rationality.

care model   The view that all of creation needs to be recognized and respected as an expression of the divine; and that we ought therefore to care for and protect both individual organisms and ecological systems as a whole with a sense of love, wonder, and awe.

Cartesian dualism   The view, associated with the philosophical work of René Descartes, that there is a strong divide between the mental and the physical, and that what is essential to a person's identity is that she is a distinct, thinking thing.

categorical imperative   The principle that rational agents always need to respect and treat each other as ends (autonomous beings with their own aims and intentions) and never merely as means. This is the fundamental principle of morality according to Immanuel Kant.

causation-correlation fallacy   The fallacy of inferring from the mere fact that two things are correlated with each other to the conclusion that one is caused by the other.

challenge of adaptation   The difficulty for human and ecological systems of adapting in response to high-rate and high-magnitude ecological change.

character ethics   The part of ethics that concerns what sort of person people ought to be or what sorts of traits they ought to have.

character traits   Dispositions to take certain types of considerations as reasons (or as motivational) for action or emotion under certain types of circumstances.

character virtue   A well-justified character trait—i.e., a disposition to respond to considerations in the world in excellent ways.

classical hedonism   The view that pleasure is good, pain is bad, and happiness is pleasure and the absence of pain.

climate injustice   The fact that those who are most responsible for causing global climate change—i.e., affluent people with high-emissions lifestyles—are least exposed to its hazards, since they have comparatively large adaptive capacity—e.g., wealth and mobility; while those who are least responsible for causing it—i.e., the global poor with low-emissions lifestyles—are most exposed to its hazards because they often depend more directly on ecological stability and/or have the fewest resources for adaptation.

climate refugees   People who have been displaced by the impacts of climate change, such as drought and sea level rise.

climate-threatened   Species and populations that are at risk due to ecological changes associated with shifting climatic background conditions.

cloning   Creating an organism that is genetically very similar to a single "parent" organism.

collective action problems   Problems that arise from the cumulative impacts of large numbers of people's seemingly insignificant actions, such as global climate change, fisheries depletion, pollution, and deforestation.

common but differential responsibility   The terminology used in United Nations climate change documents to refer to the fact that all nations have a shared responsibility to address climate change, but that the extent and form of the responsibility differs between nations.

commons problem   The challenge of managing common-pool resources, such as fisheries or water supplies, in ways that do not result in their degradation.

communitarian conception of ethics   The view that questions about ethics principally concern whether and how to moderate pursuit of one's own desires and self-interest out of respect for one's community and others in it.

concentrated animal feed operation (CAFO)   A form of animal agriculture in which large numbers of animals are concentrated in a single location and feed is brought to them; also sometimes referred to as **factory farms**.

consequentialist normative theories   Normative theories that tie the rightness and wrongness of actions, practices, and policies principally to their outcomes.

conservation cloning   Cloning animals for conservation purposes, such as increasing the genetic diversity or population size of a threatened species.

conservation dilemma   On the one hand, macroscale ecological change, particularly when driven by global climate change, will dramatically increase the number of species that are at risk of extinction; and on the other hand, macroscale ecological change, particularly when driven by global climate change, appears to undermine the effectiveness of and justifications for place-based conservation.

conservation triage   The view that under some circumstances it can be permissible to let an endangered species go extinct rather than try to save it.

conservationist   A person who believes that the protection of natural areas and resources should principally be for the benefit of people.

conspecific   A term that describes organisms that are the same species.

contingent valuation method   A method used in economics to fix the economic value of a nonmarket good by determining how much people would be willing to pay for access to it (or for it to be protected) under hypothetical scenarios.

contributory value   The value that something has in virtue of its being a part of a whole that is valuable.

convergence thesis   The thesis that what is good for human beings overall and in the long run will typically converge with what is good for nonhuman nature.

core argument for assistance   1. There is an ethical responsibility to assist people in deep poverty and suffering from chronic malnourishment if in a position to do so effectively and the costs of doing so are not overly onerous. 2. Affluent nations (and affluent individuals) can contribute to assisting people in deep poverty and suffering from chronic malnourishment in ways that are effective. 3. The costs to affluent nations (and affluent individuals) to assist people in deep poverty and suffering from chronic malnourishment are not overly onerous. 4. Therefore, affluent nations (and affluent individuals) have an ethical responsibility to assist people in deep poverty.

cost-benefit analysis   An approach to analysis and decision-making, frequently used in environmental policy and regulation, which aims to identify all the social and economic benefits and costs of the available options and determine which option has the best balance of benefits over costs.

critical habitat   The geographical areas and ecological processes crucial to a species' or population's conservation.

cultural hunting   Hunting that is connected to traditional cultural practices or that otherwise has cultural significance.

cultural theft   The use of cultural knowledge without appropriate consent or compensation, or when it is done in ways that are contrary to the culture's worldviews.

Darwinism   The theory of evolution by natural selection.

deductive inference   An argument in which it is intended that the conclusion must, by logical necessity, be true if the premises are true.

deep ecology   An approach to environmental ethics that emphasizes the interconnectedness of people with the nonhuman environment, as well as the importance of addressing the underlying ideological and systemic causes of ecological degradation.

deextinction   The use of genomic and cloning technologies to create organisms with high levels of genetic similarity to individuals of a species that has gone extinct.

denial of human superiority   The view, defended by Paul Taylor, that there is no morally relevant difference between humans and nonhumans that would justify ascribing inherent worth to humans but not nonhumans.

deontological normative theories   Normative theories that tie the rightness and wrongness of actions, practices, and policies to the principles they embody or whether they conform to the relevant rules, duties, or moral law.

descriptive claims   Claims about the way the world is.

device paradigm   Albert Borgmann's view that the tendency of modern technologies and technological systems is to provide goods and service as efficiently as possible while hiding the means of production.

directly morally considerable   Something that moral agents need to consider for its own sake.

discount rate   The rate at which welfare economics decreases the value of future goods relative to current goods.

distributive justice   A justified allocation of goods and burdens within and between societies.

dominion model   The view that human beings are distinct from and set above the rest of creation, and that we are enjoined and empowered by God to use the natural world in service of our ends.

duty of nonmaleficence   The rule, advocated by Paul Taylor, to refrain from inflicting harm on living things.

duty of restitutive justice   The rule, advocated by Paul Taylor, to "restore the balance of justice between a moral agent and a moral subject when the subject has been wronged by the agent. . . . It requires that one make amends to the moral subject by some form of compensation or reparation" (1986, 186).

ecocentric communitarianism   The view, advocated by Aldo Leopold, that we ought to be responsible members of the biotic community, and therefore should act in ways that protect and promote its ecological integrity and stability.

ecocentrism   The view that when it comes to environmental ethics, we need to prioritize what is best for the biotic community as a whole.

ecofeminism   A family of views that identify and challenge myopic, gendered, and patriarchal features of Western philosophical thought regarding nonhuman nature and animals, and emphasize the connections between the ways in which women and nonhuman nature are conceptualized, characterized, (mis)valued, and (mal)treated. Also called ecological feminism or **feminist environmental philosophy**.

ecological argument for techno-intensification   1. The more productivity that can be gotten from the areas and resources that have been appropriated for human use, the less pressure there will be to expand into additional areas and appropriate additional resources. 2. Technological innovations are crucial to increasing efficiency and productivity. 3. Therefore, proponents of biodiversity and wilderness protection ought to support techno-intensification of production.

ecological consciousness   Associated with deep ecology, having an ontologically holistic and egalitarian worldview that enables identification with all aspects of the natural world—i.e., seeing that every entity, human and nonhuman, biotic and abiotic, is fundamentally relational, an equally significant node in the interconnected fabric that constitutes reality.

ecological restoration   A variety of assisted recovery in which historical considerations are incorporated into efforts to improve a space from an ecological perspective; ecological restoration aims to improve the ecology of a place in the future by maintaining or reestablishing continuity with the past. (There is a broader use of the term "ecological restoration" on which it refers to ecological recovery more generally.)

ecological value   The value that something has in virtue of contributing to the ecological integrity or health of ecological systems.

economic value   The exchange value that something has or the value that it has in the marketplace.

eco-social sustainability   The view that human economic and social systems are not separate from or adjacent to biological and ecological systems, but are instead embedded within them, such that ecological and social sustainability are intertwined with each other.

ecosystem engineering   Intentionally designing ecological systems as we believe they ought to be, or need to be, in the future.

ecosystem nominalism   The view that ecosystems are not anything above and beyond the particular organisms, processes, and abiotic features that comprise them.

ecosystem services   The benefits that ecological processes provide to people—e.g., water purification, storm surge buffering, food provision, soil regeneration, pollination, protection from harmful solar radiation, disease and pest regulation, carbon sequestration, waste disposal, and conversion of carbon dioxide to oxygen.

ecotage   Direct environmental action that involves destroying property or disrupting economic activities.

ecoterrorism   The term critics often use to refer to direct environmental activism, particularly ecotage.

effective altruism   The view that a person ought to aim to maximize the beneficial outcomes of donating money, volunteering, and engaging in activism.

egalitarianism (regarding moral considerability)   The view that all entities that meet the standard for direct moral considerability are equally considerable.

empirical claim   A claim about the world whose truth value is determined by observational or scientific investigation.

endemic species   Species that are native to the area and not found elsewhere.

energy intensity The amount of energy used per unit of economic activity.

enlightened anthropocentrism The view that we ought to treat the environment in ways that are beneficial to all of humanity, now and in the future, even if that is different from what we currently do or would want to do.

environmental argument for reducing immigration The view that sovereign nations have a legal right to control their borders and a responsibility to their own citizens to do so in ways that protect and promote important public goods, including environmental goods, and that this can justify placing limits on immigration.

environmental benefits The commodities, experiences, and wealth whose production generates environmental burdens.

environmental burdens Hazards, land uses, facilities, or activities that diminish the quality of the environment—e.g., agricultural waste streams, air pollution, toxic waste sites, incinerators, waste transfer stations, refineries, transportation depots, mine tailings, and sewage treatment facilities.

environmental ethics The part of ethics that concerns how we ought to value and engage with nonhuman animals and the ecological environment.

environmental fascism The criticism sometimes made against ecocentric views that their subordination of the individual to the communal good leads to unacceptable implications—e.g., killing large numbers of animals or restrictive reproductive policies.

environmental injustice The fact that unequal exposure to environmental hazards very often is unjustified and caused, at least in part, by problematic social and political factors.

environmental justice movement Efforts to address the unjustified distribution of environmental hazards, as well as the social, political, and economic factors that give rise to it.

environmental pragmatism (or philosophical pragmatism) Approaches to environmental ethics that deemphasize the importance of ethical theorizing in favor of more procedural or situational approaches to characterizing environmental problems and engaging in environmental decision-making.

environmental racism The term often used to refer to environmental injustice in the United States because high-minority communities are exposed to greater levels of hazards than are low-minority communities and the explanation for this in many cases involves social and political disempowerment, economic discrimination, and structural disadvantages faced by people of color and communities of color.

environmental rights The rights that people have to environmental goods—e.g., to food or potable water—as well as the environmental conditions necessary for satisfying people's social, political, and human rights.

environmental virtue Any character trait that is justified as a virtue at least in part by environmental goods and values, that promotes environmental ends or goals, or that involves responsiveness to an environmental entity.

epistemology A theory of knowledge, particularly with respect to the standards and methods by which one distinguishes justified from unjustified beliefs.

ethical egoism The view that an action is right if it promotes the best outcomes for the agent.

ethical nihilism The view that there are not any true claims about how we ought to live.

ethical skepticism   The view that either there are not true ethical claims (ethical nihilism), ethical claims are not knowable or justifiable, or ethics does not have any special prescriptivity (amoralism).

ethical theory   An account of what sorts of things matter (or have value) and how things matter (or how we ought to consider them given their value) that is meant to give guidance for choosing well regarding actions, practices, and policies.

ethics   Inquiry into how we ought to live; ethical questions are about what actions we ought to perform, what policies we ought to adopt, what kind of people we ought to be, and what sort of society we ought to have.

etiological account of interests   The view that the nonconscious interests of organisms are established by the selection processes (i.e., etiology) that generated the teleology of their parts and processes.

etiological account of teleology   The view that an entity is goal-directed if the causal explanation for why it has the parts and processes that it does is that they were selected for (and persist in current generations) because of the role they perform in bringing about certain ends.

eudaimonistic virtue ethics   Accounts of what makes a character trait a virtue on which the virtues are character traits that a person needs to flourish or live well.

evaluative claim   A claim about something's value, particularly its goodness or badness in some respect or overall.

everyone-must-choose-their-ethical-beliefs argument   The argument that ethical skepticism is justified by the fact that each person is responsible for determining their own ethical beliefs.

evolution   The natural processes by which biological complexity and diversity arise.

***ex situ* conservation**   Conservation efforts in which a population of the target species is maintained outside of its natural habitat or historical range, such as in a zoo or aquarium.

exclusive use   When some people's interests are not taken into account (or not fully taken into account) in determining the use of a resource.

existence value   The value that something has because people value its continued existence.

experiencing subject of a life   Any being with consciousness, that can in at least in some sense care about its own welfare, or has psychological interests, desires, experiences, and memories.

explanatory claim   A claim that proposes an account of why some aspect of the world is the way it is.

extensionist argument   Any argument that aims to justify direct moral concern for an entity (or type of entity) on the grounds that there is no morally relevant difference between that entity and another entity (or type of entity) that is regarded as directly morally considerable. See also **generalization argument**.

extrinsic objections   Objections to a technology (or practice or policy) based on the expected or possible outcomes or consequences of it.

factory farms   A term often used by critics to refer to concentrated animal feed operations.

factual difference   Any descriptive difference between two things (or types of things).

fallacy of ambiguity   When an inference in an argument is invalid because the meaning of a crucial term changes between premises, and if the meaning were consistent among premises then at least one of the premises would be false. See also **fallacy of equivocation**.

fallacy of appeal to human nature   The invalid inference from "Behavior X has a biological or evolutionary basis (or humans have a proclivity toward X)" to the conclusion "We ought to do X."

fallacy of appeal to nature   The invalid inference from "Events of type X occur in nature" to the conclusion "It is permissible for us to do X."

fallacy of appeal to the crowd   The invalid inference from "Most people believe X" to the conclusion "X is true."

fallacy of appeal to tradition   The invalid inference from "There is a history of people doing X" to the conclusion "It is permissible to X."

fallacy of asserting the conclusion   When a view is stated and described, but not argued for or justified.

fallacy of assuming the conclusion   When a premise in an argument is also the conclusion of the argument; sometimes called the **fallacy of begging the question**.

fallacy of begging the question   When a premise in an argument is also the conclusion of the argument; sometimes called the **fallacy of assuming the conclusion**.

fallacy of decomposition   The invalid inference from "Entity X has property P" to the conclusion that "The parts of entity X have property P."

fallacy of equivocation   When an inference in an argument is invalid because the meaning of a crucial term changes between premises, and if the meaning were consistent among premises then at least one of the premises would be false. See also **fallacy of ambiguity**.

fallacy of hasty generalization (also called fallacy of hasty conclusion)   An invalid inference to a general conclusion from observation or consideration of too few or too unrepresentative of cases.

feminist environmental philosophy   A family of views that identify and challenge myopic, gendered, and patriarchal features of Western philosophical thought regarding nonhuman nature and animals, and emphasize the connections between the ways in which women and nonhuman nature are conceptualized, characterized, (mis)valued, and (mal)treated. Also called **ecofeminism** or ecological feminism.

fertility rate   The number of children born per woman in a defined population.

final value   The value that something has for what it is, rather than for what it does or provides. Something has final value if its instrumental value is not exhaustive of its value. Often referred to in environmental ethics as **intrinsic value**.

focal things and practices   The term used by Albert Borgmann to refer to things and activities that enrich our lives and that often provide meaning and orientation to them.

food system   The complex network of processes, infrastructures, and actors that produce the food we eat and deliver it to where we eat it; food systems involve agricultural production or capture, processing, preparation, consumption, and waste disposal.

form of life   How individuals of a biological group (e.g., species) typically strive to make their way in the world. It concerns what sorts of things they consume, how they reproduce, how (and when and whether) they move, how they avoid predators, and how they repair themselves when damaged.

form of life conception of species   An understanding of species on which they are distinguished by their distinctive forms of life.

fortress conservation   The term used by critics to refer to park and reserve management that valorizes wilderness and aims to eliminate human presence or impacts in them so far as is possible.

functional diversity   A conception of biological diversity that focuses on the role of organisms and populations in ecosystem processes.

gene drives   Genomic modifications that cause a genetic trait to spread rapidly through a sexually reproducing population; they work by increasing the rate or frequency at which a gene sequence gets passed on to offspring.

generalization argument   Any argument that aims to justify direct moral concern for an entity (or type of entity) on the grounds that there is no morally relevant difference between that entity and another entity (or type of entity) that is regarded as directly morally considerable. See also **extensionist argument**.

genetic fallacy   The invalid inference from "X was produced from an entity or process with property P" to the conclusion "X has property P."

genetically modified crops   Plant species that are used in agriculture whose genomes have been intentionally engineered by use of genomic technologies, such as recombinant DNA techniques and synthetic biology.

geoengineering (or climate engineering)   Large-scale intentional interventions in climatic and ecological processes—such as solar radiation management, ocean fertilization, and atmospheric carbon dioxide removal—to counteract the effects of climate change.

global food system   A food system in which food production and delivery networks are transnational and industrial.

global justice   Distributive and procedural justice concerns regarding people's and nations' relationships with, treatment of, and responsibilities to others around the world.

goal-directed system   Any entity that has intentions or aims, or whose parts and processes are organized in ways and for reasons to do with accomplishing things or bringing things about.

greenwashing   The use of the concept of sustainability (or other environment values or goals) to sell products, particularly in the absence of any real commitment to sustainability.

harm principle   The principle that people ought to be able to engage in whatever activities they would like so long as it does not involve harming others.

hedonistic utilitarianism   The view that pleasure is good, pain is bad, and that an action is right to the extent that it brings about the greatest balance of pleasure over pain.

historical justice argument   The argument that affluent people and nations have a responsibility to assist very poor people in less developed countries because in many places where there is significant poverty and food insecurity affluent nations contributed to creating the situation through their past activities.

holism   The view that in environmental ethics what has primary value (or should be of primary concern) are ecological collectives, such as species or ecosystems, rather than individual organisms.

hubris (environmental)   The tendency to overestimate our ability to predict and control the consequences of our alterations of complex ecological and biological systems.

human rights   The view that every human being has strong moral standing in virtue of their being human beings, regardless of what other people believe or what other people's attitudes toward them are.

ideal preferences   The preferences that people would have if they were sufficiently informed, inclusive, long-term, and rational.

***in situ* conservation**   Conservation efforts that aim to maintain populations of the target species in their natural habitats or historical ranges.

inadequacy objection   Any argument against an environmental ethic on the grounds that it will not provide a sufficient basis for advocating for and promoting environmentally sustainable practices, policies, and lifestyles

indirect consequentialism   Normative theories on which actions (and practices and policies) are not evaluated directly in terms of their consequences, but in terms of rules (or motives or virtues) that are evaluated in terms of consequences.

indirect duties   The duties that moral agents have regarding nonhuman animals and the environment (or other entities) because of their relationship to people's interests or rights— i.e., the duties are regarding nonhuman animal or the environment, but not to them.

indirectly morally considerable   When moral agents need to consider something's good or interests not for its own sake, but only because of its relationship to something else that is directly considerable or has final value.

individualism   The view that only individual organisms are morally considerable, or that the rights, welfare, and good of individuals should be the primary focus of ethical concern.

inductive inference   An argument in which it is intended that the conclusion is likely to be true if the premises are true.

inefficient use   When there is an alternative use for a resource that would better promote human welfare than its current use.

inherent worth   When something is directly considerable because it has interests that moral agents ought to care about for its own sake.

innovation presumption   The view that people should be allowed to create and adopt novel technologies—from new materials to artificial intelligences—unless good reasons are provided against their doing so.

instrumental value   The value that something has in virtue of being an effective means to a desired or sought after end.

integrating effect of virtue   The idea that those who are virtuous will take pleasure and meaning from doing the right thing, and will not see the "demands" of morality as involving large sacrifice.

intergenerational justice   What each generation is entitled to receive from the prior one and is responsible for passing on to the next one.

international order argument   The argument that affluent nations and people have a responsibility to assist those in poverty in less developed countries because international institutions are largely set up and dominated by powerful affluent nations, which frequently promote policies that serve their own economic and geopolitical interests to the disadvantage of less developed nations.

interpersonal environmental ethics   The part of environmental ethics that concerns our ethical relationships and responsibilities to other people, but involving the environment.

interpersonal ethics   The part of ethics that concerns interactions and relationships between people.

interventionist ecosystem management   Approaches to ecosystem management, such as assisted colonization and ecosystem engineering, that involve taking a more active and design-oriented approach than has generally been done in the past.

intraspecific genetic diversity   The genetic diversity within a species or population.

intrinsic objections   Objections to technologies (or practices) that are based on the features of the technology (or practice) itself, independent of whether its consequences are good or bad.

intrinsic value   Noninstrumental value, or the value that something has for what it is, rather than only what it does or provides; also sometimes referred to as **final value**.

justifying claim   A claim that supports (or is intended to support) an action, practice, or policy as being appropriate or right.

keystone species   Species that have a large ecological effect on the systems in which they occur.

land ethic   The principle, advocated for by Aldo Leopold, that a thing is right when it tends to preserve the integrity, stability, and beauty of the biotic community, and is wrong when it tends otherwise.

legal rights   Rights that are recognized within the framework of a legislative or legal system.

libertarian account of property rights   The view that a person has absolute rights over the products of her labor, as well as over anything that others freely trade with her or give to her.

lifeboat ethic   The view, defended by Garrett Hardin, that affluent nations should not send food aid to low-income nations with high levels of malnourishment, nor should they take in large numbers of immigrants from them.

logic of domination   Dichotomous (or hierarchical) conceptualizations of the world in which one side of the dichotomy is identified as superior and therefore justified in dominating or subordinating the other (or else a chain of superiority is asserted).

longitudinal collective action problems   Problems that arise from the cumulative impacts of large numbers of people's seemingly insignificant actions over a long period of time, such as global climate change and fisheries depletions.

luxury emissions   Greenhouse gas emissions that are associated with satisfying peripheral interests.

mentalistic theories of welfare   Accounts of welfare or well-being on which how well or poorly someone's life is going depends entirely upon their mental states.

metaphysical dualism   The view, associated with the philosophy of René Descartes, on which the mind and the body are distinct from each other. Also called **substance dualism**.

metaphysics   The study of the fundamental or deeper reality or nature of the world.

mind-world correspondence views of welfare   Views on which how well or poorly someone's life is going depends upon the relationship between their mental states and the world.

miniride principle   A priority principle advocated for by Thomas Regan according to which fewer rights violations are preferable to more rights violations, all other things being equal.

misanthropic   The term used to describe views or positions that take a negative view of people.

mitigation   Efforts to limit the magnitude of anthropogenic climate change by reducing greenhouse gas emissions and enhancing greenhouse sinks.

moderate anthropocentrism   The view that while all living things (or sentient beings) have inherent worth, human beings have greater worth in virtue of their humanity.

monism (regarding moral considerability)   The view that there is a single standard for direct moral considerability.

moral agency   The capacity to understand moral concepts and terms, reflect upon them, evaluate actions (or practices and policies) as right or wrong, and act on the basis of those evaluations. Also called **rational agency**.

moral hazard   Something that increases the probability of people engaging in risky behavior to the detriment of others.

moral luck argument   The argument that affluent people and nations ought to assist the poor in less developed countries because no one deserves the situation into which they are born, so it is just a matter of luck (and not desert) that some people are born into a situation of affluence while other people are born into a situation of extreme poverty.

moral patients (or moral subjects)   Individuals whose interests are directly morally considerable.

moral rights   Claims that an entity has against things being done to them, or to something to which they are entitled, no matter the current law of the land.

moral status   The ways or extent to which something is morally considerable.

moral subjects (or moral patients)   Individuals whose interests are directly morally considerable.

moral wisdom   The ability of virtuous people with the relevant experience to see things differently and better than a nonvirtuous person.

morally considerable   Anything that needs to be taken into account in deliberations regarding actions, practices, or policies that might affect them.

morally relevant differences (or morally relevant property)   A factual difference that tracks or marks something ethically significant.

narrow use   When not all of the goods and services provided by a place or resource are considered in use determinations.

natural (as the term is used here)   The extent to which something is independent of human control, impacts, or designs.

natural law tradition   The view that because humans share in God's rationality we should be able to use our rational capacities to understand the world, including how we ought to live.

natural resources   Materials or substances that occur in nature and are used by people—e.g., soil to grow crops, fossil fuels for energy, diamonds for jewelry, and trees for lumber.

natural value   The value that places or living things have in virtue of their being independent from human control, impacts, or designs.

negative rights   Claims against things being done to a person (or other entity)—e.g., to not be exploited, not be discriminated against, and not be restricted in movement, association, or speech.

no-analog systems   An ecological space in which anthropogenic activities have resulted in a system in which the biotic features (e.g., species distributions) and abiotic characteristics (e.g., soil composition) significantly depart from those of the pre-impacted system. Also called **novel systems**.

nonanthropocentrism   The view that at least some nonhumans or environmental entities possess inherent worth or other types of final value.

nonidentity problem   It is not possible to harm future people in the sense of making them worse off than they would have otherwise been, since our actions and policies determine which future people will exist.

normative theories   Theories that explicate how things matter or are to be taken into account in ethical decision-making; they provide an account of the relationship between value and right action, and supply an approach to evaluating actions, practices, and policies.

novel systems   An ecological space in which anthropogenic activities have resulted in a system in which the biotic features (e.g., species distributions) and abiotic characteristics (e.g., soil composition) significantly depart from those of the pre-impacted system. Also called **no-analog systems**.

objective final value   Any type of final (noninstrumental) value that exists independently of anyone's particular evaluative attitudes or stances.

objectivist theories of welfare   Views on which how well or poorly someone's life is going depends at least in part on considerations that are not tied to their mental states.

ontological holism and egalitarianism (or metaphysical holism)   The view that every entity, human and nonhuman, biotic and abiotic, is fundamentally relational, an equally significant node in the interconnected fabric that constitutes reality.

option value   The value that something has in virtue of its being potentially useful in ways that we cannot currently predict.

organic unity   When the interconnected components of a system make up an integrated whole that is in a significant sense distinct from or greater than the sum of its parts.

perfectionist fallacy   The invalid inference from "It is not possible to do X perfectly" to the conclusions that "X should not be done at all."

peripheral interests   Mere wants, or things that people desire to have, but do not materially impact the quality of their life.

person-affecting principle   The view that an action can be wrong only if it makes someone worse off.

philosophical method   Reason-based empirically informed inquiry, or the use of arguments, reasons, justification, and evidence with the goal of gaining knowledge.

Pleistocene rewilding   The proposal to translocate wild (or de-domesticate nonwild) tortoises, camels, cheetahs, horses, elephants, and lions from Asia and Africa, among other places, to expansive parks in the Great Plains, Western United States, Australia, and elsewhere.

pluralism (regarding moral considerability)   The view that there are different degrees, forms, or types of direct moral considerability.

pluralist ecocentrism   The view that combines an ecocentric approach to environmental ethics with respect or compassion for individuals.

polluter pays principle   The view that those who are most responsible for causing an environmental problem have the most responsibility to address it.

positive rights   Rights to something, rather than rights against something, such as the right to access potable water or a nutritionally adequate diet.

practical adequacy condition   The view that an environmental ethic should provide a basis for advocating for and promoting environmentally sustainable practices, policies, and lifestyles.

pragmatic holism   The view that we should approach environmental issues from a holistic perspective, but only because that is the best way to serve the interests of the morally considerable individuals that populate biotic systems; it is holism at the decision-making level but individualism at the value level.

precautionary principle   The view that when there is scientific uncertainty about the risks of something—e.g., when we do not adequately understand the ecological and health risks of a new technology—rather than presuming that it is acceptable, we should restrict it until it is demonstrated to be safe.

predictive claim   A claim about what is likely to happen in the future.

prescriptive claim   A claim about what ought or should be done.

preservationists   Those who believe that ecosystem management should prioritize the protection of nature rather than providing goods and services for people.

prima facie duties   Rules or duties that ought to be followed unless there is a compelling reason to violate them—i.e., they come into conflict with another, stronger duty.

prima facie wrong   Something that ought not be done unless there are overriding considerations.

principle of beneficence   The view that if you can prevent something very bad from happening with little cost to yourself, then you ought to do so.

principle of charity   The view that one should always try to interpret ideas and arguments in their strongest or most promising form when evaluating them.

principle of commensurate burdens and benefits   The view that those who enjoy the benefits of some activity should also shoulder the associated burdens, and vice versa, unless there is good justification for them not doing so.

principle of equal consideration of interests   The view, advocated by Peter Singer, that like interests should be considered alike without respect to whose interests they are.

principle of noninterference   The view that it is prima facie wrong to interfere with natural ecosystems, even if it does not cause harm—i.e. it is wrong to interfere unless there is a compelling reason for doing so.

principle of social cooperation   "Justice increases when the benefits and burdens of social cooperation are born more equally, except when moral considerations or other values justify greater inequality" (Wenz 2007, 58).

principle of species impartiality   "[E]very species counts as having the same value in the sense that, regardless of what species a living thing belongs to, it is deemed to be prima facie deserving of equal concern and consideration on the part of moral agents. . . . Subscribing to the principle of species-impartiality . . . means regarding every entity that has a good of its own as possessing inherent worth" (Taylor 1986, 155).

principle of utility   The view that something (e.g., an action or policy) is right to the extent that it brings about the greatest balance of good over bad (i.e., it maximizes utility) among the options available to the agent, considering everyone and everything impacted.

Principles of Environmental Justice   The statement on what is involved in accomplishing environmental justice that was adopted at the First National People of Color Environmental Leadership Summit in 1991.

priority principles   Principles that indicate which prima facie duties or responsibilities take precedence, and under what conditions they do so, when they come into conflict.

problem of incommensurability   The view that not all social and environmental values (particularly final values) can be fully converted to or represented by an economic value.

problem of inconsequentialism   Given that each person's contribution to addressing longitudinal collective action environmental problems is inconsequential, and may require some costs from the standpoint of their own life, why should a person make the effort to change their behavior in response to the problems?

procedural approach to ethics   The view that ethical decisions are not justified by their conforming to, expressing, or fulfilling certain norms or principles, but by the processes by which they are reached.

psychocentrism   The view that all and only sentient beings—those that have a mental life or are capable of experiencing pleasure and pain—have inherent worth. Also called **sentientism**.

psychological interests   Interests that an entity has in virtue of its intentions, desires, attitudes, or other psychological states or capacities.

pure time preference   The practice in welfare economics of discounting the value of future goods/bads just because they are in the future.

radical environmentalism   A term frequently used to refer to forms of environmentalism that advocate for or engage in direct environmental activism.

ratiocentrism   The view that all and only robustly rational beings, particularly those with the capacity for moral agency, are directly morally considerable.

reductio ad absurdum   A form of argumentation that aims to show that a principle or view is mistaken because its implications are absurd or unacceptable.

relational accounts of value   The view that moral status is not entirely determined by an entity's capacities or internal properties, but also often depends on its relationships to others.

replication argument   1. A replica ecosystem is less valuable or lacks some of the values possessed by an original ecosystem. 2. The only difference between an original ecosystem and a replica ecosystem is that the original is natural, whereas the replica is artifactual. 3. Therefore, naturalness is value adding for ecosystems.

repugnant conclusion   The implication of aggregative consequentialism that it is better to have an enormous number of people whose lives are just barely worth living than a much smaller number of people with a very high quality of life.

respect for nature   The view, advocated by Paul Taylor, that all living things are directly morally considerable, and that the primary way they ought to be considered involves treating them as ends by refraining from harming them or interfering with their pursuit of their good.

restraintful ecosystem management The view that approaches to ecosystem management ought to continue to prioritize historical continuity and human-independent ecological and evolutionary processes, rather than adopt highly interventionist strategies that involve designing ecological spaces as people believe they ought to be.

rewilding Assisted colonization and/or reintroduction of multiple species in order to restore human impacted habitats.

risk A quantitative measure of the frequency and magnitude of a hazard—i.e., the number of incidents relative to exposures, as well as how bad it is when incidents occur.

rule consequentialism A form of indirect consequentialism on which an action is right if it conforms to the rules that, if generally adopted, would bring about the greatest balance of good over bad in comparison with other possible sets of rules.

safe An activity, process, or entity with acceptable risks (not zero risk).

satisficing consequentialism A non-maximizing version of consequentialism on which an action (or policy) is right if its outcomes are sufficiently good.

secondary principles Rules or guidelines developed from experience and careful study, which in general and for the most part orient people toward right actions.

self-realization Associated with deep ecology, it is the awareness of oneself as deeply interconnected and interdependent with ecosystems, nonhuman animals, and other people, rather than conceiving of oneself as an isolated individual or ego.

sentient being An entity that has a mental life or is capable of experiencing pleasure and pain.

sentientism The view that all and only sentient beings—those that have a mental life or are capable of experiencing pleasure and pain—have inherent worth. Also called **psychocentrism**.

serious interests Interests that, if not met, will substantially diminish the quality of a person's life or the range of her opportunities.

shallow ecology (or shallow environmentalism) The term used by deep ecologists to refer to environmentalism that is oriented around treating the problematic effects of industrial activities and promoting sustainable practices, particularly insofar as they impact "the health and affluence of people in the developed countries" (Naess 1973, 95).

shared benefits argument for assistance The argument that affluent people and nations have a responsibility to assist poor people in less developed countries on the grounds that affluent nations benefit from the economic position of less developed nations in numerous ways—for example, by having access to inexpensive labor, purchasing their natural resources, displacing environmental burdens onto them, and coercing them to open their markets and commodify their agriculture.

short-term use When resources are used to satisfy people's immediate interests in ways that are overall detrimental in the long-term.

significant interests Interests that, if met, can improve a person's life or opportunities.

social contract theory (or contractarianism) The view that the basic principles of justice are those to which reasonable and self-interested people would (hypothetically) agree.

sound argument An argument with valid reasoning and true premises; sound arguments have well-justified conclusions.

speciation   The creation of new species or taxa by evolutionary processes.

species monism   The view that there is a single best way to divide organisms into species.

species pluralism   The view that there is a plurality of legitimate species concepts.

species richness   The number of species in a geographic area or system.

speciesism   Unjustified discrimination against nonhumans on the basis of factual differences that are not morally relevant.

stewardship model   The view that God has entrusted humans, rational beings with conscience created in the divine image, with caring for the rest of creation, which God also sees as good.

sport hunting   Hunting done primarily for recreational reasons.

strategic pragmatism   The view that in public discourse on environmental issues people ought to use whatever justifications or arguments are most effective in promoting environmentally acceptable practices and policies.

straw man fallacy   The invalid inference from the fact that a weak or uncharitably interpreted version of a view is mistaken to the conclusion that a more promising or charitable version is also mistaken.

strong anthropocentrism   The view that all and only human beings have inherent worth. See also **absolute anthropocentrism**.

strong sustainability   A conception of sustainability on which it requires ensuring that future generations have access to the same resources as current generations.

subjective final value (or subjective value)   The value that something has because it is valued by people for noninstrumental reasons—e.g., for its beauty, creativity, or symbolism.

subsistence emissions   Greenhouse gas emissions that are associated with satisfying serious or basic interests.

subsistence hunting   Hunting that is crucial to survival and well-being—i.e., that serves basic or serious interests.

substance dualism   The view, associated with the philosophy of René Descartes, on which the mind and the body are distinct from each other. Also called **metaphysical dualism**.

sustainability science   The use of the physical and social sciences, as well as public engagement, in order to help define what sustainability means in particular contexts and determine how to assess and promote it.

sustainable development   "Meeting the needs of the present without compromising the ability of future generations to meet their own needs" (WCED 1987).

swamping problem   If we were to consider the interests of every future person the same as we do presently existing people, then their wants and needs would completely outweigh ours, since there will be so many more of them over time.

technocratic paradigm   The identification of increases in technological power with progress, as well as faith in technological innovation to solve all our problems and provide perpetual material growth.

technofix   Responses to environmental problems that aim to use technology to treat the problematic effects, rather than address their underlying causes.

techno-optimism   The view that technological innovation, rather than systemic and behavioral change, is the best way to address most of our significant environmental, health, and social problems.

teleological account of interests   The view that an entity can be benefited or harmed directly if it is a goal-oriented system, i.e., there is something it is striving for or aiming to accomplish.

theocentric views   Views on which nature is to be used and treated according to God's will, rather than for human ends.

theoretical pluralism   The idea, associated with some pragmatist views, that we ought to recognize the legitimacy of a diversity of theories of environmental ethics and avail ourselves to whichever one is best suited to the environmental issue or situation at hand.

therapeutic hunting   Hunting done to improve the health of an animal population, to protect other species, or for ecological reasons.

they-will-be-gods problem   The view that due to the high rate of technological innovation people in the future will live much better lives than current people do, therefore it would be unjustified for us to sacrifice our interests now for their benefit later.

thought experiments   Hypothetic cases that are used in ethics in order to identify people's intuitions, generate reflection, test ideas, or encourage views.

traditional ecological knowledge (or indigenous knowledge)   Indigenous peoples' knowledge about the biological world, ecological processes, and local ecological systems.

tragedy of the commons   A situation in which there is a shared or "common" (or "common-pool") resource to which multiple agents have access, and each agent's acting in ways that are individually rationally self-interested would result in the depletion of the resource to everyone's detriment.

triple bottom line   A phrase commonly used to emphasize the interconnections between society, the environment, and economics (or people, planet, and profit), such that long-term prosperity requires accomplishing sustainability in each.

trophic cascade   The effects on processes and species within an ecosystem that occur when there are significant changes to the structure of the system—e.g., when large predators are depleted.

two-factor egalitarianism   The view, defended by Donald VanDeVeer, that adjudication of competing interests should consider both the level of the interests at stake and the psychological capacities of the individuals whose interests they are.

umbrella species   A species whose conservation will also protect many other species or other environmental goods and values.

underutilization   When a resource could produce more goods and services than it currently does, or the goods and services that it does produce are not fully utilized.

unequal exposure   The fact that minority, poor, and disempowered peoples are frequently disproportionately exposed to environmental hazards.

unknown means problem   The view that it can be difficult for us to determine what to do now to ensure that the needs of people in the distant future will be met (even if we know what their needs will be).

unknown needs problem   The view that it can be difficult to predict what goods and resources people will need in future generations, particularly given the high rate of technological change.

utilitarianism   A version of consequentialism that accepts the principle of utility—i.e., that considers everyone's interests and calls for performing the action (or enacting the policy) that has the best overall outcomes.

utility calculus   The process of determining in a concrete situation what course of action has the best overall outcomes by identifying the possible courses of action, identifying what the consequences of each of those actions would be, assigning appropriate values to those consequences, and then summing up each alternative to see which has the greatest balance of good over bad.

value axiology   Within a utilitarian (or broader consequentialist) normative framework, an account of what things are good and bad.

value realism   The view that moral properties (or final value) exist in the world independent of anyone's particular evaluative attitudes.

vice   Character traits that dispose their possessor to respond poorly in emotion and action to considerations or events in the world.

virtue   Character traits that dispose their possessor to respond excellently in emotion and action to considerations or events in the world.

virtue ethics   The area of ethical theory that concerns what sorts of character traits people ought and ought not have.

virtue-oriented normative theories   Normative theories that tie the rightness and wrongness of actions, practices, and policies to the dispositions of the agent or the character traits that they embody or express.

virtue theory   An account of what makes a character trait a virtue.

weak sustainability   A conception of sustainability on which it requires ensuring that future people have the same capacity to meet their needs as present people, even with a diminished or different resource base.

welfare economics   The branch of economics that aims to assess social and economic well-being overall or in the aggregate.

welfarism   The view that welfare or well-being is what is ultimately ethically significance.

wide reflective equilibrium   The process of developing a well-justified ethical theory by continually reassessing and revising theoretical views and particular judgments on their own merits and in light of each other.

worse-off principle   A priority principle advocate by Thomas Regan according to which one ought to prioritize avoiding greater harms when adjudicating rights conflicts.

INDEX

A

Absence-of-certainty
    argument, 33
Activism. *see* environmental
    activism
Aesthetics, 268
Aggressive mitigation, 128
Agricultural, food resources
    animal treatment, 161–63
    commons problem, 120–22
    ecofeminism on, 341–43
    ecological, social costs
        of, 125–26
    exclusive use, 122–23
    human rights violations
        and, 259
    inefficient use, 118
    meat production, 118
    monoculture *vs.* biodiversity,
        342–43
    moral considerability (*see* moral
        considerability)
    narrow use, 123–24
    short-term use, 119–20
    underutilization, 118–19
    wastage, 119–20
Alternative food movement,
    273–75
Altgeld Gardens, 364
Amoralism, 30, 31
Anangu people, 70, 79, 80*f*
Animal Liberation Front
    (ALF), 278
Animals. *see also* agricultural,
    food resources; concentrated
    animal feed operations;
    sentientism
    assisting, 47–49
    captive breeding programs,
        208–9, 232–33
    consciousness in, 145
    duty to be kind to, 110
    ethics of care for, 20

human *vs.* animal
    experimentation, 183
legal rights for, 201–3, 202*f*
moral considerability, 141–43,
    145–47, 162–63, 173
pets, 148, 161–63
research on, 217
rights, 169–74, 206–9, 216
suffering, 143–45
welfare view, 169–74
Anthropocene age, 40, 411,
    413–18, 414*f*
Anthropocenic impacts, 411–12
Anthropocentrism
    absolute, 160
    actual preference, 106–7
    arguments supporting, 96–99
    defined, 11–12, 90, 95
    enlightened (*see* enlightened
        anthropocentrism)
    as environmental ethic, 101–2,
        134–35
    group membership in, 98–99,
        138, 247–48
    ideal preference, 124–25
    indirect duties, 109–12, 315
    moderate, 160
    strong, 160
    techno-optimism, 107–9, 285
Apex predators, 253
Aquaculture, 120
Argumentation
    assistance, core argument for,
        395–97
    from disagreement, 32
    ecological restoration, 77–80
    everyone-must-choose-their-
        ethical-beliefs, 31–32
    feed-the-world, 57
    historical argument, 397
    international order
        argument, 397
    moral luck argument, 400

from participatory decision-
    making, 96–98
to preserve all species, 304–14
replication, 77–80
shared benefits argument, 397
structure of, 27–30
Artifacts, 153–55
Artifactual, 42
Artificial alternatives concern,
    68–69
Assistance, amounts of,
    400–406, 402*f*
Assistance, core argument for,
    395–97, 406–7
Assisted colonization, 320, 323
Assisted recovery, 81
Assuming the conclusion, 53
Atlantic lobster, 122

B

Bacillus thuringiensis, 55
Baier, Annette, 334–35
Banana industry, 123
Basic interests, 178–80
Basic rights, 215–17
Battery cages, 170
Baxter, William, 106
Bentham, Jeremy, 141
Beta diversity, 318
Bhopal chemical disaster, 359
Biocentric egalitarianism,
    276, 286
Biocentric pluralism, 276
Biocentrism, 95, 148, 151–52,
    155–56, 159, 175, 203–6,
    228, 266
Biodiversity
    beta diversity, 318
    conservation approaches,
        294–95
    defined, 298–99
    duty to preserve, 314–16

459